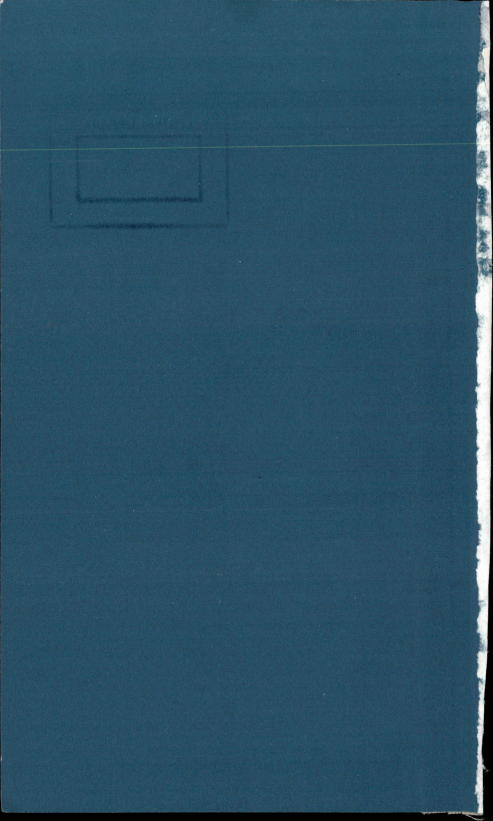

EITHER/OR
PART I

by Søren Kierkegaard

Edited and Translated
with Introduction and Notes by

Howard V. Hong and
Edna H. Hong

PRINCETON UNIVERSITY PRESS
PRINCETON, NEW JERSEY

Published by Princeton University Press,
41 William Street, Princeton, New Jersey 08540
In the United Kingdom: Princeton University Press, Guildford, Surrey

Library of Congress Cataloging in Publication Data will be
found on the last printed page of this book

ISBN 0-691-07315-5 (cloth)
ISBN 0-691-02041-8 (pbk.)

Preparation of this volume has been made possible in part by a grant from
the Division of Research Programs of the National Endowment for the Humanities,
an independent federal agency

Clothbound editions of Princeton University Press books
are printed on acid-free paper, and binding materials are
chosen for strength and durability. Paperbacks, though satisfactory
for personal collections, are not usually suitable for library rebinding

Designed by Frank Mahood

Printed in the United States of America by Princeton
University Press, Princeton, New Jersey

CONTENTS

HISTORICAL INTRODUCTION

In a journal entry from 1846, Kierkegaard stated that *Either/Or* was written "lock, stock, and barrel in eleven months. At most there was only a page (of 'Diapsalmata') prior to that time. As far as that goes, I have spent more time on all the later works. Most of *Either/Or* was written only twice (besides, of course, what I thought through while walking, but that is always the case); nowadays I usually write three times."[1] The work presumably began to germinate and to take form during the few months before Kierkegaard's departure for Berlin on October 25, 1841—the eventful months of September-October, during which he broke his engagement to Regine Olsen[2] and published and defended his dissertation, *The Concept of Irony*.[3] In his first letter from Berlin, October 31, 1841, Kierkegaard wrote to his old friend Emil Boesen: "I have much to think about and am suffering from a monstrous productivity block. I have as yet no occasion to let its *nisis* [persistent pressure] wear off . . .."[4] But on January 6, 1842, he was able to report to Boesen: "I am working hard. So that you may see that I am the same, I shall tell you that I have again written a major section of a piece, 'Either/Or.' It has not gone quickly, but that is due to its not being an expository work, but one of pure invention, which in a very special way demands that one be in the mood."[5] In November 1842,[6] the editor's preface to *Either/Or* was finished, and the two volumes were published February 20, 1843.

Before the journey to Berlin, Kierkegaard had written a draft of Judge William's "The Esthetic Validity of Marriage,"

---

[1] *JP* V 5931 (*Pap*. VII¹ A 92).
[2] October 11, 1841.
[3] Published September 16 and defended September 29, 1841.
[4] *Kierkegaard: Letters and Documents*, Letter 99, pp. 89-90, *KW* XXV.
[5] *Letters*, Letter 62, p. 123, *KW* XXV.
[6] See *JP* V 5568 (*Pap*. III B 189).

the first piece in Part II of *Either/Or*. His second piece in Part II
and most of Part I were written afterward in Berlin and Copenhagen.[7]

In February 1842, he wrote to Boesen:

> It is absolutely imperative that I return to Copenhagen
> this spring. For either I shall finish Either/Or by spring, or I
> shall never finish it. The title is approximately that which
> you know. I hope you will keep this between us. Anonym-
> ity is of the utmost importance to me. . . .
> Either/Or is indeed an excellent title. It is piquant and at
> the same time also has a speculative meaning. But for my
> own sake I will not rob you prematurely of any enjoyment.
> This winter in Berlin will always have great significance
> for me. I have done a lot of work. When you consider that I
> have had three or four hours of lectures every day, have a
> daily language lesson, and have still gotten so much written
> (and that regardless of the fact that in the beginning I had to
> spend a lot of time writing down Schelling's lectures[8] and
> making fair copies), and have read a lot, I cannot complain.
> And then all my suffering, all my monologues! I feel
> strongly that I cannot continue for long; I never expected to;
> but I can for a short while and all the more intensively.[9]

> Schelling talks endless nonsense both in an extensive and
> an intensive sense. I am leaving Berlin and hastening to Co-
> penhagen, but not, you understand, to be bound by a new
> tie, oh no, for now I feel more strongly than ever that I need
> my freedom. A person with my eccentricity should have his
> freedom until he meets a force in life that, as such, can bind
> him. I am coming to Copenhagen to complete Either/Or. It
> is my favorite idea, and in it I exist. You will see that this

---

[7] See *The Point of View for My Work as an Author, KW* XXII (*SV* XIII 569-
70 fn.); *Letters*, Letter 54, p. 104, *KW* XXV.

[8] In 1841, Friedrich Wilhelm Joseph Schelling (1775-1854) was called from
Munich to be professor of philosophy at the University of Berlin. His lectures
on the philosophy of revelation were Kierkegaard's main reason for going to
Berlin. The lectures drew auditors, including Jakob Burkhardt and Friedrich
Engels, from throughout Europe.

[9] *Letters*, Letter 68, pp. 137-38, *KW* XXV.

idea is not to be made light of. In no way can my life yet be considered finished. I feel I still have great resources within me.

I do owe Schelling something. For I have learned that I enjoy traveling, even though not for the sake of studying. As soon as I have finished Either/Or, I shall fly away again like a happy bird. I must travel. Formerly I never had the inclination for it, but first I must finish Either/Or and that I can do only in Copenhagen.[10]

Although only a few journal entries from earlier writing were used as diapsalmata in *Either/Or*,[11] the earlier writing is nevertheless present in tone and substance. The sardonic irony of Mr. A, especially in "Diapsalmata" and "Rotation of Crops," reflects the tone of a "Faustian doubter"[12] and represents the irony of despairing estheticism in contrast to what is called "Irony as a Controlled Element. The Truth of Irony" in *The Concept of Irony*.[13] On the other hand, "The Seducer's Diary"[14] is an explicit example of the romantic individualism discussed in *Irony*,[15] a particularized delineation of what Friedrich Schlegel calls life as "a work of art," an "airy dance."[16]

---

[10] Ibid., Letter 69, p. 139.

[11] "If I had not decided when publishing *Either/Or* not to use any old material, I would have found in going through my papers some aphorisms that could have been used very well. Today I found a little scrap of paper with the following written on it: 'I am so tired that I feel that I need an eternity to rest, so troubled that I feel that I need an eternity to forget my sorrows; I wish that I could sleep so long that I would wake up an old man and then could lie down again to sleep the eternal sleep' " (*JP* V 5631; *Pap.* IV A 221).

[12] This is Emanuel Hirsch's description. See Supplement, p. 453 and note 1.

[13] *KW* II (*SV* XIII 388-93).

[14] "In a review in *Forposten [Kjøbenhavnsposten*, 13, March 26, 1843], I see that it is quite properly pointed out that this narrative is not called a seducer's diary but *the* seducer's, suggesting that it is the method that is really of prime importance, not the portrayal of either Johannes or Cordelia" (*JP* V 5633; *Pap.* IV A 231).

[15] *Irony, KW* II (*SV* XIII 357-70).

[16] Friedrich v. Schlegel, *Lucinde* (Berlin: 1799), pp. 206, 299; *Friedrich Schlegel's* Lucinde *and the Fragments*, tr. Peter Firchow (Minneapolis: University of Minnesota Press, 1971), pp. 102, 129.

Kierkegaard's first use of the title phrase "either/or" is also found in *Irony* in its Latin form *aut/aut*.[17] Later, the Danish form found currency even on Copenhagen streets. As Kierkegaard remarked, "I am without authority, only a poet—but oddly enough around here, even on the street, I go by the name 'Either/Or.' "[18]

Despite the tension indicated by the very title *Either/Or* and publication in two separate volumes, Kierkegaard regarded the work as having "a plan from the first word to the last,"[19] a view hardly shared by his contemporaries. If the cohesion of the dialectically balanced volumes was overlooked at the time, it is not surprising that later readers generally failed to relate *Either/Or* to the other pseudonymous and signed works by Kierkegaard. He himself maintained that *Either/Or* has an integral wholeness and constitutes part of a larger whole: "My contemporaries cannot grasp the design of my writing. *Either/Or* divided into four parts or six parts and published separately over six years would have been all right. But that each essay in *Either/Or* is only part of a whole, and then the whole of *Either/Or* a part of a whole: that, after all, think my bourgeois contemporaries, is enough to drive one daft."[20]

Three years later, and again eighteen years later, Kierkegaard reaffirmed the integrality of the complex series of writ-

[17] *Irony, KW* II (*SV* XIII 173-74). The Latin form was used by philosophy professor Frederik Christian Sibbern in his long review of Johan Ludvig Heiberg's *Perseus, Journal for den speculative Idee, No. 1,* in *Maanedsskrift for Litteratur,* XIX, 1838, p. 432, in a section on the principle of contradiction. Bishop Jac(k)ob Peter Mynster also used the phrase in "*Rationalisme. Supernaturalisme,*" a discussion of the principle of contradiction, in opposition to Hegel, Johan Alfred Bornemann, and Johan Ludvig Heiberg. See *Tidsskrivt for Literatur og Critik,* I, 1839, p. 267, and Mynster, *Blandede Skrivter,* I-VI (Copenhagen: 1852-57), II, p. 114. See *Concluding Unscientific Postscript* to Philosophical Fragments, *KW* XII (*SV* VII 261).

[18] *JP* VI 6947 (*Pap.* XI³ B 57).

[19] *JP* V 5627 (*Pap.* IV A 214, 1843). J. L. Heiberg, in "*Vintersæd,*" *Intelligensblade,* 24, March 1, 1843, pp. 290-91, wrote (ed. tr.): "the author's unusual brilliance, learning, and stylistic facility are not united with an organizing capacity . . .." See also *Either/Or,* II, p. 411, *KW* IV (*Pap.* IV A 216).

[20] *JP* V 5905 (*Pap.* VII¹ A 118, 1846).

ings beginning with *Either/Or*, and he defined the nature of the whole. "An authorship that began with *Either/Or* and advanced step by step seeks here its consummating place of rest at the foot of the altar, where the author, personally most aware of his own imperfection and guilt, certainly does not call himself a witness to the truth but only a singular kind of poet and thinker who, 'without authority,' has had nothing new to bring but 'has wanted to read through once again, if possible in a more inward way, the original text of individual human existence-relationships, the old, familiar text handed down from the fathers' (see my postscript to *Concluding Postscript*)."[21] "What I have understood as the task of the authorship has been done. It is one idea, this continuity from *Either/Or* to Anti-Climacus, the idea of religiousness in reflection."[22] One of the latest items (1854) in Kierkegaard's papers reiterates this thought and goes beyond Anti-Climacus. The title page of the proposed summary work briefly and comprehensively reads: "My Program: Either/Or By S. Kierkegaard."[23]

As part of the whole including the pseudonymous works, *Either/Or* lacked one element, according to Kierkegaard: a narrative section or an imaginary construction[24] in the experiential mode. On the flyleaf of a copy of *Either/Or*, I, Kierkegaard wrote: "Some think that *Either/Or* is a collection of loose papers I had lying in my desk. Bravo! —As a matter of fact, it was the reverse. The only thing this work lacks is a narrative, which I did begin but omitted, just as Aladdin left a window incomplete. It was to be called 'Unhappy Love.' It was to form a contrast to the Seducer. The hero in the story acted in exactly the same way as the Seducer, but behind it was depression. He

[21] Preface to *Two Discourses at the Communion on Fridays* (1851), *KW* XVIII (*SV* XII 267). The reference to a postscript is to "A First and Last Explanation," *Postscript, KW* XII (*SV* VII [548-49]).

[22] *JP* VI 6770 (*Pap*. X⁶ B 4:3), from an unused draft of the preface to *For Self-Examination* (1851).

[23] *JP* VI 6944 (*Pap*. XI³ B 54).

[24] See *Repetition*, note to subtitle, pp. 357-62, *KW* VI.

was not unhappy because he could not get the girl he loved.
Such heroes are beneath me. He had capacities comparable to
the Seducer's; he was certain of capturing her. He won her. As
long as the struggle went on, he detected nothing; then she
surrendered, he was loved with all the enthusiasm a young girl
has—then he became unhappy, went into a depression, pulled
back; he could struggle with the whole world but not with
himself. His love made him indescribably happy at the moment; as soon as he thought of time, he despaired."[25] After the
appearance of the contemplated narrative (with appropriate
modifications) in *Stages on Life's Way*, Kierkegaard cryptically
explained its omission from the earlier work. "The imaginary
construction, however, is precisely what is lacking in *Either/
Or* (see a note in my own copy [*Pap*. IV A 215]); but before it
could be done absolutely right, an enormous detour had to be
made."[26]

In an appendix to *Concluding Unscientific Postscript*,[27] Johannes Climacus discusses in some detail the substantive relation
of *Either/Or* to the other pseudonymous works: "I mention
these books," Climacus modestly writes, "only insofar as they
constitute elements in the realization of the idea I had but
which in an ironical way I was exempted from realizing."[28]
The idea, that of "existential inwardness,"[29] involves various
"elements" of *Either/Or*: the esthetic and the ethical, immediacy and reflection, the individual and the universally human,
time and eternity, history as a given and the gaining of a personal history, the momentary and the moment, existential dialectic, the use of freedom, erotic love and ethical love, living
poetically and living responsibly, despair and hope, possibility
and actuality, choosing, immanence and transcendence, the

---

[25] *JP* V 5628 (*Pap*. IV A 215). A "sequel to 'The Seducer's Diary' " was also
contemplated, something that "must be in a piquant vein, his relation to a
young married woman" (*JP* V 5677; *Pap*. IV A 129). See also *Either/Or*, II, pp.
409-10, *KW* IV (*Pap*. IV A 181).

[26] *JP* V 5866 (*Pap*. VII¹ B 84). See also *Either/Or*, II, pp. 429-30, *KW* IV
(*Pap*. VII¹ B 83, 84).

[27] "A Glance at a Contemporary Effort in Danish Literature," *KW* XII (*SV*
VII 212-57).

[28] Ibid. (228).   [29] Ibid. (229).

inner and the outer, concealment and openness, imagination and actuality, thought and actuality, knowledge and action.

In addition to the relation of *Either/Or* to the other pseudonymous works, there is another kind of relation to the parallel series of signed works that began with *Two Upbuilding Discourses*, published (May 16, 1843)[30] three months and a day after *Either/Or* appeared. In *Point of View*, Kierkegaard characterizes himself as a poet with a leaning toward the religious. *Either/Or* was the work of the poet, and the discourses were his own.[31] This self-description accounts not only for the conscious and deliberate duplexity (differentiated parallelism) of the two writing series but also for the linear development and dynamic coherence of the entire authorship. Therefore, in a journal entry from 1848 he could write:

> Yes, it was a good thing to publish that little article. I began with *Either/Or* and two upbuilding discourses; now it ends, after the whole upbuilding series—with a little esthetic essay.[32] It expresses: that it was the upbuilding, the religious, that should advance, and that now the esthetic has been traversed; they are inversely related, or it is something of an inverse confrontation, to show that the writer was not an esthetic author who in the course of time grew older and for that reason became religious.[33]

The dialectical complexity of the pseudonymous series of writings and the duplexity of the two differentiated parallel series were Kierkegaard's way of combining Socratic maieutic

[30] This small volume was followed by *Three Upbuilding Discourses* and *Four Upbuilding Discourses* (October 13, December 6, 1843) and by *Two Upbuilding Discourses, Three Upbuilding Discourses*, and *Four Upbuilding Discourses* (March 5, June 8, August 31, 1844), which were paralleled by the publication of *Fear and Trembling* and *Repetition* (October 7, 1843), *Philosophical Fragments* (June 13, 1844), and *The Concept of Anxiety* (June 17, 1844).

[31] *KW* XXII (*SV* XIII 569).

[32] *The Crisis and A Crisis in the Life of an Actress* (1848), *KW* XVII (*SV* X 319-44). Midway between *Either/Or* and *Crisis*, Kierkegaard also wrote a piece reminiscent of *Either/Or* under the title "A Cursory Observation Concerning a Detail in *Don Giovanni*," *The Corsair Affair*, pp. 28-37, *KW* XIII (*SV* XIII 447-56).

[33] *JP* VI 6238 (*Pap.* IX A 227). See also, for example, ibid., 6356 (X[1] A 138).

indirection in the one series and the direct approach in the other. In "The Accounting," in *On My Work as an Author,* Kierkegaard explains why he used the pseudonymous approach:

> The maieutic lies in the relation between the esthetic productivity as the beginning and the religious as the τέλος [goal]. It begins with the esthetic, in which possibly the majority have their lives, and then the religious is introduced so quickly that those who, moved by the esthetic, decide to follow along, are suddenly standing right in the middle of decisive qualifications of the essentially Christian, are prompted at least to become *aware.*[34]

Kierkegaard went to great lengths to protect the pseudonymity of *Either/Or.* Not only was the transcribing of the final copy done by various hands,[35] lest the secret be detected and divulged by someone at the printing house, but he added an element to his usual practice of walking and conversing in the streets of Copenhagen.[36]

> If I wanted to tell about it, a whole book could be written on how ingeniously I have fooled people about my pattern of life.
> During the time I was reading proofs of *Either/Or* and writing the upbuilding discourses, I had almost no time to walk the streets. I then used another method. Every evening when I left home exhausted and had eaten at Mini's, I stopped at the theater for ten minutes—not one minute more. Familiar as I was, I counted on there being several gossips at the theater who would now say: Every single night he goes to the theater; he does not do another thing.

[34] *KW* XXII (*SV* XIII 496). See also, for example, *Point of View, KW* XXII (*SV* XIII 540-42).

[35] Kierkegaard mentions, for example, Peter Vilhelm Christensen (1819-1863) as a copyist. See *Letters,* Letter 188, p. 268, *KW* XXV.

[36] See Andrew Hamilton, *Sixteen Months in the Danish Isles,* I-II (London: 1852), II, p. 269: "The fact is *he walks about town all day*, and generally in some person's company . . . . When walking, he is very communicative." See also *Point of View, KW* XXII (*SV* XIII 543-56).

O, you darling gossips, thank you—without you I could never have achieved what I wanted.[37]

The pseudonymity of *Either/Or* was reinforced by a signed disclaimer, "Public Confession," in which Kierkegaard declined "the undeserved honor" of being regarded as "the author of a number of substantial, informative, and witty articles in various newspapers" and requested "the good people who show an interest in me never to regard me as the author of anything that does not bear my name."[38] A week after the publication of *Either/Or* (February 27, 1843), "Who is the Author of *Either/Or*" appeared in *Fædrelandet* over the initials A. F . . . . . .[39] A week later, the same paper carried Victor Eremita's "A Word of Thanks to Professor Heiberg,"[40] a reply to Johan Ludvig Heiberg's review of *Either/Or* in his *Intelligensblade*.[41] A few weeks later, "A Little Explanation"[42] appeared over Kierkegaard's name in response to a "fairly widespread and persistent rumor" that he was the author of the sermon at the end of *Either/Or*, II, because he had once delivered a sermon and therefore was the author of *Either/Or*. In "An Explanation and a Little More," after the first published attribution[43] of *Either/Or* and *Stages* to Kierkegaard, he declared, "If I am not the author of these books, then the rumor is a falsehood. However, if I am the author, then I am the only one authorized to say that I am that."[44] He exercised that au-

---

[37] *JP* VI 6332 (*Pap.* X⁵ A 153). See also *JP* V 5614 (*Pap.* IV A 45).

[38] *Fædrelandet*, 904, June 12, 1842; *Corsair Affair*, pp. 3, 5, *KW* XIII (*SV* XIII 397, 399).

[39] *Fædrelandet*, 1162, February 27, 1843; *Corsair Affair*, pp. 13-16, *KW* XIII (*SV* XIII 407-10).

[40] *Fædrelandet*, 1168, March 5, 1843; *Corsair Affair*, pp. 17-21, *KW* XIII (*SV* XIII 411-15).

[41] "*Litterær Vintersæd*," *Intelligensblade*, 24, March 1, 1843, pp. 288-92.

[42] *Fædrelandet*, 1236, May 16, 1843; *Corsair Affair*, pp. 22-23, *KW* XIII (*SV* XIII 416-17).

[43] *Berlingske Tidende*, 108, May 6, 1845. For an unpublished exchange between Kierkegaard and Victor Eremita, see *Either/Or*, II, pp. 388-92, *KW* IV (*Pap.* IV B 19-20).

[44] *Fædrelandet*, 1883, May 9, 1845; *Corsair Affair*, p. 24, *KW* XIII (*SV* XIII 418-19).

thority in the unnumbered pages of "A First and Last Explanation" at the end of *Concluding Unscientific Postscript*, published ten months later (February 27, 1846). An additional
reason for the pseudonymity of *Either/Or* concludes the article
by A. F. . . . . : "Most people, including the author of this article, think it is not worth the trouble to be concerned about
who the author is. They are happy not to know his identity,
for then they have only the book to deal with, without being
bothered or distracted by his personality."[45]

There was one reader, however, Regine Olsen, whom Kierkegaard wanted to discern him behind the pseudonyms, especially the writer behind the pseudonymous diary, as part of
his plan to make it easier for her to part with him. "When I left
'her,' I begged God for one thing, that I might succeed in writing and finishing *Either/Or* (this was also for her sake, because
The Seducer's Diary was, in fact, intended to repel, or as it says
in *Fear and Trembling*,[46] 'When the baby is to be weaned, the
mother blackens her breast.') . . .."[47]

But *Either/Or* did have more than a single reader. As a publication it was a "big success."[48] Christian Molbech, historian
and literary critic, wrote to Kierkegaard that the sell-out of
Either/Or was " 'a phenomenon that may need to be studied.' "[49] It was the first of the few of Kierkegaard's works to be
printed in a second edition during his lifetime.[50]

---

[45] "Who Is the Author of Either/Or," *Corsair Affair*, p. 16, *KW* XIII (*SV*
XIII 410). This was Kierkegaard's main reason for using pseudonyms, of
which there are five in *Either/Or:* (1) Victor Eremita, the editor; (2) Mr. A,
author of Part I, except for the portion by (3) Johannes, author of "The Seducer's Diary," although the editor thinks that Mr. A may have been the author; (4) Judge William, author of most of Part II; and (5) William's friend in
Jylland, author of "*Ultimatum* (A Last Word)" at the end of Part II.

[46] *Fear and Trembling*, p. 11, *KW* VI (*SV* III 64).

[47] *JP* VI 6843 (*Pap.* X⁵ A 146). See also *Either/Or*, II, pp. 443-44, *KW* IV
(*Pap.* X⁵ A 153).

[48] *JP* VI 6853 (*Pap.* X⁵ A 146). See also *Postscript, KW* XII (*SV* VII 244).

[49] *JP* V 5997 (*Pap.* VIII¹ A 84).

[50] See *Letters*, Letters 152-57, *KW* XXV. The first edition of 525 copies was
sold out within three years. The second was an edition of 750 copies. The

In keeping with the duplexity of the two series of writings, and in order to "mark the distinction between what is offered with the left hand and what is offered with the right,"[51] *The Lily of the Field and the Bird of the Air* was published on the same day (May 14, 1849) as the second edition of *Either/Or*. To reinforce the distinction, but also the connection, between the two series, Kierkegaard at different times contemplated two post-scripts to *Either/Or*. One was composed over Victor Eremita's name,[52] and the other he wrote in his own name:

What if I wrote at the back of the second edition of *Either/ Or:*

Postscript

I hereby retract this book. It was a necessary deception in order, if possible, to deceive men into the religious, which has continually been my task all along. Maieutically it certainly has had its influence. Yet I do not need to retract it, for I have never claimed to be its author.[53]

During the year of the publication of *Either/Or*, the work was reviewed in eight Danish papers and journals. Among the reviews was one by Meïer Goldschmidt in *Corsaren*,[54] laudatory in its cavalier way and mainly critical of the critics, especially the leading critic of the day, Johan Ludvig Heiberg. In his *Intelligensblade*, Heiberg stated that, "like a lightning bolt out of a clear sky, a monster of a book has suddenly plunged down into our reading public; I mean the two big, thick volumes of *Either/Or*, by Victor Eremita, consisting of fifty-four

---

other eight second editions out of thirty-six titles were of *Works of Love* (1852), *For Self-Examination* (1852), *Two Discourses at the Communion on Fridays* (1852), *The Lily of the Field and the Bird of the Air* (1854), *Practice in Christianity* (1855), *This Must Be Said* (1855), *The Moment* (1855), and *The Concept of Anxiety* (1855). In 1845, the eighteen discourses of 1843-1844 were remaindered to Philip G. Philipsen, and in 1847 the other eight books in print at the time (with the exception of *Postscript*) were remaindered to Carl A. Reitzel.

[51] *JP* VI 6407 (*Pap.* X¹ A 351).
[52] See *Either/Or*, II, pp. 414-29, *KW* IV (*Pap.* IV B 59).
[53] *JP* VI 6374 (*Pap.* X¹ A 192).
[54] No. 129, March 10, 1843.

full, closely printed sheets [864 pages] . . .. The book may be
called a monster, for it is impressive by its very mass . . .."[55]
He concluded: "One closes the book and says, 'That's enough
[*Basta*]! I have enough of *Either*; I do not want any of *Or*.' . . .
The reader whose approach to the book I have described is
'one' . . .. Some individuals may, however, be curious to
learn what sort of *Or* the author contrasts to such an *Either*, and
they will begin at least to page through the second volume."[56]
Victor Eremita's public response came in "A Word of Thanks
to Professor Heiberg,"[57] and drafts of unpublished pieces and
journal entries reflect Kierkegaard's displeasure at the uncom-
prehending superficiality of Heiberg's reading and appraisal.[58]
More substantial and reflective reviews by Johan F. Hagen and
by Hans P. Koefoed-Hansen appeared in *Fædrelandet*[59] and in
For Literatur og Kritik.[60]

Kierkegaard gives his own estimate of *Either/Or* in two
journal entries from around the time of its publication.

My Opinion of "Either/Or"

There was a young man as favorably endowed as an Alcibiades. He lost his way in the world. In his need he looked
about for a Socrates but found none among his contemporaries. Then he requested the gods to change him into one.
But now—he who had been so proud of being an Alcibiades
was so humiliated and humbled by the gods' favor that, just
when he received what he could be proud of, he felt inferior
to all.[61]

---

[55] Ibid., p. 291.

[56] Ibid.

[57] *Fædrelandet*, 1168, March 5, 1843; Corsair *Affair*, pp. 17-21, *KW* XIII (*SV* XIII 411-15).

[58] See *Either/Or*, II, pp. 397–407, *KW* IV (*Pap.* IV B 27-30, 32-33, 36-39, 41-46, 48-56; A 162). For Kierkegaard's unpublished response to the review by Claud Rosenhoff in *Den Frisindede*, 23, February 23, 1843, see *Either/Or*, II, pp. 392–97, *KW* IV (*Pap.* IV B 21-24).

[59] No. 1227-28, 1234, 1241, May 7, 14, 21, 1843. See *Either/Or*, II, pp. 426–29, *KW* IV (*Pap.* IV B 59, pp. 223-25).

[60] I, 1843, pp. 377-405.

[61] *JP* V 5613 (*Pap.* IV A 43).

Even if I proved nothing else by writing *Either/Or*, I proved that in Danish literature one can write a book, that one can work, without needing the warm jacket of sympathy,[62] without needing the incentives of anticipation, that one can work even though the stream is against one, that one can work hard without seeming to, that one can privately concentrate while practically every bungling student dares look upon one as a loafer. Even if the book itself were devoid of meaning, the making of it would still be the pithiest epigram I have written over the maundering philosophic age in which I live.[63]

---

[62] In *From the Papers of One Still Living, KW* I (*SV* XIII 72 fn.), Kierkegaard criticized the view found in Hans Christian Andersen's *Only a Fiddler* that " 'Genius is an egg that needs warmth for the fertilization of good fortune; otherwise it becomes a wind-egg' " (quoted from H. C. Andersen, *Kun en Spillemand*, I-III (Copenhagen: 1837; *ASKB* 1503), I, p. 161 (ed. tr.). In 1849, Kierkegaard sent Andersen a copy of the second edition of *Either/Or* and received the following reply (*Letters*, Letter 206, *KW* XXV):

> Copenhagen
> May 15, 1849.
>
> Dear Mr. Kierkegaard,
> You have given me really great pleasure by sending me your *Either/Or*. I was, as you can well understand, quite surprised; I had no idea at all that you entertained friendly thoughts of me, and yet I now find it to be so. God bless you for it! Thank you, thank you!
>
> Yours with heartfelt sincerity,
> H. C. ANDERSEN

[63] *JP* V 5614 (*Pap*. IV A 45).

EITHER/OR

A FRAGMENT OF LIFE

edited by
Victor Eremita

PART I

CONTAINING A'S PAPERS

Is reason then alone baptized,
are the passions pagans?

YOUNG

It may at times have occurred to you, dear reader, to doubt somewhat the accuracy of that familiar philosophical thesis that the outer is the inner and the inner is the outer.[2] Perhaps you yourself have concealed a secret that in its joy or in its pain you felt was too intimate to share with others. Perhaps your life has put you in touch with people about whom you suspected that something of this nature was the case, although neither by force nor by inveiglement were you able to bring out into the open that which was hidden. Perhaps neither case applies to you and your life, and yet you are not unacquainted with that doubt; like a fleeting shape, it has drifted through your mind now and then. A doubt such as this comes and goes, and no one knows whence it comes or whither it goes.[3] I myself have always been rather heretically minded on this philosophical point and therefore early in my life developed the habit of making observations and investigations as well as possible. For guidance, I have consulted the authors whose view I shared in this respect—in brief, I have done all I could to make up for what has been left undone in the philosophical writings. Gradually, then, hearing became my most cherished sense, for just as the voice is the disclosure of inwardness incommensurable with the exterior, so the ear is the instrument that apprehends this inwardness, hearing the sense by which it is appropriated. Consequently, every time I found a contradiction between what I saw and what I heard, my doubt was confirmed and my zeal for observation increased. A priest who hears confessions is separated by a grillwork from the person making confession; he does not see him, he only hears. As he listens, he gradually forms a picture of the other's outward appearance corresponding to what he hears; thus he finds no contradiction. It is different, however, when one sees and hears simultaneously but sees a grillwork between oneself and the speaker. My efforts to make observations along this line have been quite varied as far as results are concerned. At times I have had luck, at times not, and to obtain any returns along these paths, one needs luck. But I have never lost the desire to continue my investigations. If at times I have been about to regret my persistence, so also at times my efforts have been crowned with unexpected good fortune. It was just such unexpected good fortune that in a most curious manner put me in possession of the papers I hereby have the honor to present to the reading public. In these papers, I had an opportunity to take a look at the lives of two men, which confirmed my suspicion that the outer is not the inner. This was especially true of one of them. His exterior has been a complete contradiction of his interior. To a certain extent, it is also true of the other, inasmuch as he has hidden a more significant interior under a rather insignificant exterior.

For the sake of order, it is probably best to tell first how I happened to come into possession of these papers. It is now about seven years since I spotted in a secondhand shop here in the city a writing desk that immediately attracted my attention. It was not a modern piece of work, had been used considerably, and yet it captivated me. It is impossible for me to explain the basis of this impression, but most people presumably have had a similar experience during their lives. My daily route took me past this secondhand dealer and his writing desk, and I never let a day go by without fixing my eyes on it in passing. Gradually that desk assumed a history for me; to see it became a necessity to me, and when on a rare occasion it was necessary to make a detour for its sake, I did not hesitate. With time, as I looked at it, the desire awakened in me to own it. To be sure, I felt that it was a strange desire, since I had no use for this piece of furniture, and it would be a prodigality for me to purchase it. But desire, as is known, is very sophistical. I found a pretext for going into the secondhand shop, inquired about other things, and as I was about to leave I casually made a very low offer for the writing desk. I thought the dealer would possibly accept it. In that case, it would be a coincidence that played into my hands. It certainly was not for the sake of the money that I acted this way, but for the sake of my conscience. It misfired; the dealer was exceptionally rigid. For a time, I again walked by every day and gazed at the desk with enamored eyes. You must make up your mind, I thought. Suppose it is sold; then it is too late, and even if you managed to get hold of it again, you still would never have the same impression of it. My heart pounded when I went into the shop. I bought it and paid for it. This is the last time you are going to be so prodigal, I thought. In fact, it is really lucky that you did buy it, for every time you look at it you will be reminded of how prodigal you were; with this desk commences a new period in your life. Ah, desire is very eloquent, and good intentions are always on hand.

The writing desk was set up in my apartment, and just as in the first phase of my infatuation I had my pleasure in gazing at it from the street, so now I walked by it here at home. Gradually I learned to know its numerous features, its many drawers and compartments, and in every respect I was happy with my desk. But it was not to remain that way. In the summer of 1836, my duties allowed me to make a little journey to the country for a week. Arrangements were made with the coachman for five o'clock in the morning. The clothes I needed to take along had been packed the previous evening; everything was in order. I was already awake at four o'clock, but the picture of the beautiful countryside I was going to visit had such an intoxicating effect on me that I fell asleep again or into a dream. Presumably my servant wanted me to have all the sleep I could get, for he did not call me until six-thirty. The coachman was already blowing his horn, and although ordinarily I am disinclined to obey the orders of others, I have always made an exception of a coachman and his poetic motifs. I dressed quickly and was already at the door when the thought crossed my mind: Do you have enough money in your pocketbook? There was not much. I opened the desk to pull out the money drawer and take what happened to be at hand. But the drawer would not budge. Every expedient was futile. It was a most calamitous situation. To run into such difficulties at the very moment when the coachman's enticing tones were still ringing in my ears! The blood rushed to my head; I was furious. Just as Xerxes had the sea whipped,[4] so I decided to take dreadful revenge. A hatchet was fetched. I gave the desk a terrible blow with it. Whether in my rage I aimed wrong or the drawer was just as stubborn as I, the result was not what was intended. The drawer was shut, and the drawer stayed shut. But something else happened. Whether my blow struck precisely this spot or the vibration through the entire structure of the desk was the occasion, I do not know, but this I do know—a secret door that I had never noticed before sprung open. This door closed off a compartment that I obviously had not discovered. Here, to my great amazement, I found a mass of papers, the papers that constitute the contents of the present publication. My decision remained unchanged. At the first post house, I would borrow some money. In the greatest haste, a mahogany box that usually contained a pair of pistols was emptied and the papers deposited into it. Joy was victorious and had gained an unexpected augmentation. In my heart, I begged the desk's forgiveness for the rough treatment, while my thought found its suspicion strengthened—that the outer is certainly not the inner—and my experiential thesis was confirmed: it takes a stroke of luck to make such discoveries.

In the middle of the forenoon, I reached Hillerød,[5] straightened out my finances, and gained an overall impression of the glorious region. Right away the next morning, I began my excursions, which now took on quite another character than I originally had intended. My servant accompanied me with the mahogany box. I looked for a romantic spot in the forest where I would be as safe as possible from any surprise and there took out the documents. The innkeeper, noticing these frequent rambles in the company of a mahogany box, volunteered that perhaps I was practicing shooting with my pistols. I was much obliged to him for this remark and let him continue under that impression.

A quick look at the discovered papers readily showed me that they formed two groups, with a marked external difference as well. The one was written on a kind of letter-vellum, in quarto, with a rather wide margin. The handwriting was legible, sometimes even a bit meticulous, in one place slovenly. The other was written on full sheets of beehive paper[6] with ruled columns such as legal documents and the like are written on. The handwriting was distinct, somewhat drawn out, uniform and even; it seemed to be that of a businessman. The contents immediately appeared to be different also: the one contained a number of esthetic essays of varying lengths; the other consisted of two long studies and a shorter one, all with ethical content, it seemed, and in the form of letters. On closer inspection, this difference was entirely confirmed. The latter group does indeed consist of letters written to the author of the first group.

But it is necessary to find a more concise expression to characterize the two authors. With that in mind, I have gone through the papers very carefully but have found nothing or practically nothing. As far as the first author, the esthete, is concerned, there is no information at all about him. As far as the other, the letter writer, is concerned, we learn that his name is William and that he has been a judge, but the court is not stipulated. If I were to hold scrupulously to the historical and call him William, I would lack a corresponding designation for the first author; I would be obliged to give him an arbitrary name. For this reason, I have preferred to call the first author A, the second B.

Besides the longer pieces, a number of scraps of paper were found on which were written aphorisms, lyrical utterances and reflections. The handwriting itself indicated that they belonged to A, and the contents confirmed this.

Then I tried to organize the papers in the best manner. With B's papers it was rather easy to do. One letter presupposes the other. In the second letter, we find a quotation from the first; the third letter presupposes the two preceding ones.

Organizing A's papers was not so easy. Therefore I have let chance fix the order—that is, I have let them remain in the order in which I found them, without, of course, being able to decide whether this order has chronological value or ideal significance. The scraps of paper lay loose in the compartment, and I therefore had to assign them a place. I have placed them first, because it seemed to me that they could best be regarded as preliminary glimpses into what the longer pieces develop more coherently. I have called them Διαψάλματα[7] and added as a kind of motto: *ad se ipsum* [to himself].[8] In a way, this title and the motto are by me and yet not by me. They are by me insofar as they are applied to the whole collection, but they belong to A himself, for the word Διαψάλματα was written on one of the scraps of paper, and on two of them appear the words *ad se ipsum*. In keeping with what A himself has often done, I have also had printed on the inside of the title page a short French poem found above one of these aphorisms. Inasmuch as the majority of these aphorisms have a lyrical form, I thought it appropriate to use the word Διαψάλματα as the general title. If the reader considers this an unfortunate choice, I owe it to the truth to admit that it is my own idea and that the word certainly was used with discrimination by A himself for the aphorism over which it was found. [9]The ordering of the individual aphorisms I have left to chance. That the particular expressions often contradict one another, I found entirely appropriate, for this indeed belongs essentially to the mood; I decided it was not worth the trouble to arrange them so the contradictions were less obvious. I followed chance, and it is also chance that called my attention to the fact that the first and last aphorisms are somewhat complementary in that the one piercingly feels, as it were, the pain of being a poet, and the other relishes the satisfaction in always having the laughter on one's side.

As far as A's esthetic treatises are concerned, there is nothing about them that I would stress. They were all ready for printing, and if they contain any difficulties, I must let them speak for themselves. For my part, may I point out that to the Greek quotations found here and there I have added a translation taken from one of the better German translations.

[10]The last of A's papers is a narrative titled "The Seducer's Diary." Here we meet new difficulties, inasmuch as A does not declare himself the author but only the editor. This is an

old literary device to which I would not have much to object
if it did not further complicate my own position, since one author becomes enclosed within the other like the boxes in a
Chinese puzzle. This is not the place to explain in greater detail
what confirms me in my view; I shall only point out that the
prevailing mood in A's preface somehow manifests the poet.

It really seems as if A himself had become afraid of his fiction, [11]which, like a troubled dream, continued to make him
feel uneasy, also in the telling. If it was an actual event of
which he had secret knowledge, then I find it strange that the
preface carries no trace of A's joy over seeing the realization of
the idea he had often vaguely entertained. The idea of the seducer is suggested in the piece on the immediate erotic as well
as in "Silhouettes"—namely, that the counterpart to Don Giovanni must be a reflective seducer in the category of the interesting,[12] where the issue therefore is not how many he seduces
but how. I find no trace of such joy in the preface but indeed,
as noted previously, a trepidation, a certain horror, that presumably has its basis in his poetic relation to this idea. And A's
reaction does not surprise me, for I, too, who have nothing at
all to do with this narrative—indeed, am twice removed from
the original author—I, too, sometimes have felt quite
strangely uneasy when I have been occupied with these papers
in the stillness of the night. It seemed to me as if the seducer
himself paced my floor like a shadow, as if he glanced at the
papers, as if he fixed his demonic eyes on me, and said, "Well,
well, so you want to publish my papers! You know that is irresponsible of you; you will indeed arouse anxiety in the darling girls. But, of course, in recompense you will make me and
my kind innocuous. There you are mistaken, for I merely
change the method, and so my situation is all the more advantageous. What a flock of young girls will run straight into a
man's arms when they hear the seductive name: a seducer!
Give me half a year, and I will produce a story that will be ever
so much more interesting than everything I have so far experienced. I picture to myself a young, energetic girl of genius
having the extraordinary idea of wanting to avenge her sex on
me. She thinks she will be able to coerce me, to make me taste
the pains of unhappy love. That, you see, is a girl for me. If she

herself does not think of it profoundly enough, I shall come to her assistance. I shall writhe like the Molbos' eel.[13] And when I have brought her to the point where I want her, then she is mine."

But perhaps I have already misused my position as editor to burden the readers with my observations. The situation must be my excuse; the dubiousness of my position, owing to A's calling himself the editor and not the author of this narrative, allowed me to be carried away.

Anything else I have to add about this narrative I can do only in my role as editor. That is, I believe that in this narrative there is a specification of time. Here and there in the diary a date is given, but the year is lacking. Thus, I seem unable to go further, but I believe that by scrutinizing the dates more closely I have found a lead. Admittedly, every year has an April 7, a July 3, an August 2, etc., but it by no means follows that April 7 is a Monday every year. I have done some checking and have found out that this specification fits the year 1834. Whether A has thought of this, I cannot decide, but I hardly think so, for in that case he would not have taken as much precaution as he otherwise does. Nor does the diary say: Monday, April 7, etc. It says merely: April 7. In fact, the entry begins like this: So, on Monday—and attention is thereby diverted, but by reading through the entry under this date one sees that it must have been a Monday. I have, then, a specified time for this narrative, but every attempt I have made so far to use it to determine the time of the other treatises has failed. I could just as well have assigned it place number three, but, as I said before, I have preferred to let chance prevail, and everything remains in the order in which I found it.

As far as B's papers are concerned, they order themselves easily and naturally. But I did make one change in them: I have permitted myself to give them titles, because the letter form made it difficult for the author to give a title to these inquiries. Should the reader, therefore, after familiarizing himself with the contents, find that the titles were not felicitously chosen, I shall always be willing to put up with the pain inherent in having done something wrong when one wanted to do something well.

Occasionally there is in the margin a comment, which I have made into a footnote lest I encroach distractingly upon the text.

As far as B's manuscript is concerned, I have not permitted myself to make any changes whatsoever but have scrupulously regarded it as a document. Perhaps I could easily have deleted an occasional negligence, which is quite understandable when one considers that he is merely a letter writer. I did not wish to do so, because I feared going too far. When B supposes that out of a hundred people who go astray in the world ninety-nine are saved by women and one by divine grace,[14] it is easy to see that he is not very good in mathematics, inasmuch as he gives no place to those who are actually lost. I could easily have made a little change in the numbers, but to me there is something much more beautiful in B's miscalculation. In another place, B mentions a Greek wise man by the name of Myson and relates that he enjoyed the rare good fortune of being counted among the seven sages, when their number is set at fourteen.[15] For a while, I was perplexed about the source of B's wisdom and also about which Greek author he could be quoting. I immediately suspected that it was Diogenes Laertius,[16] and by checking Jøcher[17] and Morèri[18] I did indeed find reference to him. B's account might very well need correction, for the matter does not stand just as he relates, even though among the ancients there is some uncertainty in the designation of who the seven sages were, but I still did not think it worth the trouble; it seemed to me that his remark, even though not exactly historical, did have another value.

As early as five years ago, I had reached the point where I am at present; I had ordered the papers as they are now arranged, had decided to publish them, but nevertheless felt it was best to wait for a time. I considered five years a suitable interval. These five years are over, and I begin where I left off. Presumably I need not reassure the reader that I have not left untried any means of tracing the authors. The secondhand dealer did not keep records, which, as is commonly known, is rarely the case with secondhand dealers; he did not know from whom he had purchased that piece of furniture. He seemed to remember buying it at a mixed auction. I shall not venture to tell the reader about the many futile attempts that have cost me so much time, so much the less because recollection of them is no pleasure to me. I can share the results with the reader very briefly, for the results were nothing at all.

As I was about to carry out my decision to publish these papers, I had one particular misgiving. Perhaps the reader will permit me to speak quite candidly. The question occurred to me whether I might not become guilty of an indiscretion toward the unknown authors. But the more familiar I became with the papers, the more that misgiving diminished. The papers were of such a nature that, despite all my careful scrutiny, they yielded no information. A reader would be even less likely to find anything, since I do presume to be the equal of any reader, not in taste and sympathy and insight, but certainly in diligence and indefatigability. Therefore, if it was assumed that the unknown authors were still alive, that they lived here in the city, that they would unexpectedly recognize their own papers—nevertheless, nothing would result from the publication, provided that the authors themselves remained silent, for, in the most rigorous sense, these papers, as is ordinarily said of all printed matter, are silent.

Another misgiving I had was in and by itself less important, fairly easy to dismiss, and has been dismissed even more easily than I had expected. It occurred to me, namely, that these papers could become a financial consideration. I thought that it would be quite proper for me to accept a little honorarium for my pains as editor, but I would have to regard an author's honorarium as much too large. Just as the honest Scottish farmers in *The White Lady*[19] decide to buy the estate and cultivate it and then give it to the earls of Evenel if they should ever come back, so I decided to invest the honorarium on behalf of the unknown authors in order, if they should ever come forward, to be able to give them the whole amount together with interest and interest on the interest. If the reader has not already decided on the basis of my complete awkwardness that I am no author, nor a literary man who makes a profession of being an editor, then the naïveté of this reasoning will surely remove all doubts. This misgiving, then, was dismissed far more easily, for an author's honorarium in Denmark is no manorial estate, and the unknown authors would have to stay away a long time before their honorarium, even with interest and interest on the interest, would become a financial consideration.

All that remained was only to give these papers a title. I could call them Papers, Posthumous Papers, Found Papers, Lost Papers, etc. There is, of course, a multiplicity of variations, but none of these titles satisfied me. In determining the title, I have therefore allowed myself some freedom, a deception for which I shall attempt to give an accounting. In my continual preoccupation with these papers, it dawned on me that they might take on a new aspect if they were regarded as belonging to one person. I know very well all the objections that could be made against this view—that it is unhistorical, and that it is improbable inasmuch as it is unreasonable that one person could be the author of both parts, although the reader could easily be tempted by the pun that [20]when one has said A, one must also say B. Nevertheless I have been unable to abandon the idea. So, then, there was a person who in his lifetime had experienced both movements or had reflected upon both movements. A's papers contain a multiplicity of approaches to an esthetic view of life. A coherent esthetic view of life can hardly be presented. B's papers contain an ethical view of life. As I allowed my soul to be influenced by this thought, it became clear to me that I could let it guide me in determining the title. The title I have chosen expresses precisely this. The reader cannot lose much because of this title, for during his reading he may very well forget the title. Then, when he has read the book, he can perhaps think of the title. This will release him from every final question—whether A actually was persuaded and repented, whether B was victorious, or whether perhaps B finally came around to A's thinking. In this respect, these papers come to no conclusion. If someone finds this inappropriate, he is still not justified in calling it a defect but ought to call it a misfortune. I for my part regard it as a piece of good fortune. We sometimes come upon novels in which specific characters represent contrasting views of life. They usually end with one persuading the other. The point of view ought to speak for itself, but instead the reader is furnished with the historical result that the other was persuaded. I consider it fortunate that these papers provide no enlightenment in this respect. Whether A wrote the esthetic pieces after receiving B's letters, whether his soul subsequently continued to flounder around in its wild unruliness or whether it calmed down—I do not find myself capable of offering the slightest enlightenment about this, inasmuch as the papers contain nothing. Neither do they contain any hint as to how it went with B, whether he was able to hold fast to his point of view or not. Thus, when the book is read, A and B are forgotten; only the points of view confront each other and expect no final decision in the particular personalities.

I have nothing more to say, except that it occurred to me that the honored authors, if they were aware of my undertaking, might wish to complement their papers with a word to the reader. I shall therefore add a few words with a guided pen. A presumably would have no objection to the publication of the papers,[21] and he probably would shout to the reader, "Read them or do not read them, you will regret it either way." [22]What B would say is more difficult to determine. He perhaps would reproach me for something or other, especially with regard to the publication of A's papers; he would make me feel that he had no part in it, that he would wash his hands. Having done that, he perhaps would address the book with these words: "Go out into the world, then; avoid, if possible, the attention of the critics; visit an individual reader in a favorably disposed hour, and if you should encounter a reader of the fair sex, then I would say: My charming reader, in this book you will find something that you perhaps should not know, something else from which you will presumably benefit by

I
xvi

coming to know it. Read, then, the something in such a way that, having read it, you may be as one who has not read it;[23] read the something else in such a way that, having read it, you may be as one who has not forgotten what has been read." As editor, I shall add only the wish that the book may meet the reader in a favorably disposed hour and that the charming reader may succeed in scrupulously following B's well-intentioned advice.[24]

November 1842

EDITOR

ΔΙΑΨΑΛΜΑΤΑ[1]

ad se ipsum
[to himself][2]

Grandeur, savoir, renommée,
Amitié, plaisir et bien,
Tout n'est que vent, que fumée:
Pour mieux dire, tout n'est rien
[Greatness, knowledge, renown,
Friendship, pleasure and possessions,
All is only wind, only smoke:
To say it better, all is nothing].[3]

[4]What is a poet? An unhappy person who conceals profound anguish in his heart but whose lips are so formed that as sighs and cries pass over them they sound like beautiful music. It is with him as with the poor wretches in Phalaris's bronze bull, who were slowly tortured over a slow fire; their screams could not reach the tyrant's ears to terrify him; to him they sounded like sweet music.[5] And people crowd around the poet and say to him, "Sing again soon"—in other words, may new sufferings torture your soul, and may your lips continue to be formed as before, because your screams would only alarm us, but the music is charming. And the reviewers step up and say, "That is right; so it must be according to the rules of esthetics." Now of course a reviewer resembles a poet to a hair, except that he does not have the anguish in his heart, or the music on his lips. Therefore, I would rather be a swineherd out on Amager[6] and be understood by swine than be a poet and be misunderstood by people.[7]

It is common knowledge that the first question in the first and most compendious instruction given to a child is this: What does baby want? The answer is: Da-da.[8] And with such observations life begins, and yet we deny hereditary sin.[9] And yet whom does the child have to thank for his first thrashings, whom else but his parents.

I prefer to talk with children, for one may still dare to hope that they may become rational beings; but those who have become that—good Lord![10]

How unreasonable people are! They never use the freedoms they have but demand those they do not have; they have freedom of thought—they demand freedom of speech.

[11]I don't feel like doing anything. I don't feel like riding—
the motion is too powerful; I don't feel like walking—it is too
tiring; I don't feel like lying down, for either I would have to
stay down, and I don't feel like doing that, or I would have to
get up again, and I don't feel like doing that, either. *Summa
Summarum*: I don't feel like doing anything.

There are, as is known, insects that die in the moment of fertilization. So it is with all joy: life's highest, most splendid moment of enjoyment is accompanied by death.[12]

Tested Advice for Authors[13]

One carelessly writes down one's personal observations, has
them printed, and in the various proofs one will eventually acquire a number of good ideas. Therefore, take courage, you
who have not yet dared to have something printed. Do not despise typographical errors,[14] and to become witty by means of
typographical errors may be considered a legitimate way to
become witty.

[15]Generally speaking, the imperfection in everything human
is that its aspirations are achieved only by way of their opposites. I shall not discuss the variety of formations, which can
give a psychologist plenty to do (the melancholy have the best
sense of the comic, the most opulent often the best sense of the
rustic, the dissolute often the best sense of the moral, the
doubter often the best sense of the religious), but merely call
to mind that it is through sin that one gains a first glimpse of
salvation.

[16]In addition to my other numerous acquaintances, I have
one more intimate confidant—my depression. In the midst of
my joy, in the midst of my work, he[17] beckons to me, calls me
aside, even though physically I remain on the spot. My
depression is the most faithful mistress I have known—no
wonder, then, that I return the love.

There is a rambling of loquacity[18] that in its interminability has the same relation to the result as the incalculable lists of Egyptian kings have to the historical outcome.

Old age fulfills the dreams of youth. One sees this in Swift: in his youth he built an insane asylum; in his old age he himself entered it.[19]

[20]It is cause for alarm to note with what hypochondriac profundity Englishmen of an earlier generation have spotted the ambiguity basic to laughter. Thus Dr. Hartley[21] has observed: dass wenn sich das Lachen zuerst bei Kindern zeiget, so ist es ein entstehendes Weinen, welches durch Schmerz erregt wird, oder ein plötzlich gehemtes und in sehr kurzen Zwischenräumen wiederholtes Gefühl des Schmerzens [that when laughter first makes its appearance in the child, it is a nascent cry that is excited by pain or a suddenly arrested feeling of pain repeated at very short intervals] (see Flögel, *Geschichte der comischen Litteratur*,[22] I, p. 50). What if everything in the world were a misunderstanding; what if laughter really were weeping!

[23]There are particular occasions when one may be most painfully moved to see a person standing utterly alone in the world. The other day I saw a poor girl walking utterly alone to church to be confirmed.

[24]Cornelius Nepos tells of a general who was kept confined with a considerable cavalry regiment in a fortress; to keep the horses from being harmed because of too much inactivity, he had them whipped daily[25]—in like manner, I live in this age as one besieged, but lest I be harmed by sitting still so much, I cry myself tired.

[26]I say of my sorrow what the Englishman says of his house: My sorrow *is my castle.*[27] Many people look upon having sorrow as one of life's conveniences.

[28]I feel as a chessman must feel when the opponent says of it: That piece cannot be moved.

[29]*Aladdin*[30] is so very refreshing because this piece has the audacity of the child, of the genius, in the wildest wishes. Indeed, how many are there in our day who truly dare to wish, dare to desire, dare to address nature neither with a polite child's *bitte, bitte* [please, please] nor with the raging frenzy of one damned? How many are there who—inspired by what is talked about so much in our age, that man is created in God's image—have the authentic voice of command? Or do we not all stand like Noureddin, bowing and scraping, worrying about asking too much or too little? Or is not every magnificent demanding eventually diminished to morbid reflecting over the *I*, from insisting to informing, which we are indeed brought up and trained to do.

[31]I am as timorous as a *sheva*,[32] as weak and muted as a *daghesch lene*;[33] I feel like a letter printed backward in the line, and yet as uncontrollable as a pasha with three horse tails,[34] as solicitous for myself and my thoughts as a bank for its banknotes, indeed, as reflected into myself as any *pronomen reflexivum* [reflexive pronoun]. Yes, if it were true of miseries and sorrows as it is true of conscious good deeds—that those who do them lose their reward—then I would be the happiest person, for I take all my cares in advance, and yet they all remain behind.

The tremendous poetical power of folk literature is manifest, among other ways, in its power to desire. In comparison, desire in our age is simultaneously sinful and boring, because it desires what belongs to the neighbor. Desire in folk literature is fully aware that the neighbor does not possess what it seeks any more than it does itself. And if it is going to desire sinfully, then it is so flagrant that people must be shocked. It is not going to let itself be beaten down by the cold probability calculations of a pedestrian understanding. Don Juan still strides across the stage with his 1,003 ladyloves. Out of reverence for the venerableness of tradition, no one dares to smile. If a poet had dared to do this in our age, he would be laughed to scorn.

What a strange, sad mood came over me on seeing a poor wretch shuffling through the streets in a somewhat worn pale green coat flecked with yellow.[35] I felt sorry for him, but nevertheless what affected me most was that the color of this coat so vividly reminded me of my childhood's first productions in the noble art of painting. This particular color was one of my favorite colors. Is it not sad that these color combinations, which I still think of with so much joy, are nowhere to be found in life; the whole world finds them crude, garish, suitable only for Nürnberg prints.[36] If they are encountered occasionally, the meeting is always unfortunate, as this one is. It is always a feeble-minded person or a derelict—in short, always someone who feels alienated in life and whom the world will not acknowledge. And I, who always painted my heroes with this eternally unforgettable yellow-green tinge to their coats! Does this not happen with all the color combinations of childhood? The gleam that life had at that time gradually becomes too intense, too crude, for our dull eyes.

[37]Alas, fortune's door does not open inward so that one can push it open by rushing at it; but it opens outward, and therefore one can do nothing about it.

[38]I have, I believe, the courage to doubt everything; I have, I believe, the courage to fight against everything; but I do not have the courage to acknowledge anything, the courage to possess, to own, anything. Most people complain that the world is so prosaic that things do not go in life as in the novel, where opportunity is always so favorable. I complain that in life it is not as in the novel, where one has hardhearted fathers and nisses and trolls to battle, and enchanted princesses to free. What are all such adversaries together compared with the pale, bloodless, tenacious-of-life nocturnal forms with which I battle and to which I myself give life and existence.

I
8

[39]How sterile my soul and my mind are, and yet constantly tormented by empty voluptuous and excruciating labor pains! Will the tongue ligament of my spirit never be loosened; will I always jabber? [40]What I need is a voice as piercing as the glance of Lynceus,[41] as terrifying as the groan of the giants,[42] as sustained as a sound of nature,[43] as mocking as an icy gust of wind, as malicious as echo's heartless taunting, extending in range from the deepest bass to the most melting high notes, and modulated from a solemn-silent whisper to the energy of rage. That is what I need in order to breathe, to give voice to what is on my mind, to have the viscera of both anger and sympathy shaken. —But my voice is only hoarse like the scream of a gull or moribund like the blessing on the lips of the mute.

What is going to happen? What will the future bring? I do not know, I have no presentiment. [44]When a spider flings itself from a fixed point down into its consequences, it continually sees before it an empty space in which it can find no foothold, however much it stretches. So it is with me; before me is continually an empty space, and I am propelled by a consequence that lies behind me. This life is turned around and dreadful, not to be endured.

[45]The most beautiful time is the first period of falling in love, when, from every encounter, every glance, one fetches home something new to rejoice over.

[46]My observation of life makes no sense at all. I suppose that an evil spirit has put a pair of glasses on my nose, one lens of which magnifies on an immense scale and the other reduces on the same scale.

The doubter is Μεμαστιγομένος [one who is whipped];[47] like a spinning top, he remains on the point for a shorter or longer period depending on the strokes of the whip; he is not able to remain on the point any more than the top is.[48]

The most ludicrous of all ludicrous things, it seems to me, is to be busy in the world, to be a man who is brisk at his meals and brisk at his work. Therefore, when I see a fly settle on the nose of one of those men of business in a decisive moment,[49] or if he is splashed by a carriage that passes him in even greater haste, or Knippelsbro[50] tilts up, or a roof tile falls and kills him,[51] I laugh from the bottom of my heart. And who could keep from laughing? What, after all, do these busy bustlers achieve? Are they not just like that woman who, in a flurry because the house was on fire, rescued the fire tongs? What more, after all, do they salvage from life's huge conflagration?

[52]On the whole, I lack the patience to live. I cannot see the grass grow, and if I cannot do that, I do not care to look at it at all. My views are the superficial observations of a *"fahrender Scholastiker* [traveling scholastic]"[53] who dashes through life in the greatest haste. It is said that our Lord satisfies the stomach before the eyes. That is not what I find: my eyes are surfeited and bored with everything, and yet I hunger.

[54]Ask me what you wish; just do not ask me for reasons. A young girl is excused for not being able to state reasons; she lives in feelings, it is said. It is different with me. Ordinarily I have so many and most often such mutually contradictory reasons that for this reason it is impossible for me to state reasons. It also seems to me that with cause and effect the relation does not hold together properly. Sometimes enormous and *gewaltige* [powerful] causes produce a very *klein* [small] and insignificant little effect, sometimes none at all; sometimes a nimble little cause produces a colossal effect.

[55]And now the innocent pleasures of life. It must be granted to them that they have only one flaw—that they are so innocent. Moreover, they are to be enjoyed in moderation. When my physician prescribes a diet for me, there is some reason in that; I abstain from certain specified foods for a certain specified time. But to be dietetic in keeping the diet—that is really asking too much.

I
10

Life for me has become a bitter drink, and yet it must be taken in drops, slowly, counting.

No one comes back from the dead; no one has come into the world without weeping. No one asks when one wants to come in; no one asks when one wants to go out.

Time passes, life is a stream, etc., so people say. That is not what I find: time stands still, and so do I. All the plans I project fly straight back at me; when I want to spit, I spit in my own face.

[56]When I get up in the morning, I go right back to bed again. I feel best in the evening the moment I put out the light and pull the feather-bed over my head. I sit up once more, look around the room with indescribable satisfaction, and then good night, down under the feather-bed.

What am I good for? For nothing or for anything whatever. It is a rare ability; I wonder if it will be appreciated in life? God knows whether places are found by girls looking for a job as a general servant or, for want of that, as anything whatever.

[57]One ought to be a riddle not only to others but also to oneself. I examine myself; when I am tired of that, I smoke a cigar for diversion and think: God knows what our Lord actually intended with me or what he wants to make of me.

[58]No woman in maternity confinement can have stranger and more impatient wishes than I have. Sometimes these wishes involve the most insignificant things, sometimes the most sublime, but they all have to an equally high degree the momentary passion of the soul. At this moment I wish for a bowl of buckwheat cereal. I recall from my school days that we always had buckwheat cereal on Wednesdays. I recall how smooth and white the cereal was served, how the butter smiled at me, how warm the cereal looked, how hungry I was, how impatient to get permission to begin. Such a bowl of

buckwheat cereal! I would give more than my birthright[59] for
it.

[60]Virgilius[*sic*] the sorcerer[61] had himself hacked to pieces
and put in a caldron to be cooked for eight days in order by this
process to be rejuvenated. He arranged for someone to watch
so that no interloper would peer into the caldron. But the
watchman could not resist the temptation; it was too soon,
and Virgilius, as an infant, disappeared with a scream. I dare
say that I also peered too soon into the caldron, into the caldron of life and the historical process, and most likely will never
manage to become more than a child.

"Never lose courage! When troubles pile up most appal-
lingly about you, you will see a helping hand in the clouds"—
so said His Reverence Jesper Morten[62] at vespers recently.
Well, I am accustomed to walking a great deal under the open
sky, but I have never noticed such a thing. A few days ago
while on a walking tour, I became aware of such a phenomenon. It was really not a hand, but more like an arm, that
reached out of the cloud. I fell into contemplation, and the
thought came to me: If only Jesper Morten were here so he
could decide whether this was the phenomenon he referred to.
As I stood there lost in these thoughts, a passerby addressed
me and said as he pointed up to the clouds, "Do you see that
funnel-shaped cloud? One seldom sees such a thing in these
parts. Sometimes it carries whole houses along with it." Good
heavens, I thought, is that a funnel-shaped cloud—and took to
my heels as fast as I could. What would His Reverence Jesper
Morten have done, I wonder, in my place?

I
12

Let others complain that the times are evil. I complain that
they are wretched, for they are without passion. People's
thoughts are as thin and fragile as lace, and they themselves as
pitiable as lace-making girls. The thoughts of their hearts are
too wretched to be sinful. It is perhaps possible to regard it as
sin for a worm to nourish such thoughts, but not for a human
being, who is created in the image of God. Their desires are

staid and dull, their passions drowsy. They perform their duties, these mercenary souls, but just like the Jews, they indulge
in trimming the coins a little; they think that, [63]even though
our Lord keeps ever so orderly an account book, they can still
manage to trick him a little. Fie on them! That is why my soul
always turns back to the Old Testament and to Shakespeare.
There one still feels that those who speak are human beings;
there they hate, there they love, there they murder the enemy,
curse his descendants through all generations—there they sin.

[64]My time I divide as follows: the one half I sleep; the other
half I dream. I never dream when I sleep; that would be a
shame, because to sleep is the height of genius.

To be a perfect human being is indeed the highest. Now I
have corns—that is always of some help.

My life achievement amounts to nothing at all, a mood, a
single color. My achievement resembles the painting by that
artist who was supposed to paint the Israelites' crossing of the
Red Sea and to that end painted the entire wall red and explained that the Israelites had walked across and that the Egyptians were drowned.

I
13

Human dignity is still acknowledged even in nature, for
when we want to keep birds away from the trees we set up
something that is supposed to resemble a human being, and
even the remote resemblance a scarecrow has to a human
being is sufficient to inspire respect.

If erotic love [*Elskov*] is to have any meaning, in its hour of
birth it must be shone upon by the moon, just as Apis, in order
to be the true Apis, must have been shone upon by the moon.
The cow that gave birth to Apis is said to have been shone
upon by the moon in the moment of conception.[65]

The best demonstration of the wretchedness of life
[*Tilværelse*] is that which is obtained through a consideration
of its glory.

Most people rush after pleasure so fast that they rush right past it. They are like that dwarf who guarded a kidnapped princess in his castle. One day he took a noon nap. When he woke up an hour later, she was gone. Hastily he pulls on his seven-league boots; with one step he is far past her.

[66]My soul is so heavy that no thought can carry it any longer, no wing beat can lift it up into the ether any more. If it is moved, it merely skims along the ground, just as birds fly low when a thunderstorm is blowing up. Over my inner being broods an oppressiveness, an anxiety, that forebodes an earth-quake.

How empty and meaningless life is. —We bury a man; we accompany him to the grave, throw three spadefuls of earth on him; we ride out in a carriage, ride home in a carriage; we find consolation in the thought that we have a long life ahead of us. But how long is seven times ten years? Why not settle it all at once, why not stay out there and go along down into the grave and draw lots to see to whom will befall the misfortune of being the last of the living who throws the last three spadefuls of earth on the last of the dead?

I
14

[67]Girls do not appeal to me. Their beauty passes away like a dream and like yesterday when it is past.[68] Their faithfulness— yes, their faithfulness! Either they are faithless—this does not concern me any more—or they are faithful. If I found such a one, she would appeal to me from the standpoint of her being a rarity; but from the standpoint of a long period of time she would not appeal to me, for either she would continually re-main faithful, and then I would become a sacrifice to my ea-gerness for experience, since I would have to bear with her, or the time would come when she would lapse, and then I would have the same old story.

[69]Wretched fate! In vain do you prink up your wrinkled face like an old prostitute, in vain do you jingle your fool's bells. You bore me; it is still the same, an *idem per idem* [the same by

the same]. No variation, always a rehash. Come, sleep and death; you promise nothing, you hold everything.

[70]Those two familiar violin strains! Those two familiar violin strains here this very moment out in the street. Have I lost my mind; out of love for Mozart's music, have my ears ceased to hear? Is this a reward of the gods, to give unhappy me, who sits like a beggar at the door of the temple,[71] ears that themselves perform what they hear? Only those two violin strains, for now I hear nothing more. Just as in that immortal overture[72] they burst forth out of the deep chorale tones, so here they disentangle themselves from the noise and tumult of the street with the total surprise of a revelation. —It must be close by, for now I hear the light dance tunes. —So it is to you that I owe this joy, you two unfortunate artists. —One of them was probably seventeen years old, wearing a green Kalmuk coat with large bone buttons. The coat was much too large for him. He held the violin tightly under his chin; his cap was pulled down over his eyes. His hand was concealed in a fingerless glove; his fingers were red and blue with cold. The other one was older and wore a chenille coat. Both were blind. A little girl, who presumably guided them, stood in front of them, thrust her hands under her scarf. We gathered one by one, a few admirers of those melodies—a postman with his mailbag, a little boy, a maidservant, a couple of dock workers. The elegant carriages rolled noisily by; the carts and wagons drowned out the melodies, which emerged fragmentarily for a moment. You two unfortunate artists, do you know that those strains hide in themselves the glories of the whole world? —Was it not like a rendezvous?—

In a theater, it happened that a fire started offstage. The clown came out to tell the audience. They thought it was a joke and applauded. He told them again, and they became still more hilarious. This is the way, I suppose, that the world will be destroyed—amid the universal hilarity of wits and wags who think it is all a joke.

What, if anything, is the meaning of this life? If people are divided into two great classes, it may be said that one class works for a living and the other does not have that need. But to work for a living certainly cannot be the meaning of life, since it is indeed a contradiction that the continual production of the conditions is supposed to be the answer to the question of the meaning of that which is conditional upon their production. The lives of the rest of them generally have no meaning except to consume the conditions. To say that the meaning of life is to die seems to be a contradiction also.

Real enjoyment consists not in what one enjoys but in the idea. If I had in my service a submissive jinni who, when I asked for a glass of water, would bring me the world's most expensive wines, deliciously blended, in a goblet, I would dismiss him until he learned that the enjoyment consists not in what I enjoy but in getting my own way.

So I am not the one who is the lord of my life; I am one of the threads to be spun into the calico of life! Well, then, even though I cannot spin, I can still cut the thread.

All will be acquired in stillness and made divine in silence. It is true not only of Psyche's expected child that its future depends on her silence.

> *Mit einem Kind, das göttlich, wenn Du schweigst—*
> *Doch menschlich, wenn Du das Geheimniss zeigst*
> [With child, divine, if you are silent—
> But human, if you disclose the secret].[73]

[74]I seem destined to have to suffer through[75] all possible moods, to be required to have experiences of all kinds. At every moment I lie out in the middle of the ocean like a child who is supposed to learn to swim. I scream (this I have learned from the Greeks, from whom one can learn the purely human). Admittedly, I have a swimming belt around my waist,

but I do not see the support that is supposed to hold me up. It is an appalling way to gain experience.

It is quite striking that the two most appalling contrasts provide a conception of eternity. If I picture that unfortunate bookkeeper who went mad in his despair over having ruined a business firm by stating in the account book that seven and six are fourteen—if I picture him, indifferent to everything else, repeating to himself day in and day out, "Seven and six are fourteen," I have a symbol *of* eternity. If I imagine a lush harem beauty, reclining on a couch in all her charm and unconcerned about anything in the world, then I have again a symbol *for* eternity.

[76]What philosophers say about actuality [*Virkelighed*] is often just as disappointing[77] as it is when one reads on a sign in a secondhand shop: Pressing Done Here. If a person were to bring his clothes to be pressed, he would be duped, for the sign is merely for sale.

[78]For me nothing is more dangerous than to recollect [*erindre*].[79] As soon as I have recollected a life relationship, that relationship has ceased to exist. It is said that absence makes the heart grow fonder. That is very true, but it becomes fonder in a purely poetic way. To live in recollection is the most perfect life imaginable; recollection is more richly satisfying than all actuality, and it has a security that no actuality possesses. A recollected life relationship has already passed into eternity and has no temporal interest anymore.

[80]If anyone should keep a diary, I am the one, in order to refresh my memory [*Hukommelse*][81] a bit. It frequently happens that with the passage of time I have completely forgotten the reasons that moved me to this or that, with regard not only to trivialities but also to the most crucial steps. If the reason occurs to me, it can sometimes be so strange that I cannot even believe that it was the reason. This doubt would be removed if I had something written to refer to. On the whole, a reason is a curious thing. If I regard it with all my passion, it develops

into an enormous necessity that can set heaven and earth in motion; if I am devoid of passion, I look down on it derisively. —For some time now, I have been speculating about what really was the reason that moved me to resign as a school-teacher. When I think about it now, it seems to me that such an appointment was just the thing for me. Today it dawned on me that the reason was precisely this—that I had to consider myself completely qualified for this post. If I had continued in my job, I would have had everything to lose, nothing to gain. For that reason, I considered it proper to resign my post and seek employment with a traveling theater company, because I had no talent and consequently had everything to gain.

It takes a lot of naïveté to believe that it helps to shout and scream in the world, as if one's fate would thereby be altered. Take what comes and avoid all complications. In my early years, when I went to a restaurant, I would say to the waiter: A good cut, a very good cut, from the loin, and not too fat. Perhaps the waiter would scarcely hear what I said. Perhaps it was even less likely that he would heed it, and still less that my voice would penetrate into the kitchen, influence the chef— and even if all this happened, there perhaps was not a good cut in the whole roast. Now I never shout anymore.

I
18

Social endeavors and the associated beautiful sympathy be-come more and more widespread. In Leipzig, a committee formed out of sympathy for the sad fate of old horses has de-cided to eat them.

[82]I have only one friend, and that is echo. Why is it my friend? Because I love my sorrow, and echo does not take it away from me. I have only one confidant, and that is the si-lence of night. Why is it my confidant? Because it remains si-lent.

[83]The same thing happened to me that, according to legend, happened to Parmeniscus, who in the Trophonean cave lost the ability to laugh but acquired it again on the island of Delos

upon seeing a shapeless block that was said to be the image of the goddess Leto.[84] When I was very young, I forgot in the Trophonean cave how to laugh; when I became an adult, when I opened my eyes and saw actuality, then I started to laugh and have never stopped laughing since that time. I saw that the meaning of life was to make a living, its goal to become a councilor, that the rich delight of love was to acquire a well-to-do girl, that the blessedness of friendship was to help each other in financial difficulties, that wisdom was whatever the majority assumed it to be, that enthusiasm was to give a speech, that courage was to risk being fined ten dollars, that cordiality was to say "May it do you good"[85] after a meal, that piety was to go to communion once a year.[86] This I saw, and I laughed.

[87]What is it that binds me? From what was the chain formed that bound the Fenris wolf?[88] It was made of the noise of cats' paws walking on the ground, of the beards of women, of the roots of cliffs, of the grass of bears, of the breath of fish, and of the spittle of birds. I, too, am bound in the same way by a chain formed of gloomy fancies, of alarming dreams, of troubled thoughts, of fearful presentiments, of inexplicable anxieties. This chain is "very flexible, soft as silk, yields to the most powerful strain, and cannot be torn apart."[89]

I
19

Strangely enough, it is always the same thing that preoccupies a person throughout all the ages of life, and one always goes just so far, or, rather, one goes backwards. In grammar school, when I was fifteen years old, I wrote very suavely on demonstrations for the existence of God and the immortality of the soul, on the concept of faith, and on the meaning of miracles. For my *examen artium* [student examination],[90] I wrote a composition on the immortality of the soul, for which I was awarded *præ ceteris* [distinction or first honors];[91] later I won the prize for a composition on this subject. Who would believe that in my twenty-fifth year, after such a solid and very promising beginning, I would have come to the point of not being able to present a single demonstration for the immortality of the soul. From my school days, I especially recall that a composition of mine on the immortality of the soul was extravagantly praised and read aloud by the teacher because of the excellence of language as well as of content. Alas, alas, alas! I threw away this composition long ago. How unfortunate! My doubting soul perhaps would have been captivated by it, by the language as well as by the content. So this is my advice to parents, superiors, and teachers—that they urge the children in their charge to keep the Danish compositions written in the fifteenth year. To give this advice is the only thing I can do for the benefit of the human race.

[92]To a knowledge of the truth, I perhaps have come; to salvation, surely not.[93] What shall I do? Be active in the world, people say. Should I then communicate my sorrow to the world, make one more contribution to prove how pitiable and wretched everything is, perhaps discover a new, hitherto undetected stain [*Plet*] in human life? I could then reap the rare reward of becoming famous, just like the man who discovered the spots [*Pletter*] on Jupiter.[94] I still prefer to remain silent.

[95]How much the same human nature is! With what innate genius a little child can often show us a vivid picture of the larger scale. I was really amused today by little Ludvig. He sat in his tiny chair and looked around with visible delight. Then the nursemaid, Maren, walked through the room. "Maren!" he shouted. "Yes, little Ludvig," she answered with her customary friendliness and came over to him. He tilted his big head to one side a bit, fastened his enormous eyes on her with a certain roguishness and then said quite phlegmatically, "Not this Maren; it was another Maren." What do we adults do? We shout to the whole world, and when it approaches us in a friendly manner we say, "It was not this Maren."

My life is like an eternal night; when I die, I shall be able to say with Achilles:

I
20

Du bist vollbracht, Nachtwache meines Daseyns
[You are fulfilled, nightwatch of my life].[96]

My life is utterly meaningless. When I consider its various epochs, my life is like the word *Schnur* in the dictionary, which first of all means a string, and second a daughter-in-law. All that is lacking is that in the third place the word *Schnur* means a camel, in the fourth a whisk broom.

[97]I am just like the Lüneburger swine. My thinking is a passion. I am expert at rooting up truffles for others; I find no pleasure in them myself. I take the problems on my nose, but I can do no more with them than to throw them back over my head.

[98]In vain do I resist. My foot slips. My life nevertheless remains a poet-existence. Can anything worse be imagined? I am predestined; fate laughs at me when it suddenly shows me how everything I do to resist becomes a factor in such an existence [*Tilværelse*]. I can describe hope so vividly that every hoping individual will recognize my description as his own; and yet it is forgery, for even as I am describing it I am thinking of recollection [*Erindring*].[99]

[100]But there is yet another demonstration of the existence of God that has hitherto been overlooked. It is introduced by a servant in Aristophanes' *The Knights*, 32-35 (Demosthenes and Nicias conversing):

Δημοσθένης.

ποῖον βρέτας; ἐτεὸν ἡγεῖ γὰρ θεούς;

Νικίας.

ἔγωγε.

Δημοσθένης.

ποίῳ χρώμενος τεκμηρίῳ;

Νικίας.

ὁτιὴ θεοῖσιν ἐχθρὸς εἰμ᾽ οὐκ εἰκότως;

Δημοσθένης.

35. εὖ προσβιβάζεις με.

[DE.   Stat-at-ues is it? What, do you really think
          That there *are* gods?

NIC.   I know it.

DE.   Know it! How?

NIC.   I'm such a wretched god-detested chap.

DE.   Well urged indeed].[101]

[102]How dreadful boredom is—how dreadfully boring; I know no stronger expression, no truer one, for like is recognized only by like. Would that there were a loftier, stronger expression, for then there would still be one movement. I lie prostrate, inert; the only thing I see is emptiness, the only thing I live on is emptiness, the only thing I move in is emptiness. I do not even suffer pain. The vulture pecked continually at Prometheus's liver;[103] the poison dripped down continually on Loki;[104] it was at least an interruption, even though monotonous. Pain itself has lost its refreshment for me. If I were offered all the glories of the world or all the torments of the world, one would move me no more than the other; I would not turn over to the other side either to attain or to avoid. I am dying death.[105] And what could divert me? Well, if I managed to see a faithfulness that withstood every ordeal [*Prøvelse*], an enthusiasm that endured everything, a faith that moved mountains;[106] if I were to become aware of an idea that joined the finite and the infinite. But my soul's poisonous doubt consumes everything. My soul is like the Dead Sea, over which no bird is able to fly; when it has come midway, it sinks down, exhausted, to death and destruction.

[107]How strange! With what equivocal anxiety about losing and keeping, people nevertheless cling to this life. At times I have considered taking a decisive step compared with which all previous ones were but child's play—to set out on the great voyage of discovery. As a ship is saluted with a cannonade when it is launched, so I would salute myself. And yet. Is it courage that I lack? If a stone fell down and killed me, that would still be a way out.

[108]Tautology is and remains the highest principle, the highest maxim of thought.[109] No wonder, then, that most people use it. It is not so impoverished, either, and can well fill out a whole life. It has a jesting, witty, entertaining form; this is [the category of] infinite judgments.[110] This kind of tautology is the paradoxical and transcendental kind. It has the serious, scientific, and edifying form. The formula is as follows: when two quantities are equal in size to one and the same third quantity, they are all of equal size.[111] This is a quantitative conclusion. This kind of tautology is especially useful on podiums and in pulpits, where one must say much.

[112]The disproportion of my body is that my forelegs are too short. Like the hare from New Holland,[113] I have very short forelegs but extremely long hind legs. Ordinarily, I sit very still; if I make a move, it is a tremendous leap, to the horror of all those to whom I am bound by the tender ties of kinship and friendship.

Either/Or[114]
An Ecstatic Discourse

Marry, and you will regret it. Do not marry, and you will also regret it. Marry or do not marry, you will regret it either way.[115] Whether you marry or you do not marry, you will regret it either way. Laugh at the stupidities of the world, and you will regret it; weep over them, and you will also regret it. Laugh at the stupidities of the world or weep over them, you will regret it either way. Whether you laugh at the stupidities of the world or you weep over them, you will regret it either way. Trust a girl, and you will regret it. Do not trust her, and you will also regret it. Trust a girl or do not trust her, you will regret it either way. Whether you trust a girl or do not trust her, you will regret it either way. Hang yourself, and you will regret it. Do not hang yourself, and you will also regret it. Hang yourself or do not hang yourself, you will regret it either way. Whether you hang yourself or do not hang yourself, you will regret it either way. This, gentlemen, is the quintessence of all the wisdom of life. It is not merely in isolated moments that I, as Spinoza says, view everything *aeterno modo* [in the mode of eternity],[116] but I am continually *aeterno modo*. Many believe they, too, are this when after doing one thing or another they unite or mediate these opposites. But this is a misunderstanding, for the true eternity does not lie behind either/ or but before it. Their eternity will therefore also be a painful temporal sequence, since they will have a double regret on which to live. My wisdom is easy to grasp, for I have only one maxim, and even that is not a point of departure for me. One must differentiate between the subsequent dialectic in either/ or and the eternal one suggested here. So when I say that my maxim is not a point of departure for me, this does not have the opposite of being a point of departure but is merely the negative expression of my maxim, that by which it comprehends itself in contrast to being a point of departure or not being a point of departure. My maxim is not a point of departure for me, because if I made it a point of departure, I would regret it, and if I did not make it a point of departure, I would also regret it. If one or another of my esteemed listeners thinks there is anything to what I have said, he merely demonstrates that he has no head for philosophy. If he thinks there is any movement in what has been said, this demonstrates the same thing. But for those listeners who are able to follow me, although I do not move, I shall now elucidate the eternal truth by which this philosophy is self-contained and does not concede anything higher. That is, if I made my maxim a point of departure, then I would be unable to stop, for if I did not stop, I would regret it, and if I did stop, I would also regret it, etc. But if I never start, then I can always stop, for my eternal starting is my eternal stopping. Experience shows that it is not at all difficult for philosophy to begin. Far from it. It begins, in fact, with nothing[117] and therefore can always begin. But it is always difficult for philosophy and philosophers to stop. This difficulty, too, I have avoided, for if anyone thinks that I, in stopping now, actually stop, he demonstrates that he does not have speculative comprehension. The point is that I do not

I
24

stop now, but I stopped when I began. My philosophy, therefore, has the advantageous characteristic of being brief and of
being irrefutable, for if anyone disputes me, I daresay I have
the right to declare him mad. The philosopher, then, is continually *aeterno modo* and does not have, as did the blessed Sintenis, only specific hours that are lived for eternity.[118]

[119]Why was I not born in Nyboder,[120] why did I not die as a
baby? Then my father would himself have laid me in a little
casket, taken me under his arm, carried me out to the grave on
a Sunday morning, would himself have cast the earth on it and
in a low voice said a few words understandable only to himself. Only in the happy days of yore could people have the idea
of babies weeping in Elysium because they died so prematurely.[121]

I have never been joyful, and yet it has always seemed as if
joy were my constant companion, as if the buoyant jinn of joy
danced around me, invisible to others but not to me, whose
eyes shone with delight. [122]Then when I walk past people,
happy-go-lucky as a god, and they envy me because of my
good fortune, I laugh, for I despise people, and I take my revenge. I have never wished to do anyone an injustice, but I
have always made it appear as if anyone who came close to me
would be wronged and injured. Then when I hear others
praised for their faithfulness, their integrity, I laugh, for I despise people, and I take my revenge. My heart has never been
hardened toward anyone, but I have always made it appear, especially when I was touched most deeply, as if my heart were
closed and alien to every feeling. Then when I hear others
lauded for their good hearts, see them loved for their deep,
rich feelings, then I laugh, for I despise people and take my revenge. When I see myself cursed, abhorred, hated for my
coldness and heartlessness, then I laugh, then my rage is satisfied. The point is that if the good people could make me be actually in the wrong, make me actually do an injustice—well,
then I would have lost.

I
25

[123]My misfortune is this: an angel of death always walks at my side, and it is not the doors of the chosen ones that I sprinkle with blood as a sign that he is to pass by[124]—no, it is precisely their doors that he enters—for only recollection's love is happy.

Wine no longer cheers my heart; a little of it makes me sad—much, depressed. My soul is dull and slack; in vain do I jab the spur of desire into its side; it is exhausted, it can no longer raise itself up in its royal jump. I have lost all my illusions. In vain do I seek to abandon myself in joy's infinitude; it cannot lift me, or, rather, I cannot lift myself. Previously, when it merely beckoned, I mounted, light, hearty, and cheerful. When I rode slowly through the forest, it seemed as if I were flying. Now, when the horse is covered with lather and is almost ready to drop, it seems to me that I do not move from the spot. I am alone, as I have always been—forsaken not by men, that would not pain me, but by the happy jinn of joy, who trooped around me in great numbers, who met acquaintances everywhere, showed me an opportunity everywhere. Just as an intoxicated man collects a wanton throng of young people around him, so they flocked about me, the elves of joy, and my smile was meant for them. My soul has lost possibility. If I were to wish for something, I would wish not for wealth or power but for the passion of possibility, for the eye, eternally young, eternally ardent, that sees possibility everywhere. Pleasure disappoints; possibility does not. And what wine is so sparkling, so fragrant, so intoxicating!

I
26

Where the rays of the sun do not reach, the tones still manage to come. My apartment is dark and gloomy; a high wall practically keeps out the light of day. It must be in the next courtyard, very likely a wandering musician. What instrument is it? A reed pipe? . . . . . What do I hear—the minuet from *Don Giovanni*. Carry me away, then, you rich, strong tones, to the ring of girls, to the delight of the dance. —The pharmacist pounds his mortar, the maid scrubs her kettle, the groom curries his horse and knocks the currycomb on the cobblestones.[125] These tones are only for me; only to me do they beckon. Oh, thank you, whoever you are! Thank you! My soul is so rich, so hearty, so intoxicated with joy!

Salmon is in itself very delicious eating, but too much of it is bad for the health, inasmuch as it is a heavy food. For this reason, once when there was a great catch of salmon, the police in Hamburg ordered each master of a household to give his servants salmon not more than once a week. Would that there might be a similar police notice with regard to sentimentality.

[126]My sorrow is my baronial castle, which lies like an eagle's nest high up on the mountain peak among the clouds. No one can take it by storm. From it I swoop down into actuality and snatch my prey, but I do not stay down there. I bring my booty home, and this booty is a picture I weave into the tapestries at my castle. Then I live as one already dead. Everything I have experienced I immerse in a baptism of oblivion unto an eternity of recollection. Everything temporal and fortuitous is forgotten and blotted out. Then I sit like an old gray-haired man, pensive, and explain the pictures in a soft voice, almost whispering, and beside me sits a child, listening, although he remembers everything before I tell it.

The sun is shining brilliantly and beautifully into my room; the window in the next room is open. Everything is quiet out on the street. It is Sunday afternoon. I distinctly hear a lark warbling outside a window in one of the neighboring courtyards, outside the window where the pretty girl lives. Far away in a distant street, I hear a man crying "Shrimp for sale." The air is so warm, and yet the whole city is as if deserted. —Then I call to mind my youth and my first love— when I was filled with longing; now I long only for my first longing. What is youth? A dream. What is love? The content of the dream.

Something marvelous has happened to me. I was transported to the seventh heaven. There sat all the gods assembled.

As a special dispensation, I was granted the favor of making a wish. "What do you want," asked Mercury. "Do you want youth, or beauty, or power, or a long life, or the most beautiful girl, or any one of the other glorious things we have in the treasure chest? Choose—but only one thing." For a moment I was bewildered; then I addressed the gods, saying: My esteemed contemporaries, I choose one thing—that I may always have the laughter on my side. Not one of the gods said a word; instead, all of them began to laugh. From that I concluded that my wish was granted and decided that the gods knew how to express themselves with good taste, for it would indeed have been inappropriate to reply solemnly: It is granted to you.[127]

THE IMMEDIATE EROTIC STAGES[1]
OR
THE MUSICAL-EROTIC

From the moment my soul was first astounded by Mozart's music and humbly bowed in admiration, it has often been a favorite and refreshing occupation for me to deliberate on the way that happy Greek view of the world that calls the world a κόσμος [cosmos] because it manifests itself as a well-organized whole, as an elegant, transparent adornment for the spirit that acts upon and operates throughout it, the way that happy view lets itself be repeated in a higher order of things, in the world of ideals, the way there is here again a ruling wisdom especially wonderful at uniting what belongs together, Axel with Valborg,[2] Homer with the Trojan War, Raphael with Catholicism, Mozart with Don Juan. There is a paltry disbelief that seems to contain considerable healing power.[3] It thinks that such a connection is accidental and sees nothing more in it than a very fortunate conjunction of the various forces in the game of life. It thinks that it is accidental that the lovers find each other, accidental that they love each other. There might have been a hundred other girls with whom he could have been just as happy, whom he could have loved just as much. It considers that many a poet has lived who would have been just as immortal as Homer if that glorious subject matter had not been taken over by him, many a composer who would have been just as immortal as Mozart if the opportunity had offered itself. This wisdom contains considerable consolation and balm for all mediocrities, who thereby see themselves in a position to delude themselves and like-minded people into thinking that they did not become as exceptional as the exceptional ones because of a mistaken identification on the part of fate, a mistake on the part of the world. This produces a very convenient optimism. But it is abhorrent, of course, to every high-

minded soul, every optimate,[4] to whom it is not as important
to rescue himself in such a paltry manner as it is to lose himself
by contemplating greatness; whereas it is a delight to his soul,
a sacred joy, to see united that which belongs together. This is
good fortune, not in the sense of the accidental, and thus presupposes two factors, whereas the accidental consists in the
unarticulated interjections of fate. This is good fortune in history, the divine interplay of the historic forces, the festival period of the historic epoch. The accidental has only one factor:
It is accidental that Homer, in the history of the Trojan War,
acquired the most remarkable epic subject matter imaginable.
Good fortune has two factors: It is fortunate that this most remarkable epic subject matter came into the hands of Homer.
Here the emphasis is just as much on Homer as on the subject
matter. Here is the deep harmony that pervades every production we call classic. So also with Mozart: It is fortunate that the
perhaps sole musical theme (in the more profound sense) was
given to—Mozart.

With his *Don Giovanni*,[5] Mozart joins that little immortal
band of men whose names, whose works, time will not forget
because eternity recollects them. And although it makes no
difference, once one is in, whether one ranks highest or lowest—because in a certain sense everyone ranks equally high—
since all rank infinitely high, and although it is just as childish
to argue about first and last places here as it is to argue about
the place assigned in church on confirmation day, I am still too
much of a child, or, more correctly, I am infatuated, like a
young girl, with Mozart, and I must have him rank in first
place, whatever it costs. And I will go to the deacon and the
pastor and the dean and the bishop and the whole church council, and I will beseech and implore them to grant my request,
and I will challenge the whole congregation on the same matter, and if my appeal is not heard, my childish wish not fulfilled, then I will secede from the association, then I will divorce myself from its way of thinking, then I will form a sect
that not only places Mozart first but has no one but Mozart.
And I will beseech Mozart to forgive me that his music did not
inspire me to great deeds but made me a fool who, because of

him, lost the little sense I had and now in quiet sadness usually passes the time humming something I do not understand, and like a ghost prowls night and day around something I cannot enter. [6]Immortal Mozart! You to whom I owe everything—to whom I owe that I lost my mind, that my soul was astounded, that I was terrified at the core of my being—you to whom I owe that I did not go through life without encountering something that could shake me, you whom I thank because I did not die without having loved, even though my love was unhappy. No wonder, then, that I am much more zealous for his glorification than for the happiest moment of my own life, much more zealous for his immortality than for my own existence [*Tilvær*]. Indeed, if he were taken away, if his name were blotted out, that would demolish the one pillar that until now has prevented everything from collapsing for me into a boundless chaos, into a dreadful nothing.

Yet I certainly need not fear that any age will deny him a place in that kingdom of the gods, but I do need to be prepared for people to find it childish of me to insist that he have first place. And although I by no means propose to feel ashamed of my childishness, although it will always have more significance and value for me than any exhaustive consideration precisely because it is inexhaustible, I shall nevertheless try by way of deliberation to demonstrate his legitimate claim.

In a classic work, good fortune—that which makes it classic and immortal—is the absolute correlation of the two forces. This correlation is so absolute that a subsequent reflective age will scarcely be able, even in thought, to separate that which is so intrinsically conjoined without running the danger of causing or fostering a misunderstanding. For example, if it is said that it was Homer's good fortune that he acquired that most exceptional epic subject matter, this can lead one to forget that we always have this epic subject matter through Homer's conception, and the fact that it appears to be the most perfect epic subject matter is clear to us only in and through the transubstantiation due to Homer. If, however, Homer's poetic work in permeating the subject matter is emphasized, then one runs the risk of forgetting that the poem would never have become

what it is if the idea with which Homer permeated it was not
its own idea, if the form was not the subject matter's own
form. The poet wishes for his subject matter, but, as they say,
wishing is no art; this is quite correct and truthfully applies to
a host of powerless poetic wishes. To wish properly, however,
is a great art, or, more correctly, it is a gift. It is the inexplica-
bility and mysteriousness of genius, just as with a divining rod
[*Ønskeqvist*], which never has the notion to wish [*ønske*] except
in the presence of that for which it wishes. Hence, wishing has
a far deeper significance than it ordinarily does; indeed, to abstract reason it appears ludicrous, since it rather thinks of
wishing in connection with what is not present, not in connection with what is present.

There was a school of estheticians who, because of a one-
sided emphasis on the significance of form, were not without
guilt in occasioning the diametrically opposite misunderstanding.[7] It has often struck me that these estheticians were as a
matter of course attached to Hegelian philosophy, inasmuch as
both a general knowledge of Hegel and a special knowledge of
his esthetics give assurance that he strongly emphasizes, especially with regard to the esthetic, the importance of the subject
matter.[8] Both parts, however, essentially belong together, and
a single observation will be sufficient to show this, since otherwise a phenomenon of this sort would be inexplicable. Ordinarily, it is a single work or a single suite of works that marks
the particular individual as a classic poet, artist, etc. The same
individuality may have produced many different things, but
they are not to be compared with it. For example, Homer also
wrote a *Batrachomyomachia*[9] but did not become a classic writer
or immortal through it. To say that this is due to the unimportance of the theme is indeed foolish, since the classic consists in the balance. Now, if whatever makes a classic work
classic lies simply and solely in the producing individual, then
everything he produced would inevitably be classic, somewhat in the sense, although higher, in which bees always produce a certain kind of cell. To answer that it was due to his having been more fortunate with the one than with the other
would really say nothing. For one thing, this is merely a splen-

did tautology that all too frequently in life enjoys the honor of being regarded as an answer; for another, as an answer it pertains to a relativity other than that of the question. It throws no light on the relation between subject matter and form and at best could come under consideration if the question pertained solely to the formative activity.

It is likewise the case with Mozart that only one of his works makes him a classic composer and absolutely immortal. That work is *Don Giovanni*. Everything else he has composed can please and delight, arouse our admiration, enrich the soul, satisfy the ear, delight the heart; but no service is done to him and his immortality by throwing everything together and making it all equally great. *Don Giovanni* is his reception piece.[10] With *Don Giovanni*, he enters that eternity which lies not outside time but in the midst of it, which is not hidden from the eyes of men by any curtain, into which the immortals are not admitted once and for all but are continually being admitted, inasmuch as the generation passes by and directs its gaze toward them, is happy in its contemplation of them, goes to its grave, and the next generation in turn goes by and is transfigured in contemplating them. With his *Don Giovanni*, Mozart enters the rank of those immortals, of those visibly transfigured ones, whom no cloud takes away[11] from the eyes of men; with *Don Giovanni* he stands supreme among them. This last assertion, as I said above, I shall attempt to demonstrate.

All classic productions rank equally high, as previously noted, because each one ranks infinitely high. Consequently, if one nevertheless wants to introduce a certain order into this series, it stands to reason that it cannot be based on anything essential, for that would mean that there was an essential difference, and that in turn would mean that the word "classic" was wrongly predicated of all of them. If a classification were based on the dissimilar nature of the subject matter, one would immediately be involved in a misunderstanding, which in its wider extension would end with the annulment of the whole concept of the classic. The subject matter is an essential element, inasmuch as it is one factor, but it is not the absolute, since it is only one element. It could be pointed out that in a

sense certain kinds of classic works have no subject matter,
whereas in others, however, the subject matter plays a very
important role. The former is the case with works we admire
as classic in architecture, sculpture, music, painting—especially the first three, and even in painting, insofar as there is
any question of subject matter it has importance almost solely
as an occasion. The second is true of poetry, this word understood in its widest meaning to denote all artistic production
that is based on language and the historical consciousness. This
comment is in itself altogether correct, but it is a mistake to
base a classification on it by regarding the absence or presence
of subject matter as an advantage or a detriment to the creative
individual. If it is strictly understood, the result will be to argue the very opposite of what was really intended, as is always
the case when one moves abstractly in dialectical qualifications, where it is the case that one not only says one thing and
means something else but says something else; what one
thinks one is saying one does not say but says the opposite. So
it is when the subject matter is made the principle of division.
In speaking of it, one speaks of something entirely different:
namely, the formative activity.

But the same thing happens if one starts with the formative
activity and emphasizes it alone. In maintaining the distinction
here and emphasizing that in some respects the formative activity is creative to the degree that it creates the subject matter
in the process, whereas in other respects it receives the subject
matter, then here again, although one thinks one is speaking of
the formative activity, one is actually speaking of the subject
matter and is basing the classification on the division of the
subject matter.

The same holds for the formative activity as the point of departure in such a classification as for the subject matter. Consequently, a single aspect cannot be used as the basis for an order of rank, because it is still too essential to be sufficiently
accidental, too accidental to be a basis for an essential ranking.
But this thoroughgoing mutual permeation—which justifies
saying, if one wishes to speak clearly, that the subject matter
permeates the form and also that the form permeates the sub-

ject matter—this mutual permeation, this like-for-like in the immortal friendship of the classic, may serve to illuminate the classic from a new side and to limit it in such a way that it does not become too copious. In fact, the estheticians who one-sidedly stressed the poetic activity have broadened this concept so much that this pantheon became adorned, indeed, overdecorated, to such a degree with classic knickknacks and bagatelles that the unsophisticated notion of a cool hall with a few particular great figures utterly vanished, and instead that pantheon became a storage attic. According to this esthetic view, every artistically skillful little dainty is a classic work that is assured of absolute immortality; indeed, in this kind of hocus-pocus, such trifles are admitted first of all. Although paradoxes are otherwise detested, the paradox that the least was actually art was not dismaying. The untruth was in a one-sided emphasis on the formal activity. Therefore, such an esthetic view could last only for a certain period, that is, so long as there was no awareness that time mocked it and its classic works. In the realm of esthetics, this view was a form of the radicalism that has similarly manifested itself in so many spheres; it was an expression of the unbridled producing individual in his equally unbridled lack of substance.

Like so many others, however, this effort found its subduer in Hegel. It is a sad truth about Hegelian philosophy that on the whole it has by no means achieved the importance, neither for the past nor for the present age, that it would have achieved if the past age had not been so busy scaring people into it but had rather possessed a little more calm presence of mind in appropriating it to itself, and if the present age had not been so indefatigably active in driving people beyond it.[12] Hegel reinstated the subject matter, the idea, in its rights and thereby ousted those transient classic works, those superficialities, those twilight moths from the arched vaults of classicism. It is by no means our intention to deny these works the value that is their due, but the point is to watch out lest here, as in so many other places, the language become confused, the concepts enervated. A certain eternity may be readily attributed to them, and this is their merit, but still this eternity is actually

I
37

only the eternal moment that any true artistic production has, but not the full eternity in the midst of the shifts and changes of the times. What these productions lacked was ideas, and the more formally perfect they were, the more quickly they burned themselves out. As technical skill was more and more developed to the highest level of virtuosity, the more transient this virtuosity became and the more it lacked the mettle and power or balance to withstand the gusts of time, while more and more exalted it continually made greater claims to being the most distilled spirit. Only where the idea is brought to rest and transparency in a definite form can there be any question of a classic work, but then it will also be capable of withstanding the times. This unity, this mutual intimacy in each other, every classic work has, and thus it is readily perceived that every attempt at a classification of the various classic works that has as its point of departure a separation of subject matter and form or of idea and form is *eo ipso* a failure.

Another way might be proposed. The medium through which the idea becomes visible could be made the object of consideration. Having noted that one medium is richer and another less rich, one could base the division on this difference by finding a facilitation or an impediment in the varying richness or poverty of the medium. But the medium stands in an all too necessary relation to the whole production to keep a division based on it from becoming entangled in the above-mentioned difficulties after a few turns of thought.

I believe, however, that the following observations will open the prospect for a division that will have validity precisely because it is completely accidental. The more abstract and thus the more impoverished the idea is, the more abstract and thus the more impoverished the medium is; hence the greater is the probability that no repetition can be imagined, and the greater is the probability that when the idea has acquired its expression it has acquired it once and for all. On the other hand, the more concrete and thus the richer the idea and likewise the medium, the greater is the probability of a repetition. As I now place the various classic works side by side and, without wishing to rank them, am amazed that all stand equally high, it nevertheless will be readily apparent that one section has more works than another or, if it does not, that there is the possibility that it can have, whereas any possibility for the other is not so readily apparent.

I would like to develop this point in somewhat more detail. The more abstract the idea is, the less the probability. But how does the idea become concrete? By being permeated by the historical. The more concrete the idea, the greater the probability. The more abstract the medium is, the less the probability; the more concrete, the more. But what does it mean that the medium is concrete except that it either is, or is seen in its approximation to, language, for language is the most concrete of all media. Hence, the idea that is disclosed in sculpture is totally abstract and has no relation to the historical; the medium through which it becomes manifest is likewise abstract. Consequently, it is very probable that the section of classic works that comprises sculpture will include only a few. The witness of time and the agreement of experience bear me out on this. But if I take a concrete idea and a concrete medium, the situation is different. Homer certainly is a classic epic poet, but precisely because the idea that becomes manifest in the epic is a concrete idea and because the medium is language, it is conceivable that the section of classic works that includes the epic has many works, which are all equally classic because history continually provides new epic subject matter. Here, too, the witness of history and the agreement of experience bear me out.

If I now base a division on the completely accidental, it really cannot be denied that it is accidental. But if reproached for it, I then reply that the reproach is a mistake, for it is supposed to be just that. It is accidental that one section has or can have more works than another. But since this is accidental, it is easy to see that the class that has or can have the most works may very well be placed uppermost. At this point, I could persist in what I said before and calmly reply that this would be perfectly legitimate but that I ought to be all the more praised for my consistency because I altogether accidentally placed the opposite section uppermost. But I shall not do that. On the

I
39

other hand, I shall appeal to a circumstance that speaks in my favor—namely, the circumstance that the sections that include the concrete ideas are not closed and cannot be closed in this way. Therefore, it is more natural to place the others first and with regard to the latter group always to keep the double doors open. But if someone says that this is an imperfection, a defect in that first class, then he is plowing outside the furrows of my consideration, and I cannot pay any attention to what he says, however exhaustive it is, for it is indeed a fixed point that, viewed essentially, all are equally perfect.

But, then, which idea is the most abstract? Here, of course, the question concerns an idea that can become a theme for artistic treatment, not ideas that are suitable for scholarly-scientific presentation. Which medium is the most abstract? I will answer this question first. It is the medium that is furthest removed from language.

Before answering that question, however, may I recall that there is a circumstance related to the final solution of my task. That is, the most abstract medium does not always have the most abstract idea as its theme. Thus the medium that architecture uses is undoubtedly the most abstract, and yet the ideas that are manifest in architecture are not at all the most abstract. Architecture stands in a much closer relation to history than, for example, sculpture does. Here again appears the possibility of a new choice. For the first class in that order of precedence, I can choose either the works with the most abstract medium or those with the most abstract idea. In that respect, I prefer the idea, not the medium.

Sculpture, painting, and music have abstract media as does architecture, but this is not the place to go further into that exploration. The most abstract idea conceivable is the sensuous[13] in its elemental originality [*Genialitet*].[14] But through which medium can it be presented? Only through music. It cannot be presented in sculpture because it has a qualification of a kind of inwardness; it cannot be painted, for it cannot be caught in definite contours. In its lyricism, it is a force, a wind, impatience, passion, etc., yet in such a way that it exists not in one instant but in a succession of instants, for if it existed in one instant, it could be depicted or painted. That it exists in a succession of instants expresses its epic character, but still it is not epic in the stricter sense, for it has not reached the point of words; it continually moves within immediacy. Consequently, it cannot be presented in poetry, either. The only medium that can present it is music. Music has an element of time in itself but nevertheless does not take place in time except metaphorically. It cannot express the historical within time.

In Mozart's *Don Giovanni*, we have the perfect unity of this idea and its corresponding form. But precisely because the idea is so very abstract and because the medium also is abstract, there is no probability that Mozart will ever have a competitor. Mozart's good fortune is that he has found a subject matter that is intrinsically altogether musical, and if any other composer were to compete with Mozart, there would be nothing for him to do except to compose *Don Giovanni* all over again. Homer found a perfect epic subject matter, but because history offers more epic subject matter, many more epic poems are conceivable. Such is not the case with *Don Giovanni*. What I really mean will perhaps be seen best if I indicate the difference by reference to a related idea. Goethe's *Faust* is really a classic work, but it is a historical idea, and therefore every extraordinary time in history will have its *Faust*. *Faust* has language as its medium, and since this is a much more concrete medium, for that reason, too, many works of the same kind are conceivable. But in the same sense as the classic works of Greek sculpture, *Don Giovanni* is and remains the only one of its kind. However, since the idea of *Don Giovanni* is even much more abstract than that which constitutes the basis of sculpture, it is readily seen that whereas in sculpture there are many works, in music there is only a single work. To be sure, many more classic works in music are conceivable, but there still is only one work of which it can be said that its idea is altogether musical in such a way that the music does not help along as accompaniment but discloses its own innermost nature as it discloses the idea. Therefore Mozart with his *Don Giovanni* stands highest among those immortals.

But I shall give up this whole exploration. It is written only for those who have fallen in love. And just as it does not take much to make children happy, so it is, as is well known, that the love-enraptured often rejoice in very odd things. It is like a vehement lovers' quarrel over nothing, and yet it has its value—for the lovers.

Although the foregoing discussion has tried in every possible way imaginable or unimaginable to gain recognition for Mozart's *Don Giovanni* as supreme among all classic works, it nevertheless has made as good as no attempt to demonstrate that this work actually is classic, for the few scattered hints found here, by appearing merely as hints, simply show that the aim was not to demonstrate but occasionally to illuminate. This approach might seem more than odd. To demonstrate that *Don Giovanni* is a classic work in the strictest sense is a task for reflection, but the other endeavor is completely irrelevant to the proper domain of reflection. The movement of thought is calmed by having recognized that it is a classic work and that every classic production is equally perfect; to thinking, anything more one wants to do is suspect.

To that extent, the entire foregoing part is entangled in a self-contradiction and easily disintegrates into nothing. But this is quite proper, and such a self-contradiction is deeply rooted in human nature. The admiration, sympathy, and veneration in me, the child in me, the woman in me, demanded more than what thought could provide. Thought was calm, rested happy in its knowledge; then I went to it and begged it to bestir itself once more, to venture the ultimate. It knew very well that this was futile, but since I am usually on good terms with it, it did not refuse me. It labored in vain; egged on by me, it was continually going beyond itself and continually collapsing back into itself. It was continually looking for a foothold and finding none, continually trying to find bottom, but could neither swim nor wade. It was both a laughing and a crying matter. Therefore I did both and was very grateful that it had not denied me this service. And although I now know perfectly well that it is useless, it could still very well occur to me to ask thought to play once again the game that to me is inexhaustible material for enjoyment. Every reader who finds the game boring is, of course, not of my kind; it is meaningless to him, and here as everywhere children who are alike play together best. To him, the entire foregoing part is a superfluity; whereas to me it has such great importance that I say with Horace:

> *Exilis domus est, ubi non et multa supersunt*
> [Poor is the house where there's not much to spare].[15]

To him it is foolishness, to me wisdom; to him it is boring, to me a source of joy and merriment.

That kind of reader would therefore be incapable of appreciating my lyrical thought, which is so ecstatic that it goes beyond thought. But perhaps he would be kind enough to say, "We shall not quarrel about that; I skip that part. See now if you can come to the far more important matter of demonstrating that *Don Giovanni* is a classic work, for I admit that this would be a really appropriate introduction to the exploration proper." To what extent it would be an appropriate introduction, I shall leave in abeyance, but the trouble here for me is that I in turn cannot appreciate him, for no matter how easy it may be for me to demonstrate it, it would still never occur to me to demonstrate it. But although I always assume the matter settled, the following will many times and in many ways[16] illuminate *Don Giovanni* in this respect, just as the foregoing discussion has already contained a few hints.

The immediate task of this exploration is to show the significance of the musical-erotic and to that end in turn to indicate the various stages, which, since they are all characterized by the immediate erotic, also harmonize in this, that essentially they are all musical. What I have to say about this I owe solely to Mozart. Therefore, if anyone should be courteous enough to admit that I am right in what I aim to set forth but has some doubts whether it is in Mozart's music or whether, instead, I put it into the music, I can assure him that not only the little I am able to set forth is in Mozart's music, but infinitely much more. Yes, I can assure him that this very thought gives me the boldness to venture to try to explain a few things in Mozart's music. What one has loved with youthful infatuation, what one has admired with youthful enthusiasm, that with which one has kept secret, enigmatic company in the inwardness of the soul, that which one has hidden in the heart—one always approaches this with a certain shyness, with mixed feelings, when one knows that the purpose is to understand it. What one has come to know piece by piece, just as a bird gleans each little straw for itself, happier over each little bit than over all the rest of the world; what the loving ear, solitary, has absorbed, solitary in the great crowd, unnoticed in its secret hiding place; what the avid ear has picked up, never satisfied, what the avaricious ear has preserved, never secure, of which the faintest echo has never disappointed the sleepless attention of the reconnoitering ear; what one has lived in during the day and relived at night, what has driven away sleep and made it restless, what one has dreamed about in sleep, what one has awakened to in order awake to dream about it again, for the sake of which one has leaped out of bed in the middle of the night out of fear of forgetting it; what has made its appearance to one in the most inspired moments, what one has always had at hand like a woman's needlework, what has accompanied one on bright moonlit nights, in lonely forests by the lake, on gloomy streets, in the middle of the night, at the break of day; what has sat with one on the same horse, what has been company in the carriage; what has permeated the home, what one's room has witnessed, what has resonated in the ear, what has reverberated in the soul, what the soul has spun into its finest fabric—this now shows itself to thought. Just as in the old tales those enigmatic beings, draped in seaweed, rise up from the bottom of the sea, so this rises up from the sea of recollection, intertwined with mementos. The soul becomes sad and the heart mellow, for it is as if one were taking leave of it, as if one were parting never to meet again, neither in time nor in eternity. One feels that one is being unfaithful, that one has betrayed one's pact; one feels that one is no longer the same, not as young, not as childlike; one fears for oneself, that one will lose what made one happy, blissful, and rich; one fears for what one loves, that it will suffer in this change, will perhaps appear less perfect, that it will possibly fail to answer the many questions, alas, and then all is lost, the magic is gone, and it can never again be evoked. As for Mozart's music, my soul knows no fear, my confidence no limits. For one thing, what I have understood hitherto is only very little, and enough will always remain, hiding in the shadows of presentiment; for another, I am convinced that if Mozart ever became entirely comprehensible to me, he would then become completely incomprehensible to me.

To make the claim that Christianity brought sensuality into the world seems boldly venturesome. But as they say: Boldly ventured is half won. So it also holds here; it will become evident upon reflection that in the positing of something, the other that is excluded is indirectly posited. Since sensuality generally is that which is to be negated, it really comes to light, is really posited, first by the act that excludes it through a positing of the opposite positive. Sensuality is posited as a principle, as a power, as an independent system first by Christianity, and to that extent Christianity brought sensuality into the world. But if the thesis that Christianity has brought sensuality into the world is to be understood properly, it must be comprehended as identical to its opposite, that it is Christianity that has driven sensuality out of the world, has excluded sensuality from the world. Sensuality was first posited as a principle, as a power, as an independent system by Christianity. I could add one more qualification that perhaps most emphatically shows what I mean: sensuality was placed under the qualification of spirit first by Christianity. This is quite natural, for Christianity is spirit, and spirit is the positive principle it has brought into the world. But when sensuality is viewed under the qualification of spirit, its significance is seen to be that it is to be excluded, but precisely because it is to be excluded it is defined as a principle, as a power, for that which spirit, which is itself a principle, is supposed to exclude must be something that manifests itself as a principle, even though it does not manifest itself as a principle until the moment when it is excluded. Of course, to protest against my thesis that sensuality existed in the world prior to Christianity would be

rather foolish, inasmuch as it goes without saying that whatever is to be excluded always exists prior to that which excludes it, even though, understood in another way, it comes
into existence [*bliver til*] only when it is excluded. This in turn
occurs because it comes into existence in another sense, and
that is why I promptly said that boldly ventured is only half
won.

Consequently, the sensual certainly did exist in the world
before, but it was not qualified spiritually. How, then, did it
exist? It was qualified psychically. This was its nature in paganism, and if one wishes to look for its most perfect expression, it was in Greece. But the sensual psychically qualified is
not contrast or exclusion, but harmony and consonance. But
precisely because the sensual is posited as harmoniously qualified, it is posited not as a principle but as a consonant *encliti-
con*.[17]

This view will be of importance in illuminating the various
forms the erotic takes in various stages of the development of
world consciousness and thereby guide us to the category of
the immediate-erotic as identical with the musical-erotic. In
Greek culture, the sensuous was controlled in the beautiful individuality,[18] or, to put it more accurately, it was not controlled, for it was not an enemy to be subdued, not a dangerous insurgent to be held in check; it was liberated to life and
joy in the beautiful individuality. Thus the sensuous was not
posited as a principle. The psychical aspect constituting the
beautiful individuality was inconceivable without the sensuous; for this reason the erotic based on the sensuous was not
posited as a principle either. Erotic love [*Elskov*] was everywhere present as an element and present as an element in the
beautiful individuality. The gods, no less than men, knew its
power; the gods, no less than men, knew happy and unhappy
love affairs. But in none of them was erotic love present as a
principle; insofar as it was in them, in the single individual, it
was there as an element of erotic love's universal power,
which, however, was present nowhere and therefore not even
in the Greek conception or in the Greek consciousness.

It could be objected that Eros was indeed the god of erotic

love and that therefore erotic love must be considered present in him as a principle. But apart from the fact that here again erotic love does not rest upon the erotic in such a way that this is based solely upon the sensuous, but upon the psychical, there is also another circumstance to be noted, one that I shall now stress in somewhat more detail. Eros was the god of erotic love but was not himself in love. Insofar as the other gods or men detected the power of erotic love in themselves, they attributed it to Eros, traced it back to him, but Eros himself did not fall in love, and if it did happen to him once,[19] it was an exception; and although he was the god of erotic love, he was far behind the other gods, far behind men, in the number of his affairs. That he fell in love is as good as to say that he, too, yielded to the universal power of erotic love, which thus in a way became a power outside himself, which in being spurned by him had no place at all now where it could be sought. His erotic love is not based on the sensuous, either, but upon the psychical. It is a genuinely Greek idea that the god of erotic love is not in love himself, whereas all the others are indebted to him for their own falling in love. If I were to imagine a god or a goddess of longing, it would be genuinely Greek that, whereas everyone who knew the sweet unrest or pain of longing would trace it to this being, this being would itself know nothing of longing.

I know of no more precise way to designate what is distinctive in this relation than to say that it is the opposite of a representative relation. In the representative relation, the total power is concentrated in a single individual, and the particular individuals participate therein to the extent that they participate in the particular movements of that one. I could also say that this relation is the opposite of the one underlying incarnation. In incarnation, the full plenitude of life is in the single individual, and this is for the others only through their beholding it in the incarnated individual.

Therefore, in the Greek relation it is the reverse. That which is the god's power is not in the god but in all the other individuals, who trace it back to him; he himself is almost powerless, impotent, because he communicates his power to all the rest of

I
46

the world. The incarnated individual imbibes, as it were, power from all the others, and thus the fullness is in that one, and in the others only insofar as they behold it in this individual. This is important for what follows, just as in and by itself it is significant with regard to the categories the world consciousness uses at various times. Hence, we do not find the sensuous as a principle in Greek culture; neither do we find the erotic as a principle based upon the principle of the sensuous; and even if we had found it, we still perceive—something that is of the greatest importance in this exploration—that the Greek consciousness did not have the strength to concentrate all of it in a single individual but from a point that does not have it radiates it to all the others in such a way that this constituting point is almost recognizable by being the only one that does not have that which it gives to all the others.

So it was Christianity that posited sensuality as a principle, just as it posited the sensuous-erotic as a principle. The idea of representation was introduced into the world by Christianity. If I now imagine the sensuous-erotic as a principle, as a power, as a domain, defined in relation to spirit—that is, defined in such a way that spirit excludes it—if I imagine this principle concentrated in a single individual, then I have the concept of the sensuous-erotic in its elemental originality [*Genialitet*]. This is an idea that Greek culture did not have, that Christianity first introduced into the world, although only indirectly.

If the elemental originality of the sensuous-erotic in all its immediacy insists on expression, then the question arises as to which medium is the most suitable for this. The point that particularly must be kept in mind here is that it insists on being expressed and presented in its immediacy. In its mediacy and in being reflected in another medium, it falls within language and comes under ethical categories. In its immediacy, it can be expressed only in music. In this connection, I must ask the reader to recall something said about this in the insignificant introduction. The significance of music thereby appears in its full validity, and in a stricter sense it appears as a Christian art or, more correctly, as the art Christianity posits in excluding it from itself, as the medium for that which Christianity excludes from itself and thereby posits. In other words, music is the demonic. In elemental sensuous-erotic originality, music has its absolute theme. This, of course, does not mean that music cannot express anything else, but nevertheless this is its theme proper. Similarly, sculpture can depict something other than human beauty, and yet this is its absolute theme. Painting can depict something other than celestially transfigured beauty, and yet this is its absolute theme. In this regard, the point is to see the basic concept in each art and not to be confused by whatever else it can do. The basic concept of man is spirit, and one should not be confused by the fact that he is also able to walk on two feet. The basic concept of language is thought, and one should not be confused by the fact that a few emotional people are of the opinion that the greatest importance of language is in the production of inarticulate sounds.

At this point, may I be permitted a little insignificant interlude;[20] *praeterea censeo* [furthermore I am of the opinion][21] that Mozart is the greatest of all the classic authors, that his *Don Giovanni* deserves the highest place among all the classic works.

As to music regarded as a medium, this, of course, is always a very interesting question. Whether I am capable of saying anything adequate about it is another question. I am well aware that I do not understand music; I readily admit that I am a layman. I do not hide the fact that I do not belong to the chosen tribe of music experts, that at most I stand in the doorway as a gentile convert drawn from afar to this place by a strange, irresistible impulse—but no further. Yet it is possible that the little I have to say, if received with kindness and indulgence, may have a single comment that will be found to contain something true, even if it is concealed under a peasant's coat. I stand outside music, and from this position I observe it. That this position is very imperfect, I readily admit; that compared with the lucky ones standing inside I do not manage to see very much, I do not deny. But I go on hoping that from my position I, too, can communicate an illuminating detail, although the initiated could do it much better—indeed, to a certain degree even understand better what I say than I do myself.

If I imagined two kingdoms bordering each other, one of which I knew rather well and the other not at all, and if however much I desired it I were not allowed to enter the unknown kingdom, I would still be able to form some idea of it. I would go to the border of the kingdom known to me and follow it all the way, and in doing so I would by my movements describe the outline of that unknown land and thus have a general idea of it, although I had never set foot in it. And if this were a labor that occupied me very much, if I were unflaggingly scrupulous, it presumably would sometimes happen that as I stood with sadness at the border of my kingdom and gazed longingly into that unknown country that was so near and yet so far, I would be granted an occasional little disclosure. And even though I feel that music is an art that requires considerable experience if one is really to have an opinion on it, I comfort myself again as so often before with the paradox that also in presentiment and ignorance one can have a kind of experience. It is a comfort to me that Diana, who had not given birth herself, came to the aid of women in labor—indeed, that she had this ability from infancy as an inborn gift, so that when she was born she herself helped Latona in her labor pains.[22]

The kingdom that I know, to whose outermost boundary I shall go to discover music, is language. If the various media are ordered according to a specific process of development, language and music must be placed closest to each other, and that is also why it has been said that music is a language, which is more than a clever observation. If one is inclined to indulge in cleverness, one could say that sculpture and painting, too, are each a kind of language, inasmuch as every expression of an idea is always a language, since the essence of the idea is language. Clever folk therefore speak of the language of nature, and soft-headed clergy occasionally open the book of nature for us and read something that neither they nor their listeners understand. If the observation that music is a language did not amount to anything more than that, I would not bother with it but would let it go unchallenged and pass for what it is. But that is not the case. Not until spirit is posited is language installed in its rights, but when spirit is posited, everything that is not spirit is excluded. Yet this exclusion is a qualification of spirit, and consequently, insofar as that which is excluded is to affirm itself, it requires a medium that is qualified in relation to spirit, and this medium is music. But a medium that is qualified in relation to spirit is essentially language; now, since music is qualified in relation to spirit, it is legitimately called a language.

Language, regarded as medium, is the medium absolutely qualified by spirit, and it is therefore the authentic medium of the idea. To elaborate this more thoroughly is neither within my competence nor in the interest of this little inquiry. Just one specific comment, which again leads me into music, should find a place here. In language, the sensuous as medium is reduced to a mere instrument and is continually negated. That is not the case with the other media. Neither in sculpture nor in painting is the sensuous a mere instrument; it is rather a component. It is not to be negated continually, either, for it is continually to be seen conjointly. It would be a strangely backward consideration of a piece of sculpture or of a painting if I were to behold it in such a way that I took pains to see it independently of the sensuous, whereby I would completely cancel its beauty. In sculpture, architecture, and painting, the idea is integral to the medium, but the fact that the idea does not reduce the medium to a mere instrument, does not continually negate it, expresses, as it were, that this medium cannot speak. It is the same with nature. Therefore, it is properly said that nature is dumb, and architecture and sculpture and painting; it is properly said despite all the fine, sensitive ears that can hear them speak. Therefore, it is foolish to say that nature is a language, certainly as foolish as to say that the mute speaks, since it is not even a language in the way sign language is. But that is not the case with language. The sensuous is reduced to a mere instrument and is thus annulled. If a person spoke in such a way that we heard the flapping of his tongue etc., he would be speaking poorly; if he heard in such a way that he heard the vibrations of the air instead of words, he would be hearing poorly; if he read a book in such a way that he continually saw each individual letter, he would be reading poorly.

I
50

Language is the perfect medium precisely when everything sensuous in it is negated. That is also the case with music; that which is really supposed to be heard is continually disengaging itself from the sensuous. It has already been pointed out that music as a medium does not rank as high as language, and that is why I said that music, understood in a certain way, is a language.

Language addresses itself to the ear. No other medium does this. The ear, in turn, is the most spiritually qualified sense. Most people, I believe, will agree with me on this point. If anyone wishes more information about this, I refer him to the preface to Steffens's *Karrikaturen des Heiligsten*.[23] Apart from language, music is the only medium that is addressed to the ear. Here again is an analogy and a testimony to the sense in which music is a language. There is much in nature that is addressed to the ear, but what affects the ear is the purely sensate; therefore nature is mute, and it is a ludicrous fancy that one hears something because one hears a cow bellow or, what is perhaps more pretentious, a nightingale warble; it is a fancy that one hears something, a fancy that the one is worth more than the other, since it is all six of one and a half dozen of the other.

Language has its element in time; all other media have space as their element. Only music also occurs in time. But its occurrence in time is in turn a negation of the feelings dependent upon the senses [*det Sandselige*]. That which the other arts produce suggests their sensuousness precisely by having its continuance in space. There is, of course, much in nature that occurs in time. For example, when a brook ripples and keeps on rippling, there seems to be a qualification of time involved therein. But this is not so, and if anyone absolutely insists that the qualification of time must be present here, then one must say that it certainly is so but that it is spatially qualified. Music does not exist except in the moment it is performed, for even if a person can read notes ever so well and has an ever so vivid imagination, he still cannot deny that only in a figurative sense does music exist when it is being read. It actually exists only when it is being performed. That might seem an imperfection in this art in comparison with the other arts whose works continually exist because they have their continuance in the sensuous. But this is not so. It is indeed a demonstration that it is a higher, a more spiritual art.

Now, if I start with language in order, by a movement through it, to sound out music, as it were, the matter looks something like this. If I assume that prose is the language form that is most remote from music, I already detect in the oration, in the sonorous construction of its periods, an echo of the musical, which emerges ever more strongly at various stages in the poetic declamation, in the metrical construction, in the rhyme, until finally the musical element has developed so strongly that language leaves off and everything becomes music. Indeed, this is a pet phrase poets use to indicate that they, as it were, abandon the idea; it disappears for them, and everything ends in music. This might seem to imply that music is even closer to perfection as a medium than language. But this is one of those sentimental misconceptions that sprout only in empty heads. That it is a misconception will be pointed out later. Here I wish only to draw attention to the remarkable circumstance that by a movement in the opposite direction I once again encounter music, namely, when I descend from prose permeated by the concept until I end up with interjections, which in turn are musical, just as a child's first babbling is musical. Here the point certainly cannot be that music is closer to perfection as a medium than language, or that music is a richer medium than language, unless it is assumed that saying "Uh" is more valuable than a complete thought. But what does this mean—that where language leaves off I find the musical? This indeed expresses perfectly that language is bounded by music on all sides.

From this we also see the connection with that misconception that music is supposed to be a richer medium than language. In other words, when language leaves off, music begins; when, as is said, everything is musical, one is not progressing but retrogressing. This is why—and perhaps the experts will agree with me on this—I have never had any sympathy for the sublimated music that thinks it does not need

words. Ordinarily, it thinks itself superior to words, although
it is inferior. The objection presumably could be made that if
it is true that language is a richer medium than music, then it
is incomprehensible that an esthetic analysis of the musical involves such great difficulty, incomprehensible that here language continually shows itself to be a poorer medium than
music. But this is neither incomprehensible nor unexplainable. Music always expresses the immediate in its immediacy.
This is also the reason that in relation to language music appears first and last, but this also shows that it is a mistake to say
that music is closer to perfection as a medium. Reflection is
implicit in language, and therefore language cannot express
the immediate. Reflection is fatal to the immediate, and therefore it is impossible for language to express the musical, but
this apparent poverty in language is precisely its wealth. In
other words, the immediate is the indeterminate, and therefore language cannot grasp it; but its indeterminacy is not its
perfection but rather a defect in it. We indirectly acknowledge
this in many ways. For example, we say: I cannot really explain why I do this or that in such a way—I play it by ear. For
something that has no connection with the musical, we often
use a phrase taken from music but denote thereby the vague,
the unexplained, the immediate.

Now, if it is the immediate, qualified by spirit, that receives
its proper expression in the musical, the question may be
raised again more pointedly: What kind of immediacy is it that
is essentially the theme of music? The immediate, qualified by
spirit, can be qualified in such a way that it either comes within
the realm of spirit or is outside the realm of spirit. When the
immediate, qualified by spirit, is qualified in such a way that it
falls within the realm of spirit, it can certainly find its expression in the musical, but this immediacy still cannot be music's
absolute theme, for when it is qualified in such a way that it
will fall within the realm of spirit, this suggests that music is in
alien territory; it forms a prelude that is continually being annulled. But if the immediate, qualified by spirit, is qualified in
such a way that it is outside the realm of spirit, then music has
in this its absolute theme. For the former immediacy, it is

unessential for it to be expressed in music, whereas it is essential for it to become spirit and consequently to be expressed in language. For the latter, however, it is essential that it be expressed in music; it can be expressed only therein and cannot be expressed in language, since it is qualified by spirit in such a way that it does not come within the realm of spirit and thus is outside the realm of language. But the immediacy that is thus excluded by spirit is sensuous immediacy. This is linked to Christianity. Sensuous immediacy has its absolute medium in music, and this also explains why music in the ancient world did not become properly developed but is linked to the Christian world. So it is the medium for the immediacy that, qualified by spirit, is qualified in such a way that it is outside the realm of spirit. Of course, music can express many other things, but this is its absolute theme. It is also easy to discern that music is a more sensuous medium than language, inasmuch as considerably more emphasis is placed on the sensuous sound in music than in language.

Consequently, sensuousness in its elemental originality is the absolute theme of music. The sensuous in its essential nature is absolutely lyrical, and in music it erupts in all its lyrical impatience. That is, it is qualified by spirit and therefore is power, life, movement, continual unrest, continual succession. But this unrest, this succession, does not enrich it; it continually remains the same; it does not unfold but incessantly rushes forward as if in a single breath. If I were to describe this lyricism with a single predicate, I would have to say: It sounds—and with this I come back again to the elemental originality of the sensuous as that which in its immediacy manifests itself musically.

That on this point even I could say a good deal more, I know; that it will be easy for the experts to clear everything up in an entirely different way, I am sure. But since no one, as far as I know, has made an attempt to do so or made a move toward doing so, since they merely go on repeating that Mozart's *Don Giovanni* is the crown among operas without developing further what they mean by that, although they all say it in a way that clearly shows that they thereby mean to say

something more than that *Don Giovanni* is the best opera, that
there is a qualitative difference between it and all other operas,
which certainly cannot be looked for in anything but the absolute relation between idea, form, subject matter, and medium—since, I repeat, this is the situation, I have broken silence. Perhaps I have been too hasty; perhaps I would have
succeeded in saying it better if I had waited even longer. Perhaps. I do not know. But this I do know, that I did not hurry
in order to have the pleasure of talking, that I did not hurry because I feared that someone more expert would beat me to it—
but I hurried because I feared that if I, too, remained silent the
stones would begin to speak[24] in praise of Mozart, to the disgrace of every human being to whom the gift of speech has
been granted.

What has already been said I assume will be more or less sufficient, as far as this little exploration is concerned, since essentially it is supposed to blaze the trail for a description of the immediate erotic stages as we come to know them in Mozart.
Before turning to that, however, I wish to mention a fact that
from another side can lead our thinking to the absolute relation
between the sensuous in its elemental originality and the musical. It is well known that music has always been the object of
suspicious attention on the part of religious fervor. Whether it
is right in this or not does not concern us here, for that would
indeed have only religious interest. It is not, however, without
importance to consider what has led to this. If I trace religious
fervor on this point, I can broadly define the movement as follows: the more rigorous the religiousness, the more music is
given up and words are emphasized. The different stages in
this regard are represented in world history. The last stage excludes music altogether and adheres to words alone. I could
embellish these statements with a multiplicity of specific comments, but I shall refrain and merely quote a few words by a
Presbyterian who appears in a story by Achim v. Arnim: "Wir
Presbyterianer halten die Orgel für des Teufels Dudelsack,
womit er den Ernst der Betrachtung in Schlummer wiegt, so
wie der Tanz die guten Vorsätze betäubt [We Presbyterians regard the organ as the devil's bagpipe, with which he lulls to

sleep the earnestness of contemplation, just as dance deadens good intentions]."[25] This must be regarded as a remark *instar omnium* [worth them all]. What reason can there be to exclude music in order thereby to make words alone predominant? That words, when they are misused, can confuse the mind just as much as music, all revivalist sects will surely admit. There must, then, be a qualitative difference between them. But that which religious fervor wants to have expressed is spirit; therefore it requires language, which is the spirit's proper medium, and rejects music, which for it is a sensuous medium and thus always an imperfect medium with which to express spirit. Whether religious fervor is right in excluding music is, as stated, another question, but its view of the relation of music to language may be perfectly correct. Music need not be excluded, then, but it must be understood that in the realm of spirit it nevertheless is an imperfect medium and that consequently it cannot have its absolute theme in the immediately spiritual qualified as spirit. It by no means follows that one must regard it as the devil's work, even though our age provides many horrible proofs of the demonic power with which music can grip an individual and this individual in turn intrigues and ensnares the crowd, especially a crowd of women, in the seductive snares of anxiety by means of the full provocative force of voluptuousness. It by no means follows that one must regard it as the devil's work, even though one detects with a certain secret horror that this art, more than any other art, frequently torments its devotees in a terrible way, a phenomenon, strangely enough, that seems to have escaped the attention of the psychologists and the mass, except on a particular occasion when they are alarmed by a desperate individual's scream of anxiety. But it is quite noteworthy that in folk legends, and consequently in the folk consciousness that the legends express, the musical is again the demonic. I cite, as an example, *Irische Elfenmärchen* by Grimm, 1826, pp. 25, 28, 29, and 30.[26]

As for the immediate-erotic stages, I am indebted for what I can say about them solely to Mozart, to whom on the whole I am indebted for everything. But since the classification I shall

I
55

attempt here can only indirectly, through someone else's
interpretation, be traced back to him, I have examined myself
and the classification before beginning in earnest, lest I in any
way might spoil for myself or a reader the joy of admiring
Mozart's immortal works. Anyone who wishes to see Mozart
in his true immortal greatness must consider his *Don Giovanni*,
in comparison with which everything else is incidental, unimportant. But if one considers *Don Giovanni* in such a way
that one includes specific things from Mozart's other operas in
this point of view, then I am convinced that one will neither
disparage him nor harm oneself and one's neighbor. There
will be occasion to rejoice that the intrinsic power of music is
fully expended in Mozart's music.

I
56

Moreover, when I use the term "stage" as I did and continue
to do, it must not be taken to mean that each stage exists independently, the one outside the other. I could perhaps more
appropriately use the word "metamorphosis." The different
stages collectively make up the immediate stage, and from this
it will be seen that the specific stages are more a disclosure of a
predicate in such a way that all the predicates plunge down in
the richness of the last stage, since this is the stage proper. The
other stages have no independent existence; by themselves
they are only for representation, and from that we also see
their fortuitousness in relation to the last stage. But since they
have found a separate expression in Mozart's music, I shall discuss them separately. But, above all, they must not be thought
of as persons on different levels with respect to consciousness,
since even the last stage has not yet attained consciousness; at
all times I am dealing only with the immediate in its total immediacy.

The difficulties that always arise when music is made the
object of esthetic consideration will of course not be absent
here either. The chief difficulty in the foregoing was that,
whereas I wanted to demonstrate by way of thought that the
elemental originality of the sensuous is music's essential
theme, this still can be demonstrated properly only by music,
just as I myself also came to a knowledge of it through music.
The difficulty with which the subsequent discussion must

struggle is more particularly this: since that which music expresses, the theme under discussion here, is essentially the proper theme of music, music expresses it much better than language is capable of doing, which shows up very poorly alongside it. Indeed, if I were dealing with the different levels of consciousness, the advantage naturally would be on my side and on the side of language, but that is not the case here. Consequently, what will be developed here can have meaning only for the person who has heard and continually keeps on listening. For him it perhaps may contain a particular hint that can prompt him to listen again.

FIRST STAGE[27]

The first stage is suggested by the Page in *Figaro*. The point here, of course, is not to see a single individual in the Page, something one is so easily tempted to do when in thought or in actuality the Page is represented by a person. It then becomes difficult to avoid the intrusion of something incidental, some irrelevant idea (which more or less does happen with the Page in the play), so that he becomes more than he is supposed to be, for in a certain sense he promptly becomes that as soon as he becomes an individual. But in becoming more, he becomes less; he ceases to be the idea. This is why he cannot be given lines, but the music remains the only adequate expression, and thus it is noteworthy that *Figaro* and *Don Giovanni*, in their original form from the hand of Mozart, belong to *opera seria* [serious opera].[28] If, then, the Page is regarded in this way as a mythical character, the characteristic features of the first stage will be found expressed in the music.

The sensuous awakens, yet not to motion but to a still quiescence, not to delight and joy but to deep melancholy. As yet desire is not awake; it is intimated in the melancholy. That which is desired is continually present in the desire; it arises from it and appears in a bewildering dawning. This occurs in the sphere of the sensuous, is put at a distance by clouds and mists, and is brought closer by reflection in them. Desire possesses what will become the object of its desire but possesses it without having desired it and thus does not possess it. This is the painful, but also in its sweetness the fascinating and enchanting contradiction, which with its sadness, its melancholy, resonates through this stage. Its pain consists not in there being too little but rather in there being too much. The desire is quiet desire, the longing quiet longing, the infatuation quiet infatuation, in which the object is stirring and is so close to the desire that it is within it. That which is desired floats above the desire, sinks down into it, not because of the desire's own drawing power or because of being desired. That which is desired does not vanish, does not squirm out of desire's embrace, for then desire would indeed awaken; but without being desired, it is there for desire, which then becomes depressed precisely because it cannot begin to desire. As soon as desire awakens or, more correctly, in and with its awakening, desire and the object of desire are separated; now desire breathes freely and soundly, whereas before it could not draw its breath because of that which was desired. When desire has not awakened, that which is desired fascinates and captivates—indeed, almost causes anxiety. The desire must have air, must find escape; this occurs through their being separated. That which is desired shyly flees, bashful as a woman, and the separation occurs; that which is desired vanishes *et apparet sublimis* [and is seen aloft][29] or in any case outside desire. Painters say that a ceiling painted with figures, one alongside the other, presses down; a single figure done lightly and elusively elevates the ceiling. Such is the relation between desire and the desired in a first and a later stage.

Desire, consequently, which in this stage is present only in a presentiment of itself, is devoid of motion, devoid of unrest, only gently rocked by an unaccountable inner emotion. Just as the life of the plant is confined to the earth, so it is lost in a quiet ever-present longing, absorbed in contemplation, and still cannot discharge its object, essentially because in a more profound sense there is no object; and yet this lack of an object is not its object, for then it would immediately be in motion, then it would be defined, if in no other way, by grief and pain; but grief and pain do not have the implicit contradiction characteristic of melancholy [*Melancholi*] and depression [*Tungsin-dighed*], do not have the ambiguity that is the sweetness in melancholy. Although desire in this stage is not qualified as desire, although this intimated desire is altogether vague about its object, it nevertheless has one qualification—it is infinitely deep. Like Thor, it sucks through a horn, the tip of which rests in the ocean;[30] but the reason that it cannot suck its object to itself is not that the object is infinite, but that this infinity cannot become an object for it. Thus the sucking [*Sugen*] does not indicate a relation to the object but is identical with its sighing [*Suk*], and this is infinitely deep.

In accord with the description of the first stage given here, it is very significant that the music for the role of the Page is arranged for a woman's voice. The inconsistency in this stage seems to be suggested by this contradiction; the desire is so vague, the object so little separated from it, that what is desired rests androgynously in the desire, just as in plant life the male and female are in one blossom. The desire and the desired are joined in this unity, that they both are *neutrius generis* [of neuter gender].

Although the speaking lines belong not to the mythical Page but to the Page in the play, the poetic character Cherubino, and although consequently they cannot be considered in this connection, since for one thing they do not belong to Mozart and for another they express something entirely different from what is under discussion here, I nevertheless want to emphasize in some detail one particular line because it gives me an opportunity to characterize this stage in its analogy to a later stage. Susanna mocks Cherubino because he, too, is in a way infatuated with Marcellina, and the Page has no other answer handy than to say: She is a woman.[31] With regard to the Page in the play, it is essential that he be in love with the countess, unessential that he can fall in love with Marcellina, which is merely an indirect and paradoxical expression for the violence of the passion with which he is captivated by the countess. With regard to the mythical Page, it is equally essential that he be in love with the countess and with Marcellina, for feminin-

ity is indeed his object, and this they both have in common.
Therefore, when we later hear about Don Giovanni:

> Even coquettes as old as sixty
> He gladly records in his tally,[32]

we have the perfect analogy to this, except that the intensity
and firmness of the desire are far more developed.

Now, if I were to venture an attempt at characterizing Mozart's music with a single predicate pertaining to the Page in
Figaro, I would say: It is intoxicated with erotic love; but, like
all intoxication, an intoxication with erotic love can also have
two effects, either a heightened transparent joy of life or a concentrated obscure depression. The latter is the case with the
music here, and this is indeed proper. The music cannot explain why this is so, for it is beyond its power to do that.
Words cannot express the mood, for it is too heavy and dense
to be borne by words—only music can render it. The basis of
its melancholy lies in the deep inner contradiction we tried to
point out earlier.

We now leave the first stage, epitomized by the mythical
Page; we let him, depressed, continue to dream about what he
has, melancholy, to desire what he possesses. He never goes
further; he never moves from the spot, for his movements are
illusory, and hence there is no movement at all. The Page in
the play is another matter; with true and honest friendliness we
shall be interested in his future. We congratulate him on having become a captain; we permit him to kiss Susanna once
more in farewell. We shall not betray him with regard to the
mark on his forehead, which no one can see except the one
who knows about it.[33] But no more than this, my good Cherubino, or we shall call the count, and then it will be "Be off!
There is the door! To your regiment! After all, he is no child,
and no one knows that better than I do."

SECOND STAGE

This stage is epitomized by Papageno in *The Magic Flute*.[34]
Here again, of course, the point is to separate the essential

from the accidental, to evoke the mythical Papageno and forget the actual character in the play, and especially here, since this character in the play has become involved in all sorts of dubious nonsense. In this connection, it would not be devoid of interest to go through the whole opera to show that its theme, regarded as a theme for an opera, is a failure at its deepest level. There would also be no lack of opportunity to illuminate the erotic from a new side by observing how the attempt to put a more profound ethical view into it, in such a way that it tries its hand at all sorts of rather important dialectical engagements, is a daring venture that has ventured far beyond the boundaries of music, so that it was impossible even for a Mozart to invest it with any deeper interest. The distinguishing tendency in this opera is precisely the unmusical, and therefore, despite some perfect concert numbers and a few deeply moving, pathos-filled lines, it is by no means a classic opera. But all this cannot concern us in the present little exploration. Our only concern here is Papageno. This is a great advantage for us, if for no other reason than that we are thereby exempt from any attempt to explain the significance of Papageno's relation to Tamino, a relation that in design appears so profound and thoughtful that it practically becomes unthinkable because of its very thoughtfulness.

Such a treatment of *The Magic Flute* perhaps could seem arbitrary to one or another reader, because it sees both too much in Papageno and too little in the rest of the opera; he may not be able to sanction our conduct. This is because he does not agree with us on the point of departure for any consideration of Mozart's music. This, in our judgment, is *Don Giovanni*, and it is also our conviction—without denying the importance of making each opera the subject of a special study—that the greatest veneration of Mozart is shown if several other operas are looked at in relation to this one.

Desire awakens, and just as we always realize that we have dreamed only in the moment we awaken, so also here—the dream is over. This awakening in which desire awakens, this jolt, separates desire and its object, gives desire an object. A dialectical qualification that must be strictly maintained is this:

only when there is an object is there desire; only when there is
desire is there an object. The desire and the object are twins,
neither of which comes into the world one split second before
the other. But even though they came into the world absolutely coinstantaneously, and even though they do not have an
interval of time between them, as twins generally have, the
significance of this coming into existence [*Tilblivelse*] is not
that they are united but rather that they are separated. But this
movement of the sensuous, this earthquake, splits the desire
from its object infinitely for a moment; but just as the moving
principle shows itself for a moment as disuniting, so it manifests itself in turn as wanting to unite the separated. The result
of the separation is that desire is torn out of its substantial repose in itself, and as a consequence of this, the object no longer
falls under the rubric of substantiality but splits up into a multiplicity.

Just as the plant's life is confined to the soil, so the first stage
is captivated in substantial[35] longing. Desire awakens, the object flees, multiple in its manifestation; longing tears itself
loose from the soil and takes to wandering. The flower acquires wings and flutters, fitful and tireless, here and there.
Desire turns toward the object; it is also internally moved. The
heart beats, sound and happy; the objects swiftly appear and
vanish, but before each disappearance there is nevertheless an
instant of enjoyment, a moment of contact, short but sweet,
glowworm brilliant, fitful and fleeting as the alighting of a
butterfly, and as harmless, and there are innumerable kisses,
but so quickly enjoyed that seemingly only that is taken from
one object which is bestowed on the next. Only momentarily
is there a presentiment of a deeper desire, but this presentiment
is forgotten.

In Papageno, desire aims at discoveries. This urge to discover is the pulsation in it, its liveliness. It does not find the
proper object of this exploration, but it discovers the multiplicity in seeking therein the object that it wants to discover. In
this way desire is awakened, but it is not qualified as desire. If
it is kept in mind that desire is present in all three stages, then
it can be said that in the first stage it is qualified as *dreaming*, in

the second as *seeking*, in the third as *desiring*. That is, the seeking desire is not yet desiring desire; it is only seeking that which it can desire but does not desire it. Therefore, perhaps the most suggestive predicate for it is: it discovers. If we compare Papageno with Don Giovanni, then his journey through the world is something more than a journey of discovery; not only does he enjoy the adventure of a journey of discovery, but he is a knight who is out for victories (*veni—vidi—vice* [I came, I saw, I conquered]).[36] The discovery and the victory are identical here; indeed, in a certain sense one may say that in the victory he forgets the discovery or that the discovery lies behind him, and he therefore leaves it to his servant and secretary Leporello, who keeps a list in quite another sense than I would imagine Papageno would keep an account. Papageno selects, Don Giovanni enjoys, Leporello reviews.

I 63

As with every stage, I can represent in thought what is characteristic of this stage, but always only in the moment it has ceased to be. But even if I could describe ever so completely what is characteristic of it and give the reason for it, there would always be something left over that I cannot express and that nevertheless wants to be heard. It is too immediate to be contained in words. So it is with Papageno—it is the same song, the same melody; he begins all over again as soon as he finishes, and so on continually. The objection could be made to me that it is altogether impossible to express something immediate. In a way, this is entirely correct, but, in the first place, the immediacy of spirit has its immediate expression in language, and, in the second place, if a change occurs in it through the intervention of thought, it still remains essentially the same simply because it is a qualification of spirit. But here it is an immediacy of the sensuous, which as such has a completely different medium, where as a consequence the disparity between the media makes the impossibility absolute.

If I were to venture to characterize with a single predicate the Mozart music in the part of the play that concerns us, I would say: It is exuberant, merrily twittering, bubbling over with love. What I must emphasize particularly is the first aria and the chimes; the duet with Pamina and later with Papagena falls completely outside the qualification of the immediate-musical. But if one takes the first aria into consideration, then one presumably will approve the predicates I have used and, if one pays closer attention, will also have the opportunity to see what importance the musical has where it appears as the absolute expression for the idea and how this as a consequence is immediate-musical. As is known, Papageno accompanies his cheerful liveliness on a reed flute. Surely every ear has felt strangely moved by this accompaniment. But the more one thinks about it, the more one sees in Papageno the mythical Papageno, the more expressive and the more characteristic it proves to be. One does not weary of hearing it over and over again, for it is the absolutely adequate expression of Papageno's whole life, whose whole life is such an uninterrupted twittering, without a care twittering away uninterruptedly in complete idleness, and who is happy and contented because this is the substance of his life, happy in his work and happy in his singing. As is known, the opera is very profoundly designed in such a way that Tamino's and Papageno's flutes harmonize with each other. And yet what a difference! Tamino's flute, which nevertheless is the one the play is named after, miscarries completely, and why? Because Tamino simply is not a musical character. This is due to the misbegotten structure of the whole opera. Tamino with his flute becomes very boring and sentimental, and if all the rest of his development, his state of consciousness, is considered, then every time he takes out his flute and blows a piece on it one thinks of the peasant in Horace (*rusticus exspectat, dum defluat amnis* [the bumpkin waiting for the river to run out]),[37] except that Horace did not give his peasant a flute for pointless pastime. As a dramatic character, Tamino is completely beyond the musical, just as in general the spiritual development the play wants to accomplish is a completely unmusical idea. Tamino has simply come so far that the musical ceases, and therefore his flute playing is only a waste of time to drive away thoughts. Music is indeed excellent for driving away thoughts, even evil thoughts, as in the case of David, whose playing is said to have driven away Saul's evil mood.[38] But there is a considerable illusion here, for it does so only insofar as it leads the consciousness back into immediacy and soothes it therein. Therefore, the individual may feel happy in the moment of intoxication but becomes only all the more unhappy. Here I may be permitted a comment quite *in parenthesi*. Music has been used to cure insanity and in a certain sense this goal has been attained, and yet this is an illusion. When insanity has a mental basis, it is always due to a hardening at some point in the consciousness. This hardening must be overcome, but for it to be truly overcome the road to be taken must be the very opposite of the one that leads to music. When music is used, one is on the wrong road altogether and makes the patient even more insane, even if he seems not to be so anymore.

I
65

What I have said about Tamino's flute playing I presumably can let stand without fear of having it misunderstood. It is not at all my intention to deny what in fact has been acknowledged many times, that music may have its importance as an accompaniment when entering a foreign domain, namely, the domain of language. The defect, however, in *The Magic Flute* is that the whole piece tends toward consciousness, and as a consequence the actual tendency of the piece is to annul the music, and yet it is supposed to be an opera, and not even this idea is clear in the piece. Ethically qualified love or marital love is set as the goal of the action, and therein lies the play's basic defect, for whatever that is, ecclesiastically or secularly speaking, one thing it is not, it is not musical—indeed, it is absolutely unmusical.

The first aria, then, has its great importance musically as the immediate-musical expression of Papageno's whole life—and history, which is the absolutely adequate expression for this in the same degree that music is, is history only metaphorically. The chimes, however, are the musical expression for his activity, of which, in turn, a notion is gained only through the music; it is enchanting, tempting, alluring, just like the playing of the man who made the fish stop and listen.[39]

The spoken lines, which are either Schikaneder's or the Danish translator's,[40] are generally so lunatic and foolish that it is almost incomprehensible how Mozart has brought as much out of them as he has done. To have Papageno say of himself, "I am a child of nature,"[41] and then in the very same moment make a liar of himself, can be regarded as an example *instar omnium* [worth them all]. An exception could be made of the words in the text of the first aria, that he puts the girls he catches into his cage.[42] If one puts a little more into them than the author himself in all likelihood did, then they characterize precisely the innocence of Papageno's activity, just as we have suggested above.

We now leave the mythical Papageno. The fate of the actual Papageno cannot concern us. We wish him happiness with his little Papagena, and we gladly let him seek his joy in populating a primeval forest or a whole continent with nothing but Papagenos.[43]

THIRD STAGE

This stage is epitomized by *Don Giovanni*. Here I am not in the position, as heretofore, of having to isolate a specific portion of an opera; here the point is not to separate but to synthesize, since the whole opera is essentially the expression of the idea and, with the exception of a few particular numbers, centers essentially in this and with dramatic necessity gravitates to this as its pivot. Here again there will be occasion to see in what sense I can call the previous stages by that name when I call *Don Giovanni* the third stage. I indicated earlier that they do not have any separate existence, and since my starting point is this third stage, which actually is the whole stage, they cannot very well be regarded as one-sided abstractions or preliminary anticipations, but rather as intimations of *Don Giovanni*, except that there still is always something left over that somewhat justifies use of the word "stage"—namely, that they are one-sided intimations, that every one of them intimates only one side.

The contradiction in the first stage consisted in the inability of desire to find an object, but, without having desired, desire did possess its object and therefore could not begin desiring. In the second stage, the object appears in its multiplicity, but since desire seeks its object in this multiplicity, in the more profound sense it still has no object; it is still not qualified as desire. In *Don Giovanni*, however, desire is absolutely qualified as desire; intensively and extensively it is the immediate unity of the two previous stages. The first stage ideally desired the one; the second desired the particular in the category of multiplicity; the third stage is the unity of the two. In the particular, desire has its absolute object; it desires the particular absolutely. In this resides the seductiveness that we shall discuss later. In this stage, therefore, desire is absolutely genuine, victorious, triumphant, irresistible, and demonic. Therefore, of course, it must not be overlooked that the issue here is not desire in a particular individual but desire as a principle, qualified by spirit as that which spirit excludes. This is the idea of the elemental originality of the sensuous, as suggested above. The expression for this idea is Don Juan, and the expression for Don Juan, in turn, is simply and solely music. It is especially these two observations that will now be stressed continually from various sides, and thereby the classic significance of this opera will be indirectly demonstrated. Meanwhile, to make it easier for the reader to maintain an overview, I shall attempt to gather the scattered observations under specific themes.

To say something specific about this music is not my aim, and with the aid of all congenial spirits I shall take care not to scare up a mass of pointless but very noisy predicates or in linguistic excess to make manifest the impotence of language— and all the more so since I regard it not as an imperfection on the part of language but as a high potency, but for this reason I am more willing to acknowledge music within its boundary. What I want to do, however, is in part to illuminate the idea from as many sides as possible and its relation to language and thereby continually to encompass more and more the territory where music is at home, to provoke it, so to speak, to declare itself, without my being able to say, when it can be heard, any more than: Listen. I think that thereby I have wanted to do the best that esthetics is able to do; whether I shall be successful is another matter. In only a single place will a predicate, like an

I
67

arrest warrant, provide a description of it, but I shall not therefore forget or allow my reader to forget that the person who
has an arrest warrant in his hand has by no means thereby apprehended the person it names. Furthermore, the design of the
whole opera, its inner structure, will be discussed separately in
the appropriate place, but again in such a way that I do not permit myself to shout loudly enough for two: *Oh, bravo, schwere
Noth, Gotts Blitz, bravissimo* but just keep on tempting forth
the musical and think that thereby I have wanted to do the best
one is capable of doing purely esthetically with the musical.
Therefore, I shall not give a running commentary on the music, which essentially cannot contain anything but subjective
incidentals and idiosyncrasies and can apply only to something
corresponding in the reader. Even a commentator like Dr.
Hotho,[44] so discriminating and fertile in reflection, so copious
in expression, has been unable to avoid, on the one hand, having his interpretation deteriorate into verbiage (which is supposed to constitute recompense for Mozart's sonority or
sound like a faint echo, a pale copy of Mozart's rich, full-toned
luxuriance) and, on the other hand, having Don Giovanni at
times become more than he is in the opera, become a reflective
individual, and at times become less. The latter comes about,
of course, because the deep and absolute point of *Don Giovanni*
has escaped Hotho. For him *Don Giovanni* is still only the best
opera; it is not qualitatively different from all other operas.
But if one has not discerned this with the ubiquitous certainty
of the speculative eye, then one cannot speak worthily or val-
idly about *Don Giovanni*, even though, if one has discerned it,
one would be able to speak far more magnificently and richly
and, above all, more truthfully about it than the one who here
dares to speak.

I shall, however, continually track down the musical in the
idea, the situation, etc., explore it by listening, and when I
have brought the reader to the point of being so musically receptive that he seems to hear the music although he hears nothing, then I shall have finished my task, then I shall fall silent,
then I shall say to the reader, as I say to myself: Listen. You
friendly jinn who protect all innocent love, I commit my

whole mind to you; guard my laboring thoughts so that they may be found worthy of the subject; form my soul into a euphonious instrument; let the gentle breeze of eloquence hasten over it; send the refreshment and blessing of fruitful moods! You righteous spirits, you who guard the boundaries of the kingdom of beauty, guard me lest I, in confused enthusiasm and blind zeal to make *Don Giovanni* all in all, do it an injustice, disparage it, make it something other than what it really is, which is the highest! You powerful spirits who know how to grasp men's hearts, stand by me so that I may capture the reader, not in the net of passion or the wiles of eloquence, but in the eternal truth of conviction.

1. *The Elementary Originality of the Sensuous Qualified as Seduction*

I
69

When the idea of Don Juan emerged is not known; only this much is certain—that it is linked to Christianity and through Christianity to the Middle Ages. Even if the idea could not be traced with some certainty back to this world-historical period in the human consciousness, every doubt would be removed at once by a consideration of the inner nature of the idea. On the whole, the Middle Ages is the idea, partly conscious, partly unconscious, of representation; the totality is represented in a particular individual, yet in such a way that it is only a particular aspect that is defined as the totality and that is now manifest in a particular individual, who is therefore both more than and less than an individual. Then alongside this individual stands another individual, who just as totally represents another aspect of the content of life—for example, the knight and the scholastic, the clergyman and the layman. Here the great dialectic of life is continually exemplified in representative individuals, who are ordinarily paired opposite to each other. Life is continually approached *sub una specie* [under one form], and there is no inkling of the great dialectical unity that life possesses in unity *sub utraque specie* [under both forms].[45] The contrasts, therefore, are generally indifferent, detached from one another. Of this the Middle Ages was not aware. Thus the Middle Ages itself actualized the idea of representation unconsciously, whereas a later reflection first perceives the idea in it.

If the Middle Ages places before its own consciousness an individual as representative of the idea, then it usually places another individual alongside him in relation to him. This relation, then, is customarily a comic relation, in which one individual, as it were, makes up for the other's disproportionate magnitude in actual life. For example, the king has the fool by his side, Faust has Wagner, Don Quixote has Sancho Panza, Don Juan has Leporello. This structure also is linked essentially to the Middle Ages. Consequently the idea is linked to the Middle Ages, but in the Middle Ages it is not linked to a particular poet—it is one of those powerful, primitive ideas that emerge from the folk consciousness with autochthonic originality.

The Middle Ages had to make the discord between the flesh and the spirit that Christianity brought into the world the subject of its reflection and to that end personified each of the conflicting forces. Don Juan, then, if I dare say so, is the incarnation of the flesh, or the inspiration of the flesh by the spirit of the flesh itself. This notion has already been brought out sufficiently in the foregoing discussion; what I would like to call attention to here, however, is whether Don Juan ought to be assigned to the earlier or later Middle Ages. That he stands in an essential relation to the Middle Ages is easy for anyone to see. Either he is the contentious, mistaken anticipation of the erotic, which became manifest in the knight, or chivalry is still only a relative contrast to spirit, and not until the contrast split even more deeply did Don Juan emerge as sensuality that is mortally opposed to spirit. The erotic in the age of chivalry has a certain resemblance to that in Greek culture in that both are psychically qualified, but the difference is that its psychical qualification lies within a universal spiritual qualification or a qualification as totality. The idea of femininity is continually in motion in many ways, which was not the case in Greek culture, where everyone was just the beautiful individuality but there was no intimation of femininity. Therefore, in the consciousness of the Middle Ages, the erotic of chivalry was also in a moderately conciliatory relation to spirit, even though spirit in its zealous rigor held it suspect.

If the point of departure is that the principle of spirit is posited in the world, then, on the one hand, it may be supposed that the most striking contrast, the most scandalous separation, was the first to appear, and thereafter it was gradually mitigated. In that case, Don Juan belongs to the earlier Middle Ages. But if it is assumed that the relation gradually developed into this absolute contrast, which is also more natural inasmuch as spirit takes more and more of its shares of stock out of the united corporation in order to work alone, whereby the real σκάνδαλον [offense] comes to light, then Don Juan belongs to the later Middle Ages. Then we are led in time to the point where the Middle Ages begins to soar, where we then also meet a related idea, namely, Faust, except that Don Juan must be placed a little earlier. As spirit, qualified solely as spirit, renounces this world, feels that the world not only is not its home but is not even its stage, and withdraws into the higher realms, it leaves the worldly behind as the playground for the power with which it has always been in conflict and to which it now yields ground. Then, as spirit disengages itself from the earth, the sensuous shows itself in all its power. It has no objection to the change; indeed, it perceives the advantage in being separated and is happy that the Church does not induce them to remain together but cuts in two the band that binds them.

Stronger than ever before, the sensuous now awakens in all its profusion, in all its rapture and exultation, and—just as that hermit in nature, taciturn echo, who never speaks first to anyone or speaks without being asked, derived such great pleasure from the knight's hunting horn and from his melodies of erotic love [*Elskov*], from the baying of the hounds, from the snorting of the horses, that it never wearied of repeating it again and again and finally, as it were, repeated it very softly to itself in order not to forget it—so it was that the whole world on all sides became a reverberating abode for the worldly spirit of sensuousness, whereas spirit had forsaken the world.

I
71

In the Middle Ages, much was told about a mountain that is not found on any map; it is called Mount Venus. There sensuousness has its home; there it has its wild pleasures, for it is a kingdom, a state. In this kingdom, language has no home, nor the collectedness of thought, nor the laborious achievements of reflection; there is heard only the elemental voice of passion, the play of desires, the wild noise of intoxication. There everything is only one giddy round of pleasure. The firstborn of this kingdom is Don Juan. But it is not said thereby that it is the kingdom of sin, for it must be contained in the moment when it appears in esthetic indifference. Only when reflection enters in does the kingdom manifest itself as the kingdom of sin, but then Don Juan has been slain, then the music stops, then one sees only the desperate defiance that powerlessly resists but can find no firm ground, not even in sounds. When sensuousness manifests itself as that which must be excluded, as that with which the spirit does not wish to be involved, but when spirit has not as yet convicted it or condemned it, sensuousness takes this form, is the demonic in esthetic indifference. It is a matter of only a moment; soon all is changed, and then the music, too, is over. Faust and Don Juan are the Middle Ages' titans and giants, who in the grandness of their achievements are not different from those of antiquity, except admittedly in this, that they stand isolated, do not form an amalgamation of powers that only through amalgamation become heaven-storming; instead, all the power is concentrated in this one individual.

Don Juan, then, is the expression for the demonic qualified as the sensuous; Faust is the expression for the demonic qualified as the spiritual that the Christian spirit excludes. These ideas have an essential relation to each other and are very similar, and consequently it could be expected that they also have this in common, that both have been preserved in a legend. As is known, this is the case with Faust. There is a folk book,[46] the title of which is rather familiar even though the book itself is little used, which is especially strange in our age when everybody is so engrossed in the idea of Faust. So it goes—while every would-be assistant professor or professor thinks he will be accredited as intellectually mature by the reading public through the publication of a book about Faust, in which he faithfully repeats what all the other graduates and scholarly confirmands have already said, he thinks he dares to ignore such an insignificant little folk book. It never occurs to him how beautiful it is that true greatness is common to all, that a farmhand goes to Tribler's widow[47] or to a ballad-monger on Halmtorv[48] and reads it half aloud to himself at the same time Goethe is writing a *Faust*.[49] Indeed, this folk book deserves attention. Above all, it has what is praised as a commendable quality in wine: it has bouquet. It is a splendid vintage from the Middle Ages, and, when it is opened, such an aromatic, delicious, and distinctive fragrance flows forth that one has a very special feeling.

But enough of this. I would only point out that there is no such legend about Don Juan. No folk book, no ballad has preserved his memory by being published continually this year.[50] Presumably a legend has existed nevertheless, but in all probability it was limited to only a few hints that were perhaps even briefer than the few stanzas on which Bürger's *Lenore*[51] is based. Perhaps it contained only a number, for, unless I am greatly mistaken, the present number, 1,003,[52] does belong to a legend. A legend that has nothing else seems somewhat meager and in a way easily accounts for its not being written down, but still this number has an excellent quality, a lyrical recklessness, which many perhaps do not notice because they are so accustomed to seeing it. Although this idea has not found its expression in a folk legend, it has been preserved in another way. As is known, Don Juan existed long ago as melodrama; indeed, this was probably its first existence. But here the idea was conceived comically; moreover, it is noteworthy that just as the Middle Ages was very proficient in fitting out ideals, it was equally sure to see the comic in the preternatural magnitude of the ideal. To make Don Juan a braggart who imagined he had seduced all the girls and to have Leporello believe his lies certainly was not an altogether bad comic design. And even if that has not been the case, even if that has not been the idea, the comic twist still could never be avoided, since it is implicit in the contradiction between the hero and the arena in which he moves. Thus the Middle Ages may be allowed to tell about heroes so mightily constructed that their eyes were a foot apart,[53] but if an ordinary man were to come onstage and pretend to have eyes a foot apart, the comic would be well under way.

The above remarks about the legend of Don Juan would not have been included here if they were not closely related to the subject of this study, if they did not serve to lead our thoughts to the goal already set. The reason that this idea, compared with Faust, has such a meager past is no doubt due to something enigmatic in it as long as it was not perceived that music is its proper medium. Faust is idea, but an idea that also is essentially an individual. To conceive of the spiritual-demonic concentrated in one individual is natural to thought, whereas to conceive of the sensuous in one individual is impossible. Don Juan continually hovers between being idea—that is, power, life—and being an individual. But this hovering is the musical vibration. When the sea heaves and is rough, the seething waves in their turbulence form pictures resembling creatures; it seems as if it were these creatures that set the waves in motion, and yet it is, conversely, the swelling waves that form them. Thus, Don Juan is a picture that is continually coming into view but does not attain form and consistency, an individual who is continually being formed but is never finished, about whose history one cannot learn except by listening to the noise of the waves.

When Don Juan is comprehended in this way, there is meaning and deep significance in everything. If I imagine a particular individual, if I see him or hear him talk, then his having seduced 1,003 becomes comic; for as soon as he is a particular individual, the accent falls on an altogether different place—that is, the emphasis is on those whom he has seduced and how. The naïveté of legend and popular superstition can successfully state such things without hinting at the comic; for reflection, this is not possible. But when he is conceived in music, then I do not have the particular individual, then I have a force of nature, the demonic, which no more wearies of seducing or is through with seducing than the wind with blowing a gale, the sea with rocking, or a waterfall with plunging down from the heights. For that matter, the number of the seduced can just as well be any number whatever, a much larger number.

In translating the libretto for an opera, the translator frequently has a very difficult task to do it so accurately that not only is the translation singable but the meaning harmonizes fairly well with the text and thus with the music. I cite, as an example of its sometimes being an altogether indifferent matter, the number in the list in *Don Giovanni*, without, however, taking it as lightly as people usually would take it, thinking that nothing depends on such things. On the contrary, I view the matter with great esthetic seriousness and therefore regard it as a matter of indifference. But I do want to commend one quality of the number 1,003—namely, that it is uneven and accidental, which is by no means unimportant; it gives the impression that the list is not at all final, but rather that Don Giovanni is on the move. We almost feel sorry for Leporello, who not only, as he himself says, must hold watch outside the door but, in addition, must keep account books so complex that they would give an experienced office secretary enough to do.

The sensuous as it is conceived in Don Juan, as a principle, has never before been so conceived in the world; for this reason the erotic is here qualified by another predicate: here the erotic is *seduction*. Strangely enough, the idea of a seducer was totally lacking in Greek culture. It is not my intention to laud Greek culture in any way for this, because, as everyone knows, the gods as well as human beings were promiscuous in love affairs; neither do I censure Christianity, for, after all, it has the idea only outside itself. The reason Greek culture lacks this idea is that its whole life is qualified as individuality. Thus the psychical is predominant, or always in harmony with the sensuous. Its love was therefore psychical, not sensuous, and it is this that instills the modesty that rests over all Greek love. They fell in love with a girl, moved heaven and earth to possess her; when they succeeded, they perhaps grew weary of her and sought a new love. In their inconstancy, they certainly could have a certain resemblance to Don Juan, and, to mention just one example, Hercules undoubtedly could provide a considerable list if one bears in mind that he sometimes took interest in entire families, numbering as many as fifty maidens[54] and, as a kind of family son-in-law, polished them all off, by some accounts, in a single night. Yet he is essentially different from a Don Juan: he is no seducer. When one reflects on Greek love, it is according to its concept essentially faithful simply because it is psychical; and it is something accidental in the particular individual that he loves many; and with regard to the many he loves, it is again accidental every time he loves a new one; when he loves one, he is not thinking of the next one.

Don Juan, however, is a downright seducer. His love is sensuous, not psychical, and, according to its concept, sensuous love is not faithful but totally faithless; it loves not one but all—that is, it seduces all. It is indeed only in the moment, but considered in its concept, that moment is the sum of moments, and so we have the seducer. Chivalric love is also psychical and therefore, according to its concept, essentially faithful; only the sensuous, according to its concept, is essentially faithless. But its faithlessness manifests itself in another way also: it continually becomes only a repetition.

Psychical love contains the dialectical in two ways. For one thing, there is in it doubt and disquietude about whether it will be happy, see its desire fulfilled, and be loved. Sensuous love does not have this concern. Even a Jupiter is unsure of his victory, and this cannot be otherwise; indeed, he himself cannot wish it otherwise. This is not the case with Don Juan; he is brisk about his business and must always be regarded as completely victorious. This could seem to be to his advantage, but it is actually destitution. Furthermore, psychical love also has another dialectic in that it is different also according to the relationship with each particular individual who is the object of love. Therein lies its richness, its fullness of content.

Such is not the case with Don Juan. For this he has no time; for him everything is merely an affair of the moment. In a certain sense it can be said of psychical love that to see her and to love her are the same, but this only suggests a beginning. It holds true in a different way in connection with Don Juan. To see her and to love her are the same; this is in the moment. In the same moment everything is over, and the same thing repeats itself indefinitely. If one imagines Don Juan as having psychical love, then to place 1,003 in Spain becomes ludicrous and a contradiction that is not even in accordance with the idea. It becomes an extravagance with a disturbing effect, even if one fancied that he was conceived ideally. If there is no medium other than language to describe this love, then one is in trouble, for as soon as one has given up the naïveté that can simple-mindedly maintain that in Spain there are 1,003, something more is demanded: namely, psychical individualizing. The esthetic is not at all satisfied with tossing everything together this way and wanting to astonish with the size of the number. Psychical love moves precisely in the rich variety of the individual life, where the nuances are the really significant. Sensuous love, however, can toss everything together. For it, the essential is completely abstract femininity and at most the more sensuous difference. Psychical love is continuance in time; sensuous love is disappearance in time, but the medium that expresses this is indeed music.

Music is superbly suited to achieve this, since it is much more abstract than language and therefore articulates not the particular but the universal in all its universality, and yet it articulates this universality not in the abstraction of reflection but in the concretion of immediacy. To give an example of what I mean, I shall discuss in some detail the second servant aria: the list of those seduced. This number may be regarded as Don Juan's true epic.

If you doubt the correctness of what I say, then try an imaginary construction. Imagine a poet, one more fortunately equipped by nature than anyone preceding him. Give him richness of expression; give him mastery and authority over the powers of language; let everything that has a breath of life be obedient to him, submissive to his slightest hint; let everything wait, prepared and primed, upon his word of command; let him be surrounded by a considerable company of light skir-

I
76

mishers, fleet-footed messengers who run down thought in its
swiftest flight; let nothing escape him, not even the slightest
movement; let him lack no secret, nothing ineffable, in the entire world—then give him the task of celebrating Don Juan in
epic style, of unrolling the list of the seduced. What will be the
result: he will never finish. The defect, if you please, of the epic
is that it can go on as long as necessary; his hero, the impro-
viser, Don Juan, can go on as long as necessary. The poet will
now introduce multiplicity, and there will always be enough
in it that will please, but he will never achieve the effect Mozart
achieved, for even if he did eventually finish,[55] he still would
not have said half of what Mozart has expressed in this one
number.

Mozart did not become involved in multiplicity; there are
certain large formations that pass by. This has an adequate basis in the medium itself, in the music, which is too abstract to
express the differences. Hence the musical epic is relatively
somewhat short, and yet in an unrivaled way it has the epic
quality of being able to go on as long as necessary, since one
can always have it begin from the beginning and listen to it
again and again, simply because the universal is expressed and
is expressed in the concretion of immediacy. Here one does
not hear Don Giovanni as a particular individual; one does not
hear what he says but hears his voice, the voice of the sensuous, and hears it through the longings of femininity. Don
Giovanni can become epic only by continually finishing and
continually being able to begin all over again, for his life is the
sum of *repellerende* moments [*Momenter*][56] that have no coherence, and his life as the moment is the sum of moments and as
the sum of moments is the moment. Don Giovanni lies within
this universality, in this hovering between being an individual
and a force of nature; as soon as he becomes an individual, the
esthetic acquires completely different categories.

That is why it is quite in order and has deep inner significance that in the seduction that occurs in the play, Zerlina's seduction, the girl is an ordinary peasant girl. Pseudo-estheti-
cians, who, pretending to understand poets and composers,
contribute everything to a misunderstanding of them, will

perhaps inform us that Zerlina is an unusual girl. Anyone who believes this shows that he has totally misunderstood Mozart and that he is using incorrect categories. That he misunderstands Mozart is certainly clear, for Mozart has purposely kept Zerlina as insignificant as possible, which Hotho[57] also is aware of, without, however, perceiving the basic reason. If Don Giovanni's love had been qualified otherwise than as sensuous, if he had been a seducer in the intellectual-spiritual sense—something we shall consider later—then it would have been a basic defect in the piece to have the heroine be a little peasant girl in the seduction that engages us dramatically in the play. In that case, the esthetic would demand that he be given a more difficult task. But for Don Giovanni these differences do not apply. If I may imagine that he would speak about himself in this way, he would perhaps say, "You are mistaken. I am no husband who needs an unusual girl to make me happy; every girl has what makes me happy, and therefore I take them all." That is how the words I touched on earlier must be understood: even coquettes as old as sixty—or in another place: *pur chè porti la gonella, voi sapete quel chè fà* [if she just wears a skirt, you know well enough what he does].[58] For Don Giovanni, every girl is an ordinary girl, every love affair a story of everyday life. Zerlina is young and beautiful, and she is a woman; this is the extraordinary that she shares with hundreds of others. But it is not the extraordinary that Don Giovanni desires, but the ordinary that she shares with every woman. If this is not the case, then Don Giovanni ceases to be absolutely musical; then the esthetic demands words, lines, whereas now, since it is the case, Don Giovanni is absolutely musical.

I would like to illuminate the inner structure of the piece from another side as well. Elvira is a dangerous enemy to Don Giovanni. This is frequently emphasized in the lines by the Danish translator.[59] Certainly it is a mistake for Don Giovanni to have lines to speak, but it does not follow from this that there should not be a single good comment among them. So Don Giovanni is afraid of Elvira. Presumably some esthetician would give a thorough explanation of this by coming up with a long rigmarole about Elvira as an extraordinary girl etc. This

I
78

misses the point completely. She is dangerous to him because she has been seduced. In the same way, in entirely the same way, Zerlina is dangerous to him when she has been seduced. As soon as she has been seduced, she is raised to a higher sphere; she has a consciousness that Don Giovanni lacks. That is why she is dangerous to him. This, again, is not because of the accidental but because of the universal.

So Don Giovanni is a seducer; his eroticism is seduction. This no doubt says very much when it is understood properly, but very little when it is interpreted with a certain customary vagueness. We have already seen that with respect to Don Giovanni the concept of a seducer is essentially modified, since the object of his desire is the sensuous and this alone. This was important in order to display the musical in Don Giovanni. In antiquity, the sensuous found its expression in the mute stillness of sculpture; in the Christian world, the sensuous had to burst out in all its impatient passion. Although it can thus be truly said that Don Giovanni is a seducer, this term, which can easily confuse the weak brains of some estheticians, frequently gives occasion for misunderstanding when some random comments that could be said about such a person and have been scraped together then are automatically transferred to Don Giovanni. At times, by tracking down Don Giovanni's cunning, they have exposed their own to the light of day; at times they have talked themselves hoarse explaining his machinations and ingenuity—in short, the word "seducer" has prompted everyone to deal with him as best he could and to contribute his bit to a total misunderstanding.

Provided that it is more urgent for one to say something correct than to say anything whatsoever, one must apply the word "seducer" to Don Giovanni very cautiously. This is not because Don Giovanni is so perfect, but because he does not fall within ethical categories at all. Therefore, I would rather call him a deceiver, since there is always something more ambiguous in that term. To be a seducer always takes a certain reflection and consciousness, and as soon as this is present, it can be appropriate to speak of craftiness and machinations and subtle wiles.[60] Don Giovanni lacks this consciousness. Therefore, he does not seduce. He desires, and this desire acts seductively. To this extent he does seduce. He enjoys the satisfaction of desire; as soon as he has enjoyed it, he seeks a new object, and so it goes on indefinitely. Thus he does indeed deceive, but still not in such a way that he plans his deception in advance; it is the power of the sensuous itself that deceives the seduced, and it is rather a kind of nemesis.[61] He desires and continually goes on desiring and continually enjoys the satisfaction of desire. He lacks the time to be a seducer, the time beforehand in which to lay his plan and the time afterward in which to become conscious of his act. A seducer, therefore, ought to possess a power that Don Giovanni does not have, however well equipped he is otherwise: the power of words. As soon as we give him the power of words, he ceases to be musical, and the esthetic interest becomes a different one.

Achim v. Arnim tells somewhere[62] of a seducer with an entirely different style, a seducer who falls within ethical categories. Arnim describes him with words that in their truthfulness, boldness, and pithiness are almost a match for a stroke of the bow by Mozart. He declares that he could speak with a woman in such a way that if the devil grabbed him he would talk himself free if he could manage to speak with his dam. This is the genuine seducer; the esthetic interest here is also something else: namely, the how, the method.[63] Therefore there is something very profound (perhaps most people have not noticed it) in the fact that Faust, who reproduces Don Juan, seduces only one girl, whereas Don Giovanni seduces by the hundreds; but in intensity this one girl is seduced and destroyed in an entirely different way than all those Don Giovanni deceived—precisely because Faust as a reproduction has an intellectual-spiritual quality. The power of a seducer like that is speech: that is, the lie. A few days ago, I heard a soldier speaking with another soldier about a third one who had deceived a girl; he did not describe it in detail, and yet his expression was excellent: "He knew how to do it with lies and all that." Such a seducer is of a kind entirely different from Don Giovanni, differs from him essentially, which can also be seen in this, that he and his activities are extremely unmusical and

I
80

esthetically fall within the category of the interesting.[64] Therefore, from the properly esthetic point of view, the object of his
desire is also something more than the merely sensuous.

But what kind of power is it, then, by which Don Giovanni
seduces? It is the energy of desire, the energy of sensuous desire. He desires total femininity in every woman, and therein
lies the sensuous, idealizing force with which he simultaneously enhances and overcomes his prey. The reflection of this
immense passion enhances and develops the desired one, who
blushes in heightened beauty because of its reflection. Just as
the fire of the enthusiast envelops with a seductive luster even
those uninvolved persons who have some relation to him, so
in a far deeper sense he transfigures every girl, since his relation to her is an essential relation. This is why all the finite differences vanish for him in comparison with the main point: to
be a woman. The old ones he rejuvenates into the beautiful
middle age of womanhood; the child he almost matures in an
instant; everything that is woman is his prey (*pur chè porti la gonella, voi sapete quel chè fà*). But this must not be understood as
if his sensuousness were blindness; instinctively he knows
very well how to make distinctions, and, above all, he ideal-
izes. If I think back momentarily to a preceding stage, to the
Page, the reader will perhaps recall that already in speaking of
him I compared a remark by the Page with a remark by Don
Giovanni. I have the mythical Page remain; I have the actual
one join the army. If I now were to imagine that the mythical
Page had extricated himself and had begun to move, I would
call to mind here a comment by the Page that applies to Don
Giovanni. When Cherubino, light as a bird, boldly leaps
through the window, it affects Susanna so powerfully that she
nearly faints, and when she has recovered she cries out, "See
how he runs—oh, won't he be a success with the girls!"[65] This
is entirely appropriate for Susanna to say, and the reason for
her fainting is not simply the performance of the bold leap but
rather that he has already been a success with her. In fact, the
Page is the eventual Don Giovanni, although this must not be
ludicrously construed, as if by growing older the Page became
Don Giovanni. Now, Don Giovanni not only is a success with

the girls, but he makes the girls happy—and unhappy—yet strangely enough in such a way that that is what they want, and it would be a poor sort of girl who would not wish to become unhappy in order to have been happy once with Don Giovanni.

Therefore, even if I go on calling Don Giovanni a seducer, I nevertheless do not at all think of him slyly laying his plans, subtly calculating the effect of his intrigues; that by which he deceives is the sensuous in its elemental originality, of which he is, as it were, the incarnation. Shrewd levelheadedness is lacking in him; his life is sparkling like the wine with which he fortifies himself; his life is turbulent like the melodies that accompany his joyous repast; he is always jubilant. He needs no preparation, no plan, no time, for he is always ready; that is, the power is always in him, and the desire also, and only when he desires is he properly in his element. He sits down to dinner; happy as a god he flourishes his goblet—he rises with the napkin in his hand, ready for the attack. If Leporello awakens him in the middle of the night, he always wakes up sure of his victory. But this power, this force, cannot be expressed in words; only music can give us a notion of it; for reflection and thought it is inexpressible. The craftiness of an ethically defined seducer I can clearly put into words, and music would venture in vain to carry out this task. With Don Giovanni, it is the opposite. What kind of power is it? No one can say. Even if I asked Zerlina about it before she goes to the ball: By what power does he enthrall you?—she would answer: No one knows. And I would say: Well spoken, my child! You speak more wisely than the wise men of India; *richtig, das weisz man nicht* [correct, no one knows that], and the trouble is that I cannot explain it, either.

This power in Don Giovanni, this omnipotence, this life, only music can express, and I know no other predicate to describe it than: it is exuberant gaiety. Thus when Kruse has Don Giovanni, as he comes onstage at Zerlina's wedding, say, "Cheer up, children! You are indeed all dressed as for a wedding,"[66] he is saying something entirely appropriate and also something more than he perhaps thinks. Indeed, he himself

brings the gaiety with him, and as for the wedding, it is not
without significance that they are all dressed as for a wedding,
because Don Giovanni is the groom not only for Zerlina, but
he celebrates with games and songs the wedding of the young
girls in the whole parish. No wonder that they flock about
him, the happy maidens. Nor are they disappointed, for he has
enough for all. Flattery, sighs, bold glances, tender hand-
clasps, secret whispers, the dangerous closeness, the tempting
distance—and yet these are only the lesser mysteries, prenup-
tial gifts. It is a delight for Don Giovanni to survey such a rich
harvest; he takes care of the whole parish, and yet it perhaps
does not take him as long a time as Leporello spends at the office.

All this discussion leads again to the real subject of this investigation, that Don Giovanni is absolutely musical. He desires sensuously; he seduces with the demonic power of the
sensuous; he seduces all. Words, lines, are not suitable for him,
for then he immediately becomes a reflective individual. He
does not have that kind of continuance at all but hurries on in
an eternal vanishing, just like the music, which is over as soon
as the sound has stopped and comes into existence again only
when it sounds once again.

Therefore, if I were to raise the question of Don Giovanni's
appearance, is he handsome, young or old, approximately
how old, then it would only be a concession from my side and
what can be said about it can expect to find a place here in the
same way a tolerated sect finds a place in the state church.
Handsome he is, not exactly young; if I were to suggest his
age, I would suggest thirty-three years, which is the age of a
generation. The dubiousness of becoming involved in such investigations is that one easily loses the totality in dwelling on
the particular, as if Don Giovanni seduced with his handsomeness or anything else that could be mentioned; then one sees
him but no longer hears him, and thereby he is lost. So if I,
trying to do my part to help the reader gain a picture of Don
Giovanni, were to say: See, there he stands! See how his eyes
flame; he smiles triumphantly, so sure is he of his conquest.
See his royal countenance, claiming that which is Caesar's.[67]

See how lightly he steps in the dance, how proudly he offers his hand. Who is the lucky one to whom it is offered? Or if I were to say: Look, there he stands in the forest shadows; he is leaning against a tree and accompanies himself on a guitar, and look, over there among the trees a young maiden is disappearing, alarmed like a startled wild deer. But he is in no hurry; he knows that she is seeking him. Or if I were to say: There he rests on the lake shore in the luminous night, so handsome that the moon stands still and relives the love affair of its youth,[68] so handsome that the young maidens of the town would give everything in daring to sneak over and make use of a moment of darkness to kiss him while the moon is rising again to shine in the heavens—if I did that, the alert reader would say: See here, there he has spoiled everything for himself; he himself has forgotten that Don Giovanni is not to be seen but is to be heard. Therefore I do not do that but say: Listen to Don Giovanni—that is, if you cannot get an idea of Don Giovanni by hearing him, then you never will. Listen to the beginning of his life; just as the lightning is discharged from the darkness of the thunderclouds, so he bursts out of the abyss of earnestness, swifter than the lightning's flash, more capricious than lightning and yet just as measured. Hear how he plunges down into the multiplicity of life, how he breaks against its solid embankment. Hear these light, dancing violin notes, hear the intimation of joy, hear the jubilation of delight, hear the festive bliss of enjoyment. Hear his wild flight; he speeds past himself, ever faster, never pausing. Hear the unrestrained craving of passion, hear the sighing of erotic love, hear the whisper of temptation, hear the vortex of seduction, hear the stillness of the moment—hear, hear, hear Mozart's Don Giovanni.

2. Other Versions of Don Juan Considered in Relation to the Musical Interpretation

I
84

It is common knowledge that the idea of Faust has been the subject of numerous interpretations, but this is by no means the case with Don Juan. This might seem strange, all the more so since the second idea characterizes a far more universal period in the development of individual life than the first. But the ready explanation of this is that the Faustian idea presupposes a kind of intellectual-spiritual maturity, which much more naturally lends itself to interpretation. Besides that, as I have pointed out above with respect to the fact that there does not exist a legend of that kind about Don Juan, people obscurely felt the difficulty with respect to the medium until Mozart discovered the medium and the idea. From that moment on, the idea first gained its deserved position and in turn has more than ever filled a span of years in individual life, but so satisfyingly that the urge to condense poetically what was experienced in fantasy did not become a poetic necessity. This in turn is an indirect demonstration of the absolutely classic rank of the Mozart opera. The ideal along this line had already found its perfect artistic expression to such a degree that it could indeed be tempting, but not tempting to poetic productivity.

Mozart's music certainly has been tempting, for where is the young man who has not had a moment in his life when he would have given half his kingdom to be a Don Juan, or perhaps all of it, when he would have given half his lifetime for one year of being Don Juan, or perhaps his whole life? But that was as far as it went. The more profound natures, who were moved by the idea, found everything, even the softest breeze, expressed in Mozart's music; in its grandiose passion, they found a full-toned expression for what stirred in their own inner beings, they perceived how every mood strained toward that music just as the brook hurries on in order to lose itself in the infinitude of the sea. These natures found just as much text as commentary in the Mozartian Don Juan, and thus as they glided onward and downward in its music and relished the joy of losing themselves in this way, they also acquired the riches of admiration. The Mozartian music was in no respect too narrow; on the contrary, their own moods were expanded, took on a preternatural magnitude when they rediscovered them in Mozart. The lower natures, who have no intimation of the infinite, perceive no infinitude. The bunglers, who think themselves a Don Juan because they have pinched a peasant girl's cheek, put their arms around a waitress, or made a young girl blush, of course understand neither the idea nor Mozart, or how to produce a Don Juan themselves, except as a ludicrous freak, a family idol, who perhaps to the misty, sentimental eyes of some cousins would seem to be a true Don Juan, the epitome of all charm. In this sense, Faust has not as yet found an expression and, as noted above, never can, inasmuch as the idea is much more concrete. An interpretation of Faust can merit being called perfect, and yet a later generation will give rise to a new Faust, whereas Don Juan, because of the abstract character of the idea, lives on forever, in every age, and to wish to produce a Don Juan after Mozart will always be like wanting to write an *Ilias post Homerum* [*Iliad* after Homer] in a sense even more profound than is the case with Homer.

Now even if what has been developed here is correct, it by no means thereby follows that a particular gifted nature should not have attempted to interpret Don Juan in some other way. Everyone knows this, but not everyone may have noticed that the model for all other interpretations is essentially Molière's *Don Juan*;[69] but this, in turn, is much older than Mozart's and is also comic, and in relation to Mozart's *Don Giovanni* is like a fairy tale in Musæus's[70] interpretation in relation to a version by Tieck.[71] Therefore, I can in fact limit myself to a discussion of Molière's *Don Juan*, and as I try to make an esthetic assessment of it, I shall indirectly be assessing the other interpretations. But I make an exception of Heiberg's *Don Juan*.[72] He himself declares in the title that it is "modeled partly on Molière." This is indeed entirely true, but nevertheless Heiberg's play has a great advantage over Molière's. This no doubt is due to the sure esthetic eye with which Heiberg always comprehends his task, the taste with which he knows how to discriminate, but in the present instance it is still not impossible that Prof. Heiberg was indirectly influenced by Mozart's interpretation to see—namely, how Don Juan must be interpreted as soon as music is not made its proper expression or he is placed in completely different esthetic categories. Professor Hauch has also produced a *Don Juan*[73] that is on the verge of falling within the category of the interesting. Therefore, as I go on to discuss the other group of versions of Don Juan, I presumably need not point out to the reader that this is done not for their own sake in the present little exploration but only in order to illuminate the significance of the musical interpretation more fully than was possible in the previous discussion.

The turning point in the interpretation of Don Juan has already been designated above in this way: as soon as he is given spoken lines, everything is changed. That is, the reflection that motivates the lines reflects him out of the vagueness in which he is only musically audible. This being so, it might seem that Don Juan could be interpreted best as ballet.[74] It is indeed well known that he has been interpreted in this way. Yet this interpretation must be commended for having known its powers, and for this reason it has limited itself to the final scene, where the passion in Don Juan would be most readily visible in the pantomimic play of muscles. As a consequence, here again Don Juan is presented not in his essential passion but according to the accidental, and the poster advertising such a performance always includes more than the play; that is, it says that it is Don Juan, the seducer Don Juan, whereas the ballet presents almost nothing more than the torments of despair, the expression of which, since it has to be solely in pantomime, he shares with many others who are in despair. What is essential in Don Juan cannot be presented in ballet, and everyone readily feels how ludicrous it would be to watch Don Juan infatuating a girl by means of dance steps and ingenious gesticulations. Don Juan is an inner qualification and thus cannot become visible or appear in bodily configurations and movements or in molded harmony.

Even if Don Juan is not given speaking lines, an interpretation of Don Juan that nevertheless uses words as a medium is conceivable. And there actually is such an interpretation by Byron.[75] That Byron was in many ways particularly endowed to present a Don Juan is certain enough, and therefore one can be sure that when that undertaking failed, the reason was not in Byron but in something far deeper. Byron has ventured to bring Don Juan into existence for us, to tell us of his childhood and youth, to construct him out of the context of his finite life-relationships. But Don Juan thereby became a reflective personality who loses the ideality he has in the traditional picture.

I shall quickly explain here the change that takes place in the idea. When Don Juan is interpreted musically, I hear in him the total infinitude of passion, but also its infinite power that nothing can resist; I hear the wild craving of desire, but also the absolute victoriousness of this desire, against which any attempted opposition would be ineffectual. If thought dwells just once on the obstruction, then it is more likely to gain importance just by inciting passion than by actually creating opposition; the pleasure is increased, the victory is certain, and the obstruction is only a stimulation. In Don Juan, I have such a rudimentarily stirred life, demonically powerful and irresistible. This is his ideality, and this I can enjoy undisturbed, because to me music presents him not as a person or individual but as a power. If Don Juan is interpreted as an individual, then he is *eo ipso* in conflict with the world about him. As an individual, he feels the constraint and the fetters of these surroundings; as a great individual he may triumph over them, but one immediately feels that the difficulties of the obstructions play a different role here. The interest is preoccupied essentially with them. But Don Juan is thereby drawn under the rubric of the interesting. If by means of turgid words he were to be presented here as absolutely victorious, one would promptly feel this to be unsatisfactory, since it does not belong to an individual as such to be victorious, and one demands the crisis of conflict.

The opposition that the individual must combat can in part be something external that is not so much in the object of attention as in the surrounding world; it can in part be in the object itself. The first has been the preoccupation of nearly all the interpretations of Don Juan because they have clung to the element of the idea that as an erotic he must be triumphant. If, on the other hand, the other side is stressed, only then, I believe, is there any prospect of a significant interpretation of Don Juan that would form a counterpart to the musical Don Juan, whereas any interpretation of Don Juan that lies between these would always have imperfections. In the musical Don Juan, there would then be the extensive seducer; in the other, the intensive. So the latter Don Juan is not presented as possessing his object with one single blow—he is not the immediately qualified seducer; he is the reflective seducer.[76] That which occupies us here is the subtlety, the cunning, whereby he knows how to steal into a girl's heart, the dominion he knows how to gain over it, the enthralling, deliberate, progressive seduction. How many he has seduced is of no importance here; what occupies us is the artistry, the meticulousness, the profound cunning with which he seduces. Ultimately the enjoyment itself becomes so reflective that by comparison it becomes quite different from the musical Don Juan's enjoyment. The musical Don Juan enjoys the satisfaction; the reflective Don Juan enjoys the deception, enjoys the craftiness. The immediate pleasure is past, and reflection on the enjoyment is enjoyed more. In this respect, there is a little hint in Molière's interpretation, except that this can by no means be developed, because all the remainder of the interpretation is a hindrance. Don Juan's desire is aroused because he sees a girl happy in her relation to the one she loves; he begins to be jealous. This is an interest that in the opera would not occupy us at all, simply because Don Juan is not a reflective individual. As soon as Don Juan is interpreted as a reflective individual, an ideality corresponding to the musical ideality can be attained only when the matter is shifted into the psychological realm. What is achieved, then, is the ideality of intensity. Therefore, Byron's *Don Juan* must be regarded as a failure because it stretches out epically. The immediate Don Juan must seduce 1,003; the reflective Don Juan needs to seduce only one, and how he does it is what occupies us. The reflective Don Juan's seduction is a tour de force in which every particular little episode has its special significance; the musical Don Juan's seduction is a turn of the hand, a matter of a moment, more quickly done than said. It reminds me of a tableau I once saw. A handsome young man, a real ladies' man. He was playing with some young girls, all of them at that dangerous age when they are neither adults nor children. Among other things, they amused themselves by jumping over a ditch. He stood at the edge and helped them jump by taking them around the waist, lifting them lightly into the air, and setting them down on the other side. It was a charming

picture; I delighted in him as much as in the young girls. Then
I thought of Don Juan. They themselves run into his arms,
these young girls; then he seizes them, and just as quickly, just
as nimbly sets them down on the other side of the ditch of life.

I
89

The musical Don Juan is altogether victorious and therefore, of course, is also in complete possession of every means
that can lead to this victory, or, more correctly, he is in such
complete possession of the means that it seems as if he did not
need to use them—that is, he does not use them as means. As
soon as he becomes a reflective individual, it is apparent that
there is something called means. If the poet now gives them to
him but along with them makes the opposition and the obstruction so alarming that the victory becomes doubtful, Don
Juan then falls under the rubric of the interesting, and in this
respect many interpretations of Don Juan are imaginable, until
one reaches what we previously called intensive seduction. If
the poet denies him the means, the interpretation falls under
the rubric of the comic.

A consummate interpretation that has drawn him under the
rubric of the interesting, I have not seen; it holds true, however, of most versions of Don Juan that they approach the
comic. This is easily explained by their attachment to Molière,
in whose interpretation the comic is dormant, and it is to Heiberg's credit that he was clearly aware of this and therefore not
only calls his play a marionette show but in so many other
ways has the comic shine forth. As soon as a passion, in being
depicted, is denied the means to its satisfaction, either a tragic
or a comic turn will be produced. A tragic turn cannot very
well be produced when the idea is perceived to be wholly un-
justified, and therefore the comic is so close at hand. If I portray an individual with a passion for gambling and then give
him five rix-dollars to gamble away, the turn would be comic.
This does not entirely apply to Molière's *Don Juan*, but still
there is a similarity. If I have Don Juan be financially embarrassed, plagued by creditors, he promptly loses the ideality he
has in the opera, and the effect becomes comic. The famous
comic scene in Molière,[77] which as a comic scene is very good
and is also very appropriate in his comedy, should, of course,

never be included in the opera, where it has a totally disturbing
effect.

That Molière's version aims at the comic is apparent not
only in the comic scene just mentioned, which, if it were completely isolated, would prove nothing, but in the whole design, which bears the imprint of it. Sganarelle's first and last
lines, the beginning and the end of the whole play, more than
adequately testify to this. Sganarelle begins with a eulogy on a
pinch of snuff, from which one sees, among other things, that
he must not be so very busy in this Don Juan's service; he ends
by complaining that he is the only one who has been wronged.
If one considers that Molière also has the statue come and fetch
Don Juan and that he, although Sganarelle also has been a witness to this dreadful thing, puts these words into his mouth as
if he were saying that the statue, since, incidentally, it devoted
itself to practicing justice on earth and punishing vice, also
ought to have been ready to pay Sganarelle the wages due him
for long and faithful service to Don Juan, which his master, because of his sudden departure, did not find himself in a position to do—if one considers this, one will sense the comic in
Molière's *Don Juan*.[78] (Heiberg's version, which has the great
advantage over Molière's of being more correct, has also in
many ways produced a comic effect by putting a random kind
of learning into Sganarelle's mouth, which makes us see in
him a prattling charlatan who after attempting many things
ends up as Don Juan's servant.) The hero in the piece, Don
Juan, is anything but a hero; he is a hapless fellow who probably failed his examinations and now has chosen another ca-
reer. Indeed, we learn that he is a son of a very distinguished
man who, with a conception of his forefather's great name,
moreover is trying to inspire him to virtue and immortal
deeds,[79] but this is so unlikely in view of all his other behavior
that one is inclined to think the whole thing a lie that Don Juan
himself has invented. His conduct is not very chivalrous: we
do not see him with sword in hand carving a path through
life's difficulties; now he gives this one a clout on the ear, now
the next one—indeed, he as much as comes to blows with one
girl's fiancé.[80] So if Molière's Don Juan really is a knight, the

poet is very adept at making us forget it and strives therefore to have us see a rowdy, a common rake, who is not afraid to use his fists. Anyone who has had a chance to observe what we call a rake also knows that this class of men has a great preference for the sea. He will therefore also find it entirely appropriate that Don Juan has caught sight of a couple of skirts and immediately sets after them in a boat from Kallebostrand,[81] a Sunday adventure at sea, including the capsizing of the boat. Don Juan and Sganarelle are almost dispatched and at last are saved by Pedro and the tall Lucas,[82] who at first were betting on whether it actually was human beings out there or a stone, a bet that costs Lucas one mark, eight shillings, which is almost too much for Lucas and Don Juan. If one finds this entirely appropriate, the impression is shaken for a moment when we learn that Don Juan is also the fellow who has seduced Elvira, murdered the Commander, etc., something one finds extremely unreasonable and that in turn must be explained as a lie in order to bring about harmony. If Sganarelle is supposed to give us a notion of the passion raging in Don Juan, then his expression is such a travesty that it is impossible to keep from laughing—for example, when Sganarelle tells Gusman that Don Juan, in order to obtain the one he wants, "would gladly marry her dog or cat—yes, even worse, marry you, too."[83] Or when he makes the remark that his master is a disbeliever not only in love but also in medicine.[84]

Now, if Molière's interpretation of Don Juan, regarded as a comic version, were correct, I would not discuss it any further, since in this investigation I am dealing only with the ideal interpretation and the significance of music for it. I could then be satisfied with pointing out the noteworthy fact that only in music has Don Juan been interpreted ideally in the ideality he has in the Middle Age's traditional conception. The lack of an ideal interpretation in the medium of language could then provide an indirect proof for the legitimacy of my thesis. But here I can do more, precisely because Molière is not correct, and what prevents him from being so is that he has retained something of the ideal in Don Juan along the lines attributable to traditional conception. As I point out, it will again be apparent that this can be expressed essentially only by music, and thus once again I come back to my original thesis.

Right away in the first act of Molière's *Don Juan*, Sganarelle has a very long speech in which he attempts to give us a notion of his master's unbounded passion and the multiplicity of his adventures. This speech parallels precisely the servant's second aria in the opera. The speech produces only a comic effect, nothing more, and here again Heiberg's version has the advantage in that the comic is less heterogeneous than in Molière. This [speech], however, is an attempt to prompt in us an intimation of his power, but it is ineffective; only music can achieve this unity, because simultaneously with a description of Don Juan's conduct, at the same time as the list is unrolled for us, it makes us hear the power of the seduction.

In Molière, the statue comes in the last act to fetch Don Juan. Even though the poet, by means of an advance warning, attempted to provide a motive for the statue's stepping forth, this stone nevertheless is always a stumbling block from a dramatic point of view. If Don Juan is ideally interpreted as power, as passion, then heaven itself must intervene. If not, it is always dubious to use such strong means. Indeed, the Commander did not need to inconvenience himself, since it is far more practicable for Mr. Paaske[85] to have Don Juan put into the debtor's prison. This would be entirely in the spirit of modern comedy, which does not need such great powers in order to crush, simply because the moving powers themselves are not very grandiose. It would be quite modern to have Don Juan come to know the commonplace bounds of actuality. In the opera, it is entirely appropriate to have the Commendatore come again, but, after all, his conduct has ideal truth. The music immediately makes the Commendatore more than a particular individual; his voice is enlarged to the voice of a spirit. Therefore, just as Don Juan in the opera is interpreted with esthetic earnestness, so also is the Commendatore. In Molière, he comes with an ethical solemnity and heaviness that make him almost ludicrous; in the opera, he comes with esthetic lightness and metaphysical truth. No power in the play, no power on earth, has been able to constrain Don Juan; only a spirit, an apparition, is able to do that. Understood correctly, this in turn will illuminate the interpretation of Don Juan. A spirit, an apparition, is reproduction;[86] this is the secret implicit in the coming again. But Don Juan is capable of everything, can withstand everything, except the reproduction of life, precisely because he is immediate, sensate life, of which spirit is the negation.

Thus, Sganarelle, as interpreted by Molière, becomes unexplainable, a person with an extremely confused character. Once again, the disruptive element here is that Molière has preserved something of the traditional. Since Don Juan on the whole is a power, this is also manifest in his relation to Leporello. The latter feels drawn to him, overwhelmed by him, is assimilated by him, and becomes merely an organ for his master's will. It is precisely this vague, opaque sympathy that makes Leporello a musical person, and it is entirely appropriate that he is not capable of detaching himself from Don Juan. It is another matter with Sganarelle. In Molière, Don Juan is a particular individual, and consequently Sganarelle enters into a relation with him as an individual. Now, if Sganarelle feels indissolubly linked to him, it is no more than a reasonable esthetic demand to insist on information about how this can be explained. It does not help that Molière has him declare that he cannot detach himself from him, for the reader or spectator sees no reasonable basis for it, and whether there is a reasonable basis is precisely the issue here. Leporello's inconstancy is well motivated in the opera, because in his relation to Don Juan he is closer to being an individual consciousness, and therefore the Don Juanian life is reflected differently in him, although he still is not really able to penetrate it. In Molière, Sganarelle is also sometimes worse, sometimes better, than Don Juan, but it becomes incomprehensible that he does not leave him, since he does not even receive his wages. If anyone imagines a unity in Sganarelle comparable to the sympathetic musical vagueness Leporello has in the opera, there is no alternative except to admit that this is biased foolishness. Here again is an example of how the musical must be featured in order that Don Juan can be interpreted in his true ideality. The defect in Molière is not that he has interpreted him comically but that he has not been correct.

Molière's Don Juan is also a seducer, but the piece gives us
only a poor idea of it. That Elvira in Molière's play is Don
Juan's wife is without a doubt very appropriately designed
with a view to the comic effect. It is immediately apparent that
one is dealing with an ordinary person who uses promises of
marriage to deceive a girl. Elvira thereby loses all the ideal
stance she has in the opera, where she counters with no
weapon other than that of offended womanhood, whereas
here we imagine her with her marriage documents, and Don
Juan loses the seductive ambiguity of being a young man and
an experienced husband—that is, experienced in all ventures
outside marriage. How he deceived Elvira, by what means he
lured her out of the convent, all this we presumably are to
learn from a few of Sganarelle's lines, but since the seduction
scene that occurs in the play does not give us an occasion to
admire Don Juan's art, confidence in those reports is naturally
weakened. Insofar as Molière's Don Juan is comic, this was indeed unnecessary; but since he himself still wants to have us
understand that his Don Juan actually is the hero Don Juan,
who has infatuated Elvira and murdered the Commander,
the mistake in Molière is readily apparent. Then, however, one is
also made to reflect on whether this really was not due to the
impossibility of portraying Don Juan as a seducer without the
aid of music, unless, as noted above, one enters the psychological, which, again, cannot readily acquire dramatic interest.
Furthermore, in Molière, one does not hear him as he infat-
uates the two young girls, Mathurine and Charlotte; the infatuation occurs offstage. Since here in turn Molière has us con-
jecture that Don Juan has given them promises of marriage,
one again has only mediocre thoughts about his talent. To deceive a girl with a promise of marriage is a very inferior art,
and because someone is small enough to do that, it certainly
does not follow that he is great enough to be called Don Juan.
The only scene that seems to be intended to depict Don Juan
for us in his seductive, yet scarcely tempting, activity is the
scene with Charlotte.[87] But to tell a young peasant girl that she
is beautiful, that she has sparkling eyes, to ask her to turn
around so that one can look at her shape,[88] does not betray
anything extraordinary in Don Juan but betrays a lecherous

fellow who looks at a young girl the way a trader looks at a
horse. Admittedly the scene does have a comic effect, and if it
was supposed to have only that, I would not discuss it here.
But since this, his notorious venture, has no relation to the
many affairs he must have had, this scene in turn contributes
directly or indirectly to showing the imperfection of the comedy. Molière seems to have wanted to make something more
of him, seems to have wanted to maintain the ideal in him, but
he lacks the medium, and thus everything that actually occurs
is rather insignificant. On the whole, it may be said that in
Molière's *Don Juan* we come to know only historically that he
is a seducer; it is not made visible dramatically. The scene in
which he shows himself most active is the scene with Charlotte and Mathurine,[89] where he leads both of them on with talk
and continually makes each one think that she is the one he has
promised to marry. But what draws our interest here is not his
seductive art but a very ordinary theatrical intrigue.

In the margin: I / 95

In conclusion, I perhaps can illuminate what has been discussed here with a comment frequently heard: that Molière's
Don Juan is more moral than Mozart's *Don Giovanni*. But precisely this, properly understood, is high praise of the opera. In
the opera, not only is there talk about a seducer, but Don Juan
is a seducer, and it cannot be denied that in every detail the music often can be seductive enough. But so it ought to be, and
this is precisely its greatness. Therefore, to say that the opera
is immoral is fatuous and comes only from people who do not
understand how to interpret a totality but are trapped by details. The definitive aim of the opera is highly moral, and the
impression it leaves is altogether beneficent, because everything is large-scale, everything has genuine, unadorned pathos, the passion of desire no less than the passion of earnestness, the passion of enjoyment no less than the passion of
anger.

3. The Inner Musical Construction
of the Opera

Although the heading of this section must be regarded as already adequately enlightening, I nevertheless shall take the
precaution of noting that it naturally is not my intention at all

to make an esthetic assessment of the piece *Don Giovanni* or to
trace the dramatic structure of the text. One must always be
careful about taking something apart in this way, especially if
it is a classic production. I repeat again here what I have already
frequently emphasized in the foregoing discussion—that Don
Juan can be expressed only musically; this I myself have
learned essentially through the music, and for this reason I
ought to take care in every way lest it seem that the music
lends a hand in an extraneous manner. If the matter is treated
in that way, then for my part the music in this opera may be
admired as much as one wishes—its absolute meaning has not
been grasped. However talented Hotho's exposition is otherwise, he has not kept himself free of this kind of false abstraction, and therefore it cannot be regarded as satisfactory. His
style, his exposition, and his reproduction are lively and stirring; his categories are indefinite and nebulous; his interpretation of *Don Giovanni* is not permeated by one thought but is
disintegrated into many. For him Don Giovanni is a seducer.
But even this category is indefinite, and yet it must be specified
in what sense he is that, as I have tried to do. Many things that
are true in themselves are said about this seducer; but since
general conceptions are permitted to be much too prevalent
here, such a seducer readily becomes so reflective that he ceases
to be absolutely musical. He goes through the piece scene by
scene; his account is refreshingly leavened by his individuality,
in a few places perhaps a bit too much. When this happens,
there frequently follow sympathetic outpourings on how
beautifully and richly and profusely Mozart has expressed all
this. But this lyrical rapture over Mozart's music is not
enough, and however well it suits the man, and however
beautifully he knows how to express himself, Mozart's *Don
Giovanni* is not acknowledged in its absolute validity by this
interpretation. This acknowledgment is what I am striving
for, because this acknowledgment is identical with the proper
insight into what constitutes the subject of this investigation.
Therefore, my aim is to make the subject of consideration not
the whole opera but the opera in its totality, not to discuss the
individual parts separately but as far as possible to incorporate

them into the whole, to see them not as detached from the whole but integrated in it.

In a drama, the main interest is naturally concentrated on what is called the hero of the piece; in relation to him, the other characters take on only subordinate and relative importance. But the more the inward reflection in the drama permeates with its power of distinguishing, the more the subordinate characters also take on a kind of relative absoluteness, if I dare put it that way. This is not a defect at all but is rather a merit, just as the view of the world that can see only the few outstanding individuals and their importance in world development, but does not become aware of the subordinates, certainly ranks higher in one sense but is lower than that which includes the lesser in its equally great validity. The dramatist will succeed in this only to the degree that nothing incommensurable is left over, nothing of the mood from which the drama emerges, that is, nothing of the mood *qua* mood, but everything is converted into the dramatic sacred coin:[90] action and situation. To the degree that the dramatist is successful in this, to the same degree the total impact left by his work will be less a mood than a thought, an idea. The more the total impact of a drama is a mood, the more sure one can be that the poet himself has had a presentiment of it as mood and has successively allowed it to come into existence from that and has not apprehended it in the idea and allowed this to unfold dramatically. A drama of that kind suffers from an abnormal preponderance of the lyrical. In a drama, this is a defect, but it is by no means a defect in an opera. The unity in an opera is preserved by the dominant tone that sustains the whole.

What has been said here about the total dramatic effect holds also for the separate parts of a drama. If I were to characterize in a single word the effect of the drama insofar as this differs from the effect of any other kind of literature, I would say: Drama works through the contemporaneous. In drama, I see the mutually isolated elements together in the situation, in the unity of action. The more isolated the distinct elements are, the more profoundly the dramatic situation is permeated by reflection, the less the dramatic unity will be a mood and the more it will be a specific thought. But just as the totality of the opera cannot be permeated by reflection in a way found in drama proper, this is also the case with the musical situation, which admittedly is dramatic but nevertheless has its unity in the mood. The musical situation has the contemporaneous, as does every dramatic situation, but the effect of the forces is a consonance, a concord, a harmony, and the impact of the musical situation is the unity produced by hearing together that which sounds together. The more the drama is permeated by reflection, the more the mood is transfigured into action. The more minor the action, the more predominant the lyrical element. In opera, this is altogether appropriate. Opera does not have so much character delineation and action as its immanent objective; it is not sufficiently reflective for that. On the other hand, unreflective, substantial passion finds its expression in opera. The musical situation is constituted by the unity of mood in the discrete plurality of voices [*Stemmefleerhed*]. This is precisely the distinctive characteristic of music—that it can maintain the plurality of voices in the unity of mood. Ordinarily when we use the word "plurality," we mean a unity that is the final result; in music such is not the case.

The dramatic interest requires swift progress, a stirring tempo, what could be called the law of the immanental acceleration of a falling object. The more the drama is imbued with reflection, the more unremittingly it hastens on. If, however, the lyrical or the epic element is unilaterally dominant, this expresses itself in a kind of anesthetizing that allows the situation to fall asleep and makes the dramatic process and progress sluggish and toilsome. The opera by nature does not have this urgency; it is characterized by a kind of tarrying, a kind of self-extension in time and space. This action does not have the speed of the fall or its direction but moves more horizontally. The mood is not sublimated in character and action. Consequently, the action in an opera can be only immediate action.

If we apply all this to the opera *Don Giovanni*, it will give us occasion to see it in its true classic validity. Don Giovanni is the hero in the opera; the main interest is concentrated upon him; not only that, but he also endows all the other characters

with interest. This must not, however, be taken in any external sense, for the very secret of this opera is that its hero is also
the force in the other characters. Don Giovanni's life is the life
principle in them. His passion sets in motion the passion of the
others. His passion resonates everywhere; it resonates in and
supports the Commendatore's earnestness, Elvira's wrath,
Anna's hate, Ottavio's pomposity, Zerlina's anxiety, Mazetto's indignation, Leporello's confusion. As the hero in the opera, Don Giovanni is the denominator of the piece; as the hero
gives the name to a piece, as is usually the case, but he is
more—he is, if I may put it this way, the common denominator. Compared with his life, the lives of all the others are
only derived. If a dominant tone is required for an opera's
unity, it is easy to see that a more perfect subject for an opera
than Don Juan is unthinkable. In relation to the forces in the
play, the dominant tone can be a third force that sustains these.
I cite *The White Lady* as an example of that kind of opera, but
in relation to the opera, such a unity is an additional qualification of the lyrical. In *Don Giovanni*, the dominant tone is none
other than the basic force in the opera itself; this is Don Giovanni, but then he, in turn—precisely because he is not character but essential life—is absolutely musical. The other figures in the opera are not characters, either, but essential
passions, which are posited[91] by Don Giovanni and to that extent, in turn, become musical. In other words, just as Don
Giovanni entwines everybody, so all of them entwine Don
Giovanni; they are the external consequences that his life itself
continually posits. It is this absolute centrality of Don Giovanni's musical life in the opera that enables it to exercise an
unequaled power of illusion, to carry one away into the life
that is in the piece. Because of the ubiquity of the musical in
this music, one can enjoy a single fragment of it and yet be carried away instantly; one arrives in the middle of the performance and instantly one is in the heart of it, for this heart, which
is Don Giovanni's life, is everywhere.

It is a common experience that to strain two senses at the
same time is not pleasant, and thus it is often disruptive to have
to use the eyes a great deal at the same time as the ears are being

used. Therefore, one is inclined to shut the eyes when listening
to music. This is more or less true of all music, and *in sensu emi-
nentiori* [in an eminent sense] of *Don Giovanni*. As soon as the
eyes are involved, the impression is disrupted, for the dramatic
unity that presents itself to the eye is altogether subordinate
and deficient in comparison with the musical unity that is
heard simultaneously. My own experience has convinced me
of this. I have sat close to the front;[92] I have moved back more
and more; I have sought a remote corner in the theater in order
to be able to hide myself completely in this music. The better
I understood it or thought I understood it, the further I moved
away from it—not out of coldness but out of love, for it wants
to be understood at a distance. There has been something
strangely enigmatic about this in my life. There have been
times when I would have given everything for a ticket; now I
do not even need to pay one rix-dollar for a ticket. I stand outside in the corridor; I lean against the partition that shuts me
off from the spectators' seats. Then it affects me most powerfully; it is a world by itself, separated from me; I can see nothing but am close enough to hear and yet so infinitely far away.

Since the main characters in an opera do not need to be so
permeated by reflection that they become transparent as characters, it also follows from this, as was emphasized earlier, that
the situation cannot be perfectly developed or full-blown but
to a certain degree is sustained by a mood. The same is true of
the action in an opera. Action in the strict sense of the word,
action undertaken with a consciousness of the goal, cannot be
expressed in music, but what one could call immediate action
certainly can. Both are the case in *Don Giovanni*. The action is
immediate action; on this point may I refer to my earlier discussion of the sense in which Don Giovanni is a seducer.

Because the action is immediate action, it is also entirely appropriate that irony is so prevalent in this piece, for irony is
and remains the disciplinarian of the immediate life.[93] To cite
just one example, the Commendatore's reappearance[94] is enormously ironic, for Don Giovanni can surmount any obstruction, but a ghost, as we all know, cannot be slain.[95] The situation is sustained all the way through by the mood. On this

point, may I recall Don Giovanni's significance for the whole opera and for the commensurate existence of the other characters in relation to him.

I shall indicate what I mean by discussing a single situation in more detail. For that, I choose Elvira's first aria.[96] The orchestra plays the overture; Elvira[97] enters. The passion raging in her breast must find release, and her song avails her. But, strictly speaking, this would be far too lyrical to be a situation; her aria then would be similar to the monologue in a drama. The only difference would be that the monologue comes closest to expressing the universal individually, the aria to expressing the individual universally. But, to repeat, that would be too little for a situation. Therefore, the case is otherwise. In the background, we see Don Giovanni and Leporello in tense expectation that the woman they have already seen at the window will come forward. Now, if this were a drama, the situation would not be composed of Elvira standing in the foreground and Don Giovanni in the background but would be composed of the unexpected encounter. The interest would center in the way Don Giovanni would escape from it. In the opera, the encounter also has its significance, but a very minor one. The encounter is to be seen; the musical situation is to be heard. The unity in the situation is the concordance in which Elvira and Don Giovanni sound simultaneously. Thus it is quite proper for Don Giovanni to keep himself in the background as much as possible, for he should be unseen, not only by Elvira but also by the spectator.

I
101

Elvira's aria begins. I do not know how to describe her passion other than as love's hate, a mixed but nevertheless sonorous, resonant passion. She is inwardly agitated; she has found release. She becomes faint for a moment in the way every passionate outburst makes one weak—there is a pause in the music. But her inner agitation sufficiently indicates that her passion still has not found adequate outlet; the diaphragm of wrath must be shaken even more powerfully. But what can evoke this tremor, what provocation? It can be only one thing: Don Giovanni's mockery. Therefore Mozart has utilized the pause—would that I were a Greek, for then I would say he

used it quite divinely—to hurl in Giovanni's mockery. Now
her passion flames up more powerfully, explodes even more
violently within her, and bursts forth in sound. This is repeated once again; then her inner being trembles, then her
wrath and pain burst forth like a stream of lava in the familiar
run with which the aria ends.

Here one sees what I mean when I say that Don Giovanni
resonates in Elvira, that it is something more than a phrase.
The spectator should not see Don Giovanni, should not see
him together with Elvira in the unity of the situation; he
should hear him in Elvira, through Elvira, for it is indeed Don
Giovanni who is singing, but he sings in such a way that the
more developed the spectator's ear, the more it seems to him
as if it came from Elvira herself. Indignation, just like love,
creates its object. She is obsessed with Don Giovanni. This
pause and Don Giovanni's voice make the situation dramatic,
but the unity in Elvira's passion in which Don Giovanni resonates, while her passion is nevertheless posited by Don Giovanni, makes the situation musical.*

Viewed as a musical situation, the situation is matchless.
But if Don Giovanni is a character and Elvira equally so, the
situation is a failure; it is wrong to have Elvira pouring out her
heart[99] in the foreground and Don Giovanni mocking in the

---

* In my opinion, Elvira's aria and the situation ought to be interpreted as
follows. Don Giovanni's unparalleled irony ought not to be kept outside Elvira's substantial passion but should be concealed in it. They must be heard
together. [98]Just as the speculative eye sees things together, so the speculative
ear hears things together. I will take an example from the purely physical
world. When a person standing on a high point gazes out over a flat region and
sees several roads running parallel to one another, he will, if he lacks intuition,
see only the roads, and the fields between them will seem to disappear, or he
will see only the fields, and the roads will disappear; however, he who has an
intuitive eye will see them together, will see the whole section as striped. So
also with the ear. What I have said here applies, of course, to the musical situation; the dramatic situation has the added element that the spectator knows
that it is Don Giovanni who is standing in the background and Elvira in the
foreground. Now, if I assume that the spectator is aware of their earlier relationship (something the spectator cannot know at first), the situation gains
much, but one will also perceive that if the accent should fall here, then it
would be wrong to keep them apart so long.

background. Then it is required that I hear them together, yet without provision of the means for it, and although both of them are characters, they could not possibly harmonize that way. If they are characters, then the encounter is the situation.

It was pointed out above that in opera the dramatic haste, the acceleration of the preliminary run, is not required as in drama, that here the situation may be enlarged upon a little. But at the same time this must not deteriorate into a continuous standstill. To give an example of the true middle course, I can underline the situation I just discussed, not as if it were the only one in *Don Giovanni* or the very best—on the contrary, they are all like this and all perfect—but because the reader has this one most clearly in mind. And yet I tread on dubious ground here, for I confess that there are two arias that must be left out; however perfect they are in themselves, they nevertheless have a disruptive and delaying effect. I would just as soon keep this a secret, but it cannot be helped—the truth must come out. If they are removed, all the rest is just as perfect. The one is Ottavio's, the other, Anna's; both of them are more concert numbers than dramatic music, inasmuch as Ottavio and Anna on the whole have roles much too minor to dare to halt the movement. Remove them, and the rest of the opera has perfect musical-dramatic pace, perfect as no other is.

It would be well worth the trouble to go through each particular situation one by one, not to escort it with exclamation marks, but to show its significance, its validity as a musical situation. But this lies outside the boundary of the present little inquiry. Here it was especially important to emphasize Don Giovanni's centrality in the whole opera. Something similar recurs with respect to the particular situations.

I would like to explain somewhat more explicitly the just-mentioned centrality of Don Giovanni in the opera by considering the other characters in the piece in their relation to him. Just as in the solar system the dark bodies that receive their light from the central sun are always only half-luminous, that is, luminous on the side turned to the sun, so it is also with the characters in this piece. Only that part of life, the side that is turned toward Don Giovanni, is illuminated; otherwise they

are obscure and opaque. This must not be taken in the narrow
sense, as if each of these characters were some abstract passion,
as if Anna, for example, were hate, Zerlina, irresponsibility.
Such insipidity does not belong here at all. The passion in the
individual is concrete, but concrete in itself, not concrete in the
personality, or, to express myself more specifically, the rest of
the personality is devoured by this passion. Now this is absolutely right, because it is an opera we are discussing. This obscurity, this partly sympathetic, partly antipathetic secret af-
finity with Don Giovanni makes them all musical and makes
the whole opera harmonize in Don Giovanni. The only character in the piece who seems to constitute an exception is, of
course, the Commendatore, but therefore it is also so sagely
designed that he to some degree lies outside the piece or limits
it. The more the Commendatore would be drawn to the foreground, the more the opera would cease to be absolutely musical. Therefore, he is continually kept in the background and
as nebulous as possible. The Commendatore is the vigorous
antecedent clause and the outspoken consequent clause, between which lies Don Giovanni's intermediate clause, but the
rich content of this intermediate clause is the substance of the
opera. The Commendatore appears only two times. The first
time it is night; it is in the background of the theater; we cannot see him, but we hear him fall before Don Giovanni's rapier. Already at the very outset his earnestness, which is made
all the more manifest by Don Giovanni's caricaturing mockery, something Mozart has superbly expressed in music—already at the very outset his earnestness is too profound to be
human; before he dies, he is spirit. The second time he appears
as spirit, and the thundering voice of heaven sounds in his earnest, solemn voice. But just as he himself is transfigured, so his
voice is transfigured into something more than a human voice;
he no longer speaks, he passes judgment.

Obviously the most important character in the piece, next
to Don Giovanni, is Leporello. His relation to his master is in-
telligible precisely through the music, unintelligible without
it. If Don Giovanni is a reflective personality, then Leporello
becomes almost an even greater knave than Giovanni is, and it

becomes unintelligible that Don Giovanni can exercise so
much power over him, and the only remaining motive is that
he can pay him more than all the others, a motive that even
Molière does not seem to have wanted to use, since he allows
Don Juan to be in financial straits. But if we hold fast to Don
Giovanni as immediate life, then it is easy to understand that
he can exercise a decisive influence on Leporello, that he assimilates him so that he can almost become an organ for Don Giovanni. In a certain sense, Leporello is closer to being a personal
consciousness than Don Giovanni. In order to become that,
however, he himself would have to clarify his relation to Don
Giovanni; but he cannot do that, he cannot break the spell.
Here again it holds true that as soon as Leporello has speaking
lines he must become transparent to us. Furthermore, in Leporello's relation to Don Giovanni there is something erotic,
there is a power with which he enthralls Leporello even against
his will. But in this ambiguity he is musical, and Don Giovanni constantly resonates in him—something of which I shall
later give an example to show that this is more than a phrase.

With the exception of the Commendatore, all the characters
stand in a kind of erotic relation to Don Giovanni. He cannot
exercise any power over the Commendatore, who is consciousness; the others are in his power. Elvira loves him, and
thereby she is in his power; Anna hates him, and thereby she is
in his power; Zerlina fears him, and thereby she is in his
power. Ottavio and Mazetto go along for the sake of kinship,
for the ties of blood are tender.

Looking back for a moment over what has been developed
here, the reader will perhaps perceive how here again the relation of the idea of Don Juan to the musical has been developed from many sides, how this relation is constitutive of the
whole opera, how this is repeated in its several parts.

I could very well stop here, but for the sake of greater completeness I shall elucidate this relation by going through a few
specific parts. The choice will not be arbitrary. I choose for
this the overture, which certainly best gives the dominant tone
of the opera in a compact concentration; I choose next the
most epic and the most lyrical part in the piece in order to

I
104

show how even in the outer limits the perfection of the opera
is preserved, the musical-dramatic is sustained, how it is Don
Giovanni who musically carries the opera.

This is not the place to explain the overall importance the
overture has for the opera; here it can only be emphasized that
opera's requirement of an overture demonstrates sufficiently
the predominance of the lyrical, and that the intended effect is
to evoke a mood, something that drama cannot get involved
with, since everything there must be transparent. Therefore,
it is appropriate that the overture is composed last so that the
artist himself can be really saturated with the music. Hence,
the overture generally provides a profound glimpse into the
composer and his psychical relation to his music. If he fails to
catch in it that which is central, if he does not have a more profound rapport with the basic mood of the opera, then this will
unmistakably betray itself in the overture; then it becomes an
assemblage of the salient points interlaced with a loose association of ideas but not the totality that contains, as it really
should, the most penetrating elucidation of the content of the
music. An overture of that sort is usually also very arbitrary,
that is, it can be as long or as short as desired, and the cohesive
element, the continuity (since it is no more than an association
of ideas), can be spun out as long as desired. Therefore the
overture frequently is a dangerous temptation for minor composers; that is, they are easily prompted to plagiarize themselves, steal from their own pockets, which can have a very
disruptive effect. Although it is obvious that the overture
should not have the same content as the opera, it of course
should not contain something altogether different. Indeed, it
should have the same content as the opera, but in another way;
it should contain it in a central way, and with the full power of
what is central it should grip the listener.

In this respect, the ever admired overture to *Don Giovanni* is
and remains a perfect masterpiece, so if no other proof of the
classic quality of *Don Giovanni* could be made, it would be sufficient to make this one point, the inconceivability that the one
who had the center would not have the periphery also. This
overture is no mingling together [*Mellemhverandre*[100]] of

themes; it is not a labyrinthian interlacing of associations of ideas; it is concise, defined, strongly structured, and, above all, impregnated with the essence of the whole opera. It is powerful like a god's idea, turbulent like a world's life, harrowing in its earnestness, palpitating in its desire, crushing in its terrible wrath, animating in its full-blooded joy; it is hollow-toned in its judgment, shrill in its lust; it is ponderous, ceremonious in its awe-inspiring dignity; it is stirring, flaring, dancing in its delight. And this it has not attained by sucking the blood of the opera; on the contrary, it is rather a prophecy in its relation to the opera. In the overture, the music unfurls its total range; with a few powerful wing beats it soars above itself, as it were, floats above the place where it will descend. It is a struggle, but a struggle in the higher atmosphere. To anyone hearing the overture after he has become more familiar with the opera, it may seem as if he had penetrated the hidden workshop where the forces he has learned to identify in the opera move with a primitive power, where they wrestle with one another with all their might. The contest, however, is too uneven; before the battle one force is already the victor. It flees and escapes, but this flight is precisely its passion, its burning restlessness in its brief joy of life, the pounding pulse in its passionate ardor. It thereby sets the other force in motion and carries it along with itself. This, which at first seemed so unshakably firm that it was practically immovable, must now be off, and soon the movement is so swift that it seems like an actual conflict.

I
106

To develop this any further is not feasible; here the point is to listen to the music, for this is not a conflict of words but an elemental fury. I must only call attention to what was discussed earlier, that the interest of the opera is Don Giovanni, not Don Giovanni and the Commendatore—this is already apparent in the overture. Mozart seems to have deliberately designed it in such a way that the deep voice that rings out in the beginning gradually becomes weaker and weaker, almost loses, as it were, its majestic bearing, must hurry to keep pace with the demonic speed that evades it and yet almost attains the power to disgrace it by sweeping it into a race in the brevity of the moment. This gradually creates the transition to the opera itself. Consequently, the finale must be regarded as closely related to the first part of the overture. In the finale, the earnestness comes to itself again, whereas in the progress of the overture it seemed to be beside itself. Now there is no question of running a race with lust; earnestness returns and thereby has cut off every way of escape to a new race.

Therefore, although in one sense the overture is independent, in another sense it is to be regarded as a running start to the opera. I have tried to point this out earlier by refreshing the reader's recollection of the gradual weakening with which the one force approaches the beginning of the work. The same thing is manifest when one observes the other force—that is, it gradually increases; it begins in the overture, grows and increases. Particularly the beginning of it is admirably expressed. We hear it so faintly, so cryptically suggested. We hear it, but it is over so swiftly that it seems as if we had heard something we had not heard. It requires an alert ear, an erotic ear, to notice the first time a hint is given in the overture of the light play of this desire that is so richly expressed later in all its lavish profusion. Since I am not a music expert, I cannot punctiliously designate this place; but I am writing, after all, only for lovers, and they presumably will understand me, some of them better than I understand myself. But I am content with my allotted share, with this enigmatic love affair, and although I otherwise thank the gods that I became a man and not a woman,[101] Mozart's music has taught me that it is beautiful and refreshing and abundant to love as a woman loves.

I am no friend of figures of speech; modern literature has made them very distasteful to me. It has gone almost so far that whenever I encounter a figure of speech, an involuntary fear comes over me that its true objective is to conceal an obscurity in the thought. Therefore I shall not risk an injudicious or futile attempt to translate the overture's brisk and pithy brevity into a prolix and empty figurative language. I wish to emphasize only one point in the overture, and to draw the reader's attention to it; I shall use a figure of speech—the only means I have to establish a connection with him.

I
107

This point, of course, is none other than Don Giovanni's initial emergence, the presentiment of him and of the power
with which he later breaks through. The overture begins with
a few deep, earnest, even notes; then for the first time we hear
infinitely far away an intimation that is nevertheless instantly
recalled, as if it were premature, until later we hear again and
again, bolder and bolder, more and more clamorous, that
voice which at first subtly, demurely, and yet seemingly in
anxiety, slipped in but could not press through. So it is in nature that one sometimes sees the horizon dark and clouded; too
heavy to support itself, it rests upon the earth and hides everything in its obscure night; a few hollow sounds are heard, not
yet in motion but like a deep mumbling to itself. Then in the
most distant heavens, far off on the horizon, one sees a flash; it
speeds away swiftly along the earth, is gone in an instant. But
soon it appears again; it gathers strength; it momentarily illuminates the entire heaven with its flame. The next second, the
horizon seems even darker, but it flares up more swiftly, even
more brilliantly; it seems as if the darkness itself has lost its
composure and is starting to move. Just as the eye in this first
flash has a presentiment of a great fire, so the ear has a presentiment of the total passion in that dwindling stroke of the violin bow. There is an anxiety in that flash; it is as if in that deep
darkness it were born in anxiety—just so is Don Giovanni's
life. There is an anxiety in him, but this anxiety is his energy.
In him, it is not a subjectively reflected anxiety; it is a
substantial[102] anxiety. In the overture there is not what is commonly called—without knowing what one is saying—despair.
Don Giovanni's life is not despair; it is, however, the full force
of the sensuous, which is born in anxiety; and Don Giovanni
himself is this anxiety, but this anxiety is precisely the demonic zest for life. After Mozart has had Don Giovanni come
into existence this way, his life now develops for us in the
dancing strains of the violin, in which he lightly, fleetingly
speeds on over the abyss. When one throws a pebble in such a
way that it skims the surface of the water, it can for a time skip
over the water in light hops, but it sinks down to the bottom

I
108

as soon as it stops skipping; in the same way he dances over the abyss, jubilating during his brief span.

But if, as has been observed above, the overture can be regarded as a running start to the opera, if in the overture one descends from that higher atmosphere, then the question is: at what point is it best for one to land in the opera, or how is the begining of the opera achieved? Here Mozart saw the only right thing to do: to begin with Leporello. It might seem that this is not so very meritorious, the more so because almost all the versions of Don Juan begin with a monologue by Sganarelle. But there is a vast difference, and here again one has occasion to admire Mozart's mastery. He has placed the first servant-aria[103] in immediate connection with the overture.[104] Leporello's first aria is quite rightly reckoned as belonging to the overture. Leporello's aria corresponds to the not uncelebrated monologue by Sganarelle in Molière. We shall look more closely at the situation. Sganarelle's monologue is far from unwitty, and when it is read in Prof. Heiberg's light and flowing verse it is very diverting, but the situation itself is defective. I say this more especially with regard to Molière, for in Heiberg it is another matter, and I say it not to censure Molière but to show Mozart's merit. A monologue is always more or less a break with the dramatic, and when the poet tries to produce an effect by the wittiness of the monologue rather than by its character, he has broken the rod on himself and has relinquished the dramatic interest. Not so in opera. Here the situation is absolutely musical. I have already pointed out the difference between a dramatic and a musical-dramatic situation. In drama, chatter is not tolerated; action and situation are demanded. In opera there is repose in the situation. But then what makes this situation into a musical situation? It was emphasized earlier that Leporello is a musical character, and yet it is not he who carries the situation. If that were so, his aria would be analogous to Sganarelle's monologue, even though it would be just as certain that a quasi-situation like that is more suitable in opera than in drama. That which makes the situation musical is Don Giovanni, who is within. The center is not in Leporello, who approaches, but in Don Giovanni, whom we do not see—but whom we hear. Now, someone could very well object: But we do not hear Don Giovanni. To that I would answer: Indeed, we do, for he resonates in Leporello. For that purpose, I call attention to the transition (*vuol star dentro colla bella* [you stay inside with the pretty lady]),[105] in which Leporello is obviously reproducing Don Giovanni. But even if this were not the case, the situation nevertheless is so designed that one involuntarily gets Don Giovanni, too, that one forgets Leporello, who is standing outside, because of Don Giovanni, who is inside. On the whole, with real genius, Mozart has had Leporello reproduce Don Giovanni and thereby has achieved two things: the musical effect that whenever Leporello is alone one hears Don Giovanni, and the parodical effect that when Don Giovanni is present we hear Leporello repeat him and thereby unconsciously parody him. I cite the end of the dance as an example of this.

If one asks which part in the opera is the most epic, the answer is easy and indubitable: it is Leporello's second aria, the list.[106] In a comparison of this aria with the corresponding monologue in Molière's version, it was pointed out earlier what absolute importance the music has, that precisely by letting us hear Don Giovanni, hear the variations in him, the music produces the effect that words or lines are unable to produce. Here it is of importance to emphasize the situation and the musical in it. Now, if we look around the stage, we see the scenic ensemble consisting of Leporello, Elvira, and the faithful servant. The faithless lover, however, is not there; he is, as Leporello pointedly puts it, "Yes, he is gone."[107] This is a virtuosity that Don Giovanni has: he is—and then he is gone—and he remains just as opportunely (for himself, that is) gone as a Jeronimus[108] arrives opportunely. Since it is now obvious that he is gone, it might seem strange that I mention him and in a way bring him into the situation. On closer scrutiny, one perhaps will find it entirely appropriate and here see an example of how literally it must be understood that Don Giovanni is everywhere present in the opera, for this can hardly be more strongly expressed than by pointing out that even when he is

I
110

gone he is present. Now, however, we shall let him be gone, since later we shall see in what sense he is present.

We shall, however, consider the three characters on the stage. The presence of Elvira is naturally instrumental in bringing about a situation; for it would not do to have Leporello unroll the list for his own pastime, but her position is instrumental in making the situation embarrassing. On the whole, it cannot be denied that sometimes the ridicule made of Elvira's love is almost cruel. For example, in the second act, at the crucial moment when Ottavio finally has gathered courage in his heart and taken the rapier out of its sheath to murder Don Giovanni, she hurls herself between them and then discovers that it is not Don Giovanni but Leporello—a differentiation that Mozart has so powerfully expressed with a kind of plaintive bleat. In the situation at hand, there is likewise something painful in her having to be present in order to know that in Spain there are 1,003, and indeed, worse yet, in the German version she is told that she herself is one of them.[109] This is a German improvement that is just as foolishly improper as the German translation is ludicrously proper and utterly unsuccessful in a no less foolish way. It is for Elvira that Leporello makes an epic survey of his master's life, and it cannot be denied that it is quite in order for Leporello to recite and Elvira to listen, because both of them are exceedingly interested in it.

Therefore, just as we continually hear Don Giovanni in the whole aria, in certain places we hear Elvira, who is visibly present onstage as a witness *instar omnium* [worth them all], not because of any accidental privilege on her part but because, since the method essentially remains the same, what pertains to one pertains to all. If Leporello were a character or a personality permeated by reflection, it would be difficult to imagine such a monologue; but precisely because he is a musical figure who is absorbed in Don Giovanni, this aria has such great significance. It is a reproduction of Don Giovanni's entire life. Leporello is the epic narrator. Such a person certainly ought not to be cold or indifferent to what he is telling, but nevertheless he ought to preserve an objective attitude toward it. This

is not the case with Leporello. He is completely carried away
by the life he is describing; he loses himself in Don Giovanni.
So here I have another example of what it means to say that
Don Giovanni resonates everywhere. Hence, the situation is
not in Leporello and Elvira's conversation about Don Giovanni but in the mood that carries the whole, in Don Giovanni's invisible spiritual presence. To develop in greater detail the transition in this aria, how in the beginning it is quiet
and less stirring but becomes more and more intense as Don
Giovanni's life resonates in it more and more, how Leporello
is more and more swept away by it, wafted away and rocked
by these erotic breezes, how it is variously nuanced accordingly as the diversity of femininity that lies within Don Giovanni's range becomes audible in it—this is not the place for
that.

If one asks which part in the opera is the most lyrical, the
answer is perhaps more doubtful, but it can scarcely be open
to doubt that the most lyrical part can be accorded only to Don
Giovanni, that it would be a violation of the dramatic subor-
dination if a subsidiary character were permitted to occupy our
attention in that way. Mozart has complied here, too. This
narrows the choice considerably, and on closer scrutiny the
contenders can be only the banquet,[110] the first part of the
grand finale, or the familiar champagne aria.[111] As for the banquet scene, up to a point it may certainly be regarded as a lyrical part, and the exhilarating refreshment of the meal, the effervescing wine, the distant festive strains of the music, all
unite to heighten Don Giovanni's mood, just as his own con-
viviality casts an augmented light over the whole enjoyment,
the effect of which is so powerful that even Leporello is transfigured in this luxuriant moment, which is joy's last smile,
pleasure's farewell greeting.[112] But still it is more a situation
than a purely lyrical part. This, of course, is not due to the eating and drinking onstage, for this in itself, regarded as a situation, is very inadequate. The situation consists in Don Giovanni's being forced out to life's most extreme point. Pursued
by the whole world, this triumphant Don Giovanni now has

no other place of residence than a little out-of-the-way room. It is at this most extreme tip on life's springboard that he once again, for want of hearty companions, stirs up all the zest for life in his own breast. If *Don Giovanni* were a drama, then this internal restlessness in the situation would require that it be as brief as possible. But it is proper in the opera for the situation to be sustained, to be aggrandized with all possible luxuriance, which only sounds the wilder because for the listeners it resonates in the abyss over which Don Giovanni hovers.

The champagne aria is different. In my opinion, it would be futile to seek a dramatic situation here, but it is all the more significant as a lyrical outpouring. Don Juan is tired of the many crisscrossing intrigues, but he is by no means fagged out. His soul is just as vigorous as ever; he does not need merry company, does not need to see and hear the effervescing of the wine or to reinvigorate himself with it; his inner vitality breaks forth in him stronger and richer than ever. He is still interpreted ideally by Mozart as life, as power, but ideally in the face of an actuality; here he is ideally intoxicated, so to speak, with himself. If all the girls in the world encircled him at this moment, he would not be dangerous to them, for he is, as it were, too strong to want to infatuate them; even the most multifarious pleasures of actuality are too little for him compared with what he enjoys in himself.

What it means to say—that Don Giovanni's essential nature is music—is clearly apparent here. He dissolves, as it were, in music for us; he unfurls in a world of sounds. This aria has been called the champagne aria, and undoubtedly this is very suggestive. But what we must see especially is that it does not stand in an accidental relation to Don Giovanni. Such is his life, effervescing like champagne. And just as the beads in this wine, as it simmers with an internal heat, sonorous with its own melody, rise and continue to rise, just so the lust for enjoyment resonates in the elemental boiling that is his life. Therefore, the dramatic significance of this aria comes not from the situation but from this, that here the opera's dominant tone sounds and resonates in itself.

INSIGNIFICANT POSTLUDE

I
113

If what has been developed here is correct, then I return to my favorite theme—that Mozart's *Don Giovanni* ought to rank highest among all the classic works. Then I shall once again rejoice over Mozart's fortune [*Lykke*], a fortune that is truly enviable, both in and by itself and because it makes happy [*lykkelig*] all those with only a moderate comprehension of his fortune. I at least feel myself to be indescribably happy in having understood Mozart even remotely and having an intimation of his fortune. How much more, then, those who have understood him perfectly, how much more must they feel happy with the fortunate one.[113]

THE TRAGIC IN ANCIENT DRAMA
REFLECTED IN THE TRAGIC IN MODERN DRAMA

A VENTURE IN FRAGMENTARY ENDEAVOR

Delivered before the
Συμπαρανεκρώμενοι
[Fellowship of the Dead][1]

If someone were to say: The tragic, after all, is always the tragic, I would not have very much to urge to the contrary, inasmuch as every historical development always lies within the sphere of the concept. On the assumption that his words have meaning and that the twice-repeated word "tragic" is not intended to form meaningless parentheses around an empty nothing, then his meaning might very well be that the content of the concept did not dethrone the concept but enriched it. On the other hand, it can scarcely have escaped the attention of any observer that there is an essential difference between the tragic, ancient and modern—something that the reading and theater-going public already considers its legal possession as its dividend from the enterprises of the experts in the art. But if, in turn, someone were to affirm the distinction absolutely and, on the basis of it, at first slyly and later perhaps forcibly press this distinction between the tragic in ancient and in modern drama, his behavior would be no less unreasonable than the first person's, since he would [forget] that the foothold so indispensable to him was the tragic itself. This in turn would be so far from distinguishing between the tragic ancient and modern that, contrariwise, it would combine them. Indeed, it must be as a warning against every such one-sided effort to separate that estheticians[2] always return to the definitions of and requirements for the tragic established by Aristotle[3] as exhausting the concept. It must be as a warning, and all the more so since everyone must be gripped by a certain sadness because no matter how much the world has changed, the idea of the tragic is still essentially unchanged, just as weeping still continues to be equally natural to humankind.

As reassuring as this might seem to one who does not want any separation, least of all any break, the same difficulty that has just been dismissed appears in another and almost more dangerous form. That there is still a continual return to Aris-

totelian esthetics, not simply because of dutiful deference or
old habit, will surely be admitted by anyone who has any acquaintance with modern esthetics[4] and by this is convinced of
the scrupulous attachment to the salient points that were advanced by Aristotle[5] and that are still continually in force in
modern esthetics. But as soon as one examines them a little
more closely, the difficulty appears at once. The definitions are
of a very general kind, and one can very well agree with Aristotle in a way and yet in another sense disagree with him.

In order not to enter prematurely into the content of the following exposition by mentioning examples here, I prefer to illustrate my opinion by making a parallel observation with regard to comedy. If an ancient esthetician had said that the
presuppositions of comedy are character and situation and that
its aim is to arouse laughter, then one could very well return
to this again and again, but as soon as one pondered how different the causes of laughter are, one would soon be convinced
of what an enormous range this requirement has. Anyone who
has ever made the laughter of others and his own the object of
observation, who has had in mind, as in this project, not so
much the accidental as the universal, who has perceived with
psychological interest how different the occasion of laughter is
at every age—that person will readily be convinced that the
unchangeable requirement for comedy, that it must arouse
laughter, in itself implies a high degree of changeableness in relation to the ideas of the laughable in the varying world consciousness, yet without this difference being so diffuse that the
corresponding expression in the somatic functions would be
that laughter would manifest itself in weeping. It is the same
with respect to the tragic.

That which, generally speaking, should be the content of
this little exploration will not be so much the relation between
the tragic in ancient and in modern drama as it will be an attempt to show how the characteristic feature of the tragic in
ancient drama is incorporated in the tragic in modern drama in
such a way that what is truly tragic will become apparent. But
however much I shall try to make it apparent, I shall abstain
from any prophecy that this is what the times demand; there-

fore its becoming apparent will be devoid of consequence, and all the more so since the whole age is working more toward the comic. To a degree, existence [*Tilværelse*] is undermined by the subjects' doubt; [6]isolation continually gains the upper hand more and more, something that can best be ascertained by paying attention to the multifarious social endeavors. That they seek to counteract the isolating efforts of the age is just as much a demonstration of the isolation as is the unreasonable way they seek to counteract it. Isolation always consists in asserting oneself as number; when one wants to assert oneself as one, this is isolation; all the friends of associations will surely agree with me on that, without therefore being able or willing to see that it is altogether the same isolation when a hundred assert themselves simply and solely as a hundred. Number is always indifferent to itself, and it makes absolutely no difference whether it is 1 or 1,000, or all the inhabitants of the world defined merely numerically. In principle, then, this association-mentality is just as revolutionary as the mentality it wants to counteract. When David really wanted to feel his power and glory, he had his people counted;[7] in our age, however, it may be said that the people, in order to feel their significance over against a superior power, count themselves. But all these associations bear the stamp of arbitrariness and most often are formed for some accidental purpose, whose lord and master, of course, is the association.

These numerous associations, therefore, demonstrate the disintegration of the age and themselves contribute to speeding it up; they are the infusiora in the organism of the state that indicate that it has disintegrated. When was it that the hetairias[8] became common in Greece except at the time when the state was in the process of disintegration? And does not our age have a striking likeness to that age, which not even Aristophanes could make more ludicrous than it actually was? Has not the bond that in the political sense held the states together, invisibly and spiritually, dissolved; has not the power in religion that insisted upon the invisible been weakened and destroyed; do not our statesmen and clergymen have this in common, that they, like the augurs of old, cannot look at one another without smiling?[9]

A feature in which our age certainly excels that age in Greece is that our age is more depressed and therefore deeper in despair. Thus, our age is sufficiently depressed to know that there is something called responsibility and that this means something. Therefore, although everyone wants to rule, no one wants to have responsibility. It is still fresh in our memory that a French statesman, when offered a portfolio the second time, declared that he would accept it but on the condition that the secretary of state be made responsible.[10] It is well known that the king in France is not responsible, but the prime minister is; the prime minister does not wish to be responsible but wants to be prime minister provided that the secretary of state will be responsible; ultimately it ends, of course, with the watchmen or street commissioners becoming responsible. Would not this inverted story of responsibility be an appropriate subject for Aristophanes! On the other hand, why are the government and the governors so afraid of assuming responsibility, unless it is because they fear an opposition party that in turn continually pushes away responsibility on a similar scale. When one imagines these two powers face to face with each other but unable to catch hold of each other because the one is always disappearing and is replaced by the other, the one merely appearing in the role of the other—such a situation would certainly not be without comic power.

This indeed shows adequately that what really holds the state together has disintegrated, but the isolation resulting from this is naturally comic, and the comic consists in subjectivity's wanting to assert itself as pure form. Every isolated person always becomes comic by wanting to assert his accidentality over against the necessity of the process. No doubt it would be profoundly comic to have an accidental individual hit upon the universal idea of wanting to be the world's liberator. Christ's appearance, however, is in a certain sense the most profound tragedy (in another sense it is infinitely much more), because Christ came in the fullness of time and bore the sin of the whole world—something that I shall particularly stress in connection with what follows.

It is generally known that Aristotle gives two sources for action in tragedy, διάνοια καὶ ἦθος [thought and character],[11] but he also notes that the primary factor is the τέλος [end, purpose] and the individuals do not act in order to present characters; rather these are included for the sake of action. Here it is easy to perceive a difference from modern tragedy.[12] What specifically characterizes ancient tragedy is that the action does not proceed only from character, that the action is not subjectively reflected enough, but that the action itself has a relative admixture of suffering. Ancient tragedy, therefore, did not develop dialogue to the point of exhaustive reflection with everything merged in it; the distinct components of dialogue are actually present in the monologue and chorus. Whether the chorus comes closer to epic substantiality or to the lyrical élan, it nevertheless seems to provide "the more," so to speak, that will not merge in the individuality; the monologue, in turn, has a more lyrical concentration and has "the more" that will not merge in action and situation. In ancient tragedy, the action itself has an epic element; it is just as much event as action. This, of course, is because the ancient world did not have subjectivity reflected in itself.[13] Even if the individual moved freely, he nevertheless rested in substantial determinants, in the state, the family, in fate. This substantial determinant is the essential fateful factor in Greek tragedy and is its essential characteristic. The hero's downfall, therefore, is not a result solely of his action but is also a suffering, whereas in modern tragedy the hero's downfall is not really suffering but is a deed. Thus, in the modern period situation and character are in fact predominant. The tragic hero is subjectively reflected in himself, and this reflection has not only reflected him out of every immediate relation to state, kindred, and fate but often has even reflected him out of his own past life. What concerns us is a certain specific element of his life as his own deed. For this reason, the tragic can be exhausted in situation and lines because no immediacy is left at all. Therefore, modern tragedy has no

I
121

epic foreground, no epic remainder. The hero stands and falls entirely on his own deeds.

What is here briefly but sufficiently developed will have its importance in explaining a difference between ancient and modern tragedy that I regard as very important—the different nature of tragic guilt. It is well known that Aristotle insists that the tragic hero have ἁμαρτία [error].[14] But just as the action in Greek tragedy is something intermediate between action and the suffering, so also is guilt, and therein lies the tragic collision. But the more the subjectivity is reflective, the more Pelagianly[15] one sees the individual thrown solely upon himself, the more ethical guilt becomes. Between these two extremes lies the tragic. If the individual has no guilt whatever, the tragic interest is annulled, for in that case the tragic collision is enervated. On the other hand, if he has absolute guilt, he no longer interests us tragically. It is, therefore, surely a misunderstanding of the tragic when our age endeavors to have everything fateful transubstantiate itself into individuality and subjectivity. We want to know nothing about the hero's past; we load his whole life upon his shoulders as his own deed, make him accountable for everything, but in so doing we also transform his esthetic guilt into ethical guilt. In this way, the tragic hero becomes bad, evil actually becomes the tragic subject, but evil has no esthetic interest, and sin is not an esthetic element.

This misguided enterprise may somehow have its basis in the working of the whole age toward the comic. The comic lies precisely in the isolation; when one wants to affirm the tragic within this isolation, one has evil in its badness, not the authentic tragic guilt in its ambiguous guiltlessness.

It is not difficult to find examples if one looks at modern literature. For example, the work by Grabbe, *Faust und Don Juan*[16] (in many ways a work of genius), is built upon evil. But, rather than to argue on the basis of a single work, I prefer to show it in the common consciousness of the whole contemporary age. If one wanted to depict an individual whose unfortunate childhood had played such havoc with him that these impressions caused his downfall, such a thing would have no appeal at all to the present age—not, of course, because it was poorly done, for I take the liberty of assuming it was excellently done, but because this age applies another standard. It will have nothing to do with such coddling; it automatically makes the individual responsible for his life. Consequently, if the individual succumbs, this is not tragic, but it is bad. One would think that the generation in which I have the honor of living must be a kingdom of gods. But this is by no means so; the vigor, the courage, that wants to be the creator of its own good fortune in this way, indeed, its own creator, is an illusion, and when the age loses the tragic, it gains despair. In the tragic there is implicit a sadness and a healing that one indeed must not disdain, and when someone wishes to gain himself in the superhuman way our age tries to do it, he loses himself[17] and becomes comic. Every individual, however original he is, is still a child of God, of his age, of his nation, of his family, of his friends, and only in them does he have his truth. If he wants to be the absolute in all this, his relativity, then he becomes ludicrous. In languages, there is sometimes found a word that because of its context is so frequently used in a specific case that it eventually becomes, if you please, independent as an adverb in this case.[18] For the experts such a word has once and for all an accent and a flaw that it never lives down; if, then, this notwithstanding, it should claim to be a substantive and demand to be declined in all five cases, it would be genuinely comic. So it goes with the individual also when he, perhaps extracted from the womb of time laboriously enough, wants to be absolute in this enormous relativity. But if he surrenders this claim, is willing to be relative, then he *eo ipso* has the tragic, even if he were the happiest individual—indeed, I would say the individual is not happy until he has the tragic.

Intrinsically, the tragic is infinitely gentle; esthetically it is to human life what divine grace and compassion are; it is even more benign, and therefore I say that it is a motherly love that lulls the troubled one. The ethical is rigorous and hard. Therefore, if a criminal before the judge wants to excuse himself by saying that his mother had a propensity for stealing, especially during the time she was pregnant with him, the judge obtains

I
123

the health officer's opinion of his mental condition and decides
that he is dealing with a thief and not with the thief's mother.
Insofar as the issue here is a crime, the sinner certainly cannot
flee into the temple of esthetics, but nevertheless it will indeed
have a mitigating word for him. But it would be wrong for
him to seek refuge there, for his path takes him to the religious, not to the esthetic. The esthetic lies behind him, and it
would be a new sin on his part to seize the esthetic now. The
religious is the expression for fatherly love, for it embraces the
ethical, but it is mitigated, and by what means—by the very
same means that give the tragic its gentleness, by means of
continuity. But although the esthetic provides this repose before sin's profound discrepancy is asserted, the religious does
not provide it until this discrepancy is seen in all its frightful-
ness. At the very moment the sinner almost swoons under the
universal sin that he has taken upon himself because he felt
simply that the more guilty he became the greater would be
the prospect of being saved, at that same dreadful moment he
has the consoling thought that it is universal sinfulness that has
asserted itself also in him. But this comfort is a religious comfort, and anyone who thinks he can attain it in any other way,
by esthetic volatilization, for example, has taken the comfort
in vain, and he actually does not have it. In a certain sense,
therefore, it is a very appropriate discretion on the part of the
age to want to make the individual responsible for everything;
the trouble is that it does not do it profoundly and inwardly
enough, and hence its half-measures. It is conceited enough to
disdain the tears of tragedy, but it is also conceited enough to
want to do without mercy. And what, after all, is human life,
the human race, when these two things are taken away? Either
the sadness of the tragic or the profound sorrow and profound
joy of religion. Or is this not the striking feature of everything
that originates in that happy people[19]—a depression of spirit, a
sadness in their art, in their poetry, in their life, in their joy?

In the foregoing discussion, I have especially sought to
stress the difference between ancient and modern tragedy insofar as it is apparent in the difference in the guilt of the tragic
hero. This is the real focal point from which everything ema-

nates in its specific difference. If the hero is unequivocally guilty, monologue vanishes, fate vanishes; then thought is transparent in dialogue, and action in situation. The same thing may be stated from another side—namely, from the perspective of the mood that the tragedy evokes. It is well known that Aristotle maintains that tragedy should arouse fear and compassion [*Medlidenhed*] in the spectator.[20] I recall that Hegel in his *Esthetics*[21] picks up this comment and on each of these points makes a double observation, which, however, is not very exhaustive. When Aristotle distinguishes between fear and compassion, one presumably could rather think of the fear as the mood accompanying the particular and of the compassion as the mood that is the definitive impression. This latter mood is the one I have particularly in mind because it is the one corresponding to tragic guilt and therefore also has the same implicit dialectic as that concept. On this point, Hegel notes that there are two kinds of compassion, the usual kind that turns its attention to the finite side of suffering, and the truly tragic compassion. This observation is altogether correct but to me of less importance, since that universal emotion is a misunderstanding that can befall modern tragedy just as much as ancient tragedy. But what he adds with regard to true compassion is true and powerful: "das wahrhafte Mitleiden ist im Gegentheil die Sympathie mit der zugleich sittlichen Berechtigung des Leidenden [true sympathy, on the contrary, is an accordant feeling with the ethical claim at the same time associated with the sufferer]" (III, p. 531).[22]

Whereas Hegel considers compassion more in general and its differentiation in the difference of individualities, I prefer to stress the difference in compassion in relation to the difference in tragic guilt. To indicate this difference at once, I shall separate the *Lidende* [suffering] in the word *Medlidenhed* [compassion] and add in each instance the sympathy implicit in the prefix *med* [with], yet in such a way that I do not come to predicate something about the spectator's mood that could indicate his arbitrariness, but in such a way that in expressing the difference in his mood I also convey the difference in the tragic guilt. In ancient tragedy, the sorrow is more profound, the pain less;

in modern tragedy, the pain is greater, the sorrow less. Sorrow always has in it something more substantial[23] than pain. Pain always indicates a reflection upon the suffering that sorrow does not know. Psychologically, it is very interesting to observe a child when he sees an adult suffer. [24]The child is not sufficiently reflective to feel pain, and yet his sorrow is infinitely deep. He is not sufficiently reflective to have an idea of sin and guilt; when he sees an adult suffer, it does not cross his mind to think about that, and yet if the reason for the suffering is hidden from him, there is a dark presentiment of the reason in the child's sorrow. So it is also, but in complete and deep harmony, with the sorrow of the Greeks, and that is why it is simultaneously so gentle and so deep. On the other hand, when an adult sees a young person, a child, suffer, the pain is greater, the sorrow less. The more pronounced the idea of guilt, the greater the pain, the less profound the sorrow.

Applying this now to the relation between ancient and modern tragedy, one may say: In ancient tragedy, the sorrow is more profound, and in the corresponding consciousness the sorrow is more profound. It must continually be kept in mind that this is not in me but in the tragedy and that, in order to understand properly the profound sorrow in Greek tragedy, I must live into the Greek consciousness. Therefore, when so many admire Greek tragedy, it no doubt is often just parroting, for it is obvious that our age at least has no great sympathy for what is the truly Greek sorrow. The sorrow is more profound because the guilt has esthetic ambiguity. In modern times, the pain is greater. One could say of Greek tragedy that it is a fearful thing to fall into the hands of the living God.[25] The wrath of the gods is terrible, but still the pain is not as great as in modern tragedy, where the hero suffers his total guilt, is transparent to himself in his suffering of his guilt.

It is appropriate at this point to show, as with tragic guilt, which sorrow is true esthetic sorrow and which is true esthetic pain. The most bitter pain is obviously repentance, but repentance has ethical, not esthetic, reality [*Realitet*].[26] It is the most bitter pain because it has the complete transparency of the total guilt, but precisely because of this transparency it does not interest esthetically. Repentance has a holiness that eclipses the esthetic. It does not want to be seen, least of all by a spectator, and requires an altogether different kind of self-activity. To be sure, modern comedy has at times brought repentance onto the stage, but this only betrays a lack of judgment in the author. One is indeed reminded of the psychological interest there can be in seeing repentance depicted, but again psychological interest is not the esthetic. This is part of the confusion that manifests itself in so many ways in our day: something is sought where one should not seek it; and what is worse, it is found where one should not find it. One wishes to be edified in the theater, to be esthetically stimulated in church; one wishes to be converted by novels, to be entertained by devotional books; one wishes to have philosophy in the pulpit and a preacher on the lecture platform. This pain, then, is not esthetic pain, and yet it is obviously that which the present age is working toward as the supreme tragic interest.

This also turns out to be the case with tragic guilt. Our age has lost all the substantial categories of family, state, kindred; [27]it must turn the single individual over to himself completely in such a way that, strictly speaking, he becomes his own creator. Consequently his guilt is sin, his pain repentance, but thereby the tragic is canceled. Furthermore, suffering tragedy in the stricter sense has essentially lost its tragic interest, for the power that is the source of the suffering has lost its meaning, and the spectator shouts: Help yourself, and heaven will help you—in other words, the spectator has lost compassion, but in a subjective and also in an objective sense compassion is the authentic expression of the tragic.

For the sake of clarity, before developing this exposition further, I shall define a little more explicitly true esthetic sorrow. Sorrow and pain move in opposite directions. If one does not want to spoil this by a foolish consistency (something that I shall prevent in also another way), one may say: The greater the guiltlessness, the greater the sorrow. If this is insisted upon, the tragic will be canceled. An element of guilt always remains, but this element is not actually reflected subjectively; this is why the sorrow in Greek tragedy is so profound. To forestall premature conclusions, I shall just point out that overstatements result only in shifting the issue over into another realm. The unity of absolute guiltlessness and absolute guilt is not an esthetic category but a metaphysical one.

The real reason people have always had scruples about calling the life of Christ a tragedy is that they felt that esthetic categories do not exhaust the matter. That the life of Christ is something more than can be exhausted in esthetic categories is apparent also in another way—namely, that these neutralize themselves in this phenomenon and are rendered inconsequential. Tragic action always contains an element of suffering, and tragic suffering an element of action; the esthetic lies in their relativity. The identity of an absolute action and an absolute suffering is beyond the powers of the esthetic and belongs to the metaphysical. In the life of Christ there is this identity, for his suffering is absolute, since it is absolutely free action, and his action is absolute suffering, since it is absolute obedience.

Thus, the element of guilt that remains is not subjectively reflected, and this makes the sorrow profound. In other words, tragic guilt is more than just subjective guilt—it is hereditary guilt; but hereditary guilt, like hereditary sin, is a substantial category, and it is precisely this substantiality that makes the sorrow more profound.

The ever admired trilogy of Sophocles, *Oedipus at Colonus, Oedipus the King,* and *Antigone,* hinges essentially on this genuine tragic interest. But hereditary guilt involves the contradiction of being guilt and yet not being guilt.[28] The bond by which the individual becomes guilty is precisely [filial] piety, but the guilt that it thereby incurs has every possible esthetic amphiboly.[29] One might promptly think that the people who must have developed the profoundly tragic was the Jewish nation. For example, when it is said of Jehovah that he is a jealous God, that he visits the iniquities of the fathers upon the children to the third and fourth generations,[30] or when we hear those terrible curses in the Old Testament, one could easily be tempted to want to seek tragic material here. But Judaism is too ethically mature for that; even though they are terrible, Jehovah's curses are also righteous punishment. It was not this way in Greece; the wrath of the gods has no ethical character, only esthetic ambiguity.

In Greek tragedy itself, there is a transition from sorrow to pain, and I would cite *Philoctetes* as an example of this.[31] In a stricter sense, this is a tragedy of suffering. But here, too, a high degree of objectivity still prevails. The Greek hero rests in his fate; his fate is unalterable; of that there can be no further discussion. This element is really the component of sorrow in the pain. The first doubt with which pain really begins is this: Why is this happening to me; can it not be otherwise? To be sure, *Philoctetes*[32] has something that has always been striking to me and that essentially separates it from that immortal trilogy: a high degree of reflection[33]—the masterly depicted self-contradiction in his pain, in which there is such profound human truth, but still there is an objectivity that carries the whole. Philoctetes' reflection is not absorbed in itself, and it is genuinely Greek when he laments that no one knows his pain.[34] There is an extraordinary truth in this, and yet precisely here there is also a manifestation of the difference from the really reflective pain that always wants to be alone with its pain, that seeks a new pain in the solitude of this pain.

The true tragic sorrow, then, requires an element of guilt, the true tragic pain an element of guiltlessness; the true tragic sorrow requires an element of transparency, the true tragic pain an element of opacity. I believe this is the best way to suggest the dialectic in which the qualifications of sorrow and pain touch each other, and also the dialectic implicit in the concept: tragic guilt.

Since it is at variance with the aims of our association[35] to provide coherent works or larger unities, since it is not our intention to labor on a Tower of Babel that God in his righteousness can descend and destroy, since we, in our consciousness that such confusion justly occurred, acknowledge as characteristic of all human endeavor in its truth that it is fragmentary, that it is precisely this which distinguishes it from nature's infinite coherence, that an individual's wealth consists specifically in his capacity for fragmentary prodigality and

what is the producing individual's enjoyment is the receiving
individual's also, not the laborious and careful accomplishment or the tedious interpretation of this accomplishment but
the production and the pleasure of the glinting transiency,
which for the producer holds much more than the consum-
mated accomplishment, since it is a glimpse of the idea and
holds a bonus for the recipient, since its fulguration [*Fulguration*][36] stimulates his own productivity—since all this, I say, is
at variance with our association's inclination, indeed, since the
periodic sentence just read must almost be regarded as a serious attack on the ejaculatory style in which the idea breaks
forth without achieving a breakthrough, to which officiality is
attached in our society—therefore, after having pointed out
that my conduct still cannot be called mutinous, inasmuch as
the bond that holds this periodic sentence together is so loose
that the parenthetical clauses therein strut about aphoristically
and willfully enough, I shall merely call to mind that my style
has made an attempt to appear to be what it is not: revolutionary.

Our society requires a renewal and rebirth at every single
meeting and to that end requires that its intrinsic activity be rejuvenated by a new description of its productivity. Let us,
then, designate our intention as a venture in fragmentary endeavor or the art of writing posthumous [*efterladt*, left behind]
papers. A completely finished work is disproportionate to the
poetizing personality; because of the disjointed and desultory
character of unfinished papers, one feels a need to poetize the
personality along with them. Unfinished papers are like a ruin,
and what place of resort could be more natural for the buried?
The art, then, is to produce skillfully the same effect, the same
carelessness and fortuitousness, the same anacoluthic [*anako-
luthisk*] thought process; the art is to evoke an enjoyment that
is never present tense but always has an element of the past and
thus is present in the past. This is already expressed in the
expression "left behind." Indeed, in a certain sense everything
a poet has produced is something left behind, but it would
never occur to anyone to call a completely finished work a
work left behind, even if it had the accidental feature of not

having been published in his lifetime. I also assume it to be a
feature of all authentic human production in its truth, as we
have interpreted it, that it is property left behind, since it is not
granted to human beings to live with an eternal view like the
gods'. Consequently, I shall call what is being produced
among us property left behind [*Efterladenskab*], that is, artistic
property left behind; negligence [*Efterladenhed*], indolence, we
shall call the genius that we prize; the *vis inertiae* [force of in-
ertia] we shall call the natural law that we worship. With this I
have complied with our hallowed customs and conventions.

So, my dear Συμπαρανεκρώμενοι, come closer to me, form a
circle around me as I send my tragic heroine out into the
world, [37]as I give the daughter of sorrow a dowry of pain as
her outfit. She is my work, but still her outline is so indistinct,
her form so nebulous, that each and every one of you can *for-
liebe sig*[38] [fall in love] with her and be able to love her in your
own way. She is my creation, her thoughts are my thoughts,
and yet it is as if in a night of love I had rested with her, as if
she in my embrace had confided a deep secret to me, had
breathed it out together with her soul, as if she had then instantly changed before me, had disappeared, so that the only
trace of her actuality was the mood that remained behind, instead of the reverse situation that she is brought forth by my
mood to ever greater actuality. I put words into her mouth,
and yet it seems to me as if I abused her confidence; it seems to
me as if she were standing reproachfully behind me, and yet it
is the reverse—in her secrecy she becomes ever more visible.
She belongs to me, she lawfully belongs to me, and yet at
times it is as if I had cunningly crept into her confidence, as if
I always had to look behind me for her; and yet it is the reverse,
she is always in front of me—only as I lead her forward does
she come into existence.

Antigone[39] is her name. I shall keep this name from the ancient tragedy, to which I shall hold for the most part, although
from another angle everything will be modern. But first one
comment. I am using a female character[40] because I believe that
a female nature will be best suited to show the difference. As a
woman, she will have enough substantiality[41] for the sorrow

to manifest itself, but as one belonging to a reflective world she will have sufficient reflection to experience the pain. In order for the sorrow to be experienced, the tragic guilt must vacillate between guilt and guiltlessness, and the vehicle by which guilt enters her consciousness must always be a qualification of substantiality. But since the tragic guilt must have this indefiniteness in order for the sorrow to be experienced, reflection must not be present in its infinitude, for then it would reflect her out of her guilt, inasmuch as reflection in its infinite subjectivity cannot allow the factor of hereditary sin, which produces the sorrow, to remain. But since reflection has been awakened, it will reflect her not out of the sorrow but into it; at every moment it will transform sorrow into pain for her.

So, then, the family of Labdakos[42] is the object of the indignation of the gods:[43] Oedipus has killed the sphinx, liberated Thebes; Oedipus has murdered his father, married his mother; and Antigone is the fruit of this marriage. So it goes in the Greek tragedy. Here I deviate. With me, everything is the same, and yet everything is different. Everyone knows that he has killed the sphinx and freed Thebes, and Oedipus is hailed and admired and is happy in his marriage with Jocasta. The rest is hidden from the people's eyes, and no suspicion has ever brought this horrible dream into the world of actuality. Only Antigone knows it. How she found out is extraneous to the tragic interest, and in that respect everyone is left to his own explanation. At an early age, before she had reached maturity, dark hints of this horrible secret had momentarily gripped her soul, until certainty hurled her with one blow into the arms of anxiety. Here at once I have a definition of the tragic in modern times, for an anxiety is a reflection and in that respect is essentially different from sorrow. Anxiety is the vehicle by which the subject appropriates sorrow and assimilates it. Anxiety is the motive power by which sorrow penetrates a person's heart. But the movement is not swift like that of an arrow; it is consecutive; it is not once and for all, but it is continually becoming. As a passionately erotic glance craves its object, so anxiety looks cravingly upon sorrow. Just as the quiet, incorruptible eye of love is preoccupied with the beloved object, so anxiety's self-preoccupation is with sorrow. But anxiety has an added factor that makes it cling even harder to its object, for it both loves and fears it. Anxiety has a double function; in part it is the exploring movement that continually makes contact and by this groping discovers sorrow as it circles around it. Or anxiety is sudden; all the sorrow is lodged in one instant, yet in such a way that this instant immediately dissolves in a consecutive series. In this sense, anxiety is a genuine tragic category, and the old saying *quem deus vult perdere, primum dementat* [whom a god would destroy he first makes mad][44] is really and truly applicable here. [45]That anxiety is a reflection category is shown by language itself, for I always say that I am anxious about something, and I thereby distinguish between the anxiety and that about which I am anxious, and I can never use "anxiety" objectively; whereas when I say "my sorrow," I can be expressing as much about what I am grieving over as about my sorrow over it. Furthermore, anxiety always contains a reflection on time, for I cannot be anxious about the present but only about the past or the future, but the past and the future, kept in opposition to each other in such a way that the present vanishes, are categories of reflection. Greek sorrow, however, like all Greek life, is in the present, and therefore the sorrow is deeper, but the pain less. Anxiety, therefore, belongs essentially to the tragic. Hamlet is such a tragic figure because he suspects his mother's crime. Robert le diable[46] asks how it could happen that he does so much evil. Høgne,[47] whom his mother had conceived with a troll, accidentally comes to see his image in the water and asks his mother whence his body acquired such a form.

The difference is easy to see now. In Greek tragedy, Antigone is not occupied at all with her father's unfortunate fate. This rests like an impregnable sorrow on the whole family. Antigone, like every other young Greek girl, goes on living free from care—indeed, since her death is determined, the chorus is sorry for her because she must depart from this life at such a young age, depart from it without having tasted its most beautiful joy—obviously forgetful of the family's own profound sorrow. This by no means says that it is light-mind-

I
132

edness or that the particular individual stands all alone without concern for his relationships to the family. But this is genuinely Greek. To them, life relationships, like the horizon under which they live, are given once and for all. Even though this is dark and full of clouds, it is also unchangeable. This gives a dominant tone to the soul, and this is sorrow, not pain. In Antigone, the tragic guilt is focused upon a specific point, that she has buried her brother in defiance of the king's injunction. If this is viewed as an isolated fact, as a collision between sisterly love and piety and an arbitrary human injunction, *Antigone* would cease to be a Greek tragedy; it would be an altogether modern tragic theme. What provides the tragic interest in the Greek sense is that Oedipus's sad fate resonates in the brother's unfortunate death, in the sister's conflict with a specific human injunction; it is, as it were, the afterpains, Oedipus's tragic fate, spreading out into each branch of his family. This totality makes the spectator's sorrow so very profound. It is not an individual who goes under, but a little world; it is the objective grief, unloosed, that now strides ahead, like a force of nature, in its own terrible consistency, and Antigone's sad fate is like the echo of her father's, an intensified sorrow. Therefore, when Antigone, in defiance of the king's injunction, decides to bury her brother, we see in this not so much a free act as a fateful necessity, which visits the iniquities of the fathers upon the children. There is indeed enough freedom in it to enable us to love Antigone for her sisterly love, but in the inevitability of fate there is also a higher refrain, as it were, that encompasses not only Oedipus's life but also his family.

Whereas the Greek Antigone goes on living so free from care that, if this new fact had not come up, one could imagine her life as even happy in its gradual unfolding, our Antigone's life, on the other hand, is essentially at an end. [48]I have not endowed her parsimoniously, and, as is said, a good word in the right place is like golden apples in a silver bowl;[49] so also I have placed the fruit of grief in the bowl of pain. Her endowment is not vainglorious pomp that moth and rust can consume;[50] it is an eternal treasure. Thieves cannot break in and steal it; she herself is too alert for that. Her life does not unfold like the Greek Antigone's; it is turned inward, not outward. The stage is inside, not outside; it is a spiritual stage.

My dear Συμπαρανεϰρώμενοι, have I not managed to capture your interest for such a maiden, or shall I resort to a *captatio benevolentiae* [procedure aimed at gaining the favorable disposition of the judge or listener]? She, too, does not belong to the world in which she lives; although healthy and flourishing, her real life is nevertheless hidden. She, too, although alive, is in another sense dead; her life is quiet and concealed. The world does not hear even a sigh, for her sighing is concealed in the secrecy of her soul. I do not need to remind you that she is by no means a weak and morbid woman; on the contrary, she is proud and energetic.

Perhaps nothing ennobles a person so much as keeping a secret. It gives a person's whole life a significance, which it has, of course, only for himself; it saves a person from all futile consideration of the surrounding world. Sufficient unto himself, he rests blissful in his secret; this might be said even though his secret is a most baleful one.

So it is with our Antigone. She is proud of her secret, proud that she has been selected in a singular way to save the honor and glory of the lineage of Oedipus. When the grateful nation acclaims Oedipus with praise and thanksgiving, she feels her own significance, and her secret sinks deeper and deeper into her soul, ever more inaccessible to any living being. She feels how much has been placed into her hands, and this gives her the preternatural magnitude that is necessary in order for her to engage us tragically. She must be able to interest us as a particular character. She is more than a young girl in a general sense, and yet she is a young girl; she is a bride, and yet altogether virginal and pure. [51] As a bride, woman has fulfilled her destiny, and therefore a woman generally can concern us only to the degree that she is brought in relation to this her destiny.

There are analogies to this. We speak, for example, of a bride of God; in faith and spirit she has the content in which she rests. In a perhaps still more beautiful sense, I would call

I
134

our Antigone a bride—indeed, she is almost more, she is a mother. Purely esthetically, she is *virgo mater* [virgin mother]; she carries her secret under her heart, concealed and hidden. Precisely because she is secretive, she is silence, but this turning back into oneself implicit in silence gives her a preternatural bearing. She is proud of her grief, she is jealous of it, for her grief is her love. But yet her grief is not a dead, static possession; it is continually in motion; it gives birth to pain and is born in pain. Just as when a girl resolves to sacrifice her life for an idea, when she stands there with the sacrificial wreath on her forehead, she stands as a bride, for the great animating idea transforms her, and the sacrificial wreath is like the bridal wreath. She knows not any man,[52] and yet she is a bride; she does not even know the idea that animates her, for that would be unfeminine, and yet she is a bride.

So it is with our Antigone, the bride of sorrow. She dedicates her life to sorrowing over her father's fate, over her own. A calamity such as the one that has befallen her father requires sorrow, and yet there is no one who can sorrow over it, since there is no one who knows it. And just as the Greek Antigone cannot bear to have her brother's body thrown away without the last honors, so she feels how harsh it would have been if no one had come to know this; it troubles her that not a tear would have been shed, and she almost thanks the gods because she has been selected as this instrument. Thus, Antigone is great in her pain. Here, too, I can point out a difference between Greek and modern tragedy. It is genuinely Greek for Philoctetes to lament that no one knows what he is suffering; it is a deeply human need to want others to understand it, but reflective pain does not desire this. It does not occur to Antigone to wish anyone to come to know her pain, but instead she feels the pain in relation to her father, feels the justice implicit in sorrowing, which is just as warranted esthetically as is suffering punishment when one has done wrong. Therefore, while it is first the awareness of being destined to be buried alive that extorts this outburst of grief from Antigone in the Greek tragedy,

(850) ἰὼ δύστανος,
οὔτ᾽ ἐν βροτοῖς, ἐν νεκροῖσι,
μέτοικος, οὐ ζῶσιν, οὐ θανοῦσι*
[alive to the place of corpses, an alien still,
never at home with the living nor with the dead],[53]

our Antigone can say this of herself all her life. There is a striking difference; there is a factual truth in her utterance that diminishes the pain. If our Antigone were to say the same thing,
it would be figurative, but the figurativeness is the factual
pain. The Greeks do not express themselves figuratively simply because their lives did not have the reflection required for
this. Thus, when Philoctetes laments that he lives abandoned
and solitary on a desolate island, his remark also has external
truth; when, however, our Antigone feels pain in her solitude,
it is only figuratively that she is alone, but for this very reason,
only then is her pain truly literal.

As for the tragic guilt, it is related in part to the fact that she
buries her brother and in part to the context of her father's sad
fate implied by the two previous tragedies. Here I am face to
face again with the curious dialectic that places the family's iniquities in relation to the individual. This is what is inherited.
Ordinarily, dialectic is thought to be rather abstract—one
thinks almost solely of logical operations. But life will quickly
teach a person that there are many kinds of dialectic, that almost every passion has its own. For this reason, the dialectic
that connects the iniquity of kindred or of family to the individual subject in such a way that this one not only suffers under it (for this is a natural consequence against which one
would futilely try to harden oneself) but also bears the guilt,
participates in it—this dialectic is alien to us, contains nothing
constraining for us. If, however, we were to imagine a rebirth
of ancient tragedy, then every individual would have to contemplate his own rebirth, not only in the spiritual sense but in
the finite sense of the womb of family and kindred. The di-

I
136

---

* (844) O weh, Unselige!
Nicht unter Menschen, nicht unter Todten,
Im Leben nicht heimisch noch im Tode![54]

alectic that connects the individual with family and kindred is no subjective dialectic, for that elevates the connection and the individual out of the context; it is an objective dialectic. It is essentially [familial] piety. To preserve this cannot be regarded as harmful to the individual. In our day something is deemed to hold in the sphere of nature that is not deemed to hold in the sphere of spirit. Yet one does not want to be so isolated, so unnatural, that one does not regard the family as a whole of which it can be said that when one member suffers, then they all suffer.[55] One does this spontaneously—otherwise for what reason is the particular individual so afraid that another member of the family may bring disgrace upon it except that he feels a share of the suffering from it. Obviously the individual must put up with this suffering, whether he wants to or not. But since the point of departure is the individual, not the family line, this compulsory suffering is *maximum*; one feels that the person cannot quite become master of his inherited characteristics but nevertheless desires this as far as possible. But if the individual sees the inherited characteristics as a component of his truth, then this manifests itself in the world of spirit in such a way that the individual participates in the guilt. Perhaps not many are able to comprehend this conclusion, but then they would not be able to comprehend the tragic, either. If the individual is isolated, then either he is absolutely the creator of his own fate, and then there is nothing tragic anymore, but only evil, for it is not even tragic that the individual was infatuated with or wrapped up in himself—it is his own doing; or the individuals are merely modifications of the eternal substance of life, and so once again the tragic is lost.

With respect to tragic guilt, a difference in modern tragedy is readily apparent after it has assimilated the ancient, for only then can this really be discussed. In her childlike piety, the Greek Antigone participates in her father's guilt, and so also does the modern Antigone. But for the Greek Antigone the father's guilt and suffering are an external fact, an unshakable fact, that her sorrow does not move (*quod non volvit in pectore* [something that she does not turn over in her heart]);[56] and insofar as she personally suffers, as a natural consequence, under her father's guilt, this again is in all its external factuality. But for our Antigone it is different. I assume that Oedipus is dead. Even when he was alive, Antigone knew this secret but did not have the courage to confide in her father. By her father's death, she is deprived of the only means of being liberated from her secret. To confide in any other living being now would be to dishonor her father; her life acquires meaning for her in its devotion to showing him the last honors daily, almost hourly, by her unbroken silence. But one thing she does not know, whether or not her father knew it himself. Here is the modern element: it is the restlessness in her sorrow, it is the amphiboly[57] in her pain. She loves her father with all her soul, and this love draws her out of herself into her father's guilt. As the fruit of such a love, she feels alien to humankind. She feels her guilt the more she loves her father; only with him can she find rest; as equally guilty, they would sorrow with each other. But while the father was living, she could not confide her sorrow to him, for she indeed did not know whether he knew it, and consequently there was the possibility of immersing him in a similar pain. And yet, if he had not known it, the guilt would be less. The movement here is continually relative. If Antigone had not definitely known the factual context, she would have been trivial, she would then have had nothing but a suspicion to struggle with, and that is too little to engage us tragically. But she knows everything; yet within this knowledge there is still an ignorance that can always keep the sorrow in motion, always transform it into pain. In addition, she is continually in conflict with her surrounding world. Oedipus lives in the memory of his people as a fortunate king, honored and extolled; Antigone herself has admired and also loved her father. She takes part in every commemoration and celebration of him; she is more enthusiastic about her father than any other maiden in the kingdom; her thoughts continually go back to him. She is extolled in the land as a model of a loving daughter, and yet this enthusiasm is the only way in which she can give vent to her sorrow. Her father is always in her thoughts, but how—that is her painful secret. And yet she does not dare to abandon herself to sorrow, does not dare to

I
138

mourn; she feels how much depends upon her; she fears that a clue would be given if anyone saw her suffering, and so here, too, she finds not sorrow but pain.

Developed and elaborated in this way, Antigone can engage us, I believe, and I believe that you will not reproach me for frivolousness or paternal prejudice when I believe that she might very well venture into the tragic line and appear in a tragedy. Hitherto she has been only an epic character, and the tragic in her has had only epic interest.

A context appropriate to her is not very difficult to find, either; in that respect, one can very well be satisfied with what the Greek tragedy provides. She has a sister living; I shall have her be a little older and married. Her mother could also be alive. That these two always remain subordinate characters is, of course, taken for granted, as is the fact that tragedy generally contains an epic element in the manner of Greek tragedy, although this need not be so conspicuous because of that; nevertheless, monologue will always play a leading role here, even though the situation ought to be of assistance to it. Everything must be thought of as focused on this one main point of interest that makes up the content of Antigone's life, and when the whole thing is designed in this way, then the question is: How is the dramatic interest to be produced?

As described above, our heroine is on the point of wanting to leap over an element in her life; she is beginning to want to live altogether spiritually, something that nature does not tolerate. With her depth of soul, when she ever falls in love, she is bound to love with an extraordinary passion. So here I come to the dramatic interest—Antigone is in love, and I say it with pain—Antigone is head over heels in love.[58] Here, obviously, is the tragic collision. Generally there ought to be somewhat more discrimination about what is called a tragic collision. The more sympathetic the colliding forces are, the more profound but also the more alike they are, the more momentous the collision. So she has fallen in love, and the object of her love [*Kjærlighed*] is not unaware of it. Now, my Antigone is no ordinary girl, and her dowry likewise is not ordinary—her pain. Without this dowry, she cannot belong to any man—

that, she feels, would be taking too great a risk. To conceal it from such an observant person would be impossible; to wish to have it concealed would be a breach of her love—but with it can she belong to him? Does she dare to confide it to any human being, even to the man she loves? Antigone is strong; the question is not whether for her own sake, to ease her mind, she should confide her pain to someone, for she can very well endure it without support, but can she defend this to the one who is dead? Indeed, by confiding her secret to him, she herself suffers in a way, for her life is also sadly interwoven in that secret. But this does not concern her. The question is only about her father. Consequently, from this angle the conflict is of a sympathetic nature. Her life, which previously was peaceful and quiet, now becomes violent and passionate, at all times self-contained, of course, and here her lines begin to have pathos. She struggles with herself; she has been willing to sacrifice her life for her secret, but now her love is demanded as a sacrifice. She is victorious—that is, the secret is victorious—and she loses.

Now comes the second collision, because in order for the tragic collision to be really profound, the colliding forces must be alike. The collision described above does not have this quality, for the collision is actually between her love for her father and for herself and whether her own love is not too great a sacrifice. The second colliding force is her sympathetic love for her beloved. He knows that he is loved and audaciously ventures upon his offensive. Of course, her reluctance amazes him; he perceives that there must be some very strange difficulties, but not such as to be insurmountable for him. What to him is of supreme importance is to convince her of how deeply he loves her, indeed, that his life is over if he must give up her love. Finally his passion becomes almost unveracious, but only more inventive because of this opposition. With every protestation of love, he increases her pain; with every sigh, he plunges the arrow of grief deeper and deeper into her heart. He leaves no means untried to move her. Like everyone else, he knows how dearly she loves her father. He meets her at Oedipus's grave, where she has gone to pour out her heart, where

I
140

she abandons herself to her longing for her father, even if this longing is itself mixed with pain because she does not know how she is going to meet him again, whether or not he knew of his guilt. He surprises her; he beseeches her in the name of the love she has for her father. He perceives that he is making an extraordinary impression on her; he persists, placing all his hope in this means, not knowing that he has actually worked against himself.

The focus of interest here, then, is to extort her secret from her. To have her become temporarily deranged and in that way to betray it would be of no help. The colliding forces are matched to such a degree that action becomes impossible for the tragic individual. Her pain is now increased by her love, by her sympathetic suffering with the one whom she loves. Only in death can she find peace. Thus her life is devoted to grief, and she has, so to speak, established a boundary, a dike, against the misfortune that perhaps would have fatefully propagated itself in a following generation. Only in the moment of her death can she confess the fervency of her love; only in the moment she does not belong to him can she confess that she belongs to him. [59]When Epaminondas was wounded in the battle at Mantinea, he let the arrow remain in the wound until he heard that the battle was won, for he knew that it was his death when it was pulled out.[60] In the same way, our Antigone carries her secret in her heart like an arrow that life has continually plunged deeper and deeper, without depriving her of her life, for as long as it is in her heart she can live, but the instant it is taken out, she must die. To take her secret away—this is what the lover must struggle to do, and yet it is also her certain death. At whose hand does she fall, then? At the hand of the living or the dead? [61]In a certain sense, at the hand of the dead, and what was predicted to Hercules,[62] that he would be murdered not by a living person but by a dead one, applies to her, inasmuch as the cause of her death is the recollection of her father; in another sense, at the hand of the living, inasmuch as her unhappy love is the occasion for the recollection to slay her.[63]

SILHOUETTES
PSYCHOLOGICAL DIVERSION[1]

Delivered before the
Συμπαρανεκρώμενοι
[Fellowship of the Dead][2]

ı

Abgeschworen mag die Liebe immer seyn;
Liebes-Zauber wiegt in dieser Höhle
Die berauschte, überraschte Seele
In Vergessenheit des Schwures ein.

Gestern liebt' ich,
Heute leid' ich,
Morgen sterb' ich;
Dennoch denk' ich
Heut' und Morgen
Gern an Gestern

[Foresworn may love at all times be;
Love-magic lulls down in this cave
The soul surprised, intoxicated,
In forgetfulness of any oath.

Yesterday I loved,
Today I suffer,
Tomorrow I die,
Yet today and tomorrow
I like to think
Of yesterday].[3]

We celebrate in this hour the founding of our society; we rejoice anew that the happy occasion has repeated itself, that the
longest day is over and night begins to triumph. We have
waited all the day long; just a moment ago we sighed over its
length, but now our despair is transformed into joy. To be
sure, the victory is not great, and the preponderance of day
will last for a long time, but that its domination has been broken does not escape our attention. Therefore, we do not postpone our celebration over the victory of the night until it is
plain to all; we do not postpone it until the torpid bourgeois
life reminds us that day is declining. No, as a young bride impatiently awaits the coming of night, so we longingly wait for
the first onset of night, the first announcement of its coming
victory, and the more we have been inclined to despair over
our being able to hold out if the days were not shortened, the
greater our joy and surprise.

A year has gone by, and our society still survives. Should
we rejoice over that, dear Συμπαρανεκρώμενοι, rejoice that its
existence mocks our doctrine of the downfall of everything, or
should we not lament instead that it survives and rejoice that
in any case it has only one year left to continue, for if it has not
vanished within that time, was it not our decision to dissolve
it ourselves? In founding it, we did not make farsighted plans;   I
too familiar with the wretchedness of life and the perfidious-   146
ness of existence, we resolved to come to the aid of universal
law and obliterate ourselves if it does not forestall us. A year
has gone by and our society is still intact; as yet no one has been
released, no one has released himself, since every one of us is
too proud for that, because we all regard death as the greatest
good fortune. Should we rejoice over this and not rather be sad

and take pleasure only in the hope that life's confusion will soon split us up, that the storms of life will soon carry us off! Surely these thoughts are better suited to our society, are more in agreement with the festivity of the moment, with the entire setting. For is it not ingenious and significant that the floor of this little room is strewn, as is the local custom, with foliage, as if for a funeral; and is not nature itself giving us its approval when we take note of the wild storm raging around us, when we pay heed to the wind's powerful voice? Yes, let us be silent for a moment and listen to the music of the storm, its spirited course, its bold challenge, and the defiant roar of the sea and the uneasy sighing of the forest and the desperate crashing of the trees and the faint sibilating of the grass. To be sure, people do say that the voice of the divine is not in the driving wind but in the soft breeze,[4] but our ears, after all, are constructed not to pick up the soft breezes but to swallow the uproar of the elements. And why does it not rage even more violently and put an end to life and the world and this short speech, which at least has the merit exceeding everything else that it is soon ended. Yes, would that the vortex, which is the world's core principle,[5] even if people are not aware of it but eat and drink, marry and propagate themselves with carefree industriousness, would that it might erupt with deep-seated resentment and shake off the mountains and the nations and the cultural works and man's clever inventions; would that it might erupt with the last terrible shriek that more surely than the trumpet of doom announces the downfall of everything; would that it might stir and spin this bare cliff on which we stand as light as thistledown before the breath in its nostrils. The night, however, is being victorious, the day is shortening, and hope is growing! So fill your glasses once again, fellow topers; with this goblet I toast you, silent night, the eternal mother of everything! From you comes everything; to you everything returns. Have mercy again on the world; open up once again to gather in everything and keep us all safe in your womb! I greet you, dark night, I greet you as the victor, and this is my comfort, for in eternal oblivion you shorten everything, day and time and life and the irksomeness of recollection!

Since the time when Lessing defined the boundaries between poetry and art in his celebrated treatise *Laokoon*,[6] it no doubt may be regarded as a conclusion unanimously recognized by all estheticians that the distinction between them is that art is in the category of space, poetry in the category of time, that art depicts repose, poetry motion.[7] For this reason, the subject for artistic portrayal must have a quiet transparency so that the interior rests in the corresponding exterior. The less this is the case, the more difficult becomes the task for the artist, until the distinction asserts itself and teaches him that this is no task for him at all.

If we apply to the relation between sorrow and joy that which has been casually stated but not developed here, it is easy to perceive that joy is far easier to depict artistically than sorrow. By no means does this deny that grief can be depicted artistically, but it certainly does say that there comes a point where it is essential to posit a contrast between the interior and the exterior, which makes a depiction of it impossible for art. This in turn is due to the singular nature of sorrow. By nature, joy wishes to disclose itself; sorrow wishes to conceal itself, indeed, at times even to deceive. Joy is communicative, sociable, open, wishes to express itself. Sorrow is inclosingly reserved [*indesluttet*], silent, solitary, and seeks to return into itself. Surely no one who has made life the object of any observation at all will deny the correctness of this. There are people whose make-up is so constituted that when their emotions are stirred the blood rushes to the surface of the skin, and in this way the interior motion becomes visible in the exterior; others are so constituted that the blood recedes, withdraws into the heart chamber and the inner parts of the organism. It is somewhat like this with respect to the mode of expressing joy and sorrow. The first make-up described is much easier to observe than the second. In the first, one sees the manifestation; the interior motion is visible in the exterior. In the second, one has an intimation of the interior motion. The exterior pallor is, as it were, the interior's good-bye, and thought and imagination hurry after the fugitive, which hides in the secret recesses. This applies particularly to the kind of sorrow I shall consider more

I
148

explicitly here, what could be called reflective sorrow. Here the exterior has at most only a suggestion that puts one on the track, sometimes not even that much. This sorrow cannot be depicted artistically, for the interior and the exterior are out of balance, and thus it does not lie within spatial categories. In yet another respect it cannot be depicted artistically, for it does not have inner stillness but is constantly in motion; even if this motion does not enrich it with new effects, the motion itself is nevertheless the essential. Like a squirrel in its cage, it turns around in itself, yet not as uniformly as does that animal, but with a continual alternation in the combination of the interior elements of sorrow. What excludes reflective sorrow as the subject for artistic depiction is that it lacks repose, is not at one with itself, does not come to rest in any one definite expression. Just as the patient in his pain tosses from one side to the other, so reflective sorrow is tossed about in order to find its object and its expression. If the sorrow is in repose, the interior of sorrow will gradually work its way outward, become visible in the exterior, and in this way become a subject for artistic depiction. If sorrow has inner repose and rest, the motion begins outward from the inside; reflective sorrow moves inward, like blood rushing from the outer surface, and lets one have an intimation of it only because of the fleeting pallor. Reflective sorrow does not involve any essential change in the exterior; even in the first moment of sorrow it hurries inward, and only the more careful observer has an intimation of its disappearance; later it carefully sees to it that the exterior is as inconspicuous as possible.

By withdrawing inward in this way, it finally finds an inclosure, an innermost retreat, where it thinks it can remain, and now it begins its uniform movement. Like the pendulum in a clock, it swings back and forth and cannot find rest. It continually begins from the beginning and deliberates anew, interrogates the witnesses, checks and examines the various statements, something it has already done hundreds of times, but it is never finished. In the course of time, the uniformity has something anesthetizing about it. Just as the uniform dripping of rain from the roof, the uniform whirring of a spinning wheel, and the monotonous sound of a man pacing back and forth with measured steps on the floor above have an anesthetizing effect, so reflective grief eventually finds solace in this motion, which as an illusory motion becomes a necessity for it. At last there is a kind of balance; the need to give vent to the grief, insofar as it may ever have asserted itself at all, ceases; the exterior is calm and quiet; and deep within, in its little nook, grief lives like a well-guarded prisoner in an underground prison, who lives on year after year in his uniform movement, walking to and fro in his cubbyhole, never weary of traveling the long or short road of sorrow.

Reflective sorrow can be occasioned in part by the individual's subjective quality, in part by the objective sorrow or the occasion of the sorrow. A morbidly reflective individual will transform every sorrow into a reflective sorrow; his individual make-up and structure render it impossible for him to assimilate the sorrow right away. But this is a morbidity that cannot be of particular interest to us, because in that way every accidentality can undergo a metamorphosis by which it becomes a reflective sorrow. It is another matter when the objective sorrow or the occasion of the sorrow in the individual himself fosters the reflection that makes the sorrow into a reflective sorrow. This is everywhere the case when the objective sorrow in itself is not finished, when it leaves a doubt, whatever its nature is. Here at once a great multiplicity appears for thought, greater according to the richness of one's life and experience or one's inclination to engage one's keenness in such imaginary constructions.

But it is by no means my intention to go through the whole multiplicity; I want to single out only one aspect as it has appeared for my observation. If the occasion for sorrow is a deception, then the objective sorrow itself is of such a quality that it engenders reflective sorrow in the individual. That a deception is actually a deception is often very difficult to determine clearly, and yet everything depends upon that. As long as this is debatable, the sorrow will find no repose but must continue to ramble back and forth in reflection. Furthermore, if this deception does not involve anything external but a person's whole inner life, his life's innermost core, the probability of the continuance of the objective sorrow becomes greater and greater. But what can more truthfully be called a woman's life than her love? Consequently, if the sorrow of an unhappy love is due to a deception, we have unconditionally a reflective sorrow, whether it continues for a lifetime or the individual conquers it. Unhappy love is in itself undoubtedly the deepest sorrow for a woman, but it does not follow from this that every unhappy love engenders a reflective sorrow. If, for example, the beloved dies, or she perhaps does not find her love returned at all, or her life situation makes the fulfillment of her wish impossible, this certainly is an occasion for sorrow, but not a reflective sorrow, except to the extent that the person concerned was morbid before, and then she thereby lies outside our interest. But if she is not morbid, then her sorrow becomes an immediate sorrow and as such can also become the subject of artistic portrayal, whereas on the other hand it is impossible for art to express and portray the reflective sorrow or the point of it. In other words, immediate sorrow is the immediate imprint and expression of the sorrow's impression, which, just like the picture Veronica[8] preserved on her linen cloth, is perfectly congruous, and sorrow's sacred lettering is stamped on the exterior, beautiful and clear and legible to all.

Reflective sorrow, then, cannot become a subject for artistic portrayal. For one thing, it is never really present but is continually in the process of becoming; for another, the exterior, the visible, is a matter of unimportance and indifference. So if art will not limit itself to the naïveté (examples are found in old books) in which a figure is portrayed that can represent almost anything, but one discovers on its breast a plaque, a heart or something similar, on which one may read everything, especially when the figure's posture draws a person's attention to it, even points to it, an effect that could just as well be achieved by writing above it "Please note!"—if art will not do this, it will be obliged to reject pictures of that kind and leave reflective grief to poetic or psychological treatment.

It is this reflective sorrow that I aim to single out and, as far as possible, have emerge in a few pictures. I call them silhouettes [*Skyggerids*],⁹ partly to suggest at once by the name that I draw them from the dark side of life and partly because, like silhouettes, they are not immediately visible. If I pick up a silhouette, I have no impression of it, cannot arrive at an actual conception of it; only when I hold it up toward the wall and do not look at it directly but at what appears on the wall, only then do I see it. So it is also with the picture I want to show here, an interior picture that does not become perceptible until I see through the exterior. Perhaps there is nothing striking about the exterior, but when I look through it, only then do I discover the interior picture, which is what I want to show, an interior picture that is too delicate to be externally perceptible, since it is woven from the soul's faintest moods. If I look at a sheet of paper, it perhaps has nothing remarkable about it for immediate inspection, but as soon as I hold it up to the light of day and look through it, I discover the subtle interior picture,¹⁰ too psychical, as it were, to be seen immediately.

I
151

So fasten your gaze, dear Συμπαρανεκρώμενοι, on this interior picture; do not let yourselves be distracted by the exterior, or, more correctly, do not produce it yourselves, for I shall continually draw it aside in order to penetrate better into the interior. But presumably I do not need to encourage this society, of which I have the honor to be a member, to do this, for although we are young, we nevertheless are all old enough not to let ourselves be deceived by the exterior or to stop with that. Would I be indulging in a vain hope if I believed that you will do these pictures the honor of your attention, or would my efforts be foreign and of no consequence to you, not in harmony with the interest of our society, a society that knows but one passion, namely, sympathy with sorrow's secret.

As a matter of fact, we, too, form an order; we, too, now and then go out into the world like knights-errant, each his own way, not to fight monsters or come to the aid of innocence or be tried in amorous adventures. All this is of no concern to us, not even the last, for the arrow in a woman's eye does not wound our hardened breasts, and the cheery smiles of happy maidens do not move us, but rather the secret hint of grief. Let others be proud that no girl anywhere can resist their

erotic power; we envy them not. We shall be proud that no secret sorrow escapes our attention, that no solitary sorrow is so
prudish and so proud that we do not succeed in penetrating its
innermost hideout! Which contest is the most dangerous,
which requires the most skill and provides the greatest pleasure, we shall not investigate. Our choice is made: we love only
sorrow. We are in quest only of sorrow, and wherever we find
its trail, we follow it, fearlessly, unwaveringly, until it discloses itself. For this fight we equip ourselves; we practice
fighting daily.

I
152

It is true that sorrow sneaks about in the world so very secretively that only the person who has sympathy for it gains
an intimation of it. One walks down the street; one house
looks like the other. Only the experienced observer suspects
that in this particular house things are quite otherwise at the
midnight hour; then an unhappy person paces about, one who
found no rest; he goes up the stairs, and his footsteps echo in
the stillness of the night. People pass one another in the street;
one person looks just like the next, and the next one is like almost everyone else. Only the experienced observer suspects
that deep within that one's head resides a lodger who has nothing to do with the world but lives out his solitary life in quiet
home-industry work.

The exterior, then, is indeed the object of our scrutiny but
not of our interest. In the same way, the fisherman sits and
looks fixedly at the float; the float, however, does not interest
him at all, but rather the movements down at the bottom.
Therefore the exterior does indeed have significance for us,
but not as a manifestation of the interior, but rather as a telegraphic report that there is something hidden deep within.

When one looks long and attentively at a face, sometimes
another face, as it were, is discovered within the face one sees.
Ordinarily this is an unmistakable sign that the soul is hiding
an emigrant who has withdrawn from the exterior face in order to watch over a buried treasure, and the route for the operation of observation is suggested by the fact that the one face
seems to be within the other, which indicates that one must try
to penetrate inward if one wants to discover anything. The

face, which usually is the mirror of the soul, here takes on an ambiguity that cannot be artistically portrayed and that usually lasts only for a fleeting moment. It takes a special eye to see it, a special vision to pursue this unerring indication of secret sorrow. This vision is avid and yet so scrupulous, alarming, and compelling, and yet so sympathetic, persevering, and cunning, and yet so honest and well disposed; it lulls the individual into a sort of pleasant lassitude in which he finds a sensual pleasure in pouring out his sorrow, similar to the sensual pleasure in bleeding to death. The present is forgotten, the exterior is penetrated; the past is resurrected, sorrow's breathing is eased. The person who is grieving finds relief, and the sympathetic knight of grief rejoices over having found what he sought, for we seek not the present but the past, not joy, for it is always present, but sorrow, for its nature is to pass by, and in the present moment we see it just as we see a person when we catch sight of him for just a moment and then he turns down another street and disappears.

I
153

But sometimes the sorrow conceals itself even better, and the exterior allows us to suspect nothing, not the slightest. It can elude our attention for a long time, but when by chance a look, a word, a sigh, a tone in the voice, a hint in the eyes, a trembling of the lips, or a blunder in the handshake treacherously betrays what has been carefully concealed—then passion is aroused, then the struggle begins. Then it is a matter of having vigilance and perseverance and sagacity, for who is as inventive as secret sorrow, but a solitary lifetime prisoner has adequate time to think up many things, and who is as swift to find concealment as secret sorrow, for no young girl can cover in greater anxiety and haste a bosom she has exposed than hidden sorrow when it is surprised. Then unshakable dauntlessness is required, for the struggle is with a Proteus,[11] but he must give up if one only holds out. Even if like that sea god he assumed every shape in order to escape, such as a snake twisting in our hands, a lion terrifying us with its roaring, changed into a tree that whispers with its leaves or into roaring water or a crackling fire—at last he must nevertheless prophesy, and sorrow must disclose itself at last. See, these adventures are our delight, our diversion; to try ourselves in them is our knighthood. For that purpose, we arise in the middle of the night like robbers; this is why we risk everything, for no passion is as wild as the passion of sympathy. And we need not fear that there will be a lack of adventures for us but rather fear collision with opposition that is too hard and impregnable, for just as natural scientists report that in blasting boulders that have defied the centuries they have found deep within a living creature that, undiscovered, has maintained life, so also it is indeed possible that there are human beings whose exterior is a firm-as-rock hill that guards their forever hidden life of sorrow. This, however, will not temper our passion or cool our zeal; on the contrary, it will inflame it, because our passion, after all, is not curiosity that satisfies itself with the exterior and the superficial but is a sympathetic anxiety that searches the minds[12] and hidden thoughts, conjures forth what is hidden by means of witchcraft and invocations, even that which death has withheld from our gaze. It is said that Saul, before the battle, came in disguise to a fortune teller and demanded that she show him Samuel's image.[13] It surely was not only curiosity that impelled him, not a desire to see Samuel's visible image, but he wanted to know his thoughts, and he undoubtedly waited uneasily until he heard the rigorous judge's censorious voice. Likewise it surely will not simply be curiosity that moves one or another of you, my dear Συμπαρανεϰρώμενοι, to contemplate the pictures I am going to show you. Although I designate them with specific poetic names, by no means is it suggested thereby that it is only these poetic figures who appear before you, but the names must be regarded as *nomina appellativa* [common nouns], and from my side there is nothing to hinder any one of you, if you feel inclined, from giving a particular picture another name, a more appealing name, or a name that perhaps comes more naturally to you.

1. Marie Beaumarchais

The girl taken as our subject is known to us in Goethe's *Clavigo*,[14] except that we shall follow her a little further in time, when she has lost dramatic interest, when the accompaniments of sorrow have gradually abated. We shall continue to follow her, for we, knights of sympathy, have just as much innate gift as acquired skill in being able to keep step in procession with sorrow.

Her story is brief: Clavigo became engaged to her; Clavigo left her. This information is enough for the person who is in the habit of observing the phenomena of life as one observes rarities in a curio cabinet; the shorter the better, the more one can manage to see. In the same way, it could be told very briefly that Tantalus thirsts and that Sisyphus rolls a stone up the mountain.[15] If someone is in a hurry, it would indeed be a delay to dwell on it any further, since one cannot learn any more than one already knows, which is the whole thing. Whatever is to claim more attention must be of another kind. A group of intimates is gathered around the tea table. The samovar is singing its last verse, and the hostess asks the mysterious stranger to unburden his heart. With that in mind, she has sugar-water and jam brought in, and now he begins. It is a long, prolix story. So it goes in novels, and it is also something quite different: a prolix story and such a brief little announcement. Whether it is a brief story for Marie Beaumarchais is another question. One thing is sure; it is not prolix, for a prolix story nevertheless has a measurable length, but a short story sometimes has the mysterious quality that despite all its brevity it is longer than the most prolix.

In what has been stated in the foregoing discussion, I have already pointed out that reflective grief does not become visible in the exterior, that is, it does not find its beautiful, composed expression therein. The interior unrest does not permit this transparency, and the exterior is more likely to be consumed thereby; insofar as the interior would declare itself in the exterior, it would likely be a kind of morbidity, which can never become a subject for artistic portrayal, since it does not have the interest of the beautiful. Goethe has suggested this by a few particular hints.[16] But even if there is agreement on the correctness of this observation, there could be a temptation to regard it as something incidental, and not until one is assured, by deliberating purely poetically and esthetically, that what

I
155

the observation states has esthetic truth, not until then will one gain a deeper consciousness. Now, if I were to imagine a reflective sorrow and asked if it could not be portrayed artistically, it would immediately be apparent that the exterior is altogether incidental to it; but if this is true, then artistic beauty is abandoned. Whether she is large or small, significant or insignificant, beautiful or not so beautiful, this is of no consequence; to deliberate on whether it would be more proper to have her incline her head to this side or to that or toward the ground, to have her gaze gloomily or sadly fix her eyes on the ground—all this is utterly inconsequential; the one expresses the reflective sorrow no more adequately than the other. In comparison with the interior, the exterior has become insignificant and inconsequential. The point in reflective sorrow is that the sorrow is continually seeking its object; this seeking is the sorrow's restlessness and its life. But this seeking is a continual fluctuation, and if at every moment the exterior were a perfect expression of the interior, then there would have to be a whole series of pictures in order to portray reflective sorrow; but no particular picture would express the sorrow, and no particular picture would have real artistic value, since it would be not beautiful, but true. These pictures must be looked at in the way one looks at the second hand of a watch; one does not see the works, but the interior movement expresses itself continually in the continually changing exterior. But this changeableness cannot be portrayed artistically, and yet this is the point of the whole thing.

If, for example, unhappy love is due to a deception, then its pain and suffering are that the grief cannot find its object. If the deception is proved and the person concerned has perceived that it is a deception, the sorrow certainly does not cease, but then it is an immediate sorrow, not a reflective sorrow. Here the dialectical difficulty is obvious, for what is she sorrowing over? If he was a deceiver, then it was indeed good that he left her, the earlier the better; she should rejoice over it instead and sorrow because she had loved him, and yet it is a deep sorrow that he was a deceiver. But whether it is a deception is the restlessness in sorrow's *perpetuum mobile*. To establish certainty for the external fact that a deception is a deception is always very difficult, and yet that by no means ends the matter or stops the movement. For love [*Kjærlighed*], a deception is indeed an absolute paradox, and therein lies the necessity of a reflective grief. The different factors in love may be amalgamated in the individual in very different ways, and thus love in one person may not be the same as in another; the egotistical may be dominant, or the sympathetic. But whatever the love is in its separate elements and also in its totality, a deception is a paradox that it cannot think, and yet one that it eventually wants to think. Indeed, if the egotistic or the sympathetic element is present absolutely, the paradox is canceled; that is, in the power of the absolute, the individual is beyond reflection. To be sure, he does not think the paradox in the sense that he cancels it by a reflective "how," but he is saved precisely by not thinking it; he is not concerned with reflection's busy reports or confusions—he reposes in himself. Because of its pride, the egotistically proud love regards a deception as impossible; it is not concerned with finding out what can be said for or against, how the person concerned can be defended or excused; it is absolutely sure, because it is too proud to believe that anyone would dare to deceive it. Sympathetic love possesses the faith that can move mountains;[17] for it, any defense is nothing compared with its unshakable conviction that it was no deception. Every charge proves nothing to the advocate, who explains that it was no deception, explains it not this way or that—but absolutely. But a love like that is seldom seen in this life, or perhaps never. Usually both factors are present in love, and this brings it into relation to the paradox. In the two instances described, the paradox indeed exists for love but does not concern it; in the latter instance, the paradox exists for love. The paradox is unthinkable, and yet love wants to think it, and, in accordance with the momentary predominance of the various factors, it makes an approach in order to think it, often in contradictory ways, but it does not succeed. This path of thinking is infinite and does not end until the individual arbitrarily breaks it off by affirming something else, by a determination of the will; but the individual thereby enters into ethical qual-

I
157

ifications and does not engage us esthetically. By a resolve, it attains what it cannot attain on the road of reflection: an end, repose.

This holds for every unhappy love that is due to a deception. What may evoke reflective grief even more in Maria Beaumarchais is that it is only an engagement that has been broken. An engagement is a possibility, not an actuality; but precisely because it is only a possibility, it may seem that the effects of being broken are not so great, that it is far easier for the individual to bear this blow. This may indeed be the case at times, but on the other hand the circumstance that it is only a possibility that is destroyed entices much more reflection. When an actuality is shattered, the break is usually far more radical; every nerve is cut, and the break as a break has an implicit completeness. When a possibility is shattered, the momentary pain may not be as great, but frequently it also leaves a little ligament or two whole and undamaged, which remains a constant occasion for continued pain. The destroyed possibility appears transfigured in a higher possibility, whereas the temptation to conjure up a new possibility such as this is not as great when it is an actuality that has been shattered, because the actuality is higher than the possibility.

So Clavigo has left her, has perfidiously severed the connection. Accustomed to leaning on him, she does not have the strength to stand when he thrusts her away, and she collapses weakly into the arms of those around her. This seems to be Marie's situation. However, another beginning is also conceivable; it is conceivable that immediately at the outset she had sufficient strength to transform her sorrow into reflective sorrow, that she—either to avoid the humiliation of hearing others talk about her having been deceived or because she nevertheless still thought so highly of him that it would hurt her to hear him denounced again and again as a deceiver— promptly severed all connections with others in order to consume the sorrow in herself and to consume herself in the sorrow.

We follow Goethe. Those around her are not unsympathetic; they feel her pain with her, and in feeling it they say:

This will be the death of her. Esthetically speaking, this is altogether correct. An unhappy love may be of such a nature that suicide may be regarded as esthetically proper, but then it must not have been due to a deception. If that is the case, then the suicide would lose all loftiness and involve a concession that pride must refuse to give. If, however, it is the death of her, this is the same as saying that he has murdered her. This expression harmonizes entirely with her powerful inner agitation; she finds alleviation in it.

But life does not always follow precisely esthetic categories, does not always obey an esthetic norm, and she does not die. This places those around her in an awkward position. They sense that it is inappropriate to go on declaring that she is going to die when she continues to live; in addition, they do not feel able to do it with the same pathos-filled energy as at the beginning, and yet this was a prerequisite if there was to be any solace for her. So they change their method. He was a villain, they say, a deceiver, an abominable person not worth dying for. Forget him; don't give this thing another thought; it was only an engagement. Blot this incident out of your recollection, and once again you are young, can hope again. This incites her, for this pathos of wrath harmonizes with her other moods; her pride finds satisfaction in the vengeful idea of changing the whole thing into a nothing. It was not because he was an extraordinary person that she loved him, far from it; she was very aware of his faults, but she believed he was a good man, a faithful man, and that was why she loved him. It was out of compassion, and therefore it will be easy to forget him, because she never really needed him.

Marie and those around her are once again in tune, and the duet between them goes beautifully. Those around her do not find it difficult to believe that Clavigo was a deceiver, for they had never loved him, and therefore there is no paradox. Insofar as they perhaps had liked him (something Goethe suggests with respect to the sister),[18] this very interest arms them against him, and this kindly disposition, which perhaps was little more than kindness, becomes superb inflammable stuff to sustain the flames of hate. Nor do those around her find it

I
159

difficult to blot out the recollection of him, and therefore they demand that Marie do the same. Her pride breaks forth in hate; those around her add fuel to the flames. She finds relief in violent words and vigorous, drastic intentions and becomes self-intoxicated with them. Those around her are pleased. They do not perceive—something she will scarcely admit to herself— that in the next moment she is weak and listless; they do not perceive that she is gripped by the anxious presentiment that the energy she has at a particular moment is an illusion. This she carefully hides and confesses to no one. Those around her continue their theoretical exercises successfully but nevertheless begin to want to see tokens of practical effects. They fail to appear.

Those around her continue to incite her; her words manifest interior strength, and yet they have a suspicion that there is something wrong. They become impatient, risk the extreme; they drive the spurs of ridicule into her side in order to drive her from cover. It is too late. Misunderstanding has entered in. That he actually was a deceiver entails no humiliation for those around her, but it certainly does for Marie. The revenge offered her, to scorn him, does not really mean very much, because in order for it to mean something he would have to love her, but that he certainly does not do, and her contempt becomes a check that no one will cash. On the other hand, in Clavigo's being a deceiver there is nothing painful for those around her, but there certainly is for Marie, and he still does not totally lack a defender in her inner being. She feels that she has gone too far; she has hinted at a strength she does not possess; she will not admit it. And what consolation is there in scorning him? Then it is better to grieve. In addition, she has in her possession a secret note or two of great importance for clarification of the text but also of such a nature as to place him in a more favorable or more unfavorable light according to the circumstances. She has not, however, initiated anyone into this and does not wish to do so, for if he was not a deceiver, then it would still be conceivable that he would repent of this step and come back or, even more glorious, that he perhaps would not need to repent of it, that he could completely justify

I
160

himself or explain everything. In that case, it might become an offense if she had made use of it; then the old relationship could never be re-established, and it would be her own fault, for it was she who had shared with others his love's most secret growth with others. And if she could really be convinced that he was a deceiver, well, then nothing mattered anyway, and in any case it would be most gracious of her not to make use of it.

In this way, those around her have been instrumental, against their will, in developing a new passion in her, jealousy for her own sorrow. Her decision is made; on every score those around her lack the energy to harmonize with her passion—she takes the veil. She does not enter the convent, but she takes the veil of sorrow, which hides her from every alien glance. Outwardly she is quiet. The whole affair is forgotten; her words give no hint. She herself takes the vow of sorrow, and now she begins her lonely, hidden life. At the same moment, everything is changed; previously it seemed to her as if she could speak with others, but now she is not only bound by the vow of silence that her pride extorted from her with the consent of her love, or that her love required and her pride sanctioned, but now she does not know at all where she is to begin, or how, and this is not because new factors have intervened but because reflection has triumphed. If anyone were now to ask her what she was sorrowing over, she would have nothing to reply, or she would reply in the same way as that sage[19] who was asked what religion is, and he asked for time to think, and more time to think, and thus the reply was always due. Now she is lost to the world, lost to those around her, immured alive; sadly she closes the last opening. She feels that even at this moment it was perhaps possible to become open; the next moment she is forever removed from them. But it is decided, unshakably decided, and she does not need to fear—as is usual with one who is immured alive—that when the scanty ration of bread and water provided her is used up she will perish, for she has nourishment for a long time. She does not need to fear boredom; she indeed does have something to occupy her. Her exterior is quiet and calm, has nothing remarkable about it, and yet her inner being is not the in-corruptible essence of a quiet spirit[20] but the barren busyness of a restless spirit. She seeks solitude or its opposite. In soli-tude, she relaxes from the strain always required in forcing her exterior into a particular form. Just as someone who has been standing or sitting for a long time in a forced position pleas-urably stretches his body, just as a branch that has long been bent by force and then, when the bond is broken, joyfully takes its natural position again, so also does she find refresh-ment. Or she seeks the opposite, noise and diversion, in order to be safely preoccupied with herself while everyone else's at-tention is led to other things, and what is going on around her, the sounds of music, the noisy conversation, sounds so distant that it seems as if she were sitting in a little room by herself, remote from the whole world. And if she perhaps cannot force back the tears, then she is sure to be misunderstood; then per-haps she cries herself out, for when one lives in an *ecclesia pressa* [persecuted church], it is truly a joy that one's divine service harmonizes in its mode of expression with the public mode. She fears only the quieter sociality, for here she is less un-guarded; here it is so easy to make a blunder, so difficult to pre-vent its being noticed.

Outwardly, then, there is nothing to be detected, but in-wardly there is bustling activity. Here an interrogation is tak-ing place that with perfect right and special emphasis may be called the third degree; everything is brought out and scrupu-lously examined—his figure, his facial expression, his voice, his words. It is said that it has sometimes happened that an in-terrogator, during a third degree such as this, has been capti-vated by the beauty of the accused, has halted the interroga-tion, and has been unable to continue it. The court expectantly awaits the result of his interrogation, but it fails to come, and yet it is not at all because the interrogator is neglecting his duty. The jailer can testify that he reports every night, that the accused is brought in, that the interrogation lasts several hours, that during his term there has never been an interroga-tor as persevering as this official. The court draws the conclu-sion from all this that it must be a very complicated case. So it goes with her—not just once, but again and again. Everything is presented just as it happened, trustworthily; it demands justice—and love.

The accused is summoned: "There he comes, he is turning the corner, he is opening the wicket. See how he hurries; he has longed for me; it is as if he threw everything aside in order to come to me as soon as possible. I hear his quick footsteps, faster than my heartbeats; he is coming, there he is"—and the interrogation: it is postponed.

I
162

"Good Lord, that little phrase—I have repeated it so often to myself, recalled it amid many other things, but I have never paid attention to what is really concealed in it. Yes, it explains everything. He is not in earnest about leaving me; he is coming back. What is the whole world compared with this little phrase. People became tired of me. I did not have a friend, but now I have a friend, a confidant, a little phrase that explains everything. —He returns; he does not look down; he looks at me half reproachfully and says: O you of little faith,[21] and this little phrase is poised like an olive leaf[22] on his lips—he is there"—and the interrogation is postponed.

Under such circumstances, it is quite in order that there are enormous difficulties involved in passing judgment. A young girl, of course, is not a jurist, but it by no means follows that she cannot pass judgment, and yet this young girl's judgment will always be such that although at first glance it is a judgment, it also contains something more that shows that it is no judgment, and also shows that the very next moment a completely opposite judgment may be passed. "He was no deceiver, because in order to be that, he would have had to be conscious of it himself from the beginning, but that he was not; my heart tells me that he loved me." If the concept of a deceiver is advanced in this way, then perhaps, when all is said and done, a deceiver has never lived. To acquit him for this reason shows an interest in the accused that is incompatible with strict justice and cannot stand up against a single objection. "He was a deceiver, an abominable person, who coldly and heartlessly has made me inordinately unhappy. Before I knew him, I was satisfied. Yes, it is true that I had no idea that

I could be so happy or that there was such a wealth in joy as he taught me, but neither did I have any idea that I could become as unhappy as he has taught me to be. Therefore I will hate him, abominate him, curse him. Yes, I curse you, Clavigo; in the secrecy of my soul I curse you. No one must know it; I cannot allow anyone else to do it, for no one but me has the right to do it. I have loved you as no one else has, but I also hate you, for no one knows your cunning as I do. You good gods, to whom revenge belongs, entrust it to me for a little while; I will not misuse it, I will not be cruel. Then I will steal into his soul when he wants to love another—not in order to kill this love; that would be no punishment, for I know that he loves her just as little as he loved me. He does not love people at all; he loves only ideas, thoughts, his powerful influence at court, his intellectual power—I cannot imagine how he can love all these things. I will take it all away from him; then he will learn to know my pain. When he is on the verge of despair, I will give it all back to him again, but he will have me to thank for it—and then I shall be avenged.

"No, he was no deceiver. He did not love me anymore; that is why he left me, but that, after all, was no deception. If he had stayed with me without loving me, then he would have been a deceiver; then like a pensioner I would have lived on the love he once had had, lived on his pity, on the mite he perhaps even generously had thrown to me, lived as a burden to him and a torture to myself. Shame on you, wretched, cowardly heart; hold yourself in contempt; learn to be great, learn it from him; he has loved me better than I have understood how to love myself. And I should be angry with him? No, I will go on loving him because his love was stronger, his thoughts prouder, than my weakness and my cowardliness. And perhaps he even still loves me—yes, it was for love of me that he left me.

"Yes, now I see it; now I no longer doubt—he was a deceiver. I saw him: he looked proud and exultant; he surveyed me with a mocking glance. At his side was a Spanish girl, luxuriant in beauty. Why was she so beautiful—I could murder her—why am I not just as beautiful? And was I not? —I did not know it, but he taught it to me—and why am I no longer beautiful? Who is to blame for it? Curse you, Clavigo! If you had stayed with me, I would have become even more beautiful, for my love and, along with it, my beauty increased through your words and your assurances. Now I am faded; now I thrive no longer. Compared with a word from you, what power does the tenderness of the whole world have? Oh, would that I were beautiful once again; would that I could please him once again, because only for that reason do I want to be beautiful. Oh, would that he were no longer able to love youth and beauty; then I shall lament more than before, and who can lament as I do!

"Yes, he was a deceiver. Otherwise, how could he stop loving me? Have I, then, stopped loving him? Is there not the same law for a man's love as for a woman's? Or is a man supposed to be weaker than the weak? Or did he perhaps make a mistake; was it perhaps an illusion that he loved me, an illusion that disappeared like a dream—is this befitting in a man? Or was it fickleness; is it befitting for a man to be fickle? Why, then, did he assure me in the beginning that he loved me so much? If love cannot last, what, then, can last? Yes, Clavigo, you have robbed me of everything, my faith, my faith in love, not just in your love!

"He was no deceiver. What snatched him away, I do not know; I do not know that dark power, but it pained him personally, pained him deeply. He did not want to initiate me into his pain; therefore he pretended to be a deceiver. Indeed, if he had taken up with another girl, then I would say he was a deceiver, then no power on earth would bring me to believe anything else, but that he has not done. He thinks perhaps that making himself appear to be a deceiver will diminish the pain for me, will arm me against him. Therefore he appears now and then with young girls, therefore he looked at me so mockingly the other day—to make me furious and thereby to liberate me. No, surely he was no deceiver, and how could that voice deceive? It was so calm and yet so agitated; it sounded from an inwardness, the depth of which I could scarcely suspect, as if it were breaking a path through masses of rock. Can

I
164

that voice deceive? What is the voice, then—is it a stroke of the tongue, a noise that one can produce as one wishes? But it must have a home somewhere in the soul; it must have a birth-place. And that it did, in the innermost recess of his heart it had its home; there he loved me, there he loves me. To be sure, he had another voice also; it was cold, chilling; it could murder every joy in my soul, squelch every joyous thought, make even my kiss cold and abhorrent to me. Which was the true voice? He could deceive in every way, but this I feel—that tremulous voice in which his whole passion throbbed—that was no deceit; it is impossible. The other was a deception. Or there were evil forces that gained control of him. No, he was no deceiver; that voice that has shackled me to him forever—that is no deception. A deceiver he was not, even though I never understood him."[23]

The interrogation she will never finish, nor the judgment, either—the interrogation, because there are always interrup-tions; the judgment, because it is only a feeling. Once this movement begins, it can go on as long as it pleases, and there is no end in sight. Only by a break can it be brought to a halt—that is, by her cutting short this whole movement of thought; but this cannot happen, for the will is continually in the service of reflection, which energizes the momentary passion.

When at times she wants to tear herself away from all this, wants to reduce it to nothing, this is again only a mood, a mo-mentary passion, and reflection continually goes on being the victor. Mediation is impossible; if she wants to begin so that this beginning in one way or another is a result of the opera-tions of reflection, then at the same moment she is swept away. The will must be altogether impartial, must begin in the power of its own willing; only then can there be any question of a beginning. If this happens, then she certainly can begin, but then she falls outside our concern entirely, then we gladly turn her over to the moralists or to whoever else wants to take an interest in her. We wish her an honorable marriage and promise to dance on her wedding day, when fortunately the changed name will bring us to forget that it was the Marie Beaumarchais of whom we have spoken.

But we return to Marie Beaumarchais. As stated above, her sorrow is characterized by the restlessness that prevents her from finding the object of her sorrow. Her pain cannot find quiet; she lacks the peace that is necessary for any life if it is to be able to assimilate its nourishment and be refreshed by it; no illusion overshadows her with its quiet coolness as she absorbs the pain. She lost childhood's illusion when she acquired that of erotic love; she lost erotic love's illusion when Clavigo deceived her; if it were possible for her to acquire sorrow's illusion, she would be helped. Then her grief would attain masculine maturity, and she would be compensated for her loss. But her sorrow does not thrive, for she has not lost Clavigo—he has deceived her. Her sorrow always remains a tiny wailing infant, a fatherless and motherless child, for if Clavigo had been taken from her, then the child would have had a father in the recollection of his faithfulness and love and a mother in Marie's ardor. She has nothing on which she can bring it up, because what she experienced was beautiful, to be sure, but it had no significance in and by itself but only as a foretaste of the future. And she cannot hope that this child of pain will be transformed into a son of joy; she cannot hope that Clavigo will return, for she will not have the strength to endure a future. She has lost the happy trust with which she would have accompanied him dauntlessly into the abyss, and she has acquired instead a hundred misgivings; at most she would only be able to live through the past with him once again. At the time Clavigo left her, a future lay before her, a future so beautiful, so enchanting, that it almost confused her thoughts; it obscurely exerted its power over her. Her metamorphosis had already begun; then the process was interrupted, her transformation stopped. She had had intimations of a new life, had sensed its powers stir within her; then it was broken off and she was repulsed, and there is no recompense for her, neither in this nor in the future world. That which was to come smiled upon her very generously and mirrored itself in the illusion of her erotic love, and yet everything was so natural and direct. Perhaps a weak reflection has sometimes painted for her a weak illusion that does not affect her temptingly but probably

_I
166

is soothing for a moment. Time will go on for her in this way—until she has consumed the very object of her sorrow, which was not identical with her sorrow but the occasion for her continually seeking an object of her sorrow.

If a person possessed a letter that he knew or believed contained information about what he had to consider his life's happiness, but the characters were thin and faint and the handwriting almost illegible, then, presumably with anxiety and agitation, he would read it most passionately again and again and at one moment derive one meaning, at the next moment another, according to how he would explain everything by a word he believed that he had deciphered with certainty, but he would never progress beyond the same uncertainty with which he had begun. He would stare, more and more anxiously, but the more he stared, the less he would see. His eyes would sometimes be filled with tears, but the more frequently this happened to him, the less he would see. In the course of time, the writing would become fainter and less legible; finally the paper itself would crumble away, and he would have nothing left but tear-filled eyes.

2. Donna Elvira

We come to know this girl through the opera *Don Giovanni*, and it will not be unimportant to our subsequent exploration to note in the piece the clues to her earlier life. She was a nun; it is from the peacefulness of a convent that Don Giovanni has snatched her.[24] This suggests the staggering intensity of her passion. This was no silly molly from a finishing school who has learned to love at school, to flirt at parties; whether such a one is seduced is not very important. Elvira, on the other hand, has been brought up under the discipline of the convent, which has not succeeded in rooting out her passion but presumably has taught her to suppress it and thereby to make it even more violent as soon as it is allowed to burst forth. She is sure prey for a Don Giovanni; he will know how to coax out the passion—wild, ungovernable, insatiable, to be satisfied only in his love. In him she has all, and the past is nothing; if she leaves him, she loses all, the past also. She had renounced the world; then there appeared a figure she cannot renounce, and that is Don Giovanni. From now on, she renounces everything in order to live with him. The more meaningful that was which she leaves, the more firmly must she cling to him; the more firmly she has embraced him, the more terrible becomes her despair when he leaves her. From the very outset, her love is a despair; nothing has meaning for her, neither in heaven nor on earth, except Don Giovanni.

Elvira is of interest to us in the opera only insofar as her relation to Don Giovanni is of significance to him. If I were to suggest her significance in a few words, I would say that she is Don Giovanni's epic fate, and the Commendatore is his dramatic fate. There is in her a hatred that will seek out Giovanni in every nook, a flame of fire that will illuminate the darkest hiding place, and if she should still not discover him, then there is in her a love that will find him. She joins the others in pursuing Don Giovanni, but if I imagined that all the forces were neutralized, that his pursuers' endeavors canceled one another so that Elvira was alone with Don Giovanni and he was in her power, the hate would arm her to murder him. But her love would forbid it, not out of compassion, because to her he is too great for that, and thus she would continually keep him alive, for if she killed him she would kill herself. Consequently, if there were in the piece no forces in motion against Don Giovanni except Elvira, it would never end, for Elvira herself would prevent, if possible, even the lightning from striking him, in order to take revenge herself, and yet again she would be unable to take revenge. Such is her interest for us in the piece, but here we are concerned only with her relation to Don Giovanni insofar as it has meaning for her. She is the object of interest to many, but in very different ways. Don Giovanni is interested in her before the opera begins; the spectator bestows on her his dramatic interest; but we friends of grief, we accompany her not only to the nearest cross street, not only in the moment when she walks across the stage—no, we accompany her on her solitary way.

So, then, Don Giovanni has seduced Elvira and has forsaken her; this is speedily done, as quickly "as the tiger breaks a

I
168

lily."[25] If there are 1,003 in Spain alone, one is able to see that Don Giovanni is in a hurry and can more or less reckon the speed of the operation. Don Giovanni has forsaken her, but there is no circle of friends into whose arms she can collapse in a swoon. She need not fear that they will surround her too closely—indeed, they know very well how to open ranks in order to expedite her departure. She need not fear that anyone will argue her out of her loss—instead someone may take it upon himself to demonstrate it. She stands alone and forsaken, and no doubt tempts her; it is clear that he was a deceiver who has divested her of everything and abandoned her to infamy and disgrace. Esthetically speaking, however, this is not the worst for her; for a brief time, it rescues her from reflective sorrow, which is surely more painful than immediate grief. Here the fact is indubitable, and reflection cannot come along and change it now to this and now to that. A Marie Beaumarchais may have loved a Clavigo just as ardently, just as wildly and passionately; in relation to her passion, it may be an altogether accidental circumstance that the worst has not happened; she can almost wish that it had, for then there would be an end to the story, then she would be far better armed against him, but that did not happen. The fact she has before her is far more doubtful; its real nature always remains a secret between her and Clavigo. When she thinks of the cold cunning, the shabby commonsensicality it took to deceive her in such a way that it does not look so bad in the eyes of the world, so that she becomes prey to the sympathy that says, "Well, good Lord, it isn't so terrible," she is shocked, she can almost go insane at the thought of the proud superiority for which she has meant nothing at all, which has set a limit for her and said, "Up to here and no further." And yet the whole thing can also be explained in another, a more beautiful, way. But as the explanation changes, the fact itself also changes. Thus, reflection immediately has plenty to do, and reflective sorrow is inescapable.

Don Giovanni has forsaken Elvira; everything is clear to her at once. No doubt coaxes sorrow into reflection's parlor;[26] she falls silent in her despair. With a single pulsebeat it streams through her, and its streaming is outward; in a blaze the passion shines through her and becomes visible externally. Hate, despair, revenge, love—all burst forth to manifest themselves visibly. At this moment she is pictorial. We immediately see a picture of her in our imagination, and here the exterior is not without significance, reflection over it is not without substance, and its activity is not without meaning as it sorts and chooses.

Whether she herself at this moment is a subject for artistic portrayal is another matter, but this much is certain: at this moment she is visible and can be seen—not, of course, in the sense that this or that actual Elvira can actually be seen, which frequently is tantamount to not being seen, but the Elvira we imagine is visible in her essentiality. Whether art is capable of depicting the nuances of expression in her face to such a degree as to make visible the substance of her despair, I shall not decide; but she can be described, and the picture that emerges becomes not merely a burden for memory, which does not matter one way or another, but has its validity.

And who has not seen Elvira! It was early one morning that I started a walking tour in one of Spain's romantic regions. Nature was waking up. The trees in the forest shook their heads, and the leaves rubbed, so to speak, the sleep out of their eyes; one tree leaned toward the other to see whether it was out of bed yet, and the whole forest undulated in the cool, fresh breeze. A light fog rose from the earth; the sun snatched it away as if it were a blanket under which the earth had rested at night and now like a fond mother gazed down on the flowers and every living thing and said: Get up, dear children; the sun is already shining. As I wound my way through a deep mountain pass, my eyes fell on a cloister high up on the top of the mountain, to which a footpath led with many bends. My mind lingered on it—there it lies, I thought, like a house of God firmly grounded on the rock. My guide told me it was a convent known for its strict discipline. My pace slackened and my thoughts also, and what indeed is there to hurry after when one is so near the cloister? I probably would have come to a complete stop if I had not been aroused by a rapid movement

I
170

nearby. Involuntarily I turned around; it was a knight who hastened past me. How handsome he was, his step so light and yet so vigorous, so royal and yet so fugitive; he turned his head to look back, his face so captivating and yet his glance so restless. It was Don Giovanni. Is he hurrying to a rendezvous, or is he coming from one!

But soon he disappeared from my eyes and was gone from my thoughts; my gaze concentrated upon the cloister. Once again I was absorbed in contemplation of the lust of life and the serene peace of the cloister, when high up on the mountain I saw a female figure. In great haste she came running down the footpath, but the way was steep, and she continually seemed about to plunge down the mountain. She came closer. Her face was pallid, but her eyes were frightfully ablaze. Her body was exhausted; her bosom rose and fell violently, and yet she hurried faster and faster. Her ruffled hair flew loosely in the wind, but even the brisk morning air and her hurried pace were not able to bring color to her cheeks. Her nun's veil was torn and fluttered behind her; her thin white dress would have betrayed much to a profane gaze if the passion in her face had not drawn to itself the attention of even the most corrupt of men. She rushed past me; I did not dare speak to her—her brow was too majestic, her glance too royal, her passion too highborn for that. Where did this girl belong? In the cloister? Do these passions belong there—in the world? This dress—why is she running? Is it to hide her shame and disgrace, or to catch up with Don Giovanni? She runs into the forest, and it closes around her and hides her, and I see her no more but hear only the sighing of the forest. Poor Elvira! Have the trees found out—and yet the trees are better than people, for trees sigh and are silent: people whisper.

In this first moment, Elvira can be portrayed, and even if art does not really deal with such things because it will be difficult to find a unity of expression that also has all the multiplicity of her passions, the soul nevertheless demands to see her. I have tried to suggest this by the little picture I outlined above; it was not that I thought she was thereby portrayed, but I wanted to

I
171

suggest that her being described was quite correct, that it was not a capricious whim on my part but a valid claim of the idea. But this is only one element, and therefore we must accompany Elvira further.

The movement nearest at hand is a movement in time. Through a series of moments in time, she keeps herself at the almost picture-like peak suggested above. She thereby acquires dramatic interest. With the speed whereby she rushed past me, she catches up with Don Giovanni. This, too, is quite appropriate, for he did forsake her, but he has swept her along into the momentum of his own life, and she must reach him. If she does reach him, all her attention is once again directed outward, and we still do not have reflective sorrow. She has lost all—heaven when she chose the world, the world when she lost Giovanni. Therefore she has nowhere to turn except to him; only by being in his presence can she hold off despair, either by stifling the inner voices with the uproar of hate and rage, which sound in full force only when Don Giovanni is personally present, or by hoping. The latter already hints that the elements of reflective sorrow are present, but as yet they are unable to find time to consolidate inwardly. "First she must be cruelly convinced," so it says in Kruse's adaptation,[27] but this requirement completely betrays the inner disposition. If what has happened has not convinced her that Giovanni was a deceiver, then she will never be convinced. But as long as she demands additional evidence, she will succeed in avoiding the inner turmoil of quiet despair by means of a restless roving life perpetually engaged in a pursuit of Don Giovanni. The paradox is already there before her soul, but as long as she can keep her soul in a state of agitation by means of external evidence that is not supposed to explain the past but throw light on Don Giovanni's present condition, she does not have reflective grief. Hate, bitterness, curses, entreaties, and beseeching alternate, but her soul has still not returned into itself in order to repose in the thought that she has been deceived. She is expecting an explanation from the outside. When, therefore, Kruse has Don Giovanni say:

> are you now disposed to hear,
> To take my word—you who suspect me;
> Then I can almost say, almost improbable
> Appears the cause that compelled etc.,

we must guard against thinking that what sounds like mockery to the spectator's ear has the same effect on Elvira. To her, these words are refreshing, for she demands the improbable, and she will believe it precisely because it is improbable.

If we now have Don Giovanni and Elvira collide, then we have the choice between having Don Giovanni be the stronger or Elvira. If he is the stronger, then her whole behavior means nothing. She demands "evidence in order to be cruelly convinced"; he is sufficiently gallant not to let it fail to appear. But she naturally is not convinced and demands new evidence, because demanding evidence is a relief, and the uncertainty is refreshing. She then becomes just one more witness to Don Giovanni's achievements. But we could also imagine Elvira as the stronger. That seldom happens, but out of gallantry toward the fair sex we shall do it. She is, then, still in her full beauty— it is true that she has wept, but the tears have not quenched the gleam in her eyes; and it is true that she has sorrowed, but sorrow has not ravaged her youthful luxuriance; and it is true that she has grieved, but her grief has not gnawed away at the vitality of her beauty; and it is true that her cheeks have become pallid, but the expression is therefore all the more soulful; and it is true she does not move with the lightness of childlike innocence, but she does step forth with the energetic firmness of feminine passion.

This is how she encounters Don Giovanni. She has loved him more than the whole world, more than her soul's salvation; she has cast away everything for him, even her honor, and he was unfaithful. Now she knows only one passion— hate; only one thought—revenge. Thus, she is just as great as Don Giovanni, because seducing all the maidens means for the man the same as for the woman—to let herself be seduced once and for all, heart and soul, and then to hate—or, if you please, to love her seducer with an energy that no married woman has. This is how she encounters him. She does not lack the courage to venture out against him; she is not fighting for moral principles, she is fighting for her love, a love she does not base on respect; she is not fighting to become his mate, she is fighting for her love, and this is not satisfied with a contrite faithfulness but demands revenge. Out of love of him, she has cast away her salvation—if it were offered her again, she would again cast it away in order to avenge herself.

Such a character can never fail in its desired effect upon Don Giovanni. He knows the pleasure of inhaling the finest and most fragrant flower of early youth; he knows that it is just for a moment, and he knows what comes later; too often he has seen these pallid figures wither so quickly that it was almost visible. But here something wondrous has happened; the laws for the usual course of existence have been broken. He has seduced a young girl, but her life has not been extinguished, her beauty has not faded—she is transformed and is more beautiful than ever. He cannot deny it; she enthralls him more than any other girl has, more than Elvira herself, for despite all her beauty, the innocent nun was just another girl, his infatuation just another experience—but this girl is the only one of her kind. This girl is armed; she does not hide a dagger in her breast,[28] but she does wear armor—not visible, for her hate is not satisfied by speeches and declamations, but invisible, and it is her hatred. Don Giovanni's passion is aroused; she must be his once again, but this does not happen. Indeed, if she who hated him were a girl who knew his villainy, although she herself had not been deceived by him, then Don Giovanni would conquer. But this girl he cannot win; all his seduction is powerless. Even if his voice were more insinuating than his own voice, his advances craftier than his own advances, he would not move her; even if the angels pleaded for him, even if the Mother of God were to be the bridesmaid at the wedding, it would be futile. Just as in the underworld Dido herself turns away from Aeneas,[29] who was unfaithful to her, so she certainly will not turn away from him but will face him even more coldly than Dido.

But this meeting of Elvira and Don Giovanni is only a transitional moment; she walks across the stage, the curtain falls, but we, dear Συμπαρανεκρώμενοι, we quietly follow her, for only now does she really become the true Elvira. As long as she is in the vicinity of Don Giovanni, she is beside herself; when she comes to herself, it is appropriate to think about the paradox. Despite all the assurances of modern philosophy and the rash courage of its young ascribers, there are always great difficulties involved in thinking a contradiction.[30] Presumably a young girl will be forgiven for finding it difficult, and yet this is the task assigned her—to think that the one she loves was a deceiver. She has this in common with Marie Beaumarchais, and yet there is a difference in the way in which each of them comes to the paradox. The fact Marie had for her starting point was intrinsically so dialectical that reflection, with all its concupiscence, had to grasp it at once. As for Elvira, the factual evidence that Don Giovanni was a deceiver seems so obvious that it is hard to see how reflection can take hold of it. Therefore, it grasps the matter from another angle. Elvira has lost everything, and yet a whole life lies before her, and her soul requires money for living expenses.

Here two possibilities become apparent—either to enter into ethical and religious categories or to keep her love for Giovanni. If she does the first, she is outside our interest; we will gladly have her enter a home for fallen women or whatever else she wants. But this probably will also be difficult for her, because in order for that to be possible she must first despair; she has once known the religious, and the second time it makes great demands. On the whole, the religious is a dangerous power with which to become involved; it is jealous of itself and does not allow itself to be mocked. When she chose the convent, her proud soul perhaps found rich satisfaction in it, because, say what you will, no girl makes as brilliant a match as she who espouses heaven; but now, on the other hand, now she will have to return penitently, in repentance and contrition. Furthermore, there is always the question whether she can find a priest who can proclaim the gospel of repentance and contrition with the same pithiness as Don Giovanni has proclaimed the glad tidings of pleasure. Consequently, to save

herself from this despair, she must cling to Don Giovanni's
love, which is all the easier for her to do since she does still love
him.

A third possibility is unthinkable; that she could be able to
find consolation in another man's love would be even more
dreadful than the most dreadful. So for her own sake, therefore, she must love Don Giovanni; it is self-defense that bids
her do it. And this is the stimulus of reflection that forces her
to stare at this paradox: whether she is able to love him even
though he deceived her. Every time despair is about to seize
her, she takes refuge in the memory of Don Giovanni's love,
and in order really to feel comfortable in this refuge, she is
tempted to think that he is no deceiver, even though she does
this in various ways. A woman's dialectic is remarkable, and
only the person who has had the opportunity to observe it can
imitate it, whereas the greatest dialectician who ever lived
could speculate himself crazy trying to produce it.

I have been fortunate enough, however, to know a few outstanding examples of this and through them have had a complete course in dialectics. Oddly enough, one would expect to
find them most likely in the metropolis, for the noise and the
throngs of people conceal much, but that is not the case—that
is, if one wishes to have the perfect type. The finest ones are to
be found in the provinces, in small towns, in country houses.
The one I am thinking about in particular was a Swedish lady,
a maiden of noble birth. Her first lover could not have desired
her more ardently than I, her second lover, tried to pursue the
thought processes of her heart. But I owe it to the truth to admit that it was not my keenness and ingenuity that gave me the
clue, but an accidental circumstance that is too complicated to
tell here. She had lived in Stockholm and there had come to
know a French count to whose faithless charm [*Elskværdighed*]
she became a victim. I can still see her vividly. The first time I
saw her, she really did not make any impression on me. She
was still lovely, proud and aristocratic of bearing; she did not
say very much, and I probably would have gone away no
wiser than I came if chance had not made me a party to her secret. From that moment on, she was important to me; she

gave me such a vivid picture of an Elvira that I could never weary of looking at her.

One evening I was at a large party with her. I had arrived before she did, had already been waiting some time when I stepped to the window to see whether she was coming, and a moment later her carriage stopped at the door. She stepped out, and immediately her attire made a singular impression on me. She was wearing a thin, light silk coat, much like the domino in which Elvira appears at the dance in the opera. She entered with a grand dignity that was really impressive. She was wearing a black silk gown; she was dressed with the utmost taste and yet quite simply. No jewels embellished her; her neck was unadorned; and since her skin was whiter than snow, I have hardly ever seen so beautiful a contrast as that between her black dress and her white bosom. One frequently sees an unadorned neck, but seldom does one see a girl who really has a bosom. She curtsied to all the guests, and when the master of the house came forward to greet her, she curtsied very low to him; although her lips parted in a smile, I did not hear a word from her. To me her conduct was very fitting, and I, who shared her secret, silently associated with her the words about the oracle: οὔτε λέγει οὔτε κρύπτει, ἀλλὰ σημαίνει [neither speaks nor conceals but indicates].[31]

I have learned much from her and, among other things, have had confirmed my frequently made observation that people who conceal a sorrow acquire in the course of time a single phrase or a single idea with which they are able to signify everything to themselves and to the individual they have initiated into it. Compared with the prolixity of sorrow, such a phrase or idea is like a diminutive, like a pet name one employs for daily use. Frequently it has an entirely accidental relation to what it is supposed to signify and almost always owes its origin to an accidental circumstance. Having won her confidence, having succeeded in overcoming her mistrust of me because a chance event had placed her in my power, having had her tell me everything, I frequently went through the whole scale of moods with her. But if she was not so disposed and yet wanted to give me a hint that her soul was engrossed in her grief, she would take me by the hand, look at me and say: *I was more slender than a reed, he more glorious than the cedars of Lebanon.*[32] Where she had found these words I do not know, but I am convinced that whenever Charon comes with his boat to take her over to the underworld, he will find not the required obol[33] in her mouth but these words on her lips: I was more slender than a reed, he more glorious than the cedars of Lebanon!

So, then, Elvira cannot find Don Giovanni, and now, all by herself, she must manage to discover the way out of the complication in her life; she must come to herself. She has changed her environment, and thus the help is gone that perhaps would have contributed to drawing out her sorrow. Her new environment knows nothing of her earlier life, suspects nothing, for there is nothing striking or remarkable about her external appearance, no mark of sorrow, no sign that announces to people that there is sorrowing here. She can control every expression, for the loss of her honor can very well teach her that; and even though she does not prize people's opinions very highly, she at least can spare herself their condolences.

So now everything is in order, and she can be rather sure of going through life without arousing the suspicions of the curious populace, who ordinarily are just as stupid as they are curious. She has legitimate and unchallenged possession of her sorrow, and only if she were to be so unfortunate as to encounter a professional smuggler, only then would she have to fear a closer interrogation. What is going on within her? Is she sorrowing? Of course, she is! But how is this grief to be characterized? I would call it care for the necessities of life, because a person's life, after all, does not consist only of food and drink. The soul, too, requires sustenance. She is young, and yet the reserves of her life are used up, but from this it does not follow that she will die. In this respect, she is concerned every day about the next day. She cannot stop loving him, and yet he deceived her, but if he deceived her, then her love has indeed lost its nourishing power. Yes, if he had not deceived her, if a higher power had torn him away, then she would have been as well provided as any girl could wish, for the memory

I
177

of Don Giovanni was a good deal more than many a living husband. But if she gives up her love, then she is brought to the state of beggary, then she must return to the convent to ridicule and disgrace. Yes, if only she could buy his love again with this! In this way she goes on living. Today, this present day, she still thinks that she can endure, that there is still a little something left to live on, but the next day, that she fears. She deliberates again and again, grasps at every escape, and yet she finds none, and thus she never comes to grieve coherently and healthfully, for she continually searches for the way she is going to grieve.

"Forget him, that is what I want; rip his picture out of my soul; I want to ransack myself like a consuming fire, and every thought that belongs to him must be burned up; only then can I be saved; it is in self-defense. If I do not rip out every thought of him, even the most remote, I am lost; only in this way can I protect myself. Myself—what is this myself—wretchedness and misery. I was unfaithful to my first love, and now should I make up for it by being unfaithful to my second?

"No, I will hate him; that is the only way to satisfy my soul, the only way I can find rest and something to occupy me. I will braid a garland of curses out of everything that reminds me of him, and for every kiss I say: Cursed be you! And for every time he has embraced me: Ten times cursed be you! And for every time he swore he loved me, I will swear that I will hate him. This is going to be my work, my labor; to this I dedicate myself. After all, I became accustomed to praying my rosary in the convent, and so I will still remain a nun who prays early and late. Or should I perhaps be satisfied that he once loved me? I should perhaps be a prudent girl and not throw him away in proud contempt now when I know that he is a deceiver; I should perhaps be a good housewife who, with economic sense, knows how to stretch as far as possible the little that she has. No, I will hate him; only in that way can I tear myself away from him and show myself that I do not need him. But am I not indebted to him at all when I hate him? Am I not living off him? For what is it that nourishes my hatred except my love for him?

I
178

"He was no deceiver; he had no idea of what a woman can suffer. If he had had that, he never would have forsaken me. He was a man who was to himself enough. Is that, then, a consolation for me? Indeed it is, for my suffering and anguish prove to me how happy I was, so happy that he has no idea of it. Why, then, do I complain because a man is not like a woman, not as happy as she is when she is happy, not as unhappy as she is when she is boundlessly unhappy because her happiness knew no bounds.

"Did he deceive me? No! Did he promise me anything? No! My Giovanni was no suitor, no poor chicken thief; a nun does not debase herself for such. He did not ask my hand in marriage; he stretched out his hand, and I grasped it; he looked at me, I was his; he opened his arms, I belonged to him. I clung to him; I entwined myself around him like a climbing plant; I rested my head on his breast and gazed into that all-powerful countenance, with which he ruled the world, and which nevertheless rested upon me as if I were the whole world to him; like a suckling infant I imbibed fullness and richness and bliss. Can I demand more? Was I not his? Was he not mine? And if he was not, was I therefore the less his? When the gods wandered upon the earth and fell in love with women, did they remain faithful to their beloveds? And yet it occurs to no one to say that they deceived them! And why not? Because we want a girl to be proud of having been loved by a god. And what are all the gods of Olympus compared with my Giovanni? [34]And should I not be proud—should I disparage him, should I insult him in my thought, allow it to force him into the narrow, wretched laws that apply to ordinary men? No, I will be proud that he has loved me; he was greater than the gods, and I will honor him by making myself into a nobody. I will love him because he belonged to me, love him because he forsook me, and I will go on being his, and I will keep what he throws away.

"No, I cannot think about him; every time I recall him, every time my thoughts approach the hiding place in my soul where his memory lives, then it is as if I committed a new sin. I feel an anxiety, an unspeakable anxiety, an anxiety such as I

I
179

felt in the convent when I sat in my solitary cell and waited for
him and my thoughts terrified me: the prioress's intense scorn,
the convent's terrible punishment, my offense against God.
And yet was not this anxiety part of it? What was my love for
him without it? Indeed, he was not married to me; we had not
received the blessing of the Church; the bell had not rung for
us; no hymn was sung—and yet what was all the music and
celebration of the Church; how would it be able to put me in a
mood comparable to this anxiety! —But then he came, and the
disharmony of my anxiety dissolved into the most blissful harmony of security, and only faint tremblings voluptuously
stirred my soul. Should I fear this anxiety, then; does it not remind me of him; is it not the announcement of his coming? If
I could recollect him without this anxiety, then I would not
recollect him. He is coming; he asks for silence; he controls the
spirits that want to tear me away from him; I am his, blissful
in him."

If I were to imagine a person in distress at sea, unconcerned
about his life, remaining on board because there was something he wanted to save and could not save because of perplexity about what to save, I have an image of Elvira. She is in distress at sea; her destruction is imminent, but it does not
concern her; she is not aware of it; she is perplexed about what
she should save.

3. Margarete

We know this girl from Goethe's *Faust*. She was a little middle-class girl, not destined, like Elvira, for the convent, but
still she was brought up in the fear of the Lord, even though
her soul was too childlike to feel the earnestness, as Goethe so
incomparably says:

> *Halb Kinderspiel[e],*
> *Halb Gott im Herzen*
> [Half sport of childhood,
> Half God within thee].[35]

What we particularly love about this girl is the charming
simplicity and humility of her pure soul. The first time she sees

Faust, she immediately feels much too inferior to be loved by him, and it is not out of curiosity to know whether Faust loves her that she picks the petals of the daisy—it is out of humility, for she feels too inferior to choose and therefore submits to the oracular bidding of an enigmatic power. Yes, lovable Margarete! Goethe betrayed how you plucked the petals and recited the words: He loves me, he loves me not.[36] Poor Margarete! You can indeed continue this activity and merely change the words: He deceived me, he deceived me not. In fact, you can cultivate a little piece of ground with this kind of flower and you will have manual labor for your whole life.

Commentators have remarked on the striking fact that whereas the legend of Don Juan tells of 1,003 seduced in Spain alone, the legend of Faust speaks of only one seduced girl. It may be worth the trouble not to forget this observation, inasmuch as it will be of significance in what follows and will help us characterize what is distinctive in Margarete's reflective sorrow. At first glance, it might seem that the only difference between Elvira and Margarete was the difference between two different individualities who have experienced the same thing. But the difference is far more essential and yet is due not so much to the difference in the two feminine natures as to the essential difference between a Don Juan and a Faust. From the very start, there must be a difference between an Elvira and a Margarete, since a girl who is to make an impression on a Faust must be essentially different from a girl who makes an impression on a Don Juan. Yes, even if I supposed that it was the same girl who engaged the attention of both, it would be something different that appealed to each of them. By being brought into relation with a Don Juan or a Faust, the difference that was present only as a possibility would develop into a full actuality. Faust is admittedly a reproduction of Don Juan, but his being a reproduction is precisely what makes him essentially different from him, even in the stage of life in which he can be called a Don Juan, for to reproduce another stage does not mean only to become that but to become that with all the elements of the preceding stage in it. Therefore, even if he desires the same as a Don Juan, he nevertheless desires it in a different way. But in order for him to be able to desire it in a different way, it must also be present in a different way. He has features that make his method different, just as Margarete has features that make another method necessary. His method in turn depends upon his desire, and his desire is different from Don Juan's, even if there is a basic similarity between them.

Generally, people think they are saying something very sagacious when they emphasize that Faust ends up by becoming a Don Juan, and yet it does not say very much, for the point is, in what sense does he become that. Faust is a demonic figure, just like a Don Juan, but a superior one. Sensuousness does not acquire importance for him until he has lost a whole previous world, but the consciousness of this loss is not blotted out; it is always present, and therefore he seeks in the sensuous not so much pleasure as distraction. His doubting soul finds nothing in which it can rest, and now he grasps at erotic love [*Elskov*], not because he believes in it but because it has an element of presentness in which there is a momentary rest and a striving that diverts and that draws attention away from the nothingness of doubt. His pleasure, therefore, does not have the *Heiterkeit* [cheerfulness] that characterizes a Don Juan. His visage is not smiling, his brow not unclouded, and joy is not his escort; the young girls do not dance into his embrace, but he scares them to himself. What he is seeking, therefore, is not only the pleasure of the sensuous but the immediacy of the spirit. Just as ghosts in the underworld, when a living being fell into their hands, sucked his blood and lived as long as this blood warmed and nourished them, so Faust seeks an immediate life whereby he will be rejuvenated and strengthened. And where can this better be found than in a young girl, and how can he more completely imbibe this than in the embrace of erotic love? Just as the Middle Ages had tales of sorcerers who knew how to prepare a rejuvenating potion and used the heart of an innocent child for it, so this is the strengthening his emaciated soul needs, the only thing that can satisfy him for a moment. His sick soul needs what could be called the first greening of a young heart, and to what else could I compare the early youth of an innocent feminine soul? If I said it is like a flower, I would say too little, for it is more than that; it is a flowering. The vitality of hope and faith and trust burgeons and blossoms in rich multiplicity; gentle yearnings stir in the delicate shoots, and dreams shade their flourishing. In this way it stirs a Faust; it beckons his restless soul like an island of peace in the calm ocean. That it is ephemeral, no one knows better than Faust; he does not believe in it any more than in anything else, but that it exists, of that he assures himself in the embrace of erotic love. Only the plenitude of innocence and childlikeness can refresh him for a moment.

In Goethe's *Faust*, Mephistopheles has Faust see Margarete in a mirror. His eyes delight in gazing at her, but nevertheless it is not her beauty that he desires, although he takes that in addition. What he desires is the pure, undisturbed, rich, immediate joy of a feminine soul, but he desires it sensually, not spiritually. In a certain sense, then, he does desire as does Don Juan, but still he desires in an entirely different way. At this point, some assistant professor or other, convinced of having been a Faust himself, since otherwise he certainly could not possibly have managed to become an assistant professor, would point out that Faust requires intellectual development and refinement in a girl who is to arouse his desire. Perhaps a larger number of assistant professors would consider this a brilliant observation, and their respective wives and sweethearts would nod approval. But it would miss the point completely, for Faust would desire nothing less. A so-called refined girl would fall within the same relativity as he himself, although this would have no significance for him, would amount to nothing. With her smattering of refinement, she perhaps would tempt this old master of doubt to take her along out into the current, where she would quickly despair. An innocent young girl, however, is within another relativity and thus, in a certain sense, is nothing compared with Faust and yet, in another sense, is enormously much, since she is immediacy. Only in this immediacy is she a goal for his desire, and therefore I said that he desires immediacy not spiritually but sensually.

Goethe understood all this perfectly well, and therefore

Margarete is a little middle-class girl, a girl one could almost
be tempted to call insignificant. Since it is important with respect to Margarete's grief, we shall now consider more closely
how Faust presumably must have affected her. Of course, the
particular features Goethe has emphasized are of great value,
but I nevertheless believe that for the sake of completeness a
little modification must be made. In her innocent simplicity,
Margarete soon perceives that with respect to faith there is
something wrong with Faust. In Goethe, this appears in a little
catechization scene,[37] which is unquestionably a superb invention by the poet. The question now is what results this examination may have for their relation to each other. It is apparent
that Faust is a doubter, and it seems that Goethe, inasmuch as
he does not suggest anything more in this respect, wanted to
have Faust continue to be a doubter also in his relation to Margarete. He has tried to draw her attention away from all such
probing and to fasten it simply and solely upon the reality of
love [*Kjærlighedens Realitet*]. But I think, for one thing, that
once the problem has come up this would be difficult for
Faust, and, for another, I do not think it is psychologically correct. I shall not dwell longer on this point, for Faust's sake, but
for Margarete's sake I certainly shall, for if it is not apparent to
her that he is a doubter, then her grief has an added element.

So, then, Faust is a doubter, but he is no vain fool who wants
to make himself important by doubting what others believe;
his doubt has an objective foundation in him. To Faust's
credit, this has to be said. But as soon as he wants to press his
doubt upon others, a spurious passion can very easily enter in.
As soon as doubt is pressed upon others, there is an envy involved that rejoices in wresting from them what they regarded
as certain. But in order for this passion of envy to be aroused
in the doubter, there must be the possibility of opposition in
the individual concerned. The temptation ceases either where
there is none whatever or where it would even be unbecoming
to suppose it. The latter is the case with a young girl. Face to
face with her, a doubter is always in an awkward position. To
wrest her faith from her is no task at all for him; on the contrary, he feels that it is only through her faith that she is the

great person she is. He feels humbled, for there is in her a natural claim on him to be her supporter if she herself begins to waver. Of course, a clumsy fool of a doubter, a dabbler, presumably could find satisfaction in wresting faith from a young girl and joy in scaring women and children since he cannot terrify men. But this is not the case with Faust; he is too great for that.

Consequently, we can agree with Goethe that Faust betrays his doubt the first time, but I hardly believe it will happen with him a second time. This is very important with respect to the interpretation of Margarete. Faust readily perceives that Margarete's entire significance hinges on her innocent simplicity. If this is taken from her, she is nothing in herself, nothing to him. This, then, must be preserved. He is a doubter, but as such he has all the elements of the positive within himself, for otherwise he would be a sorry doubter. He lacks the point of conclusion, and thereby all the elements become negative. She, however, has the point of conclusion, has childlikeness and innocence. Therefore, nothing is easier for him than to equip her. He has learned from experience that what he talked about as doubt often impressed others as positive truth. So now he finds his joy in enriching her with the opulent content of a way of looking at things; he takes out all the finery of immediate faith and finds joy in embellishing her with it, for it is very becoming to her, and she thereby becomes more beautiful in his eyes. In so doing, he has the added advantage that her soul attaches itself ever more tightly to his. She really does not understand him at all; like a child she attaches herself tightly to him; what for him is doubt is unswerving truth for her. But at the same time that he is building up [*opbygge*] her faith in this way, he is also undermining it, for he himself finally becomes the object of faith for her, a god and not a human being.

But here I must try to prevent a misunderstanding. It might seem that I am making Faust into a base hypocrite. That is not at all the case. Margarete herself is the one who has brought up the whole matter; with half an eye he appraises the glory she believes is hers and sees that it cannot withstand his doubt, but he does not have the heart to destroy it and even behaves with a certain amiability toward her. Her love gives her significance for him, and yet she becomes practically a child; he condescends to her childlikeness and has his joy in seeing how she appropriates everything. This, however, has the most regretable consequences for Margarete's future. If it had become apparent to her that Faust was a doubter, she perhaps could have saved her faith later. In all humility, then, she would have recognized that his high-flying, bold thoughts were not for her; she would have clung fast to what she had. But now she is indebted to him for the content of faith, and yet when he has forsaken her she perceives that he himself has not believed in it. As long as he was with her, she did not discover the doubt; now when he is gone, everything is changed for her, and she sees doubt in everything, a doubt she cannot control since she always includes in her thinking the fact that Faust himself was unable to master it.

That whereby Faust, also according to Goethe's interpretation, captivates Margarete is not Don Juan's seductive talent but his prodigious superiority. Therefore, as she herself endearingly expresses it, she really cannot comprehend at all what Faust can see in her that is favorable.[38] Her first impression of him, then, is completely overwhelming; in relation to him, she feels her nothingness. Hence, she does not belong to him the way Elvira belongs to Don Giovanni, for that is still the expression of independent existence in relation to him, but Margarete completely disappears in Faust; neither does she break with heaven in order to belong to him, for that would imply a justification in relation to him; imperceptibly, without the slightest reflection, he becomes everything to her. But just as from the beginning she is nothing, so she becomes, if I dare say so, less and less the more she is convinced of his almost divine superiority; she is nothing, and at the same time she exists only through him. What Goethe said somewhere about Hamlet,[39] that his soul in relation to his body was an acorn planted in a flower pot, with the result, therefore, that it bursts the container, is true of Margarete's love. Faust is far too great for her, and her love must end by shattering her soul. And the moment for this cannot be far distant, for Faust is well aware that she cannot remain in this immediacy; he does not take her into the higher regions of the spirit, for it is that, after all, from which he is fleeing; he desires her sensually—and forsakes her.

So Faust has forsaken Margarete. Her loss is so terrible that, because of it, even those around her momentarily forget what they otherwise find difficult to forget—that she is dishonored. She collapses completely and is not even able to think about her loss; even the energy to comprehend her misfortune has been drained out of her. If this condition could continue, it would be impossible for reflective sorrow to commence. But little by little the consolation of those around her brings her to herself, nudges her thought into motion again; but as soon as it is in motion again, it is apparent that she is unable to hold fast to a single one of their observations. She listens to it as if it were not speaking to her, and nothing it says arrests or accelerates the unrest in her thought process. The problem for her is the same as for Elvira—to think that Faust was a deceiver— but it is still more difficult, for she is far more deeply influenced by Faust. He was not merely a deceiver, but he was in fact a hypocrite; she has not sacrificed anything for him, but she owes him everything, and to a certain degree she still has this everything, except that now it proves to be a deception. But is what he said less true because he himself did not believe it? By no means, and yet for her it is, because she believed in it through him.

It might seem that reflection would have a more difficult time starting in Margarete; that which frustrates it is the feeling that she was nothing at all. Nevertheless there is a prodigious dialectical elasticity here. If she could sustain the thought that in the strictest sense she was nothing, then reflection would be precluded, and then she would not have been deceived, either, for if one is nothing, there is no relationship, and where there is no relationship, there cannot be a deception, either. To that extent she is at rest. This thought, however, cannot be sustained but suddenly turns into its opposite. The thought that she was nothing expresses only that all the finite differences of love are negated, and therefore it is precisely the expression for the absolute validity of her love, on

I
186

which, in turn, her absolute justification is based. His conduct, therefore, is not only a deception but an absolute deception, because her love was absolute. And in this she will again be unable to rest, because, since he has been everything to her, she will not even be able to sustain this thought except through him, but she cannot think it through him, because he was a deceiver.

As those around her steadily become more and more alien to her, the inner motion begins. Not only has she loved Faust with her whole soul, but he was her life force; through him she came into existence [*blev til*]. As a result, her soul certainly does not become less agitated in mood than Elvira's, but her particular moods are less agitated. She is on the way to having a basic mood, and the particular mood is like a bubble that rises from the depths and does not have the power to endure; neither is it displaced by a new bubble but is dissolved in the general mood that she is nothing. This basic mood, moreover, is a condition that is felt and does not find expression in any specific outburst; it is unutterable, and the attempt the particular mood makes to lift it, to raise it, is futile. Thus the total mood always resonates in the particular mood; as weakness and powerlessness, it constitutes the resonance for it. The particular mood expresses itself, but it does not mitigate, does not relieve. It is, to borrow a saying from my Swedish Elvira that is definitely very expressive, even if a man does not completely understand it, it is a false sigh, which deceives, and not a genuine sigh, which is a strengthening and beneficial motion. The particular mood is not even full-toned or energetic; her expression is too burdened for that.

"Can I forget him? Can the brook, however long it keeps on running, forget the spring, forget its source, sever itself from it? If so, it would just have to stop flowing! Can the arrow, however swiftly it flies, forget the bowstring? If so, its flight would just have to come to an end! Can the raindrop, however far it falls, forget the heaven from which it fell? If so, then it would just have to disintegrate! Can I become someone else, can I be born again of a mother who is not my mother? Can I forget him? Then I would just have to cease to be!

"Can I bring him to mind? Can my recollection call him forth now that he has vanished, I who myself am only my recollection of him? This pale, hazy image—is this the Faust I worshipped? I recollect his words, but I do not possess the resonance in his voice! I remember his talks, but my breath is too faint to give them expression. Meaningless, they fall on deaf ears!

"Faust, O Faust! Come back, satisfy the hungry, clothe the naked, revive the languishing, visit the lonely one![40] I certainly know that my love had no meaning for you, but, after all, neither did I demand that. My love lay down humbly at your feet; my sigh was a prayer, my kiss a thank offering, my embrace adoring worship. Will you forsake me for this? Did you not know it beforehand? Or is it not, then, a reason to love me—that I need you, that my soul languishes when you are not with me?

"God in heaven, forgive me for loving a human being more than I loved you, and yet I still do it; I know that it is a new sin that I speak this way to you. O Eternal Love, let your mercy hold me, do not thrust me away; give him back to me, incline his heart to me[41] again; have mercy on me, God of mercy, that I pray this way again!

"Can I curse him, then? What am I that I dare to be so bold? Can the clay pot be presumptuous toward the potter?[42] What was I? Nothing! Clay in his hands, a rib from which he formed me![43] What was I? A poor insignificant plant, and he stooped down to me; he lovingly raised me [*opelskede*];[44] he was my all, my god, the origin of my thoughts, the food of my soul.

"Can I grieve? No, no! Sorrow broods like nocturnal fog over my soul. O come back, I will give you up, never claim to belong to you. Just sit with me; look at me so that I can gain enough strength to sigh; speak to me, tell about yourself as if you were a stranger, and I will forget that it is you; speak, so the tears may burst forth. Am I nothing at all, then, not even able to weep except through him!

"Where shall I find peace and rest? Thoughts rise up in my soul; the one rises against the other; the one confuses the other. When you were with me, they obeyed your suggestions; then

I played with them as a child; I braided a wreath of them and put them on my head; I let them flow like my hair, ruffled in the wind. Now they twine themselves terrifyingly around me, twist themselves around me like snakes and crush my anguished soul.

"And I am a mother! A living being demands nourishment from me. Can the hungry satisfy the hungry, the feeble from thirst refresh the thirsty? Shall I become a murderer, then? O Faust, come back; save the child in the womb even if you do not want to save the mother!"

—Thus she is agitated, not by mood but in mood, but the particular mood is no mitigation for her, because it dissolves in the total mood she cannot banish. Indeed, if Faust had been taken away from her, Margarete would not seek any calming, her fate would indeed have been enviable in her eyes—but she is deceived. She lacks what could be called the situation of grief, for she is incapable of sorrowing alone. Indeed, if, like poor Florine in the fairy tale,[45] she could find entry into a cave of echoes, from which she knew that every sigh, every lament, would be heard by her lover, then she would not, like Florine, spend only three nights there, but she would stay there day and night; but in Faust's palace there is no cave of echoes, and he has no ear in her heart.

I
189

Perhaps, dear Συμπαρανεκρώμενοι, I have already held your attention too long on these pictures, all the more so because, however much I have said, nothing visible has appeared to you. But this, of course, is due not to fraudulence in my presentation but to the subject itself and to the subtlety of sorrow. When the favorable opportunity is offered, then what is hidden discloses itself. This we have in our power. And now in parting we shall unite these three women betrothed to sorrow; we shall have them embrace one another in the harmony of sorrow; we shall have them form a group before us, a tabernacle, where the voice of sorrow is never silent, where sighs do not cease, because more carefully and faithfully than vestal virgins they keep watch over the observance of the sacred ceremonies. Should we interrupt them in this; should we wish for them the return of what was lost; would that be an advantage for them? Have they not already received a higher initiation? And this initiation will unite them and envelop their union in beauty and provide mitigation in union, for only the person who has been bitten by snakes knows what one who has been bitten by snakes must suffer.[46]

THE UNHAPPIEST ONE

AN INSPIRED ADDRESS TO THE
ΣΥΜΠΑΡΑΝΕΚΡΩΜΕΝΟΙ

Peroration at the Meeting on Fridays

As is well known, there is said to be a grave somewhere in
England that is distinguished not by a magnificent monument
or a mournful setting but by a short inscription—"The Unhappiest One."[1] It is said that the grave was opened, but no
trace of a corpse was found. Which is the more amazing—that
no corpse was found or that the grave was opened? It is indeed
strange that someone took the time to see whether anyone was
in it. When one reads a name in an epitaph, one is easily
tempted to wonder how he passed his life on earth; one might
wish to climb down into the grave for a conversation with
him. But this inscription—it is so freighted with meaning! A
book can have a title that prompts a desire to read the book,
but a title in itself can be so thought-laden, so personally appealing, that one will never read the book.[2] This inscription is
in truth very freighted with meaning—shocking or gratifying
according to one's mood—for anyone who perhaps secretly in
his heart pledged his troth to the thought that he was the most
unhappy one. But I can imagine a person whose soul has never
been preoccupied in that way and for whose curiosity there
was the task of finding out whether anyone was in that grave.
And look, the grave was empty! Has he perhaps risen from the
dead; does he perhaps want to mock the poet's words:

> —In the grave there is peace,
> Its silent occupant does not know sorrow.[3]

Did he find no rest, not even in the grave; is he perhaps still
fitfully wandering over the earth; has he left his house, his
home, leaving behind only his address! Or has he still not been
found—he, the unhappiest one, whom not even the Furies are
pursuing until he finds the door of the temple[4] and the humble
petitioner's bench, but whom sorrows keep alive and sorrows
follow to the grave!

If he has not been found, then let us like crusaders, dear Συμπαρανεκρώμενοι, commence a pilgrimage—not to that sacred sepulchre in the happy East, but to that mournful grave in the unhappy West. At that empty grave, we shall seek him, the unhappiest one, certain of finding him, for just as the longing of the believers yearns for the sacred sepulchre, so the unhappy ones are drawn toward the West to that empty grave, and each one is absorbed in the thought that it is destined for him.

Or may it be that such deliberation is not a worthy subject for consideration by us, whose activity, in compliance with our society's sacred custom, is a venture in aphoristic, occasional devotion—we who do not think and talk aphoristically but live aphoristically; we who live ἀφορισμένοι and *segregati*,[5] as aphorisms in life, without association with men, having no share in their griefs and their joys; we who are not consonants in the clamor of life but are solitary birds in the stillness of night, assembled together on only one occasion to be edified by representations of the wretchedness of life, of the length of the day, and of the endless duration of time; we, dear Συμπαρανεκρώμενοι, who do not believe in the game of gladness or the happiness of fools; we who believe in nothing but unhappiness.

See how they press forward in countless numbers, all the unhappy ones. Yet many are they who think themselves called; few are the chosen.[6] A separation must be made between them—one word, and the crowd vanishes; specifically excluded are the uninvited guests, all those who think that death is the greatest calamity, who became unhappy because they feared death; for we, dear Συμπαρανεκρώμενοι, we, like the Roman soldiers, do not fear death;[7] we know a worse calamity, and first and last, above all—it is to live. Indeed, if there were a human being who could not die, if what the legend tells of the Wandering Jew is true, why should we have scruples about pronouncing him the unhappiest one? Then why the grave was empty could be explained—namely, to indicate that the unhappiest one was the person who could not die, who could not slip down into a grave. That would settle the matter, the answer would be easy, for the unhappiest one of all would be the person who could not die, the happy one the person who could. Happy is the one who died in old age; happier is the one who died in youth; happiest is the one who died at birth; happiest of all the one who was never born. But this is not the way it is; death is the common fate of all human beings, and inasmuch as the unhappiest one has not been found, he must be sought within these confines.

See, the crowd vanished; the number is reduced. I do not say: Give me your attention, for I know that I have it; I do not say: Lend me your ears, for I know that they belong to me. Your eyes are sparkling; you lean forward in your seats. It is a contest well worth your participation, a struggle even more terrible than if it were a matter of life and death, for we do not fear death. But the reward—yes, it is more magnificent than any other in the world, and more certain, for the person who is sure that he is the unhappiest one does not need to fear fortune; he will not taste the humiliation of having to shout in his final hour: Solon, Solon, Solon![8]

So, then, we are inaugurating an open competition, from which no one will be excluded, neither because of rank nor because of age. No one will be excluded except the happy ones and the person who fears death—every worthy member of the community of the unhappy is welcome; a seat of honor is designated for every really unhappy person, the grave for the unhappiest one. My voice rings out in the world; listen to it, all you who call yourselves unhappy in the world but who do not fear death. My voice rings back into the past, for we do not want to be so sophistical as to exclude the dead and departed because they are dead, for they have in fact lived. Forgive me, I beseech you, for disturbing your repose momentarily; let us meet here by this empty grave. Three times I shout it loudly to the world: Hear this, you unhappy ones, for it is not our intention to decide this matter among ourselves here in a nook of the world. The place has been found where it must be decided before the whole world!

But before we commence interrogating them one by one, let us make ourselves qualified to sit here as worthy judges and fellow contestants. Let us strengthen our minds, arm them against the inveiglement of the ear, for what voice is so ingratiating as that of the unhappy one, what voice so bewitching as that of the unhappy one when he is speaking about his own unhappiness. Let us make ourselves worthy to sit as judges and fellow contestants so that we do not lose the overall view, are not confused by the particulars, for the eloquence of grief is infinite and infinitely inventive. We shall divide the unhappy into specific groups, and only one from each will be heard. We shall not deny that no particular individual is the unhappiest one; it is rather a class, but we shall not therefore have scruples about awarding the representative of this class the title of the unhappiest one, shall not have scruples about awarding him the grave.

In all of Hegel's systematic works there is one section that discusses the unhappy consciousness.[9] One always comes to the reading of such investigations with an inner uneasiness and palpitation of the heart, with a fear that one will learn too much or too little. "The unhappy consciousness" is a phrase that can almost make the blood run cold, the nerves shiver, if it is merely introduced casually into the course of a discussion, and then, uttered deliberately, it can, like that cryptic sentence in a story by Clemens Brentano: *tertia nux mors est* [the third nut is death],[10] make a person tremble like a sinner. Ah, happy is the one who has nothing more to do with the subject than to write a paragraph about it; even happier the one who can write the next. The unhappy one is the person who in one way or another has his ideal, the substance of his life, the plenitude of his consciousness, his essential nature, outside himself. The unhappy one is the person who is always absent from himself, never present to himself. But in being absent, one obviously can be in either past or future time. The whole territory of the unhappy consciousness is thereby adequately circumscribed. For this firm limitation, we thank Hegel, and now, since we are not only philosophers who view this kingdom at a distance, we shall as natives consider more closely the various stages contained therein.

So, then, the unhappy one is absent. But one is absent when one is in either past or future time. This expression must be insisted upon, for it is obvious, as philology also teaches us, that there is a *tempus* [tense] that is present in a past time and a *tempus* that is present in a future time, but this same science also teaches us that there is a *tempus* that is *plus quam perfectum* [more than perfect: pluperfect, past perfect], in which there is no present, and a *futurum exactum* [future perfect] with the same feature. There are the hoping and the recollecting[11] individualities. If, generally, only the person who is present to himself is happy, then these people, insofar as they are only hoping or only recollecting, are in a sense certainly unhappy individualities. But, strictly speaking, one cannot call an individuality unhappy who is present in hope or in recollection. The point to stress here is that he is present in it. We also see from this that one blow, be it ever so hard, cannot possibly make a person into the unhappiest one. That is, one blow can only either rob him of hope and thereby make him present in recollection or rob him of recollection and thereby make him present in hope. We shall now proceed and see how the unhappy individuality may be defined more precisely.

First we shall consider the hoping individuality. When, as one who hopes (and consequently to that extent is unhappy), he is not present to himself, he becomes unhappy in the stricter sense of the word. A person who hopes for eternal life is certainly in a sense an unhappy individuality, insofar as he renounces the present; but strictly speaking he is nevertheless not unhappy, because he is present to himself in this hope and does not come into conflict with the particular elements of finiteness. If, however, he cannot become present to himself in hope but loses his hope, then hopes again, etc., then he is absent from himself, not merely in present but also in future time, and thus we have a form of unhappiness. If we consider the recollecting individuality, we find the same thing. If he can become present to himself in past time, then, strictly speaking, he is not unhappy; but if he cannot do this but is continually absent from himself in past time, then we have a form of unhappiness.

Recollection is above all the distinctive element of the unhappy ones, which is natural, because past time has the notable characteristic that it is past; future time, that it is to come. In a sense, therefore, one can say that future time is closer to the present than is the past. In order for the hoping individuality to become present in future time, it must have reality [*Realitet*][12] or, more correctly, it must acquire reality for him; in order for the recollecting individuality to become present in past time, it must have had reality for him. But when the hoping individuality wants to hope for a future time that nevertheless can acquire no reality for him, or the recollecting individuality wants to recollect a time that has had no reality, then we have essentially unhappy individualities. The former might not be thought possible or might be regarded as sheer madness; but that is not so, because the hoping individuality certainly does not hope for something that does not have reality for him, but he hopes for something that he himself knows cannot be realized. That is, if a person, in losing hope, continues to hope instead of becoming a recollecting individuality, then we have this form. If an individuality in losing recollection or in having nothing to recollect will not become a hoping individuality but continues to be one who recollects, then we have a form of unhappiness. If, for example, an individual became absorbed in antiquity or in the Middle Ages or in any other time, but in such a way that it had a decisive reality for him, or he became absorbed in his own childhood or youth in the way that this had had decisive reality for him, then, strictly speaking, he would not be an unhappy individuality. But if I were to imagine a person who had had no childhood himself, since this age had passed him by without real meaning, but who now, for example, by becoming a teacher of children, discovered all the beauty in childhood and now wanted to recollect his own childhood, always stared back at it, he would certainly be a very appropriate example. He would discover backwards the meaning of that which was past for him and which he nevertheless wanted to recollect in all its meaning. If I were to imagine a person who had lived without grasping the joy of life or the enjoyment of it and who now at the point of death had his eyes opened to it, if I were to imagine that he did not die, which would be the best that could happen, but revived without therefore living his life over again, this person surely could

be considered when the question arises about who is the unhappiest one.

Hope's unhappy individualities never have the pain of recollection's. The hoping individualities always have a more
pleasant disappointment. Therefore, the unhappiest one will
always have to be sought among recollection's unhappy individualities.

But we shall go on. We shall imagine a combination of the
two forms described, unhappy forms in the stricter sense. The
unhappy hoping individuality could not become present to
himself in his hope; likewise the unhappy recollecting individuality. The only combination possible is one in which it is recollection that prevents him from becoming present in his hope
and it is hope that prevents him from becoming present in his
recollection. This is due, on the one hand, to his continually
hoping for that which should be recollected; his hope is continually being disappointed, but he discovers that this disappointment occurs not because his objective is pushed further
ahead but because he is past his goal, because it has already
been experienced or should have been experienced and thus
has passed over into recollection. On the other hand, he is continually recollecting that for which he should hope, because he
has already encompassed the future in thought, has already experienced it in thought, and he recollects what he has experienced instead of hoping for it. Thus, what he is hoping for lies
behind him; what he recollects lies ahead of him. His life is not
backwards but is turned the wrong way in two directions. He
will soon perceive his trouble even though he does not comprehend the reason for it.

In order, however, that he will really have the opportunity
to feel it, misunderstanding intervenes and in an odd way rid-
icules him at every moment. Ordinarily, he enjoys the honor
of being regarded as being in his right mind, and yet he knows
that if he were to explain to a single person how it really is with
him, he would be declared insane. This is enough to drive one
mad, and yet this does not happen, and this is precisely his
trouble. His calamity is that he came into the world too early
and therefore continually comes too late. He is continually

I
199

very close to the goal, and at the same moment he is far from it; he then discovers that what is making him unhappy now, because he has it or because he is this way, is precisely what would have made him happy a few years ago if he had had it, whereas he became unhappy because he did not have it. His life is as meaningless as Ancaeus's, of whom it is customary to say that nothing is known except that he gave rise to the proverb

πολλὰ μεταξύ πέλει κύλικος καὶ χείλεος ἄκρου
[There is many a slip betwixt the cup and the lip],[13]

as if this were not more than enough. His life knows no repose and has no content. He is not present to himself in the moment, nor is he present to himself in the future, for the future has been experienced, nor in past time, for the past has not yet come. Thus, like Latona,[14] he is chased around in the darkness of the Hyperboreans,[15] to the bright islands of the equator, is unable to give birth, and is always like a woman in labor. Abandoned to himself, he stands alone in the wide world; he has no contemporaries to whom he can attach himself, no past he can long for, because his past has not yet come, no future he can hope for, because his future is already past. All alone, he faces the whole world as the "you" with whom he is in conflict, for all the rest of the world is for him only one person, and this person, this inseparable bothersome friend, is misunderstanding. He cannot grow old, for he has never been young; he cannot become young, for he has already grown old; in a sense he cannot die, for indeed he has not lived; in a sense he cannot live, for indeed he is already dead. He cannot love, for love is always present tense, and he has no present time, no future, no past, and yet he has a sympathetic nature, and he hates the world only because he loves it; he has no passion, not because he lacks it, but because at the same moment he has the opposite passion; he does not have time for anything, not because his time is filled with something else, but because he has no time at all; he is powerless, not because he lacks energy, but because his own energy makes him powerless.

But very soon our hearts are sufficiently hardened, our ears stopped up, though not closed. We have heard the level-headed voice of deliberation; let us be attentive to the eloquence of passion—brief, pithy, as all passion is.[16]

There stands a young girl. She complains that her lover has been unfaithful to her. This does not lend itself to reflection. But in the whole world she loved only him; she loved him with all her soul, all her heart, all her mind[17]—then let her recollect and grieve.

Is this an actual person or is it an image; is it a living person who is dying or a dead person who is living—it is Niobe.[18] She lost everything all at once; she lost that to which she gave life; she lost that which gave life to her! Look up at her, dear Συμπαρανεκρώμενοι; she is standing only a little higher than the world, like a monument on a burial mound. But no hope beckons her, no future motivates her, no prospect tempts her, no hope perturbs her—hopeless she stands, turned to stone in recollection. She was unhappy for a moment; in the same moment she became happy, and nothing can take her happiness from her; the world changes, but she knows no change, and time comes, but for her there is no future time.

Look over there, what a beautiful union! The one generation offers a hand to the other! Is it an invitation to blessing, to faithful solidarity, to a happy dance? It is the outcast [*forstødte*] family of Oedipus,[19] and the blow [*stød*] is transmitted and it crushes the last one—it is Antigone. But she is provided for; the grief of a family is enough for a human life. She has turned her back on hope; she has exchanged its fickleness for the faithfulness of recollection. Stay happy, then, dear Antigone! We wish you a long life, as meaningful as a deep sigh. May no forgetfulness rob you of anything! May the daily bitterness of sorrow be offered to you abundantly!

A powerful figure appears, but he is not alone. He has friends—how, then, does he come to be here? It is the patriarch of sorrow; it is Job[20]—and his friends. He lost everything, but not in one blow, for the Lord took away, and the Lord took away, and the Lord took away. The friends taught him to perceive the bitterness of loss; for the Lord gave, and the Lord

gave, and the Lord gave, and a foolish wife[21] into the bargain.
He lost everything, for what he kept is of no interest to us.
Honor is due him, dear Συμπαρανεκρώμενοι, for his gray hair
and his unhappiness. He lost everything, but he had possessed
it.

His hair is gray, his head is bowed down, his visage withered, his soul troubled. It is the prodigal son's father. Like Job,
he lost what to him was dearest in the world, but it was the
enemy who took it, not the Lord; he did not lose it, but he is
losing it; it is not being taken away from him, but it is vanishing. He is not sitting at home by the hearth in sackcloth and
ashes; he has gone from his home, has left everything to seek
the lost; he grasps for him, but his arm does not reach him; he
calls to him, but his voice does not catch up with him. Yet he
hopes, even if through tears; he glimpses him, even if through
mists; he catches up with him, even if in death. His hope ages
him, and nothing binds him to the world except the hope for
which he lives. His feet are tired, his eyes dim, his body craves
rest, his hope lives. His hair is white, his body decrepit, his feet
pause, his heart breaks, his hope lives. Lift him up, dear Συμπαρανεκρώμενοι; he was unhappy.

I
202

Who is that pallid figure, feeble as a ghost of one dead! His
name is forgotten; many centuries have gone by since his day.
He was a young man; he was ardent.[22] He sought martyrdom.
In his mind, he saw himself nailed to the cross and saw heaven
open, but actuality was too heavy for him; his ardor vanished;
he denied his Lord and himself. He wanted to carry a world,
but he overstrained himself on it; his soul was not crushed or
destroyed; it was broken, his spirit paralyzed, his soul crip-
pled. Congratulate him, dear Συμπαρανεκρώμενοι; he was unhappy. And yet he did indeed become happy; he did indeed become what he wished to be. He became a martyr, even though
his martyrdom was not what he wanted, being nailed to the
cross or cast to the wild animals, but was being burned alive,
slowly being consumed by a low fire.

A young girl sits yonder, so very pensive. Her lover was unfaithful to her—this does not lend itself to reflection. Young
girl, look at the serious faces of this assemblage; it has heard

more terrible calamities; its audacious soul demands something even greater. Yes, but in the whole world I loved only him; I loved him with all my soul, all my heart, all my mind.[23] —We have already heard all that once before; do not weary our impatient longing. After all, you can recollect and grieve. —No, I cannot grieve, for he perhaps was not unfaithful to me; he may not have been a deceiver. —Why can you not grieve? Come closer, chosen one among maidens; forgive this rigorous interrogator for wanting to thrust you back for a moment. You cannot grieve, but then you can hope. —No, I cannot hope, for he was an enigma. —All right, my girl, I do understand you; you stand high on the ladder of unhappiness. Look at her, dear Συμπαρανεκρώμενοι; she is poised almost at the summit of unhappiness. But you must divide yourself; you must hope during the day, grieve during the night, or grieve during the day and hope during the night. Be proud, for one is to be proud not of happiness but of unhappiness. Certainly you are not the unhappiest one, but do you not think, dear Συμπαρανεκρώμενοι, that we can award her an honorable *accessit* [second place]? We cannot award her the grave, but the place closest to it.

For there he stands, the envoy from the kingdom of sighs, the chosen favorite of suffering, the apostle of grief, the silent friend of pain, the unhappy lover of recollection, confused in his recollection by the light of hope, frustrated in his hope by the ghosts of recollection. His brow is troubled, his knees are slack, and yet he leans on himself alone. He is exhausted, and yet how full of energy; his eyes do not seem to have shed, but to have drunk, many tears, and yet they flame with a fire that could consume the whole world, but not a splinter of sorrow in his own breast; he is bowed down, and yet his youth portends a long life; his lips smile at the world, which does not understand him. Arise, dear Συμπαρανεκρώμενοι; bow down, you witnesses of sorrow, in this solemn hour. I hail you, great unknown, whose name I do not know; I hail you with your title of honor: the unhappiest one. Greetings and salutations from the community of the unhappy to you here in your home; greetings and salutations to you at the entrance to this

I
203

humble, low dwelling, which nevertheless is prouder than all the palaces of the world. See, the stone is rolled away; the shade of the grave awaits you with its delicious coolness. But perhaps the time has not yet come, perhaps the way is long, but we promise you that we will assemble here often to envy you your fortune. So accept our wish, a good wish: May no one understand you but all envy you; may no friend attach himself to you; may no girl fall in love with you; may no secret sympathy suspect your solitary pain; may no eye fathom your remote sorrow; may no ear ferret out your secret sigh! Or if your proud soul disdains such compassionate wishes, scorns this mitigation—then may the girls fall in love with you; may those who are pregnant turn to you in their anxiety; may the mothers trust you; may the dying seek consolation in you; may the young people attach themselves to you; may the men rely upon you; may the aged reach for you as for a cane—may the whole world believe that you are able to make it happy. Farewell, then, you the unhappiest one! [24]But what am I saying—"the unhappiest"? I ought to say "the happiest," for this is indeed precisely a gift of fortune that no one can give himself. See, language breaks down, and thought is confused, for who indeed is the happiest but the unhappiest and who the unhappiest but the happiest, and what is life but madness, and faith but foolishness, and hope but a staving off of the evil day, and love but vinegar in the wound.

He disappeared, and we stand again by the empty grave. So we wish him peace and rest and healing, and all possible good fortune, and a quick death, and an eternal oblivion, and no remembrance, lest the memory of him make another unhappy.

Arise, dear Συμπαρανεκρώμενοι. The night is over; the day is beginning its unflagging activity again, never, so it seems, tired of repeating itself forever and ever. [25]

THE FIRST LOVE

A COMEDY IN ONE ACT BY SCRIBE

Translated by J. L. Heiberg[1]

[2]This article was planned for publication in a journal Frederik Unsmann had planned to issue at specific times. Ah, what are all human plans!

Anyone who has ever had leanings toward productivity has
certainly also noticed that it is a little accidental external circumstance that becomes the *occasion* for the actual producing. Only the authors who in one way or another have made a final purpose into their inspiration will perhaps deny this. This, however, is to their own injury, for they are thereby deprived of the extreme poles of all true and all sound productivity. The one is what is traditionally called "invocation of the muse"; the other is the occasion. —The expression "invocation of the muse" can occasion a misunderstanding. To invoke the muse may signify, for one thing, that I invoke the muse; for another, that the muse invokes me. Any author who is either so naïve as to believe that everything depends on an honest will, on industry and effort, or so shameless as to offer for sale the products of the spirit will not be wanting in ardent invocation or brash forwardness. But not much is achieved thereby, for what Wessel once said still holds concerning the god of taste "whom all invoke," that he "so rarely comes."[3] But if we interpret this expression to mean that it is the muse who invokes—I shall not say us, but those concerned—then the matter acquires a different meaning. Whereas the authors who invoke the muse also embark without her coming, those last described, on the other hand, are in another dilemma, in that they need an extra element for an inner decision to become an outer decision; this element is what one must call the occasion.

In other words, by invoking them, the muse has beckoned them away from the world, and now they listen only to her
voice, and the wealth of thought is opened to them, but so overwhelmingly that, although every word is clear and vivid, it seems to them as if it were not their possession. When consciousness has come to itself again to the extent that it possesses the whole content, then the moment is reached that contains the possibility of actual coming into existence, and yet

something is lacking, namely, the occasion—which is just as necessary, if you please, although in another sense most insignificant. It has pleased the gods to link together the greatest contradictions in this way.[4] This is a secret implicit in actuality—an offense to the Jews and foolishness to the Greeks.[5] The occasion is always the accidental, and the prodigious paradox is that the accidental is absolutely just as necessary as the necessary. In the ideal sense, the occasion is not the accidental as, for example, when I think the accidental in the logical sense, but the occasion is the accidental in the sense of fetishism, and yet in this accidentality it is the necessary.

But there is much confusion with respect to what in use and wont is called the occasion. Both too much and too little are seen in it. Any literary productivity in the category of triviality—and, worse luck, this kind of productivity is most of all the order of the day—overlooks the occasion just as much as it overlooks inspiration. For this reason, such literary productivity believes that it is appropriate to any age—something that can be conceded to it. Therefore, it completely overlooks the significance of the occasion—that is, it sees an occasion in everything. It is like a talkative person who in the most opposite things sees an occasion to bring in himself and his story, whether one has heard it before or not. But thereby the *punctum saliens* [salient point] is lost. On the other side is the literary productivity that falls in love with the occasion. The first kind can be said to see an occasion in everything, the second to see everything in the occasion. This describes the great company of occasional authors, from the occasional poets in the deeper sense to those who in the stricter sense see everything in the occasion and therefore use the same verse, the same formulas, and yet hope that for those concerned the occasion will be a sufficient occasion for an appropriate honorarium.

In our day, the occasion, which as such is the unessential and accidental, may sometimes venture into the revolutionary. The occasion often plays the absolute master; it determines the outcome; it makes the product and the producer into something or nothing, whatever it wishes. The poet expects the occasion to inspire, and with amazement he sees that nothing happens, or he produces something that he himself secretly regards as insignificant and then sees the occasion make everything of it, sees himself honored and singled out in every possible way, and privately knows that he has the occasion alone to thank for it. So these writers fall in love with the occasion; the ones we described previously overlook it and therefore in every sense are always uncalled. They can actually be divided into two classes: those who still suggest that an occasion is necessary and those who do not even pay attention to it. Both classes are based, of course, on an exorbitant overrating of their own worth. When someone continually bandies about such locutions as "On this occasion it occurs to me," "The occasion prompts me to think," etc., one can always be sure that such a person is on the wrong track as far as he himself is concerned. He often sees in even the most trifling matter an occasion to put in his bit of comment. Those who do not even suggest the necessity of an occasion may be regarded as less conceited but more demented. Without looking to the right or the left, they spin out indefatigably the thin thread of their babbling, and they produce the same effect on life with their chatter and their writing as the mill in a fairy tale, of which it says: And while all this was happening, the mill went klip klap, klip klap.[6]

And yet even the most consummate, the most profound, and the most meaningful work has an occasion. The occasion is the tenuous, almost invisible web in which the fruit is suspended. Therefore, insofar as it sometimes seems that something essential is the occasion, this is usually a mistake, since in such a case it is likely to be only a particular edge of it. If someone will not concede that I am correct in this, it is due to a confusion of occasion with ground and cause.[7] If, for example, someone would ask me, "What is the occasion for all these comments?" and he would be satisfied if I answered, "The following," he would make himself and allow me to make myself guilty of such a confusion. But if he used the word "occasion" in his question very scrupulously, it would be very proper for me to reply, "It has no occasion." With respect to the particular parts of the whole, it would be absurd to demand that which one may properly demand with respect to the whole. That is, if these comments were to claim to be an occasion, they in themselves would have to be a small rounded-off whole, which would be an egotistic attempt on their part.

The occasion, therefore, is of the greatest significance for every literary work—yes, that is what really determines its true esthetic value. Literary works without any occasion always lack something—not outside themselves, for although the occasion belongs to it, yet in another sense it does not—but they lack something within themselves. A literary work in which the occasion is everything also lacks something. That is, the occasion is generative in the negative sense, not the positive. A creation is a production out of nothing, but the occasion is the nothing that lets everything come forth. The whole wealth of thought, the fullness of the idea, can be present, and still the occasion is lacking. Nothing new, then, comes through the occasion, but through the occasion everything comes forth. The modest meaning of occasion is, in fact, expressed in the word itself.[8]

This is something that so many people are unable to grasp, but that is due to their having no intimation of what an esthetic work really is. A lawyer can write his plea, a merchant his letter, etc., without suspecting the secret that lies in the word "occasion," despite the fact that he begins with "On the occasion of your esteemed."

Now, some may agree with what I have developed here and concede its significance for poetic works but would be very surprised if I were to bring something similar to bear on reviewers and critics. And yet I believe that it is most important precisely here and that the disregard of the significance of occasion has had the result that reviews have generally been so bungled, have been such downright hackwork. In the world of criticism, the occasion acquires heightened significance. Although this accounts for our all too frequently finding the occasion mentioned in critical reviews, it is as plain as day that little is known about how it all hangs together. The critic does not seem to need an invocation of the muse, for, after all, he is

not producing a literary work; but if he does not need an invocation of the muse, then he does not need the occasion,
either. We should not forget, however, the importance of the
old saying: Like is understood only by like.[9]

Surely the object of the esthetician's consideration is already
complete, and he is not, like the poet himself, supposed to produce. Nevertheless, the occasion has absolutely the same significance. The esthetician who regards esthetics as his profession and in turn sees in his profession the legitimate occasion is
eo ipso lost. This in no way means that he cannot perform various kinds of competent work, but he has not comprehended
the secret of all production. He is too much a Pelagian[10] auto-
crat to be able to rejoice in childlike amazement over the curious fact that strange forces seem to produce what a person
believes belongs to himself: namely, inspiration and the occasion.

Inspiration and the occasion belong inseparably together; it
is a combination frequently seen in the world: the great one,
the exalted, always has in his company an agile little person.
Such a person is the occasion, a person to whom one generally
would not tip one's hat, who does not dare to open his mouth
when he is in high society but sits silent with a mischievous
smile and inwardly regales himself without divulging what he
is smiling about or that he knows how important, how indispensable, he is; still less would he become involved in an argument about it, for he knows very well that it does not help
and that every occasion is used only to humiliate him. The occasion always has this equivocal character, and it is of no more
use to want to deny this, to want to free oneself from this
thorn in the flesh,[11] than to want to place the occasion on the
throne, for it looks very foolish in purple and with scepter in
hand, and it is immediately obvious that it was not born to
rule. It is very easy, however, to go astray in this manner, and
frequently it is the best minds that do so. In other words, when
a person has enough of an eye for life to see how the eternal
being flouts mankind by having something so insignificant
and inferior, something people are almost ashamed to talk
about in polite society, be absolutely part of it all, he is readily

tempted to want to meddle with the affair, indeed, to want to return the taunt. Just as God mocks the greatness of men by forging them into the law of the occasion, so a person in turn mocks by making the occasion into everything and the next moment into foolishness, whereby God then becomes superfluous, the concept of a wise Governance becomes a piece of folly, and the occasion becomes a wag who pokes fun at God just as much as at man, so that all existence ends in a jest, a joke, a charade.

So the occasion is simultaneously the most significant and the most insignificant, the highest and the lowest, the most important and the most unimportant. Without the occasion, nothing at all actually occurs, and yet the occasion has no part at all in what occurs. The occasion is the final category, the essential category of transition from the sphere of the idea to actuality. Logic should bear this in mind. It can immerse itself as much as it wishes in immanental thinking, plunge from nothing down into the most concrete form;[12] it never reaches the occasion and therefore never reaches actuality, either. In the idea, all actuality can be in readiness—without the occasion, it never becomes actual. The occasion is a finite category, and it is impossible for immanental thinking to grasp it; it is too much a paradox for that. We see this because that which comes out of the occasion is something quite different from the occasion itself, which is an absurdity to any immanental thinking. But for that reason the occasion is also the most amusing, the most interesting, the wittiest of all categories. Like a wren, it is everywhere and nowhere. Like the elves, it walks around in life invisible to all the schoolmasters,[13] whose gestures therefore become an inexhaustible material for laughter to the person who believes in the occasion. The occasion, then, is nothing in and by itself and is something only in relation to that which it occasions, and in relation to that it is actually nothing. That is, if the occasion were something else than nothing, it would immediately have a relative, immanental connection with what it produces and would then be either ground[14] or cause. If this is not held fast, everything is confused again.

Thus, if I were to say that the occasion for the present little review of a play by Scribe was the superb performance it received, I would insult the dramatic art, for it is certainly true that I could also write a review of it without having seen it performed, without having seen it superbly performed, yes, even if I had seen it poorly performed. In the last case, I would be more correct in calling the bad performance the occasion. But now that I have seen it performed perfectly, the theatrical performance becomes more than an occasion to me; it is a very important factor in my interpretation, whether or not it served to correct or to strengthen and confirm my views. Therefore, my respect prevents me from calling the theatrical performance the occasion; it binds me to see something more in it, to admit that without it I might not have quite understood the play. I am, therefore, not in the usual position of reviewers who are shrewd enough or stupid enough to discuss first the play and later the performance by itself. For me, the performance is itself the play, and I cannot delight enough in it in a purely esthetic sense, cannot as a patriot delight enough in it. If I were to show a stranger our stage in its full glory, I would say: Go and see *The First Love* [*Den første Kjærlighed*].[15] In Madame Heiberg, Frydendahl, Stage, and Phister,[16] the Danish theater has a four-leaf clover that is manifest here in all its beauty. I call this combination of artists a four-leaf clover, and yet I might seem to be saying too little, for a four-leaf clover is distinguished only by having four ordinary clover leaves set on one stem, but our four-leaf clover has the distinction that a single leaf all by itself is just as rare as a four-leaf clover, and yet in turn these four leaves together form a four-leaf clover.

Yet it was on the occasion of the occasion of this little review that I wanted to say something rather general about the occasion or about the occasion in general. Very fortunately, it so happens that I have already said what I wanted to say, for the more I deliberate on this matter, the more I am convinced that there is nothing in general to be said about it, because there is no occasion in general. If so, then I have come just about as far as I was when I began. The reader must not be angry with me—it is not my fault; it is the occasion's. He might perhaps think that I ought to have thought the whole thing through before I started to write, and then I ought not to have begun to say something that later turned out to be nothing. Nevertheless, I do believe that he ought to give my method its due, insofar as he has convinced himself in a more satisfying manner that the occasion in general is something that is nothing. Later on, he perhaps will come to think about this again when he has convinced himself that there is something else in the world about which one can say much under the impression that it is something, and yet it is of such a character that, once it is said, it turns out to be nothing. What is said here, then, must be regarded as a superfluity, like a superfluous title page that is not included when the work is bound. Therefore, I know no other way to conclude than in the incomparable laconic manner in which I see that Professor Poul Møller concludes the introduction of his excellent review of *Extrememe*: With this the introduction is concluded.[17]

I
214

As for the particular occasion for the present little review, it is related to my insignificant person and hence, with the ordinary quality of being insignificant, dares to commend itself to the reader. Scribe's play *The First Love* has touched my life personally in many ways and in so doing has prompted the present review, which then is the child of the occasion in the strictest sense! I, too, was young once, was an enthusiast, was in love. The girl who was the object of my longings I had known from very early on, but the dissimilar conditions of our lives led to our seeing each other only infrequently. However, we did think about each other all the more. This mutual preoccupation with each other drew us closer and at the same time put distance between us. When we did see each other, we were so bashful, so modest, that we were much further apart than when we did not see each other. Then when we were apart again and the unpleasantness of this mutual uneasiness was forgotten, our having seen each other acquired its full significance; then in our dreams we began exactly where we had stopped. So it was at least with me, and later I learned that it had been the same with my beloved. Marriage was a long way off for me; on the other hand, our understanding met with no hindrances that could have incited us, and thus we were in love in the most innocent way in the world. Before there could be any question of a declaration of my feelings, a rich uncle, whose sole heir I was, had to die. This, too, seemed beautiful to me, because in all the novels and comedies I knew I found the hero in a similar situation, and I rejoiced in the thought that I was a poetic character.

And in this way my beautiful poetic life went on. Then one day I saw in the newspaper that a play titled *The First Love* was to be performed. I did not know that such a play existed, but the title delighted me and I decided to go to the theater. The first love—that, I thought, is precisely the expression for your feelings. Have I ever loved anyone else but her, does not my love go back to my earliest recollection, shall I ever be able to think of loving another or seeing her united with another? No, she will be my bride, or I will never marry. That is why the words "the first" are so beautiful. It suggests the original in love, for it is not in the numerical sense that we speak of the first love. The poet could just as well have said "the true love" or titled it "The First Love is the True Love." This play will now help me to understand myself; it will give me the occasion to take a deep look into myself. The reason poets are called priests is that they interpret life, but they do not want to be understood by the masses but only by those natures with sensitive hearts. For them the poet is an inspired singer who points to beauty everywhere but testifies, first and last, to the beauty of love. The poetic power of this play will prompt the love in my breast to spring forth, its flower to open with a snap as the passion-flower does. Ah, I was very young at the time! I scarcely understood what I said, and yet I found it stated well. The flower of love must open with a snap: the feelings, just like champagne, must break their closure by force. It was a gallant phrase, full of passion, and I was very pleased with it. And yet what I said was stated well, for I meant that love must open as a passion-flower does. This was the good part of the observation, because love usually opens in marriage, and if one is going to call this latter a flower, it may appropriately be called a passion-flower.

I
215

¹⁸But back to my youth. The day of the performance arrived. I had my ticket, I was in a festive mood, and with a certain excitement I hurried, joyful and expectant, to the theater.
Going through the door, I glanced up at the first balcony, and
what did I see? My beloved, the mistress of my heart, my
ideal—she was sitting there. Involuntarily I stepped back into
the darkness of the parquet in order to watch her without
being seen. How had she come here? She must have come to
the city just today, and I did not know it, and now she was
here in the theater. She would see the same play. This was no
accident; it was a dispensation, a kindness on the part of the
blind god of love. I stepped forward, our eyes met, she acknowledged me. Bowing to her or conversing with her was
out of the question. In short, there was nothing that could em-
barrass me. My infatuation had free play. We met each other
halfway; like transfigured beings, we stretched out hands to
each other; we floated like phantoms, like jinn in the world of
fantasy. Her eyes rested soulfully on me, a sigh heaved her
breast; it was for me; she belonged to me, that I knew. And yet
I had no desire to rush up to her and throw myself at her feet;
that would have been embarrassing to me, but at this distance
I felt the beauty of loving her and of daring to hope that I was
loved.

The overture was over. The chandelier was raised; my eyes
followed its movement; for the last time it cast its light over
the first balcony and over her. The theater was enveloped in a
twilight that to me was even more beautiful, even more infatuating. The curtain was raised. Once again it seemed as if I
were peering into a dream when I gazed upon her. I turned
around; the play began. I wished to think only of her and of
my love; everything that was said in honor of the first love I
would apply to her and to my situation. There was perhaps no
one in the whole theater who would understand the poet's divine discourse as I would—and perhaps she. The thought of
the powerful impression made me even stronger; I felt the
courage to let my secret feelings burst forth the next day. They
must not miscarry in their effect upon her; with a single hint I
would remind her of what we had heard and seen this evening,

I
216

and in that way the poet would come to my aid and make her more receptive and me stronger and more eloquent than ever. —I looked and listened—and listened—and the curtain went down. The chandelier in turn forsook its heavenly hiding place, the twilight vanished; I looked up—all the young maidens looked so pleased, my beloved also. She had laughed so hard that there were tears in her eyes; her bosom still rose and fell in agitation; laughter had gained the upper hand. Fortunately, it was the same with me.

We saw each other the next day at my aunt's. The shy awkwardness we usually had when in the same room together had disappeared—replaced by a kind of genial delight. We laughed a little at each other; we had understood each other, and we were indebted to the poet for that. A poet is called a seer because he foresees the future. The situation provided the occasion for an explanation. But we could not decide to wipe out everything that had gone before. We pledged ourselves with a solemn promise. Just as Emmeline and Charles promise each other to contemplate the moon,[19] we promised to see this play every time it was performed. I have faithfully kept my promise. I have seen it in Danish, in German, in French, abroad and here at home, and I have never grown weary of its inexhaustible wittiness, the truth of which no one understands better than I.

This became the first occasion for the present little review. By seeing it so often, I eventually became productive with respect to this play. For the time being, this productivity remained in my head, and only a single reflection was jotted down. This occasion can then be regarded as the occasion for the ideal possibility of this review.

Very likely I would have gone no further if a new occasion had not intervened. Some years ago, an editor of one of our journals approached me and asked me to provide him with a little article. He had an unusually persuasive eloquence in inveigling people, and he inveigled a promise from me. This promise, then, was also an occasion, but it was an occasion in general and therefore had only a slight enabling effect upon me. I found myself in the awkward situation like that in which

I
217

a theological candidate would find himself if he were given the whole Bible from which to choose his own text. But I was committed by my promise. With many other thoughts, also the thought of my promise, I took a little excursion in Sjælland. When I arrived at the post house where I planned to spend the night, I did what I never fail to do—had the servant bring whatever books the innkeeper could assemble. I always observe this custom and have often benefited by it, because quite accidentally one comes upon things that otherwise might escape one's attention. But that was not the case here, for the first book brought to me was—*The First Love.* This amazed me, since out in the country the *Theater Repertoire* is seldom found. But I had lost faith in the first love and believe no more in the first. In the next town, I visited one of my friends. He was out when I arrived; I was asked to wait and was shown into his study. Walking over to his desk, I found a book lying open—it was Scribe's plays, opened to *Les premières amours.* Now the die seemed to be cast. I decided to fulfill my promise and write a review of this play. It so happened, strange to say, that my former love, my first love, who lived there in the region, had come to town, not to the capital, but to the small town where I was—and that solidified my decision. I had not seen her for a long time and now found her engaged, cheerful and happy, so much so that it was a pleasure to see. She informed me that she had never loved me but that her fiancé was her first love, and then proceeded to tell the same story as Emmeline, that only the first love is the true love. If my decision had not been firm before, it became so now. But I had to find out what first love means. My theory began to wobble, for "my first love" was immovable on the point that her present love was the first.

There were motives enough; the piece was finished short of the final period and a few parenthetical clauses that had to be inserted here and there. My friend the editor promptly put pressure on me and held me to my promise with a stubbornness that would have done honor even to an Emmeline. I explained to him that the piece was finished, that only some small details were lacking, and he expressed his satisfaction.

But as time passed these molehills turned into mountains, into insurmountable difficulties. Moreover, as I wrote, I forgot that it was going to be printed. I had already written several little articles in this fashion but never had anything printed. He grew weary of my saying I was finished when he still could not receive the manuscript. I grew weary of his everlasting requests and wished that all promises would go to the devil. Then his journal ceased publication because of too few subscribers, and I thanked the gods; I felt at ease again, unembarrassed by any promise.

This was the occasion for the birth of this review as an actuality for me, as a possibility for my friend the editor, a possibility that later changed into an impossibility. Again a year went by, and during that time I became precisely one year older. There is nothing particularly remarkable about that, for it went with me as it presumably went with most other people. But sometimes one year can be more meaningful than another, can mean more than that one becomes a year older. That was the case here. At the end of that year, I found myself in a new period of my life, in a new world of illusion that falls only to the lot of young men. That is, if a person belongs to "the readers' sect," if he in one way or another distinguishes himself as an alert and diligent reader, others begin to nurture the notion that a minor author might emerge, for as Hamann says: "aus Kindern werden Leute, aus Jungfern werden Bräute, aus Lesern werden Schriftsteller [out of children come adults, out of virgins come brides, out of readers come writers]."[20]

Now a rose-tinted life begins, much like a girl's early youth. Editors and publishers begin to pay court. It is a dangerous period, for the conversation of editors is very seductive, and soon one is in their power; but they deceive only us poor children, and then—well, then it is too late. Watch out, young man, and do not go too often to the cafés and restaurants, for that is where editors spin their webs. And when they see an innocent young man who talks straight from the shoulder,[21] fast and loose, with no idea whether what he says is worth anything or not, but merely rejoices in letting his words freely flow forth, in hearing his heart pound as he speaks, pounding in what is said—then a dark figure approaches him, and this figure is an editor. He has a subtle ear; he can hear immediately whether what is being said will look good in print or not. Then he tempts the young fellow; he shows him how indefensible it is to cast his pearls away in this manner; he promises him money, power, influence, even with the fair sex. The heart is weak, the editor's words beautiful, and soon he is trapped. Now he no longer seeks solitary places in order to yearn and sigh; he does not hurry eagerly to the happy haunts of youth to become intoxicated with talk; he is silent, for one who writes does not talk. He sits pallid and cold in his workroom; he does not change color at the kiss of the idea; he does not blush like a young rose when the dew sinks into its cup. He has no smiles, no tears; calmly he watches the pen glide across the paper, for he is an author and not young anymore.

My youth also was exposed to trials of this kind. Yet I think I dare to testify of myself that my resistance has been bold. What helped me was that I had this experience at a very young age. The editor who received my first promise was very friendly to me, but still it always seemed to me as if it were a favor, an honor, befallen to my lot, that someone would accept an article from my hand, as if people singled me out from among my peers and said: In time something may come of him; let him try his hand; it is an encouragement to him to be shown this honor. The temptation was not very great then, and yet I learned to know all the terrible consequences of a promise. For a young man, then, I was unusually armed against the temptation and dared to visit the cafés and restaurants rather frequently. So the danger had to come from another quarter, and it did not fail to come. It happened that one of my cafe acquaintances decided to become an editor; his name will be found on the title page of that journal. No sooner had he conceived this idea and discussed the essentials with the publisher than he sat down at his desk one evening and wrote all night long—letters to all possible people about contributions. I also received such a letter, drawn up in the most courteous phrases, full of the most brilliant prospects. I, however, bravely resisted but promised to be of service to him in every

way in minor editing of the articles submitted. He himself
worked indefatigably on the first article, which was to inau-
gurate the journal. He was practically finished with it and had
the kindness to show it to me. We spent a very pleasant morning; he seemed satisfied with my comments, made some
changes here and there. The mood was wonderful; we ate fruit
and candies and drank champagne. I was pleased with his article; he seemed to approve of my comments—when, as I
leaned over to take an apricot, my unlucky star made me tip
the inkwell over the whole manuscript. My friend was furious. "Everything is ruined. The first issue of my journal will
not come out on time; my credit is gone; the subscribers will
cancel. You have no idea how much work is involved in gaining subscribers, and once one has them they are disloyal and,
like mercenary soldiers, take every chance to desert. All is lost;
the only way out is that you must provide an article. I know
you have manuscripts ready; why will you not have them
printed? You have your review of *The First Love*. Let me have
it; I'll complete it. I beg you, I implore you, for the sake of our
friendship, my honor, the future of my journal."

He accepted the article, and so my inkwell became the occasion for my little review's becoming an actuality that now
is—I say it with horror—*publici juris* [public property].

If the merit of modern comedy (especially Scribe's), in relation to older comedy, were to be suggested briefly, it could
perhaps be expressed as follows: the personal substance of the
poetic character is commensurate with the dialogue; the effusions of the monologue are made superfluous; the substance
and the dramatic action are commensurate with the situation;
the novelistic details are made superfluous; and the dialogue finally becomes audible in the transparency of the situation. No
information is necessary in order to orient the spectator; no
pause in the drama is required in order to give clues and accounts. So it is in life, where one always needs explanatory
notes, but it ought not to be so in poetry. Then the spectator,
free from care, can enjoy, can absorb undisturbed, the dramatic life. Although modern drama seems to require less self-

I
220

I
221

activity on the part of the spectator, it perhaps nevertheless requires more in another way or, more correctly, does not require it but takes revenge on the forgetting of it. The less perfect the dramatic form or the structure of the drama, the more frequently the spectator is provoked out of his sleep, insofar as he is sleeping. When one is jolted on a poor country road whenever at one moment the carriage hits a stone and at another the horses are stuck in the brush, there is no good opportunity to sleep. But if the road is level and easy, then one can really have time and opportunity to look around—but also, less disturbed, to fall asleep. So it is in modern drama. Everything happens so easily and quickly that the spectator, if he does not pay a little attention, misses a great deal. It is certainly true that an older five-act comedy and a modern five-act comedy last just as long, but there is always the question whether just as much takes place.

To pursue this exploration further might be interesting, but not in this review; it could be important to demonstrate this in more detail in Scribe's dramas, but I believe that the more precise discussion of the little masterpiece that is the object of the present deliberation will be sufficient. I much prefer to dwell on the present play, since it cannot be denied that in some of Scribe's other dramas there is a lack of perfect correctness since the situations drag and the dialogue is onesidedly garrulous. *The First Love*, however, is a flawless play, so consummate that it alone is bound to make Scribe immortal.

We shall first examine more closely the characters of this play in their singularity, in order to observe later how the poet has known how to let their individualities become disclosed in lines and situation, and this even though the whole play is only a sketch.

Dervière, a wealthy iron-founder and widower, has only one daughter, "a little miss of sixteen years."[22] Certainly every reasonable claim of his to be regarded as a good, decent man who has much money must be respected, whereas every attempt to be a man, to be a father "who does not understand a joke,"[23] must be regarded as unsuccessful. It is also thwarted by his daughter, without whose permission and approval he scarcely dares to regard himself as a rational being. "She twists him around her little finger,"[24] and he shows an extraordinary talent for understanding a joke, since her capriciousness incessantly plays blindman's buff with his fatherly dignity.

His only daughter, Emmeline, is now sixteen years old. A lovely, engaging little miss, but a daughter of Dervière and brought up by Aunt Judith. The aunt has brought her up and educated her on novels,[25] and her father's wealth has made it possible to keep this education undisturbed by the actuality of life. Everyone in the house obeys her whim, the instability of which can be seen, among other places, in the servant Lapierre's monologue in the third scene.[26] Because of Judith's education, she has lived in her father's house without much acquaintance with the world and has not missed the opportunity to spin herself into a web of sentimentality. She has been brought up with her cousin Charles; he was her playmate, her everything, the requisite supplement to the aunt's novels. She has gone through the reading with him, has transferred everything to him since he left her at a very early age. Their ways parted; now they live far from each other, united only by "a sacred vow."[27]

Novel-nurturing is something Charles shares with his cousin, but not her life situation. At a very early age, he is sent out into the world, has only 3,000 francs a year (see scene 6), and quickly finds himself obliged to make his education fruitful, if possible, in the world. His endeavors in this respect do not seem to have met with success; actuality soon reduces him and his theories *in absurdum:* the hopeful Charles becomes a debauched fellow, a black sheep, a failed genius. A character such as this has so much intrinsic dramatic effectiveness that it is inconceivable that one sees it utilized so rarely. A dabbling playwright, however, is easily tempted to interpret him quite abstractly: a black sheep in a general sense. This is not the case with Scribe, but then he is no dabbler, but a virtuoso. For such a character to have interest, one must continually have an intimation of how it happened; that is, in a stricter sense than for other men, he has a pre-existence. One must catch a glimpse of this even in his failure and thus see the possibility of his depravity. But this is not as easily done as said, and one cannot sufficiently admire the virtuosity with which Scribe knows how to have it come out—not in tedious monologue but in situation. On the whole, Charles is perhaps one of the most brilliant characters Scribe has brought to the stage; every one of his lines is worth its weight in gold, and yet the poet has dashed him off in a hasty sketch. Charles is no abstraction, is not a new Charles, but one sees at once how it happened; one sees in him the consequences of the premises of his life.

The yield of being educated on novels can be twofold. The individual either becomes more and more immersed in illusion or comes out of it and loses faith in illusion but acquires faith in mystification. In illusion, the individual is hidden from himself; in mystification, he is hidden from others—but both conditions are the consequences of being brought up on romantic novels. A girl is more likely to become immersed in illusion, and this is what the poet has had happen to Emmeline, and in this respect her life is fortunate. It is otherwise with Charles. He has lost his illusions, but although he has experienced the pinch of actuality in many ways, he still has not completely sweat out his education through novels. He believes he is able to mystify. Therefore, when Emmeline speaks of sympathetic feelings that are beyond her father's comprehension,[28] one immediately hears the reader of novels, but in Charles's lines one finds no less accurate reminders of his education. He credits himself with extraordinary talent for mystifying, but this faith in mystification is just as romantic as Emmeline's visionary infatuation. "After eight years of vagabonding, he comes back incognito; he is intelligent by nature and is well read and knows that there are five or six ways to move an uncle's heart, but the main thing is to be unrecognized; that is a necessary condition."[29] One immediately hears the hero of a novel. That Charles should credit himself with sufficient competence to fool such a simpleton as his uncle is just as it should be, but this is not what Charles is thinking about; he is speaking of uncles in general, about five or six ways in general, and about the condition of being unrecognized in general. Thus his belief in mystification is just as fan-

ciful as Emmeline's illusion, and one recognizes Judith's
schooling in both. In this respect, we gain a good idea of
Charles's extravagance from his being unable, despite all these
wonderful theories, to hit upon the least thing and having to
be advised by the anything but visionary Rinville.[30] His belief
in mystification is just as unproductive as Emmeline's in illusion, and therefore the poet has had them both arrive at the
same result—namely, the opposite of what they imagined they
were working toward, for Emmeline's sympathy and
Charles's mystification have just the opposite effect of what
they believe they will have. This I shall develop later.

Although Charles, at the cost of his illusions, has gained a
belief in mystifying, he nevertheless has retained a trace of
them, and this is the other thing by which one recognizes Judith's pupil and Emmeline's playmate in the ill-fated Charles.
Despite all the wretchedness and triviality of his life, he knows
how to conceive of it in a romantic transfiguration. He con-
templates his youth, when he went out into the world "as an
extremely charming cavalier, a young man with the best of
manners, full of fire and life and grace, exposed to vigorous
pursuits by the opposite sex."[31] In his eyes, even the affair with
Pamela[32] has a romantic cast, although the spectator very correctly suspects that Charles actually has been a laughing stock.
It is easy to see why I regarded mystification as the predominant trait in Charles, for his illusion is actually an illusion
about his talent for mystifying. Here again one sees the hero of
a novel. There is an unparalleled truth in Charles. In comparison with ordinary folk, a black sheep like this has something
distinguished about him; he is stirred by the idea; his mind is
not unfamiliar with fantastic notions. Such a character, then, is
quite properly comic, for his life is under the universal, is
wretched, and yet he believes that he is accomplishing the extraordinary. He believes that the affair with Pamela is an "adventure," and yet one has the suspicion that it was she, instead,
who has hoodwinked him; one is almost tempted to believe
that he is more innocent than he himself believes, that Pamela's terrifying him "with tailor's shears" was for reasons other

than her violated love, indeed, that these reasons probably lay even outside his relation to her.

Ultimately we recognize in the black sheep the original Charles on the basis of low-comedy emotions, a softness that believes in great feelings and is moved by them. When he hears that the uncle has paid the bank note, he cries out: Yes, the bonds of blood and nature are sacred.*[33] He is really moved, his romantic heart is touched; he gives vent to his feelings, he becomes emotional. "Of course, I thought as much; either one has an uncle or one does not."[35] There is not a trace of irony in him; it is the sweetest sentimentality, but this is why the play has such a comic effect. When the cousin begs her father to forgive the supposed Charles, he cries out agitatedly, with tears in his eyes: O good cousin![36] He has not lost all his belief that in life, as in novels, there are noble feminine souls whose sublime resignation can only wring forth one's tears. Now this belief awakens with its former infatuation.

I have deliberately dwelt on Charles a little longer, because the author has penned such a perfect character that I believe I could write a whole book about him merely by concentrating on his lines. Is Emmeline perhaps regarded as the sentimental one and Charles, on the other hand, the worldly-wise? By no means. Scribe's infinite wit consists precisely in this, that Charles in his own way is just as sentimental as Emmeline, so that both of them with equal force show themselves to be pupils of Aunt Judith.

The old Dervière, his daughter, and Charles together now form an utterly fantastic world, even though in another sense they are all characters taken from life. This world has to be brought into relation with actuality, and this happens through

---

* If the reader is very familiar with the play, he will have had the chance to delight in the poetic coincidence that has Rinville, in the first scene where Rinville portrays Charles, reproduce him with such poetic authenticity that his speech becomes a kind of ventriloquism with an extremely comic effect, because it is as if the sentiment-befuddled, emotionally moved Charles were seen and heard declaiming these words: "Is the voice of blood only a figment of the imagination, then? Does it not speak to your heart? Is it not saying to you, my precious uncle . . ." (see scene 6).[34]

Mr. Rinville. Rinville is a cultured young man who has traveled abroad. He is at the age when it might seem appropriate for him to take, through marriage, a step decisive for his whole life. He has pondered the matter privately and fixed his eyes on Emmeline. He knows the world too well to be visionary; his marriage is a well-considered step that he resolves to take for several reasons.[37] First, the girl is rich and has the prospect of 50,000 francs a year in interest;[38] second, the girl's father and his father are on friendly terms; third, he has jestingly said that he would conquer this coy beauty; fourth, she really is a charming girl. This reason comes last; it is a footnote added later.

We have considered the individual characters in the play and now proceed to investigate how they must be placed in relation to one another in order to acquire dramatic interest. Here there will be good opportunity to admire Scribe. The play must be built on Emmeline; of that there can be no doubt. Emmeline is altogether in the habit of controlling, and thus it is appropriate that she is also the dominant character in the play. She has all possible qualities for becoming a heroine, not substantially, however, but negatively. She is, then, comic, and because of her the play is a comedy. She is in the habit of controlling, as befits a heroine, but that which she controls is a fool of a father, the staff of servants, etc. She has pathos, but since its content is nonsense, her pathos is essentially chatter; she has passion, but since its content is a phantom, her passion is essentially madness; she has enthusiasm, but since its content is nothing, her enthusiasm is essentially frivolity; she wants to sacrifice everything for her passion—that is, she wants to sacrifice everything for nothing. As a comic heroine, she is unparalleled. With her, everything revolves around a fantasy, and everything outside her revolves in turn around her and thereby around her fantasy. It is easy to see how thoroughly comic the whole action must become; watching it is tantamount to gazing into an abyss of the ridiculous.

Emmeline's fantasy is no more and no less than that she loves her cousin Charles, whom she has not seen since she was eight years old. The main argument with which she tries to uphold her illusion is the following: the first love is the true love, and one loves only once.

As an advocate of the absolute validity of the first love, Emmeline represents a large class of people. That it is possible to love more than once is admitted, of course, but the first love is nevertheless essentially different from every other. This can be explained in no other way than by assuming that there is a compassionate daimon who has given humankind a little gilt with which to decorate life. For the thesis that the first love is the true love is very convenient and can be of service to people in many ways. If one is not so fortunate as to obtain what one wishes, there is still the sweetness of the first love. If one is so unfortunate as to love several times, each time is nevertheless the first time. In other words, the thesis is a sophistical thesis. If one loves for a third time, one says: My present love is, nevertheless, my first true love, but the true love is the first— *ergo* this third love is my first. The sophistry consists in this, that the category *the first* is supposed to be a qualitative and a numerical category simultaneously. When a widower and a widow combine forces and each brings along five children, they nevertheless assure each other on the wedding day that this love is their first love. In her romantic orthodoxy, Emmeline would look upon such a union with detestation; to her it would be a perfidious detestableness as abominable as a marriage between a monk and a nun was to the Middle Ages. She understands the thesis numerically and so conscientiously that she believes that an impression in her eighth year is decisive for her whole life. She understands the next thesis, one loves only once, in the same way. This thesis is just as sophistical and just as elastic. One loves several times and each time denies the validity of the previous times, and in this way one still insists on the rightness of the thesis that one loves only once.[39]

So Emmeline maintains her numerically qualified thesis. No one can refute her, for anyone who risks it she declares to be devoid of sympathy. She must now learn by experience, and the experience refutes her. The question is how the poet is to be understood at this point. It turns out that she loves Rinville, not Charles. The answer to this question will be crucial

in determining whether the play is infinitely comic or finitely moralizing. As is known, the play ends with Emmeline's turn- I
228
ing away from Charles, extending her hand to Rinville, and saying, "It was a mistake; I confused the past with the future."[40] Now, if the play is moralizing in the finite sense, as it probably is generally understood to be, then it is the poet's intention to depict in Emmeline a childish, mixed-up girl who has the fixed idea that she loved no one except Charles but who now knows better, is healed of her sickness, makes a sensible match with Mr. Rinville, and lets the spectator hope for the best for her future, that she will become a diligent housewife etc. etc. If this is the intention, then *The First Love* is changed from a masterpiece to a theatrical triviality, on the assumption that the poet has somewhat motivated her improvement. Since that is not the case, the play, regarded as a whole, becomes a mediocre play, and it must be lamented that the brilliant details in it are wasted.

That Scribe in no way has motivated her improvement, I shall now show. Rinville resolves to pass himself off as Charles. He manages to deceive Emmeline. He enters completely into the sentimentality of the supposed Charles, and Emmeline is beside herself with joy. Therefore, it is not with his own person that Rinville charms her but with Charles's Sunday best. Indeed, even if it had been the real Charles instead of the pretended one, even if he had looked exactly like Rinville, the entrance of this character would have provided no new motive for loving. On the contrary, she loves him with an objective, mathematical love, because he fits the image she herself has formed. Rinville, then, has really made no impression at all on Emmeline. How powerless he is becomes manifest in her not loving him when he does not have the ring and loving him again when he does have it, from which it seems probable that for Emmeline this ring is a magic ring and that she would love anyone who showed up with this ring. When Emmeline finally learns that Charles is married, she decides to marry Rinville. Now, if this step is in any way supposed to suggest a change in her—indeed, even more, a change for the better—then, on the one hand, Rinville would have to

have succeeded in pleasing her with his own charm, which in
the play would have to be seen to be of better quality than
Charles's; on the other hand, he would have to have succeeded
in dissipating and transfiguring her theoretical stubborness
about the absolute validity of the first love. Neither of these is
the case. Rinville appears as Charles and pleases her only because he resembles him. And her picture of Charles is not a
grandiose fantasy piece that only a poetic character could satisfy—no, her ideal Charles is identified by a host of incidentals, especially by a ring on the finger. Rinville appeals to her
only because of his resemblance to Charles, and he does not
exhibit a single charm of his own that could make an impression on Emmeline. She does not see Rinville at all but only her
own Charles. She is at the point where she loves Charles and
detests Rinville; she does not decide which of them is more attractive by seeing them—that was decided long before. When
Charles appears as Rinville, she finds him "disgusting."[41] The
spectator must agree that she is right in this judgment, but it
does not seem to be the poet's intention to make much of this.
She knows that he is disgusting before she looks at him; she
has only to look at him and finds it confirmed. Instead, the
poet wants to show her judgment about the supposed Rinville
to be arbitrary and therefore lets it be parodied continually by
the father's judgment. The father finds nothing at all appealing
in the supposed Charles, but he finds the supposed Rinville
very attractive—the daughter just the reverse. He finds it so
because he wants it to be so, as she does also. That she is right
is apparent to the spectator, but her judgment is nonetheless
sheer arbitrariness, and the situation thereby acquires so much
comic power.

Rinville does not succeed in triumphing over her theory,
either. Charles is married, and consequently she cannot have
him* unless he wants to grapple with the authorities. She mar-

* Another way out, perhaps, would be for Emmeline to have the idea that
she would be content with half of Charles's love. We have, of course, seen
something like this in novels, and it is not inconceivable that the idea could
dawn on Emmeline in all its clarity. It is altogether remarkable that there is no
female counterpart to Don Quixote in all European literature. Is the age not

ries Rinville for two reasons—partly to have revenge on
Charles, partly to obey her father. These reasons do not seem
to indicate a change for the better. If she does it to have revenge
on Charles, this indeed shows that she continues to love
Charles. The theme is altogether in keeping with the logic of
the novel, and she can by no means be regarded as healed. If
she does it to obey her father, then either a seriousness must
have entered her soul, repentance and deep sorrow over having allowed herself to make fun of a father who had only one
weakness, that of being too good to her, but this would contradict the whole play—or her obedience is based on the coin-
ciding of her father's will and her whim, and then again she has
not changed.

I
230

In the play, then, there is not the slightest perceptible suggestion that her choice of Rinville is supposed to be more sensible than anything else she has done. Essentially, Emmeline is
infinitely silly, and she is just as silly at the end as at the beginning, and therefore one can be unreservedly entertained by the
comic effect of the play, an effect that originates in the continual opposition of the situation against her. She is no more improved at the end of the play than Holberg's Erasmus Montanus.[42] She is too much a theoretician, too good a dialectician
(for every person who has a fixed idea is a virtuoso on one
string), to allow herself to be persuaded empirically. Charles
has been untrue to her, and she marries Rinville, but her romantic conscience does not reproach her. If Aunt Judith were
still alive, Emmeline would dare to come up to her and calmly
declare, "I do not love Rinville, I have never loved him; I love
only Charles, and I still say that one loves only once and the
first love is the true love; but I do respect Rinville, and that is
why I have married him and obeyed my father" (see scene
14).[43] Then Judith would answer, "You are so right, my child;
in a footnote, the textbook sanctions this step. It says: When
the lovers cannot have each other, they should go on living
quietly, and even though they do not have each other their re-

---

yet mature enough for that; has not the continent of sentimentality yet been
discovered?

lationship should have the same meaning as if they did have each other, and their lives should be just as beautiful and in all respects be regarded as a life together. This I know from my own experience. My first love was a teachers college graduate, but he could not find a position. He was my first love and became my last; I died unmarried and he without a position. But when one party is untrue to the other, then the other has permission to marry, but in such a way that she does it on the basis of respect."

Therefore, since there is the choice between reducing Scribe's play to a triviality by insisting that there is something in it that cannot be established or delighting in a masterpiece by being able to explain everything, the choice seems easy.

I
231

The play is not moralizing in a finite sense but witty in an infinite sense; it has no finite purpose but is an infinite jest with Emmeline. Therefore, the play does not end. Since the new love for Rinville is motivated only by a mistaken identity, it is altogether arbitrary to have the play terminate. Now, this is either a defect in the play or a merit. Here again the choice is easy. When the spectator thinks the play is over and that he has secured a good foothold, he suddenly discovers that what he is stepping on is not something firm but, so to speak, the end of a see-saw, and as he steps upon it he tilts the whole play up and over himself. An infinite possibility for confusion becomes manifest, because Emmeline, on the basis of her novel-education, is *übergreifende* [encroaching] upon every qualification of actuality. That the real Charles was not her Charles, she has learned, but she will soon convince herself, when Rinville becomes Rinville, that he is not that, either. Clothes make the man, and it is the romantic attire that she looks at. A new character who resembles Charles may put in his appearance—and so on. If the play is interpreted in this way, then her concluding lines are even profound; whereas in the other case, to me at least, it is impossible to find any meaning in them. She denotes, then, a change in movement. Previously, her illusion lay behind her in the past; now she will seek it in the world and in the future, for she has not given up the romantic Charles; but whether she travels forward or backward, her expedition in search of the first love is comparable to the journey one takes in search of health, which, as we say, is always one post house ahead.

It will also be found appropriate that Emmeline provides no elucidation of her theory, which could otherwise be rightfully demanded. If a man changes his belief, an explanation is asked for; if he is a theoretician, one has a right to ask for it. Emmeline is no lay person; she is well read; she has a theory. By virtue of this she has loved Charles; she has advanced the thesis that the first love is the true love. How will she make her way out of this? If she says that she has never loved Charles but that Rinville is her first love, then she contradicts herself, since she actually believes that Rinville is Charles. If she says: The first love was a childish game; the second love is the true love—then one readily perceives that she slips away only through a sophism. If she says: It has nothing to do with numbers, whether it is number one or number two; true love is something else entirely—then one must ask what attraction she has found in Rinville, since the alert observer has not discovered anything other than that he was so courteous as to impersonate Charles in order to please her. If the play is really over, then it is reasonable to ask for an explanation of all this. If, however, it is the poet's intention that the play be endless, then it is unreasonable to ask for an explanation from Emmeline, since she herself has not yet arrived at a clear understanding of these things.

I
232

The interest centers on Emmeline and her illusion. To bring about a collision is easy enough. I shall now place three characters, Charles excepted, in relation to one another for a moment and see how far we are able to go in this way. The father wants to see Emmeline married and cared for. She refuses every proposal. Finally, he suggests young Rinville, recommends him more warmly than anyone else, even pretends to have made up his mind. Emmeline admits that she loves another, namely, Charles. Rinville comes, receives the letter, hits upon the idea of passing himself off as Charles.

So far, the play could manage with three characters, and we would not lose one of the most comic situations in the play—

the recognition scene. Here I can promptly take the opportunity to show how Scribe has everything come out in the situation. Emmeline never airs her sentimentality in a monologue but always in dialogue and situation. We do not hear her rave in solitude about Charles. Not until the father presses her hard must she confess, which contributes to making her sentimentality appear in a better light. We do not hear her in a monologue repeating to herself her reminiscences of love; that takes place only in the situation. Her feelings tell her at once that Rinville is Charles, and now she goes through with him all the old memories. A more comic situation can scarcely be imagined. Rinville is a man of the world, and with the help of some very few particulars about Emmeline's state of mind he quickly sees that her cousin Charles is a very nebulous and mythical character. In her imagination, she has painted a picture of Charles that can match everyone, just as the faces painted by one of the several Wehmüllers[44] match every Hungarian. The portrait of Charles is just as abstract as that painter's *National-Gesichter* [national facial types]. This portrait, some broad formulas, not to forget a little verse,[45] are the result of her novel-education. Thus the imposture is made fairly easy for Rinville and is inordinately successful.

I
233

A comedy could be constructed around these three characters and their relation to one another. Rinville had perceived that, although as Rinville he stood in high favor with the father, it was nevertheless more important to please the daughter, whose beck and call everyone in Dervière's house obeyed. So he would go on passing himself off as Charles. In that way he would secure a foothold in the family and would have the opportunity to enthrall the girl for himself. He dared to count on Emmeline's control over her father, and when she had extorted her father's consent, he would so enthrall her that she would not hesitate again.

The defect in this plot is obvious. To bring his daughter to confess her secret, Dervière must have exerted great pressure on her, for otherwise she could just as well have confessed it the first time he spoke to her at all about marriage. Consequently, the father has had many reasons for desiring Rinville

as a son-in-law. The more zealous he is, the more tense the relationship becomes and the less probable it is that he will consent to her taking Charles. On the other hand, there must be a
dramatic probability of Emmeline's making a mistake. This
the poet has achieved by having Charles expected and has so
arranged things that she herself brings the news—and at the
very same moment the supposed Charles is there. Her father's
dilemma and eagerness to conceal Charles's arrival strengthen
even more her belief that it really is Charles.

Now I shall pick up the fourth character to show the excellence of the structure and how the one situation surpasses the
other in the comic.

Charles hurries home as the prodigal son in order to cast
himself into his uncle's arms, to get rid of his cousin, and to
have his debt paid. But to accomplish all this, he must be incognito. Just as almost every situation is an infinitely witty
mockery of Emmeline's sentimentality, so almost every situation is also an equally witty mockery of Charles's mystification. He arrives home full of confidence in his talent for mystifying. He believes that it is he who is carrying on the
intrigue, he who mystifies, and yet the spectator sees that the
intrigue was afoot before Charles appeared, for Rinville has already passed himself off as Charles. So the intrigue includes
Charles; Rinville's mystification forces Charles into his mystification, and yet Charles thinks that it originates with him.
Now the play is in full swing, a crisscrossing of situations almost mad in mischievousness. All four characters are mutually mystified. Emmeline wants to have Charles; Charles
wants to be rid of her; Charles the mystifier does not know
that Rinville is impersonating him and trying in every way to
enthrall the girl. Rinville is not mindful that Charles as Rinville is disparaging him in every way; Dervière prefers Rinville, but the person he prefers is Charles; Emmeline prefers
Charles, but the person she prefers is Rinville. Thus the whole
operation disintegrates into nonsense. What the play revolves
around is nothing; what comes out of the play is nothing.

Emmeline and Charles counteract each other, and yet they

I
234

both achieve the very opposite of what they wanted: she wins Rinville, and he, who wanted to mystify, betrays everything.

At every theater where *The First Love* is performed, I daresay that there is much laughter, but I think I may assure the theater-going public that there is never laughter enough. To recall an old story,[46] if I were to say of a person who laughed very heartily that either he is mad or he is reading or, perhaps closer to the truth, he is watching *The First Love*, I do not believe I am saying too much. Sometimes one laughs at something and regrets it at almost the same moment, but the situations in this play are such that the more one becomes absorbed in them the more ludicrous, the more lunatic, they prove to be. Since the situation in itself is extremely ludicrous, the witty lines themselves show up all the more superbly.

That Scribe can write lines is too well known to need saying. Admire him for it, but he is to be admired even more for the virtuosity with which he knows how to fit them into the situation so that the lines arise out of the situation and in turn elucidate it. If on a rare occasion one of his lines is a bit less correct, he immediately buys indulgence with its wittiness. It must be remembered, however, that I am not speaking of all the plays by Scribe but only of *The First Love*.

With the introduction of the fourth character, an utterly dramatic fermentation commences in the material. One need not fear that the material will lack life but rather that the life will become too giddy and disinclined to obey the reins. Every situation must have its time, and yet the play's inner agitation must be discerned in it. In conclusion, I shall now show that Scribe is a master at this by going through the particular situations. The reader must forgive me if I become a bit too prolix; it is due to my jealousy on Scribe's behalf and to my lack of confidence in the reader. My jealousy on Scribe's behalf whispers to me that he can never be adequately understood; my lack of confidence in the reader makes me believe that in certain passages he does not see everything. The comic is commonly thought to be more a matter of the moment than is the tragic. We laugh at it and forget it, whereas we often turn back to the tragic and become immersed in it. The comic and the tragic can be either in the lines or in the situation. Some people prefer to linger over the lines, to preserve them in memory, to return to them often. Others prefer to linger over the situation and to reconstruct it for memory. The latter are the contemplative natures. Nor will they deny that a comic situation has something just as satisfying to the intuition, indeed, that the comic, if, that is, it is artistically correct, tempts one to become absorbed in it more than in the tragic. I have heard and read many tragedies, but I can remember only a very particular line, and this, too, concerns me less; on the other hand, I can sit very quietly and become absorbed in the situation. I shall take an example. When Clärchen in Goethe's *Egmont* learns that Egmont is imprisoned, she goes to talk to the Hollanders to incite them to rebellion.[47] She is convinced that her eloquence will agitate them, and yet the Hollanders stand there just like Hollanders, unmoved, thinking only of evading her. I have never been able to remember one word of her lines, but to me the situation has been unforgettable from the first time I saw it. As a tragic situation, it is perfect. The beautiful young girl, poetic in her love for Egmont, animated by Egmont's whole being—one would think her able to move the whole world, but no Hollander understands her. The soul rests with infinite sadness in a situation like that, but it does rest—contemplation is completely in repose. The comic situation, to be sure, has a similar continuance for contemplation, but at the same time reflection is in motion within; and the more it discovers—the more infinite the comic situation becomes inside itself, so to speak—the dizzier one becomes, and yet one cannot stop staring into it.

I
236

The situations in *The First Love* are precisely of this kind. Their first impact already has a comic effect, but when they are reproduced for intuition, the laughter is quieter, yet the smile is more transfigured. One can scarcely keep from thinking about it again because it seems as if there is something even more ludicrous to come. This quiet enjoyment of the situation when one gazes into it, somewhat as a man smoking tobacco gazes into the smoke, is perhaps unfamiliar to some readers.

That is not Scribe's fault; if that is the case, the reader himself is at fault vis-à-vis Scribe.

Dervière puts strong pressure on Emmeline to marry Rinville; she admits her love for Charles, confesses the very innocent understanding on which she has lived with him, persuades her father with sweet words to write a letter to Rinville containing a refusal. The servant is sent with the letter; the family refuses to see anyone; Rinville appears. Instead of instructing the servants downstairs, Lapierre has put on his riding boots. As a consequence, Rinville is admitted. Here Scribe, instead of having Mr. Rinville appear and announce himself, has from the outset achieved a not unwitty situation that contains just as much mockery of Dervière as of Emmeline. Rinville has received the letter and reads it. Here again is a situation. The letter is not, as is usually the case, one that is read to draw attention solely to its contents. It is in Mr. Dervière's house that the future son-in-law receives the refusal. Rinville makes his plan; Dervière comes in; Rinville poses as Charles.

Here we have a thoroughly comic situation. There could, of course, be no guest more unwelcome to Mr. Dervière than Charles. Rinville has no inkling of this. His whole intrigue, then, turns out to be a very unfortunate idea. The situation is a consequence not of Rinville's posing as Charles but of his having made the most unfortunate choice he could make, even though he must of necessity believe that he has chosen the best. In the next place, the situation is a consequence of Dervière's having the excellent young Rinville in his house without suspecting it.

If one now pays attention to the lines, in and by themselves poetically fitting, one will again and again come to relish the situation in a higher potentiation, because in them the ludicrousness of the situation becomes more and more apparent. Rinville starts out in a sentimental and emotional style. Whether this is artistically correct could seem doubtful. He is not acquainted with Charles and therefore cannot know which way would work the most deceptively. But he does have some conception of Dervière's household and dares to deduce from

I
237

that the character of the rest of the members of this family. If the beginning is regarded as incorrect, it cannot be denied that Scribe compensates for this weakness with the wittiness of the lines and the suspicion aroused in the spectator about the real Charles. What is incorrect about it is that Rinville's first words[48] are so emotional that it seems as if he feared being not welcome, whereas Rinville, in accordance with what has preceded, ought to believe he would be. Therefore, Rinville probably resembles the real Charles a bit too much.

Despite his stupidity otherwise, the uncle seems to have appraised Charles rather well; he thinks that with money he can rid himself of Charles and offers him six thousand francs a year instead of the earlier three thousand. This makes us involuntarily think of the real Charles. He would have deemed himself very fortunate and would have gladly accepted this offer. The whole scene would have ended just as emotionally as it began; he would have thrown himself into his uncle's arms and cried out: Yes, the bonds of nature and blood are sacred. But that is not good enough for Rinville; he continues in the tone in which he began, just as Charles would have expressed himself if he had not needed the six thousand francs. The uncle now decides to approach him amicably and win him over; he candidly tells him the true state of affairs, gives a eulogy on Rinville, which because of the situation becomes a parody. The situation reaches its consummate peak when Dervière confides to Rinville that he has been trying to devise some scheme for making Emmeline aware of Rinville without awakening her suspicions.* The contrast is superb. Dervière wants to devise a scheme, and Rinville has already devised this scheme. Rinville's scheme shapes the situation, and in this situation Dervière's lines are heard. Dervière himself admits that he is not

I
238

* Perhaps an alert reader might think the play could properly end here. For what would be simpler than that Rinville would now identify himself to old Dervière and thus sail with a double wind, being taken for Charles by Emmeline and having Dervière know who he really is—Rinville. But we cannot blame Rinville for maintaining his incognito before Dervière, since just a few words from him are sufficient to show him that, if one is going to engage in an intrigue, one should never have Dervière a party to it.

very ingenious; his scheme is very simple, if Charles will only
be so kind as to leave. If this scheme were to succeed, Dervière
would have done just about the most stupid thing he could do.

Rinville, however, does not leave; on the other hand,
Emmeline enters with the news that a certain Mr. Zacharias[49]
wishes to speak with her father about Charles, who is expected
any moment. Her father's embarrassment betrays everything,
and she recognizes Charles. With this design, the poet gains a
great deal. The first person the pretended Charles encounters
is the uncle; he must be regarded as the one who is easiest to
deceive. He is stupid, uneasy because Charles is coming, and
therefore is all too disposed to believe the certainty of this distressing event; he would never dream that anyone could think
of passing himself off as Charles. As far as he is concerned,
then, Rinville can be rather daring. But with regard to Emmeline it would be all too daring a venture, for she is always a
good deal more sly. Moreover, it would be unseemly for Rinville to disregard decorum altogether, and no less unseemly
for Emmeline. Now, however, she has in her father's embarrassment the most reliable evidence that it is Charles. The recognition takes place in her father's presence, and Rinville does
not have to do anything; instead of guarding his role, he can
remain quite calm, for now Emmeline has had her eyes
opened. She almost compels Rinville to be Charles, and to that
extent he is without blame, and she herself is without blame,
since her father is the one who has compelled her to take him
for Charles. With this design, the poet has diffused over the
situation a certain delicacy that removes anything objectiona-
ble and makes it an innocent jest.

The situation is no less comic than the preceding one. Dervière is very nervous, and yet he himself has been the occasion
of it all and has helped Rinville over the difficulty of passing
himself off as Charles to Emmeline. The situation also forms
a parody of the preceding one; the uncle could not recognize
him right away, but she can. She accounts for it by a strange
feeling that she nevertheless cannot define, but it was as if a
voice whispered to her: There he is. (This voice is undoubtedly her father's voice,[50] which betrayed everything.) She ex-

plains it by sympathetic feelings that she can explain not to her
father but presumably to Aunt Judith. Who, now, is the more
sagacious: Dervière, who did not recognize him, who had no
inkling but who now recognizes him, or Emmeline, who recognized him immediately? The longer one watches it, the
more ludicrous it becomes. Here again the lines help the spectator to become absorbed in the ludicrousness of the situation.
After Emmeline says that she had such a strange feeling, Dervière follows with: "I for my part did not have the faintest inkling, and if he had not come right out with it and told me his
name . . . ."[51] Such a line is worth its weight in gold. It is so
natural and simple, and yet perhaps not one playwright in ten
would have the presence of mind and enough of an eye for the
situation to have it appear. An ordinary playwright would
have had all the attention center on Emmeline; indeed, in the
previous scene he would have ended with the recognition between Dervière and Charles. He would not have produced this
interaction, and yet this contributes to making the situation so
witty. It is comic that Emmeline immediately recognizes
Charles in Rinville, but Dervière's presence helps make the situation ironic. He stands there like an idiot who cannot comprehend a thing. And yet, which is easier to explain, that
Emmeline had an inkling of it or that Dervière did not?

Now comes the recognition scene, one of the most felicitous
situations imaginable. But the comic is by no means in Emmeline's mistaking Rinville for Charles. After all, mistaken iden-
tities have been seen often enough on the stage. A mistaken
identity depends on an actual resemblance, whether the individual is unaware of it or has himself brought it about. If that
were the case here, then Rinville, after having passed the test,
would have to have some idea of what Charles looked like, for
Charles, after all, would have to look somewhat like himself.
But this is by no means the case; any such conclusion would be
inane. The comic, then, is in Emmeline's recognizing in Rinville someone she does not know. The comic is not in her recognizing Rinville but in the indication thereby that she does
not know Charles. As it went with Rinville, so it would have
gone with any male under the same circumstances—she would

I
239

also have taken him for Charles. So, then, she mistakes Rinville for someone she does not know, and this is undeniably a
very comical kind of mistaken identity. Therefore, the situation has a high degree of probability that one would think very
difficult to achieve. Then Rinville is also a laughingstock, inasmuch as he believes he has advanced one step further. That
is, Emmeline's Charles is an "x," a *desideratur* [something
wanted], and here one clearly sees what otherwise happens in
secret, how such a little miss acts in forming an ideal for herself. And yet she has loved Charles for eight years and will
never love anyone else.

I
240

If one comes upon a very rare line that seems a little incorrect artistically, Scribe makes up for it with a witticism, for example, Rinville's line "God be praised, I was afraid I had gone
further than I wanted to."[52]

So Emmeline recognizes Charles, or, more accurately, she
discovers him. Whereas Rinville does not, as one would rather
have expected, come to find out what Charles looks like,
Emmeline does, and this is very deftly designed, since she did
not know it in advance. The situation is so lunatic that it is
doubtful whether one should say it is Rinville who deceives
Emmeline or Emmeline who deceives Rinville, for indeed he
is deceived in a way, inasmuch as he thought there actually
was a Charles. But amid all this the point, and it is inexhaustible, is that the scene is a recognition scene. The situation is
just as lunatic as would be the comment from a man who had
never seen his own image and then saw it in a mirror for the
first time: I recognize myself right away.

Emmeline and the supposed Charles have come to the point
in the recognition scene where they were interrupted by
Charles's departure; then the uncle interrupts them once more
by his presence. From Mr. Zacharias, he has learned something about Charles that is not especially pleasant. This now
recoils upon Rinville. The situation is essentially the same as
before, but we shall see what the poet has gained. Charles's ex-
ploits are of such a kind that if they were told bluntly they
would interfere with the total impact of the play. It is a matter
of giving them a certain light touch so that they do not have

too earnest an effect. The poet has achieved this in two ways. The first information we obtain about Charles's life is in scene nine. Here it recoils upon Rinville, who is passing himself off as Charles. The spectator's attention is led away from the details in the narrative to the mistaken identity; instead of thinking about the specific episodes, one thinks only of stupid antics in general and of Rinville's embarrassment and the comic situation in his being asked for more detailed information. Complete information comes from Charles's own mouth in scene sixteen, but one does not forget that Charles is passing himself off as Rinville. What would become far too earnest or too brash if Charles were telling it in his own person now comes to have a comic, almost hilarious, touch by his telling it in the person of Rinville, using his incognito to make it as fantastic as possible. If he told the story of his life in his own person, he would be required to have an awareness of it, and it would be regarded as exceedingly immoral if he did not have it. But now that he is telling everything in the person of someone else, indeed, in order to disturb Emmeline, we find the fantastic tinge of his narrative poetically correct in a double sense.

So Dervière has obtained information that the supposed Charles is unable to rectify or complete. Then Emmeline discovers "that he is no longer the same."[53] This is somewhat precipitous after she had been absolutely positive that he is completely the same old Charles. Here Emmeline is really in her element; whatever she says is all sheer prattle. The remark itself deserves closer scrutiny, because it provides the occasion for reveling all the more in the situation, which in all its ludicrousness is illuminated from a new angle. Just the sound of the words "the same" has the effect of a new titillating ingredient in the madness of the situation. One laughs involuntarily because one involuntarily asks: The same as who? The same as the one he appeared to be in the testing scene. One thinks, then, of how deficient that test was. The same as who? As Charles, whom she did not know? Moreover, when I say of a person that he is the same or that he is not the same, I can mean this in either an outer or inner sense, with respect either to his exterior or to his inner being. One would assume that the lat-

I
241

ter would be especially important to the lover. Now, however, it is discovered that the test was not concerned with this
at all, and yet he had been found to be the same. Quite by
chance, Emmeline begins to wonder whether Charles has not
changed with respect to his character, and now she discovers
that he is not the same. The denial that he is the same morally
also implies an affirmation that in all other respects he is the
same. Yet Emmeline explains herself more explicitly. She
looks for the change not in Charles's having become a wastrel
and maybe something even worse but in his no longer confiding everything to her as she was accustomed to having him do.
This must be one of her ideas from novels, which most likely
must be interpreted to mean that she was accustomed to prattle about everything to him, as in the recognition scene. That
Charles made a habit of confiding everything to her, she knew
not at all from experience but from novels, from which one
learns that lovers ought to have no secrets from each other. She
would not be upset if Charles were a runaway convict, if only
her erotic curiosity were satisfied by his confiding it to her.
The attempt Emmeline makes to convince herself of Charles's
identity through an observation of his character must then be
regarded as prattle, which in part illuminates her whole being,
in part all the rest of her prattle. Therefore, she abandons this
line of thought and obtains far more positive evidence that he
is not the same the very moment she discovers that he does not
have the ring. Now she needs no further testimony against
him. She admits, therefore, that he could have done anything
he wanted to, the wildest things, or, in other words, could
have changed as much as he wanted to—he would still have remained the same—but that he does not have the ring testifies
against him.[54] Emmeline is characterized by a singular kind of
abstract thinking. But what she retains after and through all
this abstraction is not so much Charles's unalloyed nature as
the ring. Emmeline is to be regarded as the jinni of the ring,
who obeys the one "who has the ring in his hand."[55]

Lapierre announces a new stranger. All are agreed that it
must be Rinville. Emmeline is ordered to spruce herself up and
bursts out, "How tiresome. Must I go and dress up for the

sake of a strange man I already know in advance I can't stand!"[56] With this line the spectator is made aware in due time of the irony in one of the situations to follow. On the whole, Emmeline can flatter herself that she is irony's darling. It favors her everywhere and afterward makes fun of her. She wants the supposed Charles to be a handsome young man, and irony favors her; Dervière cannot see it, and he appears the fool; Emmeline comes off with flying colors, and yet she is the biggest fool. She wants the supposed Rinville to be a man she cannot stand, although her father informs her that he is supposed to be an excellent young man. Here again irony favors her, and yet in such a way that it makes a fool of her.

Scene eleven is a monologue by Rinville.[57] It might seem better to have omitted this monologue, since the effect is an interference in every way. Insofar as it was all right to leave Rinville in possession of the field of battle and be the first one to receive Charles, his monologue could have been shortened. Nor would it then have been without effect. In the words of the poet, the monologue could then say, "Bravo! It is going superbly! Quarreling with the father, quarreling with the daughter—I certainly have to admit that it is an auspicious plan." This monologue would then contain a kind of objective reflection on the course of the play. If the poet considered it necessary to make the monologue a little longer in order to give Charles time to arrive, he could, after all, have Rinville make a little joke with himself about the fact that, in the long run, he perhaps would have been smarter to come in his own character, and about the drollery of thus being transmuted from badness to badness as new dispatches about Charles came in. Then it would have been best to have his deliberations be interrupted by Charles's lines spoken in the wings. As Scribe ends the monologue, we feel too strongly that the monologue is now over and that a new person must come. If Rinville's monologue were interrupted in this way, a new light would be thrown on Charles's incredible haste, on the importunity that always marks his behavior, also on the breathless foolishness with which the poet has so incomparably stamped his first lines.[58]

I
243

But this is less important. The main defect in this monologue is that Rinville's proposed procedure turns out to be just
talk, a merely feigned movement. Rinville explains that he is
no longer playing the role of Charles in fun. As a matter of
fact, it never was that; on the contrary, in the beginning he
himself gave three solid reasons for his desire to bring about
his marriage to Emmeline. Next he explains that he wants to
prevent Emmeline from confusing him with Charles; he
wants to convince himself that he is the one she loves and not
the recollection of Charles. This is of the utmost importance
for the whole play, because it is this that decides (as advanced
previously) whether it is in the finite sense moralizing or in the
infinite sense witty. His procedure, then, must aim at letting
his own (to him distinctive) charm become visible through the
person of Charles. But this does not happen, and if it had, the
play would have been entirely different.

For Emmeline, everything revolves around the ring; when
he shows up with it in scene fifteen,[59] she restores him to favor,
acknowledges him to be the same, etc. For the sake of the
overall impact of the play, Rinville generally must in no way
be interpreted as a poetic character, nor could this be demonstrated by the few sidelights that are given about him. He is a
man who has arrived at the age of discretion, who has solid
reasons for what he does. Now and then he appears in a comic
light, because it turns out that his solid reasons and his sensibleness would help him very little in capturing such a romantic
little gazelle as Miss Emmeline. Even if he were an absolutely
charming man and dangerous for a young girl's heart, he
would have no power over Emmeline; she is invulnerable.
The only way he can influence her is by coming in touch with
her fixed idea, that is, by means of the ring. But since the main
interest of the play would neutralize his actual charm, it is not
right to accentuate his charm, something the poet has never
done, either, except in this one monologue. In the scene where
Rinville has the most to do with Emmeline,[60] there can, of
course, be no mention at all of any opportunity for him to
manifest his personal charm. When a young miss has a liking
for a man to the degree that Emmeline has for him and she by

her own yielding continually provides him with every opportunity to slip into her heart, Rinville would indeed have to be
a total bungler if he could not come to her assistance. That this
scene can be assumed to be designed for the purpose of showing Rinville's charm is so far from the case that instead it seems
to place him in a somewhat comic light. Rinville is obviously
an intellectualist; in an earlier monologue he has been a bit
pompous, has let the spectator and also his friends in Paris understand that he is indeed the man to tame a little miss like this.
He does in fact succeed, it is true; but if his friends in Paris
could see how it happens, they would have no occasion to admire his talents. His good sense tells him it is feasible to pass
himself off as Charles. To that extent, he must be granted his
due. Now it has happened; now he must manifest his charm.
Now, one thinks, now he will have his hands full, and then it
turns out that he has nothing at all to do. The fleet-footed
Emmeline, hurrying back into childhood recollections, takes
Mr. Rinville along, and any man who is not a complete clod
would be able to emulate his masterstroke.

What has been advanced here about Rinville's character is,
in my opinion, of absolute importance for the whole play. In
it there must not be a single character, not a single stage situation, that could claim to survive the downfall that irony from
the outset prepares for each and all in it. When the curtain falls,
everything is forgotten, nothing but nothing remains, and that
is the only thing one sees; and the only thing one hears is a
laughter, like a sound of nature, that does not issue from any
one person but is the language of a world force, and this force
is irony.

Charles enters and meets Rinville. The fact that Charles, this
schemer, arrives too late, not only in relation to Mr. Zacharias
but above all in relation to the intrigue in the play, is the basis
of the comic in the situation. His lines, here as everywhere, are
masterly, simultaneously just as characteristic of him as they
are adapted to the situation. Rinville advises Charles to pass
himself off as Rinville. He has completely sketched the idea for
it when Charles, who cannot possibly allow anyone else to
teach him anything about mystification, interrupts him and

I
245

gives the impression that he himself is the one who is contriving the whole thing. Yet it promptly turns out that he is not a
man who thinks of the slightest thing; he would also have
overlooked the ring if Rinville had not called his attention to
it. Rinville obtains the ring.

Charles introduces himself to the family as Mr. Rinville,
and his reception is conditioned by that. Dervière finds him
younger and handsomer than Charles; Emmeline finds him repulsive. Both opinions are equally untrustworthy, and one
may very well presume to think that Emmeline has not even
felt it worth the trouble to look at him but knows it on the basis of an inspiration. So also with the father. Therefore, there
is in the situation a profound mockery of Charles, who presumably attributes this propitious reception to his cleverness
and expects that everything will be successful if he only maintains his incognito.

Now comes a monologue in which Emmeline consults her
heart and learns that she will never forget Charles but will
marry Rinville.

Rinville comes to take his leave and to deliver the ring. They
are reconciled again. We are already acquainted with these situations.

Now comes the most splendid situation in the whole play.
It has an aura about it, a transfiguration; it has a festive for-
mality of its own. One could almost wish to see Aunt Judith
in the background as a spirit who gazes down at her two pupils. Emmeline decides to confide in the supposed Rinville and
to disclose everything. This situation completely exposes
Emmeline and Charles. Emmeline's faithfulness becomes utter parody. Not for the whole world will she give him up; she
will not be frightened by fire or water; Charles's dilemma
grows by leaps and bounds, since he wants to be rid of her.
Such faithfulness is quite as it should be, for a little miss like
Emmeline is usually most faithful when the beloved wishes to
be rid of her.

Charles, who was positive that he was clever enough to rescue himself from this whole mess, since he had learned that
Mr. Zacharias had not divulged the worst,[61] now becomes the

one who betrays everything. The opportunity is much too tempting. He can become the troubadour of his own life and hopes in this way to be rid of his cousin. It was pointed out earlier that the situation gains lightness because Charles's excesses take on a comic touch. One has a vivid idea of his irresponsibility and his intellectual confusion but does not become indignant, as one would if he told everything the same way in his own person, and yet one suspects that he probably would do these things. One suspects this, but one does not hear it. But Charles does not accomplish a thing; he pleases only himself. Emmeline's faithfulness knows no limits. Finally Charles confesses that he is married. The deftness with which the poet is able to present Emmeline ironically is unbelievable. She hears that he is married, and she becomes furious. Some spectators might think the reason for her being incensed with Charles was that she now had learned about all his bad escapades. Not at all, dear friend! You misunderstand her. She will take Charles if only she can get him. But he is married. To be sure, she would find it more appropriate if he had not looked at any other girl during the eight years but had conscientiously contemplated the moon. She, however, knows how to ignore such things. Let him have seduced ten girls, she will take him, take him *à tout prix* [at any price], but if he is married she cannot take him. *Hinc illae lacrymae* [Hence these tears].[62] If that was not what the poet meant, he would have had Emmeline interrupt Charles somewhat earlier. Charles has explained that he has been subjected to many pursuits by the opposite sex, that he has had various amorous adventures, that perhaps sometimes he has gone too far in being charming.[63] She does not interrupt him, promises to do everything to reconcile him with her father and to have him herself, for it is very apparent that if she cannot have him (as soon as she hears that he is married), she is not one to forget to sound the alarm in camp. Charles begins the story about Pamela; she listens calmly. Now comes the terrible thing—that he is married;[64] there burst the kingdom of Norway.[65]

The profound irony in this situation arises from Emmeline's inviolable faithfulness, which at no price can give up Charles,

I
247

since it would cost her life, and also from Charles's mounting dilemma in not being able to be rid of her. The whole scene is like a licitation process whereby the ideal Charles is awarded to Emmeline. Finally, the whole thing ends at the point where it is clear that she cannot have Charles and Charles cannot run away from his stupid escapades.

Emmeline cries out; the father arrives on the scene, and he vows that he will never forgive Charles.

Now the supposed Charles enters. Emmeline has begged her father not to fly into a rage; she herself will hear his confession. Here as everywhere we must admire the poet's discretion. The scene is bound to remain ludicrous and the situation ironic when we see on the supposed Rinville the impression that the thundering denunciation should make on the supposed Charles—that is, the actual Charles has the pleasure of being personally present when he is being executed *in effigie*. It would have been a poetic injustice if the poet had assigned the delivery of this speech to Dervière. The uncle has been Charles's benefactor and has a legitimate claim not to be made a fool of in front of Charles. To be sure, the uncle is not as bright as the chit of a girl, but his benefactions over a series of years give him an advantage over Charles that is quite different from the rash promise of marriage he has given Emmeline. But since everything else that Emmeline says turns out to be prattle, the marriage vow included, it is quite in order that this philippic also turns out that way. Her old love for Charles is drivel, and her new love for Rinville is also drivel; her enthusiasm is drivel, and her rage is also drivel; her defiance is drivel, and her good resolve is also drivel.

Emmeline vents her wrath, and the supposed Rinville parodies the effect of her speech with the facial expressions and gestures of the actual Charles. Emmeline's admission that she actually has loved Charles can be regarded as the climactic point in this situation. The confusion here is complete. That is, the one she by her own admission has loved these eight years is Rinville, in whom through her feelings she had promptly recognized Charles, and who she later was convinced was not the same, but then in turn she soon recognized him by the ring.

In the end, the mistaken identity is cleared up. It turns out that she now has Rinville instead of Charles. With this the play is finished—or, more correctly, it is not finished. This I have already discussed earlier; here I shall once again merely elucidate in a few words what has been advanced. If it is the intention of the play to show that Emmeline has become a sensible girl who in choosing Rinville is making a sensible choice, then the accent of the whole play falls in the wrong place. In that case, we shall be less interested in finding out exactly in what sense Charles is a black sheep. What we do require, however, is enlightenment as to Rinville's charm. Just because Charles has become a rake, it by no means follows that Emmeline should choose Rinville, unless Scribe is derogated to a dramatic dabbler who respects the dramatic convention that every young miss ought to be married, and if she does not want to have the one she must then take the other. If, however, the play is understood as I have understood it, then the jest is altogether aimless, the wittiness infinite, the comedy a masterpiece.

The curtain falls; the play is over. Nothing remains but the large outline in which the fantastic *Schattenspiel* [shadow-play] of the situation, directed by irony, discloses itself and remains afterward for contemplation. The immediately actual situation is the unreal situation; behind it appears a new situation that is no less awry, and so on. One hears the dialogue in the situation, and when it is most sensible it turns out to be most lunatic, and just as the situation regresses, so also does the dialogue, more and more meaningless despite its sensibleness.

In order to enjoy the irony in this play contemplatively, one must not read it but see it; one must see it again and again, and if one is then so fortunate as to be contemporary with the four talented dramatic artists[66] in our theater who in every way contribute to disclosing and intimating to us the transparency of the situation, the enjoyment becomes greater and greater every time one sees it.

The lines in this play may be ever so witty—one will forget

them. Once one has seen the situations, they are unforgettable. Once they have become familiar, the next time one sees the play one will learn to appreciate the dramatic performance. I know of no higher praise for the performance of the play than to say that it is so consummately done that it makes one altogether unappreciative the first few times because what one has is the play, no more, no less. I know a young philosopher[67] who once discoursed for me on some part of the doctrine of essence. The whole thing was so easy, so simple, so natural, that when he was finished I almost shrugged my shoulders and said: Is that all there is to it? When I arrived home, I wanted to reproduce the logical progression, but it turned out I could not even begin. Then I perceived that other factors must also be involved. I felt how much his virtuosity and his superiority were above me; I felt it almost as mockery that he had done it so well that I became unappreciative. He was a philosophical artist, and the same thing happened to him that happens to all great artists, the good Lord included.

As it was with me and my philosophical friend, so it also was with me and the performance of *The First Love*. Now, however, that I have seen it performed again and again, also on other stages, only now am I properly appreciative of our dramatic artists. Therefore, if I were to show a stranger our stage, I would take him to the theater when this play is being performed, and then, assuming that he was familiar with this play, I would say to him: Look at Frydendahl;[68] now turn your eyes away, shut them, imagine him standing before you. Those pure, noble features, that aristocratic bearing—how can this be the object of laughter? Open your eyes and look at Frydendahl.

Look at Madame Heiberg;[69] lower your eyes, for perhaps Emmeline's charm might become dangerous to you; hear the girl's sentimental languishing in the voice, the childish and capricious insinuations, and even if you were dry and stiff like a bookkeeper, you still must smile. Open your eyes—how is it possible? Repeat these movements so quickly that they become almost simultaneous in the moment, and you will have a conception of what is being performed. Without irony, an artist can never sketch; a stage artist can produce it only by contradiction, for the essence of a sketch is superficiality. Where character portrayal is not required, the art is to transform oneself into a surface, which is a paradox for the stage performance, and it is given to only a few to solve it. A spontaneous comedian can never play Dervière, for he has no character. Emmeline's whole nature is a contradiction and therefore cannot be represented spontaneously. She must be charming, for otherwise the effect of the whole play is lost; she must not be charming, but extravagant, for otherwise the total effect of the whole play is lost in another sense.

Look at Phister;[70] it almost hurts when you fix your eyes upon the infinitely insipid stupidity that is stamped on his face. And yet this is not a spontaneous stupidity; his look still has an enthusiasm that in its foolishness calls to mind a past. No one is born with such a face; it has a history. I can remember that when I was little my nursemaid explained to me that we must not make distorted faces, and as a warning to me and other children she told a story of a man with a preposterous face, which served him right, for he had made distorted faces. It so happened, strange to say, that the wind changed and the man kept his preposterous face. Phister lets us see a preposterous face such as this; there is still a trace of the romantic grimaces, but when the wind changed it remained somewhat twisted. Phister's portrayal of Charles has less irony, but more whimsy. This is altogether proper, for the contradiction in his nature is not as conspicuous. He is not supposed to be Rinville except in the eyes of Dervière and Emmeline, who are equally biased although in different ways.

Look at Stage;[71] delight in this handsome, manly bearing, this cultured personality, this slight smile that betrays Rinville's fancied superiority over Dervière's fantastic family, and then see this representative of good sense swept along in the confusion that arises, like a rushing wind, from Emmeline's inane passion.

ROTATION OF CROPS

A VENTURE IN A THEORY
OF SOCIAL PRUDENCE

Χρεμύλος.
189. . . . . . . ἐστὶ πάντων πλησμονί.
190. ἔρωτος.

Καρίων.
ἄρτων.

Χρεμύλος.

μουσικῆς.

Καρίων.
                                        τραγημάτων.
Χρεμύλος.
191. τιμῇς.

Καρίων.
πλακούντων.

Χρεμύλος.

ἀνδραγαθίας.
Καρίων.
ἰσχάδων.
Χρεμύλος.
192. φιλοτιμίας.

Καρίων.
μάζης.

Χρεμύλος.
στρατηγίας.

Καρίων.
φακῆς.

See *Aristophanis Plutus*, v. 189 ff.[1]

CHREMYLOS.

. . . . . . an Allem bekommt man endlich Ueberdruss.

An Liebe [at last one has too much of everything. Of love],

KARION.

Semmel [rolls],

CHREMYLOS.

Musenkunst [the arts],

KARION.
und Zuckerwerk [and sweets].

CHREMYLOS.

An Ehre [Of honor],

KARION.

Kuchen [cakes],

CHREMYLOS.

Tapferkeit [bravery],

KARION.
und Feigenschnitt [and dried figs].

CHREMYLOS.

An Ruhm [Of fame],

KARION.
an Rührei [of scrambled eggs],

CHREMYLOS.
am Kommando [of authority],

KARION.
am Gemüs' [of vegetables].

See Aristophanes, *Plutos*, in Droysen's translation.[2]

People with experience maintain that proceeding from a basic principle is supposed to be very reasonable; I yield to them and proceed from the basic principle that all people are boring. Or is there anyone who would be boring enough to contradict me in this regard? This basic principle has to the highest degree the repelling force always required in the negative, which is actually the principle of motion.[3] It is not merely repelling but infinitely repulsive, and whoever has the basic principle behind him must necessarily have infinite momentum for making discoveries. If, then, my thesis is true, a person needs only to ponder how corrupting boredom is for people, tempering his reflections more or less according to his desire to diminish or increase his *impetus*, and if he wants to press the speed of the motion to the highest point, almost with danger to the locomotive, he needs only to say to himself: Boredom is the root of all evil. It is very curious that boredom, which itself has such a calm and sedate nature, can have such a capacity to initiate motion. The effect that boredom brings about is absolutely magical, but this effect is one not of attraction but of repulsion.

How corrupting boredom is, everyone recognizes also with regard to children. As long as children are having a good time, they are always good. This can be said in the strictest sense, for if they at times become unmanageable even while playing, it is really because they are beginning to be bored; boredom is already coming on, but in a different way. Therefore, when selecting a nursemaid, one always considers essentially not only that she is sober, trustworthy, and good-natured but also takes into esthetic consideration whether she knows how to entertain children. Even if she had all the other excellent virtues, one would not hesitate to give her the sack if she lacked this qualification. Here, indeed, the principle is clearly acknowledged, but things go on so curiously in the world, habit and boredom have gained the upper hand to such a degree, that justice is done to esthetics only in the conduct of the nursemaid. It would be quite impossible to prevail if one wanted to demand a divorce because one's wife is boring, or demand that a king be dethroned because he is boring to behold, or that a clergyman be exiled because he is boring to listen to, or that a cabinet minister be dismissed or a journalist be executed because he is frightfully boring.

Since boredom advances and boredom is the root of all evil, no wonder, then, that the world goes backwards, that evil spreads. This can be traced back to the very beginning of the world. The gods were bored; therefore they created human beings. Adam was bored because he was alone; therefore Eve was created.[4] Since that moment, boredom entered the world and grew in quantity in exact proportion to the growth of population. Adam was bored alone; then Adam and Eve were bored together; then Adam and Eve and Cain and Abel were bored *en famille.* After that, the population of the world increased and the nations were bored *en masse.* To amuse themselves, they hit upon the notion of building a tower so high that it would reach the sky.[5] This notion is just as boring as the tower was high and is a terrible demonstration of how boredom had gained the upper hand. Then they were dispersed around the world, just as people now travel abroad, but they continued to be bored. And what consequences this boredom had: humankind stood tall and fell far, first through Eve, then from the Babylonian tower.

On the other hand, what was it that delayed the fall of Rome? It was *panis* [bread] and *circenses* [games].[6] What is being done in our day? Is consideration being given to any means of amusement? On the contrary, our doom is being expedited. There is the idea of convening a consultative assembly. Can anything more boring be imagined, both for the honorable delegates as well as for one who will read and hear about them? The country's financial situation is to be improved by economizing. Can anything more boring be imagined? [7]Instead of increasing the debt, they want to pay it off in installments. From what I know about the political situation, it would be easy for Denmark to borrow fifteen million rix-dollars. Why does no one think of this? Now and then we hear that someone is a genius and does not pay his debts; why should a nation not do the same, provided there is agreement? Borrow fifteen million; use it not to pay off our debts but for public entertainment. Let us celebrate the millennium with fun and games. Just as there currently are boxes everywhere for contributions of money, there should be bowls everywhere filled with money. Everything would be free: the theater would be free, prostitutes would be free, rides to Deer Park[8] would be free, funerals would be free, one's funeral eulogy would be free. I say "free," for if money is always available, everything is free in a way.

No one would be allowed to own any property. An exception should be made only for me. I shall set aside for myself one hundred rix-dollars a day deposited in a London bank, partly because I cannot manage on less, partly because I am the one who provided the idea, and finally because no one knows if I will not be able to think up a new idea when the fifteen million is exhausted.

[9]What would be the result of this prosperity? All the great would stream to Copenhagen: the greatest artists, actors, and dancers. Copenhagen would become another Athens. What would be the result? All the wealthy would settle in this city. Among others, the emperor of Persia and the king of England would undoubtedly also come here. Here is my second idea: kidnap the emperor. Someone may say that then there would be a revolution in Persia, a new emperor placed on the throne—it has frequently happened before—and the price of the old emperor would slump. In that case, my idea is that we should sell him to the Turks. They will undoubtedly know how to make money out of him.

In addition, there is yet another circumstance that our politicians seem to ignore entirely. Denmark holds the balance of power in Europe. A more propitious position is inconceivable. This I know from my own experience. I once held the balance of power in a family. I could do as I wished. I never suffered, but the others always did.

O may my words penetrate your ears, you who are in high places to counsel and control, you king's men and men of the people, you wise and sensible citizens of all classes! You just watch out! Old Denmark is foundering—it is a matter of life and death; it is foundering on boredom, which is the most fatal of all. In olden days, whoever eulogized the deceased most handsomely became the king.[10] In our age, the king ought to be the one who delivers the best witticism and the crown prince the one who provides the occasion for the best witticism.

But how you do carry me away, beautiful stirring enthusiasm! Should I raise my voice this way in order to address my contemporaries, to initiate them into my wisdom? Not at all, for my wisdom is really not *zum Gebrauch für Jedermann* [for use by everyman], and it is always most prudent to be silent about rules of prudence. Therefore, I want no followers, but if someone were standing beside my deathbed and if I were sure it was all over for me, then in a fit of philanthropic delirium I might whisper my doctrine into his ear, not quite sure whether I would have done him a favor or not.[11] There is so much talk about man's being a social animal,[12] but basically he is a beast of prey, something that can be ascertained not only by looking at his teeth. Therefore, all this chatter about sociality and community is partly inherited hypocrisy and partly studied perfidy.

All human beings, then, are boring. The very word indicates the possibility of a classification. The word "boring" can designate just as well a person who bores others as someone who bores himself. Those who bore others are the plebians, the crowd, the endless train of humanity in general; those who bore themselves are the chosen ones, the nobility. How remarkable it is that those who do not bore themselves generally bore others; those, however, who bore themselves entertain others. Generally, those who do not bore themselves are busy in the world in one way or another, but for that very reason they are, of all people, the most boring of all, the most unbearable. [13]Certainly this class of animals is not the fruit of man's appetite and woman's desire. Like all lower classes of animals, it is distinguished by a high level of fecundity and propagates beyond belief. It is incomprehensible, too, that nature should need nine months to produce such creatures, which presumably could rather be produced by the score. The other class of human beings, the superior ones, are those who bore themselves. As noted above, they generally amuse others—at times in a certain external way the masses, in a deeper sense their co-initiates. The more thoroughly they bore themselves, the more potent the medium of diversion they offer others, also when the boredom reaches its maximum, since they either die of boredom (the passive category) or shoot themselves out of curiosity (the active category).

I
261

Idleness, we are accustomed to say, is the root of all evil. To prevent this evil, work is recommended. But it is just as easy to see from the dreaded occasion as from the recommended remedy that this whole view is of very plebian extraction. Idleness as such is by no means a root of evil; on the contrary, it is a truly divine life, if one is not bored. To be sure, idleness may be the occasion of losing one's property etc., but the noble nature does not fear such things but does indeed fear being bored. The Olympian gods were not bored; happy they lived in happy idleness. A female beauty who neither sews nor spins nor irons nor reads nor plays an instrument is happy in idleness, for she is not bored. Idleness, then, is so far from being the root of evil that it is rather the true good. Boredom is the root of evil; it is that which must be held off. Idleness is not the evil; indeed, it may be said that everyone who lacks a sense for it thereby shows that he has not raised himself to the human level. There is an indefatigable activity that shuts a person out of the world of spirit and places him in a class with the animals, which instinctively must always be in motion. There are people who have an extraordinary talent for transforming everything into a business operation, whose whole life is a business operation, who fall in love and are married, hear a joke, and admire a work of art with the same businesslike zeal with which they work at the office. The Latin proverb *otium est pulvinar diaboli* [idleness is the devil's pillow] is quite correct, but the devil does not find time to lay his head on this pillow if one is not bored. But since people believe that it is man's destiny to work, the antithesis idleness/work is correct. I assume that it is man's destiny to amuse himself, and therefore my antithesis is no less correct.

Boredom is the demonic pantheism. It becomes evil itself if one continues in it as such; as soon as it is annulled, however, it is the true pantheism. But it is annulled only by amusing oneself—*ergo*, one ought to amuse oneself. To say that it is annulled by working betrays a lack of clarity, for idleness can certainly be canceled by work, since this is its opposite, but boredom cannot, as is seen in the fact that the busiest workers of all, those whirring insects with their bustling buzzing, are the most boring of all, and if they are not bored, it is because they do not know what boredom is—but then the boredom is not annulled.

Boredom is partly an immediate genius, partly an acquired immediacy. [14]On the whole, the English nation is the model nation. The true genius of indolence is seldom encountered; it is not found in nature; it belongs to the world of spirit. At times one meets an English tourist who is an incarnation of this genius, a heavy, inert woodchuck whose total resource of language consists of a single monosyllable, an interjection[15] with which he indicates his highest admiration and his deepest indifference, for admiration and indifference have become undifferentiated in the unity of boredom. No nation other than the English produces such oddities of nature; every individual belonging to another nation will always be a bit more lively, not so altogether stillborn. The only analogy I know is the apostle of empty enthusiasm, who likewise travels through life on an interjection, people who make a profession of being enthusiastic everywhere, who are present everywhere and, no matter whether what happens is something significant or insignificant, shout: Oh! or Ah! because the difference between what is important and unimportant is undifferentiated in the emptiness of blind, clamorous enthusiasm.

The boredom that comes later[16] is usually a fruit of a misguided diversion. It seems doubtful that a remedy against boredom can give rise to boredom, but it can give rise to boredom only insofar as it is used incorrectly. A mistaken, generally eccentric diversion has boredom within itself, and thus it works its way up and manifests itself as immediacy. Just as a distinction is made between blind staggers and mad staggers in horses, but both kinds are called staggers, so also a distinction can be made between two kinds of boredom that nevertheless are both joined in the category of boredom.

Pantheism ordinarily implies the qualification of fullness; with boredom it is the reverse: it is built upon emptiness, but for this very reason it is a pantheistic qualification. [17]Boredom rests upon the nothing that interlaces existence [*Tilværelsen*]; its dizziness is infinite, like that which comes from looking down into a bottomless abyss. That the eccentric diversion is based upon boredom is seen also in the fact that the diversion sounds without resonance, simply because in nothing there is not even enough to make an echo possible.

Now, if boredom, as discussed above, is the root of all evil, what then is more natural than to seek to conquer it? But here, as everywhere, it is primarily a matter of calm deliberation, lest, demonically possessed by boredom in an attempt to escape it, one works one's way into it. All who are bored cry out for change. In this, I totally agree with them, except that it is a question of acting according to principle.

My deviation from popular opinion is adequately expressed by the phrase "rotation of crops." There might seem to be an ambiguity in this phrase, and if I were to find room in this phrase for a designation of the ordinary method I would have to say that rotation of crops consists in continually changing the soil. But the farmer does not use the expression in this way. For a moment, however, I will use it in this way to discuss the rotation of crops that depends upon the boundless infinity of change, its extensive dimension.

This rotation of crops is the vulgar, inartistic rotation and is based on an illusion. [18]One is weary of living in the country and moves to the city; one is weary of one's native land and goes abroad; one is *europamüde* [weary of Europe] and goes to America etc.; one indulges in the fanatical hope of an endless journey from star to star. Or there is another direction, but still extensive. One is weary of eating on porcelain and eats on silver; wearying of that, one eats on gold; one burns down half of Rome[19] in order to visualize the Trojan conflagration. This method cancels itself and is the spurious infinity.[20] What, after all, did Nero achieve? No, then the emperor Antoninus was wiser; he says: ἀναβιῶναί σοι ἔξεστιν ἴδε πάλιν τὰ πράγματα, ὡς ἑώρας· ἐν τούτῳ γὰρ τὸ ἀναβιῶναι (Βιβλίον Z., 6.) [You can begin a new life. Only see things afresh as you used to see them. In this consists the new life (Book VII, 2)].[21]

The method I propose does not consist in changing the soil but, like proper crop rotation, consists in changing the method of cultivation and the kinds of crops. Here at once is the principle of limitation, the sole saving principle in the world. The more a person limits himself, the more resourceful he becomes. A solitary prisoner for life is extremely resourceful; to him a spider can be a source of great amusement. Think of our school days; we were at an age when there was no esthetic consideration in the choosing of our teachers, and therefore they were often very boring—how resourceful we were then![22] What fun we had catching a fly, keeping it prisoner under a nutshell, and watching it run around with it! What delight in cutting a hole in the desk, confining a fly in it, and peeking at it through a piece of paper! How entertaining it can be to listen to the monotonous dripping from the roof! [23]What a meticulous observer one becomes, detecting every little sound or movement. Here is the extreme boundary of that principle that seeks relief not through extensity but through intensity.

The more resourceful one can be in changing the method of cultivation, the better, but every particular change still falls under the universal rule of the relation between *recollecting* and *forgetting*. It is in these two currents that all life moves, and therefore it is a matter of having them properly under one's control. Not until hope has been thrown overboard does one begin to live artistically; as long as a person hopes, he cannot limit himself. It is indeed beautiful to see a person put out to sea with the fair wind of hope; one may utilize the chance to let oneself be towed along, but one ought never have it on board one's craft, least of all as pilot, for it is an untrustworthy ship-master. For this reason, too, hope was one of Prometheus's dubious gifts; instead of giving human beings the foreknowledge of the immortals, he gave them hope.[24]

[25]To forget—this is the desire of all people, and when they encounter something unpleasant, they always say: If only I could forget! But to forget is an art that must be practiced in advance. To be able to forget always depends upon how one remembers, but how one remembers depends upon how one experiences actuality. The person who runs aground with the speed of hope will recollect in such a way that he will be unable to forget. Thus *nil admirari* [marvel at nothing][26] is the proper wisdom of life. No part of life ought to have so much meaning for a person that he cannot forget it any moment he wants to; on the other hand, every single part of life ought to have so much meaning for a person that he can remember it at any moment. The age that remembers best is also the most forgetful: namely, childhood. The more poetically one remembers, the more easily one forgets, for to remember poetically is actually only an expression for forgetting. When I remember poetically, my experience has already undergone the change of having lost everything painful. In order to be able to recollect in this way, one must be very much aware of how one lives, especially of how one enjoys. If one enjoys indiscriminately to the very end, if one continually takes the utmost that enjoyment can give, one will be unable either to recollect or to forget. That is, one has nothing else to recollect than a satiation that one only wishes to forget but that now torments with an involuntary recollection. Therefore, if a person notices that enjoyment or a part of life is carrying him away too forcefully, he stops for a moment and recollects. There is no better way to give a distaste for going on too long. From the beginning, one curbs the enjoyment and does not hoist full sail for any decision; one indulges with a certain mistrust. Only then is it possible to give the lie to the proverb that says that one cannot eat one's cake and have it, too. It is true that the police forbid carrying secret weapons, and yet there is no weapon as dangerous as the art of being able to recollect. It is

I
265

a singular feeling when in the midst of enjoyment one looks at it in order to recollect it.

When an individual has perfected himself in the art of forgetting and the art of recollecting in this way, he is then able to play shuttlecock with all existence.

A person's resiliency can actually be measured by his power to forget. He who cannot forget will never amount to much. Whether or not a Lethe[27] wells up anywhere, I do not know, but this I do know—that this art can be developed. But it by no means consists in the traceless disappearance of the particular impression, because forgetfulness is not identical with the art of being able to forget. What little understanding people generally have of this art is readily seen, for they usually want to forget only the unpleasant, not the pleasant. This betrays a total one-sidedness. Indeed, forgetting is the right expression for the proper assimilation that reduces experience to a sounding board. The reason nature is so great is that it has forgotten that it was chaos, but this thought can appear at any time. Since forgetting is usually thought of in relation to the unpleasant, it is generally conceived of as a wild force that stifles. But forgetting, on the contrary, is a quiet pursuit, and it ought to be related to the pleasant just as much as to the unpleasant. Furthermore, the pleasant as a bygone, specifically as a bygone, has an intrinsic unpleasantness with which it can awaken a sense of loss; this unpleasantness is canceled by forgetting. The unpleasant has a sting—everyone admits that. This, too, is removed by forgetting. But if one behaves as many do who dabble in the art of forgetting, who brush the unpleasant away entirely, one will soon see what good that is. In an unguarded moment, it often surprises a person with the full force of the sudden. This is completely at odds with the well-ordered pattern in an intelligent head. No misfortune, no adversity is so unfriendly, so deaf that it cannot be flattered a little; even Cerberus[28] accepted honey cakes, and it is not only young maidens one beguiles. One talks around it and thereby deprives it of its sharpness and by no means wishes to forget it— but forgets it in order to recollect it. Indeed, even with reminiscences of such a kind that one would think eternal forget-

fulness would be the only means against them, one allows
oneself such cunning, and the fakery is successful for the adept. Forgetting is the scissors with which one snips away what
cannot be used, but, please note, under the maximal supervi-
sion of recollection. In this way, forgetting and recollecting
are identical, and the artistically achieved identity is the Archimedean point with which one lifts the whole world.[29] When
we speak of writing something in the book of oblivion, we are
indeed suggesting that it is forgotten and yet at the same time
is preserved.

[30]The art of recollecting and forgetting will also prevent a
person from foundering in any particular relationship in life—
and assures him complete suspension.

[31]Guard, then, against *friendship*. How is *a friend* defined? A
friend is not what philosophy calls the necessary other[32] but
the superfluous third. What are the rituals of friendship? One
drinks *dus*;[33] one opens an artery, mingles one's blood with the
friend's. Just when this moment arrives is difficult to determine, but it proclaims itself in a mysterious way; one feels it
and can no longer say *De* to the other. Once this feeling is present, it can never turn out that one has made a mistake such as
Gert Westphaler made when he drank *dus* with the execu-
tioner.[34] —What are the sure signs of friendship? Antiquity
answers: *idem velle, idem nolle, ea demum firma amicitia* [agree-
ment in likes and dislikes, this and this only is what constitutes
true friendship][35] —and is also extremely boring. What is the
meaning of friendship? Mutual assistance with counsel and action. Two friends form a close alliance in order to be everything to each other, even though no human being can be anything for another human being except to be in his way. [36]Well,
we can help each other with money, help each other into and
out of our coats, be each other's humble servants, gather for a
sincere New Year's congratulation, also for weddings, births,
and funerals.

[37]But just because one stays clear of friendship, one will not
for that reason live without contact with people. On the contrary, these relationships can take a deeper turn now and then,
provided that one always—even though keeping the same

I
267

pace for a time—has enough reserve speed to run away from them. It may be thought that such conduct leaves unpleasant recollections, that the unpleasantness consists in the diminishing of a relationship from having been something to being nothing. This, however, is a misunderstanding. The unpleasantness is indeed a piquant ingredient in the perverseness of life. Moreover, the same relationship can regain significance in another way. One should be careful never to run aground and to that end always to have forgetting in mind. The experienced farmer lets his land lie fallow now and then; the theory of social prudence recommends the same thing. Everything will surely come again but in a different way; what has once been taken into the rotation process remains there but is varied by the method of cultivation. Therefore, one quite consistently hopes to meet one's old friends and acquaintances in a better world but does not share the crowd's fear that they may have changed so much that one could not recognize them again. One fears, instead, that they may be altogether unchanged. It is unbelievable what even the most insignificant person can gain by such sensible cultivation.

[38]Never become involved in *marriage*. Married people pledge love for each other throughout eternity. [39]Well, now, that is easy enough but does not mean very much, for if one is finished with time one is probably finished with eternity. If, instead of saying "throughout eternity," the couple would say "until Easter, until next May Day," then what they say would make some sense, for then they would be saying something and also something they perhaps could carry out. What happens in marriage? First, one of them detects after a short time that something is wrong, and then the other one complains and screams: Faithlessness! Faithlessness! After a while, the other one comes to the same conclusion and a state of neutrality is inaugurated through a balancing of accounts by mutual faithlessness, to their common satisfaction and gratification. But it is too late now, anyway, because a divorce involves all kinds of huge problems.

Since marriage is like that, it is not strange that attempts are made in many ways to shore it up with moral props. If a man wants to be separated from his wife, the cry goes up: He is a mean fellow, a scoundrel, etc. How ridiculous, and what an indirect assault upon marriage! Either marriage has intrinsic reality [*Realitet*], and then he is adequately punished by losing it, or it has no reality, and then it is unreasonable to vilify him because he is wiser than others. If someone became weary of his money and threw it out the window, no one would say he is a mean fellow, for either money has reality, and then he is adequately punished by not having it anymore, or it has no reality, and then, of course, he is indeed wise.

[40]One must always guard against contracting a life relationship by which one can become many. That is why even friendship is dangerous, marriage even more so. They do say that marriage partners become one, but this is very obscure and mysterious talk. If an individual is many, he has lost his freedom and cannot order his riding boots when he wishes, cannot knock about according to whim. If he has a wife, it is difficult; if he has a wife and perhaps children, it is formidable; if he has a wife and children, it is impossible. Admittedly, there is the example of a gypsy woman who carried her husband on her back[41] throughout life, but for one thing this is a great rarity and, for another, it is very tiring in the long run—for the husband. Moreover, through marriage one falls into a very deadly continuity with custom, and custom is like the wind and weather, something completely indeterminable. To the best of my knowledge, it is the custom in Japan for the husbands also to be confined during childbirth. Perhaps the time is coming when Europe will import the customs of foreign lands.

[42]Even friendship is dangerous; marriage is still more dangerous, for the woman is and will be the man's ruination as soon as he contracts a continuing relationship with her. Take a young man, spirited as an Arabian horse; let him marry and he is lost. At the outset, the woman is proud, then she is weak, then she swoons, then he swoons, then the whole family swoons. A woman's love is only pretense and weakness.

Just because one does not become involved in marriage, one's life need not for that reason be devoid of the erotic. The erotic, too, ought to have infinity—but a poetic infinity that can just as well be limited to one hour as to a month. When two people fall in love with each other and sense that they are destined for each other, it is a question of having the courage to break it off, for by continuing there is only everything to lose, nothing to gain. It seems to be a paradox, and indeed it is, for the feelings, not for the understanding. In this domain it is primarily a matter of being able to use moods; if a person can do that, an inexhaustible variation of combinations can be achieved.

Never take any *official post*. If one does that, one becomes just a plain John Anyman, a tiny little cog in the machine of the body politic. The individual ceases to be himself the manager of the operation, and then theories can be of little help. One acquires a title, and implicit in that are all the consequences of sin and evil. The law under which one slaves is equally boring no matter whether advancement is swift or slow. A title can never be disposed of; it would take a criminal act for that, which would incur a public whipping, and even then one cannot be sure of not being pardoned by royal decree and acquiring the title again.

Even though one stays clear of official posts, one should nevertheless not be inactive but attach great importance to all the pursuits that are compatible with aimlessness; all kinds of unprofitable pursuits may be carried on. Yet in this regard one ought to develop not so much extensively as intensively and, although mature in years, demonstrate the validity of the old saying: It doesn't take much to amuse a child.

Just as one varies the soil somewhat, in accordance with the theory of social prudence (for if one were to live in relation to only one person, rotation of crops would turn out badly, as would be the case if a farmer had only one acre of land and therefore could never let it lie fallow, something that is extremely important), so also must one continually vary oneself, and this is the real secret. To that end, it is essential to have control over one's moods. To have them under control in the sense that one can produce them at will is an impossibility, but prudence teaches us to utilize the moment. Just as an experienced sailor always scans the sea and detects a squall far in advance, so one should always detect a mood a little in advance. Before entering into a mood, one should know its effect on oneself and its probable effect on others. The first strokes are for the purpose of evoking pure tones and seeing what is inside a person; later come the intermediate tones. The more practice one has, the more one is convinced that there is often much in a person that was never imagined. When sentimental people, who as such are very boring, become peevish, they are often amusing. [43]Teasing in particular is an excellent means of exploration.

Arbitrariness is the whole secret. It is popularly believed that there is no art to being arbitrary, and yet it takes profound study to be arbitrary in such a way that a person does not himself run wild in it but himself has pleasure from it. One does not enjoy the immediate object but something else that one arbitrarily introduces. One sees the middle of a play; one reads the third section of a book. One thereby has enjoyment quite different from what the author so kindly intended. One enjoys something totally accidental; one considers the whole of existence [*Tilværelse*] from this standpoint; one lets its reality run aground on this. I shall give an example. There was a man whose chatter I was obliged to listen to because of the circumstances. On every occasion, he was ready with a little philosophical lecture that was extremely boring. On the verge of despair, I suddenly discovered that the man perspired exceptionally much when he spoke. This perspiration now absorbed my attention. I watched how the pearls of perspiration collected on his forehead, then united in a rivulet, slid down his nose, and ended in a quivering globule that remained suspended at the end of his nose. From that moment on, everything was changed; I could even have the delight of encouraging him to commence his philosophical instruction just in order to watch the perspiration on his brow and on his nose.

Baggesen[44] tells somewhere that a certain man is no doubt a very honest fellow but that he has one thing against him: nothing rhymes with his name. It is very advantageous to let the realities of life be undifferentiated in an arbitrary interest like that. Something accidental is made into the absolute and as

I
271

such into an object of absolute admiration. This is especially effective when the feelings are in motion. For many people, this method is an excellent means of stimulation. Everything in life is regarded as a wager etc. The more consistently a person knows how to sustain his arbitrariness, the more amusing the combinations become. The degree of consistency always makes manifest whether a person is an artist or a bungler, for up to a point everyone does the same. [45]The eye with which one sees actuality must be changed continually. The Neoplatonists assumed that people who fell short of perfection on earth became after death more or less perfect animals according to their merits; those who, for example, had practiced social virtues on a minor scale (punctilious people) turned into social creatures—for example, bees. Such a view of life, which here in this world sees all human beings transformed into animals or plants (Plotinus also believed this—that some were changed into plants)[46] offers a rich multiplicity of variation. The artist Tischbein[47] has attempted to idealize every human being as an animal. His method has the defect that it is too serious and tries to discover an actual resemblance.

The accidental outside a person corresponds to the arbitrariness within him. Therefore he always ought to have his eyes open for the accidental, always ought to be *expeditus* [ready] if something should come up. The so-called social pleasures for which we prepare ourselves a week or a fortnight in advance are of little significance, [48]whereas even the most insignificant thing can accidentally become a rich material for amusement. To go into detail here is not feasible—no theory can reach that far. Even the most elaborate theory is merely poverty compared with what genius in its ubiquity easily discovers.

THE SEDUCER'S DIARY[1]

Sua passion' predominante
e la giovin principiante
[His predominant passion
is the youthful beginner].[2]
Don Giovanni, aria no. 4

Hide from myself, I cannot; I can hardly control the anxiety
that grips me at this moment when I decide in my own interest
to make an accurate clean copy of the hurried transcript I was
able to obtain at the time only in the greatest haste and with
great uneasiness. The episode confronts me just as disquiet-
ingly and just as reproachfully as it did then. Contrary to his
usual practice, he had not locked his desk; therefore everything
in it was at my disposal. But there is no use in wanting to gloss
over my conduct by reminding myself that I had not opened
any of the drawers. One drawer stood open. In it was a mass
of loose papers, and on top of them lay a large quarto volume,
exquisitely bound. On the upper side was placed a vignette of
white paper on which he had written in his own hand: *Com-
mentarius perpetuus* [Running commentary] *no. 4*.[3] There is no
use, however, in trying to delude myself into thinking that if
the top of the book had not been turned up, and if the striking
title had not tempted me, I would not have fallen into temptation or at least would have offered resistance.

The title itself was curious, yet more because of the items
around it than the title itself. From a hasty glance at the loose
papers, I learned that they contained impressions of erotic situations, intimations of some relationship or other, drafts of
letters of a particular kind, with which I later became familiar
in their artistically completed, calculated nonchalance. Now,
having seen through the contriving heart of that corrupt man,
when I recall the situation, now, with my eyes opened to all
the cunning, so to speak, when I approach that drawer, I feel
the same way a policeman must feel when he enters a forger's
room, goes through his things, and finds a mass of loose papers in a drawer, specimens of handwriting; on one there is a
little decorative design, on another a monogram, on a third a
line of reversed writing. It readily shows him that he is on the
right track, and his delight over this is mixed with a certain ad-

miration for the effort and diligence obvious here. Since I am
less accustomed to detecting crimes and am not armed with a
policeman's badge, I would have reacted differently. I would
have felt the double weight of the truth that I was on an unlawful path. At that time I lacked ideas as much as I lacked words,
which is usually the case. One is awestruck by an impression
until reflection once again breaks loose and with multifarious
deft movements talks and insinuates its way to terms with the
unknown stranger. The more developed reflection is, the
more quickly it can collect itself; like a passport officer checking foreign travelers, it comes to be so familiar with the sight
of the most fabulous characters that it is not easily taken aback.
Although my reflection is indeed very highly developed, I
nevertheless was greatly amazed at first. I recall so well that I
turned pale, that I was close to fainting, and therefore how
anxious I was. Suppose that he had come home, had found me
in a swoon with the drawer in my hand—a bad conscience can
indeed make life interesting.[4]

In itself, the title of the book did not startle me. I took it to
be a collection of excerpts, which to me seemed quite natural,
since I knew that he had always taken to his studies with zeal.
But it contained something altogether different. It was neither
more nor less than a diary, painstakingly kept. On the basis of
my former acquaintance with him, I did not consider that his
life was in great need of a commentary, but according to the
insight I now had, I do not deny that the title was chosen with
great discernment and much understanding, with truly esthetic, objective mastery of himself and of the situation. The
title is in perfect harmony with the entire contents. His life has
been an attempt to accomplish the task of living poetically.[5]
With a sharply developed organ for discovering the interesting
in life, he has known how to find it and after having found it
has continually reproduced his experiences half poetically.
Therefore, his diary is not historically accurate or strictly narrative; it is not indicative but subjunctive. Although his experiences were of course recorded after they were experienced,
sometimes perhaps even a long time afterward, they nevertheless are frequently described as if they were taking place right

now and with such dramatic vividness that it sometimes seems as if everything were taking place before one's eyes. It is highly improbable that he did this because he had some other purpose with this diary; it is obvious that in the strictest sense it had only personal importance for him, and to assume that I have before me a poetic work, perhaps even intended for publication, is excluded by the whole as well as by its parts. It is true that he would not need to fear anything personally in publishing it, for most of the names are so odd that it is altogether improbable that they are historical. My only suspicion has been that the first name is historically accurate, and in this way he has always been sure of identifying the actual person, whereas every interloper would be misled by the family name. At least this is the case with the girl I knew, Cordelia, on whom the main interest centers; she was very correctly named Cordelia[6] but not, however, Wahl.

How then can it be explained that the diary nevertheless has taken on such a poetic tinge? The answer to this is not difficult; it is easily explained by his poetic nature, which is not abundant enough or, if you please, not deficient enough to separate poetry and actuality from each other. The poetic was the plus he himself brought along. This plus was the poetic he enjoyed in the poetic situation of actuality; this he recaptured in the form of poetic reflection. [7]This was the second enjoyment, and his whole life was intended for enjoyment. In the first case, he personally enjoyed the esthetic; in the second case, he esthetically enjoyed his personality. The point in the first case was that he egotistically enjoyed personally that which in part actuality has given to him and which in part he himself had used to fertilize actuality; in the second case, his personality was volatilized, and he then enjoyed the situation and himself in the situation. In the first case, he continually needed actuality as the occasion, as an element; in the second case, actuality was drowned in the poetic. Thus, the fruit of the first stage was the mood from which the diary emerged as the fruit of the second stage, with these words taken in a somewhat different sense in the second case than in the first. In this way he has continually possessed the poetic through the ambiguity in which his life elapsed.

[8]Behind the world in which we live, far in the background, lies another world, and the two have about the same relation to each other as do the stage proper and the stage one sometimes sees behind it in the theater. Through a hanging of fine gauze, one sees, as it were, a world of gauze, lighter, more ethereal, with a quality different from that of the actual world. Many people who appear physically in the actual world are not at home in it but are at home in that other world. But a person's fading away in this manner, indeed, almost vanishing from actuality, can have its basis either in health or in sickness. The latter was the case with this man, whom I had once known without knowing him. He did not belong to the world of actuality, and yet he had very much to do with it. He continually ran lightly over it, but even when he most abandoned himself to it, he was beyond it. But it was not the good that beckoned him away, nor was it actually evil—even now at this moment I dare not say that of him. He has suffered from an *exacerbatio cerebri* [exacerbation of the brain],[9] for which actuality did not have enough stimulation, at most only momentarily. He did not overstrain himself on actuality, he was not too weak to bear it; no, he was too strong, but this strength was a sickness. As soon as actuality had lost its significance as stimulation, he was disarmed, and the evil in him lay in this. He was conscious of this at the very moment of stimulation, and the evil lay in this consciousness.

I knew the girl whose story constitutes the main content of the diary. Whether he has seduced others, I do not know, [10]but that seems to be borne out by his papers. He appears also to have been practiced in a different kind of procedure, which is altogether typical of him, for he was much too endowed intellectually to be a seducer in the ordinary sense. One sees from the diary that what he at times desired was something totally arbitrary, a greeting, for example, and would accept no more at any price, because that was the most beautiful thing about the other person. With the help of his intellectual gifts, he knew how to tempt a girl, how to attract her without caring to possess her in the stricter sense. I can picture him as knowing how to bring a girl to the high point where he was sure that she would offer everything. When the affair had gone so far, he broke off, without the least overture having been made on his part, without a word about love having been said, to say nothing of a declaration, a promise. And yet it had happened, and for the unhappy one the consciousness of it was doubly bitter because she did not have the least thing to appeal to, because she was continually agitated in a dreadful witches' dance of the most varied moods as she alternately reproached herself, forgave him, and in turn reproached him. And now, since the relationship had possessed actuality only figuratively, she had to battle continually the doubt whether the whole affair was not a fantasy. She could not confide in anyone, because she did not really have anything to confide. When a person has dreamed, he can tell his dream to others, but what she had to tell was indeed no dream; it was actuality, and yet as soon as she was about to tell it to another to ease her troubled mind, it was nothing. She was fully aware of it herself. No one could grasp this, scarcely she herself, and yet it weighed upon her as a disquieting burden.

[11]Such victims were, therefore, of a very special kind. They were not unfortunate girls who, as outcasts or in the belief that they were cast out by society, grieved wholesomely and intensely and, once in a while at times when the heart was too full, ventilated it in hate or forgiveness. No visible change took place in them; they lived in the accustomed context, were respected as always, and yet they were changed, almost unaccountably to themselves and incomprehensibly to others. Their lives were not cracked or broken, as others' were, but were bent into themselves; lost to others, they futilely sought to find themselves. In the same sense as it could be said that his journey through life was undetectable (for his feet were formed in such a way that he retained the footprint under them—this is how I best picture to myself his infinite reflectedness into himself), in the same sense no victim fell before him.[12] He lived much too intellectually to be a seducer in the ordinary sense. Sometimes, however, he assumed a parastatic

I
279

body and then was sheer sensuousness. Even his affair with Cordelia was so intricate that it was possible for him to appear as the one seduced—indeed, even the unhappy girl can at times be perplexed on this score; and then, too, his footprints here are so indistinct that any proof is impossible. For him, individuals were merely for stimulation; he discarded them as trees shake off their leaves—he was rejuvenated, the foliage withered.

But how may things look in his own head? Just as he has led others astray, so he, I think, will end by going astray himself. He has led the others astray not in the external sense but in the interior sense with respect to themselves. There is something shocking about a person's directing a hiker, uncertain of his way, to the wrong path and then abandoning him in his error; but what is that compared with causing a person to go astray within himself. The lost hiker still has the consolation that the scenery is continually changing around him, and with every change there is fostered a hope of finding a way out. He who goes astray within himself does not have such a large territory in which to move; he soon perceives that it is a circle from which he cannot find an exit. I think that he himself will have the same experience on an even more terrible scale. I can think of nothing more tormenting than a scheming mind that loses the thread and then directs all its keenness against itself as the conscience awakens and it becomes a matter of rescuing himself from this perplexity. The many exits from his foxhole are futile; the instant his troubled soul already thinks it sees daylight filtering in, it turns out to be a new entrance, and thus, like panic-stricken wild game, pursued by despair, he is continually seeking an exit and continually finding an entrance through which he goes back into himself. Such a person is not always what could be called a criminal; he very often is himself frustrated by his own schemes, and yet he is stricken with a more terrible punishment than is the criminal, for what is even the pain of repentance compared with this conscious madness? His punishment has a purely esthetic character, for even the expression "the conscience awakens" is too ethical to use about him; conscience takes shape in him merely as a higher consciousness that manifests itself as a restlessness that does not indict him even in the profounder sense but keeps him awake, allows him no rest in his sterile restlessness. Nor is he insane, for his multitude of finite thoughts are not fossilized in the eternity of insanity.

Poor Cordelia—for her, too, it will prove difficult to find peace. She forgives him from her heart of hearts, but she finds no rest, for then the doubt awakens: she was the one who broke the engagement; she was the occasion of the calamity; it was her pride that craved the unusual. Then she repents, but she finds no rest, for then the accusing thoughts acquit her of the charges: he was the one who with his cunning instilled this plan into her soul. Then she hates; her heart finds relief in curses, but she finds no repose. Once again she reproaches her-self—reproaches herself because she has hated, she who herself is a sinner, reproaches herself because regardless of how cunning he was she nevertheless always remains guilty. It is op-pressive for her that he has deceived her, but still more oppres-sive, one is almost tempted to say, that he has awakened multiple-tongued reflection, that he has so developed her es-thetically that she no longer listens humbly to one voice but is able to hear the many voices at the same time. Then recollec-tion awakens in her soul, and she forgets blame and guilt; she recollects the beautiful moments, and she is dazed in an unnat-ural exaltation. At such moments, she not only recalls him, she perceives him with a *clairvoyance* that only shows how highly developed she is. Then she does not see the criminal in him, but neither does she see the noble person—she feels him only esthetically. [13]She once wrote me a letter in which she comments on him. "He was sometimes so intellectual that I felt myself annihilated as a woman; at other times he was so wild and passionate, so desiring, that I almost trembled before him. At times I was like a stranger to him; at times he surren-dered completely. Then when I threw my arms around him, everything changed, and I embraced a cloud.[14] I knew this expression before I knew him, but he taught me to understand it; when I use it, I always think of him, just as every thought I think is only through him. I have always loved music; he was a matchless instrument, always sensitive; he had a range such as no other instrument has. He was the quintessence of all feelings and moods, no thought was too sublime for him, none too desperate. He could roar like an autumn storm; he could whisper inaudibly. Not a word of mine was without effect, and nevertheless I cannot say that my words did not fall short in their effect, because it was impossible for me to know what they would do. With an indescribable but cryptic, blissful, unnameable anxiety, I listened to this music I myself had evoked and yet did not evoke; always there was harmony, always I was enraptured by him."

Terrible it is for her; more terrible it will be for him—this I can conclude from the fact that I myself can scarcely control the anxiety that grips me every time I think about the affair. I, too, am carried along into that kingdom of mist, into that dreamland where one is frightened by one's own shadow at every moment. Often I futilely try to tear myself away from it; I follow along like an ominous shape, like an accuser who cannot speak. How strange! [15]He has spread the deepest secrecy over everything, and yet there is an even deeper secrecy, that I myself am in on the secret and that I came to know it in an unlawful way. To forget the whole thing is not possible. I have sometimes thought of talking to him about it. But what would be the use—he would either disclaim everything and insist that the diary was a literary venture, or he would enjoin me to silence, something I cannot deny him in view of the way in which I came to know about it. There is nothing that involves so much seduction and so much malediction as a secret.

From Cordelia I have received a collection of letters. Whether it is all of them, I do not know, although it seemed to me that she once gave me to understand that she herself had confiscated some. [16]I have copied them and shall interleave them in my fair copy. Admittedly, they are not dated, but even if they were it would not help me much, since the diary becomes more and more sparse as it proceeds. In fact, at last with only a single exception it abandons dates altogether, as if the story in its development became so qualitatively significant that, although historically actual, it came so close to being idea that specifications of time became unimportant. What did help me, however, was that I found here and there in the diary some words that I did not grasp at first. But by relating them to the letters I perceived that they are the themes in them. Thus it will be easy for me to interleave them in the right places, since I shall always insert the letter where there is an allusion to the theme. If I had not discovered these guiding clues, I would have been guilty of a misunderstanding, for it probably would not have occurred to me—as the diary now seems to indicate—that at times the letters succeeded one another at such short intervals that she seems to have received several in one day. If I had pursued my own thinking, I would probably have dispersed them more evenly and not suspected the effect he achieved through the passionate energy with which he used this and every means to hold Cordelia at the pinnacle of passion.

In addition to the complete information about his relation to Cordelia, the diary has several little word pictures interwoven here and there. Wherever such a piece is found, there is an "NB" in the margin. These word pictures have nothing at all to do with Cordelia's story but have given me a vivid idea of the meaning of an expression he often used, even though I formerly understood it in another way: One should always have a little line out on the side. If an earlier volume of this diary had fallen into my hands, I probably would have encountered several of these, which in the margin he himself calls: *actiones in distans* [actions at a distance],[17] for he himself declares that Cordelia occupied him too much for him really to have time to look around.

[18]Shortly after he had left Cordelia, he received from her a couple letters that he sent back unopened. These were among the letters Cordelia turned over to me. She herself had broken the seal, and I take the liberty of making a copy of them. She has never spoken of their contents to me, but whenever she mentioned her relation to Johannes she used to recite a little verse, from Goethe as far as I know—a verse that seemed to mean something different to her according to the difference of her mood and the varied diction conditioned thereby.

I
283

Gehe,	[Go,
Verschmähe	Scorn
Die Treue,	Faithfulness,
Die Reue	Regret
Kommt nach	Will follow].[19]

The letters read as follows:

Johannes,

Never will I call you "my Johannes," for I certainly realize you never have been that, and I am punished harshly enough for having once been gladdened in my soul by this thought, and yet I do call you "mine": my seducer, my deceiver, my enemy, my murderer, the source of my unhappiness, the tomb of my joy, the abyss of my unhappiness. I call you "mine" and call myself "yours," and as it once flattered your ear, proudly inclined to my adoration, so shall it now sound as a curse upon you, a curse for all eternity. Do not look forward to my planning to pursue you or to arm myself with a dagger in order to provoke your ridicule! Flee where you will, I am still yours; go to the ends of the earth,[20] I am still yours. Love a hundred others, I am still yours—indeed, in the hour of death, I am yours. The very language I use against you must demonstrate to you that I am yours. You have had the audacity to deceive a person in such a way that you have become everything to me, so that I would rejoice solely in being your slave. Yours I am, yours, yours, your curse.

Your CORDELIA

Johannes,

There was a rich man; he had great flocks and herds of livestock large and small. There was a poor little maiden; she possessed but a single lamb;[21] it ate from her hand and drank from her cup. You were the rich man, rich in all the glories of the world; I was the poor one who possessed only my love. You took it, you delighted in it. Then desire beckoned you, and you sacrificed the little that I possessed—you could sacrifice nothing of your own. There was a rich man; he possessed great flocks and herds. There was a poor little maiden, she possessed only her love.

Your CORDELIA

Johannes,

Is there no hope at all, then? Might your love never awaken again? That you did love me, I know, even though I do not know what it is that makes me sure of it. I will wait, however long the time is for me; I will wait, wait until you are tired of loving others. Then your love for me will rise again from its grave; then I will love you as always, thank you as always, as before, O Johannes, as before! Johannes, is your heartless coldness toward me, is it your true nature? Was your love, your rich love, a lie and a falsehood; are you now yourself again! Have patience with my love; forgive me for continuing to love you. I know that my love is a burden to you, but there will still come a time when you will come back to your Cordelia. Your Cordelia! Hear this imploring word! Your Cordelia.

Your CORDELIA

Even though Cordelia did not possess the admired range of her Johannes, it is clear that she was not without modulation. Her mood is clearly impressed upon every one of the letters, even though she was somewhat lacking in clarity of exposition. This is especially true of the second letter, where one suspects rather than actually understands her meaning, but for me this deficiency makes it very moving.

I
285

---

[22]April 4

[23]Take care, my beautiful stranger! Take care! To step out of a carriage is not such a simple matter; at times it is a decisive step. I could lend you a novel by Tieck[24] in which you would see that in dismounting from a horse a lady became so involved in a complicated situation that this step became definitive for her entire life. Indeed, carriage steps usually are so ill-contrived that one is almost compelled to abandon all grace

I
286

and to hazard a desperate leap into the arms of the coachman and servant. Yes, what a good deal a coachman and servants have! I do believe I shall try to find a job as a servant in a house where there are young girls; a servant easily comes to know the secrets of such a little miss. —But for God's sake don't leap, I beg of you. It is very dark; I shall not disturb you. I am simply going to stand under this street light; then you will be unable to see me, and invariably one is embarrassed only to the degree that one is seen, but invariably one is seen only to the degree that one sees. Therefore, out of concern for the servant, who perhaps will not be able to withstand such a leap, out of concern for the silk dress, also out of concern for the lace fringes, out of concern for me, let this charming tiny foot, whose daintiness I have already admired, let it try itself in the world, risk reliance upon it; it will certainly find firm footing, and if you shudder for a moment because it seems as if your foot sought in vain something to rest upon, if you still shudder after it has found it, then quickly put the other foot down beside it. Who, after all, would be so cruel as to leave you suspended in this position, who so ungracious, so slow to respond to the revelation of beauty. Or do you still fear some outsider—but certainly not the servant, or me, either, for indeed I have already seen the tiny foot, and since I am a natural scientist I have learned from Cuvier[25] how to draw conclusions from it with certainty. So please hurry! How this anxiety does enhance your beauty! But anxiety in and by itself is not beautiful; it is so only when at the same time one sees the energy that overcomes it. There! How firmly this tiny foot is standing now. I have noticed that girls with tiny feet usually stand more firmly than the more pedestrian big-footed ones.

Now who would have thought it? It goes against all experience; the danger of a dress catching is not nearly as great when one steps out as when one leaps out. But then it is always precarious for girls to go driving in a carriage; they end up staying in it. The lace and trimmings are lost, and that's that. No one has seen anything. True, a dark figure appears, enveloped to the eyes in a cape. It is not possible to see where he is coming from, for the light is shining right in one's eyes. He passes by you just as you are entering the front door. At precisely the crucial moment a sidelong glance falls on its object. You blush; your bosom is too full to unburden itself in a single breath. There is indignation in your glance, a proud contempt. There is a plea, a tear in your eye; both are equally beautiful. I accept them both with equal right, for I can just as well be the one as the other.

But I am being mean. What is the number of the house? What do I see? A public display of fancy articles. My beautiful stranger, it may be shocking on my part, but I am following the bright path. . . . . . She has forgotten what happened— ah, yes, when one is seventeen years old, when one goes shopping in this happy age, when every single large or little object picked up gives unspeakable delight, then one readily forgets. As yet she has not seen me; I am standing at the other end of the counter, far off by myself. There is a mirror on the opposite wall; she is not contemplating it, but the mirror is contemplating her. How faithfully it has caught her image, like a humble slave who shows his devotion by his faithfulness, a slave for whom she certainly has significance but who has no significance for her, who indeed dares to capture her but not to hold her. Unhappy mirror, which assuredly can grasp her image but not her; unhappy mirror, which cannot secretly hide her image in itself, hide it from the whole world, but can only disclose it to others as it now does to me. What torture if a human being were fashioned that way. And yet are there not many people who are like that, who possess nothing except at the moment when they are showing it to others, who merely grasp the surface, not the essence, lose everything when this is going to show itself, just as this mirror would lose her image if she were to disclose her heart to it by a single breath. And if a person were unable to possess an image in recollection at the very moment of presence, he must ever wish to be at a distance from beauty, not so close that the mortal eyes cannot see the beauty of that which he holds in his embrace and which the external eyes have lost, which he, to be sure, can regain for the external vision by distancing himself from it, but which he can, in fact, have before the eye of his soul when he cannot see

I
288

the object because it is too close to him, when lips are clinging to lips. . . . . . How beautiful she is! Poor mirror, it must be tormenting—it is good that you do not know jealousy. Her head is perfectly oval; she tilts it a little, thereby accentuating her forehead, which rises pure and proud without any delineation of the powers of understanding. Her dark hair rings her forehead softly and gently. Her countenance is like a fruit, every angle fully rounded; her skin is transparent, like velvet to the touch—that I can feel with my eyes. Her eyes—yes, I have not even seen them; they are hidden by lids armed with silken fringes that are bent like barbs, dangerous to anyone who wishes to meet her glance. Her head is a Madonna head, purity and innocence its mark. She is bowed down like a Madonna, but she is not lost in contemplation of the One; this causes the expression in her face to vary. [26]What she is contemplating is multiplicity, the multiplicity over which earthly pomp and glory cast a reflection. She takes off her glove to show to the mirror and me a right hand as white and shapely as that of an ancient statue, without any ornaments, not even a flat gold ring on the fourth finger[27]—bravo! She raises her eyes—how changed everything is, and yet the same—the forehead a little less high, the face a little less uniformly oval but more vital.[28] She is speaking with the store clerk; she is lively, cheerful, talkative. She has already chosen one, two, three articles; she picks up a fourth. She is holding it in her hand; her eyes look down again; she is asking what it costs. She lays it aside under the glove; it must surely be a secret, intended for— a sweetheart? But she is not engaged. Ah, but there are many who are not engaged and yet have a sweetheart, many who are engaged and yet do not have a sweetheart. . . . . . Should I relinquish her? Should I leave her undisturbed in her delight? She wants to pay but she has lost her purse—presumably she is giving her address. I do not wish to hear it; I do not wish to deprive myself of the surprise. I certainly shall meet her again sometime; I certainly shall recognize her, and she may recognize me—my sidelong glance is not forgotten so easily. Then when I am taken by surprise upon meeting her in surroundings I did not expect, her turn will come. If she does not know me, if her glance does not immediately convince me of that, then I certainly shall find occasion to look at her from the side—I promise that she will recall the situation. No impatience, no greediness—everything will be relished in slow draughts; she is selected, she will be overtaken.

[29]The fifth

This I do like: alone in the evening on Østergade. Yes, I do see your servant following along. Now, do not believe that I think so ill of you as to imagine that you would go walking all alone; do not believe that I am so inexperienced that in my survey of the situation I have not immediately observed this portentous figure. But why, then, the hurry? You are indeed a little uneasy; you feel a certain beating of the heart, not because of an impatient longing to go home but because of an impatient fear running through your whole body with its sweet disquietude, and therefore the quick tempo of the feet. But nevertheless it is marvelous, inestimably so, to go walking alone— with the servant in tow. . . . . . One is sixteen years old; one is well read—that is, in novels; in walking through the brothers' room by chance one has overheard some words in a conversation between them and their acquaintances, something about Østergade. Later one scurried through several times to pick up more information, if possible. But in vain. Yet one should—as befits a big, grown-up girl—know a little bit about the world. If one could just go walking without any fuss and with the servant following behind. Yes, that's all very fine— but Father and Mother would surely look askance at that, and what reason can one give? When one is going to a party, there is no chance for it; it is a bit too early, because I overheard August say around nine or ten o'clock. When it is time to go home, it is too late, and usually there has to be a gentleman escort to drag along. Thursday evening when we leave the theater would really be an excellent opportunity, but then I always have to ride in the carriage and have Mrs. Thomsen and her charming cousins packed in with me. If I could just ride alone, then I could open the window and look around a little. But often the unhoped for happens. Today Mother said to me: I do

not think you will be finished with what you are sewing for
your father's birthday. In order to be entirely undisturbed,
you may go over to Aunt Jette's and stay until tea time, and
Jens will come and fetch you. It really was not exactly pleasant
news, for it is very boring at Aunt Jette's, but then I shall be
walking home alone at nine o'clock with the servant. Then
when Jens comes, he will have to wait until a quarter past nine,
and then we'll be off. Only I might meet my brother or August—but that would not be so good, for then I probably
would be escorted home. Thanks, but we would rather be free
of that—freedom—but if I could catch sight of them without
being seen. . . . . . Well, my little miss, what do you see,
then, and what do you think I see? In the first place, the little
cap you are wearing is very becoming and harmonizes completely with the haste of your whole demeanor. It is neither a
hat nor a bonnet, but a kind of hood. But you could not possibly have had that on when you went out this morning.
Could the servant have brought it, or did you borrow it from
Aunt Jette? —Perhaps you are incognito. —But the veil should
not be allowed to drop all the way down when you are going
to look around. Or perhaps it is not a veil but only a wide piece
of lace? It is impossible to tell in the dark. Whatever it is, it
hides the upper part of your face. Your chin is rather lovely, a
bit too pointed. Your mouth is small, open—that is because
you are walking too fast. Your teeth, white as snow. So it
should be. Teeth are extremely important; they are a body-
guard concealed behind the seductive softness of the lips. Your
cheeks are glowing with health. —If you tilt your head a little,
it might be possible to penetrate up under this veil or this piece
of lace. Be careful; such a glance from below is more dangerous than one that is *gerade aus* [direct]! It is like fencing; and
what weapon is as sharp, as penetrating, as gleaming in its
movement and thereby as illusive as the eye? You feint a high
quarte, as the fencer says, and then lunge instantaneously; the
more swiftly the lunge can follow upon the feint, the better. It
is an indescribable moment, the instant of the feint. The opponent feels, as it were, the cut; he is struck; and so he is, but
in a place quite different from what he thought. . . . . . Un-
daunted, she walks on, fearless and flawless. Watch out! There

comes a man—drop your veil; do not let his profane glance defile you. You have no notion of it; for a long time it perhaps would be impossible for you to forget the repulsive uneasiness with which it moved you—you do not notice, but I do, that he has surveyed the situation. The servant is marked out as the closest object. —Well, now you see the consequence of walking alone with the servant. The servant has fallen down. Really, it is ludicrous, but what are you going to do now? To turn back and help him up on his feet is out of the question; to walk with a muddy servant is unpleasant; to walk alone is precarious. Watch out; the monster is approaching. . . . . . You do not answer me. [30]Just look at me—is my external appearance anything to be afraid of? I do not make the slightest impression on you; I seem to be a nice man from quite another world. There is nothing in what I say that disturbs you, nothing that reminds you of the situation, no movement that even remotely encroaches upon you. You are still a little apprehensive; you have not yet forgotten that *unheimliche* [disquieting] character's approach toward you. You feel rather kindly disposed toward me; my shyness, which prevents me from looking at you, gives you the upper hand. It delights you and makes you safe; you could almost be tempted to make sport of me a little. I wager that right now you would have the courage to take my arm if it occurred to you. . . . . . So you live on Stormgade. You curtsey to me coldly and casually. Do I deserve this, I who helped you out of all that unpleasantness? You have a change of mind, you turn back, thank me for my kindness, offer me your hand—why are you turning pale? Is not my voice the same as before, my attitude the same, my eyes just as calm and quiet? This handclasp? Can a handclasp mean anything? Indeed, much, very much, my little miss. Within a fortnight, I shall explain it all to you; until then you will remain in the contradiction: I am a nice man who came like a knight to the assistance of a young girl, and I can also press your hand in no less than a gentle manner.[31]

April 7

[32]"Monday, then, one o'clock, at the exhibition." Very good, I shall have the honor of turning up at a quarter to one.

A little rendezvous. On Saturday, I finally cut the matter short and decided to pay a visit to my much-traveled friend Adolph Bruun. With that in mind, about seven o'clock in the evening I started out on Vestergade, where someone told me he was supposed to live. But he was not to be found, not even on the fourth floor, where I arrived all out of breath. As I was about to go down the stairs, my ears picked up a melodious female voice saying in an undertone, "Monday, then, one o'clock, at the exhibition; at that time the others are out, but you know that I never dare to see you at home." The invitation was not meant for me but for a young man who—one, two, three— was out of the door so fast that my eyes, let alone my feet, could not catch up with him. Why do they not have a gaslight in stairways; then I might have been able to see whether it was worth the trouble to be so punctual. But if there had been a light, I perhaps would not have managed to hear anything. The established order is still the rational,[33] and I am and remain an optimist. . . . . . Now who is it? The exhibition, to use Donna Anna's expression, swarms with girls.[34] It is precisely a quarter to one. My beautiful stranger! Would that your intended might be as punctual in every way as I am, or do you wish instead that he may never arrive fifteen minutes early? As you wish—I am at your service in every way. . . . . . "Enchanting troll woman, fairy, or witch, dispel your fog," show yourself. You are probably here already but invisible to me; make yourself known, for otherwise I certainly do not dare to expect a revelation. Are there perhaps several up here on the same errand as she? Very possibly. Who knows the ways of an individual, even when he is attending an exhibition? —There comes a young girl through the foyer, hurrying faster than a bad conscience after a sinner. She forgets to hand over her ticket; the man in a red uniform stops her. Good heavens, what a rush she is in. It must be she. Why such premature vehemence? It is not one o'clock yet. Do remember that you are supposed to meet your beloved. Does it make any difference how one looks on such an occasion, or is this an occasion when one must put one's best foot forward, as they say? When such an innocent young thing is keeping an appointment, she goes at it in a frenzy. She is as nervous as can be. I, however, sit here most comfortably in my chair and contemplate a lovely rural landscape. . . . . . She is a very daughter of the devil; she storms through all the rooms. You must still try to hide your eagerness a bit; remember what was said to Miss Elizabeth: Is it seemly for a young girl to be so eager to become involved with someone?[35] But your involvement, of course, is one of the innocent ones.

A rendezvous is usually regarded by lovers as the most beautiful moment. I myself still recall as clearly as if it were yesterday the first time I hurried to the appointed place with a heart as full as it was unacquainted with the joy awaiting me. The first time I knocked three times; the first time a window was opened; the first time a little wicker gate was opened by the invisible hand of a girl who concealed herself by opening it; the first time I hid a girl under my cape in the luminous summer night. But in this opinion there is a considerable admixture of illusion. A neutral third party does not always find the lovers to be most beautiful at this moment. I have witnessed trysts in which, although the girl was lovely and the man handsome, the total impression was almost revolting and the meeting itself far from beautiful, although it undoubtedly seemed so to the lovers. In a way, one gains in becoming more experienced, for admittedly one loses the sweet disquietude of impatient longing but gains the poise to make the moment really beautiful. It annoys me to see a male become so confused on such an occasion that out of sheer love he has *delirium tremens*. What, indeed, do peasants know about cucumber salad! Instead of having the composure to enjoy her disquietude, to let it inflame her beauty and make it incandescent, he brings about only an ungainly confusion, and yet he goes home happy, imagining that it was something glorious.

—But where the devil is the man? It is now almost two o'clock. Well, they are a splendid tribe, these lovers! What a scoundrel—to let a young miss wait for him! No, but of course I am a much more dependable person! It is probably best to speak to her now as she passes me for the fifth time. "Forgive my boldness, lovely lady; you are presumably looking for your family here. You have hurried by me several times, and as my eyes followed you I noticed that you always stop in the next to the last room. Perhaps you do not know that there is still another room beyond that. There you will possibly find the ones you are looking for." She curtseys to me; it is very becoming to her. The opportunity is propitious. I am glad that the man is not coming—the fishing is always best in troubled waters. When a young miss is agitated, one can successfully risk much that otherwise would miscarry.

I have bowed to her as politely and formally as possible; I am once again sitting on my chair looking at my landscape and keeping my eye on her. To follow her immediately would be risking too much; it might seem as if I were obtrusive, and then she would be on her guard at once. Now she is of the opinion that I spoke to her out of sympathy, and I am in her good favor. —I know for sure that there is not a soul in the last room. Solitude will have a favorable effect upon her; as long as she sees many people around her, she is uneasy; if she is alone, she no doubt will subside. Quite right—she is staying in there. In a while, I will *en passant* [casually] come in; I have the right to say one line more—after all, she does owe me as much as a greeting.

She has sat down. Poor girl, she looks so sad; she has been crying, I think, or at least she has had tears in her eyes. It is shocking—to force such a girl to tears. But be calm, you shall be avenged; I will avenge you; he will find out what it is to wait. —How beautiful she is now that the various squalls have calmed down and she is at rest in one mood. Her bearing is a harmonious blend of sadness and pain. She is really attractive. She sits there in her traveling clothes, and yet it was not she who was going to travel; she put them on to go out looking for joy, and now they are a symbol of her pain, for she is like one from whom joy is traveling away. She looks as if she had taken leave of her beloved forever. Let him go! —The situation is propitious; the moment beckons. The thing to do now is to express myself in such a way that it will appear as if I were of the opinion that she was looking for her family or a party of friends up here, and yet so warmly that every word is suggestive to her feelings, so I will have the opportunity to insinuate myself into her thoughts.

Damn the scoundrel—there a fellow comes full speed into the room; no doubt it is he. Oh, no, what a clumsy fool, now when I have just got the situation the way I wanted it. Oh, well, I shall probably be able to turn this to advantage. I must come into casual contact with them, manage to be brought into the situation. When she sees me, she will involuntarily smile at me, who thought she was looking for her family out here, whereas she was looking for something entirely different. This smile will make me her confidant, which is always something. —A thousand thanks, my child; that smile is worth much more to me than you think; it is the beginning, and the beginning is always the hardest. Now we are acquaintances; our acquaintance is established in a piquant situation—for the time being it is enough for me. You no doubt will stay here scarcely more than an hour; in two hours I will know who you are—why else do you think the police keep census records?

I
295

The ninth

Have I become blind? Has the inner eye of the soul lost its power? I have seen her, but it is as if I had seen a heavenly revelation—so completely has her image vanished again for me. In vain do I summon all the powers of my soul in order to conjure up this image. If I ever see her again, I shall be able to recognize her instantly, even though she stands among a hundred others. Now she has fled, and the eye of my soul tries in vain to overtake her with its longing. —I was walking along Langelinie,[36] seemingly nonchalantly and without paying attention to my surroundings, although my reconnoitering glance left nothing unobserved—and then my eyes fell upon her. My eyes fixed unswervingly upon her. They no longer obeyed their master's will; it was impossible for me to shift my gaze and thus overlook the object I wanted to see—I did not look, I stared. As a fencer freezes in his lunge, so my eyes were fixed, petrified in the direction initially taken. It was impossible to look down, impossible to withdraw my glance, impossible to see, because I saw far too much. The only thing I have retained is that she had on a green cloak, that is all—one could call it capturing the cloud instead of Juno;[37] she has escaped me, like Joseph from Potiphar's wife,[38] and left only her cloak behind. She was accompanied by an elderly woman, who appeared to be her mother. Her I can describe from top to toe, even though I did not really look at her at all but at most included her *en passant*. So it goes. The girl made an impression on me, and I forgot her; the other made no impression, and her I can remember.

The eleventh

My soul is still caught in the same contradiction. I know that I have seen her, but I also know that I have forgotten it again, yet in such a way that the remnant of the recollection that is left does not refresh me. With a restlessness and vehemence, my soul, as if my welfare were at stake, demands this image, and yet it does not appear; I could tear out my eyes to punish them for their forgetfulness. Then, when I have chafed in impatience and have calmed down, it is as if presentiment and recollection were weaving an image that still cannot take definite shape for me, because I cannot make it stand still in context; it is like a pattern in a fine weaving—the pattern is lighter than the background, and by itself it cannot be seen because it is too light. —This is a strange state to be in, and yet it has its pleasure intrinsically and also because it assures me that I am still young. This I also am able to learn from another observation—namely, that I continually seek my prey among young girls, not among young women. A woman is less natural, more coquettish; a relationship with her is not beautiful, not interesting; it is piquant, and the piquant is always the last. — I had not expected to be able to taste once again the first fruits of falling in love. I have gone under in love-rapture; I have been given what swimmers call a ducking. No wonder that I am a little dazed. So much the better, so much the more do I promise myself out of this relationship.

The fourteenth

I scarcely know myself. My mind roars like a turbulent sea in the storms of passion. If someone else could see my soul in this state, it would seem to him that it, like a skiff, plunged prow-first down into the ocean, as if in its dreadful momentum it would have to steer down into the depths of the abyss. He does not see that high on the mast a sailor is on the lookout. Roar away, you wild forces, roar away, you powers of passion; even if your waves hurl foam toward the clouds, you still are not able to pile yourselves up over my head—I am sitting as calmly as the king of the mountain.[39]

I am almost unable to find a foothold; like a water bird, I am seeking in vain to alight on the turbulent sea of my mind. And yet such turbulence is my element. I build upon it as the *Alcedo ispida* builds its nest upon the sea.[40]

Turkey cocks ruffle their feathers when they see red. So it goes with me when I see green, every time I see a green cloak, and since my eyes often deceive me, all my expectations sometimes run aground on a porter from Frederik's Hospital.

I
297

The twentieth

One must limit oneself—that is the primary condition for all enjoyment. It does not seem that I shall soon find out anything about the girl who so fills my soul and my mind that the lack is amplified. Now I am going to stay quite calm, for this state, this obscure and indefinite but nevertheless powerful emotion, also has its sweetness. I have always liked to lie in a boat on a clear moonlit night out on one of our beautiful lakes. I haul in the sails, take in the oars, unship the rudder, lie down full length, and gaze up at the vault of heaven. When the waves rock the boat on their breast, when the clouds swiftly drift before the wind, making the moon disappear for a moment and then reappear, I find rest in this restlessness. The motion of the waves lulls me; their slapping against the boat is a monotonous lullaby; the clouds' hasty flight and the variation in lights and shadows intoxicates me so that I dream wide awake. I lie the same way now, haul in the sails, unship the rudder. Longing and impatient expectancy toss me in their arms; longing and expectancy become quieter and quieter, more and more blissful: they coddle me like a child. Over me arches the heaven of hope; her image drifts past me like the moon's, indistinct, now blinding me with its light, now with its shadow. How enjoyable to ripple along on moving water this way—how enjoyable to be in motion within oneself.[41]

The twenty-first

The days go by; I am still making no headway. The young misses delight me more than ever, and yet I have no desire to enjoy. I look for her everywhere. Often it makes me unreasonable, befuddles my vision, enervates my enjoyment. [42]That beautiful season will soon be here when one can buy up in the public streets and lanes the small claims that cost dearly enough during the social life in the winter season, for a young girl can forget much, but not a situation. It is true that social life does put a person in touch with the fair sex, but it is no good for beginning an affair. In social life, every girl is armed; the situation is unsatisfactory and occurs again and again—she receives no sensuous jolt. In the street, she is on the open sea, and therefore everything affects her more, and likewise everything is more enigmatic. I would give a hundred rix-dollars for a smile from a young girl in a street situation, and not ten for a hand squeeze at a party—that is an entirely different kind of currency. When the affair has started, one looks for the person concerned at parties. One has a secret communication with her that is tempting; it is the most energetic stimulation I know. She does not dare to talk about it, and yet she thinks about it; she does not know whether one has forgotten it or not; now one misleads her in this way, now in another. This year my ingathering has been small; this girl preoccupies me too much. In a certain sense, my profits are meager, but then I do indeed have the prospect of the grand prize.

The fifth

[43]Cursed chance! Never have I cursed you because you made your appearance; I curse you because you do not make your appearance at all. Or is this perhaps supposed to be a new invention of yours, you incomprehensible being, barren mother of everything, the only remnant remaining from [44]that time

when necessity gave birth to freedom, when freedom let itself
be tricked back into the womb again? Cursed chance! You, my
only confidant, the only being I deem worthy to be my ally
and my enemy, always similar to yourself in dissimilarity; always incomprehensible, always an enigma! You whom I love
with all the sympathy of my soul, in whose image I form myself, why do you not make your appearance? I do not beg, I do
not humbly plead that you will make your appearance in this
manner or that; such worship would indeed be idolatry,
would not be pleasing to you. I challenge you to a fight—why
do you not make your appearance? Or has the balance wheel
in the world structure stopped, is your enigma solved, and so
you, too, have plunged into the sea of eternity? Terrible
thought—then the world will come to a halt out of boredom!
Cursed chance, I am waiting for you! I do not want to vanquish you by means of principles or what foolish people call
character—no, I shall be your poet! I do not want to be a poet
for others; make your appearance, and I shall be your poet. I
shall eat my own poem, and that will be my food. Or do you
find me unworthy? Just as a temple dancer dances to the honor
of the god [*Guden*], so I have consecrated myself to your service; light, thinly clad, limber, unarmed, I renounce everything. I own nothing; I desire to own nothing; I love nothing;
I have nothing to lose—but have I not thereby become more
worthy of you, you who long ago must have been tired of depriving people of what they love, tired of their craven snivel-
ing and craven pleading. Surprise me—I am ready. No
stakes—let us fight for honor. Show her to me, show me a
possibility that seems to be an impossibility; show her to me
among the shades of the underworld, and I shall bring her
back.[45] Let her hate me, scorn me, be indifferent to me, love
someone else—I do not fear; but stir up the water,[46] break the
silence. To starve me this way is mean of you, you who nevertheless fancy yourself stronger than I.

I
299

May 6

Spring is here. Everything is burgeoning, the young girls
also. Their cloaks are laid aside; presumably my green one,

too, has been hung up. This is the result of making a girl's acquaintance in the street, not in society, where one is immediately told her name, her family, where she lives, whether she
is engaged. The last is extremely important information for all
sober and steady suitors, to whom it would never occur to fall
in love with an engaged girl. Such an ambler would then be in
mortal distress if he were in my place; he would be utterly
demolished if his efforts to obtain information were crowned
with success and with the bonus that she was engaged. This,
however, does not bother me very much. An engagement is
nothing but a comic predicament. I fear neither comic nor
tragic predicaments; the only ones I fear are the *langweilige*
[boring] ones. So far, I have not come up with a single bit of
information, although I certainly have left nothing untried and
many times have felt the truth of the poet's words:

> *Nox et hiems longaeque viae, saevique dolores*
> *Mollibus his castris, et labor omnis inest*
> [Night, storm, long journeys, cruel pains
> All kinds of pains are in this dainty camp].[47]

Perhaps she does not live here in the city at all; perhaps she is
from the country, perhaps, perhaps—I can fly into a rage over
all these perhapses, and the angrier I become, the more the perhapses. I always have money at hand in order to be able to set
out upon a journey. In vain do I look for her at the theater, at
concerts, at dances, on the promenades. In a certain sense, I am
pleased; a young girl who participates in such amusements a
great deal is usually not worth conquering; she most often
lacks the originality that for me is and remains the *conditio sine
qua non* [indispensable condition]. It is not as incomprehensible
to find a Preciosa[48] among the gypsies as in the market places
where young girls are offered for sale—in all innocence—good
heavens, who says otherwise!

The twelfth

[49]Now, my child, why do you not remain standing quite
calmly in the doorway? There is absolutely nothing against a
young girl's entering a doorway during a shower. I do it my-

self when I have no umbrella, sometimes even when I have one, as now, for example. Moreover, I could mention several estimable ladies who have not hesitated to do it. Just be calm, turn your back to the street; then the passersby cannot even tell whether you are just standing there or are about to enter the building. But it is indiscreet to hide behind the door when it is standing half open, chiefly because of the consequences, for the more you are concealed, the more unpleasant it is to be surprised. But if you have concealed yourself, then stand very still, commending yourself to your good guardian spirit and the care of all the angels; especially avoid peeking out to see whether the rain is over. If you really want to be sure of it, take a firm step forward and look up gravely at the sky. But if you stick your head out somewhat inquisitively, self-consciously, anxiously, uncertainly, quickly draw it back—then any child understands this movement; it is called playing hide-and-seek. And I, who always join in games, should I hold back, should I not answer when asked? . . . . . Do not think I am harboring any disrespectful thoughts about you; you did not have the slightest ulterior motive in sticking your head out—it was the most innocent thing in the world. In return, you must not affront me in your thoughts; my good name and reputation will not tolerate it. Moreover, it was you who started this. I advise you never to speak to anyone about this incident; you are in the wrong. What do I propose to do other than what any gentleman would do—offer you my umbrella. —Where did she go? Splendid! She has hidden herself down in the porter's doorway. What a darling little girl, cheerful, contented. —"Perhaps you could tell me about a young lady who this very moment stuck her head out of this door, obviously in need of an umbrella. She is the one I am looking for, I and my umbrella." —You laugh. —Perhaps you will allow me to send my servant to fetch it tomorrow, or do you recommend that I call a carriage? —Nothing to thank me for; it is only common courtesy. —That is one of the most delightful girls I have seen in a long time; her glance is so childlike and yet so saucy, her manner so lovely, so chaste, and yet she is inquisitive. —Go in peace, my child. If it were not for a green cloak, I might have

I
301

wished to establish a closer acquaintance. —She walks down along Store Kjøbmagergade. How innocent and full of confidence, not a trace of prudery. See how lightly she walks, how pertly she tosses her head—the green cloak requires self-denial.

The fifteenth

Thank you, kind chance; accept my thanks! Erect was she and proud, mysterious and abounding in thought like a spruce tree, one shoot, one thought, which deep from the interior of the earth shoots up toward heaven, unexplained, unexplainable to itself, a unity that has no parts. The beech tree puts on a crown; its leaves tell what has occurred beneath it. The spruce has no crown, no history, is a riddle to itself—she was like that. [50]She herself was hidden in herself; she herself rose up out of herself; there was a recumbent pride in her like the spruce's bold escape—although it is riveted to the earth. A sadness surrounded her, like the cooing of the wood dove, a deep longing that was lacking nothing. She was an enigma that enigmatically possessed its own solution, a secret, [51]and what are all the secrets of the diplomats compared with this, a riddle, and what in all the world is as beautiful as the word that solves it? How suggestive, how pregnant, the language is: to solve [*at løse*]— what ambiguity there is in it, with what beauty and with what strength it pervades all the combinations in which this word appears! Just as the soul's wealth is a riddle as long as the cord of the tongue is not loosened [*løst*] and thereby the riddle is solved [*løst*], so also a young girl is a riddle.

Thank you, kind chance; accept my thanks! If I had been able to see her in the wintertime, she no doubt would have been wrapped in the green cloak, benumbed with cold perhaps, and the harshness of nature would have diminished her beauty. But now—what luck! I saw her the first time at the most beautiful time of the year, in the early part of summer in the afternoon light. Of course, winter also has its advantages. A brilliantly lighted ballroom may very well be a flattering setting for a girl dressed for a dance. But for one thing she seldom shows up to her best advantage here precisely because everything requires her to do so—a requirement that has a disturbing effect on her whether she complies with it or does just the opposite. For another, everything is reminiscent of transitoriness and vanity and evokes an impatience that makes the enjoyment less refreshing. There are certain times when I admittedly would not want to be deprived of a ballroom, deprived of its expensive luxury, its priceless overabundance of youth and beauty, its multiple play of powers, but I do not enjoy it as much as I revel in possibility. It is not a particular beauty who captivates me, but a totality; a visionary picture floats past me in which all these feminine beings blend with one another and all these movements are seeking something, seeking repose in a picture that is not seen.[52]

It was on the footpath between Nørreport and Østerport.[53] It was about half past six. The sun had lost its vigor; only a recollection of it was preserved in a soft glimmering that spread over the landscape. Nature breathed more freely. The lake was still, smooth as a mirror. The pleasant, friendly buildings of Blegdam[54] were reflected on the water, which further out was as dark as metal. The path and the buildings on the other side were illuminated by the faint rays of the sun. The sky was clear and open; only a single light cloud glided hazily across it, best observed when one stared fixedly at the lake, over whose smooth brow it disappeared. Not a leaf was stirring. —It was she. My eyes had not deceived me, even though the green cloak had done so. Although I had been prepared for this for a long time, it was impossible for me to control a certain restlessness, a rising and falling like that of the lark as it rises and falls in its song over the nearby fields.

She was alone. Once again I have forgotten what she was wearing, and yet I do have an image of her now. She was alone, preoccupied, obviously not with herself but with her own thoughts. She was not thinking, but the quiet revolving of her thoughts wove an image of longing for her soul that had a presentiment as unexplainable as a young girl's many sighs. She was in her most beautiful age. A young girl does not develop in the sense that a boy does; she does not grow, she is born. A boy begins to develop immediately and takes a long time to do it; a young girl takes a long time to be born and is born full-grown. In this lies her infinite richness; the moment she is born, she is full-grown,[55] but this moment of birth comes late. [56]Therefore she is born twice: the second time when she marries or, more correctly, at that moment she stops being born—only at that moment is she born. It is not only Minerva[57] who springs full-grown out of Jupiter's forehead, it is not only Venus[58] who rises up out of the sea in her full beauty—every young girl is like this if her femininity has not been spoiled by what is called developing. She does not awaken gradually, but at once; on the other hand, she dreams that much longer, that is, if people are not so unreasonable as to awaken her too soon. But this dreaming is an infinite richness.

She was preoccupied not with herself but within herself, and this preoccupation was a boundless peace and repose within herself. In this way a young girl is rich; to embrace this richness makes oneself rich. She is rich, although she does not realize that she possesses anything; she is rich—she is a treasure. A quiet peacefulness rested upon her, and a trace of sadness.[59] She was light to lift with the eyes, as light as Psyche,[60] who was carried away by the jinn, even lighter, for she carried herself. Let the teachers of the Church argue about the assumption of the Madonna; it does not seem incomprehensible to me, for she no longer belonged to the world, but the lightness of a young girl is incomprehensible and mocks the law of gravity.

She did not notice anything and for that reason believed that she was not noticed either. I remained at a distance and imbibed her image. She was walking slowly; no sense of haste marred her peace or the tranquillity of the surroundings. A boy sat by the lake and fished; she stood still and watched the mirror of the water and the little float. Although she had not been walking fast, she nevertheless wanted to cool off. She loosened a little scarf tied around her neck under her shawl; a gentle breeze from the lake fanned a bosom as white as snow, yet warm and full. The boy did not seem pleased to have a witness to his fishing; he turned and observed her with a rather apathetic look. He really looked ludicrous, and I do not blame her for laughing at him. How youthfully she laughed; if she had been alone with the boy, I believe she would not have been afraid to scrap with him. Her eyes were large and glowing; when one looked into them, they had a dark luster, intimating an infinite depth, since it was impossible to penetrate into them; pure and innocent they were, gentle and calm, full of roguishness when she smiled. Her nose was delicately arched; when I saw her from the side, it seemed to draw back into her forehead and thereby became a bit shorter and a bit more saucy.

She walked on; I followed. Fortunately there were several strollers on the path. Exchanging a few words with one person and another, I let her get ahead a little and soon caught up with her again and in that way saved myself the need of having to walk at a distance just as slowly as she did. She walked in the direction of Østerport. I wished to see her closer at hand without being seen. On the corner there was a house from which I might be able to do that. I knew the family and thus needed only to pay them a visit. With a quickened pace, I hurried past her as if I did not notice her in the remotest way. Having gone far ahead of her, I greeted the family all around and then took possession of the window that looked out on the footpath. She came walking along; I looked and looked, while at the same time I spun out chitchat with the tea company in the living room. The way she walked quickly convinced me that she had not had much training in dance, and yet there was a pride in it, a natural nobility, but an absence of self-consciousness. I managed to see her one more time than I had actually counted on. From the window, I could not see far down the path, but I could see a dock that ran out into the lake, and to my great amazement I spied her again out there. It occurred to me that perhaps she lived out here in the country; perhaps her family had taken rooms for the summer.

I was already beginning to regret my visit, fearing that she would turn around and I would lose sight of her, indeed, that her appearance at the far end of the dock was a sign that she was vanishing from my sight—and then she appeared nearby.

She was walking past the house; I hastily grabbed my hat and
my cane with the intention of passing by her and dropping behind her again many times until I discovered where she lived—
when in my haste I jolted a woman's arm just as she was offering tea. There was a frightful shriek; I stood there with hat and
cane, wanting only to be off and if possible to give the incident
a turn and motivate my retreat. I cried out with pathos: I shall
be exiled like Cain from this place that saw this tea spilled! But
just as if everything had conspired against me, my host had the
dismaying idea of following up my comment and declared
loudly and solemnly that I would not be allowed to go before
I had enjoyed a cup of tea and had made restitution for the
spilled tea by serving the ladies myself. Since I was convinced
that in the present situation my host would regard it as a courtesy to use force, there was nothing to do but remain. —She
had disappeared.

I
305

The sixteenth

How beautiful it is to be in love; how interesting it is to
know that one is in love. This, you see, is the difference. I can
become furious at the thought that she disappeared before me
the second time, and yet in a certain sense I am glad of it. The
image I have of her hovers indefinitely somewhere between
her actual and her ideal form. I now have this image before me,
but precisely because either it is actuality or actuality is indeed
the occasion, it has a singular magic. I feel no impatience, for
she must live here in the city, and at this moment that is
enough for me. This possibility is the condition for the proper
appearance of her image—everything will be enjoyed in slow
drafts. And should I not be calm—I, who can regard myself as
a favorite of the gods, I, whose lot was the rare good fortune
of falling in love again. This is something that cannot be elic-
ited by skill or study—it is a gift. But if I have succeeded in
stirring up an erotic love again, I do want to see how long it
can be sustained. I coddle this love as I never did my first. The
opportunity falls to one's lot rarely enough—therefore the
point is truly to utilize it if it does come along, for it is dismaying that it is no art to seduce a girl but it is a stroke of good

fortune to find one who is worth seducing. —Love is full of mysteries, and this first falling in love is also a mystery, even though a minor one. Most people rush ahead, become engaged or do other stupid things, and in a turn of the hand everything is over, and they know neither what they have won nor what they have lost. Two times she has appeared before me and has disappeared; that means she will appear more often. When Joseph had interpreted Pharaoh's dream, he added: But the fact that you dreamed twice means that it will be fulfilled soon.[61]

I
306

Yet it would be interesting if one could discern somewhat ahead of time the forces whose emergence forms the content of life. At present she is living in all her tranquil peace; she does not have even an inkling of my existence, even less of what is going on within me, to say nothing of the assurance with which I gaze into her future, for my soul is demanding more and more actuality, and it is becoming stronger and stronger. If at first sight a girl does not make such a deep impression on a person that she awakens the ideal, then ordinarily the actuality is not especially desirable; but if she does, then no matter how experienced a person is he usually is rather overwhelmed. I always advise the person who is not sure of his hand, his eye, and his victory to venture the attack in this first state, in which, precisely because he is overwhelmed, he has supranatural powers—for being overwhelmed is a curious mixture of sympathy and egotism. He will, however, miss out on an enjoyment, for he does not enjoy the situation since he himself is wrapped up in it, hidden in it. Which is the more beautiful is difficult to decide—which is the more interesting is easy. It is, however, always best to come as close as possible to the line. This is the real enjoyment, and what others enjoy I do not know for sure. Mere possession is very little, and the means such lovers use are usually paltry enough; they do not even reject money, power, alien influence, sleeping potions, etc. But what pleasure is there in love if absolute abandon is not intrinsic to it, that is, from the one side—but ordinarily that takes spirit, and such lovers generally do not have that.

The nineteenth

Cordelia, then, is her name! Cordelia! It is a beautiful name, and that, too, is important, since it can often be very disturbing to have to name an ugly name together with the most tender adjectives. I already recognized her a long way off; she was walking with two other girls on her left. The movement of their walking seemed to indicate that they were about to stop. I stood on the corner and read the posters, while I continually kept my eye on my strangers. They parted. The two presumably had gone a little out of their way, for they went in a different direction. She came along toward my corner. When she had walked a few steps, one of the young girls came running after her and cried loudly enough for me to hear it: Cordelia! Cordelia! Then the third one joined them; they put their heads together for a privy council meeting whose secrets I futilely strained my ears to hear. Thereupon they all three laughed and hurried away at a somewhat quicker pace in the direction the two had taken. I followed them. They entered a house on Stranden.[62] I waited for a while, since there was a strong probability that Cordelia would soon come back alone. But that did not happen.

Cordelia! That is really a splendid name—indeed, the same name as that of King Lear's third daughter, that remarkable girl whose heart did not dwell on her lips, whose lips were mute when her heart was full.[63] So also with my Cordelia. She resembles her, of that I am certain. But in another sense her heart does dwell on her lips, not in the form of words but in a more heartfelt way in the form of a kiss. How ripe with health her lips! I have never seen lips more beautiful.

That I actually am in love I can tell partly by the secrecy with which I treat this matter, almost even with myself. All love is secretive, even the faithless kind, if it has the appropriate esthetic element within it. It has never occurred to me to wish for confidants or to boast of my adventures. Thus it almost makes me happy that I did not come to know where she lives but the place where she frequently visits. Perhaps I thereby may also have come even closer to my goal. I can make my observations without arousing her attention, and from this firmly established point it will not be difficult for me to gain admission into her family. But should this situation turn out to be a difficulty—*eh bien* [well, now]!—then I will put up with the difficulty alone. Everything I do I do *con amore* [with love], and so I also love *con amore*.

The twentieth

Today I learned something about the house into which she disappeared. It belongs to a widow with three lovely daughters. Information in abundance is to be had there—that is, provided they have any. The only difficulty is to understand these details raised to the third power, for they all three speak at once. Her name is Cordelia Wahl, and she is the daughter of an officer in the Royal Navy. He has been dead for some years—the mother, too. He was a very severe and strict man.[64] She now lives with her aunt, her father's sister, who is supposed to be like her brother but otherwise is a very respectable woman. Now that is all very fine, but in other respects they know nothing about this household; they never visit there, but Cordelia visits them frequently. She and the two girls take a course in the royal kitchen. Therefore, she generally visits there early in the afternoon, sometimes in the morning, never in the evening. They keep very much to themselves.

So this is the end of the story; it is apparent that there is no bridge over which I can steal into Cordelia's house.

Consequently, she does have a conception of the pains in life, of its dark side. Who would have said this of her. Yet these recollections probably belong to an earlier period; this is a horizon under which she has lived without really being aware of it. That is fine—it has saved her femininity; she is not warped. On the other hand, it will also have significance in elevating her, if one really knows how to call it forth. All such things usually teach pride, provided they do not break one, and she is far from being broken.

The twenty-first

She lives near the embankment; the locality is not the best, no neighbors whose acquaintance one could make, no public places where one can make observations unnoticed. The em-

I
308

bankment itself is not very suitable; one is too visible. If one walks below on the street, one cannot very well walk on the side next to the embankment, because no one walks there, and it would be too conspicuous, or one would have to walk close to the houses, and then one can see nothing. It is a corner house. Since the house has no neighboring house, the windows to the courtyard are also visible from the street. Presumably her bedroom is there.

The twenty-second

Today I saw her for the first time at Mrs. Jansen's. I was introduced to her. She did not seem to make anything of it or pay any attention to me. I kept myself as unobtrusive as possible in order to observe her all the better. She stayed only a moment; she had come only to fetch the daughters, who were to go to the royal kitchen. While the two Jansen girls were putting on their coats, we two were alone in the room, and I, with a cold, almost supercilious apathy, said a few casual words to her, to which she replied with undeserved politeness. Then they went. I could have offered to accompany them, but that already would have sufficed to indicate the gallant suitor, and I have convinced myself that she is not to be won that way. — On the contrary, I chose to leave right after they had gone and to walk faster than they, but along other streets, yet likewise heading toward the royal kitchen so that when they turned onto Store Kongensgade I passed them in the greatest haste without greeting them or anything—to their great astonishment.

The twenty-third

It is necessary for me to gain entrance to the house, and for that, as they say in military language, I am prepared. It looks, however, as if that will be a fairly protracted and difficult matter. I have never known any family that lived so much apart. It is only she and her aunt—no brothers, no cousins, not a thread to grab onto, no far-removed connection to contact. I walk around continually with one arm available. Not for anything in the world would I walk with someone on each arm at this time. My arm is a grappling hook that must always be kept in readiness; my arm is intended for the potential yield— if far off in the distance a very distant relative or friend should appear whom I from afar could catch hold of, then I make a grab. Moreover, it is not right for a family to live so isolated; the poor girl is being deprived of the opportunity to learn to know the world, to say nothing of the other possible dangerous consequences it may have.[65] That always has its revenge. It is the same with proposing. To be sure, such isolation does protect one from petty thievery. In a very sociable house, opportunity makes the thief. But that does not matter greatly, for there is not much to steal from such girls; when they are sixteen years old, their hearts are already a filled autograph album, and I never care to write my name where many have already written. It never occurs to me to scratch my name on a window pane or in a tavern, or on a tree or a bench in Frederiksberg gardens.[66]

The twenty-seventh

The more I see of her, the more convinced I am that she is an isolated person. This a man ought never to be, not even a young man, because, since his development depends essentially upon reflection, he must have contact with others. Therefore, a young girl should not be interesting either, for the interesting always involves a reflecting on oneself, just as for the same reason the interesting in art always includes an impression of the artist. A young girl who wants to please by being interesting will, if anything, please herself. From the esthetic side, this is the objection to all kinds of coquetry. It is quite different with what is inappropriately called coquetry, which is nature's own gesture—for example, feminine modesty, which is always the most beautiful coquetry. An interesting girl may very well be successful in pleasing, but just as she herself has surrendered her womanliness, so also the men whom she pleases are usually just as unmasculine. Such a young girl first becomes interesting in her relation with men. The woman is the weaker sex, and yet it is much more important for her to stand alone in her youth than for the man; she must be sufficient unto herself, but that by which and in which she is sufficient unto herself is an illusion; it is this dowry with which nature has endowed her like a king's daughter. But it is precisely this resting in illusion that isolates her.

I have often pondered why it is that there is nothing more corrupting for a young girl than associating a great deal with other young girls. Obviously the reason is that this association is neither one thing nor another; it unsettles the illusion but does not clarify it. The woman's fundamental qualification is to be company for the man,[67] but through association with her own sex she is led to reflection upon it, which makes her a society lady instead of company. The language itself is very suggestive in this respect; the man is called "master," but the woman is not called "maidservant" or anything like that—no, a definition of essence is used: she is company, not company-maid. If I were to imagine an ideal girl, she would always stand alone in the world and thereby be assigned to herself, but mainly she would not have friends among the girls. It is certainly true that the Graces were three, but it certainly never occurred to anyone to think of them as talking together; in their silent trinity they form a beautiful feminine unity. In this respect, I could almost be tempted to recommend the virgins' bower [*Jomfrubuur*][68] again, if this constraint were not in turn damaging in its effects. It is always best that a young girl be allowed her freedom, but that the opportunity not be provided. She thereby becomes beautiful and is rescued from becoming interesting. To give a virgin's veil or a bridal veil to a young girl who spends much time in the company of other girls is futile, but he who has sufficient esthetic sensitivity will always find that an innocent girl in the deeper and best sense of the word is brought to him veiled, even if it is not the custom to use a bridal veil.

She has been brought up strictly; I honor her parents in their graves for that; she leads a very reserved life, and in thanks I could hug her aunt for that. She has not become acquainted with worldly delights, has not become jaded through indulgence. She is proud; she spurns what delights other girls, and this is as it should be. It is a falseness that I shall know how to turn to my advantage. Frills and finery do not appeal to her as they do to other girls; she is somewhat polemic, but this is necessary for a girl with her romanticism. She lives in a world of fantasy. If she fell into the wrong hands, it might bring out something very unwomanly in her precisely because there is so much womanliness in her.

The thirtieth

Everywhere our paths cross. Today I met her three times. I know about her every little outing, when and where I shall come across her, but I do not use this knowledge to contrive an encounter with her—on the contrary, I am prodigal on a frightful scale. A meeting that often has cost me several hours of waiting is wasted as if it were a bagatelle. I do not approach her, I merely skirt the periphery of her existence. If I know that she is going to Mrs. Jansen's, I prefer not to encounter her unless it is important for me to make a particular observation. I prefer to come to Mrs. Jansen's a little early and, if possible, to pass her at the door as she is coming and I am going, or on the steps, where I nonchalantly pass by her. This is the first web into which she must be spun. On the street, I do not stop her, or I exchange a greeting with her but never come close, but always strive for distance. Presumably our repeated encounters are clearly noticeable to her; presumably she does perceive that on her horizon a new planet has loomed, which in its course has encroached disturbingly upon hers in a curiously undisturbing way, but she has no inkling of the law underlying this movement. She is tempted instead to look around to the right and to the left to see whether she can discover the point that is the goal; she is just as unaware that it is she as her antipode is. Just as those around me are inclined to do, she believes that I have a host of business affairs; I am constantly on the go and say, like Figaro: One, two, three, four schemes at a time[69] — that is my pleasure. Before I begin my attack, I must first become acquainted with her and her whole mental state.

The majority enjoy a young girl as they enjoy a glass of champagne, at one effervescent moment—oh, yes, that is really beautiful, and with many a young girl that is undoubtedly the most one can attain, but here there is more. If an individual is too fragile to stand clarity and transparency, well, then one enjoys what is unclear, but apparently she can stand it. The more devotedness one can bring to erotic love, the more interesting. This momentary enjoyment is a rape, even if not outwardly but nevertheless mentally, and in a rape there is only imagined enjoyment; it is like a stolen kiss, something nondescript. No, if one can bring it to a point where a girl has but one task for her freedom, to give herself, so that she feels her whole happiness in this, so that she practically begs for this devotedness and yet is free—only then is there enjoyment, but this always takes a discerning touch.

Cordelia! It is indeed a glorious name! I sit at home and practice saying it to myself like a parrot. I say: Cordelia, Cordelia, my Cordelia, you my Cordelia. I cannot help smiling at the thought of the plan according to which sometime at the crucial moment I shall pronounce these words. One should always make preparatory studies; everything must be properly arranged. No wonder poets are always describing this *dus*-moment,[70] that most beautiful moment when the lovers, not by sprinkling (to be sure, there are many who go no further) but by immersion in the sea of love, strip themselves of the old man and rise up from this baptism and only then really recognize each other as old acquaintances, although they are only one moment old. For a young girl, this is always the most beautiful moment, and to enjoy it properly one ought to be on a somewhat higher level—not just as someone being baptized but also as the priest. A little irony makes the moment following this moment one of the most interesting—it is a spiritual disrobing. One must be poetic enough not to interfere with the ceremony, and yet the rogue in oneself must always be on the watch.

June 2

She is proud—that I saw long ago. When she is together with the three Jansens, she speaks very little. Their chatter obviously bores her; a certain smile on her lips seems to indicate that. I am building upon that smile. —At other times, to the amazement of the Jansens, she can abandon herself to an almost boyish wildness. When I consider her life as a child, it is not unaccountable to me. She had only one brother, a year older than she. She knew only the father and brother, witnessed some earnest episodes that make ordinary silly chatter disgusting. Her father and mother did not live together happily; that which generally more or less clearly or obscurely beckons to a young girl does not beckon to her. It might well be that she is puzzled about what a young girl is. Maybe at particular moments she wishes that she were not a girl but a man.

She has imagination, spirit, passion—in short, all the essentials, but not subjectively reflected. An incident today convinced me of this. I knew from the Jansen house that she does not play an instrument—it goes against her aunt's principles. I have always regretted this, for music is always a good means of communication with a young girl if one, please note, is careful not to appear to be a connoisseur. Today I went over to Mrs. Jansen's. I had partially opened the door without knocking, a rudeness that frequently works to my advantage and that I remedy, when necessary, by the foolishness of knocking on the open door. She was sitting there alone at the piano—she seemed to be playing furtively. It was a little Swedish melody. She did not play well; she became impatient, but then the strains came again, more softly. I shut the door and remained outside, listening to the change in her moods. At times there was a passion in her playing that reminded me of the maid Mettelil,[71] who struck the golden harp so that milk spouted from her breasts. —There was something sad but also something dithyrambic in her playing. —I could have rushed forward, seized this moment: that would have been foolish. — Recollection is a means not only of conserving but also of augmenting; something that is permeated by recollection has a double effect. —Frequently in books, especially hymnbooks, one finds a little flower—the occasion for its being placed there was a beautiful moment; the recollection is even more beautiful. Obviously she conceals the fact that she plays, or perhaps

I
314

she plays only this little Swedish melody—does it perhaps have a special interest for her? I know nothing about this, but for that reason this event is of great importance to me. Sometime when I can speak more confidentially with her, I shall very covertly lead her to this point and let her fall down through this trapdoor.

June 3

Still I cannot make up my mind how to understand her; this is why I keep so quiet, so much in the background—indeed, like a soldier on vedette duty who throws himself on the ground and listens to the faintest reverberation of an advancing enemy. I do not actually exist for her, not in the sense of a negative relationship but in the sense of no relationship at all. As yet I have risked no venture. —To see her was to love her, as the novels say—yes, that would be true enough if love did not have a dialectic, but what, indeed, does one come to know about love from novels? Sheer lies—which helps to shorten the task.

According to everything I have now learned about her, when I think back on the impression that first meeting made on me, my conception of her is certainly modified, but to her advantage as well as to mine. It is not exactly the order of the day for a young girl to walk all alone this way, or for a young girl to sink into herself this way. She was tested according to my rigorous critique: lovely. But loveliness is a very volatile element that vanishes like yesterday when it is over.[72] I had not thought of her in the setting in which she lives, least of all so unreflectively acquainted with the storms of life.

[73]But I would like to know the state of her feelings. Surely she has never been in love; her spirit is too free-ranging for that. Least of all is she one of those theoretically experienced maidens who, long in advance, are so facile in imagining themselves in the arms of a lover. The real-life people she has met have simply not been able to confuse her about the relation between dream and actuality. Her soul is still nourished by the divine ambrosia of ideals. But the ideal hovering before

her is certainly not a shepherdess or a heroine in a novel, a mistress, but a Joan of Arc or something like that.

The question always remains whether her womanliness is sufficiently strong to reflect itself, or whether it will be enjoyed only as beauty and loveliness; the question is whether one dares to bend the bow to greater tension. It is in itself something great to find a purely immediate womanliness, but if one dares to risk altering it, one has the interesting. In that case, it is best to saddle her with a plain and simple suitor. That this would harm a young girl is a superstition people have. — Indeed, if she is a very choice and delicate plant who has only one crowning feature in her life—loveliness—then it is always best that she has never heard love mentioned. But if that is not the case, then it is an advantage, and I would never hesitate to produce a suitor if there was none. This suitor must not be a caricature either, for nothing is gained thereby; he must be a respectable young man, even charming if possible, but still inadequate for her passion. She looks down on such a person; she acquires a distaste for love; she becomes almost diffident about her own reality [*Realitet*] when she senses her destiny and sees what actuality [*Virkelighed*] offers. If to love, she says, is nothing else, then it does not amount to much. She becomes proud in her love. This pride makes her interesting; it illuminates her being with heightened color, but it also brings her closer to her downfall—but all this makes her ever more interesting. It is nevertheless best to make sure of her acquaintances first, in order to see if there might be such a suitor. There is no opportunity at home, for practically no one ever visits there, but she does go out, and probably such a person could be found there. It is always precarious to provide such a person before knowing this. Two suitors, each inconsequential in himself, could have a harmful effect because of their relativity. I shall now find out whether there is such a lover in secret who does not have the courage to storm the house, a chicken thief who sees no chance in such a cloister-like house.

Consequently, the strategic principle, the law for every move in this campaign, is always to have tangential contact with her in an interesting situation. Consequently, the interesting is the territory in which the struggle is to be carried on; the potency of the interesting must be exhausted. If I am not much mistaken, her whole nature is designed for this, so that what I ask for is precisely what she gives—indeed, what she asks for. What it all depends on is to keep watch on what the individual can give and what she requires as a consequence of that. My love affairs, therefore, always have a reality [*Realitet*] for me personally; they amount to a life factor, an educational period that I definitely know all about, and I often even link with it some skill or other. For the sake of the first girl, I learned to dance; for the sake of the little dancer, I learned to speak French. At that time, like all fools, I went to the market and was often cheated. Now I buy before the market opens. Perhaps she has exhausted one aspect of the interesting; her inclosed life seems to indicate that. The point, then, is to find another aspect that at first glance may not seem so to her but that precisely because of this impediment becomes interesting to her. To that end, I choose not the poetic but the prosaic. So this is the beginning. First of all, her womanliness is neutralized by prosaic common sense and ridicule, not directly but indirectly, at the same time by the absolutely neutral, namely, intellect. She almost loses the feeling of being a woman, but in this state she is not able to stand out alone; she throws herself into my arms, not as if I were a lover—no, still completely neutrally. Now her womanliness is aroused; one coaxes it forth to its extreme point of elasticity, allows her to offend against some actual validity or other. She goes beyond it; her womanliness reaches almost supranatural heights; she belongs to me with a world of passion.

The fifth

Well, I did not need to go far. She visits at the home of Mr. Baxter the wholesaler. Here I found not only her but also a person who for me appeared just as opportunely. Edward,[74] the son of the house, is head over heels in love with her—it takes but half an eye to see it when one looks into his eyes. He is in the business, in his father's office, a good-looking fellow, very pleasant, a bit shy, and I believe this last trait does not damage him in her eyes.

Poor Edward! He does not have the slightest idea how to proceed with his love. When he knows she is going to be there in the evening, he dresses for her sake alone, puts on his new black suit for her sake alone, his fancy cuffs for her sake alone—and thus cuts an almost ludicrous figure among the other daily company in the drawing room. His bashfulness verges on the unbelievable. If it were a guise, then Edward would be a dangerous rival to me. It takes great art to use bashfulness, but one does achieve a great deal with it. How often I have used bashfulness to trick a little miss! Ordinarily, young girls speak very harshly about bashful men, but secretly they like them. A little bashfulness flatters a teenage girl's vanity, makes her feel superior; it is her earnest money. When they are lulled to sleep, then at the very time they believe you are about to perish from bashfulness, you show them that you are so far from it that you are quite self-reliant. Bashfulness makes a man lose his masculine significance, and therefore it is a relatively good means for neutralizing the sex relation. Therefore, when they perceive that it was only a guise, they become so abashed that they blush inwardly, feel very strongly that in a way they have overstepped their limits; it is just as if they continued to treat a boy as a child too long.

The seventh

So now we are friends, Edward and I. There is between us a true friendship, a beautiful relationship, such as has not existed since the most beautiful days of Greece. We were on intimate terms at once when, after having involved him in a multiplicity of observations about Cordelia, I managed to make him confess his secret. Of course, when all the secrets come out together, then this one can come along. Poor fellow, he has been pining for a long time already. He spruces himself up every time she comes, then escorts her home in the evening; his heart pounds at the thought of her arm resting on his. They walk home, looking at the stars. He rings her doorbell; she disap-

I
318

pears; he despairs—but has hopes for the next time. As yet he has not had the courage to step across her threshold, he who has such a superb opportunity. Although I cannot refrain from secretly deriding Edward, there is nevertheless something beautiful in his childlikeness. Although I ordinarily fancy myself to be fairly conversant with the whole sum and substance of the erotic, I have never noticed this state in myself, this anxiety and trembling of infatuation, that is, to the degree that it deprives me of my composure, for at other times I know it all right, but with me it is such that it makes me stronger instead. Perhaps someone would say that I have never really been in love—maybe so. I have taken Edward to task; I have encouraged him to depend upon my friendship. Tomorrow he will take a decisive step, go in person to her and invite her. I managed to lead him to the preposterous idea of inviting me to go along; I promised him to do so. He takes it as an extraordinary show of friendship. The situation is just as I want it; it amounts to bursting unexpectedly through the door into the room. Should she have the remotest doubt about the significance of my appearance, my appearance will in turn confuse everything.

Previously it has never been my habit to prepare myself for my conversations; now it has become a necessity for me in order to entertain the aunt. In other words, I have now taken on the respectable commission of conversing with her and thereby covering Edward's infatuated approaches to Cordelia. Earlier, the aunt lived out in the country, and I am making considerable progress in knowledge of and competence in the subject through the aunt's communications based on her experience as well as through my own careful study of works in agronomy.

I am scoring a big success with the aunt; she regards me as a stable and steady person, someone with whom it is really a pleasure to associate, not like some of our stylish young dandies. I do not seem to stand very well with Cordelia. To be sure, she is too purely and innocently womanly to require that every man pay his respects to her, but she still feels far too much the rebelliousness in my character.

When I am sitting this way in the cozy drawing room, when she, like a good angel, is spreading loveliness everywhere, over all with whom she comes in touch, over good and evil, I at times lose patience inwardly and am tempted to rush out of my hiding place, for although I am sitting before the eyes of all in the drawing room, I am still on watch. I am tempted to seize her hand, to enfold the girl in my arms, to hide her inside me for fear that someone might take her away from me. Or when Edward and I take our leave of them in the evening, when she extends her hand in farewell and I hold it in mine, I find it very difficult at times to let the bird slip out of my hand. Patience— *quod antea fuit impetus, nunc ratio est* [what was impulse then is science now][75]—she must be spun into my web in a totally different way, and then suddenly I shall let the full force of love burst forth. We have not spoiled that moment for ourselves by spooning, by premature anticipations—you can thank me for that, my Cordelia. I am working to develop the contrast; I am pulling the bow of love tighter in order to wound all the deeper. Like an archer, I slacken the string, pull it tight again, listen to its song; it is my martial music, but as yet I do not aim—as yet I do not place the arrow to the string.

When a small number of people often come together in the same room, a tradition readily develops as to where each individual has his place, his station; it becomes a kind of picture a person can unroll for himself when he so desires, a map of the terrain. So it is also with us in the Wahl house—together we form a picture. We drink tea there evenings. The aunt, who until now has been sitting on the sofa, usually moves to the little sewing table, which place Cordelia in turn vacates. She then goes over to the tea table in front of the sofa; Edward follows her, and I follow the aunt. Edward strives for an air of mystery. He wants to whisper and usually does it so well that he becomes entirely mute; I make no secret of my effusions to the aunt—market prices, an estimate of how many quarts of milk it takes for one pound of butter through the medium of cream and the dialectic of the butter churn. Indeed, it is not only something any young girl can listen to without harm, but, what is far more unusual, it is a solid and fundamental and edifying conversation that is equally ennobling to the head and the heart. I usually turn my back to the tea table and to Edward's and Cordelia's romance; I romance with the aunt. And is not nature magnificent and wise in what she produces, what a precious gift is butter, what a glorious accomplishment of nature and art! The aunt would surely not be able to hear what was being said between Edward and Cordelia, assuming that something really was being said—this I had promised Edward, and I always keep my word. I, however, can hear perfectly every single word that is exchanged, hear every movement. It is very important to me, because what a person may venture in his despair cannot be known. The most circumspect and most timid people at times dare to do the most extreme things. Although I do not have the slightest to do with the two isolated people, I nevertheless can readily perceive in Cordelia that I am always invisibly present between her and Edward.

But it is a curious picture we four make together. I presumably could find an analogy if I were to think of well-known types, and then I might think of myself as Mephistopheles, but the difficulty is that Edward is no Faust. If I make myself Faust, then the difficulty again is that Edward certainly is no Mephistopheles. Nor am I a Mephistopheles, least of all in Edward's eyes. He regards me as the good jinni of his love, and in that he is right; at least he can be sure that no one watches over his love more carefully than I do. I have promised him to engage the aunt in conversation, and I carry out this respectable duty most earnestly. The aunt almost vanishes before our eyes in pure agronomy; we go into the kitchen and the cellars, up into the attic, look at the chickens and ducks, geese, etc. All this offends Cordelia. She, of course, cannot comprehend what I really want. I remain an enigma to her, but an enigma that does not tempt her to guess but that exasperates, indeed, makes her indignant. She senses very well that her aunt is becoming almost ludicrous, and yet she is such a respectable lady that she certainly does not deserve it. On the other hand, I do it so well that she is fully aware that it would be futile for her to try to sway me. Sometimes I carry it so far that I make Cordelia very secretly smile at her aunt. These are exercises that must be done. It is not as if I were doing this in conjunction with Cordelia—far from it; then I would never bring her to smile at her aunt. I remain unchanged, earnest, thorough, but she cannot help smiling. This is the first false teaching: we must teach her to smile ironically, but this smile applies to me just as much as to the aunt; for she does not know at all what to think of me. But it could just be that I was the kind of young man who became old prematurely; it is possible; there could be a second possibility, a third, etc. Having smiled at her aunt, she is indignant with herself; I turn around and, while I continue to speak with the aunt, I look very gravely at her, whereupon she smiles at me, at the situation.

I
321

Our relationship is not the tender and trusting embrace of understanding, not one of attraction; it is the repulsion of misunderstanding. There is actually nothing at all in my relationship with her; it is purely intellectual, which for a young girl is naturally nothing at all. The method I employ has nevertheless its extraordinary conveniences. A person who plays the gallant arouses suspicions and stirs up resistance to himself; I am exempt from all that. I am not being watched; on the contrary, I am marked rather as a dependable man fit to watch over the young girl. The method has only one defect, which is that it is slow, but for that reason it can be used successfully against individuals only when the interesting is to be gained.

What a reinvigorating power a young girl has—not the freshness of the morning air, not the sighing of the wind, not the coolness of the sea, not the fragrance of wine, its aroma—nothing in the world has this reinvigorating power.

I hope that soon I shall have brought her to the point where she hates me. I have assumed completely the character of a confirmed bachelor. I talk about nothing else than sitting comfortably, lying at ease, having a trusty servant, a friend with good footing so that I can rely on him when we walk arm in arm. Now, if I can persuade the aunt to forsake her agricultural observations, I can lead her in this direction in order to have a more direct occasion for irony. One may laugh at a bachelor, indeed, have little pity for him; but a young man who (although not devoid of intelligence) by such behavior outrages a young girl—all the significance of her sex, its beauty and its poetry, is annihilated.

In this way the days go by. I see her but do not speak with her; I speak with the aunt in her presence. Occasionally at night, it may cross my mind to pour out my love. Then, wrapped in my cape, with my hat pulled down over my eyes, I go and walk outside her windows. Her bedroom faces the courtyard but is visible from the street, since the place is on a corner. Sometimes she stands at the window for a moment, or she opens it and looks up at the stars, unseen by all but the one by whom she would least of all think to be noticed. In these nocturnal hours, I walk around like a ghost; like a ghost I inhabit the place where her dwelling is. Then I forget everything, have no plans, no reckonings, cast understanding overboard, expand and fortify my chest with deep sighs, a motion I need in order not to suffer from my systematic conduct. Others are virtuous by day, sin at night; I am dissimulation by day—at night I am sheer desire. If she saw me here, if she could look into my soul—if.

If this girl is willing to understand herself, she must admit that I am a man for her. She is too intense, too deeply moved, to be happy in marriage; it would be too meager for her to let herself fall for an outright seducer; when she falls for me, she will rescue the interesting out of the shipwreck. In relation to me, she must, as the philosophers say with a play on words: *zu Grunde gehn* [fall to the ground].[76]

She really is weary of listening to Edward. Just as always, when cramped limits are set for the interesting, one discovers all the more. Sometimes she listens to my conversation with the aunt. When I notice it, far off on the horizon there comes a flashing intimation from a quite different world, to the astonishment of the aunt as well as of Cordelia. The aunt sees the lightning but hears nothing; Cordelia hears the voice but sees nothing. But at the same moment everything is in its quiet order; the conversation between the aunt and me proceeds in its uniform way, like post horses in the stillness of the night; the sad hum of the samovar accompanies it. At such moments, it can sometimes be uncomfortable in the drawing room, especially for Cordelia. She has no one she can talk with or listen to. If she turns to Edward, she runs the risk that he will do something stupid in his bashfulness; if she turns to the other side, toward the aunt and me, the assurance dominant here, the monotonous hammer stroke of the rhythmical conversation, produces the most disagreeable contrast with Edward's lack of assurance. I can well understand that it must seem to Cordelia as if the aunt were bewitched, so perfectly does she move to the tempo of my rhythm. She cannot participate in this conversation either, because one of the means I have also used to outrage her is that I allow myself to treat her just like a child. It is not as if I for that reason would allow myself any liberties whatever with her, far from it. I well know the upsetting effects such things can have, and the point is that her womanliness must be able to rise up pure and beautiful again. Because of my intimate relationship with the aunt, it is easy for me to treat her like a child who has no understanding of the world. Her womanliness is not insulted thereby but merely neutralized, for the fact that she does not know market prices cannot insult her womanliness, but the supposition that this is the ultimate in life can certainly be revolting to her. With my powerful assistance on this score, the aunt is outdoing herself. She has become almost fanatic—something she can thank me for. The only thing about me that she cannot stand is that I have no position. Now I have adopted the habit of saying whenever a vacancy in some office is mentioned: "There is a position for me," and thereupon discuss it very gravely with her. Cordelia always perceives the irony, which is precisely what I want.

Poor Edward! It is a shame that he is not called Fritz.[77] Every time I ponder my relationship with him, I always think of Fritz in *The Bride*.[78] Moreover, like his prototype, Edward is

I
323

a corporal in the civic militia. To be honest, Edward is also rather boring. He is doing it all wrong, always arrives so formal and spruced up. Out of friendship for him, *unter uns gesagt* [just between us], I come visiting dressed as negligently as possible. Poor Edward! The one thing that almost makes me feel bad is that he is so infinitely obliged to me that he hardly knows how he will thank me. For me to be thanked for it—that is too much.

Why can't you just be nice and quiet? What have you done all morning but shake my awnings, tug at my window street-mirror and the cord on it, play with the bellpull wire from the fourth floor, push against the windowpanes—in short, proclaim your existence in every way as if you wanted to beckon me out to you? Yes, the weather is fine enough, but I have no inclination; let me stay home. [79]—You playful, exuberant zephyrs, you happy lads, go by yourselves; have your fun as always with the young girls. Yes, I know, no one knows how to embrace a young girl as seductively as you. It is futile for her to try to wriggle away from you; she cannot extricate herself from your snares—nor does she wish to, for you cool and refresh and do not agitate. Go your own way! Leave me out of it. But then you think you have no enjoyment in it; you are not doing it for your own sake. Well, then, I shall go along with you, but on two conditions. —Number one. On Kongens Nytorv there lives a young girl; she is very lovely but also has the effrontery to be unwilling to love me—yes, what is worse, she loves someone else, and it has gone so far that they go walking together arm in arm. I know he goes to fetch her at one o'clock. Now promise me that the strongest winds among you will remain hidden somewhere nearby until the moment he comes through the street door with her. The very moment he is about to turn down Store Kongensgade, this detachment will rush out and in the most courteous way take the hat off his head and carry it at a steady speed exactly one yard ahead of him—not any faster, for then it is conceivable that he would go home. He continually expects to grab it the next second; he does not even let go of her arm. In that manner you will lead

him and her through Store Kongensgade along the wall to
Nørreport, to Høibroplads. —How long will that take? I think
just about a half hour. Exactly at half past one, I shall approach
from Østergade. Now, when the detachment has led the lovers out into the middle of the square, a powerful attack will be
made on them in which you will also snatch off her hat, di-
shevel her curls, carry off her shawl, while all this time his hat
is jubilantly rising aloft higher and higher. In short, you will
produce such a confusion that not only I but the very honored
public will burst into roars of laughter, the dogs will begin to
bark, the tower watchman to toll. You will contrive to have
her hat soar over to me, who will be the lucky fellow who
hands it over to her. —Number two. The unit that accompanies me will obey my every suggestion, keep within the
bounds of propriety, insult no pretty girl, take no more liberties than will allow her childlike soul, during the entire joke,
to preserve its delight, her lips their smile, her eyes their calm-
ness, and her heart to remain without anxiety. If one of you
dares to act in any other way, may your name be cursed. —
And now be off to life and gladness, to youth and beauty.
Show me what I so often have seen, what I never grow weary
of seeing; show me a beautiful young girl and unfurl her
beauty to me in such a way that she herself becomes even more
beautiful; examine her in such a way that she finds joy in the
examination! —I choose Bredgade, but remember, I have at
my disposal only the time until half past one.—

There comes a young girl, all starched and dressed up—to
be sure, it is Sunday today. —Cool her off a bit, fan her, stroke
her with gentle breezes, embrace her with your innocent
touch! What delicate reddening of her cheeks I detect! Her lips
become more vividly colored; her bosom rises. —Is it not
true, my girl, that it is indescribable, that it is blissful pleasure
to breathe this fresh air? The little collar flutters like a leaf.
How healthy and full her breathing. Her pace slackens, she is
almost carried along by the gentle breeze—like a cloud, like a
dream. —Blow a little harder, in longer drafts! —She pulls
herself together, draws her arms closer to her bosom, which
she covers more carefully lest a puff of wind be too indiscreet

I
325

and sneak in agilely and coolly under this light covering. —
Her color rises, her cheeks become full, her eyes clearer, her
step more rhythmic. All opposition enhances a person's
beauty. Every young girl ought to fall in love with a zephyr,
for no man knows how to heighten her beauty the way it does
when it skirmishes with her. —Her body leans forward a bit;
she is looking down at the toes of her shoes. —Stop for a
while! You are blowing too hard, and her body hunches up
and loses its beautiful slimness. —Cool her off a little! —Isn't
it refreshing, my girl, when you are warm and then feel these
cooling shivers? You could fling out your arms in gratitude, in
joy over existence. —She turns sideways—now, quickly, a
powerful puff so that I can have a hint of the beauty of her
form. —A bit stronger so that the folds cling more closely. —
It is too much! Her bearing becomes ungraceful; her light foot-
step is thrown off. She turns around again. —Blow, now, let
her prove herself! —That is enough, that is too much: one of
her curls has tumbled down. —Control yourselves, please! —
There comes a whole regiment marching:

Die eine ist verliebt gar sehr;
Die andre wäre es gerne
[The one is very much in love;
The other would very much like to be].[80]

Yes, it is undeniably a bad employment in life to go walking
with a prospective brother-in-law on his left arm. For a girl, it
is just about the same as it is for a man to be a supplementary
clerk. —But the supplementary clerk can advance; moreover,
he has his place in the office, is present on special occasions—
this is not the sister-in-law's fate. But then in compensation
her advancement is not so slow—when she advances and is
moved into another office. —Blow a little harder now! If you
have something firm to hold onto, you can offer resistance all
right. —The center presses forward vigorously; the wings are
unable to follow. —He stands firmly enough. The wind cannot budge him; he is too heavy for that—but also too heavy for
the wings to be able to lift him from the earth. He charges
ahead to show—that he is a heavy body. But the more un-

moved he remains, the more the girls suffer from it. —My beautiful ladies, may I not be of service with some good advice: Leave the prospective husband and brother-in-law out of it; [81]try to walk all alone, and you will have much more enjoyment out of it. —Blow more gently now, please! —How they toss about in the waves of wind; now they are performing dance steps sideways down the street—can any dance music evoke a livelier cheerfulness? And yet the wind does not exhaust them; it strengthens. —Now, side by side, they sweep along down the street in full sail—can any waltz sweep a young girl along more seductively, and yet the wind is not tiring but sustaining. Now they turn around and face the husband and brother-in-law. —Isn't it true that a little resistance is pleasant? You willingly struggle in order to come into possession of what you love, and very likely you will attain what you are fighting for. There is a higher Governance that comes to the aid of love; that is why the man has the wind in his favor. —Did I not organize it right: if you have the wind on your own back, you can easily rush past the beloved, but when it is against you, you are pleasantly stimulated; then you fly to the beloved's side, and the puffing of the wind makes you healthier, more tempting, more seductive, and the puffing of the wind cools the fruit of your lips, which is enjoyed best when cold, because it is so hot, just as champagne inflames when it almost chills. —How they laugh and talk—and the wind carries the words away; is there really anything to talk about? — And they laugh again and lean against the wind and hold on to their hats and watch their feet. —Better stop now, lest the young girls become impatient and angry with us or afraid of us!

That's right, resolutely and powerfully, the right foot before the left. —How boldly and saucily she looks around at the world. —If I am seeing right, she is indeed holding on to the person's arm and therefore is engaged. Let me see what present you received on life's Christmas tree, my child. —Ah, yes! He really seems to be a very solid fiancé. So she is in the first stage of the engagement; she loves him—maybe so, but her love, broad and copious, nevertheless flutters loosely about him. She still possesses the cloak of love that can cover a multitude.[82] —Blow a little harder! —Well, if you walk so fast, it is no wonder that the ribbons on your hat stretch against the wind, making it look as if these, like wings, were carrying this light creature—and her love—and it, too, follows like a fairy veil the wind plays with. Yes, when love is looked at in this way, it seems so copious, but when one is to be dressed in it, when the veil is to be sewed into a housedress—then there is not material for many puffs.[83] —Good heavens! If you have the courage to risk a step decisive for your whole life, should you not have the heart to go straight against the wind? Who doubts it? Not I—but no temper tantrum, my little miss, no temper tantrum. Time is a hard disciplinarian, and the wind is not so bad either. —Tease her a little! —What happened to the handkerchief? All right, you have it again. There went one of the ribbons from your hat. —It is really very embarrassing for the prospective one who is present. —There comes a girl friend you must greet. It is the first time she has seen you as a fiancée; of course, it is to make an appearance as a fiancée that you are here on Bredgade and intend to go out on Langelinie. As far as I know, it is the custom for the newlyweds to go to church the first Sunday after the wedding; the newly engaged, however, walk on Langelinie. Well, generally an engagement does have much in common with Langelinie. —Watch out, now, the wind is taking your hat. Hang on to it, bend your head down. —It is really too bad that you did not manage to greet your girl friend at all, did not gain the composure to greet her with the superior air an engaged girl is supposed to assume before the not-engaged. —Blow more gently now! — Good days are coming now.

How she clings to her beloved; now she is far enough ahead of him to turn her head and look up at him and rejoice in him, her wealth, her good fortune, her hope, her future. —O my girl, you make too much of him. —Or does he not have me and the wind to thank that he looks so vigorous? And do you yourself not have me and the soft breezes, which now healed you and made you cast your pain into oblivion, to thank that

you yourself look so exuberant, so full of longing and anticipation?

> I do not want a student
> Who lies and reads at night,
> But I do want an officer
> Who goes with feathers in his hat.[84]

One sees it in you at once, my girl; there is something in your
look. —No, a student is by no means good enough for you. —
But why exactly an officer? A university graduate [85]all
through with his studies—would he not serve just as well? —
But right now I can provide you with neither an officer nor a
university graduate. But I can provide some tempering cool
breezes. —Blow a little now! —That was fine. Toss the silk
scarf back over the shoulder; walk very slowly so that your
cheeks become a bit more pale, the glow of your eyes not so
intense. —Just so. Yes, a little exercise, especially in such delightful weather as today, and then a little patience, and you
will surely have your officer.

There go two who are destined for each other. What rhythm
in their step, what assurance, built on mutual trust, in their
whole bearing; what *harmonia praestabilita* [preestablished har-
mony][86] in all their movements, what self-sufficient solidity.
They are not light and graceful in posture; they are not dancing
with each other. No, there is durability about them, a boldness
that awakens an infallible hope, that inspires mutual respect. I
wager that their view of life is this: life is a road. And they do
seem determined to walk arm in arm with each other through
life's joys and sorrows. [87]They are so harmonious that the lady
has even surrendered her claim to walk on the flagstones. —
But, you dear zephyrs, why are you so busy with that couple?
They do not seem to be worth the attention. Is there anything
in particular to look at? [88]—But it is half past one—off to Høibroplads.

I
329

One would not believe it possible to plot so entirely accurately the history of the development of a psyche. It shows
how sound Cordelia is. Truly, she is a remarkable girl. To be

sure, she is quiet and modest, unassuming, but yet there is unconsciously within her an enormous claim. —This struck me today when I saw her go into her house. The little resistance that a puff of wind can give seems to arouse all the forces within her, but there nevertheless is no inner conflict. She is not an insignificant little girl who vanishes between one's fingers, so frail that one is almost afraid that she will break in two when looked at, but neither is she a pretentious ornamental flower. Therefore, like a physician, I can delight in observing all the symptoms in this health record.

In my attack, I am beginning to close in on her gradually, to shift into a more direct attack. If I were to indicate this change on my military map of the family, I would say: I have turned my chair so that I am now turned sideways toward her. I am involved with her more; I address her, elicit her response. Her soul has passion, intensity, and, without being brought to the point of oddity by vain and foolish reflections, she has a need for the unusual. My irony over the foolishness of people, my ridicule of their cowardliness, of their tepid torpidity, captivate her. She likes to drive the sun chariot across the arch of heaven and to come close enough to earth to scorch people a little. But she does not trust me; as yet I have prevented every approach, even in an intellectual sense. She must be strengthened within herself before I let her find support from me. Now and then it may seem as if I were seeking to make her my confidante in my freemasonry, but that is only momentary. She herself must be developed within herself; she must feel the resilience of her soul; she must come to grips with the world and lift it. In her eyes and in what she says, it is easy for me to see the progress she is making; only once have I seen a devastating wrath there. She must owe me nothing, for she must be free. Only in freedom is there love; only in freedom are there diversion and everlasting amusement. Although I am making arrangements so that she will sink into my arms as if by a necessity of nature and am striving to make her gravitate toward me, the point nevertheless is that she should not fall like a heavy body but as mind should gravitate toward mind. Although she will belong to me, yet it must not be in the unbeautiful way of resting upon me as a burden. She must be neither an appendage in the physical sense nor an obligation in the moral sense. Between us two, only freedom's own game will prevail. She must be so light to me that I can carry her on my arm.

Almost too much does Cordelia preoccupy me. I am losing my balance again—not face-to-face with her when she is present, but when I am alone with her in the strictest sense. I may yearn for her, not in order to speak with her but merely to have her image float past me; when I know she has gone out, I may stealthily follow her, not to be seen but to see. The other evening, we left the Baxter house together; Edward escorted her. I parted from them in the greatest haste, hurried over to another street where my servant was waiting for me. In no time at all, I had changed my clothes and met her again without her suspecting it. Edward was just as mute as ever. I certainly am in love, but not in the ordinary sense, and one must be extremely careful about that; it always has dangerous consequences, and, after all, one is that way only once. But the god of love is blind, and if one is clever, he can surely be fooled. The art is to be as receptive as possible to impressions, to know what impression one is making and what impression one has of each girl. In that way, one can be in love with many girls at the same time, because one is in love in a different way with each one. To love one girl is too little; to love all is superficiality; to know oneself and to love as many as possible, to let one's soul conceal all the powers of love inside itself so that each receives its specific nourishment while the consciousness nevertheless embraces the whole—that is enjoyment, that is living.

I
331

July 3

Edward really cannot complain about me. As a matter of fact, I want Cordelia to fall in love with him so that through him she will acquire a distaste for plain and simple love and thereby go beyond her own limits, but that requires in particular that Edward not be a caricature, for that is of no help. Now, Edward is not only a good match in the bourgeois sense, which does not mean anything to her—a girl of seventeen does not care about such things—but he has several appealing personal qualities that I try to help him show in the most advantageous light. Like a lady's maid or a decorator, I deck him out as well as the resources of the house allow—in fact, I sometimes hang a little borrowed finery on him. When we go together over there, it seems very strange to me to walk along at his side. To me it is as if he were my brother, my son, and yet he is my friend, my contemporary, my rival. He can never become dangerous to me. Hence, the higher I can elevate him, since he is bound to fall, the better it is, the more it awakens in Cordelia a consciousness of what she disdains, the more intense the presentiment of what she desires. I lend him a helping hand, I recommend him—in short, I do everything a friend can do for a friend. In order to set my own coldness in relief, I almost rant against Edward. I characterize him as a dreamer. Since Edward does not know how to help himself at all, I have to push him forward.

Cordelia hates and fears me. What does a young girl fear? Intellect [*Aand*]. Why? Because intellect constitutes the negation of her entire womanly existence. Masculine handsomeness, prepossessing nature, etc. are fine resources. One can also make a conquest with them but never win a complete victory. Why? Because one is making war on a girl in her own sphere of power, and in her own sphere of power she is always the stronger. With these resources, one can make a girl blush, drop her eyes, but one can never generate the indescribable, captivating anxiety that makes her beauty interesting.

> *Non formosus erat, sed erat facundus Ulixes,*
> *Et tamen aequoreas torsit amore Deas*
> [Ulysses was not comely, but he was eloquent,
> Yet he fired two goddesses of the sea with love].[89]

Now, everyone ought to know his own powers. But something that has often shocked me is that even those who have talents act like such bunglers. A person actually ought to be able to see immediately in any young girl who has become a victim to another's love—or, more correctly, to her own—in what way she has been deceived. The practiced killer uses a particular stab, and the experienced policeman immediately recognizes the criminal when he sees the wound. But where does one meet such systematic seducers, such psychologists? For most people, to seduce a young girl means to seduce a young girl, period—and yet a whole language is concealed in this thought.

Being a woman—she hates me; being a talented woman— she fears me; being a good mind—she loves me. This conflict I have now established in her soul as the first step. My pride, my defiance, my cold ridicule, my callous irony tempt her— not as if she would want to love me—no, there is certainly not the slightest trace of any such feelings in her, least of all for me. She wants to compete with me. What tempts her is the proud independence in relation to people, a freedom like that of the desert Arabs. My laughter and eccentricity neutralize every erotic expression. She is fairly free with me, and insofar as there is any reserve, it is more intellectual than womanly. She is so far from seeing a lover in me that our relationship is only that of two good minds. She takes me by the hand, clasps my hand, laughs, pays a certain attention to me in the purely Greek sense. Then when the ironist and the ridiculer have duped her long enough, I follow the instructions in an old verse: the knight spreads out his cape so red and bids the beautiful maiden sit on it.[90] I spread out my cape—not in order to sit on the greensward with her but to vanish into the air with her in a flight of thought. Or I do not take her along but set myself astride a thought, wave at her, throw her a kiss, and become invisible to her, only audible in the hum of winged words; I, unlike Jehovah,[91] become not more and more visible in the voice, but less and less, for the more I speak the higher I ascend. Then she wants to go along, away on this bold flight of thought. But it is just for a moment; the next instant I am cold and arid.[92]

There are various kinds of womanly blushes. There is the dense brick-red blush. [93]This is the one novelists always have in good supply when they have their heroines blush *über und über* [through and through]. There is the delicate blush; it is the spirit's sunrise-red. In a young girl it is priceless. The fleeting blush that accompanies a happy thought is beautiful in a man, more beautiful in a youth, lovely in a woman. It is a flash of lightning, the summer lightning of the spirit. It is most beautiful in a youth, lovely in a girl, because it manifests itself in its virginal purity and thus also has the modesty of surprise. The older one grows, the more this kind of blush disappears.

Sometimes I read something aloud to Cordelia—for the most part very trivial things. As usual, Edward has to be an unwitting instrument—that is, I have pointed out to him that lending a girl books is a very good way to establish rapport with her. Indeed, he has gained in various ways thereby, for she is much obliged to him for it. I am the one who gains the most, for I determine the choice of books and continually stay in the background. Here I have a wide playground for making my observations. I can give Edward whichever books I want to; literature is not his line; I can try what I wish, to any extreme whatsoever. Now when I visit her in the evening, I pick up the book as if by chance, leaf through it a little, read half aloud, commend Edward for his attentiveness. Last evening, by means of a test, I wanted to assure myself of the resilience of her soul. I was puzzled about whether I should have Edward lend her Schiller's *Gedichte* so that I could accidentally come across Thekla's song[94] to recite, or Bürger's *Gedichte*.[95] I selected the latter, especially because his "Lenore" is somewhat highflown, however beautiful it is otherwise. I opened it to "Lenore" and read this poem aloud with all the pathos I could muster. Cordelia was moved; she sewed hurriedly, as if it were she Vilhelm came to fetch. I stopped; the aunt had listened without very much sympathy. She has no fear of any Vilhelms living or dead and, moreover, does not know German well, but she found herself quite in her element when I showed her the beautifully bound copy and started a conversation about bookbinding work. [96]My intention was to destroy in Cordelia the impression of pathos the very moment it was awakened. She became a little anxious, but it was apparent to me that this anxiety did not have a tempting effect on her but made her *unheimlich* [uncomfortable].

Today my eyes have rested upon her for the first time. It is said that sleep can make the eyelids so heavy that they close by themselves; perhaps this glance would be capable of something similar. Her eyes close, and yet dark forces stir within her. She does not see that I am looking at her; she feels it, feels it through her entire body. Her eyes close, and it is night, but within her it is bright day.

Edward must go. He is at the last extremity; I can expect that at any moment he will go and make a declaration of love to her. No one knows that better than I, his confidant, who with diligence keep him overwrought so that he can influence Cordelia all the more. But to let him confess his love is too risky. I know very well that he will receive a "No," but that will not be the end of the story. He will certainly take it very hard. This perhaps will move and agitate Cordelia. Although in that case I need not fear the worst, that she would change her mind, nevertheless her soul's pride will possibly suffer from this unalloyed compassion. If that happens, my whole intention with Edward will be a complete failure.

My relationship with Cordelia is beginning to take a dramatic course. Something has to happen; whatever it is, I can no longer have a relationship simply as an observer without letting the moment slip by. She must be surprised; it is necessary, but if I wish to surprise her, I must be at my post. That which ordinarily would surprise perhaps would not affect her in that way. She must be really surprised in such a way that at the very beginning that which is close to being the cause of her surprise is something that happens quite ordinarily. It must gradually become manifest that nevertheless something surprising was implicit in it. This is always the law for the interesting, and this in turn is the law for all my moves with regard to Cordelia. If one just knows how to surprise, one always

wins the game. The energy of the person involved is temporarily suspended; one makes it impossible for her to act, and
this happens whether extraordinary or ordinary means are
used. I still remember with a certain self-satisfaction a rash
venture with a woman of a rather aristocratic family. For some
time, I had been covertly prowling around her looking for an
interesting contact, but to no avail, and then one noon I met
her on the street. I was certain that she did not recognize me or
know that I lived here in the city. She was walking alone. I
slipped by her and thus managed to meet her face-to-face. I
stepped aside for her; she stayed on the flagstones. Just at that
moment, I cast a sorrowful look at her; I believe I almost had
tears in my eyes. I took off my hat. She stopped. With a shak-
ing voice and a dreamy look, I said: Do not be angry, gracious
lady; you have such a striking resemblance to a creature whom
I love with all my soul, but who lives far away from me, that
you will forgive my strange conduct. She believed I was a
dreamer, and a young girl may very well like a little dreaminess, especially when she also feels her superiority and dares to
smile at one. Sure enough, she smiled, which was indescribably becoming to her. With aristocratic condescension, she
greeted me and smiled. She continued her walk; I accompanied her for a few steps. I met her a few days later; I ventured
to greet her. She laughed at me. —Patience is still a precious
virtue, and he who laughs last laughs best.

Various means of surprising Cordelia are conceivable. I
could try to raise an erotic storm capable of tearing up trees by
the roots. By means of it, I could see if it is possible to lift her
off the ground, to lift her out of the historical context, and
through secret meetings to generate her passion in this unsettled state. It is not inconceivable that it could be done. A girl
with her passion can be made to do anything one pleases. But
it would be esthetically incorrect. I do not relish romantic gid-
diness, and this state is to be commended only when one is
dealing with girls who are able to acquire a poetic afterglow in
no other way. Moreover, one easily loses out on the real enjoyment, for too much turmoil is also damaging. On her, it

would completely fail in its effect. In a couple of drafts, I would have imbibed what I could have had the use of for a long time—indeed, worse yet, what I with circumspection could have enjoyed more fully and richly. Cordelia is not to be enjoyed in a state of elation. If I were to behave in that manner, she perhaps would be taken by surprise at first, but she would soon be sated, precisely because this surprise would lie too close to her audacious soul.

A plain and simple engagement is the best of all means, the most suitable for the purpose. She will perhaps believe her own ears even less when she hears me make a prosaic declaration of love, also ask for her hand, even less than if she listened to my ardent eloquence, imbibed my poisonous intoxicating potion, heard her heart pound at the thought of an elopement.[97]

The banefulness of an engagement is always the ethical in it. The ethical is just as boring in scholarship as in life. What a difference! Under the esthetic sky, everything is buoyant, beautiful, transient; when ethics arrives on the scene, everything becomes harsh, angular, infinitely *langweiligt* [boring].[98] But in the strictest sense an engagement does not have ethical reality [*Realitet*] such as a marriage has; it has validity only *ex consensu gentium* [by universal consensus]. This ambiguity can be very advantageous for me. It has just enough of the ethical in it so that in due time Cordelia will gain the impression that she is transgressing the boundaries of the universal; moreover, the ethical in it is not so earnest that I have to fear a more serious jolt.

I have always had a certain respect for the ethical. I have never made a promise of marriage to any girl, not even nonchalantly; insofar as it might seem that I am doing it here, it is merely a simulated move. I shall very likely manage things in such a way that it is she herself who breaks the engagement. My chivalrous pride has contempt for making promises. I have contempt when a judge entices a culprit into a confession with the promise of freedom. A judge like that renounces his power and his talent. In my practice, there is even the additional circumstance that I desire nothing that in the strictest sense is not freedom's gift. Let vulgar seducers use such means. What do they gain anyway? He who does not know how to encircle a girl so that she loses sight of everything he does not want her to see, he who does not know how to poetize himself into a girl so that it is from her that everything proceeds as he wants it—he is and remains a bungler. [99]I shall not envy him his enjoyment. Such a person is and remains a bungler, a seducer, which I can by no means be called. I am an esthete, an eroticist, who has grasped the nature and the point of love, who believes in love and knows it from the ground up, and I reserve for myself only the private opinion that no love affair should last more than a half year at most and that any relationship is over as soon as one has enjoyed the ultimate. All this I know; I also know that the highest enjoyment imaginable is to be loved, loved more than anything else in the world. To poetize oneself into a girl is an art; to poetize oneself out of her is a masterstroke. But the latter depends essentially on the former.

There was the possibility of another way. I could do everything to get her engaged to Edward. I would then become a family friend. Edward would trust me unconditionally, for I would be the one to whom he would more or less owe his good fortune. I would thereby acquire a better camouflage. But it will not do. She cannot become engaged to Edward without her being diminished in one way or another. Add to that the fact that my relationship with her would become more engagingly provocative than interesting. The infinite prosiness of an engagement is precisely the sounding board for the interesting.

Everything is becoming more momentous at the Wahl house. One clearly perceives that underneath the everyday routines there stirs a secret life that soon must proclaim itself in a corresponding disclosure. The Wahl household is making preparations for an engagement. A merely superficial observer might think that the couple would be the aunt and I. What could not such a marriage do for the propagation of agronomical knowledge in the next generation! So then I would be

I
337

Cordelia's uncle. I am a friend of freedom of thought, and no thought is so absurd that I do not have the courage to stick to it. Cordelia is apprehensive of a declaration of love from Edward; Edward is hoping that such a declaration will decide everything. Indeed, he can be sure of that. But to spare him the unpleasant consequences of such a step, I shall steal a march on him. I hope to dismiss him soon; he is actually standing in my way. I really felt that today. Does he not look so dreamy and drunk with love that one may very well fear that he will suddenly rise up like a sleepwalker and in front of the whole assembly confess his love from such an objective point of view that he will not even approach Cordelia. I looked daggers at him today. Just as an elephant picks up something with its trunk, I picked him up with my eyes, the whole of him, and tossed him over backward. Although he remained seated, I believe that he nevertheless had a corresponding sensation in his entire body.

Cordelia is not as self-confident in relation to me as she was before. She has always approached me with womanly assurance; now she is a little unsteady. But it does not mean very much, and it would not be difficult for me to put everything on the old footing. But that I shall not do. Just one more exploration and then the engagement. There can be no difficulties in this. In her surprise, Cordelia will say "Yes," the aunt a fervent "Amen." She will be beside herself with joy to have such an agronomist for a son-in-law. Son-in-law! How thick as thieves we all become when we venture into this domain! I shall not actually become her son-in-law, but only her nephew or, more correctly, *volente deo* [God willing], none of these.

The twenty-third

Today I harvested the fruit of a rumor I had started going around—that I was in love with a young girl. With Edward's help, it also reached Cordelia's ears. She is curious; she watches me, but she does not dare to inquire. And yet it is not unimportant for her to find out definitely, partly because it seems unbelievable to her, and partly because she almost sees in it a precedent for herself, because if such a cold scoffer as I can fall in love, then presumably she can also, without needing to be ashamed. Today I broached the subject. To tell a story in such a way that the point is not lost is, I believe, right up my alley—also, in such a way that it is not divulged prematurely. It is my delight to keep the listeners to my story *in suspenso* by means of minor actions of an episodic nature to ascertain how they want it to turn out, and then in the course of the telling to fool them. My art is to use amphibolies so that the listeners understand one thing from what is said and then suddenly perceive that the words can be interpreted another way. If one really wants to have a chance to make investigations of a particular kind, one must always deliver a speech. In a conversation, the person in question can be more evasive, can, through questions and answers, better conceal the impression the words are making.

With ceremonial earnestness, I began my speech to the aunt. "Shall I attribute this to the kindness of my friends or to the malice of my enemies, and who does not have too many of both the one and the other?" Here the aunt made a comment that I did everything in my power to spin out in order to keep Cordelia, who was listening, in suspense, a suspense she could not dispel since it was the aunt with whom I was talking, and my mood was very ceremonial. I continued: "Or shall I attribute it to chance, the *generatio aequivoca* [spontaneous generation]" (Cordelia obviously did not understand this phrase; it merely confused her, all the more since I gave it a false emphasis, saying it with a sly look as if the point lay there) of a rumor "that I who am accustomed to live hidden from the world have become the subject of discussion inasmuch as they claim I am engaged." Cordelia obviously still lacked my interpretation. I continued, "Shall I attribute it to my friends, since it is always regarded as a great good fortune to have fallen in love" (she was startled); "to my enemies, since it must always be regarded as extremely ludicrous if this good fortune fell to my lot" (a countermove); "or to chance, since there is no foundation to it at all; or to the *generatio aequivoca* of the rumor, since the whole thing must have originated in an empty mind's thoughtless association with itself." With feminine curiosity, the aunt hastened to find out the identity of this woman to whom rumor had been pleased to engage me. I parried every question along that line. The whole story made an impression on Cordelia; I almost believe that Edward's stock went up a few points.

The crucial moment is approaching. I could communicate with the aunt in writing and ask for Cordelia's hand. After all, that is the usual procedure in affairs of the heart, as if it were more natural for the heart to write than to speak. The very philistinism of such a move just might make me decide to do it. If I choose it, I lose the real surprise, and that I cannot relinquish. —If I had a friend, he would perhaps say to me: Have you pondered well this very serious step you are taking, a step that is crucial to all the rest of your life and to another creature's happiness. This is the advantage of having a friend. I have no friend; whether this is an advantage I shall leave undecided, but I regard being free from his advice as an absolute advantage. As for the rest, I have certainly thought through the whole matter in the strictest sense of the word.

On my side there is nothing to hinder the engagement now. So I go a'courting; who would think it to look at me? Soon my insignificant person will be seen from a higher point of view. I shall cease to be a person and become—a match—yes, a good match, the aunt will say. The one I almost feel most sorry for is the aunt, for she loves me with such a pure and upright agronomical love; she almost worships me as her ideal.

Now, I have made many declarations of love in my life, and yet here all my experience is of no help at all, for this declaration must be made in an altogether distinctive way. Primarily what I must drum into myself is that the whole thing is merely a simulated move. I have practiced various steps to see what the best approach might be. To make the moment erotic would be dubious, since this might easily anticipate what should come later and sequentially unfold. To make it very earnest is dangerous—for a young girl, such a moment is of such great significance that her whole soul can be concentrated in it, just as a dying person is concentrated in his last wish. To make it hearty, low comedy would not be in harmony with the mask I have used up to now or with the new one I intend to put on and wear. To make it witty and ironic is too great a risk. If my principal concern, as it commonly is for most people in such a situation, were to lure forth the little "Yes," then it would be as easy as falling off a log. To be sure, this is of importance to me, but not of absolute importance, for even though I reserved this girl for myself, even though I have devoted considerable attention, indeed, all my interest, to her, there nevertheless are conditions under which I would not accept her "Yes." I do not care at all to possess the girl in the external sense but wish to enjoy her artistically. Therefore the beginning must be as artistic as possible. The beginning must be as nebulous as possible; it must be an omnipossibility. If she promptly sees a deceiver in me, then she misunderstands me, for I am no deceiver in the ordinary sense; if she sees a faithful lover in me, then she also misunderstands me. It is a matter of having her soul be determined as little as possible by this episode. At such a moment, a girl's soul is as prophetic as a dying person's.[100] This must be prevented. My dear Cordelia! I am defrauding you of something beautiful, but it cannot be otherwise, and I shall give you all the compensation I can. The whole episode must be kept as insignificant as possible, so that when she has given her consent she will be unable to throw any light whatever on what may be concealed in this situation. It is precisely this infinite possibility that is the interesting. If she is able to predict anything, then I have gone about it the wrong way and the whole relationship loses significance. That she would give her consent because she loves me is unthinkable, for [101]she does not love me at all. The best thing to do is to transform the engagement from an act to an event, from something she does to something that happens to her, something about which she is compelled to say: God alone knows how it really came about.

The thirty-first

Today I wrote a love letter for a third party. For me that is always a great pleasure. In the first place, it is always very interesting to place myself so vividly into the situation, and yet in complete comfort. I fill my pipe and hear about the relationship; the letters from the other party are submitted. How a young girl writes is always a very important subject to me! He sits there head over heels in love like a rat in cheese; he reads her letters aloud, interrupted by my laconic comments: She writes very well; she has feeling, taste, prudence; she has certainly been in love before etc. In the second place, what I am doing is a good deed. I am helping a couple of young people to come together; now I am settling the account. For every happy couple, I select a victim for myself; I make two people happy, at most only one unhappy. I am honest and reliable, have never deceived anyone who has confided in me. It goes without saying that there is always a little joking, but that, after all, is a legitimate perquisite. [102]And why do I enjoy this confidence? Because I know Latin and do my homework, and because I always keep my little stories to myself. And do I not deserve this confidence? After all, I never abuse it.

August 2

[103]The moment had arrived. I caught a glimpse of the aunt on the street and thus knew that she was not at home. Edward was at the customhouse. In all likelihood, Cordelia was home alone. And so she was. She was sitting at the sewing table busy with some handiwork. Rarely did I visit the family in the morning; therefore, she was a little flustered at seeing me. The situation became almost too emotional. She was not to blame for that, for she regained her composure rather easily, but I myself was at fault, for despite my armor plating, she made an unusually powerful impression upon me. How lovely she was in her plain, blue-striped calico housedress, with a freshly picked rose on her bosom. A freshly picked rose—no, the girl herself was like a freshly picked blossom, so fresh was she, so recently arrived! Indeed, who knows where a young girl spends the night—in the land of illusions, I believe—but every morning she returns, and this explains her youthful freshness. She looked so young and yet so fully developed, as if nature, like a tender and luxuriant mother, had this very moment released her from her hand. To me it was as if I were a witness to

I
342

this farewell scene; I saw how that fond mother embraced her once again in farewell, and I heard her say, "Go out into the world now, my child; I have done everything for you. Take now this kiss as a seal upon your lips. It is a seal that guards the sanctuary; it cannot be broken by anyone if you yourself do not want it to be, but when the right one comes you will know him." And she pressed a kiss upon her lips, a kiss, unlike a human kiss, which subtracts something, but rather a divine kiss, which gives everything, which gives the girl the power of the kiss. Wonderful nature, how profound and enigmatic you are! To man you give words, and to the girl the eloquence of the kiss! This kiss was upon her lips, and the farewell upon her brow, and the joyous greeting in her eyes—therefore she simultaneously looked so much at home, for she was the child of the house, and so much the stranger, for she did not know the world but only the fond mother who invisibly watched over her. She was truly lovely, young as a child, and yet adorned with the noble-minded virginal dignity that inspires respect.

Soon, however, I was dispassionate again and solemnly obtuse, as is befitting when one is about to cause something full of meaning to happen in such a way as to make it mean nothing. After a few general remarks, I drew a bit closer to her and came out with my petition. A person who talks like a book is extremely boring to listen to, but sometimes it is rather expedient to talk that way. [104]That is, a book has the remarkable characteristic that it can be interpreted as one pleases. If a person talks like a book, his talking also has the same characteristic. I kept very strictly to the usual formulas. [105]She was surprised, as I had expected; that is undeniable. It is difficult for me to give an account of how she looked. Her expression was multifarious—indeed, just about like the still unpublished but announced commentary on my book, a commentary that contains the possibility of any and every interpretation. One word, and she would have laughed at me; one word, she would have been moved; one word, she would have escaped me—but no word passed my lips; I remained solemnly obtuse and kept precisely to the ritual. —"She had known me for such a short time." Good lord, such difficulties are encountered only on the narrow path of an engagement, not on the flowery path of love.

Very strange. When I was deliberating on the matter during the preceding days, I was resolute enough about it and sure that in her surprise she would say "Yes." There one sees how much all the preparations help; the matter did not turn out that way, for she said neither "Yes" nor "No" but referred me to her aunt. I should have foreseen that. But luck was actually with me, for this result was even better.

The aunt gives her consent; of that I have never entertained the remotest doubt. Cordelia follows her advice. As for my engagement, I shall not boast that it is poetic, for in every way it is utterly philistine and bourgeois. The girl does not know whether she should say "Yes" or "No"; the aunt says "Yes," the girl also says "Yes," I take the girl, she takes me—and now the story begins.

The third

[106]So now I am engaged; so is Cordelia, and that is just about all she knows concerning the whole affair. If she had a girl friend to whom she would talk honestly, she would very likely say, "What it all means, I really do not understand. There is something about him that draws me to him, but I cannot make out what it is. He has a strange power over me, but love him, that I do not and perhaps never shall, but I shall surely be able to endure living with him and thus also be quite happy with him, for he will probably not demand too much if one only sticks it out with him." My dear Cordelia! Perhaps he will require something more, and in return less endurance. —Of all ludicrous things an engagement is still the most ludicrous. [107]There is at least meaning in a marriage, even if this meaning does not suit me. An engagement is a purely human invention and is no credit whatsoever to its inventor. It is neither one thing nor the other and has as much to do with love as the ribbon the beadle wears down his back has to do with a professor's academic gown. Now I am a member of this re-

spectable society. [108]It is not without significance, for as Trop says: Not until you become an artist yourself do you earn the right to judge other artists. [109] And is not an engaged man also a Dyrehaug artist?[110]

Edward is beside himself with indignation. He is letting his beard grow, has hung up his black suit—which tells much. He wants to speak with Cordelia, wants to describe for her all my cunning. It will be a shocking scene: Edward unshaven, disheveled, and speaking loudly with Cordelia. If he will only not dislodge me with his long beard. I try futilely to bring him to reason; I explain that it is the aunt who arranged the match, that Cordelia perhaps still entertains feelings for him, that I shall be willing to bow out if he can win her. [111]For a moment, he hesitates about whether he should have his beard trimmed a new way, buy a new black suit—the next moment, he heaps abuse upon me. I do everything to keep up appearances with him. However angry he is with me, I am sure he will take no step without consulting me; he does not forget what benefit he has had from me as his mentor. And why should I tear his last hope from him, why break with him? He is a good man; who knows what may happen in time.

What I have to do now is, on the one hand, to organize everything so that the engagement is broken in such a way that I thereby secure a more beautiful and significant relationship to Cordelia; on the other hand, I must utilize the time to the best of my ability to delight in the loveliness, all the lovableness, with which nature has so abundantly equipped her, delight in it, but nevertheless with the restraint and circumspection that forestall the anticipation of anything. When I have brought her to the point where she has learned what it is to love and what it is to love me, then the engagement will break like a defective mold and she will belong to me. Others become engaged when they have arrived at this point and have the good prospect of a boring marriage for all eternity. That is their business.

Everything is still *in statu quo*, but scarcely any engaged person can be happier than I; no miser who has found a gold coin is happier than I. I am intoxicated with the thought that she is in my power. Pure, innocent womanliness, as transparent as the sea, and yet just as deep, with no idea of love [*Kjærlighed*]! But now she is going to learn what a powerful force erotic love [*Elskov*] is. Just like a king's daughter who has been elevated from the dust to the throne of her forefathers, so she will be enthroned in the kingdom to which she belongs. And this will take place through me; and in learning to love, she will learn to love me; as she develops the rule, the paradigm will sequentially unfold, and this I am. As she in love becomes alive to her entire meaning, she will apply this to loving me, and when she suspects that she has learned it from me, she will love me twofold. The thought of my joy overwhelms me to such a degree that I am almost losing my senses.

Her soul is not diffused or slackened by the vague emotions of erotic love, something that keeps many young girls from ever learning to love, that is, definitely, energetically, totally. In their minds they have a vague, foggy image that is supposed to be an ideal by which the actual object is to be tested. From such incompleteness emerges a something whereby one may help oneself properly through the world. —As erotic love now awakens in her soul, I see into it, I learn to know it by listening to all the voices of erotic love in her. I make sure of the shape it has taken in her and form myself in likeness to it; and just as I already am spontaneously included in the story that love is running through in her heart, so I come again to her from the outside as deceptively as possible. After all, a girl loves only once.

Now, then, I am in legitimate possession of Cordelia and have the aunt's consent and blessing, the congratulations of friends and relatives; surely it will last. So now the troubles of war are over and the blessings of peace begin. What foolishness! As if the aunt's blessing and the friends' congratulations were able to give me possession of Cordelia in the more profound sense; as if love made such a distinction between times of war and times of peace and did not instead—as long as it exists—announce itself in conflict, even though the weapons are different. The difference is actually in whether the conflict is *cominus* [close at hand] or *eminus* [at a distance]. The more the conflict in a love relationship has been *eminus*, the more distressing it is, for the hand-to-hand combat becomes all the more trifling. Hand-to-hand combat involves a handshake, a touching with the foot—something that Ovid,[112] as is known, recommends just as much as he most jealously rants against it, to say nothing of a kiss, an embrace. The person who fights *eminus* usually has only the eyes[113] on which to depend, and yet, if he is an artist, he knows how to use this weapon with such virtuosity that he achieves almost the same result. He can let his eyes rest on a girl with a desultory tenderness that has the same effect as if he casually touched her; he can grasp her just as firmly with his eyes as if he held her locked in his arms. But it is always a mistake or a disaster if one fights *eminus* too long, for such fighting is always only a symbol, not the enjoyment. Not until one fights *cominus* does everything acquire its true meaning. If there is no combat in love, then it has ceased. I have almost never fought *eminus*, and this is why I am now not at the end but at the beginning; I am taking out my weapons. I am in possession of her, that is true, that is, in the legal and bourgeois sense, but that means nothing at all to me—I have much purer concepts. She is engaged to me, that is true, but if from that I were to draw the conclusion that she loves me, it would be an illusion, for she does not love at all. I am in legitimate possession of her, and yet I am not in possession of her, just as I can very well be in possession of a girl without being in legitimate possession of her.

> *Auf heimlich erröthender Wange*
> *Leuchtet des Herzens Glühen*
> [On a secretly blushing cheek
> Shines the glow of the heart].[114]

She is sitting on the sofa by the tea table, I on a chair at her side. This position has a confidentiality and yet a dignity that distances. A great deal depends upon the position, that is, for one who has an eye for it. Love has many positions—this is the first. How royally nature has equipped this girl: her clean soft figure, her profoundly feminine innocence, her clear eyes—all this intoxicates me. —I have greeted her. She approached me, happy as usual, yet a little embarrassed, a little uncertain— after all, the engagement must make our relationship somewhat different, but how, she does not know; she took my hand, but not with the usual smile. I responded to the greeting with a slight, almost unnoticeable pressure of the hand; I was gentle and friendly, yet without being erotic. —She is sitting on the sofa by the tea table, I on a chair at her side. A transfiguring ceremoniousness sweeps over the scene, a soft morning light. She is silent; nothing breaks in upon the stillness. My eyes glide softly over her, not desiringly—that would truly be brazen. A delicate fleeting blush, like a cloud over the meadow, fades away, heightening and fading. What does this blush signify? Is it love, is it longing, hope, fear, for is not red the color of the heart? By no means. She wonders, she really wonders—not at me, for that would be too little to offer her; she is amazed—not at herself but within herself. She is being transformed within herself. This moment craves stillness; therefore no reflection is to disturb it, no noise of passion is to disrupt it. It is as if I were not present, and yet it is my very presence that is the condition for this contemplative wonder of hers. My being is in harmony with hers. In a state such as this, a girl is adored and worshiped, just as some deities are, by silence.[115]

[116]It is fortunate that I have my uncle's house. If I wanted to impart to a young man a distaste for tobacco, I would take him into some smoking room or other in Regensen;[117] if I want to impart to a young girl a distaste for being engaged, I need only to introduce her here. Just as no one but tailors frequents the tailors' guildhall, so here only engaged couples come. It is an appalling company in which to become involved, and I cannot blame Cordelia for becoming impatient. When we are gathered *en masse*, I think we put ten couples on the field, besides the annexed battalions that come to the capital for the great festivals. Then we engaged ones really enjoy the delights of being engaged. [118]I report with Cordelia at the assembly ground in order to give her a distaste for these amo-

rous tangibilities, these bunglings of lovesick workmen. [119]Incessantly, all night through, one hears a sound as if someone were going around with a fly swatter—it is the lovers' kissing. In this house, one has an amiable absence of embarrassment; one does not even seek the nooks and corners—no, people sit around a large round table. I, too, make a move to treat Cordelia in the same way. To that end, I really have to force myself. It would really be shocking if I allowed myself to insult her deep womanliness in this way. I would reproach myself even more for this than when I deceive her. On the whole, I can guarantee perfect esthetic treatment to any girl who entrusts herself to me—it only ends with her being deceived, but this, too, is part of my esthetics, for either the girl deceives the man or the man deceives the girl. [120]It would certainly be interesting if some literary drudge could be found to count up in fairy tales, legends, folk ballads, and myths whether a girl is more often faithless or a man.

Repent of the time Cordelia is costing me, I do not, even though she is costing me a great deal. Each meeting often requires long preparations. I am experiencing with her the emergence of her love. I myself am almost invisibly present when I am sitting visible at her side. My relationship to her is like a dance that is supposed to be danced by two people but is danced by only one. That is, I am the other dancer, but invisible. She moves as in a dream, and yet she is dancing with another, and I am that other one who, insofar as I am visibly present, is invisible, and insofar as I am invisible, is visible. The movements require another. She bows to him; she stretches out her hand to him. She recedes; she approaches again. I take her hand; I complete her thought, which nevertheless is completed within itself. She moves to the melody in her own soul; I am merely the occasion for her moving. I am not erotic; that would only arouse her; I am flexible, supple, impersonal, almost like a mood. [121]

What do engaged people ordinarily talk about? As far as I know, they are very busy mutually weaving each other into the boring context of the respective families. No wonder the erotic vanishes. If a person does not know how to make erotic love the absolute, in comparison with which all other events vanish, then he should never let himself become involved in loving, even if he marries ten times. Whether I have an aunt named Marianne, an uncle named Christopher, a father who is a major, etc. etc., all such public information is irrelevant to the mysteries of love. Yes, even one's own past life is nothing. Ordinarily a young girl does not have much to tell in this regard; if she does, it may very well be worth the trouble to listen to her—but, as a rule, not to love her. [122]I for my part am not looking for stories—I certainly have enough of them; I am seeking immediacy. The eternal in erotic love is that [123]in its moment individuals first come into existence for each other.

I
349

A little confidence must be awakened in her, or, more correctly, a doubt must be removed. I do not exactly belong to the aggregate of lovers who out of respect love each other, out of respect marry each other, out of respect have children together, but nevertheless I am well aware that erotic love, especially as long as passion is not set in motion, demands of the one who is its object that he not esthetically offend against morality. In this regard, erotic love has its own dialectic. For example, while my relationship with Edward is far more censurable from the moral standpoint than my conduct toward the aunt, it will be much easier to justify the former to Cordelia than the latter. It is true that she has not said anything about it, but nevertheless I found it best to explain the necessity of my acting in that way. The cautiousness I have used flatters her pride; the secretiveness with which I handled everything captures her attention. Surely it might seem that here I have already betrayed too much erotic polish, so that when I am obliged later to insinuate that I have never been in love before I shall be contradicting myself, but that makes no difference. I am not afraid of contradicting myself if only she does not detect it and I achieve what I wish. Let it be the ambition of learned doctoral candidates to avoid every contradiction; a young girl's life is too abundant to have no contradictions and consequently makes contradictions inevitable.

She is proud and also has no real conception of the erotic. Although now she probably submits to me intellectually to some degree, it is conceivable that when the erotic begins to assert itself she might take it into her head to turn her pride against me. From all that I can observe, she is perplexed about woman's real significance. Therefore it was easy to arouse her pride against Edward. But this pride was completely eccentric, because she had no conception of erotic love. If she acquires it, then she will acquire her true pride, but a remnant of that eccentric pride might easily supervene. It is then conceivable that she would turn against me. Although she will not repent of having consented to the engagement, she will nevertheless readily perceive that I obtained it at a rather good price; she will see that the beginning was not made correctly from her side. If this dawns on her, she will dare to stand up to me. Good! Then I shall be convinced of how profoundly she is stirred.

I
350

Sure enough. Even from far down the street, I see this lovely little curly head leaning out of the window as far as possible. It is the third day I have noticed it. —A young girl certainly does not stand at the window for nothing; presumably she has her good reasons. —But I beg you for heaven's sake not to lean so far out of the window; I wager that you are standing on the rung of a chair—I can tell from your posture. Think how terrible it would be if you fell down, not on my head, because I am keeping out of this affair until later, but on his, his, because there certainly must be a he. —No! What do I see! Way off there, my friend Hansen, the licentiate, is coming down the middle of the street. There is something unusual about his behavior. It is a rather uncustomary conveyance; if I judge rightly, it is on the wings of longing that he is coming. Could it be that he is a regular visitor to the house and I do not know it? —My pretty little miss, you disappear; I suppose you have gone to open the door to receive him. —You can just as well come back; he is not coming into the house at all. —How can it be that you know better? Well, I can assure you—he said it himself. If the carriage that passed had not made so much noise, you yourself could have heard it. I said, just *en passant:* Are you going in here? To which he answered with a clear word: No. —So you may as well say good-bye, for the licentiate and I are going out for a walk. He is embarrassed, and embarrassed people generally are talkative. I am going to talk with him about the pastoral appointment he is seeking. — Good-bye, my pretty miss, we are on our way to the customhouse. When we arrive there, I shall say to him: What a damned nuisance—you have taken me out of my way. I am supposed to go to Vestergade.

Look, here we are again. —What constancy! She is still standing at the window. A girl like that is sure to make a man happy. —And why am I doing all this, you ask. Because I am a vile fellow who has his fun by teasing others? By no means. I am doing it out of consideration for you, my charming girl. In the first place, you have been waiting for this licentiate, longing for him, and thus he is doubly handsome when he comes. In the second place, when he comes through the door now, he will say, "We damned near let the cat out of the bag when that confounded fellow was at the door as I was about to visit you. But I was smart; I inveigled him into a long chat about the appointment I am seeking; I walked him here and there and finally way out to the customhouse. I assure you that he did not notice a thing." And what then? [124]So you are fonder of your licentiate than ever, for you have always thought that he had an excellent way of thinking, but that he was clever—well, now you see it for yourself. And you have me to thank for that. —But something occurs to me. Their engagement must not have been announced yet—otherwise I would know about it. The girl is lovely and delightful to look at, but she is young. Perhaps her discernment is not mature yet. Was it not conceivable that she would go and rashly take a most serious step? That must be prevented; I must speak with her. I owe it to her, for she certainly is a very charming girl. I owe it to the licentiate, for he is my friend; as far as that goes, I owe it to her because she is my friend's intended. I owe it to the family, for certainly it is a very respectable family. [125]I owe it to the whole human race, for it is a good deed. The whole hu-

man race! What a tremendous thought, what uplifting sport—
to act in the name of the whole human race, to be in possession
of a general power of attorney. —But now to Cordelia. I can
always make use of mood, and the girl's beautiful longing has
really stirred me.

So now begins the first war with Cordelia, in which I retreat
and thereby teach her to be victorious as she pursues me. I continually fall back, and in this backward movement I teach her
to know through me all the powers of erotic love, its turbulent
thoughts, its passion, what longing is, and hope, and impatient expectancy. As I perform this set of steps before her, all
this will develop correspondingly in her. It is a triumphal
procession in which I am leading her, and I myself am just as
much the one who dithyrambically sings praises to her victory
as I am the one who shows the way. She will gain courage to
believe in erotic love, to believe it is an eternal force, when she
sees its dominion over me, sees my movements. She will believe me, partly because I rely on my artistry, and partly because at the bottom of what I am doing there is truth. If that
were not the case, she would not believe me. With my every
move, she becomes stronger and stronger; love is awakening
in her soul; she is being enthroned in her meaning as a woman.
[126]Until now I have not proposed [*friet*] to her, as it is called
in the bourgeois sense; now I shall do it. I shall make her free
[*fri*]; only in that way shall I love her. That she owes this to me,
she must never suspect, for then she will lose her confidence in
herself. Then when she feels free, so free that she is almost
tempted to want to break with me, the second struggle will
begin. Now she has power and passion, and the struggle has
significance for me—let the momentary consequences be what
they may. Suppose that in her pride she becomes giddy, suppose that she does break with me—all right!—she has her freedom, but she will still belong to me. That the engagement
should bind her is silly—I want to possess her only in her freedom. Let her leave me—the second struggle is nevertheless beginning, and in this second struggle I shall be victorious as
surely as it was an illusion that she was victorious in the first

one. The greater the abundance of strength she has, the more interesting for me. The first war is a war of liberation; it is a game. The second is a war of conquest; it is a life-and-death struggle.

Do I love Cordelia? Yes! Sincerely? Yes! Faithfully? Yes—in the esthetic sense, and surely this should mean something. What good would it have been if this girl had fallen into the hands of a clumsy oaf of a faithful husband? What would have become of her? Nothing. They say that it takes a bit more than honesty to make one's way through the world. I would say that it takes a bit more than honesty to love such a girl. That more I do have—it is deceitfulness. And yet I do love her faithfully. Strictly and abstinently, I keep watch on myself so that everything in her, the divinely rich nature in her may come to full development. I am one of the few who can do this, and she is one of the few qualified for it; so are we not suited to each other?[127]

Is it sinful of me not to look at the pastor but instead fasten my eyes on the beautiful embroidered handkerchief you are holding in your hand? Is it sinful of you to hold it in just that way? —There is a name in the corner. Your name is Charlotte Hahn? It is so seductive to come to know a woman's name in such an accidental way. It is as if there were an obliging spirit who secretly introduced me to you. Or perhaps it is not accidental that the handkerchief is folded in such a way that I am able to see the name? —You are moved, you wipe a tear from your eye. —The handkerchief is hanging loosely once again. —It seems strange to you that I am looking at you and not at the pastor. You look at the handkerchief and notice that it has betrayed your name. It is indeed a most innocent thing; one can easily find out a girl's name. —Why must the handkerchief suffer? Why must it be crumpled up? Why become angry with it? Why become angry with me? What is that the pastor is saying: "Let no one lead a person into temptation. Even the person who does it unknowingly bears a responsibility; he, too, has a debt to the other that he can pay off only by increased

I
353

kindness." —Now he says Amen. Outside the door of the church, you will probably let the handkerchief fly loosely in the wind. —Or have you become afraid of me? What have I done? —Have I done more than you can forgive, than what you dare to remember—in order to forgive?

A double-movement[128] is necessary in relation to Cordelia. If I just keep on retreating before her superior force, it would be very possible that the erotic in her would become too dissolute and lax for the deeper womanliness to be able to hypostatize itself. Then, when the second struggle begins, she would be unable to offer resistance. To be sure, she sleeps her way to victory, but she is supposed to do that; on the other hand she must continually be awakened. If for one moment she thinks her victory would in turn be wrested from her, she must learn to will to hold onto it tightly. Her womanliness will be matured in this conflict. I could use either conversation to inflame her or letters to cool her off, or vice versa. The latter is preferable in every way. I then enjoy her most extreme moments. When she has received a letter, when its sweet poison has entered her blood, then a word is sufficient to make her love burst forth. At the next moment, irony and hoarfrost make her doubtful, but not so much that she nevertheless does not continually feel her victory, feel it augmented by the receipt of the next letter. Nor can irony be used very well in a letter without running the risk that she would not understand it. Only traces of ardor can be used in a conversation. My personal presence will prevent ecstasy. If I am present only in a letter, then she can easily cope with me; to some extent, she mistakes me for a more universal creature who dwells in her love. Then, too, in a letter one can more readily have free rein; in a letter I can throw myself at her feet in superb fashion etc.— something that would easily seem like nonsense if I did it in person, and the illusion would be lost. The contradiction in these movements will evoke and develop, strengthen and consolidate, the erotic love in her—in one word: tempt it.

These letters, however, must not take on a strongly erotic color too soon. In the beginning, it is best that they bear a more universal stamp, contain a single clue, remove a single doubt. Occasionally they may suggest the advantage an engagement has, insofar as people can be deflected by mystifications. Whatever drawbacks it has otherwise, she will not lack opportunities to become aware of them. [129]In my uncle's house I have a caricature that I can always place alongside. Without my help, she cannot produce the erotic inwardness. If I deny her this and let this burlesque image plague her, then she will surely become bored with being engaged, yet without really being aware that it is I who have made her bored with it.

A little epistle today describing the state of my soul will give her a clue to her own inner state. It is the correct method, and method I do have. I have you to thank for that, you dear girls I have loved in the past. I owe it to you that my soul is so in tune that I can be what I wish for Cordelia. I recall you with thanks; the honor belongs to you. I shall always admit that a young girl is a born teacher from whom one can always learn—if nothing else, then to deceive her—for one learns that best from the girls themselves. No matter how old I become, I shall still never forget that it is all over for a man only when he has grown so old that he can learn nothing from a young girl.

My Cordelia,

You say that you had not imagined me like this, but neither did I imagine that I could become like this. Is not the change in you? For it is conceivable that I have not actually changed but that the eyes with which you look at me have changed. Or is the change in me? It is in me, for I love you; it is in you, for it is you I love. In the calm, cold light of the understanding, I considered everything. Proud and unmoved, I was terrified by nothing. Nothing surprised me; even if a ghost had knocked at the door, I would have calmly picked up the candelabrum[130] and opened it. But see, it was not ghosts for whom I unlocked the door, not pale, feeble shapes—it was for you, my Cordelia; it was life and youth and health and beauty that approached me. My arm shakes; I cannot hold the light steady. I fall back from you, and yet I cannot keep from looking at you, cannot

I
355

keep from wishing I could hold the light steady. I am changed, but why, how, what is the nature of this change? I do not know; I know of no more explicit definition to add, no richer predicate to use than this when I altogether enigmatically say of myself: I have changed.[131]

Your JOHANNES

[132]My Cordelia,

Erotic love loves secrecy—an engagement is a disclosure; it loves silence—an engagement is a public announcement; it loves whispering—an engagement is a loud proclamation, and yet, with my Cordelia's help, an engagement will be a superb way to deceive the enemies. On a dark night, there is nothing more dangerous for other ships than to hang out a lantern, which is more deceptive than the darkness.[133]

Your JOHANNES

[134]She is sitting on the sofa by the tea table; I am sitting at her side. She is holding my arm; her head, heavy with many thoughts, is resting on my shoulder. She is so near and yet still so far; she is devoted to me, and yet she does not belong to me. There is still some resistance, but it is not subjectively reflected; it is the common resistance of womanliness, for woman's essence is a devotedness that takes the form of resistance. —She is sitting on the sofa by the tea table; I am sitting at her side. Her heart is beating, but without passion; her bosom rises and falls, but not in agitation; at times her color changes, but with soft shading. Is it love? By no means. She listens; she understands. She listens to the familiar saying; she understands it. She listens to another person's talking; she understands it as her own. She listens to another person's voice as it resonates within her; she understands this resonance as if it were her own voice that discloses to her and to another.

What am I doing? Am I beguiling her? By no means—that would be of no avail to me. Am I stealing her heart? By no means—in fact, I prefer that the girl I am going to love should keep her heart. What am I doing, then? I am shaping for myself a heart like unto hers. An artist paints his beloved; that is now his joy; a sculptor shapes her. This I, too, am doing, but in an intellectual sense. She does not know that I possess this image and therein really lies my falsification. I obtained it secretively, and in that sense I have stolen her heart, just as it is told of Rebecca that she stole Laban's heart when she took his household gods away from him in a cunning manner.[135]

Surroundings and setting do have a great influence upon a person and are part of that which makes a firm and deep impression on the memory [*Hukommelse*] or, more correctly, on the whole soul, and for this reason cannot be forgotten either. No matter how old I may become, it will nevertheless always be impossible for me to think of Cordelia in surroundings other than this little room. When I come to visit her, the maid usually lets me in by the door to the large drawing room; Cordelia herself enters from her room, and as I open the door to enter the small drawing room, she opens the other door, so that our eyes meet in the doorway. This drawing room is small, cozy, is almost the size of a private room. Although I have now seen it from many different angles, I am most fond of seeing it from the sofa. She sits there at my side; before us stands a round tea table, over which a tablecloth is spread in rich folds. On the table stands a lamp shaped in the form of a flower, which rises up vigorously and copiously to bear its crown, over which in turn hangs a delicately cut veil of paper, so light that it cannot remain still. The form of the lamp is reminiscent of the Orient, the movement of the veil reminiscent of the gentle breezes in that region. The floor is covered by matting woven of a special kind of willow, a work that immediately betrays its foreign origin.

At moments, I let the lamp be the motif in my landscape. I sit with her then, stretched out on the ground under the flower of the lamp. At other times, I let the willow matting call up the image of a ship, of an officer's stateroom—we are sailing out in the middle of the great ocean. When we are sitting far from the window, we look directly into the sweeping horizon of the sky. This, too, augments the illusion. When I am sitting at her side, I let such things appear like an image that hastens as elusively over actuality as death crosses a person's grave.

The surroundings are always of great importance, especially for the sake of recollection [*Erindring*].[136] Every erotic relationship must always be lived through in such a way that it is easy for one to produce an image that conveys all the beauty of it. To be able to do this successfully, one must be attentive to the surroundings. If they are not found to be as desired, then they must be made so. For Cordelia and her love, the surroundings are entirely appropriate. But what a different image presents itself to me when I think of my little Emily, and yet, again, were not the surroundings appropriate? I cannot imagine her or, more correctly, I want to recall her only in the little room opening onto the garden. The doors stood open; a little garden in front of the house cut off the view, compelled the eyes to be arrested there, to stop before boldly following the road that vanished into the distance. Emily was lovely but of less significance than Cordelia. The surroundings were also designed for that. The eyes remained earthbound, did not rush boldly and impatiently ahead, rested on that little foreground. The road itself, even though it romantically wandered off into the distance, had no other effect than that the eyes glanced over the stretch before it and then returned home in order to glance over the same stretch again. The room was earthbound. Cordelia's surroundings must have no foreground but rather the infinite boldness of the horizon. She must not be earthbound but must float, not walk but fly, not back and forth but eternally forward.

[137]When a person himself becomes engaged, he is at once effectually initiated into the antics of the engaged. Some days ago, licentiate Hansen showed up with the charming young girl to whom he has become engaged. He confided to me that she was lovely, which I knew before, that she was very young, which I also knew; he finally confided to me that he had chosen her precisely so that he himself could form her into the ideal that had always vaguely hovered before him. Good lord, what a silly licentiate—and a healthy, blooming, cheerful girl.

Now, I am a fairly old hand at the game, and yet I never approach a young girl other than as nature's *Venerabile* [something worthy of veneration] and first learn from her. Then insofar as I may have any formative influence upon her, it is by teaching her again and again what I have learned from her.

Her soul must be stirred, agitated in every possible direction—not piecemeal and by spurts, but totally. She must discover the infinite, must experience that this is what lies closest to a person. This she must discover not along the path of thought, which for her is a wrong way, but in the imagination, which is the real line of communication between her and me, for that which is a component for the man is the whole for the woman. She must not labor her way forward to the infinite along the irksome path of thought, for woman is not born to labor, but she will reach it along the easy path of the imagination and the heart. For a young girl, the infinite is just as natural as the idea that all love must be happy. Everywhere, wherever she turns, a young girl has the infinite around her, and the transition is a leap,[138] but, please note, a feminine, not a masculine, leap. Why are men ordinarily so clumsy? When they are going to leap, they have to take a running start, make many preparations, measure the distance with the eyes, make several runs—shy away and turn back. Finally they leap and fall in. A young girl leaps in a different way. In mountainous country, one often comes upon two towering mountain peaks. A chasmic abyss separates them, terrible to look down into. No man dares to risk this leap. But a young girl, so say the natives in the region, did dare to do it, and it is called the Maiden's Leap. I am fully prepared to believe it, just as I believe everything remarkable about a young girl, and it is intoxicating to me to hear the simple natives talk about it. I believe it all, believe the marvelous, am amazed by it only in order to believe; as the only thing that has amazed me in the world, a young girl is the first and will be the last. And yet for a young girl such a leap is only a hop, whereas a man's leap always becomes ludicrous because no matter how far he stretches out, his exertion at the same time becomes minuscule compared with the distance between the peaks and nevertheless provides a kind of yardstick. But who would be so foolish as to imagine a young girl taking a running start? One can certainly imagine her running, but this running is itself a game, an enjoyment, a display of her loveliness, whereas the idea of a running start separates what in woman belongs together; that is, a running start has in itself the dialectical, which is contrary to woman's nature. And now the leap—who again would be graceless enough here to dare to separate what belongs together! Her leap is a gliding. And once she has reached the other side, she stands there again, not exhausted by the effort, but more beautiful, more soulful than ever; she throws a kiss over to us who stand on this side. Young, newborn, like a flower that has shot up from the root of the mountain, she swings out over the abyss so that everything almost goes black before our eyes. — What she must learn is to make all the motions of infinity, to swing herself, to rock herself in moods, to confuse poetry and actuality, truth and fiction, to frolic in infinity. Then when she is familiar with this tumult, I shall add the erotic; then she will be what I want and desire. Then my duties will be over, my work; then I shall haul in all my sails; then I shall sit at her side, and under her sails we shall journey forward. In fact, as soon as this girl is erotically intoxicated, I shall have enough to do sitting at the helm in order to moderate the speed so that nothing happens too soon or in an unbecoming manner. Once in a while one punctures a little hole in the sail, and the next moment we rush along again.

[139]In my uncle's house, Cordelia becomes more and more indignant. She has requested several times that we do not go there anymore, but it is to no avail; I always know how to think up evasions. When we were leaving there last night, she shook my hand with an unusual passion. She probably has really felt very distressed there, and no wonder. If I did not always find amusement in observing these unnatural affectations, I could not possibly hold out. This morning, I received a letter from her in which she makes fun of engagements with more wit than I had given her credit for. I kissed the let-

ter; it is the most cherished one I have received from her. Just right, my Cordelia! That is the way I want it.

[140]It so happens, rather oddly, that on Østergade there are two coffee shops directly opposite each other. On the second floor, left side, lives a young miss or a young lady. Usually, she is concealed behind a vertical venetian blind covering the window by which she sits. The blind is made of very thin material, and anyone, if he has good eyes, who knows the girl or has seen her frequently will easily be able to identify every feature, whereas to the person who does not know her and does not have good eyes she will appear as a dark figure. In some measure, the latter is the case with me; the former with a young officer who every day, precisely at twelve o'clock, shows up in the offing and turns his gaze up toward that venetian blind. Actually it was the venetian blind that first directed my attention to that fine telegraphic connection. There are no blinds on the other windows, and a solitary blind such as that, covering only one window, is usually a sign that someone sits behind it regularly.

One morning, I stood in the window of the pastry shop on the other side. It was exactly twelve o'clock. Paying no attention to the people passing by, I kept my eyes on that venetian blind, when suddenly the dark figure behind it began to move. The profile of a woman's head appeared in the next window in such a way that it turned in a strange manner in the same direction as the venetian blind. Thereupon the owner of the head nodded in a very friendly way and again hid behind the venetian blind. I concluded first and foremost that the person she greeted was a man, for her gesture was too passionate to be prompted by the sight of a girl friend; second, I concluded that the one to whom the greeting applied ordinarily came from the other side. She had placed herself just right in order to be able to see him some distance away, in fact, hidden by the venetian blind, she could even greet him. —Quite so! At precisely twelve o'clock, the hero in this little love episode, our dear lieutenant, comes along. I am sitting in the coffee shop on the ground floor of the building in which the young lady lives on the second floor. The lieutenant has already spied her. Be careful, my good friend; it is not such an easy matter to pay one's respects gracefully to the second floor. Incidentally, he is not bad—slender, well built, a handsome figure, a curved nose, black hair—the cocked hat is very becoming. Now the pinch. His legs begin to knock a little, to become too long. This makes a visual impression comparable to the feeling a person has when he has a toothache and the teeth become too long for the mouth. If one is going to concentrate all the energy in the eyes and direct them toward the second floor, one is likely to draw too much strength from the legs. Pardon me, Mr. Lieutenant, for halting this gaze in its ascension. It is a piece of impertinence, I know very well. This gaze cannot be said to say very much; rather, it says nothing at all, and yet it promises very much. But obviously these many promises are mounting too powerfully to his head; he is reeling, or to use the poet's words about Agnes: he staggered, he fell.[141]

It is too bad, and if the matter had been left to me, it would never have happened. He is too good for that. It is really unfortunate, for if one is going to impress the ladies as a gallant, one must never fall. Anyone wishing to be a gallant must be alert to such things. But if someone appears merely as an intelligent being, all such things are of no importance; one is deeply absorbed in oneself, one droops, and if one actually does fall down, there is nothing striking about it. —What impression did this incident probably make on my little miss? It is too bad that I cannot be simultaneously on both sides of this Dardanelles street. I could, it is true, have an acquaintance posted on the other side, but for one thing I always prefer to make the observations myself, and for another, one can never know what may come out of this affair for me. In such a case, it is never good to have someone in on the secret, for then one must waste a good deal of time wresting from him what he knows and making him puzzled.

I am really becoming bored with my good lieutenant. Day in and day out, he marches past in full uniform. It is indeed a terrible kind of steadfastness.[142] Is this befitting for a soldier? Good sir, do you not carry side arms? Should you not take the house by storm and the girl by force? Of course, if you were a student, a licentiate, a curate, who keeps himself alive by hope,[143] that would be another matter. [144]But I forgive you, for the girl pleases me the more I see her. She is beautiful; her brown eyes are full of roguishness. When she is awaiting your arrival, her countenance is transfigured by a higher beauty that is indescribably becoming to her. Therefore, I conclude that she must have great imagination, and imagination is the natural cosmetic of the fair sex.

I
362

My Cordelia,

What is longing [*Længsel*]? Language and poets rhyme [*rime*] it with the word "prison [*Fængsel*]". How unreasonable [*urimelig*]! As if only the person sitting in prison could long. As if one could not long if one is free. Suppose that I were free—how I would long! And on the other hand, I am certainly free, free as a bird, and yet how I do long! I long when I am going to you; I long when I leave you; even when I am sitting at your side, I long for you. Can one, then, long for what one has? Indeed, if one considers that the next moment one may not have it. My longing is an eternal impatience. Only if I had lived through all eternities and assured myself that you belonged to me every moment, only then would I return to you and live through all eternities with you and certainly not have enough patience to be separated from you for one moment without longing but have enough assurance to sit calmly at your side.

Your JOHANNES

My Cordelia,

Outside the door there stands a little cabriolet, to me larger than the whole world, since it is large enough for two, hitched to a pair of horses, wild and unruly like the forces of nature, impatient like my passions, bold like your thoughts. If you wish, I shall carry you off—my Cordelia! Do you command it? Your command is the password [*Løsen*] that lets loose [*løsne*] the reins and the pleasure of flight. I am carrying you away, not from some people to others, but out of the world.

—The horses rear; the carriage rises up; the horses are standing upright almost over our heads. We are driving through the clouds up into the heavens; the wind whistles about us; is it we who are sitting still and the whole world is moving, or is it our reckless flight? Are you dizzy, my Cordelia? Then hold fast to me; I do not become dizzy. Intellectually one never becomes dizzy if one thinks of only one thing, and I think only of you. Physically one never becomes dizzy if one looks fixedly at only one object, and I look only at you. Hold tight; if the world passed away, if our light carriage disappeared beneath us, we would still cling to each other, floating in the harmony of the spheres.[145]

                                             Your JOHANNES

[146]It is almost too much. My servant has waited six hours, I myself two in the wind and rain, just to waylay that dear child Charlotte Hahn. She usually visits an old aunt of hers every Wednesday between two and five. Precisely today would have to be the day she did not come, precisely today when I did so much want to meet her. Why? Because she puts me in a very particular mood. I greet her; she curtseys in a way that simultaneously is indescribably terrestrial and yet so heavenly. She almost stops; it is as if she were about to sink into the earth, and yet she has a look as if she were about to be elevated into the heavens. When I look at her, my mind simultaneously becomes solemn and yet desiring. Otherwise, the girl means nothing to me; all I ask is this greeting, nothing more, even if she were willing to give it. Her greeting puts me in a mood, and in turn I squander this mood on Cordelia. —And yet I wager that she has slipped past us in one way or another. Not only in comedies but also in actual life is it difficult to keep watch on a young girl; one must have an eye on each finger. There was a nymph, Cardea,[147] who spent her time fooling the menfolk. She lived in a wooded area, lured her lovers into the thicket, and vanished. She was going to fool Janus, too, but he fooled her, because he had eyes in the back of his head.

My letters are not failing of their intention. They are developing her mentally, even though not erotically. For that purpose, letters cannot be used, but notes. The more the erotic emerges, the shorter they become, but all the more unerringly they seize the erotic point. For in order not to make her sentimental or soft, irony stiffens the feelings again but also makes her crave the sustenance of which she is most fond. Distantly and indefinitely, the notes give a presentiment of the highest. The moment this presentiment begins to dawn in her soul, the connection is broken. Through my resistance, the presentiment will take form within her soul as if it were her own thought, the impulse of her own heart. This is just what I want.

My Cordelia,

Somewhere in the city there lives a little family consisting of a widow and three daughters. Two of them go to the royal kitchen to learn how to cook. One afternoon in early summer, about five o'clock, the door to the drawing room opens softly, and a reconnoitering glance surveys the room. No one is there except a young girl sitting at the piano. The door is slightly ajar, so one can listen without being observed. The one playing is no great artist, for then the door would surely have been entirely closed. She is playing a Swedish melody; it is about the brief duration of youth and beauty. The words mock the girl's youth and beauty; the girl's youth and beauty mock the words. Which is right—the girl or the words? The music sounds so hushed and melancholy, as if sadness were the arbitrator that would settle the controversy. —But it is in the wrong, this sadness! What communion is there between youth and these reflections! What fellowship between morning and evening! The piano keys quiver and quake; the spirits of the soundboard spring up in confusion and do not understand one another. —My Cordelia, why so vehement! Why this passion!

I
365

How distant must an event be from us in time in order for us to recollect it; how distant so that recollection's longing can no longer grasp it? In this respect, most people have a limit; they cannot recollect what is too close in time, nor can they recollect what is too distant. I know no limit. Yesterday's experience I push back a thousand years in time and recollect it as if it were experienced yesterday.

Your JOHANNES

My Cordelia,

I have a secret to confide to you, my confidante. To whom should I confide it? To echo? It would betray it. To the stars? They are cold. To human beings? They do not understand it. Only to you do I dare to confide it, for you know how to keep it. There is a girl, more beautiful than the dream of my soul, purer than the light of the sun, deeper than the springs of the sea, prouder than the flight of the eagle—there is a girl—O incline your head to my ear and to my words so that my secret can steal into it. —This girl I love more than my life, for she is my life; more than all my desires, for she is my only desire; more than all my thoughts, for she is my only thought; more warmly than the sun loves the flower, more intimately than grief loves the privacy of the troubled mind, more longingly than the burning sand of the desert loves the rain. I cling to her more tenderly than the mother's eye to her child, more confidently than the entreating soul to God, more inseparably than the plant to its root. —Your head grows heavy and full of thoughts; it sinks down upon your breast; your bosom rises to come to its aid—my Cordelia! You have understood me, you have understood me correctly, literally; not one jot or tittle has escaped you! Shall I strain every nerve of my ears and let your voice convince me of it? Would I be able to doubt? Will you keep this secret? Dare I depend upon you? Tales are told of people who by dreadful crimes initiated each other into mutual silence.[148] To you I have confided a secret that is my life and the content of my life—have you nothing to confide to me that is so significant, so beautiful, so chaste that supranatural forces would be set in motion if it were betrayed?

Your JOHANNES

My Cordelia,

The sky is cloudy—dark rain clouds scowl like black eyebrows above its passionate countenance; the trees of the forest are in motion, tossed about by troubled dreams. You have disappeared from me into the forest. Behind every tree I see a feminine creature that resembles you; if I come closer, it hides behind the next tree. Do you not wish to show yourself to me, collect yourself? Everything is confused to me; the various parts of the forest lose their distinctive contours; I see everything as a sea of fog, where feminine creatures resembling you appear and disappear everywhere. I do not see you; you are continually moving in a wave of perception, and yet I am already happy over every single resemblance to you. What is the reason—is it the copious unity of your nature or the scanty multiplicity of my nature? —To love you, is it not to love a world?

Your JOHANNES

It would be of real interest to me if it were possible to reproduce very accurately the conversations I have with Cordelia. But I easily perceive that it is an impossibility, for even if I managed to recollect every single word exchanged between us, it nevertheless is out of the question to reproduce the element of contemporaneity, which actually is the nerve in conversation, the surprise in the outburst, the passionateness, which is the life principle in conversation. Ordinarily, I am not prepared in advance, of course, for this is at variance with the essential nature of conversation, especially erotic conversation. But I continually bear *in mente* [in mind] the content of my letters, always keep my eye on the mood they may have evoked in her. Of course, it could never occur to me to ask whether she has read my letter. It is easy to ascertain that she has read it. Nor do I ever speak directly with her about it, but I maintain secret communication with them in my conversations, partly in order to fix more firmly in her soul some impression or other, partly in order to wrest it from her and

I
367

make her perplexed. Then she can read the letter again and gain a new impression from it and so forth.

A change has taken place and is taking place in her. If I were to designate the state of her soul at this moment, I would say that it is pantheistic boldness. The expression in her eyes betrays it at once. It is bold, almost reckless, in expectations, as if it asked for the extraordinary at every moment and was prepared to see it. Like the eye that gazes in the distance, this look sees beyond what immediately appears to it and sees the marvelous. It is bold, almost reckless, in its expectancy—but not in self-confidence, and therefore it is rather dreaming and imploring, not proud and commanding. She is seeking the marvelous outside herself; she will pray that it might make its appearance, as if it were not in her power to call it forth. This must be prevented; otherwise I shall gain the upper hand too soon. Yesterday she told me there was something royal in my nature. Perhaps she wants to defer to me, but that absolutely will not do. To be sure, dear Cordelia, there is something royal in my nature, but you have no inkling of the kind of kingdom I have dominion over. It is over the tempests of moods. Like Aeolus,[149] I keep them shut up in the mountain of my personality and allow one and now another to go out. Flattery will give her self-esteem; the distinction between what is mine and what is yours will be affirmed; everything will be placed upon her. Flattery requires great care. Sometimes one must place oneself very high, yet in such a way that there remains a place still higher; sometimes one must place oneself very low. The former is more proper when one is moving in the direction of the intellectual; the latter is more proper when one is moving in the direction of the erotic.

Does she owe me anything? Not at all. Could I wish that she did? Not at all. I am too much a connoisseur, understand the erotic too well, for such foolishness. If this actually were the case, I would try with all my might to make her forget it and to lull to sleep my own thoughts about it. When it comes to the labyrinth of her heart, every young girl is an Ariadne;[150] she holds the thread by which one can find the way through—

but she possesses it in such a way that she herself does not know how to use it.

My Cordelia,

Speak—I obey. Your desire is a command; your entreaty is an omnipotent adjuration; your every most evanescent wish is a boon to me, for I do not obey you as a ministering spirit, as if I stood outside you. When you command, your will comes into existence, and I along with it, for I am a disarray of soul that simply awaits a word from you.

Your JOHANNES

My Cordelia,

You know that I very much like to talk with myself. I have found in myself the most interesting person among my acquaintances. At times, I have feared that I would come to lack material for these conversations; now I have no fear, for now I have you. I shall talk with myself about you now and for all eternity, about the most interesting subject with the most interesting person—ah, I am only an interesting person, you the most interesting subject.

Your JOHANNES

My Cordelia,

You find the time I have loved you to be so short; you almost seem to fear that I could have loved before. There are manuscripts in which the fortunate eye quickly sees faintly an older writing that in the course of time has been supplanted by trivial inanities. With caustic substances, the later writing is erased, and now the older writing is distinct and clear. In the same way, your eye has taught me to find myself in myself. I allow forgetfulness to consume everything that does not touch on you, and then I discover a pristine, a divinely young, primitive text; then I discover that my love for you is just as old as I myself.

Your JOHANNES

I
369

My Cordelia,

How can a kingdom survive that is in conflict with itself;[151] how can I survive if I am in conflict with myself? About what? About you—in order if possible to find repose in the thought that I am in love with you. But how am I to find this repose? One of the conflicting forces will continually convince the other that it is indeed the one most deeply and fervently in love; at the next moment, the other will. It would not concern me so much if the conflict were outside myself, if there were someone who dared to be in love with you or dared to desist— the crime is equally great—but this conflict within me consumes me, this one passion in its duplexity.

Your JOHANNES

Just vanish, my little fisherman's daughter; just hide among the trees; just pick up your load, for bending over is so becoming to you—yes, this very minute you are bending over with a natural grace under the bundle of brushwood you have gathered. How is it that such a creature should have to carry such loads! Like a dancer, you betray the beauty of your form— small of waist, full of bosom, burgeoning in development— any recruiting officer must admit that. You perhaps think these are trifles; you believe that society women are far more beautiful. Alas, my child, you do not know how much falseness there is in the world! Just set out upon your walk with your bundle into the enormous woods that presumably stretch many, many miles into the country to the border of the blue mountains. Perhaps you are not actually a fisherman's daughter but an enchanted princess; you are a troll's domestic servant, and he is cruel enough to make you pick up firewood in the woods. So it always goes in the fairy tale. Otherwise, why do you walk deeper into the forest? If you are really a fisherman's daughter, you will walk past me with your firewood down to the fishing village that lies on the other side of the road.

Just take the footpath that winds easily among the trees; my eyes will find you. Just turn around and look at me; my eyes will follow you. You cannot make me move; longing does not carry me away; I am sitting calmly on the railing and smoking my cigar. —Some other time, perhaps. —Yes, when you turn back your head halfway in that manner, the expression in your eyes is roguish; your light step is beckoning. Yes, I know, I understand where this path leads—to the solitude of the forest, to the whispering of the trees, to the abundant stillness. Look, the sky itself favors you. It hides itself in the clouds; it darkens the background of the forest, as if drawing the curtains for us. —Farewell, my beautiful fisherman's daughter, take care of yourself! Thanks for your favor. It was a beautiful moment, a mood, not strong enough to move me from my firm seat on the railing but still abundant in inner motion.

When Jacob had bargained with Laban about the payment for his service, when they agreed that Jacob should tend the white sheep and as reward for his work have all the motley-colored lambs born in his flock, he set rods in the watering troughs and had the sheep look at them[152]—in the same way I place myself before Cordelia everywhere; her eyes see me continually. To her it seems like sheer attentiveness from my part, but on my side I know that her soul thereby loses interest for everything else, that there is being developed within her a mental concupiscence that sees me everywhere.

My Cordelia,
I
371
As if I could forget you! Is my love, then, a work of memory [*Hukommelse*]? Even if time erased everything from its blackboards, even if it erased memory itself, my relationship with you would remain just as alive, you would still not be forgotten. As if I could forget you! What, then, should I recollect [*erindre*]? After all, I have forgotten myself in order to recollect you, so if I forgot you, I would then recollect myself, but the moment I remembered myself I would have to recollect you again. As if I could forget you! What would happen then? There is a painting from ancient times that shows Ariadne leaping up from her couch and anxiously watching a ship speeding away under full sail.[153] At her side stands Cupid

with an unstrung bow and dries his eyes. Behind her stands a winged female figure with a helmet on her head. The figure is usually assumed to be Nemesis.[154] Imagine this picture; imagine it slightly changed. Cupid is not weeping and his bow is not unstrung, or would you then have become less beautiful, less triumphant, because I had gone out of my mind. Cupid smiles and draws the bow. Nemesis does not stand idle at your side; she, too, draws her bow. In that old painting, we see on the ship a manly figure busy at his work. Presumably it is Theseus. Not so in my picture. He is standing in the stern; he is looking back longingly. He is stretching out his arms; he has repented of it or, more correctly, his madness has left him, but the ship is carrying him away. Cupid and Nemesis both aim, an arrow flies from each bow, they accurately hit the mark; we see and we understand that both have hit one spot in his heart to symbolize that his love was the Nemesis that avenged.

Your JOHANNES

My Cordelia,

I am in love with myself, people say of me. That does not surprise me, for how would it be possible for them to see that I can love, since I love only you? How could anyone else suspect it, since I love only you? I am in love with myself. And why? Because I am in love with you; for you I love and you alone and everything that truly belongs to you, and thus I love myself because this self of mine belongs to you, so that if I stopped loving you, I would stop loving myself. Therefore, what is an expression of the utmost egotism in the world's profane eyes is in your initiated eyes an expression of the purest sympathy; what is an expression of the most prosaic self-preservation in the world's profane eyes is in your sanctified sight an expression of most inspired self-annihilation.

Your JOHANNES

What I feared most was that the whole process would take me too long a time. I see, however, that Cordelia is making great progress, yes, that it will be necessary, in order to keep her inspired, to set everything in motion. She must not for all the world become listless ahead of time, that is, before that time when her time is up.

When in love, one does not take the highway. It is only marriage that is right in the middle of the king's highway. If one is in love and walks from Nøddebo, one does not go along Esrom Lake, even though the path is really only a hunting path, but it is a beaten path, and love prefers to beat its own path. One proceeds deeper into Gribs forest.[155] And when a couple wanders arm in arm in this way, each understands the other; that which obscurely delighted and pained before becomes clear now. There is no hint of anyone's presence. —So this lovely beech tree becomes a witness to your love; under its crown you two confessed it for the first time. You recollected everything so clearly—the first time you saw each other, the first time you took each other's hands in the dance, when you parted toward morning, when you would not admit anything to yourselves, let alone to each other. —It really is beautiful to listen to these love rehearsals. —They fell on their knees under the tree; they swore unbreakable love to each other; they sealed the pact with the first kiss. —These are productive moods that must be squandered on Cordelia. —So this beech tree became a witness. Oh, well, a tree is a quite suitable witness, but nevertheless it is too little. Presumably you two are thinking that heaven, too, was a witness, but heaven as such is a very abstract idea. Therefore, you see, there was still another witness. —Should I stand up and let them see that I am here? No, they may know me, and then the game is over. When they are some distance away, should I stand up and let them know someone was present? No, that is pointless. Silence must rest over their secret—as long as I want it to. They are in my power; I can separate them when I want to. I know their secret; only from him or from her can I have found it out— from her personally, that is impossible; consequently from him, it is detestable—bravo! And yet it is indeed almost malice. Well, I shall see. If I can gain a definite impression of her that I otherwise cannot obtain in the ordinary way, which I prefer, then there is nothing else to do.

My Cordelia,

Poor am I—you are my wealth; dark—you are my light; I own nothing, need nothing. Indeed, how should I be able to own anything; it is indeed a contradiction that a person who does not own himself can own something. I am happy like a child who cannot and must not own anything. I own nothing, for I belong only to you. I am not; I have ceased to be, in order to be yours.

Your JOHANNES

My Cordelia,

"My"—what does the word designate? Not what belongs to me, but what I belong to, what contains my whole being, which is mine insofar as I belong to it. After all, my God is not the God who belongs to me, but the God to whom I belong, and the same when I say my native land, my home, my calling, my longing, my hope. If there had been no immortality before, then the thought that I am yours would break through nature's usual course.

Your JOHANNES

My Cordelia,

What am I? The humble narrator who follows your triumphs, the dancer who bows under you as you soar in lovely buoyancy, the branch upon which you momentarily rest when you are tired of flying, the bass voice[156] that interjects itself under the soprano's ebullience to make it ascend even higher—what am I? I am the earthly force of gravity that keeps you captive to the earth. What am I, then? Body, substance, earth, dust, and ashes. —You, my Cordelia, you are soul and spirit.

Your JOHANNES

I
374

My Cordelia,

Love is everything; therefore, for one who loves everything ceases to have intrinsic meaning and has meaning only through the interpretation love gives to it. Thus, if some other engaged man became convinced that there was another girl he cared for, he probably would stand there like a criminal, and she would be outraged. But you, I know, you would see esteem in such a confession, for you know that it is impossible for me to love another—it is my love for you that casts a luster over all of life. So if I care for another, it is not to convince myself that I do not love her but only you—that would be presumptuous—but since my whole soul is full of you, life acquires another meaning for me—it becomes a myth about you.

Your JOHANNES

My Cordelia,

My love consumes me; only my voice remains,[157] a voice that has fallen in love with you, that whispers everywhere to you that I love you. Oh! Does it weary you to hear this voice? It surrounds you everywhere; I wrap my thoroughly reflective soul, like a manifold mobile frame, around your pure, deep being.

Your JOHANNES

My Cordelia,

We read in old stories that a river fell in love with a maiden.[158] Just so is my soul like a river that loves you. It is still at times and reflects your image deeply and calmly. At times it fancies that it has taken your image captive and tosses up its waves to prevent you from escaping again; then it ripples its surface gently and plays with your image. At times it has lost it, and then its waves become dark and despairing. — Just so is my soul—like a river that has fallen in love with you.

Your JOHANNES[159]

To be honest, it does not take unusually vivid imaginative power to conceive of a conveyance that is more convenient, comfortable, and, above all, more consistent with one's station in life. To ride with a peat cutter—that attracts attention but not in the desirable sense. But in an emergency, one accepts it with thanks. You walk some distance out in the country. You climb up, ride a mile, and encounter nothing; two miles, and everything goes well. You begin to feel safe and secure; the scenery actually is better than usual from this level. Almost three miles have gone by—who would ever have expected to meet a Copenhagener way out on a country road? And he is a Copenhagener, that you can see well enough. He is not from the country; he has an altogether singular way of looking at things—so definite, so observant, so appraising, and so little given to derision. Well, my dear girl, your position is by no means comfortable; you look as if you were sitting on a tray. The cart is so flat that it has no recess for the feet. —But it is, of course, your own fault. My carriage is entirely at your service; I take the liberty of offering you a much more comfortable seat, if it will not be too uncomfortable for you to sit beside me. In that case, I shall place the whole carriage at your disposal and sit in the driver's box myself, happy to be allowed to drive you to your destination. —The straw hat does not even shield you sufficiently from a sidelong glance. It is futile for you to bow your head; I still admire your beautiful profile. —Is it not annoying that the peasant bows to me? But, after all, it is proper for a peasant to bow to a distinguished man. —You are not getting off so lightly. Well, here is a tavern, a post house, and a peat cutter is much too pious in his way to neglect his devotions. Now I shall take care of him. I have an extraordinary talent for fascinating peat cutters. Oh, would that I might also succeed in pleasing you! He cannot resist my invitation, and once he has accepted it, he cannot resist the effects of it. If I cannot, then my servant can. —He is going into the barroom now; you are alone in the wagon in the shed. —God knows what kind of girl this is! Could this be a little middle-class miss, perhaps the daughter of a parish clerk? If so, she is unusually pretty and unusually well dressed for a parish clerk's daughter. The parish clerk must have a good salary. It occurs to me: Could she perhaps be a little blueblood miss who is tired of driving in a fine carriage, who perhaps is taking a little hike out to the country house and now also wants to try her hand at a little adventure? Quite possibly, such things are not unheard of. —The peasant does not know anything; he is a clod who only knows how to drink. Yes, yes, go on drinking, my good man; you are welcome to it.

But what do I see—it is none other than Miss Jespersen, Hansine Jespersen, daughter of the wholesaler. Good heavens, we two know each other. It was she I once met on Bredgade. [160]She was riding backwards; she could not raise the window. I put on my glasses and had the enjoyment of following her with my eyes. It was a very awkward situation; there were so many in the carriage that she could not move and presumably did not dare to make any outcry. The present situation is even more awkward. We two are destined for each other; that is obvious. She must be a romantic little miss; she is definitely out on her own initiative. —There comes my servant with the peat cutter. He is dead drunk. It is disgusting. They are a depraved lot, these peat cutters. Alas, yes! And yet there are even worse people than peat cutters. —See, now you are in a pretty mess. Now you yourself will have to drive the horses—how romantic! —You refuse my offer; you insist that you are a good driver. You do not deceive me; I perceive very well how crafty you are. When you have gone a little way you are going to jump out; in the woods one can easily find a hiding place. — My horse will be saddled; I shall follow on horseback. —You see, now I am ready, now you can be safe against any attack. —Please do not be so terribly afraid; then I shall turn back at once. I merely wanted to make you a little uneasy and give you an occasion for the heightening of your natural beauty. After all, you do not know that it is I who caused the peasant to get drunk, and I certainly have not taken the liberty of one offensive word to you. Everything can still be all right; I daresay that I shall give the affair such a turn that you can laugh at the whole episode. I just want a little unsettled account with you. Never think that I take any girl by surprise. I am a friend of freedom, and I do not care for anything I do not receive freely. —"You will certainly see for yourself that it will not do to continue the journey this way. I myself am going hunting; therefore I am on horseback. But my carriage is harnessed at the tavern. If you give the order, it will catch up with you at once and take you wherever you wish. I myself, I regret, cannot have the pleasure of escorting you; I am committed to a hunting engagement, and they are sacred." —But you accept. — Everything will promptly be in order. —See, you have no need at all to be embarrassed by seeing me again, or in any case no more embarrassed than is very becoming to you. You can be amused by the whole affair, laugh a little, and think about me a little. I ask no more. It might seem to be very little, but for me that is enough. It is a beginning, and I am especially good at the principles of beginnings.

Yesterday evening there was a little party at the aunt's. I knew Cordelia would take out her knitting. I had hidden a little note in it. She dropped it, picked it up, was stirred, wistful. One should always make use of the situation in this way. It is unbelievable what advantage can be derived from it. An intrinsically insignificant little note, read under such circumstances, becomes enormously significant for her. She had no chance to talk to me, for I had arranged things so that I had to escort a lady home. She was obliged to wait, therefore, until today. This is always a good way to drill the impression all the deeper into her soul. It always seems as if I were the one who paid attention to her; the advantage I have is that I am placed in her thoughts everywhere, that I surprise her everywhere.

I
378

[161]Erotic love does have its distinctive dialectic. There was a young girl with whom I was once in love. At the theater in Dresden[162] last summer, I saw an actress who bore a remarkable resemblance to her. Because of that, I wanted to make her acquaintance, and did succeed, and then realized that the dissimilarity was rather great. Today on the street I meet a lady who reminds me of that actress. This story can be continued as long as you wish.

My thoughts surround Cordelia everywhere. I send them like angels around her. Just as Venus in her chariot is drawn by doves, so she sits in her triumphal chariot, and I harness my thoughts in front like winged creatures. She herself sits there happy, exuberant like a child, omnipotent like a goddess; I walk along at her side. Truly, a young girl is and remains the *Venerabile* [something worthy of veneration] of nature and of all existence! No one knows that better than I. But what a pity that this glory lasts such a short time. She smiles at me, she greets me, she beckons to me—as if she were my sister. A glance reminds her that she is my beloved.

Erotic love has many gradations. Cordelia is making good progress. She is sitting on my lap; her arm, soft and warm, winds around my neck. Light, without physical weight, she rests against my chest; her soft curves scarcely brush against me. Like a flower, this lovely creature entwines me, free as a bow. Her eyes hide behind her lashes; her bosom is as dazzling white as snow, so smooth that my eyes cannot rest; they would slide off if her bosom did not move. What does this stirring mean? Is it love? Perhaps. It is the presentiment of love, the dream of love. As yet it lacks energy. She embraces me encompassingly, as the cloud embraces the transfigured one, lightly as a breeze, softly as one cups a flower; she kisses me as vaguely as the sky kisses the sea, as gently and quietly as the dew kisses the flower, as solemnly as the sea kisses the image of the moon.

I
379

At this moment, I would call her passion a naïve passion. When the turn is made and I begin to pull back in earnest, then she will summon up everything in order really to take me captive. She has no other means for that than the erotic itself, except that this will now manifest itself on an entirely different scale. Then it will be a weapon in her hand that she swings against me. Then I will have reflected passion. She will struggle for her own sake, because she knows I have the erotic in my possession; she will fight for her own sake in order to vanquish me. She herself needs a higher form of the erotic. What I taught her to sense by inciting her, my coldness will now

teach her to comprehend, but in such a way that she will believe that she herself discovers it. She will take me by surprise
with it; she will think that she has outdone me in boldness and
thereby has taken me captive. Then her passion will be definite, energetic, [163]determined, dialectical; her kissing will be
consummate, her embrace not hiatic. —In me she is seeking
her freedom, and the more firmly I encircle her, the better she
will find it. The engagement will break. When this has happened, she will need a little rest, lest something unlovely come
out in this wild turmoil. Her passion will rally once again, and
she will be mine.

Just as even in poor Edward's time I indirectly looked after
her reading, now I do so directly. What I am offering is what I
regard as the best nourishment: mythology and fairy tales. Yet
here as everywhere she has her freedom; I learn everything
about her by listening to her. If it is not there already, then I
put it there first.[164]

[165]When the servant girls go to Deer Park in the summer, it
usually affords scant pleasure. They go there only once a year,
and therefore they expect to have as much as possible from it.
So they must wear a hat and shawl and disfigure themselves in
every way. The merriment is wild, graceless, lascivious. No,
then I prefer Frederiksberg Gardens. Sunday afternoons they
go there, and I also. Here everything is seemly and decent; the
merriment itself more quiet and refined. On the whole, the
man who has no sense for servant girls loses more by it than
they lose. The great host of servant girls is actually the most
beautiful militia we have in Denmark. If I were king, I know
what I would do—I would not review the regular troops. If I
were one of the city's thirty-two men,[166] I would promptly petition for the establishment of a committee of public safety that
would try by every means—by insight, counsel, admonition,
appropriate rewards—to encourage servant girls to dress with
care and taste. Why should their beauty go to waste? Why
should it go through life unnoticed? [167]Let it at least be seen
once a week in the light under which it appears at its best! But

above all, good taste, restraint. A servant girl should not look like a lady—there *Politivennen*[168] is right, but the reasons this respected newspaper gives are entirely fallacious. If we then may dare to anticipate such a desirable flowering of the maid-servant class, would not this in turn have a beneficial effect on the daughters in our homes? Or is it rash of me to catch a glimpse along this particular road of a future for Denmark that truly can be called matchless? If only I myself might be allowed to be contemporary with this golden age,[169] then with good conscience I could spend the whole day walking around the streets and lanes and delight in the pleasures of the eyes! — How bold and spacious are my teeming thoughts, how patriotic! But here I am, of course, out in Frederiksberg where the servant girls come on Sunday afternoon and I, too.

First come the peasant girls holding hands with their sweethearts, or in another pattern, all the girls in front holding hands and the fellows behind, or in another pattern, two girls and one fellow. This flock forms the frame; they usually stand or sit under the trees in the great square in front of the pavilion. They are healthy and lively; the color contrasts are a bit too strong—their clothing as well as their complexions. Inside come the girls from Jylland and Fyn—tall, straight, a little too powerfully built, their clothing somewhat mixed. Here there would be much for the committee to do. Nor is a representative of the Bornholm division lacking here either: clever kitchen girls but rough customers both in the kitchen and here in Frederiksberg—there is something proudly repelling in their nature. Thus by contrast their presence here is not without effect, and I would be loath to do without them, but I seldom become involved with them.

Now come the select troops—the Nyboder girls, less tall, well rounded and filled out, delicate in complexion, merry, happy, quick, talkative, a bit coquettish, and, above all, bareheaded. Their attire may often approximate a lady's except for two things: they wear scarves and not shawls, and no hats—at most a little fluttering cap, but preferably they should be bareheaded. —Well, good day, Marie! So we meet out here. It is a long time since I saw you. Are you still at the councilor's?

"Yes." It is a very good place, I imagine. "Yes." But you are
so alone out here, have no one to go with—no sweetheart—or
perhaps he has no time today, or you are waiting for him. —
What, you are not engaged? Impossible! The prettiest girl in
Copenhagen, a girl who works at the councilor's, a girl who is
an ornament and a model for all servant girls, a girl who
knows how to dress so neatly and—so sumptuously. That is
indeed a pretty handkerchief you are holding in your hand,
made of the finest linen. And what do I see, edged with em-
broidery? I wager it cost ten marks. There is many a fine lady
who does not own its equal. French gloves, a silk umbrella—
and such a girl is not engaged. It is indeed preposterous. [170]If I
remember correctly, Jens thought a good deal of you—you
know whom I mean—Jens, the wholesaler's Jens, the one up
there on the third floor. —You see, I hit it on the head. Why
didn't you become engaged? After all, Jens was a handsome
fellow, had a good job; perhaps with a little pull on the part of
the wholesaler, in time he could have become a policeman or a
fireman; it wouldn't have been such a bad match. —You must
be to blame yourself; you must have been too hard on him.
"No! But I found out that Jens had been engaged once before
to a girl he did not treat very well at all." —What am I hearing?
Who would have thought that Jens was such a bad fellow? —
Yes, those guardsmen, those guardsmen, they are not to be
trusted. —You did absolutely right; a girl like you is much too
good to be thrown to just anybody. —You will surely make a
better match, I can vouch for that. —How is Miss Juliane? I
have not seen her for a long time. Would my pretty Marie be
so kind as to enlighten me about a few things. —Because one
has been unhappy in love, one should not therefore be unsympathetic toward others. —There are so many people here. —I
dare not speak with you about it; I am afraid someone might
spy on me. —Please listen for a moment, my pretty Marie.
Look, here is a place on this shaded path where the trees are
entwined together to hide us from others, where we see no
one, hear no human voices, only the soft echo of the music.
Here I dare speak about my secret. Is it not true, if Jens had not
been a bad fellow you would have walked with him here, arm

in arm, listened to the jolly music, even enjoyed a still
more. . . . . . Why are you so agitated—forget Jens. —Do
you want to be unfair to me? It was to meet you that I came
out here. It was to see you that I visited the councilor's. You
must have noticed—every time I had a chance I always went to
the kitchen door. You are going to be mine. The banns will be
read from the pulpit. Tomorrow evening I will explain everything to you—up the kitchen stairway, the door to the left, directly opposite the kitchen door. —Good-bye, my pretty
Marie. Do not mention to anyone that you have seen me out
here or spoken with me. Now you know my secret. She is
very lovely; something could be done with her. Once I get a
foothold in her room, I can read the banns from the pulpit myself. I have always tried to develop the beautiful Greek αὐτάϱ-
κεια [self-sufficiency] and in particular to make a pastor superfluous.

If I could manage to stand behind Cordelia when she receives a letter from me, it would be of great interest to me.
Then it would be easy for me to find out to what extent she has
in the most proper sense appropriated them erotically. On the
whole, letters are and will continue to be a priceless means of
making an impression on a young girl; the dead letter of writing often has much more influence than the living word.[171] A
letter is a secretive communication; one is master of the situation, feels no pressure from anyone's actual presence, and I do
believe a young girl would prefer to be all alone with her ideal,
that is, at certain moments, and precisely at those moments
when it has the strongest effect on her mind. Even if her ideal
has found an ever so perfect expression in a particular beloved
object, there nevertheless are moments when she feels that in
the ideal there is a vastness that the actuality does not have.
These great festivals of atonement must be permitted her, except that one must be careful to use them properly so that she
comes back to the actuality not fatigued but strengthened. In
this, letters are an aid; they help one to be invisibly and mentally present in these moments of sacred dedication, while the

I
383

idea that the actual person is the author of the letter forms a
natural and easy transition to the actuality.[172]

Could I become jealous of Cordelia? Damn it, yes! And yet
in another sense, no! That is, if I saw that her nature would be
disordered and not be what I want it to be—even though I won
in the clash with another—then I would give her up.

An ancient philosopher has said that if a person carefully
chronicles all his experiences, he is, before he knows where he
is, a philosopher.[173] For a long time now, I have lived in association with the fellowship of the engaged. Such a connection
certainly ought to yield some harvest. I have thought of gathering material for a book titled: *A Contribution to a Theory of the
Kiss*, dedicated to all doting lovers.[174] Incidentally, it is curious
that there is no book on this topic. If I manage to finish it, I
shall also fill a long-felt need. Can the reason for this deficiency
in the literature be that philosophers do not think about such
things or that they do not understand them? —I am already in
a position to offer some hints. A perfect kiss requires that the
agents be a girl and a man. A man-to-man kiss is in bad taste,
or, worse yet, it tastes bad. —In the next place, it is my opinion that a kiss comes closer to the idea when a man kisses a girl
than when a girl kisses a man. When over the years the distinction has been lost in this relationship, the kiss has lost its meaning. That is the case with the conjugal domestic kiss, by which
husband and wife, for want of a napkin, wipe each other's
mouth while saying "May it do us good [*Velbekom's*]."

If the age gap is very great, the kiss lies outside the idea. I
recall a special expression used by the senior class of an outly-
ing girls' school—"to kiss the councilor"—an expression with
anything but agreeable connotations. It began this way. The
teacher had a brother-in-law living in the house. He was an
elderly man, formerly a councilor, and because of his age he
took the liberty of kissing the young girls.

The kiss must be the expression of a particular passion.
When a brother and sister who are twins kiss each other, it is
not an authentic kiss. The same holds for a kiss paid in Christmas games, also for a stolen kiss. A kiss is a symbolic act that

I
384

is meaningless if devoid of the feeling it is supposed to signify, and this feeling can be present only under specific conditions.

[175]If one wants to try to classify kisses, numerous possible principles of classification come to mind. The kiss can be classified according to sound. Unfortunately, language does not have an adequate range for my observations. I do not believe all the languages of the world have the stock of onomatopoeiea necessary to designate the variations I have come across just in my uncle's house. Sometimes it is a smacking sound, sometimes whistling, sometimes slushy, sometimes explosive, sometimes booming, sometimes full, sometimes hollow, sometimes like calico, etc. etc.

The kiss can be classified according to touch—the tangential kiss, the kiss *en passant*, and the clinging kiss.

The kiss can be classified according to time as short or long. In the category of time, there is another classification, really the only one I like. A distinction is made between the first kiss and all the others. What is under consideration here cannot be used as the measure of what appears in the other classifications—it has nothing to do with sound, touch, time in general. The first kiss is qualitatively different from all others. Very few people think about this. It would be a shame if there were not even one who thinks about it.

My Cordelia,

A good answer is like a sweet kiss, says Solomon.[176] As you know, I have a weakness for asking questions; I may almost be censured for it. This happens because people do not understand what I am asking about, for you and you alone understand what I am asking about, and you and you alone know how to answer, and you and you alone know how to give a good answer, for, as Solomon says, a good answer is like a sweet kiss.

YOUR JOHANNES

I
385

There is a difference between the mental erotic and the earthly erotic. Until now, I have tried mainly to develop the mental kind in Cordelia. My personal presence must be different now, not just the accompanying mood; it must be tempting. These days, I have been continually preparing myself by reading the well-known passage in the *Phaedrus*[177] about erotic love. It electrifies my whole being and is an excellent prelude. Plato really had knowledge of the erotic.[178]

My Cordelia,

[179]The Latinist says of an attentive pupil that he hangs on his teacher's lips. For love, everything is a symbol; in recompense, the symbol in turn is actuality. Am I not a diligent, attentive pupil? But you do not say a word.

                                        Your JOHANNES

If anyone other than I were directing this development, he presumably would be too sagacious to let himself direct. If I were to consult an initiate among those who are engaged, he would no doubt say with a great flourish of erotic audacity: In these gradations of love, I seek in vain for the Chladni figure[180] in which the lovers converse about their love. I would answer: I am pleased that you look in vain, for the figure does not belong within the scope of the essentially erotic, not even when the interesting is drawn into it. Erotic love is much too substantial to be satisfied with chatter, the erotic situations much too significant to be filled with chatter. They are silent, still, definitely outlined, and yet eloquent, like the music of Memnon's statue.[181] Eros gesticulates, does not speak; or if he does, it is an enigmatic intimation, symbolic music. The erotic situations are always either sculptural or pictorial, but two people speaking together about their love is neither sculptural nor pictorial. But the solid engaged couple always begin with such chitchat, which goes on to become the thread that holds their loquacious marriage together. This chitchat is also the beginning of the dowry Ovid mentions: *dos est uxoria lites* [the dowry of a wife is quarreling][182] and the guarantee that their marriage will not lack it. —If there must be speaking, it is sufficient that one person does it. The man should do the speaking and therefore ought to possess some of the powers in the girdle of Venus[183] with which she beguiled: conversation and sweet flattery, that is, the power to ingratiate. —It by no means follows that Eros is mute, or that it would be erotically improper to converse, provided that the conversation itself is erotic and does not wander off into edifying observations on life's prospects etc. and that the conversation is actually regarded as a respite from the erotic action, a diversion, not as the ultimate. Such a conversation, such a *confabulatio* [fantasizing together], is entirely divine by nature, and I can never become bored conversing with a young girl. That is, I can become weary of a particular young girl, but never of conversing with a young girl. That is just as impossible for me as it is to become weary of breathing. What is really the distinctive characteristic of such speaking together is the vegetative flowering of conversation. The conversation keeps contact with the earth, has no actual subject; the accidental is the law of its movements—but daisy [*Tusindfryd*, thousand delights] is its name and the name of what it produces.

My Cordelia,

"My—Your"—those words, like parentheses, enclose the paltry content of my letters. Have you noticed that the distance between its arms is becoming shorter? O my Cordelia! [184]It is nevertheless beautiful that the emptier the parenthesis becomes the more momentous it is.

Your JOHANNES

My Cordelia,
Is an embrace a struggle?[185]

Your JOHANNES

Usually Cordelia keeps silent. This has always made me happy. She has too deep a womanly nature to pester one with hiatuses, a mode of speaking especially characteristic of women and unavoidable when the man who should supply the preceding or succeeding circumscribing consonant is just as

I
387

feminine. But at times a single brief remark betrays how much dwells within her. Then I assist her. It is as if behind a person, who with an unsure hand hastily made a few strokes in a drawing, there stood another person who every time made something vivid and finished out of it. She herself is surprised, and yet it is as if it belonged to her. This is why I watch over her, over every chance remark, every casual word, and as I give it back to her it always becomes something more significant, which she both recognizes and does not recognize.

Today we were at a party. We had not exchanged a word with each other. We rose from the table; then a servant came in and told Cordelia that there was a messenger who wished to speak with her. This messenger was from me, bringing a letter alluding to a remark I had made at the table. I had managed to introduce it into the general dinner conversation in such a way that Cordelia, although she sat some distance from me, was bound to hear it and misunderstand it. The letter was composed with this in mind. If I had been unable to turn the dinner conversation in that direction, I would have been present at the designated time to confiscate the letter. She came in again and had to tell a little white lie. Such things consolidate the erotic secretiveness without which she cannot walk the path assigned to her.

I
388

My Cordelia,

Do you believe that the person who pillows his head on an elf-hillock sees the image of an elf-girl in his dreams? I do not know, but this I do know—when I rest my head upon your breast and then do not close my eyes but look up, I see an angel's face. Do you believe that the person who leans his head against an elf-hillock cannot lie quietly? I do not think so, but this I do know—that when my head inclines upon your bosom it is too deeply stirred for sleep to alight upon my eyes.

Your JOHANNES[186]

Jacta est alea [The die is cast].[187] Now the turn must be made. I was with her today but was completely engrossed in thinking about an idea that totally occupied me. I had neither eyes nor ears for her. The idea itself was interesting and captivated her. Furthermore, it would have been incorrect to begin the new operation by being cold in her presence. After I have gone and the thought no longer occupies her, she will easily discover that I was different from what I have usually been. Because she discovers this change in her solitude, the discovery will be much more painful for her, will work its effect more slowly but all the more penetratingly. She cannot promptly flare up, and when she does have a chance she will already have thought out so much to say that she cannot say it all at once but will always retain a remnant of doubt. The disquietude mounts, the letters stop coming, the erotic rations are diminished, erotic love is mocked as something ludicrous. Perhaps she goes along with it for a time, but in the long run she cannot endure it. Then she will want to make me captive with the same means I have employed against her—with the erotic.

I
389

[188]On the subject of breaking an engagement, every little miss is a great casuist, and although in the schools there is no course on the subject, every little slip of a girl is superbly informed when the question is under what circumstances an engagement should be broken. This really ought to be the standing question in the senior examination, and although I know that generally the papers written in girls' schools are very much the same, I am sure that there would be no lack of variety here, since the issue itself opens a wide field to a girl's acuteness. And why should a young girl not be given the opportunity to use her acuteness in the most brilliant manner? Or will she not precisely thereby have the opportunity to show that she is mature enough—to become engaged? I once witnessed a situation [189]that interested me very much. One day, the parents in a family I sometimes visited were absent; however, the two daughters of the household had invited a circle of girl friends for morning coffee. There were eight in all, between the ages of sixteen and twenty. Very likely they had not expected a visit—in fact, the maid even had orders to say they were not at home. But I went in and clearly perceived that they

were somewhat surprised. God knows what eight young girls like that discuss in such a solemn synodical meeting. At times, married women also convene in similar meetings. Then they discourse on pastoral theology, discussing in particular such important questions as: under what circumstances it is all right to allow a maidservant to go to market alone; whether it is better to have a charge account at the butcher's or to pay cash; the likelihood that the kitchenmaid has a sweetheart; how to eliminate all this sweetheart traffic that delays the cooking.

[190]I found my place in this beautiful cluster. It was very early in the spring. The sun sent out a few odd shafts of light as express messengers of its arrival. Inside the apartment, everything was wintry, and for that very reason the sun's rays were so portentous. The coffee shed fragrance at the table, and the young girls themselves were happy, healthy, blooming—and hilarious, for their anxiety had quickly subsided. What was there to be afraid of, after all; in a way they were strong in manpower. I managed to direct their attention and conversation to the question: under what circumstances should an engagement be broken. While my eyes delighted in flitting from one flower to the next in this circle of girls, delighted in resting now on this beauty, now on that one, my outer ears delighted in reveling in the enjoyment of the music of their voices, and my inner ears delighted in listening closely to what was said. A single word was frequently enough for me to gain a deep insight into such a girl's heart and its history. How seductive are the ways of love, and how interesting to explore how far along the way the individual is. I continually fanned the flames; brilliance, wit, esthetic objectivity contributed to making the situation more relaxed, and yet everything remained within the bounds of the strictest propriety. While we jested this way in the regions of light conversation, there slumbered the possibility of putting the good maidens into a disastrously awkward situation with a single word. This possibility was in my power. The girls did not comprehend this, had scarcely an inkling of this. It was kept submerged at all times by the easy play of conversation, just as Scheherazade[191] held off the death sentence by telling stories.

Sometimes I led the conversation to the edge of sadness; sometimes I let flippancy break loose; sometimes I tempted them out into a dialectical game. Indeed, what subject contains greater multiplicity, all according to how one looks at it. I continually introduced new themes.[192] —I told of a girl whom the parents' cruelty had forced to break an engagement. The unhappy collision almost brought tears to their eyes. —I told of a man who had broken an engagement and had given two grounds: that the girl was too big and that he had not knelt before her when he confessed his love. When I protested to him that they could not possibly be regarded as adequate grounds, he replied, "Well, they are quite adequate to achieve what I want, for no one can give a reasonable reply to them." —I submitted a very difficult case for the assembly's consideration. A young girl broke her engagement because she felt sure that she and her sweetheart were not compatible. The lover sought to bring her to her senses by assuring her how much he loved her; whereupon she answered: Either we are compatible and there is a real sympathy, and in that case you will perceive that we are not compatible, or we are not compatible, and in that case you will perceive that we are not compatible. It was amusing to see how the girls cudgeled their brains to grasp this enigmatic talk, and yet I clearly noticed that there were a couple of them who understood it superbly, for on the subject of breaking an engagement every young miss is a born casuist. —Yes, I really do believe it would be easier for me to argue with the devil himself than with a young girl when the topic is: under what circumstances should an engagement be broken.

I
391

Today I was with her. Precipitously, with the speed of thought, I immediately turned the conversation to the same subject with which I had occupied her yesterday, once again trying to make her enraptured. "Yesterday, after I had gone, I thought of something I would have said." It worked. As long as I am with her, she enjoys listening to me; after I am gone, she perceives very well that she is being deceived, that I am different. In this way one withdraws one's shares of stock. It is a disingenuous method but very expedient, as are all indirect

methods. She can very well understand that something such as
we are discussing can occupy me; indeed, she herself finds it
interesting at the moment, and yet I am cheating her of the essentially erotic.¹⁹³

Oderint, dum metuant [Let them hate me, so they but fear
me],¹⁹⁴ as if only fear and hate belong together, whereas fear
and love have nothing to do with each other, as if it were not
fear that makes love interesting. With what kind of love do we
embrace nature? Is there not a secretive anxiety and horror in
it, because its beautiful harmony works its way out of lawless-
ness and wild confusion, its security out of perfidy? But precisely this anxiety captivates the most. So also with love, if it
is to be interesting. Behind it ought to brood the deep, anxious
night from which springs the flower of love. Thus the *nym-
phaea alba* [white water lily] rests with its calyx on the surface
of the water, while thought is anxious about plunging down
into the deep darkness where it has its root. —I have noticed
that she always calls me "my" when she writes to me but does
not have the courage to say it to me. Today, with as much insinuating and erotic warmth as possible, I beseeched her to do
so. She began to do so; an ironic look, briefer and swifter than
it takes to say it, was enough to make it impossible for her, although my lips did their utmost to encourage her. This mood
is normal.

She is mine. This I do not confide to the stars, according to
custom; I really do not see of what concern this information
can be to those remote globes. Neither do I confide it to any
human being, not even to Cordelia. This secret I keep to myself alone, whisper it, as it were, into myself in the most secretive conversations with myself. Her attempted resistance to
me was not particularly great, but the erotic power she displays is admirable. How interesting she is in this profound
passionateness, how great she is—almost larger than life! How
agile she is in escaping, how adroit in insinuating herself wherever she discovers a weak point! Everything is set in motion,
but I find myself right in my element in this rioting of the elements. And yet even in this agitation she is by no means unbeautiful, not torn to pieces in moods, not split up into frag-

ments. She is always an Aphrodite, except that she does not rise up in naïve loveliness or in *unbefangen* [disinterested] tranquillity but is stirred by the strong pulsebeat of erotic love, although she nevertheless is unity and balance. Erotically, she is fully equipped for battle; she fights with the arrows of her eyes, with the command of her brow, with the secretiveness of her forehead, with the eloquence of her bosom, with the dangerous enticements of her embrace, with the appeal of her lips, with the smile of her cheeks, with the sweet longing of her whole being. There is a power in her, an energy, as if she were a Valkyrie, but this erotic plenitude of power is tempered in turn by a certain pining languor that suffuses her. —She must not be kept too long at this pinnacle where only anxiety and uneasiness support her and keep her from plunging down. Emotions such as these will soon make her feel that the engagement is too constricted, too hampering. She will herself become the temptress who seduces me into going beyond the boundary of the universal; in this way she will become conscious of it herself, and for me that is primary.

Quite a few remarks dropped from her side to indicate that she is tired of the engagement. They do not pass my ear unnoticed; they are the reconnoiterers of my enterprise in her soul that give me informative clues; they are the ends of the threads by which I am spinning her into my plan.

My Cordelia,

You complain about the engagement; you think that our love does not need an external bond, which is only a hindrance. I thereby recognize at once my excellent Cordelia! I truly do admire you. Our outward union is still only a separation. There is still a partition that keeps us apart like Pyramus and Thisbe.[195] There is still the disturbance of having others share our secret. Only in contrast is there freedom. Only when no alien suspects our love, only then does it have meaning; only when all outsiders think that the lovers hate each other, only then is love happy.

Your JOHANNES

Soon the bond of the engagement will be broken. She herself will be the one who dissolves it, in order by this dissolution to captivate me even more, if possible, just as flowing locks captivate more than those that are bound up. If I broke the engagement, I would miss out on this erotic somersault, which is so seductive to look at and such a sure sign of the audacity of her soul. For me, that is primary. Moreover, the whole incident would create for me some unpleasant consequences in connection with other people. I shall become unpopular, detested, loathed, although unjustly so, for would not many people derive some advantage from it? There is many a little miss who, failing to become engaged, would still be quite content to have been close to it. After all, it is something, even though, to tell the truth, exceedingly little, for just when one has elbowed forward this way in order to obtain a place on the waiting list [*Exspectance-List*], the prospects [*Exspectance*] are dim; the higher one moves up, the further one advances, the dimmer the prospects. In the world of love, the principle of seniority does not hold with respect to advancement and promotion. In addition, such a little miss is bored by holding undivided possession of the property; she wants her life to be stirred by some event. But what can compare with an unhappy love affair, especially when, in addition, one can take the whole thing so lightly. So one makes oneself and the neighbors believe that one is among the victimized, and, not qualified to be accepted into a home for fallen women, one takes lodging next door as a wailer. People are duty-bound to hate me.

In addition, there is still a class of those whom someone has deceived totally, one-half, or three-quarters. There are many gradations here, from those who have a ring as evidence to those who hang their hats on a handclasp in a square dance. Their wound is torn open again by the new pain. I accept their hate as a bonus. But, of course, all these haters are the same as crypto-lovers to my poor heart. A king without any territory is a ludicrous character, but a war of succession among a mob of pretenders to a kingdom without any territory goes beyond even the most ludicrous. Thus I really ought to be loved and cared for by the fair sex as a pawnshop is. [196]A person who is actually engaged can take care of only one, but such an extensive potentiality can take care of, that is, up to a point take care of, as many as you please. [197]I escape all this finite nonsense and also have the advantage of being able to appear to others in a totally new role. The young girls will feel sorry for me, pity me, sigh for me. I play in the very same key, and in this way one can also make a catch.

[198]Strangely enough, right now I note with distress that I am getting the sign of denunciation Horace wished upon every faithless girl—a black tooth,[199] moreover, a front one. How superstitious one can be! The tooth really disturbs me; I dislike any reference to it—it is a weak point I have. Although I am fully armed everywhere else, here even the biggest lout can give me a jolt that goes far deeper than he thinks when he refers to the tooth. I do everything to whiten it, but in vain. I say with Palnatoke:

> I am rubbing it by day, by night,
> But cannot wipe out that black shadow.[200]

I
395

Life does indeed have extraordinarily much that is enigmatic. Such a little circumstance can disturb me more than the most dangerous attack, the most painful situation. I would have it pulled out, but that would affect my speaking and the power of my voice. But if I do have it pulled out, I will have a false one put in—that is, it will be false to the world; the black one was false to me.

[201]It is superb that Cordelia takes exception to an engagement. Marriage still is and will continue to be an honorable institution, even though it does have the wearisome aspect of enjoying already in its youth a share of the honor that age provides. An engagement, however, is a strictly human invention and as such is so significant and so ludicrous that on the one hand it is entirely appropriate that a young girl in the tumult of passion overrides it, and yet on the other hand she feels its significance, perceives the energy of her soul as a higher blood system everywhere present in herself. The point now is

to guide her in such a way that in her bold flight she entirely loses sight of marriage and the continent of actuality, so that her soul, as much in pride as in her anxiety about losing me, will destroy an imperfect human form in order to hurry on to something that is superior to the ordinarily human. But in this regard, I need have no fear, for her movement across life is already so light and buoyant that actuality has already been lost sight of to a large extent. Moreover, I am indeed continually on board and can always stretch out the sails.

[202]Woman still is and will continue to be an inexhaustible subject for contemplation for me, an everlasting overabundance for observations. The person who feels no need for this study can be whatever he wants to be in the world as far as I am concerned, but one thing he is not, he is no esthetician. What is glorious and divine about esthetics is that it is associated only with the beautiful; essentially it deals only with belles lettres and the fair sex. It can give me joy, it can joy my heart, to imagine the sun of womanhood sending out its rays in an infinite multiplicity, radiating into a confusion of languages, where each woman has a little share of the whole kingdom of womanhood, yet in such a way that the remainder found in her harmoniously forms around this point. In this sense, womanly beauty is infinitely divisible. But the specific share of beauty must be harmoniously controlled, for otherwise it has a disturbing effect, and one comes to think that nature intended something with this girl, but that nothing ever came of it.

My eyes can never grow weary of quickly passing over this peripheral multiplicity, these radiating emanations of womanly beauty. Every particular point has its little share and yet is complete in itself, happy, joyous, beautiful. Each one has her own: the cheerful smile, the roguish glance, the yearning eye, the tilted head, the frolicsome disposition, the quiet sadness, the profound presentiment, the ominous depression, the earthly homesickness, the unshriven emotions, the beckoning brow, the questioning lips, the secretive forehead, the alluring curls, the concealing eyelashes, the heavenly pride, the earthly modesty, the angelic purity, the secret blush, the light step, the lovely buoyancy, the languorous posture, the longing dreaminess, the unaccountable sighing, the slender figure, the soft curves, the opulent bosom, the curving hips, the tiny feet, the elegant hands.

Each one has her own, and the one does not have what the other has. When I have seen and seen again, observed and observed again, the multiplicity of this world, when I have smiled, sighed, flattered, threatened, desired, tempted, laughed, cried, hoped, feared, won, lost—then I fold up the fan, then what is scattered gathers itself together into a unity, the parts into a whole. Then my soul rejoices, my heart pounds, passion is aroused. This one girl, the one and only in all the world, she must belong to me; she must be mine. Let God keep his heaven if I may keep her.[203] I know very well what I am choosing; it is something so great that heaven itself cannot be served by sharing in this way, for what would be left in heaven if I kept her? The hopes of believing Mohammedans would be disappointed if in their paradise they embraced pale, feeble shadows, because they would not be able to find warm hearts, since all the warmth of the heart would be concentrated in her breast; they would despair inconsolably when they found pale lips, lusterless eyes, an inert bosom, a weak handclasp, for all the redness of the lips and fire of the eye and restlessness of the bosom and promise of the handclasp and intimation of the sighing and seal of the lips and quivering of the touch and passion of the embrace—all—all would be united in her, who squandered on me what would be sufficient for a world both here and to come.

I have often thought on the matter in this way, but every time I think thus I always become warm because I imagine her as warm. Although warmth is generally considered a good sign, it does not follow from this that my mode of thinking will be conceded the honorable predicate that it is sound. Therefore, for variety, I, myself cold, shall imagine her as cold. I shall attempt to consider woman categorically. In which category is she to be placed? In the category of being-for-other.[204] But this is not to be taken in the bad sense, as if one who is for me is also for an other. Here one must, as always in abstract thinking, abstain from every consideration of experience, for otherwise in the present instance I would in a curious way have experience both for and against me. Here as everywhere, experience is a curious character, for its nature is always to be both for and against. So she is being-for-other. Here in turn, from a different angle, we must not let ourselves be disturbed by experience, which teaches us that very seldom do we meet a woman who is truly being-for-other, since the great majority usually are not entities at all, either for themselves or for others. She shares this qualification with all nature, with all femininity in general. All nature is only for-other in this way, not in the teleological sense, in such a way that one specific segment of nature is for a different specific segment, but the whole of nature is for-other—is for spirit. It is the same again with the particular. Plant life, for example, in all naïveté unfolds its hidden charms and is only for-other. Likewise, an enigma, a charade, a secret, a vowel, etc. are merely being-for-other. This explains why God, when he created Eve, had a deep sleep fall upon Adam, for woman is man's dream. The story teaches us in another way that woman is being-for-other. That is, it says that Jehovah took one of man's ribs. If he had, for example, taken from man's brain, woman would certainly have continued to be being-for-other, but the purpose was not that she should be a figment of the brain but something quite different. She became flesh and blood, but precisely thereby she falls within the category of nature, which essentially is being-for-other. Not until she is touched by erotic love does she awaken; before that time she is a dream. But in this dream existence two stages can be distinguished: in the first, love dreams about her; in the second, she dreams about love.

As being-for-other, woman is characterized by pure virginity. That is, virginity is a being that, insofar as it is being-for-itself, is actually an abstraction and manifests itself only for-other. Feminine innocence has the same characteristic. Therefore, it can be said that woman in this state is invisible. It is well known that there was no image of Vesta,[205] the goddess who most closely represented true virginity. In other words, this form of existence is esthetically jealous of itself, just as Jehovah is ethically jealous,[206] and does not want any image to exist or even any idea of one. This is the contradiction—that which is for-other *is* not and, so to speak, first becomes visible through the other. Logically, this contradiction is entirely in order, and one who knows how to think logically will not be disturbed by it but will rejoice over it. But one who thinks illogically will imagine that whatever is being-for-other *is* in the same finite sense as one can say of a particular thing: That is something for me.

Woman's being (the word "existence"[207] already says too much, for she does not subsist out of herself) is correctly designated as gracefulness, an expression that is reminiscent of vegetative life; she is like a flower, as the poets are fond of saying,[208] and even the intellectual [*aandelige*] is present in her in a vegetative way. She belongs altogether to the category of nature and for this reason is free only esthetically. In the deeper sense, she first becomes free [*fri*] through man, and therefore we say "to propose [*at frie*]," and therefore man proposes. If he proposes properly, there can be no question of any choice. To be sure, woman chooses, but if this choice is thought of as the result of a long deliberation, then that kind of choosing is unwomanly. Therefore, it is a disgrace to be rejected, because the individual involved has overrated himself, has wanted to make another free without having the capacity to do so.

In this relation there is profound irony. That which is for-other has the appearance of being dominant; man proposes, woman chooses. According to her concept, woman is the vanquished and man, according to his concept, the victor, and yet the victor submits to the defeated one; nevertheless this is altogether natural, and it is sheer boorishness, stupidity, and lack of erotic sensitivity to disregard that which follows directly as a matter of course. This also has a deeper basis, namely, that woman is substance, man is reflection. Therefore, she does not choose without further ado; rather, man proposes, she chooses. But man's proposal is a questioning; her choosing is actually an answer to a question. In a certain sense, man is more than woman, in another sense infinitely much less.

This being-for-other is the pure virginity. If it makes an attempt itself to be in relation to another being that is being-for-it, then the opposite manifests itself in an absolute coyness, but this opposite also shows that woman's true being is being-for-other. The diametrical opposite of absolute devotedness is absolute coyness, which conversely is invisible as the abstraction against which everything breaks, although the abstraction does not therefore come to life. Womanliness now assumes the quality of abstract cruelty, which is the caricaturing extreme of essential virginal *Sprödigkeit* [coyness]. A man can never be as cruel as a woman. A search of mythology, folktales, legends will confirm this. If a representation is to be given of a principle of nature that in its ruthlessness knows no limits, then it is a feminine creature. Or one is terrified to read about a young girl who callously has her suitors liquidated, as one so frequently reads in the fairy tales of all peoples. On the wedding night, a Bluebeard kills all the girls he has loved, but he does not enjoy the killing of them; on the contrary, the enjoyment was antecedent, and therein lies the concretion—it is not cruelty for the sake of cruelty alone. A Don Juan seduces them and abandons them, but he has enjoyment not in abandoning them but rather in seducing them; therefore, it is in no way this abstract cruelty.

The more I deliberate on the matter, the more I see that my practice is in complete harmony with my theory. My practice, namely, has always been imbued with the conviction that woman is essentially being-for-other. The moment is so very significant here because being-for-other is always a matter of the moment. A longer or shorter time may pass before the moment arrives, but as soon as it has arrived, then that which originally was being-for-other assumes a relative being, and with that everything is finished. I am well aware that husbands sometimes say that woman is being-for-other in a quite different sense, that she is everything for them for the whole of life. Allowances must be made for husbands. I do believe that this is something that they make each other believe. Every class in life ordinarily has certain conventional ways and especially certain conventional lies. This traveler's tale must be reckoned as one of those. To have an understanding of the moment[209] is not such an easy matter, and the one who misunderstands it is doomed to boredom for life. The moment is everything, and in the moment woman is everything; the consequences I do not understand. One such consequence is having a child. Now, I fancy myself to be a fairly consistent thinker, but even if I were to go mad, I am not the man to think that consequence. I do not understand it at all—it takes a married man for such things.

I
400

[210]Yesterday, Cordelia and I visited a family at their summer home. The people spent most of the time in the garden, where we amused ourselves with all kinds of physical exercise. One of the games we played was quoits [*Ring*]. When another gentleman who had been playing with Cordelia left, I seized the opportunity to take his place. What a wealth of loveliness she displayed, even more seductive in the graceful exertions of the game! What lovely harmony in the self-contradictions of her movements! How light she was, like a dance across the meadow! How vigorous, yet without needing resistance; how deceptive until her balance accounted for everything! How dithyrambic her demeanor, how provocative her glance! Naturally, the game itself had a special interest for me. Cordelia did not seem to notice it. An allusion I made to one of those present about the beautiful custom of exchanging rings struck her soul like a lightning bolt. From that moment, a higher explanation pervaded the whole situation, a deeper significance permeated it, a heightened energy inflamed her. I had both rings on my stick; I paused for a moment, exchanged a few words with those standing around us. She understood this pause. I tossed the rings to her again. A moment later, she caught both of them on her stick. She tossed both of them straight up into the air simultaneously, as if inadvertently, so that it was impossible for me to catch them. This toss was accompanied by a look filled with unbounded daredeviltry. There is a story of a French soldier who had been in the Russian campaign and had to have his leg amputated because of gangrene. The very

moment the agonizing operation was over, he seized the leg by
the sole of the foot, tossed it up into the air, and shouted: *Vive
l'empereur* [Long live the emperor]. With a look such as that,
she, even more beautiful than ever before, tossed both rings up
into the air and said to herself: Long live erotic love. I deemed
it inadvisable, however, to let her run riot in this mood or to
leave her alone with it, out of fear of the letdown that often
comes on its heels. Therefore, I remained very cool, as if I had
noticed nothing, and with the help of those present con-
strained her to keep on playing. Such behavior only gives her
more elasticity.

[211]If any sympathy with explorations of this kind could be
expected in our age, I would pose this question for a prize essay: From the esthetic point of view, who is more modest, a
young girl or a young wife, the inexperienced or the experienced; to whom does one dare to grant more freedom? But
such things do not concern our earnest age. In Greece, such an
investigation would have prompted universal attention; the
whole state would have been set in motion, especially the
young girls and the young wives. Our age would not believe
this, but neither would our age believe it if it were told of the
celebrated contest held between two Greek maidens[212] and the
very painstaking investigation it occasioned, for in Greece
such problems were not treated casually and light-mindedly,
and yet everyone knows that Venus has an extra name on account of this contest and that everyone admires the statue of
Venus that has immortalized her.

A married woman has two periods of her life in which she is
interesting: her very earliest youth and again at long last when
she has become very much older. But she also has a moment,
and this must not be denied her, when she is even lovelier than
a young girl, inspires even more honor. But this is a moment
that seldom occurs in life; it is a picture for the imagination that
does not need to be seen in life and perhaps is never seen. I
imagine her as healthy, blooming, amply developed; in her
arms she is holding a child, to whom all her attention is given,
in the contemplation of whom she is absorbed. It is a picture

that must be called the loveliest that human life has to display; it is a nature myth, which therefore may be seen only in artistic portrayal, not in actuality. There must be no more figures in the picture either, no setting, which only interferes. If one goes to our churches, one will often have occasion to see a mother appear with a child in her arms. Apart from the disquieting crying of the child, apart from the uneasy thought about the parents' expectations for the little one's future based upon this crying of the infant, the surroundings in themselves interfere so much that even if everything else were perfect the effect would nevertheless be lost. The father is visible—a huge defect, since that cancels the myth, the charm. The earnest chorus of sponsors is visible—*horrenda refero* [I report dreadful things][213]—and one sees nothing at all. Presented as a picture for the imagination, it is the loveliest of all. I do not lack the boldness and dash, or the brashness, to venture an assault—but if I were to see such a picture in actuality, I would be disarmed.

I
402

[214]How Cordelia preoccupies me! And yet the time will soon be over; my soul always requires rejuvenation. I already hear, as it were, the rooster crowing in the distance. Perhaps she hears it, too, but she believes it is heralding the morning. —Why does a young girl have such beauty, and why does it last such a short time? That thought could make me very melancholy, and yet it is really none of my business. Enjoy—do not chatter. Ordinarily, people who make a profession of such deliberations do not enjoy at all. But it does no harm to think about it, because this sadness—not for oneself but for others— usually makes one a bit more handsome in a masculine way. A sadness that like a veil of mist deceptively obscures manly strength is part of the masculine erotic. A certain depression in woman corresponds to this.

[215]As soon as a girl has devoted herself completely, the whole thing is finished. I still always approach a young girl with a certain anxiety; my heart pounds, for I sense the eternal power that is in her nature. It has never occurred to me face to face with a married woman. The little bit of resistance she artfully seeks to make is nothing. It is like saying that the married

woman's housecap is more impressive than the young girl's uncovered head. [216]That is why Diana[217] has always been my ideal. This pure virginity, this absolute coyness, has always occupied me very much. But although she has always held my attention, I have also always kept a suspicious eye on her. That is, I assume that she actually has not deserved all the eulogies upon her virginity that she has reaped. She knew, namely, that her game in life is bound up with her virginity; therefore it is preserved. To this is added that in a philological nook of the world I have heard murmurings that she had some idea of the terrible birth pangs her mother had experienced. This had frightened her, and for that I cannot blame Diana. I say with Euripides: I would rather go into battle three times than give birth once.[218] I really could not fall in love with Diana, but I do not deny that I would give a lot for a talk with her, for what I would call a candid conversation. She must have a bag full of all kinds of tricks. Obviously my good Diana in one way or another has knowledge that makes her far less naïve than even Venus. I would not bother to spy on her in her bath, by no means, but I would like to spy on her with my questions. If I were sneaking off to a rendezvous where I had fears for my victory, I would prepare myself and arm myself, activate the spirits of the erotic by conversing with her.

[219]A question that has frequently been the subject of my consideration is: which situation, which moment, may be regarded as the most seductive? The answer, of course, depends upon what and how one desires and how one is developed. I claim that it is the wedding day, and especially a particular moment. When she is standing there adorned as a bride, and all her splendor nevertheless pales before her beauty, and she herself in turn grows pale, when the blood stops, when the bosom is motionless, when the glance falters, when the foot hesitates, when the maiden trembles, when the fruit matures; when the heavens lift her up, when the solemnity strengthens her, when the promise carries her, when the prayer blesses her, when the myrtle crowns her; when the heart trembles, when the eyes drop, when she hides within herself, when she does not belong

to the world in order to belong to it entirely; when the bosom swells, when the creation sighs, when the voice fails, when the tear quivers before the riddle is explained, when the torch is lit, when the bridegroom awaits—then the moment is present. Soon it is too late. There is only one step left, but this is just enough for a stumble. This moment makes even an insignificant girl significant; even a little Zerlina[220] becomes something. Everything must be gathered together, the greatest contrasts united in the moment; if something is lacking, especially one of the primary opposites, the situation promptly loses part of its seductiveness. There is a well-known etching that portrays a penitent.[221] She looks so young and so innocent that one is almost embarrassed for her and the father confessor— what can she really have to confess? She lifts her veil slightly and looks out at the world as if she were seeking something that she perhaps could have the opportunity of confessing on a later occasion, and obviously it is nothing more than an obligation out of solicitude for—the father confessor. The situation is very seductive, and since she is the only figure in the picture there is nothing to prevent imagining the church in which all this takes place as being so spacious that several and very dissimilar preachers could preach there simultaneously. The situation is very seductive, and I have no objection to introducing myself into the background, especially if this slip of a girl has nothing against it. But it nevertheless remains a very minor situation, for the girl seems to be but a child in both respects, and consequently it will take time for the moment to arrive.

[222]In my relation to Cordelia, have I been continually faithful to my pact? That is, my pact with the esthetic, for it is that which makes me strong—that I continually have the idea on my side. It is a secret like Samson's hair, one that no Delilah can wrest from me.[223] Plainly and simply to deceive a girl, for that I certainly would not have the stamina; but the fact that the idea is present in motion, that I am acting in its service, that I dedicate myself to its service—this gives me rigorousness toward myself, abstinence from every forbidden pleasure. Has

I
404

the interesting been preserved at all times? Yes—I dare to say
that freely and openly in this secret conversation. The engagement itself was the interesting precisely because it did not yield
that which is commonly understood as the interesting. It preserved the interesting precisely through the contradiction between the outward appearance and the inner life. If I had had a
secret connection with her, it would have been interesting
only to the first power. But this is the interesting raised to the
second power, and therefore only then is it the interesting for
her. The engagement is broken, but she herself breaks it in order to soar into a higher sphere. So it should be; this is precisely the form of the interesting that will occupy her the most.

September 16

The bond has broken—full of longing, strong, bold, divine,
she flies like a bird that now for the first time is allowed to
spread its wings. Fly, bird, fly![224] Truly, if this regal flight
were a retreat from me, it would pain me very deeply. For me
it would be the same as if Pygmalion's beloved were changed
to stone again.[225] Light have I made her, light as a thought, and
should then this thought of mine not belong to me! It would
be enough to despair over. A moment before, it would not
have occupied me; a moment later, it will not concern me, but
now—now—this now that is an eternity for me. But she is not
flying away from me. Fly, then, bird, fly, rise proudly on your
wings, glide through the delicate aerial kingdom; soon I shall
be with you, soon I shall hide myself with you in deep solitude.

The aunt was rather astonished at this news. But she is too
broad-minded to want to coerce Cordelia, even though I have
made some attempt to engage her interest on my behalf—
partly to lull her into a deeper sleep and partly to tease Cordelia
a little. She is, however, very sympathetic toward me; she
does not suspect how much reason I have to decline all sympathy.

She has received permission from her aunt to spend some
time out in the country; she will visit a family. Fortunately, it
so happens that she cannot immediately surrender to a glut of

moods. For some time yet, she will be kept in tension by all kinds of resistance from without. I keep up a slight communication with her through letters; in that way our relationship is coming to life again. She must now be made strong in every way; in particular it is best to let her make a couple of flourishes of eccentric contempt for men and for the universal. Then when the day for her departure arrives, a trustworthy fellow will show up as the driver. Outside the city gate, my highly trusted servant will join them. He will accompany them to their destination and remain with her to wait on her and help her in case of need. Next to myself, I know of no one better suited for that than Johan. I have personally arranged everything out there as tastefully as possible. Nothing is lacking that in any way can serve to beguile her soul and pacify it in luxuriant well-being.

My Cordelia,

Yet the cries of "Fire!" in individual families have not joined in a universal Capitolinian confusion of citywide shrieking.[226] Probably you have already had to put up with a few solos. Imagine the whole gaggle of teatime talebearers and coffee gossips; imagine a presiding chairwoman, a worthy counterpart to that immortal President Lars in Claudius,[227] and you have a picture of and a notion of and a measure of what you have lost and with whom: the opinion of good people.

Enclosed is the celebrated engraving that depicts President Lars.[228] I was unable to purchase it separately, so I bought the complete Claudius, tore it out, and threw the rest away—for why should I venture to inconvenience you with a gift that means nothing to you at this moment; why should I not summon everything to provide what could please you for just one moment; why should I permit more to be mixed up in a situation than belongs to it? Nature has such a complexity, as does the person who is a slave to life's finite relations, but you, my Cordelia, you will in your freedom hate it.

Your JOHANNES

I
406

Spring is indeed the most beautiful time to fall in love, autumn the most beautiful to attain the object of one's desire.
Autumn has a sadness that corresponds exactly to the movement whereby the thought of the fulfillment of a desire flows
through a person. Today I myself have been out at the country
house where in a few days Cordelia will find a setting that harmonizes with her soul. I myself do not wish to participate in
her surprise and in her joy over it; such erotic episodes would
only weaken her soul. But if she is alone in it, she will dream
away; she will see hints everywhere, clues, an enchanted
world. But all this would lose its significance if I were at her
side; it would make her forget that for us the time is past when
something like this enjoyed together had significance. This
setting must not narcotically entrap her soul but continually
allow it to soar aloft as she views it all as a game that means
nothing compared with what is to come. During the days still
remaining, I myself plan to visit this place more often in order
to keep myself in the mood.

My Cordelia,
Now I truly call you *my*; no external sign reminds me of my
possession. —Soon I shall truly call you *my*. And when I hold
you clasped tightly in my arms, when you enfold me in your
embrace, then we shall need no ring to remind us that we belong to each other, for is not this embrace a ring that is more
than a symbol? And the more tightly this ring encircles us, the
more inseparably it knits us together, the greater the freedom,
for your freedom consists in being mine, as my freedom consists in being yours.

Your JOHANNES

My Cordelia,
While he was hunting, Alpheus[229] fell in love with the
nymph Arethusa. She would not grant his request but continually fled before him until on the island of Ortygia she was
transformed into a spring. Alpheus grieved so much over this
that he was transformed into a river in Elis in the Peloponne-

sus. He did not, however, forget his love but under the sea united with that spring. Is the time of transformations past? Answer: Is the time of love past? To what can I compare your pure, deep soul, which has no connection with the world, except to a spring? And have I not told you that I am like a river that has fallen in love? And now when we are separated, do I not plunge under the sea in order to be united with you? There under the sea we shall meet again, for only in the deeps of the sea shall we really belong together.

Your JOHANNES

My Cordelia,

Soon, soon you will be mine. [230]When the sun shuts its vigilant eye, when history is over and the myths begin, I will not only throw my cloak around me but I will throw the night around me like a cloak and hurry to you and listen in order to find you—listen not for your footsteps but for the beating of your heart.

Your JOHANNES

During these days when I cannot be with her personally when I want to be, the thought has troubled me that it may occur to her at some moment to think about the future. It has never occurred to her before, because I have known too well how to anesthetize her esthetically. There is nothing more unerotic imaginable than this chattering about the future, which is due mainly to having nothing with which to fill up present time. If only I am with her, I have no fear about such things; no doubt I shall make her forget both time and eternity. If a man does not know how to establish rapport with a girl's soul to that extent, he should never become involved in trying to beguile, for then it will be impossible to avoid the two reefs, questions about the future and catechizing about faith. [231]Therefore, it is entirely appropriate for Gretchen in *Faust*[232] to conduct a little examination of him, since Faust had been injudicious enough to disclose the knight in him, and against such an assault a girl is always armed.

I
408

I
409

Now I believe that everything is arranged for her reception; she will not lack opportunity to admire my memory, or, more correctly, she will not have time to admire it. Nothing has been forgotten that could have any significance for her; on the other hand, nothing has been introduced that could directly remind her of me, although I am nevertheless invisibly present everywhere. But in large part the effect will depend upon how she happens to see it the first time. In that regard, my servant has received the most precise instructions, and in his way he is a perfect virtuoso. He knows how to drop a remark casually and nonchalantly if directed to do so; he knows how to be ignorant—in short, he is invaluable to me.

The location is just as she would like it. Sitting in the center of the room, one can look out on two sides beyond everything in the foreground; there is the limitless horizon on both sides; one is alone in the vast ocean of the atmosphere. If one moves nearer to a row of windows, a forest [*Skov*] looms far off on the horizon like a garland, bounding and inclosing. So it should be. What does erotic love [*Elskov*] love? —An enclosure. Was not paradise itself an enclosed place, a garden facing east?[233] —But it hedges one in too closely, this ring. One moves closer to the window—a calm lake hides humbly within the higher surroundings. At the edge there is a boat. A sigh out of the heart's fullness, a breath from the mind's unrest. It works loose from its mooring, glides over the surface of the lake, gently moved by the soft breeze of ineffable longing. Rocked on the surface of the lake, which is dreaming about the deep darkness of the forest, one vanishes in the mysterious solitude of the forest. —One turns to the other side, where the sea spreads out before one's eyes, which are stopped by nothing and are pursued by thoughts that nothing detains. What does erotic love love? Infinity. —What does erotic love fear? Boundaries.

Beyond this large room lies a smaller room or, more correctly, a private room, for this was what the drawing room in the Wahl house approximated. The resemblance is striking. Matting woven of a special kind of willow covers the floor; in front of the sofa stands a small tea table with a lamp upon it, the mate to the one there at home. Everything is the same, only more sumptuous. This change I think I can permit myself to make in the room. In the large room there is a piano, a very plain one, but it brings to mind the piano at the Jansens. It is open. On the music holder, the little Swedish melody lies open. The door to the hall is slightly ajar. She comes in through the door in the back—Johan has been instructed about that. Then her eyes simultaneously take in the private room and the piano; recollection is aroused in her soul, and at the same moment Johan opens the door. —The illusion is perfect. She enters the private room. She is pleased; of that I am convinced. As her glance falls on the table, she sees a book; at that very instant, Johan picks it up as if to put it aside as he casually remarks: The gentleman must have forgotten it when he was out here this morning. From this she learns for the first time that I had already been there the day before, and then she wants to see the book. It is a German translation of the well-known work by Apuleius: *Amor and Psyche*.[234] It is not a poetic work, but it should not be that either, for it is always an affront to a young girl to offer her a book of real poetry, as if she at such a moment were not herself sufficiently poetic to imbibe the poetry that is immediately concealed in the factually given and that has not first gone through someone else's thought. Usually one does not think of this, and yet it is so.[235] —She wants to read this book, and with that the goal is reached. —When she opens it to the place where it was last read, she will find a little sprig of myrtle, and she will also find that this means a little more than to be a bookmark.

My Cordelia,

What, fear? When we stay together, we are strong, stronger than the world, even stronger than the gods themselves. As you know, there once lived a race upon the earth who were human beings, to be sure, but who were self-sufficient and did not know the intensely fervent union of erotic love [*Elskov*]. Yet they were powerful, so powerful that they wanted to assault heaven. Jupiter feared them and divided them in such a way that one became two, a man and a woman.[236] If it sometimes happens that what was once united is again joined in love [*Kjærlighed*], then such a union is stronger than Jupiter; they are then not merely as strong as the single individual was, but even stronger, for the union of love [*Kjærlighed*] is an even higher union.

Your JOHANNES

September 24
[237]The night is still—the clock strikes a quarter to twelve—the hunter at the city gate blows his benediction out across the countryside, and it echoes from Blegdam; he enters the gate—he blows again, and it echoes from still farther away. —Everything sleeps in peace, but not erotic love [*Elskov*].[238] Arise, then, you mysterious powers of erotic love, concentrate yourselves in this breast! The night is silent—a solitary bird breaks this silence with its cry and the beat of its wings as it sweeps over the misty field toward the slope of the embankment; no doubt it, too, is hastening to a rendezvous—*accipio omen* [I accept the omen]![239] —How ominous all nature is! I take auguries from the flight of the birds, from their cries, from the frolicsome slap of the fish on the surface of the water, from their vanishing into the depths, from the faraway baying of a dog, from the rattling of a carriage in the distance, from footsteps echoing far off. At this hour of the night, I do not see ghosts; in the bosom of the lake, in the kiss of the dew, in the fog that spreads out over the earth and hides its fertile embrace, I do not see what has been but what is to come. Everything is a metaphor; I myself am a myth about myself, for is it not as a myth that I hasten to this tryst? Who I am is irrelevant; everything finite and temporal is forgotten; only the eternal remains, the power of erotic love, its longing, its bliss. How responsive is my soul, like a taut bow, how ready are my thoughts, like arrows in my quiver, not poisoned, and yet able to blend with blood. How vigorous, sound, and happy is my soul, as present as a god.

She was beautiful by nature. I thank you, marvelous nature! Like a mother, you have watched over her. Thank you for your solicitude. Unspoiled she was. I thank you, you human beings to whom she owed this. Her development—that was my work—soon I shall enjoy my reward. —How much I have gathered into this one moment that is now at hand! Damned if I should fail now!

As yet I do not see my carriage. —I hear the crack of the whip; it is my driver. —Drive on for dear life, even if the horses collapse, but not one second before we reach the place.

I
412

September 25

Why cannot such a night last longer? If Alectryon[240] could forget himself, why cannot the sun be sympathetic enough to do so? But now it is finished, and I never want to see her again. When a girl has given away everything, she is weak, she has lost everything, for in a man innocence is a negative element, but in woman it is the substance of her being. Now all resistance is impossible, and to love is beautiful only as long as resistance is present; as soon as it ceases, to love is weakness and habit. I do not want to be reminded of my relationship with her; she has lost her fragrance, and the times are past when a girl agonizing over her faithless lover is changed into a heliotrope.[241] I shall not bid her farewell; nothing is more revolting than the feminine tears and pleas that alter everything and yet are essentially meaningless.[242] I did love her, but from now on she can no longer occupy my soul. If I were a god, I would do for her what Neptune did for a nymph: transform her into a man.[243]

Yet it would really be worth knowing whether or not one could poetize oneself out of a girl in such a way as to make her so proud that she imagined it was she who was bored with the relationship. It could be a very interesting epilogue, which in and by itself could have psychological interest and besides that furnish one with many erotic observations.[244]

SUPPLEMENT

KEY TO REFERENCES

Marginal references alongside the text are to volume and page [I 100] in *Søren Kierkegaards Samlede Værker*, I-XIV, edited by A. B. Drachman, J. L. Heiberg, and H. O. Lange (1 ed., Copenhagen: Gyldendal, 1901-06). The same marginal references are used in Sören Kierkegaard, *Gesammelte Werke*, Abt. 1-36 (Düsseldorf: Diederichs Verlag, 1952-69).

References to Kierkegaard's works in English are to this edition, *Kierkegaard's Writings* [*KW*], I-XXV (Princeton: Princeton University Press, 1978-). Specific references to the *Writings* are given by English title and the standard Danish pagination referred to above [*Stages, KW* XI (*SV* VI 100)].

References to the *Papirer* [*Pap.* I A 100; note the differentiating letter A, B, or C, used only in references to the *Papirer*] are to *Søren Kierkegaards Papirer*, I-XI³, edited by P. A. Heiberg, V. Kuhr, and E. Torsting (1 ed., Copenhagen: Gyldendal, 1909-48), and 2 ed., photo-offset with two supplemental volumes, XII-XIII, edited by Niels Thulstrup (Copenhagen: Gyldendal, 1968-70), and with index, XIV-XVI (1975-78), edited by N. J. Cappelørn. References to the *Papirer* in English [*JP* II 1500] are to the volume and serial entry number in *Søren Kierkegaard's Journals and Papers*, I-VII, edited and translated by Howard V. Hong and Edna H. Hong, assisted by Gregor Malantschuk (Bloomington: Indiana University Press, 1967-78).

References to correspondence are to the serial numbers in *Breve og Aktstykker vedrørende Søren Kierkegaard*, I-II, edited by Niels Thulstrup (Copenhagen: Munksgaard, 1953-54), and to the corresponding serial numbers in *Kierkegaard: Letters and Documents*, translated by Henrik Rosenmeier, *Kierkegaard's Writings*, XXV [*Letters*, Letter 100, *KW* XXV].

References to books in Kierkegaard's own library [*ASKB* 100] are based on the serial numbering system of *Auktionsprotokol over Søren Kierkegaards Bogsamling* (Auction-catalog of

Søren Kierkegaard's Book-collection), edited by H. P. Rohde (Copenhagen: Royal Library, 1967).

In the Supplement, references to page and lines in the text are given as: 100:1-10.

In the notes, internal references to the present work are given as: p. 100.

Three periods indicate an omission by the editors; five periods indicate a hiatus or fragmentariness in the text.

Enten — Eller.

Et Livs-Fragment

udgivet

af

Victor Eremita.

––––––––––

Første Deel

indeholdende A.'s Papirer.

––––––––––

Er da Fornuften alene døbt,
ere Lidenskaberne Hedninger?

Young.

Kjøbenhavn 1843.

Faaes hos Universitetsboghandler C. A. Reitzel.

Trykt i Bianco Lunos Bogtrykkeri.

Either - Or.

A Fragment of Life

edited

by

Victor Eremita.

———————

Part One

containing A's Papers.

———————

Is reason then alone baptized,
are the passions pagans?

Young.

———————————————————

Copenhagen 1843.

Available at University Bookseller C. A. Reitzel's.

Printed by Bianco Luno Press.

SELECTED ENTRIES FROM
KIERKEGAARD'S JOURNALS AND PAPERS
PERTAINING TO
EITHER/OR, PART I

Copenhagen, June 1, 1835[1]

I
A 72
45

I
A 72
46

You know how inspiring I once found it to listen to you[2] and how enthusiastic I was about your description of your stay in Brazil, although not so much on account of the mass of detailed observations with which you have enriched yourself and your scholarly field as on account of the impression your first journey into that wondrous nature made upon you: your paradisical happiness and joy. Something like this is bound to find a sympathetic response in any person who has the least feeling and warmth, even though he seeks his satisfaction, his occupation, in an entirely different sphere, but especially so in a young person who as yet only dreams of his destiny. Our early youth is like a flower at dawn with a lovely dewdrop in its cup, harmoniously and pensively reflecting everything that surrounds it. But soon the sun rises over the horizon, and the dewdrop evaporates; with it vanish the fantasies of life, and now it becomes a question (to use a flower metaphor once more) whether or not man is able to produce—by his own efforts as does the *nereum*—a drop that may represent the fruit of his life. This requires, above all, that one be allowed to grow in the soil where one really belongs, but that is not always so easy to find. In this respect there exist fortunate creatures who have such a decided inclination in a particular direction that they faithfully follow the path once it is laid out for them without ever falling prey to the thought that perhaps they ought to have followed an entirely different path. There are others who let themselves be influenced so completely by their surroundings that it never becomes clear to them in what direction they are really striving. Just as the former group has its own implicit categorical imperative, so the latter recognizes an explicit categorical imperative. But how few there are in the former group, and to the latter I do not wish to belong. Those who get to experience the real meaning of Hegelian dialectics in their lives are greater in number. Incidentally, it is altogether natural for wine to ferment before it becomes clear; nevertheless this process is often disagreeable in its several stages, although regarded in its totality it is of course agreeable, provided it does in the end yield its relative results in the context of the usual doubt. This is of major significance for anybody who has come to terms with his destiny by means of it, not only because of the calm that follows in contrast to the preceding storm, but because one then *has life* in a quite different sense than before. For many, it is this Faustian element that makes itself more or less applicable to every intellectual development, which is why it has always seemed to me that we should concede cosmic significance to the *Faust* concept. Just as our ancestors worshipped a goddess of yearning, so I think that Faust represents doubt personified. He need be no more than that, and Goethe probably sins against the concept when he permits Faust to convert, as does Mérimée[3] when he permits Don Juan to convert. One cannot use the argument against me that Faust is taking a positive step at the instant he applies to the Devil, for right here, it seems to me, is one of the most significant elements in the Faust legend. He surrendered himself to the Devil for the express purpose of attaining enlightenment, and it follows that he was not in possession of it prior to this; and precisely because he surrendered himself to the Devil, his doubt increased (just as a sick person who falls into the hands of a medical quack usually gets sicker). For although Mephistopheles permitted him to look through his spectacles into man and into the secret hiding places of the earth, Faust must forever doubt him because of his inability to provide enlightenment about the most profound intellectual matters. In accordance with his own idea he could never turn to God because in the very instant he did so he would have to

I
A 72
47

admit to himself that here in truth lay enlightenment; but in that same instant he would, in fact, have denied his character as one who doubts.

But such a doubt can also manifest itself in other spheres. Even though a man may have come to terms with a few of these main issues, life offers other significant questions. Naturally every man desires to work according to his abilities in this world, but it follows from this that he wishes to develop his abilities in a particular direction, namely, in that which is best suited to him as an individual. But which is that? Here I am confronted with a big question mark. Here I stand like Hercules—not at a crossroads—no, but at a multitude of roads, and therefore it is all the harder to choose the right one. Perhaps it is my misfortune in life that I am interested in far too many things rather than definitely in any one thing. My interests are not all subordinated to one but are all coordinate.

I shall attempt to show how matters look to me.

1. *The natural sciences.* (In this category I include all those who seek to explain and interpret the runic script of nature, ranging from him who calculates the speed of the stars and, so to speak, arrests them in order to study them more closely, to him who describes the physiology of a particular animal, from him who surveys the surface of the earth from the mountain peaks to him who descends to the depths of the abyss, from him who follows the development of the human body through its countless nuances to him who examines intestinal worms.) First, when I consider this whole scholarly field, I realize that on this path as well as on every other (but indeed primarily here) I have of course seen examples of men who have made names for themselves in the annals of scholarship by means of enormous diligence in collecting. They master a great wealth of details and have discovered many new ones, but no more than that. They have merely provided the substratum for the thought and elaboration of others. These men are content with their details, and yet to me they are like the rich farmer in the gospel;[4] they have gathered great stores in their barn, yet science may declare to them: "Tomorrow I demand your life," inasmuch as it is that which determines the

I
A 72
48

significance of each particular finding for the whole. To the extent that there is a sort of unconscious life in such a man's knowledge, the sciences may be said to demand his life, but to the extent that there is not, his activity is comparable to that of the man who nourishes the earth by the decay of his dead body. The case differs of course with respect to other phenomena, with respect to those scholars in the natural sciences who have found or have sought to find by their speculation that Archimedean point that does not exist in the world and who from this point have considered the totality and seen the component parts in their proper light. As far as they are concerned, I cannot deny that they have had a very salutary effect on me. The tranquillity, the harmony, the joy one finds in them is rarely found elsewhere. We have three worthy representatives here in town: an Ørsted,[5] whose face has always seemed to me like a chord that nature has sounded in just the right way; a Schouw,[6] who provides a study for the painter who wanted to paint Adam naming the animals; and finally a Hornemann,[7] who, conversant with every plant, stands like a patriarch in nature. In this connection, I also remember with pleasure the impression you made upon me as the representative of a great nature which also ought to be represented in the National Assembly. I have been and am still inspired by the natural sciences; and yet I do not think that I shall make them my principal field of study. By virtue of reason and freedom, life has always interested me most, and it has always been my desire to clarify and solve the riddle of life. The forty years in the desert before I could reach the promised land of the sciences seem too costly to me, and the more so as I believe that nature may also be observed from another side, which does not require insight into the secrets of science. It matters not whether I contemplate the whole world in a single flower or listen to the many hints that nature offers about human life; whether I admire those daring designs on the firmament; or whether, upon hearing the sounds of nature in Ceylon,[8] for example, I am reminded of the sounds of the spiritual world; or whether the departure of the migratory birds[9] reminds me of the more profound yearnings of the human heart.

I
A 72
49

I
A 72
50

2. *Theology.* This seems to be what I have most clearly chosen for my own,[10] yet there are great difficulties here as well.
In Christianity itself there are contradictions so great that they
prevent an unobstructed view, to a considerable extent, at any
rate. As you know, I grew up in orthodoxy, so to speak. But
from the moment I began to think for myself, the gigantic colossus began to totter. I call it a gigantic colossus advisedly, for
taken as a whole it does have a good deal of consistency, and
in the course of many centuries past, the component parts have
become so rightly fused that it is difficult to come to terms
with them. I might now agree with some of its specific points,
but then these could only be considered like the seedlings one
often finds growing in rock fissures. On the other hand, I
might also see the inconsistencies in many specific points, but
I would still have to let the main basis stand *in dubito* for some
time. The instant *that* changed, the whole would of course assume an entirely different cast, and thus my attention is drawn
to another phenomenon: rationalism, which by and large cuts
a pretty poor figure. There is really nothing to object to in rationalism, as long as reason consistently pursues its own end
and—in rendering an explanation of the relation between God
and the world—again comes to see man in his most profound
and spiritual relation to God. In this respect, rationalism from
its own point of view considers Christianity that which for
many centuries has satisfied man's deepest need. But then it is
in fact no longer rationalism, for rationalism is given its real
coloring by Christianity. Hence it occupies a completely different sphere and does not constitute a system but a Noah's
Ark (to adopt an expression Professor Heiberg[11] used on another occasion), in which the clean and the unclean animals lie
down side by side. It makes roughly the same impression as
our Citizens' Volunteer Company of old would have made
alongside the Royal Potsdam Guards. Therefore it attempts
essentially to ally itself with Christianity, bases its arguments
upon Scripture, and in advance of every single point dispatches a legion of Biblical quotations that in no way penetrate
the argument. The rationalists behave like Cambyses,[12] who
in his campaign against Egypt dispatched the sacred chickens

and cats in advance of his army, but they are prepared, like the Roman Consul, to throw the sacred chickens overboard when they refuse to eat.[13] The fallacy is that when they are in agreement with Scripture, they use it as a basis, but otherwise not. Thus they adopt mutually exclusive points of view.

Nonnulla desunt [something missing].[14]

As to minor discomforts I will merely say that I am now studying for my theological qualifying examinations, an occupation that holds no interest for me at all and which accordingly does not proceed with the greatest efficiency. I have always preferred the free and thus perhaps somewhat indefinite course of study to that service offered at a pre-set table where one knows in advance the guests one will meet and the food one will be served every single day of the week. Nevertheless, it is a necessity, and one is scarcely permitted out onto the scholarly commons without having been branded. In my present state of mind, I also consider it useful for me to do so and furthermore, I also know that in this way I can make Father very happy (for he thinks that the true land of Canaan[15] lies beyond the theological qualifying examinations, but at the same time, as Moses once did, he climbs Mount Tabor and reports that I will never get in—but I do hope that his prophecy will not come true this time), so I suppose I must get to work. How fortunate you are to have found in Brazil a vast field of investigation where every step offers strange new objects and where the cries of the rest of the learned republic cannot disturb your peace. To me the learned theological world seems like the Strandvej[16] on a Sunday afternoon in the season when everybody goes to Bakken in Dyrehven: they tear past each other, yell and scream, laugh and make fun of each other, drive their horses to death, overturn, and are run over. Finally, when they reach Bakken covered with dust and out of breath—well, they look at each other—and go home.

As far as your returning is concerned, it would be childish of me to hasten it, as childish as when the mother of Achilles[17] attempted to hide him in order that he might avoid a speedy honorable death. —Take care of yourself!—*Pap*. I A 72 June 1, 1835; *Letters*, Letter 3, *KW* XXV.

The proximity of the tragic to the comic (an observation particularly attributable to Holberg's use of comedy—for example, his *Jeppe paa Bjerget, Erasmus Montanus, den Stundesløse*, etc.) seems to account also for the fact that a person *can laugh until he begins to cry*.

January 19, 1835

On the other hand, the comic lies so close to the tragic that, for example, in Goethe's *Egmont*, act 5, scene 1, we are inclined to smile at the Hollanders.—*JP* IV 4823 (*Pap*. I A 34) *n.d.*, 1835

I would have been very happy if Goethe had never continued *Faust*; I would then have called it a miracle; but here human frailty has overcome him. It takes a certain strength to see the hero of a piece get the worst of it in his struggle, in this case despairing over his doubt; but it is precisely this which gives Faust greatness, that is, it is his reformation which draws him down into the common everyday life. His death is the ultimate reconciliation in the work, and we could very well sit and weep over his grave but never think of lifting the curtain which at death made him invisible to our eyes.—*JP* II 1178 (*Pap*. I A 104) November 1, 1835

It is interesting that Faust (whom I perhaps more properly place in the third stage as the more mediate) embodies both Don Juan and the Wandering Jew (despair).—

It must not be forgotten, either, that Don Juan must be interpreted lyrically (therefore with music), the Wandering Jew epically, and Faust dramatically.—*JP* I 1179 (*Pap*. I C 58) December, 1835

When I notice that my head is beginning to act up. —The poet should have what the Northmen expected in Valhalla—a pig from which a piece can always be cut and which always restores itself.

Shoot a bullet in the head: three, two, one, now the tale is done; eight, nine, ten, now another can begin.—*JP* V 5140 (*Pap.* I A 156) *n.d.*, 1836

I have just now come from a gathering where I was the life of the party; witticisms flowed out of my mouth; everybody laughed, admired me—but I left, yes, the dash ought to be as long as the radii of the earth's orbit_____

_____

_____and wanted to shoot myself.—*JP* V 5141 (*Pap.* I A 161) *n.d.*, 1836

Blast it all, I can abstract from everything but *not from myself*; I cannot even forget myself when I sleep.—*JP* V 5142 (*Pap.* I A 162) *n.d.*, 1836

A strange apprehensiveness—every time I woke up in the morning after having drunk too much, [what it was about] eventually came true.—*JP* V 5146 (*Pap.* I A 179) *n.d.*, 1836

Someone who went insane because he was constantly aware that the earth was going around.—*JP* V 5147 (*Pap.* I A 182) *n.d.*, 1836

Does not Goethe's treatment of Faust really lack the enthusiasm for knowledge that nevertheless must be regarded as characteristic of Faust? —Something I have expressed on another occasion is no doubt true—that Faust embodies Don Juan; yet his love life and his sensuality can never be like Don Juan's. With Faust the latter has already become indirect, something into which he plunges himself, driven by despair.—*JP* II 1180 (*Pap.* I A 227) August 25, 1836

What does it mean and to what extent is it true that every age has its Faust etc.? —No, in the development of the world there is only *one* Faust, only *one* Don Juan, but for the single individual just as for the individual nation in the development of the world there naturally is one for each. Precisely for that reason Faust, for example, can in a certain sense reform, in which case this is the new period's interpretation—which, please note, is not a conception of Faust but is the idea of this age.—*JP* I 1181 (*Pap.* I A 292) *n.d.*, 1836

At the moment the greatest fear is of the total bankruptcy toward which all Europe seems to be moving and men forget the far greater danger, a seemingly unavoidable bankruptcy in an intellectual-spiritual sense that waits at the door, a confusion of language[18] far more dangerous than that (typical) Babylonian confusion, than the confusion of dialects and national languages following that Babylonian attempt of the Middle Ages—that is, a confusion in the languages themselves, a mutiny, the most dangerous of all, of the words themselves, which, wrenched out of man's control, would despair, as it were, and crash in upon one another, and out of this chaos a person would snatch, as from a grab-bag, the handiest word to express his presumed thoughts.* In vain do individual great men seek to mint new concepts and to set them in circulation—it is pointless. They are used for only a moment, and not by many either, and they merely contribute to making the confusion even worse, for one idea seems to have become the fixed idea of the age: to surpass one's superior. If the past may be charged with a certain indolent self-satisfaction in rejoicing over what it had, it would indeed be a shame to make the same charge against the present age (the minuet of the past and the galop of the present). Under a curious delusion, the one cries out incessantly that he has surpassed the other, just as the Copenhageners, with philosophic visage, go out to Dyrehaugen[19] "in order to see and observe," without remembering that they themselves become objects for the others, who have also gone out simply to see and observe. Thus there is the continuous leap-frogging[20] of one over the other—"on the basis of the immanent negativity of the concept," as I heard a Hegelian say

I
A 328
138

I
A 328
139

---

* One would speak according to the association of ideas (the words' *Selbstsucht* [self-seeking]).

recently, when he pressed my hand and made a run preliminary to jumping. —When I see someone energetically walking
along the street, I am certain that in his joy he will shout to me,
"I have gone further than,"—but unfortunately I did not hear
who had been surpassed (this actually happened); I will leave a
blank for the name, so everyone can fill in an appropriate
name.* If older critics have been charged with always seeking
in their retrogression an older writer whom they could use as
a model in order to censure later writers, it would be wrong to
charge contemporaries with this, for now when the critic sets
about to write there is hardly a writer left to provide the ideal,
and instead of this the publisher who is supposed to promote
the critic's work sees in amazement a counter-criticism of the
criticism not yet written.** Most systems and viewpoints also
date from yesterday, and the conclusion is arrived at as easily
as falling in love is accomplished in a novel where it says: To
see her and to love her were synonymous†—and it is through
curious circumstances that philosophy has acquired such a
long historical tail from Descartes to Hegel, a tail, however,
which is very meager in comparison with that once used, beginning with the creation of the world, and perhaps is more
comparable to the tail that man has, according to the natural
scientists. But when one sees how necessary it has become in a
later age to begin every philosophical work with the sentence:
"There once was a man named Descartes,"²¹ one is tempted to
compare it with the monk's well-known practice.²² But now
if only a few gifted men can more or less save themselves, it
seems all the more dangerous for those who must be dependent on others for their living. They must clutch at the drifting
terminology rushing by them, with the result that their
expression becomes so mixed and motley (a kind of *Blumenlese*
[anthology]) that, just as in French a foreigner may say something with a double meaning, they often say the same thing

I
A 328
140

---

* Just as some people, with an instinctive vehemence, rub writing paper to
flatten it, so too there are those who, having heard a name, have promptly
gone further.

** [See *Pap.* I A 329.]

† [See *Pap.* I A 330.]

throughout a whole book, but with different expressions from different systems. As a result of this, a phenomenon* has arisen that is quite similar to the famous dispute between a Catholic and a Protestant who convinced each other, inasmuch as men can very easily convince one another because of the vague and indefinite meanings of the words. But in this wild hunt for ideas, it is still very interesting to observe the felicitous moment when one of these new systems achieves supremacy.** Now everything is set in motion, and principally this also involves making the system popular—*per systema influxus physici*,[23] it lays hold of all men. How Kant was treated in his time is well known, and therefore I need only mention the infinite mass of lexicons, summaries, popular presentations, and explanations for everyman, etc. And how did Hegel fare later, Hegel, the one who of all modern philosophers, because of his rigorous form, would most likely command silence? Has not the logical trinity been advanced in the most ludicrous way? And therefore it did not astound me that my shoemaker had found that it could also be applied to the development of boots, since, as he observes, the dialectic, which is always the first stage in life, finds expression even here, however insignificant this may seem, in the squeaking, which surely has not escaped the attention of some more profound research psychologist. Unity, however, appears only later, in which respect *his* shoes far surpass all others, which usually disintegrate in the dialectic, a unity that reached the highest level in that pair of boots Carl XII wore on his famous ride, and since he as an orthodox shoemaker proceeded from the thesis that the immediate (feet without shoes—shoes without feet) is a pure abstraction, he took it [the dialectical] as the first stage in the development.[24] And now our modern politicians! By veritably taking up Hegel, they have given a striking example of the way one can serve two masters, in that their revolutionary striving is paired with a life-outlook that is a rem-

I
A 328
141

---

* Which, together with barenecked Danish bluffness, has made the polemic equally useless and nauseating.

** The result presumably will be that philosophy is put up for auction; at the moment there really seem to be no buyers.

edy for it, an excellent remedy for lifting part of the illusion that is necessary for encouraging their fantastical striving. And the actuality of the phenomenon will surely not be denied if one recalls that the words "immediate or spontaneous unity" occur just as necessarily in every scientific-scholarly treatise as a brunette or a blonde in every well-ordered romantic household. At the happy moment each one received a copy of sacred scripture in which there was, however, one book that was almost always very brief and sometimes almost invisible, and this was, I regret—the Acts of the Apostles. And how curious it is to note that the present age, whose social striving is trumpeted quite enough, is ashamed of the monks and nuns of the Middle Ages, when at the same time, to confine ourselves to our own native land, a society[25] has been formed here that seems to embrace almost the entire kingdom and in which a speaker began thus: Dear Brothers and Sisters. How remarkable to see *them* censure the Jesuitry of the Middle Ages, since precisely the liberal development, as does every one-sided enthusiasm, has led and must lead to that. And now Christianity—how has it been treated? I share entirely your disapproval of the way every Christian concept has become so volatilized, so completely dissolved in a mass of fog, that it is beyond all recognition. To the concepts of faith, incarnation, tradition, inspiration, which in the Christian sphere are to refer to a particular historical fact, the philosophers have chosen to give an entirely different, ordinary meaning, whereby faith[26] has become the immediate consciousness, which essentially is nothing other than the *vitale Fluidum* of mental life, its atmosphere, and tradition has become the content of a certain experience of the world, while inspiration has become nothing more than the result of God's breathing of the life-spirit into man, and incarnation no more than the presence of one or another idea in one or more individuals. —And I still have not mentioned the concept that has not only been volatilized, like the others, but even profaned: the concept of redemption, a concept that journalism in particular has taken up with a certain partiality and now uses for every one, from the greatest hero of freedom to the baker or butcher who redeems his quarter of the city by selling his wares a penny cheaper than the others. And now what is to be done about this? Undoubtedly it would be best if one could get the carillon-clock of time to be silent for a while, but since this presumably will not be achieved, we shall at least join with our banking people[27] and cry out to them: Savings, hefty and sweeping economies. Of course, to overbid one's predecessors can be of no help, and instead of following the novelist who, in his indignation that a full facial blush of a girl in a novel was not a sign of her being a decent girl, swore that every girl in his novels should blush far down her back—instead of following him in making such an attempt, we wish rather to bring to mind a happier phenomenon: the move from cursing to simple statements. —We would also wish that powerfully equipped men might emerge who would restore the lost power and meaning of words, just as Luther restored the concept of faith for his age. In everything there is the trace of the invention so characteristic of the period: the pressure for speed, even in the curious reflection the age has gotten into, with the result that the age, continually limiting its expression by reflection, actually never manages to say anything. This curious prolixity has also crowded out time-and-talk-saving pithy aphorisms and in their place has allowed the appearance of a certain oratorical jabbering that has taken over even our mealtimes. Only when this economizing, together with the restoration of the language's prodigal sons, has been introduced, can there be hope for better times. And here it occurs to me, to touch again upon your letter,[28] that there really is merit in Grundtvig's attempt to vivify the old Church-language and to advance his theory of the Living Word,[29] although I still cannot omit reminding you that just as we use the word "scribbling" to designate bungled writing, we also have a particularly good expression to characterize muddled speaking: "hot air"—and that this should really be more effective than writing. I do not maintain, despite Pastor Grundtvig's claim that the written word is powerless and dead, despite the court judgment[30] confirming his theories by a strange irony of fate: that his (written) words were dead and powerless—I still

I
A 328
143

do [not] believe I dare maintain that.—*JP* V 5181 *(Pap.* I A 328) *n.d.*, 1836-37

Addition to Pap. I A 328, *p. 139:*

**Because of this rush, the generation does not get much solid content; in spite of all its efforts it becomes a kind of *Schattenspiel an der Wand* [shadow play on the wall] and thereby it becomes a myth, yes, not even criticism, as Görres rightly observes (see *Die christliche Mystik*,[31] I, preface, p. vii, bottom—the passage should be quoted).[32] —Finally the theater becomes actuality and actuality comedy.—*JP* V 5182 *(Pap* I A 329) *n.d.*, 1836-37

Addition to Pap. I A 328, *p. 139:*

†Thus the talk that suicide is cowardice is for most men nothing but a leap over a stage—those shrewd and proud fellows who have never known that it requires courage! Only he who has had the courage to commit suicide can say that it was cowardly to have done it.[33]—*JP* V 5183 *(Pap.* I A 330) *n.d.*, 1836-37

I
A 331
144

Sorrow has come to me since I last wrote to you.[34] You will note this from the black sealing wax I am obliged to use—although as a rule I hate such external symbols—since there is nothing else to be had in this tragic family. Yes, my brother[35] is dead, but oddly enough I am not actually grieving over *him*; my sorrow is much more over my brother[36] who died several years ago. On the whole I have become aware that my sorrow is not momentary but increases with time, and I am sure that when I get old I will come to think rightly of the dead,[37] not—as it says in the rhetoric of consolation—to rejoice over the thought of meeting them yonder, but properly to feel that I have lost them. As far as my brother is concerned, I am sure it will take a long time for my grief to awaken. —At first there are so many ridiculous situations that I find it impossible not to laugh. For example, today my [brother's] brother-in-law,

I
A 331
145

the business agent—I have spoken of him before and will describe him in more detail some day—makes a visit to console his sister. In his frail, strangely grating voice, a superb parody of the gentlemanly he tries to express in his appearance, he bursts out: *Ja! Was ist der Mensch* [Well! What is man]? A clarinet, I answered; whereupon he immediately fell out of his role and tried to explain to me that the proper gentleman does not have a voice like a bear but a sonorous and melodious voice. All this time he stood before the mirror and smoothed his hair or plucked out the occasional hair that had become a little gray or reminded him a bit too much of its original color—red— and for this he had a special instrument, a pair of tweezers, on his dressing table—and I really believe that it can truthfully be said of the hairs of his head what the gospel says of all hair, that they are numbered.[38] The undertaker came then to inquire if they wished to have more than ham, salami, and Edam cheese to be served, and offered to make all the arrangements; my brother-in-law the business agent declined, explaining that it would be good for his broken-hearted sister to have something to think about so as to forget the emptiness and stillness prevailing around her now that her "sainted husband" was gone. (It is terrible how quickly people learn to say *that*, that is, the husband who as sainted no longer needs me, and it naturally follows that I do not need him either. I always notice how speedily people begin to say "my sainted husband, my sainted wife." Similarly, the quicker a woman is to scold, the less modesty she has. Consider how in the beginning children respond to the question "What does the child want?"—one of the questions put to every child in the concise epitome of knowledge inflicted upon them—by saying "Da-Da," and with such melancholy observations the child's first and yet most innocent period begins—and yet people deny hereditary sin!)[39]

Since it was, in fact, moving time, he advised her to move to another place and the sooner the better, in order "to avoid sorrowful memories." Yes, really: "to avoid sorrowful memories." That fits the pronouncement in the newspaper that "One has lost everything." —Not so, for the memories of one who has lost everything are precious, gratifying, for he can never, after all, live more happily than in the past.[40] One thing is sure, that on such an occasion what most people lose is memory. —I shall pass over the intervening days. Then came the day of the funeral. Great quantities of the already mentioned cheese, sausage, and ham are served; there is no lack of a variety of wines and cakes. —No one is seen eating anything—alas, *so* great is the grief! Here the rule of the book "about good manners"[41]—that no one is to begin to eat before his neighbor—is carried out literally. God help us, what if it were carried out literally at every meal! In the old days the natural association of ideas led one on such occasions to recall the true dictum that without beer [*Øl*] and food the hero is nothing, and therefore there was a funeral feast [*Gravøl*], but nowadays this has become a gravediggers' feast [*Graverøl*], for the funeral director, the pallbearers, the gravediggers, etc. are the ones who eat for all of us. On such occasions I always develop a fearful appetite and despite good manners I begin first—but no one follows my example anyway.—*JP* V 5184 (*Pap.* I A 331) *n.d.*, 1836-37

On the wedding day[42] came a letter from her brother; he was a captain in the Brazilian army. It was handed to her, and since we were eager to hear from him, I read it aloud:

"Dear Sister! What he was to you I will not speak of; you yourself know it too well. I will just say that although over here I see 100 die daily, I nevertheless truly feel that death is a universal fate, but also that I have had only one brother-in-law, just as you no doubt also feel that he was your first and last love.

Your Brother $\dfrac{+}{1}$

Postscript
Excuse the short reply; you no doubt have had to put up with enough tedious talk, and I have just received orders to battle and must take off. Take care of yourself and remember

that the short time was when the pole-star was at its apparent height, and thank God that it lasted as long as it did; as is the apparent height, so is the quotient of the true.[43]

Your————"

—*JP* V 5185 (*Pap*. I A 332) *n.d.*, 1836-37

December 2[44]

I will no longer converse with the world at all;[45] I will try to forget that I ever did. I read of a man who lay abed[46] for fifty years, never speaking to anyone; like Queen Gudrun[47] after she had quarreled with O————, I shall go to bed after quarreling with the world. Or I will run away to a place where no one knows, no one understands my language, or I theirs, where, like a Caspar Hauser[48] the Second, I can stand in the middle of a Nürnberg street without really knowing how it all happened. I
A 333
147

The trouble is that as soon as a person has thought up something, he becomes that himself. The other day I told you[49] about an idea for a Faust, but now I feel that *it was myself* I described; I barely read or think about an illness before I have it. I
A 333
148

Every time I want to say something, someone else says it at the same time. It is just as if I were a double-thinker and my other *I* continually anticipated me, or while I stand and talk everyone believes it is someone else, so that I may justifiably raise the question the bookseller Soldin[50] put to his wife: Rebecca, is it I who is speaking? —I will run away from the world, not to the monastery—I still have vigor—but in order to find myself (every other babbler says the same thing), in order to forget myself, but not over there where a babbling brook meanders through the grassy glen. —I do not know if this verse is by some poet, but I wish some sentimental poet or other would be compelled by inexorable irony to write it, but in such a way that he himself would always read something else. Or the echo—yes, Echo,[51] you grand-master of irony, you who in yourself parody the loftiest and the most profound on earth: the word, which created the world, while you give only the outline, not the fullness—yes, Echo, take revenge upon all the sentimental rubbish that hides in woods and fields, in churches and theaters, and that every once in a while breaks away from *there* and drowns out everything for me. I do not hear the trees in the forest tell old legends and the like— no, they whisper to *me* about all the stuff and nonsense they have witnessed too long, beseech *me* in God's name to chop them down and free them from the babbling of those nature worshippers. —Would that all those muddled heads sat on one neck; like Caligula,[52] I know what I would have to do. I see that you are beginning to fear that I will end on the scaffold. No, mark well, the muddle-head (I mean the one who embraces them all) would certainly like to have brought me there, but you forgot that such a wish does no actual harm in the world. Yes, Echo—you whom I once heard chastise an admirer of nature when he burst out: Listen to that infatuated nightingale singing its solitary flute-like notes in the light of the moon—and you answered: -oon-loon-lunatic[53] (revenge, yes, take revenge)—*you* are the man![54]

I
A 333
149

No, I will not leave the world—I will go into an insane asylum,[55] and I will see if the profundity of insanity will unravel the riddle of life for me. Fool, why didn't I do it long agò, why has it taken me so long to understand what it means when the Indians honor the insane, step aside for them. Yes, into an insane asylum—do you not believe that I will end up there?

—However, it is fortunate that language has a section of expressions for chitchat and nonsense. If it did not, I would go mad, for what would it prove except that everything said is nonsense. It is lucky that language is so equipped, for now one can still hope to hear rational discourse sometimes.

It is called a tragedy when the hero gives his whole life to an idea—folly! (Then I commend the Christians for calling the day the martyrs died their birthdays, because in this way they connected with them the festive notion men usually have about birthdays.) —No, a misunderstanding! On the contrary, I grieve when a child is born[56] and wish that at least it may not live to be confirmed! I weep when I see or read *Erasmus Montanus*;[57] he is right and succumbs to the *masses*.[58] Yes, that is the trouble. When every confirmed glutton is entitled to vote, when the majority decides the matter—is this not succumbing to the masses, to fatheads? —Yes, the giants, did they not also succumb to the masses? And yet—and this is the only comfort remaining!—and yet every once in a while they terrify the Hottentots trotting over them by drawing in their breath and giving vent to a flaming sigh—not to complain—no, all condolences declined—but to frighten.

I want—no, I don't want anything at all.[59] Amen!

And when one meets at twentieth-hand and more an idea that has sprung fresh and alive from an individual's head—how much truth remains? At most one can reply with the old saying: "But at least it does taste like fowl," said the old crone who had made a soup out of a branch on which a crow had sat.—*JP* V 5186 (*Pap.* I A 333) *n.d.*, 1836-37

I
A 333
150

This is the road we all must walk—over the Bridge of Sighs into eternity.—*JP* I 28 (*Pap.* I A 334) *n.d.*, 1836-37

It is these trifling annoyances[60] that so often spoil life. I can cheerfully struggle against a storm until I almost burst a blood vessel, but the wind blowing a speck of dust into my eye can irritate me so much that I stamp my foot.

These small annoyances—they are like flies—just when a person is about to carry out a great work, a tremendous task, crucially important to his own life and the life of many others—a gadfly lands on his nose.[61]—*JP* V 5187 (*Pap.* I A 335) *n.d.*, 1836-37

One thought succeeds another; just as it is thought and I want to write it down, there is a new one—hold it, seize it— madness—dementia!—*JP* V 5188 (*Pap.* I A 336) *n.d.*, 1836-37

If there is anything I hate it is these smatterers—often when I go to a party I deliberately sit down to talk with some old spinster who lives on telling news of the family, and I listen most earnestly to everything on which she can hold forth.—*JP* V 5189 (*Pap.* I A 338) *n.d.*, 1836-37

I prefer to talk with old women who chatter about their families, next with demented people—and lastly with very sensible people.[62]—*JP* V 5190 (*Pap.* I A 339) *n.d.,* 1836-37

Something about Hamann

I
A 340
151
It is most interesting right now in our time when the recognized achievement of thought holds that the important thing is to live for one's age, and that the abstract immortality which men previously rejoiced in was an illusion—it is most interesting right now to see that there nevertheless is something to living for a posterity[63] and being misunderstood by contemporaries. People move continually between these two extremes. Whereas a few stand isolated in the world, balancing with the agility of a Simeon Stylites,[64] or at most beating their wings like tame geese, admired, or more correctly, stared at by the gaping crowd, despised by the philistines, served by angels, there are, on the other hand, enormous numbers who are living totally in the present age, who, so to speak, are to the body politic much like the brass hammers of a clavichord that swing at the slightest touch and cannot possibly maintain a definite impression; they are like certain patients who always get a little attack of every epidemic, a class of people so numerous that they have brought a kind of spiritual ventriloquism into the whole society. One hears a confused sound and scarcely knows whether it is oneself speaking or someone else, and is easily tempted to say with Soldin: Rebecca, is it I who is speaking?[65] To live in the age and die in the age in *this* fashion is not particularly inspiring, and yet there is not much left for the majority of men who have, for better or for worse, pawned their reason for the motto: Conform to the age. Certainly *this* has not been the idea of the few great men who first expressed this view of life, but the tragedy is that whenever a rational man opens his mouth there immediately are millions ready posthaste—to misunderstand him. Well, God help them. If in military fashion he should hear the password again from the last generation (there is a password that God delivered in Adam's ear, that one generation is supposed to deliver to the next

I
A 340
152

and that shall be demanded of them on judgment day)—God help him, it must be frightful!

So much for that misunderstanding, and I also hope that it will be apparent that every man who in the proper sense is to fill out a period in history must always begin polemically, precisely because the subsequent stage is not purely and simply the result of the previous one. Was this not the case with Holberg, was it not the case with Goethe, was it not the case with Kant, and so on? And must it not be this way? Must it not be, as in a procession (the new that is to come), that the law court officials go first to clear the way? Here, again, so much depends upon how quickly the new follows on the heels of the polemic, and whether it is the truth that must be fought for day after day for years or is merely one insignificant modification or another.—*JP* II 1541 (*Pap.* I A 340) *n.d.*, 1836-37

How very unfortunate we human beings are, how few the things that give us enduring and solid pleasures. I had hoped by this time through my perseverance to have come into "possession of the maiden"—. O excellent Holberg! How delightful to see a phraseologist like Mr., as I informally call him, Leander parody himself with a single phrase—his solid pleasures—his—"possession of the maiden"![66]—*JP* V 5191 (*Pap.* I A 341) *n.d.*, 1836-37

What is friendship without intellectual interaction, a refuge for weak souls who are not able to breathe in the atmosphere of intelligence but only in the atmosphere of animal exhalations? How wretchedly it drags itself along in spite of all the external means with which one tries to patch it up (by drinking *dus*[67] etc.). What a caricature it is, except for those who straightforwardly admit that friendship is nothing else than mutual insurance.[68] How disgusting to hear those insipid stereotyped screeds about mutual understanding, about friendship. Certainly understanding is part of friendship, but not the kind that makes the one continually aware of what the other is going to say. No, it is essential to friendship that the one never knows what the other is going to say; when that point is reached, friendship is past. But that kind of understanding

II
A 22
24

leads such persons to believe that they understand everyone
else, too. Out of this comes the self-satisfaction with which
they say that they expected one to answer precisely as he did
answer, etc., which frequently is not true and has its base in
their presuming that everyone's conversation is just like their
own, insipid, trivial, and pointless, and they have no intimation of the whole host of individualizing traits etc. that make
every observation interesting. It is always well to avoid such
people, since in spite of all their understanding, they always
misunderstand. How distressing for someone who is having
doubts to hear from such a "one of a dozen" that "he has experienced the same thing." If the conversation is about a great
man, he promptly has a little man whom he thinks to be just
as great; naturally all phenomena are fetched out of his duo-
decimo horizons* (a good example: *Raketten med Stjerner* com-
plained that Sibbern was now beginning to write and found
this doubly regrettable because it was at the very same time
that Messrs. Blok Tøxen and Lange laid down their pens).[69] If
the conversation is about a great thinker, he promptly has an
opinion because he perhaps has heard the man's name at some
time. As the years pass, as far as their conversation is concerned, people generally tend to become more and more like
hand-organs, mobile automatons (including their expressions
and movements), something like ship captains, who, even
with the opportunity to walk the longest and most beautiful
avenue, nevertheless prefer their standard skipper walk.[70]—*JP*
II 1279 (*Pap.* II A 22) *n.d.*, 1837

In margin of Pap. II A 22:

*The basis is that they, too, naturally are moved by the train
of events and by the mightier spirits, and they reproduce them
by way of parody, just as tame geese and ducks beat their
wings, cry out, and quiver for a moment when a wild goose
or duck flies over them.—*JP* II 1280 (*Pap.* II A 23) *n.d.*, 1837

All true love is grounded in this, that one loves another in a
third[71]—all the way from the lowest stage, for example, where
they love one another in a third, to the Christian teaching that

the brothers should love one another in Christ.—*JP* III 2380
(*Pap.* II A 24) *n.d.*, 1837

In margin of Pap. II A 24:

If there were no higher individuality in whom the single individual rests and through whom spiritual reciprocity is realized, the same would happen with individuality in this love as
happened at one time with Catholics and Protestants who dis-
puted and persuaded one another: namely, the one would become the other, just as the Catholic became Protestant and the
Protestant Catholic.—*JP* III 2381 (*Pap.* II A 25) *n.d.*, 1837

A thesis: great geniuses are essentially unable to read a book.
While they are reading, their own development will always be
greater than their understanding of the author.—*JP* II 1288
(*Pap.* II A 26) *n.d.*, 1837

That the Faust who is now supposed to represent the age is
essentially different from the earlier Faust and from the Faust
of every other age is so evident that one needs only to be reminded of it. But how? If we look at the age, we find a host of
men who in the elemental Greek sense are really πραϰτιϰοί [fit
for doing], whom Aristotle[72] has already assigned to the lowest level of development—preoccupied by their chores of cul-
tivating their land and, as it is called, bringing up their children—that is, as "confirmed consumers" they go on living
carefree lives and even in death do something practical for the
world—by decaying and enriching the earth. In them something Faustian will hardly develop. On the other hand, there is
a great number of men who have either turned their heads to
investigate a vanished past or immerse themselves in investi-
gating nature. Because of their busyness, the Faustian does not
appear in them either, inasmuch as the appearance of the Faustian requires first of all that this energetic life be paralyzed in
some way or other. —But now there finally appears the type
of men we need to observe, namely, those who seek by intuition to comprehend the multiplicity of nature, of life, and of
history in a totality-view. But here, too, there is something

II
A 29
27

unfortunate, for much is already unrolled before their vision and more appears every day; but under all this knowledge of many things dozes the feeling of how infinitely small this knowledge is, and it is this feeling that paralyzes their activity, and now the Faustian appears as despair over not being able to comprehend the whole development in an all-embracing to- tality-view in which every single nuance is also recognized for its full value, that is, its absolute worth. —But wherein lies the difference? The original Faust's despair was more practical. He had studied, but his studies had not yielded him any return (whereas the other [Faust] at least gained something from what he had seen, even though infinitely little compared with what he wished; Faust's profit from knowledge was a nothing, because in the last resort it was not this question he wanted an- swered, but rather the question: *what he himself* should do). On the basis of the far more elementary state of the sciences at that time, by means of a survey he could more easily have thought himself convinced of their emptiness, and on account of the special character of the age—enthusiastic action in order to re- alize its ideal—the question had to be moved over into this area; he had to reconcile life with [that] knowledge. For our time, this question must recede much further since, naturally, as the world becomes older, the intuitive tendency must take precedence, and the question consequently becomes: how can true intuition enter in despite man's limited position. But that which drives men on to this demand for a perfect and true in- tuition is a despair over the relativity of everything. While he himself uses a rather high criterion (his conviction about this corroborated by having to listen daily to complaints over how fantastical it is), by associating with people who use all possi- ble infinite gradations of a criterion all the way from decimals to the diameter of the heavenly orbit, all the way from those who are inspired by the greatest world-historical personages to those for whom the pastor and the deacon are hitherto un- surpassed and unrivalled ideals, all the way from those who have intensely felt and have intensely experienced all the tem- pestuous emotions of the heart to those who, because once upon a time they were impressed by a juggler, now let us know with a self-assured smile that "they have outgrown

II
A 29
28

those childish tricks" etc.—by associating with such people he gets the idea that he himself in turn is using a much too relative criterion and begins to fear that he is sinking down and losing himself in a bourgeois, philistine mentality. He hears of a discovery that opens vistas over a vast unknown world, that will probably force him to graduate his criterion in quite another way and make vanishing magnitudes of his heroes and his sufferings. He discerns how the most gifted of his contemporaries squeeze out a little yield (speculative abstracting or historical sketching), and he has a secret fear that this possibly may not be what they assume it to be—the most important—but merely what *they* succeed in comprehending and fathoming. He longs for a view that abolishes all relativities and shows him the absolute worth of even the most insignificant thing, because for the true (i.e., divine) view everything has the same magnitude. That such a Faust does not lack Wagners is certainly obvious. Herein now lies the despair. The way all of life alters for him now also shows him to be quite different from the first Faust, for while that one with his activist tendency sank into sensuality, this one will back out of everything, forget, if possible, that he ever knew anything, and watch the cows—or perhaps, out of curiosity, transport himself into another world.—*JP* II 1182 (*Pap*. II A 29) March 19, 1837

II
A 29
29

Christianity has a certain settling power by affirming the highest degree of relativity, by presenting an idea, an ideal, that is so great that all others disappear alongside it (the romantic and humorous aspect of Christianity). Therefore, it is always far more enjoyable to converse with a Christian, because he has a criterion that is definite; he has a fullness in comparison with which the infinite differences in capacities, occupations, etc. are nothing. From this comes the stance which, if it does not degenerate into arrogance, is very worthy of respect.—*JP* I 422 (*Pap*. II A 30) *n.d.*, 1837

A Preface

Most people usually go about reading a book with a notion of how they themselves would have written it, how someone else has written or would have written, just as a similar prejudice occurs when they are to see someone for the first time, and as a result very few people really know how the other person looks. Here begins the first possibility of not being able to read a book, which thereupon goes through innumerable nuances until on the highest level—misinterpretation—the two most opposite kinds of readers meet, the most stupid and the most brilliant, who share in common the inability to read a book—the first because of vacuity and the second because of a wealth of ideas. Therefore I have given this work a very ordinary title (it should be called "Letters") in order to do my part in preventing what is frequently* a loss for the author and sometimes for the readers—misinterpretation.

In margin: *I say *frequently*, for it sometimes happens that through misinterpretation one finds good things in a wretched book.—*JP* I 131 (*Pap.* II A 46) *n.d.*, 1837

Insofar as Hegel was fructified by Christianity, he sought to eliminate the humorous element that is in Christianity (something about this is found elsewhere in my papers [*Pap.* I A 207]), and consequently reconciled himself completely with the world, with quietism as a result. The same thing happened with Goethe in his *Faust*, and it is curious that the second part came so late. He could easily produce the first part, but the problem was how to calm the storm once it was aroused. The second part, therefore, has a far more subjective character (indeed, on the whole Goethe has sufficiently expressed how his experience occasioned one or another work of art); it seems as if he makes this confession of faith in order to calm himself down.—*JP* II 1568 (*Pap.* II A 48) *n.d.*, 1837

Hegel's subsequent position swallows up the previous one, not as one stage of life swallows another, with each still retaining its validity, but as a higher title or rank swallows up a lower title.—*JP* II 1569 (*Pap.* II A 49) *n.d.*, 1837

In connection with a little essay by Johannes M. . . . . . . (Martensen) on Lenau's *Faust*,[73] in which it is told that the piece ends with Faust's killing himself and Mephistopheles' giving an epilog, I began to ponder to what extent, after all, it is appropriate to let a work of this kind end in such a way. And here I believe that Goethe was right in ending Part One with Mephistopheles' "Heinrich! Heinrich!" A suicide would make too much of a character out of the idea; it should be the counterweight of the whole world that crushes him, as with D. Juan. —Or end in despair (the Wandering Jew). Despair is romantic—not punishment, as it was in the case of Prometheus.—*JP* II 1183 (*Pap*. II A 50) *n.d.*, 1837

Faust may be paralleled with Socrates. Just as the latter expresses the individual's emancipation from the state, Faust expresses the individual after the abrogation of the Church, severed from its guidance and abandoned to himself; this is an indication of his relationship to the Reformation and is a parody of the Reformation insofar as it one-sidedly emphasizes the negative aspect.—*JP* II 1968 (*Pap*. II A 53) *n.d.*, 1837

It is touching to go past the most ordinary of bookstores and see *Den Ærke Troldkarl Faust*[74] etc., see the most profound [books] offered for sale to the most ordinary people.—*JP* V 5216 (*Pap*. II A 54) *n.d.*, 1837

Don Juan has never become as popular as Faust—why?
—*JP* I 769 (*Pap*. II A 55) *n.d.*, 1837

Faust cannot commit suicide. As the idea hovering over all its actual forms, he must complete himself in a new idea (the Wandering Jew).—*JP* II 1184 (*Pap*. II A 56) *n.d.*, 1837

Reflection can wind itself around a person in the most curious way. I can imagine someone's wanting to make a theatrical presentation of the fallaciousness of the age; but when he himself sits among the spectators he sees that no one, after all, takes it to heart except to detect the fallacy in his neighbor; he makes one more attempt and stages this very scene in the theater, and people laugh at it saying: Isn't it terrible how most people can see the faults of others and not their own, etc. etc.

In margin: With them it is just as with King David, who did not understand the prophet's parable before he said: You are the man, O King![75]—*JP* III 3698 (*Pap.* II A 57) *n.d.*, 1837

Philosophy is life's dry-nurse, who can take care of us—but not suckle us.—*JP* III 3252 (*Pap.* II A 59) *n.d.*, 1837

The *bourgeois* always skip over one part of life, and from this comes their parodying relationship to those who outrank them. [. . . . .][76] To them morality is supreme, far more important than intelligence, but they have never felt enthusiasm for the great, for the talented, even in its extraordinary form. Their *morality* is a brief summary of the various police posters; the most important thing for them is to be a useful member of the state and to make after-dinner talk at a club—they have never felt homesickness for an unknown, remote something or for the profundity that is rooted in being nothing at all, in walking through Nørreport with four pennies in one's pocket and a slender cane in one's hand; they have no idea of the view of life (which a gnostic sect[77] made its own): learn to know the world through sin—and yet they too say one must sow one's wild oats (*"Wer niemals hat ein Rausch gehabt, er ist kein braver Mann* [He who has never been drunk is not a real man]),"[78] they have never caught a glimpse of the idea that lies underneath when we are pushed through the hidden, mysterious door, open in all its terror only to presentiment, into this dark realm of sighs—when we see the crushed sacrifices of seduction and deception and the coldness of the tempter.—*JP* I 219 (*Pap.* II A 127) July 14, 1837

II
A 127
74

The Don Juanian life is really musical,[79] and thus it is very proper for Lenau in his *Faust*, at the moment Faust begins to portray Don Juan, to have Mephistopheles *start the music*.[80] — Martensen has not seen the deeper significance of the circumstance.[81]—*JP* I 5226 (*Pap.* II A 598) *n.d.*, 1837

The idea, the philosophy of life, of knowing all evil, which a sect of gnosticism[82] embraced, is profound; only one must have a predisposition for it, which is suggested in legends by the ability of the unbaptized to see things that others do not see.—*JP* V 5227 (*Pap.* II A 599) *n.d.*, 1837

Why is there so much talk about—or, more correctly, what after all is the source of the idea of talking about the devil's **great-grandmother**.—*JP* V 5229 (*Pap.* II A 601) *n.d.*, 1837

Someone dies just as he has proved that there is eternal damnation, trapped in his own theory. Remarkable transition from theory to practice.—*JP* V 5230 (*Pap.* II A 602) *n.d.*, 1837

Yes, I believe I would surrender to Satan so that he could show me every abomination, every sin, in its most dreadful form—it is this penchant, this taste, for the secret of sin.[83]—*JP* V 5231 (*Pap.* II A 603) *n.d.*, 1837

Although I[84] rail against the others for studying compendiums instead of the sources, I myself live a compendium—although I am able to win every argument, I am saddled with a ghost from my own imagination that I cannot argue away.— *JP* V 5232 (*Pap.* II A 607) *n.d.*, 1837

Now and then I see myself hemmed in by an appalling, phrase-laden figure—I would call it a compendium of a human being—a brief resume of emotions and ideas—a *belieblich* [agreeable] long, thin man whom nature, however, has arrested, so to speak, in every development—he should have long arms, but the upper arm is extremely long and the lower arm very short, the same with his fingers, face, etc.; every communication begins with a very promising introductory phrase so that one hopefully applies a prodigious criterion, but then it comes to nothing.—*JP* V 5233 (*Pap.* II A 609) *n.d.*, 1837

The Hottentots always cut off the head of a snake they have killed, fearing that someone may accidentally step on it and be bitten, since they believe that even after its death the snake can do injury with its poison.—*JP* V 5235 (*Pap.* II A 613) *n.d.*, 1837

Situation
    A person wants to write a novel in which one of the characters goes insane; during the process of composition he himself gradually goes insane and ends it in the first person.—*JP* V 5249 (*Pap.* II A 634) *n.d.*, 1837

    Every flower of my heart turns into a frost flower.—*JP* V 5253 (*Pap.* II A 641) *n.d.*, 1837

    My[85] ideas suffer the same fate as parents who do indeed bear healthy children but forget to have them baptized in time; along come the subterranean spirits and put a changeling in their place (native gifts are not lacking, but solicitous care and nurture).—*JP* V 5254 (*Pap.* II A 642) *n.d.*, 1837

    It seems as if I[86] were the hero in a story, a *wild* shoot who should be displayed in a novel.—*JP* V 5255 (*Pap.* II A 644) *n.d.*, 1837

    It seems as if I[87] were a galley slave chained together with death; every time life stirs, the chain rattles and death makes everything decay—*and that takes place every moment.*—*JP* V 5256 (*Pap.* II A 647) *n.d.*, 1837

    Everything human lies, hope as well as despair—I read this as a quotation in an old devotional book.—*JP* V 5257 (*Pap.* II A 648) *n.d.*, 1837

    The fate of my ideas and their fulfillment is much like fishing during certain months of the year—the fish nibble—there are plenty of nibbles, but no fish.—*JP* V 5259 (*Pap.* II A 653) *n.d.*, 1837

    I am a two-faced Janus: with one face I laugh, with the other I cry.[88]—*JP* V 5260 (*Pap.* II A 662) *n.d.*, 1837

Unfortunately my real spirit frequently is present in me only κατά κρύψιν [in the form of concealment].—*JP* V 5261 (*Pap*. II A 164) September 20, 1837

I would like to write a novella that begins with an unqualified still life, until through the medium of the Don Giovanni music a new light is suddenly ushered in, and then the whole thing is drawn into an utterly fantastic world.—*JP* V 5314 (*Pap*. II A 732) *n.d.*, 1838

Most of what is written is nothing more than *asserta* [assertions] on plain paper—I, however, write on a stamped paper.—*JP* V 5379 (*Pap*. II A 413) *n.d.*, 1839

When I[89] open my eyes these days, they lift a great load of weights (visualize a mass of crazy ideas), which promptly settle down again; so too it is with my hope, for the door through which it is granted me at times to look into brighter regions (my daily environment and atmosphere are like the view and climate in a Greenland cave, and for that reason I receive very few visits in this my winter residence, since only missionaries have the courage to creep on all fours into such a cave—hope, the missionary of heaven—rarely sends out a gleam) is not a door that stays open once it is opened, nor is it a door that shuts again slowly so that one still might have the hope of stealthily peeking through it a few times before it shuts; no, it shuts promptly again, and the dreadful thing about it is that one almost forgets what one saw.—*JP* V 5382 (*Pap*. II A 416) May 11, 1839

The trouble with me is that I[90] immediately use up in one single desperate step the tiny bit of happiness and reassurance I slowly distill in the dyspeptic process of my toilsome intellectual life.—*JP* V 5400 (*Pap*. II A 509) July 22, 1839

The reason I[91] find so little joy in life is that when a thought of something awakens in my soul it awakens with such energy, larger than life, that I actually overstrain myself with it, and for me the ideal anticipation is so far from explaining life that instead I am debilitated when I depart from it to find something equivalent to the idea. I am too disturbed and, so to speak, nerve-shattered to rest in it.—*JP* V 5402 (*Pap.* II A 512) July 25, 1839

There are animals that cannot eat as long as anyone is watching them, animals that get their nourishment in the most amazing and cunning ways—so it is with my moods: what I[92] seem to despise, I absorb secretly and unnoticed.—*JP* I 802 (*Pap.* III A 219) *n.d.*, 1840

I[93] live constantly on the border between felicitous Arabia and desert Arabia.—*JP* V 5503 (*Pap.* III A 142) *n.d.*, 1841

The older one gets, the more one feels at certain times like shouting: Allah is great, somewhat as the Arabs do on almost every occasion in life. Today a paper was missing; it was extremely important for me to know whether or not it still existed; if it did, it could destroy the entire point of a very elaborate piece of work—looking for some other things, I opened a secret drawer, and there it was—and I shouted: Allah is great.[94]—*JP* V 5554 (*Pap.* III A 220) *n.d.*, 1840-42(?)

My Umbrella, My Friend

It never forsakes me; it did that only once. It was during a terrible storm; I stood all alone on Kongens Nytorv, forsaken by everybody, and then my umbrella turned inside out. I was at a loss as to whether or not I should abandon it because of its faithlessness and become a misanthrope. I have acquired such an affection for it that I always carry it, rain or shine; indeed, to show it that I do not love it merely for its usefulness, I sometimes walk up and down in my room and pretend I am outside, lean on it, open it up, rest my chin on the handle, bring it up to my lips, etc.—*JP* V 5555 (*Pap.* III A 221) *n.d.*, 1840-42(?)

In the old days, as is well known, they wrote one word after the other without a break, one sentence after another without any separation. One shudders to think of reading such writing! Now we have gone to the opposite extreme. We write nothing but punctuation marks, no words, no meaning, but simply exclamation and question marks.—*JP* III 2319 (*Pap.* III A 222) *n.d.*, 1840-42(?)

If I did not know that I am a genuine Dane, I could almost be tempted to explain the contradictions moving within me by supposing that I am an Irishman. For the Irish do not have the heart to immerse their children totally when they have them baptized; they want to keep a little paganism in reserve. Generally the child is totally immersed under water, but they leave the right arm free, so that he will be able to wield a sword with it, embrace the girls.—*JP* V 5556 (*Pap.* III A 223) *n.d.*, 1840-42(?)

My head is as empty and dead as a theater when the play is over.—*JP* V 5559 (*Pap.* III A 224) *n.d.*, 1840-42(?)

. . . . . after one has lived a dozen years in this appalling still life, this wretched, meager life has yielded just about as much cream as one can swallow in one single instant without overeating. I cannot march to that tempo.—*JP* V 5558 (*Pap.* III A 225) *n.d.*, 1840-42(?)

What is sin: the pact of an evil conscience with the devil—and what has a memory like that of an evil conscience?—*JP* IV 4005 (*Pap.* III A 226) *n.d.*, 1840-42(?)

From sketch:

I am well aware that most people do not, like guarantors and sureties, dare to admit what they think; therefore they put their refractoriness in the mouth of a fictitious character and then think themselves blameless—I say it loudly and clearly before the whole parish, that is, to you— —*Pap.* III B 179:5 *n.d.*, 1841-42

From sketch:

. . . . . it was the manorial right I preferred to have—*jus primae noctis.*[95]—*Pap.* III B 179:6 *n.d.*, 1841-42

From sketch:

You ask me what I do in the world—answer: I amuse myself—what do you think of that—I know very well that my occupation is the opposite of most other people's, for they are bored.—*Pap.* III B 179:7 *n.d.*, 1841-42

From sketch:

You say I am in love, and I have to agree with you, but not with what you go on to say, that I should get married. My love is a world-historical passion that demands sacrifices.— *Pap.* III B 179:11 *n.d.*, 1841-42

From sketch:

All I am qualified to do is to converse with crazy people and to offer them my hand.—*Pap.* III B 179:21 *n.d.*, 1841-42

From sketch:

The other evening I went to the theater and saw *Don Giovanni.* I seldom talk with anyone on such an occasion; accidentally I met a man who for thirty years has seen *D. G.* every time it was performed. In this way, the one generation shakes the hand of the next generation in admiring this immortal music.—*Pap.* III B 180:1 *n.d.*, 1841-42

From sketch:

Do you recollect the first time you stole away to a rendezvous, how your heart was so full, so moved by vague ideas of what was in store for you—do you recollect how you longed for the sun to go down—do you recollect the first time you knocked on the little wicket gate——do you recollect the first time you hurried to hear *D. G.*, do you recollect when the chandelier was raised and the piece had not yet begun, do you recollect the first time the mysterious three taps behind the curtains signaled to the conductor, do you recollect the first time he rapped three times with his baton.—*Pap.* III B 180:2 *n.d.*, 1841-42

From sketch:

There are beasts of prey that cannot assimilate their food if someone is watching.—*Pap.* III B 180:3 *n.d.*, 1841-42

From sketch:

For me the most intolerable relationship in life is any relationship involving love or a personal relationship; it has an incommensurability that one can never terminate. Just as naturalists inject liquid wax into the veins of animals, which are thereby arrested and the vein shows up more clearly; just so I inject money into every life situation of that nature, thereby killing it. One puts on heavy clothes in cold weather, armor in battle—so do I attire myself in money in order to protect myself against the cunning onset of all these personal relationships.—*Pap.* III B 180:4 *n.d.*, 1841-42

From sketch:

It is the most beautiful moment in my life—when I stand down there in one of the bathhouses stripped—the door is open—the wide horizon—the air is hazy—I have nothing more to do with the world—I am split naked—leap out into the water.—*Pap.* III B 180:5 *n.d.*, 1841-42

From sketch:

I am rich—in order that financial worries will not divert and cool my hot head; I can always smile—in order better to guard against the inner weeping and the stifled sighs of the soul; I have knowledge—in order that my sick soul will not lack the material in which to clothe itself; I have many friends—in order to prevent myself from confiding in one person.—*Pap.* III B 180:6 *n.d.*, 1841-42

From sketch:

Everyone has his ideal, and most often one becomes its caricature. My ideal has always been a stout, fat basement dweller. I recall this figure from my earliest childhood, when he stood there in his basement door in the afternoon light and smoked his pipe—indeed, I am actually a caricature!—*Pap.* III B 180:7 *n.d.*, 1841-42

From sketch:

III
B 180:8
213

All sorrow is fantasy. If people did not believe that they ought to sorrow dutifully because it is tradition and custom, it would cease. If it were tradition and custom to laugh on sorrowful occasions, everyone would do that. Only when a per-

III
B 180:8
214

son's circumstances are so complex that he is always compelled to hide one passion with another, only then would one, if one could see into hearts, be able to see who was sorrowing and who was not.—*Pap.* III B 180:8 *n.d.*, 1841-42

From sketch:

It must be a wonderful thing to earn something; the only thing I have earned up until now is a gentle warmth flowing through my whole body when I have walked or ridden horseback, but how pleasant it is! I cannot say that I earn my bread by the sweat of my brow, but in the sweat of my brow I earn the sweat of my brow, and this earning is indescribably pleasant. In a way, I eat my bread in the sweat of my brow, and thus it always does me the most good.—*Pap.* III B 180:9 *n.d.*, 1841-42

From sketch:

I have shouted my pain out in the wide world—to see if I could scream it away or if Echo could steal it from me, but Echo is too conscientious for that. —I have sunk it deep in the abyss of my soul; I am like a stone sunk deeper and deeper in my own depths; I have hidden myself in the noise of the world, mislaid myself in its diversions and delights—I have entangled myself in myself.—*Pap.* III B 180:10 *n.d.*, 1841–42

From sketch:

Modern tragedy has taken the comic into itself; the more one thinks about it, the more one is tempted to cancel the difference between the tragic and the comic in the unity of the tragic. Both obviously depend upon a misrelation between idea and actuality, and the two ways people have always sought to allay it have been either by laughing or by crying, but the misrelation itself is obviously the tragic, which thus becomes the unity of the tragic and the comic.—*Pap.* III B 180:11 *n.d.*, 1841–42

From sketch:

To be consistent is not worth the trouble; it is much too boring. Nor are there any more boring people than the consistent.—*Pap.* III B 180:12 *n.d.*, 1841–42

From sketch:

The Stoics say that all pain resides in the idea—stop imagining it and it ceases. As an Epicurean, I imitate them. All pleasure resides in the idea—evoke it and you have pleasure. In other words, the idea is the breath through which one appropriates the one as much as the other, that by which it actually comes into existence [*bliver til*]. Therefore, continually keep yourself in motion; true enjoyment does not consist in rest but in control over unrest. You expect something from a thing, and quite rightly so, for you ought to see the thing in order to desire it. Your expectation is disappointed; that is not bad but good, for thereby it acquires a reality [*Realitet*] for you that it otherwise would not have acquired.—*Pap.* III B 180:13 *n.d.*, 1841-42

From sketch:

The sky viewed through a ventilator in a stagecoach: it is past midnight—a soft breeze passes through the little window, and from this one's thoughts take occasion to move in the opposite direction, out from this narrow little passageway into the wide world. The sky is restless, moved by great thoughts; the moon tries in vain to regain its composure. —The stagecoach proceeds slowly, slowly in comparison with the swift flight of the clouds—and yet it is drawn by four horses, and yet it is hastened by the various passengers' various thoughts, wishes, and longings, which, however different they are, nevertheless have this in common, that all of them are restlessness, haste. —Here is one of the instances in which actuality has its significance. One could easily imagine all sorts of ingenious combinations of ways in which these very different individuals could be brought together, but it has no reality. I have traveled with a poor widow from Nain,[96] who suddenly received news that her son had become ill and who now was riding fifty miles to see him. She cried a good deal. In the same carriage was a man who had traveled halfway around the world.—*Pap.* III B 180:14 *n.d.*, 1841-42

From sketch:

In order properly to feel the slowness of time, I have lying before me a little calendar, the smallest edition of it obtainable, where each day is but an infinitely small magnitude, whereas for me it is an infinitely large magnitude.—*Pap.* III B 180:15 *n.d.*, 1841-42

From sketch:

And at times she nevertheless knelt before me and stretched her hands up to me!—*Pap*. III B 180:16 *n.d.*, 1841-42

From sketch:

If only one could forget oneself—and yet there is only one way to do it, and that is to love.—*Pap*. III B 180:17 *n.d.*, 1841-42

From sketch:

Every classification has lost its meaning for my life, has become an illusion. I can remember visiting a house where they had a clock that struck, but very slowly, usually at intervals of a quarter hour. When it was supposed to strike twelve, it took three hours to strike the twelve strokes; meanwhile it had become three o'clock. It was behind and became more and more so; finally it was not possible for it to finish—consequently it struck and by its striking tried to create a division of time, but this was not enlightening but thoroughly confusing.—*Pap*. III B 180:18 *n.d.*, 1841-42

Disjecta Membra [Dismembered Limbs][97]
—*JP* V 5561 (*Pap*. III A 227) May 1842

. . . . . and if the bitter cup of suffering is handed to me, I will ask that, if possible, it be taken away, but if it is not possible, I will take it cheerfully, and I will not look at the cup but at the one who hands it to me, and I will not look at the bottom of the cup to see if it is soon empty, but I will look at him who hands it to me, and while I trustingly raise the goblet I will not say to any other man: Here's to your health, as I myself am savoring it, but I will say: Here's to my health, and empty its bitterness, to my health, for I know and am convinced that it is for my health that I empty it, for my health, as I leave not one drop behind.—*JP* V 5562 (*Pap*. III A 228) *n.d.*, 1840

. . . . . and it was the delight of his eyes and his heart's desire. And he stretched out his arm and took it, but he could not
keep it; it was offered to him, but he could not possess it—alas,
and it was the delight of his eyes and his heart's desire. And his
soul verged on despair, but he preferred the greater anguish,
losing it and giving it up, to the lesser of having it wrongfully,
or, to speak more exactly, as one should do in this holy place,
he chose the lesser anguish to avoid the greater one of possessing it with a soul at strife . . . . . and oddly enough it turned
out to be the best for him.—*JP* V 5563 (*Pap.* III A 229) *n.d.*,
1842

It certainly would not be appalling that I should suffer punishment that I deserved because I had done wrong; but it
would be appalling if I or any man should be able to do wrong
and no one punished it. It would not be appalling that I should
wake up in anxiety and horror to the deceit of my heart; it
would be appalling if I or any man should be able to deceive
his heart in such a way that no power could awaken it . . . . .
I will conduct myself at this moment as I consider best, but
then I beseech you, O God, that, if I have acted wrongly, your
judgment will not give me peace until I have realized my delusion, for it is not important that I go free but that the truth
take place. It is not that I would hide or hide my action from
myself; I know and I want to know what I have done; and even
if I awakened in the middle of the night I still would want to
be able to say definitely what I had done. I do not want to deceive myself; I want to know clearly and specifically what will
at some later time be either to my shame, yes, to my horror,
or to my peace and joy.—*JP* I 890 (*Pap.* III A 230) *n.d.*, 1842

There are men who say with a certain pride: I am indebted
to no other human being; I am self-taught. There are others
who say: This great philosopher is my teacher, this outstanding general, and I count it an honor to be his pupil, to have
fought under him—but what would you think if a person were
to say: God in heaven was my teacher, and I count it an honor
to be his pupil, that he educated me.—*JP* I 785 (*Pap.* III A 231)
n.d., 1842

Therefore my voice will shout for joy, louder than the voice of a woman who has given birth, louder than the angels' glad shout over a sinner who is converted, more joyful than the morning song of the birds, for what I have sought I have found, and if men robbed me of everything, if they cast me out of their society, I would still retain this joy; if everything were taken from me, I would still continue to have the best—the blessed wonder over God's infinite love, over the wisdom of his decrees.—*JP* II 2184 (*Pap.* III A 232) *n.d.*, 1842

The nature of hereditary sin has often been explained, and still a primary category has been lacking—it is *anxiety* [*Angst*]; this is the essential determinant. Anxiety is a desire for what one fears, a sympathetic antipathy; anxiety is an alien power that grips the individual, and yet he cannot tear himself free from it and does not want to, for he fears, but what he fears he desires. Anxiety makes the individual powerless, and the first sin always occurs in weakness; therefore it apparently lacks accountability, but this lack is the real trap.—*JP* I 94 (*Pap.* III A 233) *n.d.*, 1842

Addition to Pap. III A 233:

Women are more anxious than men; therefore it was she whom the serpent chose for his attack, and it deceived her through her anxiety.—*JP* I 95 (*Pap.* III A 234) *n.d.*, 1842

Addition to Pap. III A 233:

In volume VI, p. 194, of his works, Hamann makes an observation that I can use, although he neither understood it as I wish to understand it nor thought further about it: "However, this *Angst* [anxiety] in the world is the only proof of our heterogeneity. If we lacked nothing, we should do no better than the pagans and the transcendental philosophers, who know nothing of God and like fools fall in love with lovely nature, and no homesickness would come over us. This impertinent disquiet, this holy hypochondria . . . . ."—*JP* I 96 (*Pap.* III A 235) *n.d.*, 1842

When you were happy, have you ever said to yourself that you could easily go through life alone? When you were heavy-hearted, have you ever said that it seemed as if even God in heaven was not able to help you?—*JP* II 1985 (*Pap*. III A 236) *n.d.*, 1842

. . . . . Perhaps you express yourself more as a child; perhaps you say: God, to be sure, is all-powerful; it's an easy matter for him and for me it is so very important that I get my wish; my future, my joy, and everything depend on it. It is charming of you not to lose your childlikeness even though sufferings threaten; you captivate us. And yet is it not true that you could not wish to captivate God in the same way, for if you obtained what you wanted, you would obtain it as a child does, and you could not love God with your whole heart, could not love him with all your passion—but only this love is becoming to a man, only this love makes him happy.—*JP* III 2395 (*Pap*. III A 237) *n.d.*, 1842

. . . . . When everything is lost, when that which to you is dearest of all is denied you, when there is not one remaining doubt that can keep the soul breathing, when it wants to sink down in stagnation and death "because there is nothing left to do"—could there really be absolutely nothing left? I do know of one thing still—before you lay yourself down to die, even though you keep on living, ask yourself: Do I still love God as deeply as before? If you have to admit that you do not, then your soul will not have time to fall asleep but will have much to do; and if you sense that you do, then you will be so happy that you will feel more alive than ever.—*JP* I 742 (*Pap*. III A 238) *n.d.*, 1842

. . . . . the magnitude of the suffering and pain cannot always be judged by the shriek and the noise.—*JP* IV (*Pap*. III A 239) *n.d.*, 1842

. . . . . and discover that it is a mystery deeper than any thought that has ever arisen within a man's heart,[98] that God is one who hates all ceremonies, that one dares without further ado (*ex tempore*) to speak with him without an appointment etc. in the joy of life, during sorrow-filled nights; that one always has occasion to thank him, and that when one forgets this, he is loving enough to remind one of it. I meditate upon how proportionately God shares with man, for it must be far more difficult for him to love a human being in such a way that he is not crushed by God's love, far more difficult for him to make himself so small that a human being really can love him.[99]

And when one does not have a single human being who understands one, then he is willing to listen and he can remember far better than any man, even better than one can oneself. And when one's thoughts are so confused that one does not know whether one is coming or going, God has not forgotten even the slightest thing one has prayed him to remember; and if it were not so, everything would be a matter of indifference, whether one could remember it oneself or not.—*JP* II 1508 (*Pap.* III A 240) *n.d.*, 1842

. . . . . And when you had become utterly weary of the world, when you wanted to give your passion the outlet of one single statement, you perhaps said: "Let the world pass away and the lust thereof."[100] But at the same moment your soul was reminded that it was an old saying, and involuntarily you began to repeat what from your childhood followed next: God's word endures forever. At first you said it quite indifferently, but finally it became everything to you.—*JP* I 743 (*Pap.* III A 241) *n.d.*, 1842

Just to have been the object of more severe judgment even once is something that cannot be forgotten, even though one has improved.—*JP* II 1773 (*Pap.* III A 242) *n.d.*, 1842

The only thing to fear is that it could occur to the prostituted women to deny her wish, for then all would be lost; they would have gained an appearance of truth, and the girl would have lost everything.—*Pap.* III A 243 *n.d.*, 1842

The Skeptic

Just as the seducer was meant to give a reflected picture of the abortive endeavor that wished to carry out its purpose in relation to "woman," so also the skeptic in relation to man as an attempt to wrench everything away from him.—*JP* III 3286 (*Pap*. III A 244) *n.d.*, 1842

Page from a Street Inspector's Diary

It was April 1, 1830, that I became district inspector below the stock exchange.

(a) Reflections on a fish tank by one of the fishing boats, the enormous horizon, still life in contrast

(b) A Laplander—idyll

the coal market the old market

the straw market

   the tale of a gutter plank

   deluge

The editor has been unable to restrain himself from slipping in a few observations.

It is Sunday afternoon—all so quiet—a shrimp-seller cries his wares—

A man with plantain—the out-of-the-way place where it grows—

A woman selling oranges—harbinger of spring—

A little love story in the district—

       —*JP* V 5564 (*Pap*. III A 245) *n.d.*, 1842

The tale of the rat that became a misanthrope.—*JP* V 5565 (*Pap*. III A 246) *n.d.*, 1842

From sketch; see 3-15:

Preface

It may at times have occurred to you, dear reader, to wish for yourself the possibility of really being able to see into a person's innermost being, to see how he is when he is alone with himself; indeed, you may even have wished more, to know how he is when he is alone with his God, in order to see what a person truly is—it has perhaps struck you that when two people have lived together for a long time neither of them perhaps knew what dwelt in the other; they perhaps went to the Lord's Supper together; they confessed the same faith etc.—

Kind lady reader, certainly you, too, have often wished—not so much from ordinary human interest—to see what dwelt in a person.

I have always had a decided bent toward such reflections.—*Pap.* III B 185:1 *n.d.*, 1842

In margin of Pap. III B 185:1:

If a person has experienced much, has much interior history, then he has an authentic interpretation of everything.

. . . . . even if you could do without the help of others, as it seems to you, you perhaps felt the pain deepest because of your being unable to help others.

Love no longer united people, but anxiety separated them—
—*Pap.* III B 185:2 *n.d.*, 1842

In margin of Pap. III B 185:1:

. . . . . . and I imagine you so vividly—my confession of love cannot disturb you—you do not know who I am—I do not know who you are—and yet there can be an understanding between us, and every time I see a pretty young girl I think that she perhaps has read it, she perhaps has felt a faint shiver—and I ask whether she has read it— —*Pap.* III B 185:3 *n.d.*, 1842

From sketch; see 3-15:

Preface

The wish may at times have occurred to you, dear reader, to be able really to see into a person's innermost being in order to see how he is when he is alone with himself. You perhaps may

III
B 187:1
223

not entirely trust the accuracy of the philosophical thesis that the inner is the outer.* You may at times have happily felt that it was possible for you to hide your life's deepest secret from others in order to brood over it undisturbed, either because it seems to you too good, too fortunate, to communicate to others, or too sad and crushing to allow others to share, at times may have wished it were possible, at times may have painfully felt that it was possible, for others to avoid even your sharpest and most attentive scrutiny. Such thoughts come and go and no one knows from whence they come or whither they go; but they seize the mind with a strange anxiety because the great and beautiful family of mankind is thereby disintegrated into an infinite variety of isolated lives, because faith in working together for world historical achievements just as for the most insignificant private enterprise thereby dissolves like an illusion, because trust and confidence appear to you as foolishness, love and the human race appear to historical observation, like the milky way to astronomical observation, as a multitude of pinpoints having nothing at all to do with each other—the countries appear just as accidental as the figures astronomers have named as constellations.

III
B 187:1
224

. . . . . and even if the embrace is ever so tender, they still do not become one—no more than a jumper who can jump ever so high can therefore fly. That is to say, there remains a qualitative difference, and out of this difference comes a third being that brings its secret with it into the world.—*Pap.* III B 187:1 *n.d.*, 1842

Addition to Pap. III B 187:1:

*Or you perhaps have held such a Proteus in your arms, who continually changed himself, assumed the most ridiculous shapes in order to slip away from you, in order that in the moment of laughter you would forget to hold onto him; you may not have had the strength to hold out with him and doubted whether eventually there would come a midnight hour when everyone has to take off his mask.—*Pap.* III B 187:2 *n.d.*, 1842

From draft; see 4:16-9:7:

These papers have come into my possession—I know nothing at all about his way of life, his outward circumstances—
usually one comes to know most about these—thus he is anon-
ymous and yet everything adds up to a definite personality—
therefore, I hear his confessions but like the confessor am separated by a partition from the one confessing, whom I cannot
see. —Should I not wish to form a conception of the person.
When I sit and listen and hear a trembling, youthful, female
voice confess sins, choked with sobs, I immediately form a
picture—or a youthful, happy, confident, buoyant voice. —
Therefore, even though I lack the external image, the confessions are all the more lively; he does not speak at a definite
hour what comes to his mind—it is momentary, sometimes
when sleep refused to come, sometimes when it suddenly left
him, at times in the middle of a tumult of joy, at times in the
middle of deepest solitude. Therefore the confessions have a
freshness, an aroma— —*Pap.* III B 185:4 *n.d.*, 1842

From draft; see 4:16-6:24:

How I happened to come into possession of them— —*Pap.* III B
185:5 *n.d.*, 1842

From draft; see 7:35-10:31:

I cannot find even any historical development in them—
with respect only to erotic factors, he seems at times to be in
love for the first time—at times to have been that for a long
time and many times, at times even to be experienced in all the
secret depths of erotic love—whether it is illusions—moods—
or actual data—I do not know—I let everything take its course
with the most diplomatic exactitude—perhaps it is an accident
that has arranged them in this way—perhaps his plan—he presumably has been afraid that these pages might sometime fall
into strangers' hands—he has never mentioned any name—he
himself understood this—it is a laudable caution and by no

means unnecessary, as one sees *in casu.* —The date of the year is utterly lacking; occasionally there is a date, but without the year it is meaningless—the only information is found in the letters from Edward, which are included. One sees from these that his name was Johannes. However, one cannot be completely sure of that, for it would certainly be possible that, given his caution, even the letters were written under fictitious names. This is supported by the fact that in one of the letters the name is changed to Johannes—so it is just as possible that Johannes is the right name as the fictitious name—where he has lived is very difficult to determine—he seems to have traveled a good deal—at times he writes: here in the city, but one does not know which city is meant—presumably he himself could easily call to mind as to what city it was or perhaps it was of no interest to him at all to remember mere externals. —That the letters which follow are actually from someone is demonstrated by the difference in the handwriting. It is very striking—the loose pages are all written very disconnectedly—the letters are calm and sensible, at times even beautiful, always carefully written—the pages often lack meaning, although in another sense the meaning is clear enough if one just adds a single word or inserts a comma or reads it aloud.—*Pap.* III B 185:6 *n.d.,* 1842

From sketch; see 8:35-10:31:

The Seducer's **Diary** [**Dagbog**]

III
B 188:1
225

Time. —A poem. —He himself has become anxious.

moral—seducer (—not the hero of a novel).

The girl herself has guilt. (the rarity.) One sees also from this that it is fiction, for he would never have been able to find a girl who would do it.

The estheticist has wanted to exhaust the potentiality of the interesting (see the note about Don Giovanni) [*Pap.* III B 41:26; *Either/Or,* II, p. 377, *KW* III (*Pap.* III B 41:26)]. *The Method.*

to seduce only *one*

In novels it is a matter of either to see her and to love her being one and the same or a seduction happening so easily that it tempts. Here one sees that it is not so easy—a seduction in which the girl herself does not have an element of guilt has no true esthetic worth.

The schism: something is true in poetry that is untrue in life, is canceled. All romantic love is essentially deceit. The seducer does not lack the erotic, wants to sacrifice everything for his idea, but he does not believe in the durability of love, it is his heresy; but the same is true of any hero in a novel, only we do not come to see it.

"The Seducer's Diary" thus forms the transition to the ethicist and is very far from being immoral.—*Pap.* III B 188:1 *n.d.*, 1842

III
B 188:1
226

From draft; see 8:35-10:5:

And just as it made A uneasy to be involved with these papers (see note marked in red crayon [*Pap.* III B 47:1]), so it has also made me anxious when I copied them in the stillness of the night. It seemed to me as if the seducer paced the floor like a ghost, glanced at the papers, fixed his demonic eyes on me, and said: Well, well, so you want to publish my papers. That is, you know, irresponsible, for you will arouse anxiety in the darling girls. But, on the other hand, you will, of course make me innocuous. Dear friend, you are mistaken. I merely change the method. Now I am known as Seducer. I will not mention the large flock of young girls who will fly straight into the light when they hear this seductive name—but give me just half a year and I shall provide a new story more daring than all the rest: a girl who gets the idea that she will avenge the whole sex on me, will teach me to taste all the pains of unhappy love. If she does not think of it herself, I shall poetize it into her. I shall writhe like an eel and when I have brought her to the point where I want her, then it is over. What do you think of that story.—*Pap.* III B 188:2 *n.d.*, 1842

From draft; see 9:9-10:

. . . . . the whole narrative is to be regarded as a troubled and dark dream.—*Pap.* III B 188:3 *n.d.*, 1842

From sketch; see 10:12-31:

. . . . . it is not easy to decide how long a time has passed, since the whole movement is, like a nightmare ride, indeterminable as to time.—*Pap.* III B 185:7 *n.d.*, 1842

From draft; see 13:22-23:

. . . . . he who has said A must also say B; however, this is not always the case in life.—*Pap.* III B 187:3 *n.d.*, 1842

From sketch; see 14:24-25:

If A knew it, he would undoubtedly say: Read it or do not read it, you will regret it either way.—*Pap.* III B 187:6 *n.d.*, 1842

From draft; see 14:26-15:25:

If B knew that it was being published, he would perhaps end his preface thus: Go out into the world, then; go quietly and unobserved; avoid, if possible, the attention of every critic; and should it fall into the hands of a female reader, then I would say: My charming reader, in this book you will find much that you perhaps should not know, something by which you presumably can benefit from knowing it; therefore read a great deal in such a way that, having read it, you may be as one who has not read it, and read the something in such a way that, having read it, you may be as one who has not forgotten what has been read.—*Pap.* III B 187:5 *n.d.*, 1842

III
B 187:5
224

III
B 187:5
225

From page preceding final draft of "The Seducer's Diary"; see 15:6:

In the preface to the whole work, that is, in the editor's preface, it should read: If anyone should think he recognizes the editor, if anyone should be of the opinion that the whole thing resembles him personally, then I will always say that it is impossible except insofar as it would be true, spiritually speaking, that the child ought to resemble not only the father but also the godfather. III B 169 186

In the same way in the first preface: it occurs to me that the whole thing might be a hoax; maybe someone wants to make fun of me. Well, the world is full of hoaxes.—*Pap.* III B 169 *n.d.*, 1842 III B 169 187

From page preceding final draft of "The Seducer's Diary"; see 15:6:

Victor Eremita's Dedication

This work is dedicated
to Mr. X

At a happy party, it sometimes happens that everyone joins in giving one specific toast to one specific person; at other times, one joins in drinking a toast, while each person thinks of whatever he so wishes. The former is a loud toast, the latter a silent homage. Which homage is the more beautiful. As I let this work go out into the world, I am thinking of you, dear Mr. X; my thoughts address you, you to whom I owe so much.—*Pap.* III B 171 *n.d.*, 1842

From sketch; see 17:1:

Διαψαλματα.

Some of these are not here but are partly among various papers in the thin green book, and partly in other places.[101]

Others found here were not printed.
—*Pap.* III B 178 *n.d.*, 1842

See 17:2:

1839
ad se ipsum [to himself][102]—

Pap. II A 340 *n.d.*, 1839

From sketch; see 17:1-2:

Under the title:

Refrains

ad se ipsum

all the separate observations that are already worked out may
well be collected. They are scattered elements of a view of life
that is not only personal but also scholarly, yet precisely because of this duplexity, cancels itself and once again ends in
either/or.—*Pap.* III B 175 *n.d.*, 1842

Addition to Pap. III B 175:

. . . . . there frequently are contradictions in them, his
moods have been this way. The single mood is intensified as
mood, and one would expect him not to have other moods.—
Pap. III B 176 *n.d.*, 1842

From sketch; see 19:1-18:

The first sentence in the refrains should read thus:

What is a poet?

The unhappiness in this is described, and it ends with: least of
all I wished to be a poet.—*Pap.* III B 179:2 *n.d.*, 1841–42

From draft; see 19:2-16:

. . . . . of all the senses I like hearing the most. I listen, just
like the Catholic Church—and I know how to find an interesting side to even the most tragic and painful sound, just as

the unhappy wretches who despaired in Phalarus's bull became virtuosos by means of its construction—

At times my ear swallows what is heard and it vanishes exceedingly deep within; at times a venetian blind is drawn before it and the trembling words are sifted through it—what a remarkable thing is the ear—the eye— —*Pap.* III B 187:4 *n.d.*, 1842

The first διαψαλμα is really the task of the entire work, which is not resolved until the last words of the sermon. An enormous dissonance is assumed, and then it says: Explain it. A total break with actuality is assumed, which does not have its base in futility but in mental depression and its predominance over actuality.

The last διαψ. tells us how a life such as this has found its satisfactory expression in laughter. He pays his debt to actuality by means of laughter, and now everything takes place within this contradiction. His enthusiasm is too intense, his sympathy too deep, his love too burning, his heart too warm to be able to express himself in any other way than by contradiction. Thus A himself would never have come to a decision to publish his papers.—*JP* V 5629 (*Pap.* IV A 216) *n.d.*, 1843

Deleted from final copy; see 19:26:

All of the numerous discussion group leaders, assistant professors, and survey people who nowadays in Germany take it upon themselves to introduce people to philosophy and to characterize philosophy's present position are just as distasteful to me with their devoid-of-all-pathos newspaper information about the situation of philosophy as dull, sleepy billiard-game scorekeepers with their monotonous cry: *dixe à ons*. And strangely enough, philosophy advances steadily, and despite the fact that in the whole crowd of philosophers there is not one single player but simply scorekeepers. I wait in vain for a man to appear who would have the power to say: *à point* [nothing, no score]. In vain—we are already far along in *quarant*, and the game will soon be over and all the enigmas explained. If only the German philosophers could explain the enigma that the game goes on although there is no one who plays. —What wonder then, when this is the situation with the Germans, that I set my hopes on Danish philosophy. My barber, too, an older but well-read man, who has followed the movements of modern Danish philosophy with energy and interest, maintains that Denmark has never had such philosophers as it has now; the beginning of Danish philosophy should now be at hand. The other day he was so good as to utilize the ten minutes he uses for my shave to give me a short survey of modern Danish philosophy. He assumes that it begins with *Riegels, Horrebov,* and *Boie.* He knew Riegels intimately; he was his friend and *dus*-brother, a little square-built man, always cheerful and contented. He remembers distinctly what a sensation his debut aroused. He advanced many remarkable truths. What they were my barber has forgotten—it was many years ago; yet he remembers as vividly as if it were yesterday what a sensation he made. Horrebov and Boie always came to his barber shop, where he then had the opportunity to become familiar with their philosophy. These three men must be regarded as the coryphi in modern Danish philosophy. Riisbrigh should also be mentioned, although his work as a teacher at the University of Copenhagen was quieter and less noticed. On the whole, however, he stood outside the great movements in modern Danish philosophy. But what my barber could not recall without deep emotion was that through untimely death Denmark should lose the most gifted philosopher it had. The man is now forgotten. Many people perhaps do not know he ever lived. His name is Niels Rasmussen, and he was a contemporary of the three great philosophers. He had conceived the eminent idea that all European philosophy might unite around the Danish, and this again around his philosophy. To that end he worked energetically on a subscription plan; but the work took all his strength to the extent that he died of overexhaustion. If, said my barber, if his subscription plan had been finished, if the work it heralded had been finished, if it had been read, if it had been translated, if it had been understood by the European philosophers, then without any doubt the hopeful Niels Rasmussen would have brought Denmark to the heights it does not occupy even in this moment. But—

he died, Denmark's philosophical hope. —The barber and I offered him a tear, whereupon he continued to shave my beard as well as to communicate a survey of modern Danish philosophy. What Riegels in a jovial moment had confided to him, what Horrebov, Boie, and he had whispered about in the barber shop—this he spread all around the country. —He paused a moment in his barbering to wipe off some lather; he used the moment to show me on a map which hung on the wall how modern Danish philosophy in its grand movements spread across Sjælland, yes, pushed way up into Norway as far as Trondhjem. Everyone justifiably dared to expect something extraordinary from this great stir, but then came the unhappy years of the war, which shattered everything. But now once again he had gained the courage to hope. The present epoch in Danish philosophy showed clearly that it stood in an essential relation to the previous epoch in modern Danish philosophy; it had contact with it and forsook its conclusion only to find one higher. The first epoch worked toward a sound understanding of man and achieved it as well; philosophy today abandons more and more this relative superficiality in order to reach something higher. It has perhaps discovered that there is something more and something different, something it provisionally calls the anterior Innermost or that which is behind the Innermost Being. As soon as it has discovered what this is or, as my barber more correctly put it, as soon as it has gotten back there behind, it will gain the European reputation which Niels Rasmussen had intended it to have. My barber is of the opinion that one may safely dare hope so, confident in the extraordinary powers of Danish philosophy.—*JP* III 3288 (*Pap.* III B 191:4, same as 192) *n.d.*, 1842

See 20:1-6:

I don't feel like doing anything. I don't feel like walking—it is tiring; I don't feel like lying down, for either I would lie down for a long time, and I don't feel like doing that, or I would get up right away, and I don't feel like that either—I don't feel like riding—the motion is too vigorous for my apathy; I don't feel like doing anything except just taking a drive, indolently, smoothly undulating along, letting objects in abundance glide by, pausing at every beautiful spot merely to feel my listlessness—my ideas and impulses are just as barren as a eunuch's desire. —I seek in vain for something to stimulate me—not even the pithy language of the Middle Ages is able to destroy the emptiness that prevails in me—now I really feel the meaning of the expression about Christ's words[103] that they are life and spirit—to be brief: I do not feel like writing what I have written here, and I do not feel like erasing it either.—*JP* V 5251 (*Pap.* II A 637) *n.d.*, 1837

See 20:11-17:

Tested Advice for Unwitty Authors
Price: 5 rix-dollars

One carelessly writes down one's personal observations. Later, by way of all the various proofs, one eventually acquires a fair number of good ideas. Therefore, take courage, you who have not yet dared to have something printed; do not despise typographical errors, and do not let on that they are typographic errors. Besides, no one can wrench your property away from you, since it really belongs to no one. The only problem is that you must have the help of a good friend who knows how to decide what is witty, so that you do not acquire new stupidities.—*JP* I 142 (*Pap.* III A 111) *n.d.*, 1841

See 20:18-26:

Generally speaking, the imperfection in everything human is that its aspirations are achieved only by way of their opposites. I shall not discuss the variety of formations, which can give psychologists plenty to do (the melancholy have the best sense of the comic, the most opulent often the best sense of the rustic, the dissolute often the best sense of the moral, the doubter often the best sense of the religious), but it is through sin that one gains a first glimpse of salvation. Therefore, the imperfection consists not so much in the opposite as in one's not being able to see one thing and its opposite *simultaneously*.—*JP* I 700 (*Pap.* III A 112) *n.d.*, 1841

See 20:27-32:

In addition to my other numerous acquaintances, with whom, on the whole, I have a very formal relationship, I have also one intimate confidante—my depression, and in the midst of my joy, in the midst of my work, she beckons to me, calls me aside, even though physically I remain on the spot. It is the most faithful mistress I have known—no wonder, then, that I must be prepared to follow at any moment.—*JP* V 5496 (*Pap. III A 114*) *n.d.*, 1841

See 21:7-19:

I am strangely alarmed when I note the hypochondriac profundity with which Englishmen of an earlier generation have spotted the ambiguity basic to laughter, as Dr. Hartley has observed:* What if laughter were completely misunderstood, what if the world were so bad and existence so unhappy that laughter really is weeping? What if it were a misunderstanding—a misunderstanding caused by a compassionate genius or a mocking demon—?

*"Dass wenn sich das Lachen zuerst bey Kindern zeiget, so ist es ein entstehendes Weinen, welches durch Schmerz erregt wird, oder ein plötzlich gehemmtes und in sehr kurzen Zwischenraumen wiederholtes Gefühl des Schmerzens [that when laughter first makes its appearance in the child, it is a nascent cry that is excited by pain or a suddenly arrested feeling of pain repeated at very short intervals]." (See *Geschichte der komischen Literatur*, by Flögel, I, p. 50.)[104]—*JP* V 5371 (*Pap. II A 373*) February 21, 1839

See 21:20-23:

There are certain occasions when a person especially feels how hard it is to stand utterly alone* in the world. The other day I saw a poor girl walking utterly alone to church to be confirmed. And I saw an old man whose whole family had died out—he was carrying his little grandson, his last comfort, in a coffin under his arm, and some time later I saw him in the cemetery sitting like a cross on a family grave.—*JP* II 1979 (*Pap*. II A 400) April 28, 1839

In margin of Pap. II A 400:

*God knows where the expression *mutters-alene* actually comes from.[105]—*JP* II 1980 (*Pap*. II A 401) *n.d*.

See 21:24-29:

Cornelius Nepos tells of a general who was kept confined in a fortress with a considerable cavalry regiment; to keep the horses from getting sick because of too much inactivity, he had them whipped daily to put them in motion—in like manner I live in my room as one besieged—I prefer to see no one, and every moment I fear that the enemy will try an assault— that is, someone will come and visit me. I would rather not go out, but lest I be harmed by sitting still so much—I cry myself tired.—*JP* V 5380 (*Pap*. II A 414) May 10, 1839

See 21:30-32:

I say of my sorrow what the Englishman says of his house: My sorrow *is mey castle* [*Min sorg* is mey castle]. —But there are many men who, when they have occasion for sorrow (wear crepe around the hat), ask for sympathy not so much to alleviate the sorrow as to be petted and pampered a bit, and thus basically look upon having sorrow as one of life's conveniences.—*JP* V 5384 (*Pap*. II A 421) May 12, 1839

See 22:1-2:

I live and feel these days somewhat as a chessman must feel when the opponent says: That piece cannot be moved—like a useless spectator, since my time has not yet come.—*JP* V 5388 (*Pap*. II A 435) May 21, 1839

See 22:3-15:

Aladdin is so very refreshing because of the audacity of the child, of the genius, in the wildest wishes. For how many are there in our day who truly dare to wish, dare to desire, dare to demand, dare to address nature neither with a *polite* child's *"bitte, bitte* [please, please]" nor with the raging frenzy of one damned? How many are there who—inspired by what is talked about so much in our age, that man is created in God's image, is his natural representative—have the authentic voice of command, the authentic, divinely official style, or do we not all stand like Nourredin, bowing and scraping, worrying about asking too much or too little? Or is not this magnificent demanding gradually diminished to morbid reflecting over the *I*, from insisting to *informing*, which from the outset the child is indeed *brought up* to do.—*JP* IV 4928 (*Pap.* II A 451) June 10, 1839

See 22:16-24:

. . . . . I am as timorous as a *scheva*, as weak and muted as a *daghesch lene*; I feel like a letter printed backward in the line, as uncontrollable as a pasha with three horsetails.* Yes, if thinking about one's miseries removed them just as those who are conscious of their good deeds lose their reward, how happy a hypochondriac of my format would be, for I take all my troubles in advance and yet they all remain behind.

August 24, 1839

In margin: *as solicitous for myself and my scribblings as the National Bank is for its own, generally as reflexive as any pronoun.—*JP* V 5407 (*Pap.* II A 540) August 24, 1839

From sketch; see 23:21-23:

. . . . . For the door of fate does not open inward so that one can push it open by rushing at it, but it opens outward so that the individual first has to stand back (resignation).—*Pap.* III B 179:3 *n.d.*, 1841–42

See 23:24-34:

I have, I believe, the courage to doubt everything; I have, I believe, the courage to fight against everything; but I do not have the courage to acknowledge anything, the courage to possess, to own anything. Most people complain that the world is so prosaic that things do not go in life as in novels, where the lovers are so fortunate. I complain that life is not as it is in novels, where one has hardhearted fathers to struggle against, maidens' bowers to force open, convent walls to storm. I have only the pale, bloodless, tenacious-of-life nocturnal forms to struggle against, to which I myself give life and existence.—*JP* I 801 (*Pap.* III A 218) November 16, 1840

See 24:1-14:

The sad thing about me is that my whole life is an interjection and has nothing nailed down (everything is movable—nothing immovable, no *real property*)—my sorrow is a despairing wail—my joy an overly lyrical tra-la-la.—*JP* V 5372 (*Pap.* II A 382) March 13, 1839

See 24:23-25:

The most interesting time is the period of falling in love, when, after the first magical sweeping sensation, one fetches something home from every encounter, every glance (however fleetingly the soul hides, so to speak, behind the eyelid), just like a bird busily fetching one stick after the other to its nest and yet always feeling overwhelmed by the great wealth.—*JP* III 2382 (*Pap.* II A 273) October 11, 1838

See 24:26-29:

I would like to write a novel in which the main character would be a man who had obtained a pair of glasses, one lens of which reduced images as powerfully as an oxyhydrogen microscope[106] and the other magnified on the same scale, so that he perceived everything relatively.—*JP* V 5281 (*Pap*. II A 203) December 10, 1837

See 24:26-29:

Precisely because humor wants to have the absolute without the relative, it fumbles about in the most desperate leaping, always within the most appalling relativity—

The same glass magnifies (a blade of grass is worth more than all ingenuity) and diminishes (rather hear wisdom from the mouth of a Pharisee against his will than from an apostle)—[107]—*JP* II 1722 (*Pap*. III A 49) *n.d*., 1840

See 25:1-11:

Irony no longer stands out the way it used to. I have often thought it was a kind of irony of the world when, for example, a horsefly sat on a man's nose the very moment he made his last running leap to throw himself into the Thames, when in the story of Loki and the dwarf,[108] after Eitri has gone away and Brock stands by the bellows, a fly settles on his nose three times—here the ironical appears as one of Loki's intrigues to prevent him from winning the wager, and in the other case it is a grandiose human plan that is horridly ridiculed by a horsefly.—*JP* II 1697 (*Pap*. II A 112) July 8, 1837

See 25:6-7:

One who walked along contemplating suicide—at that very moment a stone fell down and killed him, and he ended with the words: Praise the Lord!—*JP* II 1672 (*Pap*. I A 158) *n.d*., 1836

From sketch; see 25:12-18:

On the whole, I lack the patience to live; to acquire children seems ridiculous to me; where would I find time to wait for them to grow up—I cannot see the grass grow, but if I cannot do that, I do not care to look at it. My views are the superficial observations of a *"fahrende Skolastisker* [traveling scholastic]" who dashes through life in the greatest haste. It is said that our Lord satisfies the stomach before the eyes; it is not so with me—my eyes are surfeited and bored with everything, although I hunger—*Pap*. III B 179:8 *n.d.*, 1841-42

From sketch; see 25:19-28:

Above all, do not ask me for reasons—a young girl is usually excused for not being able to give reasons; she lives too much in feelings—with me it is different. Ordinarily, I have so many and most often such mutually contradictory reasons that it is impossible for me to enunciate them, least of all simultaneously in pairs, as is proper. In addition, very frequently a little trifle determines the issue. So you see that for this reason it is impossible for me to give reasons. —It also seems to me that with cause and effect the relation is not right, for sometimes enormous *gewaltige* [powerful] causes produce a very *klein* [small] and slight little effect—indeed, sometimes no effect at all; sometimes a nimble little cause produces a colossal effect, a mouse a mountain.—*Pap*. III B 179:9 *n.d.*, 1841-42

From sketch; see 25:29-35:

. . . . . and these innocent pleasures . . . . . they have only one flaw, that they are so innocent, and particularly that they are to be enjoyed in moderation. —My physician sometimes prescribes a diet. There is some reason in that; one abstains from certain specified things, but to be dietetic in keeping the diet is indeed all too dreadful.—*Pap*. III B 179:10 *n.d.*, 1841-42

See 26:10-14:

I am so unhappy at present that in my dreams I am indescribably happy.—*JP* V 5381 (*Pap*. II A 415) *n.d.*, 1839

From sketch; see 26:19-22:

A riddle—one ought always be that not in the substantial sense but subjectively—my life knows no law and therefore is unpredictable. Not only am I a riddle to people, but I am that to myself. It is absolutely splendid. I examine myself and tease myself, and if I am tired of that, I smoke a cigar for diversion and think: God knows what our Lord actually intended with me or what he wants to make of me.—*Pap.* III B 179:13 *n.d.,* 1841-42

From sketch; see 21:23-27:2:

No woman in maternity confinement can have stranger and more impatient wishes than I have. And if I am not like a woman in confinement, I am continually experiencing the sensual rapture and pain of childbirth. —Sometimes these wishes involve the most insignificant things, sometimes the most sublime, but all with the momentary wildness of the soul. I can wish for a certain food—not with Esau's starving hunger,[109] but with the sensual rapture of a woman in confinement. I can wish to see through the deep things of God with the same passion. At this moment I wish for—a bowl of buckwheat cereal. I can remember from my school days that we always had buckwheat cereal on Wednesdays and Wednesday afternoons we had recess from school. I recall how smooth and white the cereal was served, how the butter smiled at me, how warm it was, how impatient I was to get permission to begin. At this moment, I would give everything for a bowl of buckwheat cereal.—*Pap.* III B 179:14 *n.d.,* 1841-42

See 27:3-11:

One must not be in too much of a hurry with one's rebirth, lest it go as it did with the sorcerer Virgilius when he was going to rejuvenate himself and to that end had let himself be put to death (hacked to pieces), and then, through the careless-ness of the one who was supposed to watch the kettle, it was

opened too soon, and Virgilius, who at this point had just become an infant, disappeared with a doleful wail.—*JP* IV 4399
(*Pap*. II A 152) August 31, 1837

See 27:3-11:

You well know the story about the sorcerer Vergilius, who
wanted to rejuvenate himself—bear it in mind. (In order to
mystify the readers, this story must not be developed further.
On the whole, more must be done in this respect.)—*Pap*. III B
41:7 *n.d.*, 1841

From sketch; see 27:3-11:

Like the sorcerer Virgilius (he appears in Hagen's
Märchen),[110] I hack myself to pieces, put myself into a caldron
and let myself cook in order to be rejuvenated. Virgilius also
did the same. He arranged for someone to hack him to pieces,
to put him in a caldron, and now he was supposed to cook for
eight days, and the other person was supposed to see to it that
no interloper came to peer into the caldron. But the watchman
himself could not resist the temptation; he peered in, and too
soon, and Virgilius, as an infant, disappeared with a scream.
So also with me; I have peered too soon into the caldron, into
the machinery of life and its historical process, and now I rescue only my childhood—with a scream.—*Pap*. III B 179:15
n.d., 1841-42

From sketch; see 27:29-28:9:

. . . . . even though our Lord keeps ever so orderly an account book according to Italian bookkeeping
It is not modern literature's shocks I need, but it is the pathos
of true passion, its drastic power. There they hate
. . . . . there the voice of love and of cursing is so loud that
it forces its way to the throne of God—there they sin.—*Pap*.
III B 179:17 *n.d.*, 1841-42

From draft; see 28:10-12:

I divide my time as follows. The one half I sleep; the other half I dream. Most people do not dream at all. That is always good insofar as they do not dream in their sleep. Sleep ought not to be disturbed by dreams. There is something of great genius about sleep. But one ought to dream when awake.—*Pap.* III B 179:18 *n.d.*, 1841-42

From sketch; see 29:6-11:

My soul is so heavy that no thought can carry it any longer, no wingbeat can lift it up into the ether any more; only rarely is it moved, and when that happens it does not rise toward the higher regions but skims along the ground, just as birds fly low in distressed flight when a thunderstorm is blowing up— and in the same way a secret anxiety broods over my whole inner being, an oppressiveness that forebodes an earthquake.—*Pap.* III B 179:24 *n.d.*, 1841-42

From sketch; see 29:21-31:

Not even girls appeal to me—their beauty passes away like a dream and like yesterday when it is past. —Their faithfulness—what shall I say about it. Either they are faithless—this does not concern me; it's all too familiar to me—or if one found a faithful [girl], then from the standpoint of an exception she certainly will appeal to me, but, on the other hand, from the standpoint of a long period of time she would not appeal to me, for either she would continually remain faithful, and it would go with me in my eagerness for experience just as it would have gone with that judge (who out of conscientiousness submitted himself to every possible punishment) if he had gone so far as to have himself executed, or there would come a time when she would lapse, and then we would come under the above.—*Pap.* III B 179:26 *n.d.*, 1841-42

From sketch; see 29:32-30:26:

Wretched fate, in vain do you prink up your wrinkled face like an old prostitute, I still recognize you; in vain do you put your hair in curls, I recognize you. You have lost; you also have your old rigamarole, your *Idem per Idem* [the same by the same]; in vain do you warm up the same story. You bore me as a fool bores his master; it is your old acrobatics, the same somersaults—*

Come, sleep and death; you promise nothing; you hold so much more.** in vain do you jingle your fool's bells—

I do not blame Nero for burning down Rome, but I wish I knew if he knew how to enjoy it. To burn Rome down because he wanted to see the show and also because he wanted to see a dove make its escape over the sea of fire—that would be a pleasure.

*There is still nothing new under the sun.[111] You are your own echo.

**I shall lay me down to sleep, and if you have found out anything new, then come and call me.—*Pap.* III B 179:30 *n.d.*, 1841-42

From sketch; see 29:32-30:2:

Come, sleep and death; you promise nothing; you hold so much more. I shall lay me down to sleep, and if you have found out anything new, then come and call me.—*Pap.* III B 179:32 *n.d.*, 1841-42

From sketch; see 30:3-29:

Those two familiar violin strains, which Mozart uses with his boundless genius to dialecticize his Don Giovanni out of morality's substantial, unexplained, mute depths, to show him vanishing or, more correctly, let him vanish far off in the horizon, in a twinkling let him run away like a shadow far beyond the farthest streak of horizon, as if there were an infinity between these two powers, as if the whole world lay between

these two worlds—those two violin strains, this very moment, here in the middle of the street—have I lost my mind?
—Is it my ears, which for love of Mozart's music have ceased
to hear? —Is this the reward of the god, to give unfortunate
me, who sits like the lame and the blind at the entrance to the
temple of music and begs from those who enter, to give me
ears which themselves present what they hear? Only those two
violin strains—for now I hear nothing more. Just as in that immortal overture they spring forth from the deep choral tones,
so here they leap at me out of the street noise and tumult with
the total surprise of a revelation. It must be close by, for now
I hear his light dance again. Those passing by probably think I
have lost my mind; I imagine that my face looks like a question
mark, asking: Don't you hear anything? Answer: I beg your
pardon? —There is of, course, a confounded racket. —Now I
see them: So it is to you, you two unfortunate artists, I owe
this surprise! —One was probably seventeen years old, wearing a green Kalmuk coat with large bone buttons; the coat itself was too large for him. He held the violin tightly under his
chin; his cap was pulled down over his eyes; his hand was concealed in a fingerless glove, and his fingers were red and blue
with cold. The other one was older and wore a chenille coat.
Both were blind. A litte girl, who presumably guided them,
stood in front of them and thrust her hands under her scarf. We
gathered one by one, a few admirers of those melodies—a
postman with his mailbag, a little boy, a couple of dock workers. The elegant carriages rolled noisily by; the carts and wagons drowned out the melodies, which occasionally emerged
fragmentarily from the engulfing noise.

For me it was a rendezvous.—*JP* III 2790 (*Pap.* III B 179:34)
n.d., 1841-42

From sketch; see 31:27-32:2:

I seem destined to run through all moods; I lie like a child
who is supposed to learn to swim—I scream—this I have
learned from the Greeks—when the support is taken away.—
Pap. III B 128 *n.d.*, 1841-42

From sketch; see 32:18-26:

For me there is nothing more dangerous than to recollect [*erindre*]. As soon as I have recollected a life relationship, it is impossible for me to have any interest in it again. It is said that absence makes the heart grow fonder; well, if in the very same moment the recollection awakens I could return with all love's youthfulness, it is not impossible; if I first have time to experience what I all too often have experienced, that recollection is more richly satisfying than all actuality—then it is all over. Then such a life relationship has already passed into eternity and has no temporal interest.—*Pap.* III B 179:46 *n.d.*, 1841-42

From sketch; see 32:27-33:12:

III
B 179:47
201
III
B 179:47
202

If anyone should keep a diary, I am the one. It frequently happens that with the passage of some time I have completely forgotten the reasons that moved me to do this or that, and it is not only trivialities in life but often the most crucial step. Then again it can happen that it suddenly occurs to me why it was, and I then have the great joy of perceiving that I did have good reason for it. I would have this joy far more often and not the opposite pain if I had everything written down; I could then check on it immediately. At times, it no doubt would happen that I could not understand my own reasons. On the whole, a reason is a poor wretch of a thing—if I regard it with all my passion, this reason develops into an enormous necessity that would set heaven and earth in motion; at other times, I walk coldly and proudly by. For example, I have been speculating for some time now about what really was the reason that moved me to resign as a schoolteacher. When I think about it now, it seems to be that such an appointment was just the thing for me. Today was my good day, and the motivating reason really dawned on me with all its convincing power. I had to live next door to another teacher, which was altogether intolerable to me. Add to that the fact that since I above all had to consider myself qualified to be a schoolteacher, I would have everything to fear if I was not eminently successful, and for that reason I considered it most proper to resign my post and seek employment with a traveling theater company. No doubt people think that one should never commit oneself to the art without an inner call as the motivation for it, but this is not correct. If one has a call to it, one always ought to keep away from it.—*Pap.* III B 179:47 *n.d.*, 1841-42

From draft; see 33:27-31:

Now I dive down once again into the depths—and there I hide myself in myself; I envelop myself within myself—
I live on depression.—*Pap.* III B 186 *n.d.*, 1842

From sketch; see 33:32-34:14:

In my life the same thing has happened to me that according to legend happened to Parmeniscus, who in the Trophonean cave lost the ability to laugh but acquired it again on the island of Delos upon seeing a shapeless block that was said to be the image of the goddess Leto. I spent my childhood in the cave of Trophonius and forgot how to laugh or never learned, but when I became an adult, when I opened my eyes and saw actuality, then I started to laugh and have never stopped laughing since that time. So it goes: some people have a happy childhood and become almost anxious about actuality—I am not afraid of actuality but of the unactual, of the kingdom of sighs into which I have peered. Actuality did not give the ideal, but the ideal of which I had a vague notion was an ideal of pain. And is it not indeed ludicrous. (Develop polemic here.)—*Pap.* III B 179:51 *n.d.*, 1841-42

See 34:15-23:

Hero legends are permeated by a very remarkable self-con-tradiction, an utterly naïve lie (which is why these stories are so easily parodied). I shall take only one example from the saga of Hervor and King Heidrek found in Rafn's *Nordiske Kœm-*

II
A 36
34

pehistorier, III. It is not simply forgetfulness of what was said previously which accounts for reporting practically every hero as the strongest etc., but also something of a quite different kind. Thus on p. 8 it tells that Svafurlame gets Tyrfing from the trolls, a sword with the special characteristic that every time it was drawn it would prove fatal to someone; he now proceeds to draw the sword, attacks the trolls, but he does not touch them and consequently should have killed himself. Further along on page 8, where Angantyr is about to do battle with Hialmar, but Odd advises him to let him go instead, because he had a silk shirt with which no steel could make contact (consequently a sword that cuts everything—and on the other hand a shirt that cannot be cut up by any sword).[*] Another contradiction in all such tales is in the conception of the way the warriors live; the stories dwell upon their great courage, passion for fighting, etc., and at the same time portray them most anxiously taking care to have not only good weapons but even enchanted weapons which would give an otherwise wretched warrior the advantage over the proudest warrior.[**] At the same time, in the story about the battle it is overlooked that only one of the warriors had this auxiliary help, and it takes a terribly long time for the victory to be decided—yes, he is just barely victorious. —In this romantic life there is an irony still slumbering in and with its immediacy. — Also related to this is the splendid naïveté in the story about the chain that bound the Fenris wolf; five things that are not to be found in this world are named, and it is said of them: Thus they are not to be found in the world. —Thor, when he is fishing for the Midgaard serpent, thrusts his legs through the boat (no doubt physically impossible) and ends up standing on the bottom of the sea.[112]

II
A 36
35

[*]*In margin:* Similarly in Ørvarodd's Saga, in the third part of *Kæmpehistorier* by Rafn, on p. 118, where he battles with Øgmund and the latter says: I smote your arm, but it was not cut, although I have a *sword that stops at nothing*.

[**]*In margin:* or a costly salve that heals every wound.—*JP*
V 5209 (*Pap.* II A 36) *n.d.*, 1837

From sketch; see 34:15-23:

And so I, while the whole world is unable to bind me,
nevertheless am bound and rage in my chains, and I am bound
with a chain that is unreal and yet is the only thing that can
hold; just as the chain that bound the Fenris wolf was woven
of things that were not (can be developed) and that nevertheless was the only chain that was able to hold this monster—just
so I am bound in the unreal and nevertheless real chains of my
gloomy fancies.—*Pap.* III B 179:52 *n.d.*, 1841-42

From sketch; see 35:13-20:

I should see about being of some use in the world, a man
said to me today. Fine. To a knowledge of the truth I presumably have come, but not to salvation. What, then, should I do?
Communicate my sorrow, my torment, to the world, make
one more contribution to prove how pitiable and wretched
everything is, perhaps discover a new, hitherto undetected
stain [*Plet*] in human life, perhaps become famous thereby, just
like those who discovered spots [*Pletter*] on Jupiter—?
If the treasure I owned were a Pandora-box—would it not
be best for me never to open it?—*Pap.* III B 179:53 *n.d.*, 1841-
42

From sketch; see 35:20-31:

It is not merely general ideas that are recollected in every individual; no, it is also moods that belong to the whole soul and
yet are merely in recollection but by means of this recollection
knit one to a past. Today I sat with little Ludvig on my lap [*defect in ms.*] I told him that I had rented a new [*defect*] described
it to him, emphasizing especially that it was an old-fashioned
sofa that had decided the matter for me, because I have had a

partiality for that time, in the same way as my [*defect*] had told it according to his grandfather. With an unusually intelligent [*defect*] he said that he also longed for those times. Consequently, he recollects through my recollection what I through my father's recollection recollect of my grandfather. And [*defect*] a paradise, a golden time, etc. No, a sofa [*defect*] is something over which to laugh and to cry.—*Pap*. III B 179:55 *n.d.*, 1841–42

Deleted from sketch; see 36:8-12:

I am just like the Lüneburger swine—my thinking is passion. Therefore I am expert at rooting up the truffles I cannot eat myself; like an elephant I cast all the problems behind me, tear them out by the roots, and it goes as fast as if that elephant were running at full speed, but it remains at that . . . . . — *Pap*. III B 123 *n.d.*, 1841–42

From sketch; see 36:13-20:

In vain do I strive to resist. Already early in my life I was seized with a certain anxiety about my life becoming a poet-existence. Indeed, is there anything worse. I resist. In vain I am swept off my feet; I am predestined, and fate laughs at me when it suddenly shows me how everything I had done in defense simply becomes a factor in the poet-existence.—*Pap*. III B 179:56 *n.d.*, 1841–42

Underlined in copy of Either/Or, *I; see 36:13-20:*

In vain do I resist. My foot slips. My life nevertheless remains a poet-existence. Can anything worse be imagined? I am predestined; fate laughs at me when it suddenly shows me *how everything I do to resist becomes a factor in such an existence*.—*JP* V 5630 (*Pap*. IV A 217) *n.d.*, 1843

In margin of copy of Either/Or, I, *see 36:21-37:6:*

In a somewhat changed form, Diogenes Laertius attributes this demonstration to Diogenes, and he also names another as the originating author.—*Pap.* IV A 218 *n.d.*, 1843

From sketch; see 37:7-28:

How dreadful boredom is—how dreadfully boring; I know no stronger expression, no truer one, for like is recognized only by like; would that there were a loftier expression, for then there would still be something to hope, still one movement. There is a picture showing a woman in a harem. It is obviously not night but day; she is resting her head on a pillow around which her arm is bent, her other hand swings limply, her fingers are idle, are not even playing with anything, and yet she probably is not observing the length of time. —Just so do I lie, but the only thing I see is emptiness; the only thing I live on is emptiness, the only thing I move in is emptiness—I do not even suffer pain. —The vulture pecked continually at Prometheus's liver; the poison dripped down continually on Loki. It was at least an interruption, a change, even though monotonous. —I suffer nothing; pain itself has lost its refreshment for me. If I were offered all the glories of the world or all the torments of the world, one would move me no more than the other; I would not turn over to the other side either to attain or avoid. —I am dying death,[113] as the Hebrews say. —Or what could divert me—well, if I managed to see a faithfulness that lasted in life (for lies and cunning and deceit and ingenious ideas: I seek in vain in them for anything surprising). —But my soul's poisonous doubt kills faithfulness midway—my soul is like the Dead Sea, over which no bird is able to fly; when it has come midway, it sinks down in a stupor to death and destruction.—*Pap.* III B 179:58 *n.d.*, 1841-42

III
B 179:58
205

III
B 179:58
206

From sketch; see 37:29-36:

How strange! With what equivocal anxiety about losing and keeping, people nevertheless cling to this life! How often I have considered taking once again a decisive step, compared with which all previous ones were but child's play—to set out on the great voyage of discovery, and as a ship is saluted with a cannonade when it is launched, so I would salute myself. — Or is it perhaps for shrewd economic reasons that I hide a registered bond as a last resort? —If a stone fell down and killed me, it would not alarm me.—*Pap.* III B 179:59 *n.d.*, 1841-42

From sketch; see 38:1-40:6:

III
B 177
189
III
B 177
190

. . . . . that which matters most to me about the whole of *Either/Or* is that it become really evident that the metaphysical meaning that underlies it all leads everything everywhere to the dilemma. The same also underlies the little philosophical essay: tautology as the highest principle of thought, namely, if the principle of contradiction is true (and it is expressed by either/or), it is (alas, but how many will understand it) the scientific expression for it, and it is the only unity into which it can be taken up and by which the system becomes possible. It would, therefore, not be esthetically correct to write a treatise on the principle of contradiction in this work; no, it is asserted personally—but the same seen from a speculative point of view, if one does not wish to go further, is an idolizing of tautology.—*Pap.* III B 177 *n.d.*, 1842

From sketch; see 38:1-11:

III
B 179:60
206

Tautology regarded as the highest principle in all science, as the only rescue from doubt, the only escape.—it is the supreme *principium cognitionis* [principle of cognition], *das höchste Denkgesetzt* [the supreme law of thought].

> its scientific expression is *idem per idem*
> [the same by the same]
> it is not as poor as one thinks
> > it has the jesting manner the witty
> > > it is infinite in judgments

the serious scientific and edifying
> when two quantities are equal in size to
> one and the same third they are all of equal size
> quantitative conclusions
> this is useful on podiums as well as
> in pulpits, where one says much
> without saying anything.
>> —*Pap*. III B 179:60 *n.d.*, 1841–42

In margin of copy of Either/Or, *I; see 38:1-2:*

*Stilpo of the Megara school of philosophy has already formulated this.—*Pap* IV A 219 *n.d.*, 1843

See 38:12:17:

My journey through life is so unsteady because in my early youth my forelegs (expectations etc.) were weakened by being overstrained.—*JP* V 5401 (*Pap*. II A 510) July 22, 1839

From sketch; see 38:18-40:6:

"Either/Or" is a talisman with which the whole world can be demolished.—*JP* I 756 (Pap. III B 179:27) *n.d.*, 1842

From sketch; see 38:18-40:6:

These words Either/Or are a double-edged dagger I carry with me and with which I can assassinate the whole of actuality [*Virkelighed*]. I just say: Either/Or. Either it is this or it is that; since nothing in life is either this or that, it does not, of course, exist. I have watched conjurers do their acts, heard them explain it, seen the crowd amazed, but all the same I have done far more singular things with my magic formula. One can explain everything away—indeed, one can help oneself superbly. That is, a person always lives in such a way that he has a few elements of everything in himself; thus no devil can make him out: either he is a deceiver, and there are some indications of that, or he is not, and there is some evidence of that—ergo, he does not exist at all. That is: ergo, we let him stand, as the peasant said of the Round Tower.—*Pap*. III B 179:62 *n.d.*, 1841-42

See 38:18-40:6:

III
B 179:63
207

From A's Papers
Either/Or

An Ecstatic Discourse

III
B 179:63
208

. . . seek wisdom, and you will regret it; shun wisdom, and you will regret it; seek wisdom or shun it, you will regret it either way; whether you seek wisdom or you shun it, you will regret it either way. . . .

III
B 179:63
209

My philosophy, therefore, has the advantageous characteristic of being brief and of being irrefutable, for if anyone disputes it, he of course thereby proves that he has not understood it.*

In margin: *Therefore, I have not like some philosophers canceled the principle [*Grundsætning*] of contradiction by going beyond, because, not to speak of the danger involved in such a step, which necessarily must give a frightful start [*Sæt*] and shock in the whole body, something not easily overcome, it is also dubious to have such a subject [*Undersaat*] or, more correctly, two subjects. To be sure, at times one does see someone riding two horses, which in itself is ingenious enough, but I have never seen anyone ride a horse and an ass, or a horse and an elephant. I am victorious over the principle of contradiction, because it cannot reach me.

III
B 179:63
210

It has two sides, length and breadth or, to express myself more concisely, shortness and narrowness. It apparently proceeds from the phenomenon just as I have shown in the first four sentences, but it is apparent, for it is beyond the phenomenon before it proceeds from it; it returns to the phenomenon apparently, for it never reaches it, since the true philosopher is continually *æterno modo* [in the eternal mode] and does not, like Professor Brorson, have only a few hours lived for eternity. — This philosophy is to be recommended also in practical respects, for it has been victorious over the most dangerous enemy, death, for death is obviously tricked when it finds me dead beforehand.—*Pap.* III B 179:63 *n.d.*, 1842-43

See 38:18-40:6:

The universalized interpretation of the particular thesis— Marry or do not marry, you will regret it either way—is, so to speak, the epitome of all the wisdom of life; and the personal relationship a teacher should always have to his pupil is best designated by: May it be to your good [*Velbekomme*]. We cannot, however, say to a person what would otherwise be considered the very best: The best thing for you is to go and hang yourself, for we have to say: Hang yourself or do not hang yourself, you will regret it either way.—*JP* III 2586 (*Pap.* III A 117) *n.d.*, 1841

In margin of copy of Either/Or, *I; see 38:20-21:*

. . . . . these words are ascribed to Socrates by Diogenes Laertius.—*Pap.* IV A 220 *n.d.*, 1843

From sketch; see 40:7-14:

One buries one's relative, rides out in a coach, rides home again in a coach—is anything more ridiculous to be imagined! For that reason alone I could wish to have died as a baby, especially if I were born in Nyboder. Then the father takes the baby in a little casket under his arm, goes out to the cemetery himself on a Sunday morning, is himself priest, gravedigger, mourner, etc.—*Pap.* III B 179:64 *n.d.*, 1842-43

From sketch; see 40:15-35:

Each one takes his own revenge on the world. I get mine by carrying my sorrows and afflictions shut up deep inside me while the laughter entertains everybody. If I see anyone suffering, I am sorry for him, console him as well as I can, listen calmly when he assures me "that *I* am happy." If I can keep on doing this until I die, I will be avenged.—*JP* V 5258 (*Pap*. II A 649) *n.d.*, 1837

From sketch; see 40:15-35:

I engage in all sorts of activities with the greatest zeal. Then when I, often by working at night, have brought it to the point that I know I can achieve just as much as the best, I stop achieving anything. Then when I hear others lauded for their achievements, I laugh, for I despise people and I take my revenge. When I see myself held in contempt, set aside, disregarded because I can do nothing, I laugh, for I despise people and take my revenge.—*Pap*. III B 179:66 *n.d.*, 1841-42

From sketch; see 41:1-5:

My misfortune is this: an angel of death always accompanies me, and it is not the doors of the chosen ones that I sprinkle with blood as a sign that he is to pass by, but it is precisely the doors of the chosen ones that lack this sign, and he kills them, for not until they are dead can I really love them.—*Pap*. III B 179:67 *n.d.*, 1841-42

From sketch; see 41:28-42:2:

A wandering musician played the minuet from *Don Giovanni* on a sort of reed pipe (since he was in another courtyard, I could not see what it was), a pharmacist pounded his medicine, and the maid scrubbed in the court* etc., and they did not notice a thing, and perhaps the flutist did not either, and I felt so wonderful.

June 10, 1836

And the groom currying his horse knocked the currycomb against a stone, and from another part of the city came the voice of the shrimp seller.—*JP* V 5144 (*Pap.* I A 169) June 10, 1836

From sketch; see 42:9-20:

And my sorrow is my baronial castle; like an eagle's nest between the clouds, it lies high up in the mountains, and no one as yet has dared to come near it. And so I swoop down into actuality and snatch my prey, but I do not stay there. I take an impression of it and weave it into the tapestries in my castle, and there I live as one already dead. And what happened yesterday is for me as if it were a 1,000 years ago, for one day is for me as 1,000 years, and this one day I use to drop between today and the day before yesterday. It is oblivion, not for forgetting, but a baptism of oblivion unto an eternal life. I have forgotten everything finite in it and remember the infinite, and up there I live like Ossian in recollections of a previous time, among old acquaintances. —And an old gray-haired man, pensive, sits and recounts in a soft voice, almost whispering, and I listen, but this man is myself.—*Pap.* III B 179:70 *n.d.*, 1841-42

On chapter title page in copy of Either/Or, I; *see 45:*

What Homer says of music is true: οἴο ακούουε, ουδε τι ιδόυε [we only hear, we know nothing]. *Iliad*, II, 486. One hears it, but one does not know, does not understand it.

See Longinus in my edition,[114] p. xxxvi., note.—*JP* I 147 (*Pap.* IV A 222) *n.d.*, 1843

On chapter title page in copy of Either/Or, *I; see 45:*

An actual love affair could not be used in the first part, for it always affects a man so profoundly that he enters into the ethical. What I could use was a variety of erotic moods. I let these link themselves to Mozart's *Don Giovanni*. Essentially they belong in the world of fantasy and find their satisfaction in music. In such a situation a girl is much too little, precisely because she is infinitely much more.—*JP* V 5632 (*Pap*. IV A 223) *n.d.*, 1843

Deleted from final draft; see 47:14:

. . . . . and actually is only a kind of despair
—*Pap*. III B 172:1 June 13, 1842

Underlined in copy of Either/Or, *I; see 49:4-9:*

Immortal Mozart! You to whom I owe everything—to whom I owe *that I lost my mind.*

this is no mere phrase; it is an expression for the wild depression of fantasy, which at the next moment manifests itself as quiet depression and thus alternates.—*JP* III 2781 (*Pap*. IV A 224) *n.d.*, 1843

See 53:23-54:17:

When certain people maintain that they have gone beyond Hegel, it must be regarded at best as a bold metaphor, by which they are trying to express and illustrate the thoroughness with which they have studied him, to describe the terrific running start they have made to get into his thought—and with their momentum they have not been able to stop but have gone beyond him.—*JP* II 1573 (*Pap*. II A 260) September 12, 1838

See 75:14-85:23:

Something about the Page in "Figaro,"
Papageno in "The Magic Flute,"
and Don Giovanni

I
C 125
303

Tonight for the first time I shall see *The Magic Flute.* It has occurred to me that it might have significance with respect to Don Giovanni and might fill out a stage between him and the Page in *Figaro.* I am of the opinion that in these three stages Mozart has perfected and perfectly presented a development of love on the level of immediacy.

I
C 125
304

(1) The Page in *Figaro* is the first level in the development. This is the level of undefined, awakening desire in an unconscious conflict with the environment: it is a play of colors from which gradually there develops a pure color: it is the level not of a given *I* but of the becoming *I* with its searching feelers. Just as all coming into existence [*Tilblivelse*] is a polemic, so also is life itself: on the first level [it is] not conscious but is a continual approximation toward consciousness. It identifies itself in a way with the world (the child's "me"),[115] but precisely because it is a life, a development, precisely for that reason there is an endless approach toward definite conscious desire, yet without its thereby appearing as a final factor, since it rather comes all at once as a new point of departure and cannot be explained by everything that has happened previously. All the abundance of life and the full range in which it is to move on the different levels of its development are given: the whole horizon of life with all its variety is given (but simply because the *I* is not given, the question could perhaps arise as a conclusion at the highest stage of approximation: Why did one not see the earth, which after all is also a celestial body in the heavens)—therefore, like the plant imprisoned at one spot, it exhales its longing, sheds forth the fragrance of its desire, but the longing and desire are not so definite that they wrench him from the earth in order to find what is sought after. On the contrary, it seems as if the objects of his desiring glide past him

in great numbers, and when he wants to grasp at a particular
one and at the same time leave it alone, it is not because it disappears before him—in such a case his desire would either be
so intense that it would suddenly wrench him loose from the
earth in which he sprouted or else he would follow the vanishing object of desire with the yearning gaze of Ingeborg—but
because something just as glorious and beautiful appears that
very moment, something which, as it too vanishes, is succeeded by something equally glorious and beautiful etc.—and
this again is not because everything in all the fully developed
abundance is equally beautiful, but because the individual at
this point has not detached himself and therefore cannot actually establish any criterion, not even that of the plant that
closes up in bad weather or at a profane touch (because the
plant does not have desire in this sense). —And how could I
better express this than to recall the Page's rapture over every
girl he sees along the way; indeed, he even reacts the same way
to old Dr. Bartholo's housekeeper. From the foregoing, the
basis of what is distinctive in the melancholy of this level
should be evident, that it arises because the whole fullness of
life presses down and, so to speak, overwhelms one; whereas
the melancholy of another level (the romantic) can express itself, inasmuch as the individual, pursuing his vanishing object,
is as if brought to a standstill by what it would call the poor,
prosaic world.

That which is not taken up into the idea is the accidental and
unessential, which results from the reception of a foreign ad-
ditive when it [the idea] is represented in a particular personality. This is the case with the Page, in that, so it seems, he is
deeply *forliebt* [infatuated] with the Countess, but this is accounted for in part by what I have just emphasized, and in part
by the fact that the Page in *Figaro* has gone a little beyond the
very middle point of that stage, and in this way a glimpse of
one side of the third stage is seen. —So it is in Papageno's duet
in the fourth act, which shows that Mozart has filled out Papageno's position with inner consciousness. (Perhaps all his

I
C 125
305

wanderings were for that purpose? Silence is imposed upon him, a sojourn with Isis and Osiris, where the flightiness must settle down.) Instead of the first and second stages being rounded out in the third stage as in Don Giovanni, Mozart has an individual at this point arrive at gratification. The Page's infatuation is to be interpreted in the same way, although it is not so obvious there.

I
C 125
306

Note: In the awakening of the Page's love is there not something unbeautiful with respect to the as yet undeveloped sensuousness? May this perhaps be explained as being more natural in Italian life?

But the longing becomes more definite or, more correctly, by means of a contradiction (a continuous desire and an all too great gratification that is still not gratification), the first stage must move into the second stage. The longing detaches itself from the home soil and takes to wandering. The heart beats faster, the objects appear and disappear more rapidly, but still before every disappearance there is an instant [*et Nu*] of pleasure, brief but happy, gleaming like a firefly, inconstant and fleeting as a butterfly, countless kisses, but so hurriedly enjoyed, as if he tore them away from one girl in order to give them to the next one, and yet with occasional darts of desire for a deeper satisfaction, which, however, never gets time to take form as such.*

(2) Papageno in *The Magic Flute*.** This is the second stage, just as the perpendicular direction of plant life is superseded by the horizontality of locomotion. Melancholy does not take form at all as on the previous level, because the desire following upon the pleasure is satisfied at once by a new pleasure—even though not completely (see above) yet in such a way that the remaining desire is again gratified by a new pleasure—even though not completely—and so on and on endlessly. It is not the melancholy stare, itself fixed, as it were, that seemingly

I
C 125

---

*It is the level found in plants with the male and female on the same stem.

**Skjærvæk in *Apothekeren og Doctoren*[116] is somewhat analogous to Papageno.

cannot forget the past object upon the presentation of the new—and so on endlessly; it is like the concentration of the soul in the eyes all at once for an instant—a single object—and then concentrating on the next, and so on endlessly, but yet in such a way that the full concentration does not take place because almost at the same instant a new pleasure presents itself.

(3) Now we approach the third stage, Don Giovanni, who is the unity of both stages and is the final stage of the development of immediacy (by calling it immediacy, I wish to indicate that as striving it has not yet reached consciousness of its relation to the world, but magnetically seeks its gratification). This stage is a unity of the two previous ones, in that the deep, infinitely melancholy draining of the whole fullness of love (like the horn from which Thor drank at Loki's, the horn with its tip in the ocean)[117] is united on one side with the exuberant variety, and therefore all the striving is infinite in intensity as well as in extensity and thus in constant contradiction with itself.[*] Moreover, I do not believe that the first aspect (intensity) is sufficiently emphasized in the adaptations we have of Don Juan, although significant clues in this respect are found, of course, in Mozart.

Just one more observation: naturally, all three stages, being immediate, are purely musical,** and any attempt in another presentation is likely to endow them with far too much consciousness.

(Note: does not the more mediated love-life begin in Faust, insofar as he reproduces Don Juan?)

Thursday afternoon, January 26, 1837

[*]*In margin*: Through this contradiction appears the significance of married life—debauchery (for there can be no question of this in the first stage).

In margin: **I mean, specifically, that the immediate (lyrical) level is completed through a steady ascent in music (prose—immediate musical verse—reflective musical verse—music). All the reflections about this are so sparse, because it is by far an *einfachere* [simpler] medium for one's expression. The significance of music in the treatment of the insane. Music completes the immediate level, just as actions another, concepts another.— —*JP* IV 4397 (*Pap.* I C 125) January 26, 1837

See 90:34-91:14:

The World-Famous
Master of the Black Arts
and
Sorcerer

Doctor
Johan Faust,

and

the Pact He Made with the Devil,
His Amazing Life and
Horrible Death
[*woodcut of bust*]

Copenhagen.

On Sale at 107 Ulkegaden. . . .
—*JP* V 5168 (*Pap.* I C 107) *n.d.*, 1836

See 99:16-22:

*During this time I have read various things by A. v. Arnim,
among others "Armuth, Reichthum, Schuld und Busse der Gräfinn
Dolores."* 2 volumes.[118]
II, p. 21, where he speaks of her seducer . . .
—*JP* V 5221 (*Pap.* II A 70) May 16, 1837

From final draft; see 105:34-36:

Prof. Hauch has also produced a D. J. It is less related to
Molière and is on the verge of falling within the category of the
interesting. We shall see later how successful the poet was.—
Pap. III B 172:2 *n.d.*, 1842

See 110:2-111:25:

It is strange to note the naïveté with which the legend given here treats Faust's relation to Mephistopheles. The inability to rise to the conception of absolute mastery over nature's powers, riches, glory, etc., is constantly manifest, and for that reason Faust is allowed to get into many scrapes, gets hold of money in all kinds of ways, accepts bribes, etc., but this of course is not conceived humorously (as it was in a certain sense in the case, for example, of Molière's *Don Juan* and, if I am not mistaken, Heiberg's *Don Juan*; the humor lies precisely in seeing a hero like that in such a scrape). Inasmuch as the folk-consciousness has been unable to detach itself from life's barriers, to that extent its position is a kind of humorous commentary on the folk-consciousness itself, which, wanting to understand such a striving, has been unable to understand it clearly.—*JP* V 5170 (*Pap.* I C 109) October 29, 1836

See 121:6:

Elvira (in *Don Giovanni*) is not really a character; she lacks the required definite and more explicit contours; she is a transparent, diaphanous figure, through which we see the finger of God, providence, which in a way mitigates the impression of the all too vindictive nemesis in the Commendatore, because it continually opens for D. G. the possibility of escaping it. Elvira is all too ethereal for a character; she is like the fairy maidens who have no back.—*JP* III 2785 (*Pap.* I A 240) September 13, 1836

See 122:27-33:

Actually, the important thing in reasoning is the ability to see the part within the whole. Most people never actually enjoy a tragedy; it falls into separate pieces for them—nothing but monologues—and an opera into arias etc. The same sort of thing happens in the physical world if, for example, I walked along a road parallel to two other roads with interspersed strips of ground; most people would only see the road, the strip of ground, and then the road, but would be unable to see the whole as being like a piece of striped cloth.—*JP* II 2245 (*Pap*. I A 111) January 7, 1836

From final draft; see 130:13:

. . . . . It is something that rarely happens; here it is completely as it should be and throws a new light on the structure of the overture. The overture seeks to stoop to find footing in the scenic actuality; the Commendatore and D. G. have already been heard in the overture; next to them, Leporello is the most important figure. He, however, cannot be elevated up into that battle in the atmosphere, and yet he belongs to that more than anyone else does. Therefore, the piece begins with him in such a way that he stands in immediate connection with the overture.—*Pap*. III B 172:3 *n.d.*, 1842

From final draft; see 135:12, end:

June 13, '42
—*Pap*. III B 172:4

See 137:4:

I was just searching for an expression to designate the kind of people I would like to write for, convinced that they would share my views, and now I find it in Lucian: παϱάνεϰϱοί.[119] (one who like me is dead), and I would like to issue a publication for παϱάνεϰϱοί.—*JP* 5295 (*Pap*. II A 690) January 9, 1838

In margin of copy of Either/Or, I; *see 137:4:*

I perhaps could also have called these Πεισιθάνατοι [persuaders of suicide] and thereby called to mind the nickname the Cyrenaic Hegesias[120] was given because he spoke so excellently about the wretchedness of life. (See Tennemann, *Gesch. d. Phil.*,[121] II, p. 106.)—*Pap*. IV A 225 *n.d.*, 1843

From sketch; see 141:4-25:

I must include hypochondria in "Either/Or" in order always to characterize the isolated elements in isolated subjectivity. This I should like to do in "Either/Or"—and then mediate in B's papers in part two.—*JP* V 5549 (*Pap.* III B 130) *n.d.,* 1842

See 144:32-33:

There are several absolutely wonderful great ideas in Grabbe's *Don Juan*, each one of which shoots up suddenly like an enormous spruce and stands before us.—*JP* V 5315 (*Pap.* II A 733) *n.d.,* 1838

Deleted from sketch; see 148:5-16:

A child's sorrow when it sees an adult suffer is deeper than an adult's; its pain is less—nature has boundlessly deep sorrow—no pain, this with respect to the spectator

Sorrow is a substantial qualification—pain a reflective—*Pap.* III B 124 *n.d.,* 1841-42

Deleted from margin of final draft; see 149:20-22:

In a certain sense it is now very correct, for by means of an everlasting "Go to the next house"[122] one attains no substantial qualification, and it would indeed be making oneself a fool if one were to seek the author of the guilt through seventeen ancestors *ins Blaue hinein* [in the distant past].—*Pap.* III B 132:2 *n.d.,* 1841-42

See 151:12-22:

As well as being interesting, *Philoctetes* borders on being drama. Philoctetes' mounting bitterness and the progressive self-contradiction in his behavior connected with it are profoundly true psychologically, but the whole thing is not classical.—*JP* V 5547 (*Pap.* III C 40) *n.d.,* 1841-42

See 151:14-22:

In *Philoctetes* even the situation itself is reflective, ll. 878, 879.—*Pap*. III C 39 *n.d.*, 1841-42

From sketch; see 153:13:14:

She wears sorrow and not just the apparel of sorrow—*Pap*. III B 83 *n.d.*, 1841-42

See 153:33:

I must get at my Antigone again. The task is a psychological development and motivation of the presentiment of guilt. With that in mind I have been thinking of Solomon and David, of the relation of Solomon's youth to David, for no doubt both Solomon's good sense (dominant in the relationship) and his sensuality are the results of David's greatness. He had had earlier intimations of David's deep agitation without realizing what guilt might rest upon him, and yet he had seen this profoundly God-fearing man give such an ethical expression to his repentance, but it would have been a quite different matter if David had been a mystic. These ideas, these presentiments, smother energies (except in the form of imagination), evoke reflection, and this combination of imagination and reflection, where the factor of the will is lacking, is sensuality proper.— *JP* V 5669 (*Pap*. IV A 114) *n.d.*, 1843

See 153:36:

No doubt I could bring my Antigone to an end if I let her be a man. He forsook his beloved because he could not keep her together with his private agony. In order to do it right, he had to turn his whole love into a deception against her, for otherwise she would have participated in his suffering in an utterly unjustifiable way. This outrage enraged the family: a brother, for example, stepped forward as an avenger; I would then have my hero fall in a duel.—*JP* V 5569 (*Pap*. III A 207) November 20, 1842

See 154:14-155:11:

It is very remarkable that the wrath of the gods pursues the family of Labdakos; it is evident in Oedipus' fate; the daughters of his unhappy marriage are Antigone and Ismene. As we see, however, Antigone is engaged to Creon's son. The family develops very tranquilly. This is Greek tragedy. Romantic tragedy could be joined to it if, for example, I had Antigone fall in love with all the energy of love, but in order to halt the vengeance of the gods she would not get married, she would regard herself as a sacrifice to the wrath of the gods because she belonged to the family of Oedipus, but she would not leave behind any family that could again become the object for the angry gods' persecution.—*JP* V 5546 (*Pap*. III C 37) *n.d.*, 1841–42

Deleted from margin of final draft; see 155:11-17:

As for the meaning of anxiety and its characteristic tragic element, there are several notes [*Pap*. II A 585] that apply to this in the little oblong book in my desk, illustrations taken from hero tales.—*Pap*. III B 132:3 *n.d.*, 1842.

See 155:24-29:

For something to be really depressing, there must develop first of all, in the midst of all possible favors, a presentiment that it might just be all wrong; one does not oneself become conscious of anything very wrong, but it must lie in the familial context; then original sin displays its consuming power, which can grow into despair and have a far more frightful effect than the particular whereby the truth of the presentiment is verified. This is why Hamlet is so tragic. This is why Robert le diable, driven by a disquieting presentiment,* asks how it could ever be that he does so much evil. —The blessing is changed into a curse. —It is an extremely poetic governance that makes the girl dumb, she who alone can comprehend what is behind Robert le diable's assumed madness (his penance).

*When Høgne, whom his mother had
conceived with a troll, sees his image in the water, he
asks her why his body is shaped that way.
See *Nordiske Kæmpehistorier* by Rafn,
II, p. 242.
                    —*JP* IV 3999 (*Pap*. II A 584) *n.d*., 1837

From sketch; see 156:32-157:7:

The fruit of sorrow in the bowls of pain, silver fruit in
golden bowls—a trousseau that is not destroyed by time—she
is, so to speak, marriageable
   Allow me now to invite your interest—*Pap*. III B 129 *n.d*.,
1841-42

From sketch:

. . . . . this clinging to life is genuinely Greek—therefore,
when someone is willing to sacrifice himself for the other, the
Greek is content with it and does not know the hollow reflection that does not want to permit it.—*Pap*. III B 125 *n.d*., 1841-
42

From sketch; see 157:32-158:6:

Woman's destiny is to be a bride—this expresses that she
lacks something—a similar expression is to hide a secret; she is
a mother; it stirs under her breast
            —God's bride, the analogy in the esthetic
      silence
                    —*Pap*. III B 126 *n.d*., 1841-42

From final draft; see 162:30:

I am not very interested in the nature of the person with
whom she is in love; I am interested only in my Antigone. She
is in love—indeed she is; I say it with pain—she is head over
heels in love.—*Pap*. III B 132:4 *n.d*., 1842

Deleted from sketch; see 164:21-28:

I feel that my life must soon end—it goes with me as with Epaminondas after the battle at Mantinea; my secret is an arrow sticking in my heart; as long as it remains sticking there I can no doubt live, but as soon as I pull it out, I must die. Now I have revealed myself; now I must die.—*Pap.* III B 179:40 *n.d.*, 1841-42

Deleted from sketch; see 164:31-37:

And just as it went with Hercules, so it goes with me. It was predicted to him that he would not be murdered by a living person but by a dead one; thus, the recollection of her murders me.—*Pap.* III B 179:41 *n.d.*, 1841-42

From final draft; see 164, end:

> January 30, '42.
> —*Pap.* III B 132:5

From final draft; see 165:1-2:

> Psychological Diversion [*changed from:*
> Venture (*Forsøg*) in the Black Arts].
> —*Pap.* III B 173:1 *n.d.*, 1842

See 166:5-10:

A Spanish Song	(Lessing, vol. XVII, p. 281
Gestern liebt ich,	[Yesterday I loved,
Heute leid' ich,	Today I suffer,
Morgen sterb' ich,	Tomorrow I die,
Dennoch denk' ich,	Yet, today and tomorrow,
Heut' und morgen,	I like to think
Gern an gestern	Of yesterday].

> —*JP* II 2369 (*Pap.* III A 200) *n.d.*, 1842

See 203:27-34:

Lines of a Girl Who Has Been Seduced
. . . . . spare me your pity—you understand neither my
sorrow nor my joy—I still love him so much that I have but
one wish: to be young again in order to be seduced by him
once again.—*JP* V 5498 (*Pap.* III A 116) *n.d.*, 1841

From final draft; see 215, end:

July 25, '42
—*Pap.* III B 173:2

See 219:1-5:

Somewhere in England there is a gravestone with only these
words on it: The Unhappiest One. I can imagine that someone
would read it and think that no one at all lies buried there but
that it was destined for him.—*JP* V 5447 (*Pap.* III A 40) *n.d.*,
1840

From final draft; see 227:1-4:

Let us with hushed voice sing out the scale of unhappiness;
each note is in itself precise and brief, and yet constantly without interruption it sounds in life's perpetual repetition.—*Pap.*
III B 174:1 *n.d.*, 1842

From final draft; see 228:24:

. . . . . but his ardor was not a smoke that rises freely toward heaven but was pressed down.—*Pap.* III B 174:2 *n.d.*,
1842

Underlined in copy of Either/Or, I; *see 230:18-21:*
But what am I saying—"the unhappiest"? I ought to say
"the happiest," *for this is indeed precisely a gift of fortune that no
one can give himself.*
Addition: One may think that this exclamation "the unhap-

piest one is the happiest" is a rhetorical turn. By no means, it is a turn in the thought; for to be the unhappiest person is actually a gift that no one can give himself. I may be able to make myself the guiltiest of persons, but in the esthetic sense I cannot make myself into the unhappiest—the contrast is found in Part II, p. 246, at the bottom of the page, "if I dared to call myself the greatest tragic hero," which I cannot possibly make myself, since that involves an element of fate.—*Pap.* IV A 227 *n.d.*, 1843

From final draft; see 232:1-3:

This review was planned to be the first esthetic article in a periodical I had planned to publish at unspecified times. Ah, but what are all human plans!—*Pap.* III B 40 *n.d.*, 1841

From sketch; see 242:1-243-9:

A scene or two may also be taken from the theater. —The moment the curtain rises, when the chandelier slowly rises and in farewell once again throws light on the young girls in the first balcony.—*Pap.* III B 95 *n.d.*, 1841-42

See 260:17:19:

Previously the tendency was to make fractional men out of human beings; today they are changed into an abstraction. Everybody looks exactly alike ("venturesome, sensitive, enthusiastic Danes"), and now it becomes easy for a Wehmaler to come forward and paint Hungarian and Danish national facial types, portraits that are painted before seeing the individual. Everything is directed toward getting everyone a national physiognomy, just as one has a national costume.—*JP* I 1967 (*Pap.* I A 337) *n.d.*, 1836-37

From draft; see 286:36-38:

Instead of increasing the debt, they want to pay it off and even do it all at once. The state is heading for disaster, that is clear; if it survives the next consultative assembly, it will assuredly receive its death wound!

In margin: Everything retrogresses; even the theater is changed for the intelligent by its striving to be not only for pleasure, an alarming tendency toward the other side.—*Pap.* III B 122:1 *n.d.*, 1841-42

From draft; see 287:21-38:

All the artists from Paris, London, America would stream here; in all probability the Queen of England and the Emperor of Russia would come also. I propose that we kidnap one of these majesties beloved of their people and release them for enormous sums of money. What would they do to us? Denmark is the happiest country in all Europe. It holds the balance of power; it is a secret.—*Pap.* III B 122:2 *n.d.*, 1841-42

From draft; see 288:37-38:

This class of animals I believe actually results from a *generatio æquivoca* [spontaneous generation]; they do not even have the privileged marriage-bed sultriness to thank for their origin; even less are they the fruit of man's appetite and woman's desire. This accounts for the widespread folk-saying that the stork brings babies. The stork as a rule stays in swampy, marshy areas, and what can such areas produce except torpid, useful creatures, whose torpidity is demonstrated especially by their busyness.—*Pap.* III B 122:3 *n.d.*, 1841-42

From draft; see 290:17-19:

. . . . . it is found especially among Englishmen—(it can be described in a few lines.—)—*Pap.* III B 122:4 *n.d.*, 1841-42

From draft; see 291:10-13:

. . . . . the nothing from which God creates, the nothing the devil chews on in vain, the nothing—*Pap.* III B 122:5 *n.d.*, 1841-42

From draft; see 291:34-292:9:

Most people attempt this by traveling*—one is *europamüde* [weary of Europe] and goes to America—or by another kind of extensity, for example, Nero, by burning Rome**

In margin: *With regard to boredom, they do what according to Horace the merchant does with regard to poverty and with the same restlessness, as the verse so excellently depicts: *per mare pauperiem fugiens per saxa per ignes* [fleeing poverty through sea, through rocks, through flames].[123]

In margin: **The great emperor Anthony was wise in an entirely different way. He says: Restoration to life is in your power; look at things in another way than you have looked at them until now, for in this consists the restoration to life.

see *ad se ipsum*, translation, VII, 2, end.[124]

—*Pap*. III B 122:6 *n.d.*, 1841-42

In margin of draft; see 292:19:

. . . . . it is a durability similar to the durability of cloth in the old days, when it was not unheard of to have a dress coat turned three times.—*Pap*. III B 122:7 *n.d.*, 1841-42

From draft; see 292:24-26:

. . . . . I shall not speak of more important things, for example, when a pretty girl lives right across the street and sometimes appears at the window. What a meticulous observer one becomes then; the least little expression does not escape one, and while here the external change is very slight, the greater is the change one can experience in oneself, and this little externality continually reflects itself in it.—*Pap*. III B 122:8 *n.d.*, 1841-42

In margin of draft; see 293:5-7:

Recollection is in every way to be preferred to hope; in recollection a person is sure. He can always turn back to it; he can let it explain itself to him.—*Pap*. III B 122:9 *n.d.*, 1841-42

From draft; see 295:5-10:

The Archimedean point from which one lifts the world. Forgetting possesses the same as recollecting, somewhat as the stage in darkness exhibits the same as the stage when it is illuminated.—*Pap.* III B 122:10 *n.d.*, 1841-42

From draft; see 295:11-13:

Consequently, it is the law for all rotation, the movement between forgetting and recollecting. The person who has become a virtuoso in this art has around the breast that triple copper that Horace speaks of, that he had who first ventured out upon the sea in a boat.[125] And to what indeed can the art of living be better compared than to the art of navigation.—

In order, however, to keep this current continually fresh, one must make sure not to get stuck in any single life relationship.—*Pap.* III B 122:11 *n.d.*, 1841-42

From draft; see 295:14-16:

Guard, therefore, against *friendship*. What is a friend? A friend is not what the philosophers call the necessary other but the superfluous other.

N.B. At this point comes a polemic that I have essentially ready in the red book at home.—*Pap.* III B 122:12 *n.d.*, 1841-42

See 295:14-16:

. . . . . A friend is not what we philosophers call the necessary other but the superfluous other.—*JP* II 1282 (*Pap.* III A 119) *n.d.*, 1841

From draft; see 295:30-34:

. . . . . help a man up from the gutter, raise the hat respectfully to each other, be the humble servant to each other etc.— one thinks it is pride to learn this point of view—on the contrary, it is humility, whereas it is pride to fancy that one ac-

tually can be something for another person.—*Pap*. III B 122:13
n.d., 1841-42

In margin of draft; see 295:35-36:

Faithless men of that sort are often described by the faithful
as negative, while they fancy themselves to be positive. This
can indeed be granted them. Portable organs [*Positiver*] they
are, at least barrel organs, but of all instruments they are also
the most boring to play.—*Pap*. III B 122:14 *n.d.*, 1841-42

From draft; see 296:21:

Stay clear of **marriage**. Of all ludicrous things, marriage is
the most ludicrous. Add to this what is most doubtful of all,
that it has intrinsic ethical qualifications.—*Pap*. III B 122:15
n.d., 1841-42

See 296:22-28:

Many people are afraid of eternity—if we can only endure
time, certainly we can cope with eternity. Therefore when one
hears the lovers swear mutual love for all eternity, it does not
mean nearly as much as when they pledge love for time, because one who pledges love for eternity can always answer:
You will have to excuse me for time.—*JP* I 835 (*Pap*. III A 124)
n.d., 1841

From draft; see 297:11-28:

For marrying, I have no time, for having children, even less.
Everything would depend upon whether two persons actually could become one, but I shall have to think about that
first. If it were such an easy matter, then why all the moral earnestness with which marriage is saturated. Nature is able to do
it, but since nature is temporality subject to a sequence, this
unity is only momentary. Moreover, very soon an unsettled
account comes between the happy married couple, if nothing
else, then children, two, three, etc. according to time and op-

portunity, which now the couple quite inconsistently regard as a great good fortune, without considering that the unity is more and more endangered. One also sees the ludicrousness implicit in family life in the solidarity with which families seek to create a phalanx against the mockers, therefore the avidity and greediness with which they grasp at every engagement and seek by all kinds of shock methods to prevent a backsliding.

But if it is impossible to become one in marriage, then neither can one stroll about on highways and byways. If one has a wife, it is difficult, although there are examples of gypsy women who have carried their husbands on their backs—and yet this will not do. If one has a wife and perhaps children, it is even more difficult; if one has a wife and children, it is impossible. It is all very fine to walk with someone on one's arm, but it must always be a casual relationship, not—what a dreadful thought!—a *lebenslänglich* [life-long] one.

And if it were possible to become one in marriage, then of course there would be the danger that the husband would have to lie in confinement, as is indeed the custom in some societies.

As a married man, one is subjected to the whole bourgeois atmosphere, new customs.—*Pap.* III B 122:16 *n.d.* 1841-42

From draft; see 297:29-35:

Nothing corrupts a man more than falling in love. Take a young man, spirited as an Arabian horse; let him fall in love and he is lost. At the outset, the woman is proud, later she is weak, then she cries, then he cries with her, and then the family blubbering is in full swing. Thereupon the poets and married men come forward and say: Ah, no one can love like a woman, which is true in the same sense as no big dog is as watchful as a little dog, and this is because the little dog is afraid. Only a man is able to love; a woman's love is weakness. And dissimulation, just like the screams of a woman in labor, which according to the doctors are not because of the pain but because she prevents the pain with this scream; therefore one must never believe a woman's scream, and the best thing to do is to let them scream.—*Pap.* III B 122:17 *n.d.*, 1841-42

III
B 122:17
172

III
B 122:17
173

From draft; see 299:9-10:

Teasing is on the whole an excellent means of exploration. Families and certain individuals who in and by themselves are far too soft must be provided with a little stimulation. One ignores them, for example, and then suddenly without any ceremony one returns to the attack. At times one intervenes masculinely in existence, at times femininely.—*Pap.* III B 122:18 *n.d.*, 1841-42

From draft; see 300:8-9:

The eye with which one sees actuality must be changed continually. At times one sees it ideally. It is a divine world in which we live; in that light it becomes especially ludicrous. Or one sees it caricatured. Sometimes one sees it through an infinite magnifying glass, at times through an equally infinitely reducing glass—all in order to have a disturbing effect. One thereby always shocks people, and it is exceedingly laughable to see their expressions.—*Pap.* III B 122:19 *n.d.*, 1841-42

From draft; see 300:22-31:

. . . . . the most insignificant thing can accidentally become worth more than all the well-prepared joys put together. I was walking one day, sunk in my own thoughts, came to a standstill, almost depressed, when as I look up my eyes fall on a sign that says: Role-casting Done Here.[126] The effect was boundless.—*Pap.* III B 122:20 *n.d.*, 1841-42

Underlined in copy of Either/Or, *I; see 301:*

The Seducer's Diary

Addition:
In a review in *Forposten*, I see that it is quite properly pointed out that this narrative is not called a seducer's diary but *the* seducer's, suggesting that the method really is of prime impor-

tance, not the portrayal of either Johannes or Cordelia.—*JP* V
5633 *(Pap.* IV A 231) [March 26], 1843

Deleted from final draft; see 302:1-5:

> sa passione præ*dominante*
> est la principiante
>   from *Don Giovanni* in the second
>   great servant-aria (must
>   be checked)
>   —*Pap.* III B 67 *n.d.*, 1841-42

Deleted from the page preceding the final draft of "The Seducer's Diary"; see 303:14:

In Victor Eremita's preface to "The Seducer's Diary," it
should be remarked: If Denmark had a very cultivated esthetician, I would ask him to answer the question whether he
believes that this work has been produced by a happy or
an unhappy individuality, whether it is on the basis of an
observation of a happy or an unhappy love, whether he was
an extraordinarily faithful or an absolutely faithless person.
—*Pap.* III B 170 *n.d.*, 1842

From final draft; see 304:18:

. . . . . ; no wonder that persons in despair clutch at this last
means of diversion.—*JP* I 806 *(Pap.* III B 45:1) *n.d.*, 1841-42

Deleted from margin of final draft; see 305:24-25:

. . . . . this vampyric tendency of his. Just as the shadows in
the underworld sucked the blood out of the real human beings
and lived so long, so did he.
. . . . . it is shameful to misuse the spirit's flight in order to
serve the flesh; but it will also have its revenge, just as it happened to Bellerophon,[127] who misused Pegasus to visit a
woman and plunged into the sea.—*Pap.* III B 45:2 *n.d.*, 1841

From final draft; see 306:3-27:

III
B 45:3
136

Just as in the theater the same play is often performed on both stages, so these two worlds always relate to each other. That other world has nothing whatsoever that does not appear in the actual world, but the actual world of course does have something or other that does not appear in that world. That other world is a picture of it, yet not artistically executed, but an idealized imprint woven into the delicate, almost invisible fabric of this world, just like the Veronica picture of Christ's face, imprinted in the fine cloth when she wiped the sweat from his face. Now, there are many people who have no eye at all for that world, and in a certain sense one has to be a Sunday's child in order to see it. One does not see in that world everything that appears in the actual world; for example, in that world one always sees only those who themselves see it. It is impossible for another person to detect in it the individual who does not himself see it, for to see and to be seen are identical. Now, if someone sees that world—something that to external observation will ordinarily appear in such a way that it seems as if one did not see it at all—then he will also in that world be able to discover the actual world surrounding him; he will be able to recognize even individuals. [*Deleted:* They all appear as shadows, but some so pale and elusive that it is almost impossible to recognize them; others are more distinctly developed, all in relation to how they see this world. The more they live for actuality, the more faintly they appear in this world; the less, the more they make their appearance in that. The few who are almost palpable actuality appear as shadow pictures with almost three-dimensional effect. These individuals, however, appear in the actual world almost as shadows.]

III
B 45:3
137

But a person's fading away and practically disappearing from actuality can have two bases—it is either a sickness or a soundness, a difference that is also manifest to the person who pays attention to that world. That is, some shadows, although clear and with sharp outlines, appear as pale and faint, indescribably beneficial to the eye, just like the dull work in metals; an even softness is shed over the whole. These are the good ones. Others appear with equally definite outlines, but dark and spiteful; these are the evil.—*Pap.* III B 45:3 *n.d.*, 1841-42

From final draft; see 306:29-307:1:

. . . . . but it is very likely that he, even after she, whom he actually has loved, if I dare use that word about him, has become meaningless to him, that he now is wilder than ever before. Earlier his seduction seems to have been more subtle. His actual practice has been . . . . . —*Pap.* III B 45:4 *n.d.*, 1841-42

Deleted from sketch; see 307:22-308:8:

The Seducer—
either so young that they had only a presentiment of love [*Kjærlighed*]—or an awkward venture in the prosaic erotic— —*Pap.* III B 33 *n.d.*, 1841

From sketch; see 307:22-308:8:

The Seducer and the Seduced

One should not expect to see here a list of seduced girls who have been excluded from human society by the loss of their honor. On the contrary, no change in them was visible to those around them; only he and she knew it; he had infatuated them, knew that they would sacrifice everything for him, and with that he was content—
either they were so young that they only had a presentiment of love [*Kjærlighed*] or daydreamed about love, or he let an outright suitor intervene. When that one had given them a distaste for love, he followed, but he did not speak of love; on the contrary, he did everything to neutralize it, developed the intellectual side for them so that they even became capable of comprehending love ironically. During all this, he maintained a high degree of intellectual superiority. It was as if he were totally insensitive to the sensuous, until suddenly, one single word, a look, like a dagger stab, made them blush; now he

III
B 34
126

III
B 34
127

shared their secret—they felt his superiority and had no one to turn to but him—all sorts of mystifications—*Pap.* III B 34 *n.d.*, 1841

Addition to Pap. IV B 34:

. . . . . and the fact that I love someone is a secret that may be betrayed only in the stillness of the night, may never be repeated to the same person, and woe to the one who would force this admission out of me. This is the crowning moment, and how could it be repeated without sounding like a flagrant parody.—*Pap.* III B 35 *n.d.*, 1841

Deleted from final draft; see 307:37-38:

He was like one of those long-legged spiders—briskly and easily and with shrewd eyes, he hurried across life.—*JP* I 807 (*Pap.* III B 45:5) *n.d.*, 1841-42

From final draft; see 309:30-31:

I once received a letter from her that was written in a smilar frame of mind. I have kept it; it reads as follows:

Deleted from margin: The letter [*Pap.* III B 38] may be found among my papers. I had worked it out before my journey.— *Pap.* III B 45:7 *n.d.*, 1842-43

From sketch; see 309:30-310:11:

Letter from **the one seduced**
—He was sometimes so intellectual that I felt my womanly existence annihilated before him, at times so sensual that I trembled before him, and then when he surrendered to me and I embraced him, held him in my arms, he was gone, and I embraced the cloud—to recollect an expression of his, not as if I did not know this expression before he taught me to know it,

but he has captured me, has taken possession of me so that all my thinking is really of him. . . . —*Pap.* III B 38 *n.d.*, 1841

In margin of draft; see 310:19-28:

In the editor's preface there will be some corresponding ironic reflections on the comic in A's situation, how he is in hot water with the other's secret; there ought to be a bank in which one could deposit secrets.—*Pap.* III 47:1 *n.d.*, 1841-42

From draft; see 310:32-311:16:

. . . . . interleave them according to their stated dates, in order thereby to obtain, if possible, a totality. A cursory inspection already shows me that they more or less correspond to one another as far as the dates are concerned; on the other hand, the contents of the diary and of the letters naturally often completely contradict each other.—*Pap.* III B 47:2 *n.d.*, 1841-42

Deleted from draft; see 311:1:

When I turned over the diary, I found that it had also been written in from the back toward the front. It contained a piece entitled: Woman viewed categorically.—*Pap.* III B 48 *n.d.*, 1841-42

Deleted from margin of Pap. III B 48:

N.B. it is best to make the little investigation into an element in the diary itself.—*Pap.* III B 49 *n.d.*, 1841-42

Deleted from sketch; see 311:26-27; 313:28-315:5:

N.B. It probably would be best to have the so-called *actiones in distans* keep pace in between; that will provide the correct

elucidation and show the nature of his passion.—*Pap*. III B 51
n.d., 1841-42

Deleted from sketch; see 311:26-27; 313:28-315:5:

N.B. The diary must not begin with Cordelia's story but
with the first *actio in distans*, which is in the blue book.
—*Pap*. III B 52 *n.d.*, 1841-42

In margin in copy of Either/Or, *I; see 311:26-27; 313:28-315:5:*
("actiones in distans'"*):

*See p. viii of preface to the volume of Schelling published
by Rosenkrantz in 1843.[128]—*Pap*. IV A 232 *n.d.*, 1843

Deleted from sketch; see 311:30-313:9:

1. N.B. it is best to have three or four letters from Cordelia
to Edward come after the seduction, letters that express her
various moods: She has shown them to me but also has assured
me that she has never been able to decide to send them to him
because she could never make up her mind how she should regard him.

2. Edward [*changed to:* Johannes],
I do not call you "my"; I know very well that you are not. I
call you only my seducer, my enemy, my murderer—I call
myself yours, and just as it once flattered your ears, now it
shall be a curse for all eternity. Flee where you will—I am still
yours, you cannot get rid of me. Indeed, the fact that I use this
bold language demonstrates that I am yours. You have made
yourself guilty of the most dreadful rebellion of all, you have
perverted a human being from a free being to your slave.

3. Edward [*changed to:* Johannes],
The story of the rich man who slaughtered the poor man's
lamb.

4. Edward [*changed to:* Johannes],
Is there no hope for me at all. Will your love for me never

awaken; for you have loved me, that I know, without really being able to explain what makes me sure of it.—*Pap.* III B 50:1-4 *n.d.*, 1841-42

III
B 50:4
140

From final draft: see 313:27:

From The Seducer's Diary. No. 1

In margin: actio in distans [action at a distance].
$\qquad$—*Pap.* III B 68:1 *n.d.*, 1841-42

From final draft; see 316:15-17:

But what engages her attention is indeed multiplicity, yet multiplicity with a certain higher light on it, [*deleted:* for, just like the Christmas season, Christmas gifts also have something ceremonious, a nobility,] which brings them closer to heaven.
In margin: a reflection of earthly pomp and glory.—*Pap.* III B 68:2 *n.d.*, 1841-42

From final draft; see 316:23:

. . . . . vital; it is for the eye what it is for the ear when a little wooded area is hushed and quiet and suddenly a nightingale warbles and the area comes to life.—*Pap.* III B 68:3 *n.d.*, 1841-42

In margin of final draft; see 317:6:

No. 2
$\qquad$—*Pap.* III B 70:1 *n.d.*, 1841-42

From final draft; see 319:12-15:

Consider only my external appearance. They have nothing to fear from me; I not only look like a nice man, but I do not look at all like a cavalier. My figure cannot, of course, make any impression, and does not demand it either; they can easily see on me that I am a thinker accustomed to live in the world of abstraction, and to that a young girl certainly forms a perfect contrast.—*Pap.* III B 70:2 *n.d.*, 1841-42

From final draft; see 319:35:

You disappear—no doubt we shall see each other again, but for a time this handclasp will be a puzzle to you, difficult to reconcile with all the rest of my behavior.—*Pap.* III B 70:3 *n.d.*, 1841-42

From draft; see 319:37-320:1:

Monday, then, one o'clock, at the exhibition. Very good, I shall have the honor. A little rendezvous. I am downright curious, for it was quite dark and I was unable to distinguish the features of any of them. All the better, all the better for my observations. I will show up at half-past twelve.

In margin: No. 3.

—*Pap.* III B 73 *n.d.*, 1841-42

See 325:11-12:

One has achieved tranquillity when, like the *Alcedo ispida* [kingfisher] (ice-bird), one can build one's nest upon the sea.— *JP* I 1023 (*Pap.* II A 612) *n.d.*, 1837

In margin of final draft; see 325:11-12:

. . . . . the name of this bird must be in my excerpts in the oblong book at home—*Pap.* III B 55:1 *n.d.*, 1841-42

From final draft; see 326:4:

. . . . . thus to paddle one's own canoe.

In margin: I collect myself within myself, say a prayer just as soldiers do before the battle, but the collecting within oneself is no work but a pleasure, an ambiguity implicit in the Latin *colligere se* [collect oneself].—*Pap.* III B 55:2 *n.d.*, 1841-42

From draft; see 326:10-19:

Now I must again go out into society. Gradually I have been buying up a lot of small claims, now the time of payment is here. —In this respect, too, my principle will always be able to hold its own. One must not seek them first at social gatherings, in families, etc.; there they are always to a certain degree armed. But casual contacts first—later comes the harvesting. The more surprises one can manage, the better.—*Pap.* III B 84 *n.d.*, 1841-42

Deleted from sketch; see 326:32-327:28:

You barren mother of a countless brood—the only thing left when those ancient gods were conquered, when eternity gave birth to time, when time gave birth to eternity, but you escaped.

III
B 179:28
196

Cursed chance, you my only confidant, the only one I deem worthy of being my ally and my enemy, always like yourself, always incomprehensible, always an enigma, you whom I love with all the sympathy of my soul, I who am created in your image. Cursed chance, why do you not make your appearance. I do not beg, I do not humbly plead that you will make your appearance in this manner or that; I challenge you to a fight. Why do you not show your bare neck, or has the balance wheel [*Uro*] in the world structure, the restless [*urolig*] balance wheel, also become still [*rolig*]?* I am seized with anxiety; I believe the world is coming to a standstill from boredom. Cursed chance, I am waiting for you: I do not want to be so foolish as to want to vanquish you by means of principles, by what people call character. No, I want to wrestle with you. I am like a temple dancer;** I have consecrated myself to your service. Light, thinly clad, limber, unarmed, without preparation, I own nothing in the world, I care to own nothing,† I have nothing to lose, but I want to wrestle with you. I do not come with long incantations. Show yourself, surprise me, I still want to wrestle with you. What shall we fight about? I have nothing at stake, and yet I offer the proudest condition that may have been offered you—let us fight for honor.

III
B 179:28
197

*or has your riddle perhaps been solved; have you plunged yourself into the sea of eternity.

**I have nothing to do; I renounce everything in order to serve you, in order to dance to your honor.

†and you no doubt are also accustomed to such a battle.

—*Pap*. III B 179:28 *n.d.*, 1841–42

In margin of final draft; see 326:36-327:2:

. . . . . that proud time when mankind ruled the world, when eternity gave birth to time, the only remnant that remained, when time again sank down into eternity, but you escaped.

In margin: that time when necessity gave birth to freedom, when freedom let itself be tricked back into the womb again in order to be born anew.—*Pap*. III B 55:3 *n.d.*, 1841–42

From final draft; see 328:16-19:

Ovid's [*in margin: de arte amandi*, II, v. 235.][129]
—*Pap*. III B 55:4 *n.d.*, 1841–42

From sketch:

Good morning, Madam! Are you going to the market to do the buying yourself. —She is pleased with my conversation. She is accompanied by a very beautiful maidservant with a market basket on her arm. Maidservants have always delighted me. They are such small diverting conquests—he who has no taste for maidservants shows *eo ipso* that he is culturally retarded.—*Pap*. III B 77 *n.d.*, 1841–42

From draft; see 328:34-329:6:

Now, why do you not remain standing in the doorway; why did you peek out? There is nothing offensive or peculiar about standing in a doorway during a shower. Moreover, one cannot even tell that you are not entering the building. But now that I have seen you I know that in the strictest sense you are standing behind the door.—*Pap.* III B 78 *n.d.*, 1841-42

From final draft; see 330:14-16:

The bird builds its nest in the beech tree; no bird builds its nest in the spruce except the wood dove—she was like that. . . . . —*Pap.* III B 56:1 *n.d.*, 1841-42

From sketch; see 330:19-21:

. . . . . and yet what are all the diplomatic secrets of the world compared with a young girl's secret.—*Pap.* III B 36 *n.d.*, 1841

From final draft; see 331:13:

The best thing at a dance is all the small advantages the dancers enjoy. The conventional freedoms do not signify much precisely because they are conventional and because a male dancer ordinarily does not have anything special in his favor, and ordinarily it is a very ambiguous compliment to a man when a girl says he is a good dancer.—*Pap.* III B 56:2 *n.d.*, 1841-42

In margin of final draft; see 332:3:

I could wish that I were a painter, for this moment in a girl's life, precisely because it is only a moment, actually can only be painted; since it presupposes no development, it cannot be described.—*Pap.* III B 56:3 *n.d.*, 1841-42

From final draft; see 332:4-6:

Therefore, a woman is born twice; when she marries, her maiden name is said to be this or that. Actually it is only one birth, of course, but it is so long that it forms a period of its own.—*Pap.* III B 56:4 *n.d.*, 1841-42

From final draft; continuation of 320:20:

. . . . . but she was not emptied by sentimentality or embellished with sentimentality like those fancied rich whom one seeks in vain to embrace, since their content has evaporated.— *Pap.* III B 56:5 *n.d.*, 1841–42

Deleted from final draft; see 337:14:

. . . . . who by his hot temper so embittered his only son that the latter, after many scenes, emigrated to America. The mother is also dead;—*Pap.* III B 56:7 *n.d.*, 1841–42

Deleted from final draft; see 339:81:

Look what happened to Tønder.[130] Would he have died so wretchedly if he had not lived so isolated?—*Pap.* III B 56:8 *n.d.*, 1841–42

Deleted from margin of final draft; see 344:28-345:2:

If I were to tell my life story, I do not believe I would have many satisfied readers; they would no doubt soon be a bit irritated because they would go away hungry from a table where so much enjoyment continually went past their noses.—*Pap.* III B 56:9 *n.d.*, 1841–42

From final draft; see 346:34:

Edward; *changed from:* Fritz
—*Pap.* III 56:10 *n.d.*, 1841–42

From sketch; see 354:15-23:

. . . . . such really jolly zephyrs—you frisky fauns, play nicely with the young girls—but what good would it be for you if I do not join you in it, what joy would you then have from it?—*Pap*. III B 89 *n.d.*, 1841-42

From draft; see 354:15-23:

. . . . . the road is slippery today and it is windy. You jolly fauns, what joy would you have playing your game if there were no one who was enjoying it?—*Pap*. III B 85 *n.d.*, 1841-42

From draft; see 356:20-15:

> *Die eine ist verliebt gar sehr*
> *die Andre wär' es gerne*
> [The one is very much in love
> the other would very much like to be]

Indeed, it is hard to have to walk alongside, at most in the evening to be allowed to take her future brother-in-law by the arm, and even then by his left arm.—*Pap*. III B 72 *n.d.*, 1841-42

From final draft; see 357:4-5:

Just so, resolute and *gewaltig* [powerful].
Several little features[131] from the blue book can be used here. It must be checked.—*Pap*. III B 135:1 *n.d.*, 1841-42

From draft; see 358:9:

. . . . . then it often becomes rather scanty; there is nothing available for many tucks and folds. You are beautiful, my girl; your lips, what health they breathe, your eyes, how shining, how pure. When you open them, it is like the fog lifting from the ocean in an instant and the shining dark sea reflecting the sky, like a dark cloud hiding the moon and now suddenly disappearing and the moon is twice as bright because the cloud has polished it.—*Pap.* III B 69 *n.d.*, 1841–42

From draft; see 359:9-10:

. . . . . a university graduate. —What is the use if he in fact has no job, if he perhaps has to break off again, but with a little coolness—*Pap.* III B 93 *n.d.*, 1842–43

From final draft; see 359:28-32:

. . . . . there is a uniformity that renders superfluous even the courtesy that the woman walks on the flagstones. They do not seem designed for other erotic positions. Both bend their knees a little. One does not often see a man who walks with such a long stride, less often a woman—indeed, he can count himself fortunate; he has found a life-companion.

Incidentally, there is something about her. *In margin:* But you dear zephyrs, why are you so busy with that couple; they do not seem to be worth the attention—there must certainly be something in particular—why do you tug at the little scarf—quite true, it is indeed an unusually lovely neck.—*Pap.* III B 91 *n.d.*, 1841–42

From final draft; see 359:32-33:

Now I have no more time; now I must go up to Høibroplads.—*Pap.* III B 135:2 *n.d.*, 1842

Deleted from sketch:

So, on Vandkunsten lives a beauty like that—and I am ignorant of it—Fritz, my boots—in order to bear in mind at all times my principal adventure, I have started to call my servant Fritz—his mere name then reminds me indirectly—*Pap.* III B 92 *n.d.*, 1841–42

From final draft; see 362:31-34:

> Nec levis, ingenuas pectus coluisse per artes,
> Cura sit, et linguas edidicisse duas.
> Non formosus erat, sed erat facundus Ulixes,
> Et tamen aequoreas torsit amore Deas.
> O! Quoties illum doluit properare Calypso;
> Remigioque optas esse negavit aquas

> [Nor let it be a slight care to cultivate your mind in liberal arts, or to learn the two languages well. Ulysses was not comely, but he was eloquent, yet he fired two goddesses of the sea with love. Ah, how oft did Calypso grieve that he was hasting, and say that the waters were not fit for oars]!
> *de arte amandi, Lib.* II, l. 121
> —*Pap.* III B 43 *n.d.*, 1843

From final draft; see 363:37:

There are various ways of intoxicating a woman bacchanticly; mine is the surest.—*Pap.* III B 58:1 *n.d.*, 1841-42

From final draft; see 364:2-4:

. . . . . This is the one novelists always have in good supply on their palette and at every opportunity smear it all over the poor girls, back and front. It finally ends with having them blush over the entire body.—*Pap.* III B 58:2 *n.d.*, 1841-42

From final draft; see 365:1-5:

My intention was to destroy the whole impression and then if possible take away from her the pathos and replace it with irony. It was too soon; I have let myself be carried away. I would give anything not to have done it. She became anxious, but her anxiety had nothing tempting for her; it was only *unheimlich* [uncomfortable]. Anxiety is always a trustworthy means, but it must tempt and lure like the song of the Lorelei, not deter. I must take stronger measures to awaken the pathos; as yet she is not sufficiently developed to go out on the depths; if only this episode does not make her afraid of water.—*Pap.* III B 58:3 *n.d.*, 1841–42

From final draft; see 367:15:

. . . . . that a carriage and horses awaited us. She would more easily compose herself in this unusual situation than in the conventional one. But, an engagement is a special matter. It is a public demonstration; I make an avowal that perhaps can involve someone in many consequences. Once one is engaged, it is soon public knowledge, and all the rest of one's life one bears the stamp of having been engaged, something that always denounces one as a person who has traveled on these waters and that in the future makes all mystifications difficult for one. Moreover, it is not so easy to extricate oneself. This, however, I fear less: it depends on how one conducts oneself. Above all, one must guard against coming in contact with the ethical, and an engagement can so easily take on an ethical character.—*Pap.* III B 58:4 *n.d.*, 1841–42

From final draft; see 368:6-18:

. . . . . And I shall never envy him his conquests, since they are all based upon a lie and thus esthetically have no meaning. He does not know what joy it is to be loved, loved more than everything in the world. It always becomes more difficult to poetize oneself out of it again, and yet it must be possible to do it, but it ought to happen so subtly that she does not even dare claim that she is deceived. We shall see. I shall do for the girl what I have never done for any other; I shall become engaged to her. It is a considerable venture I am making. I am well aware of that, but I still hope to receive the principal and interest again. I must have a relationship to her that gives me the peace to enjoy her development, which does not giddily seize the highest.—*Pap*. III B 58:5 *n.d*., 1841-42

From final draft; see 372:31:

. . . . . she certainly does not love me, and if I were at this moment to bring her to do so, I would have to overwhelm her all too powerfully. For her to surrender to me out of fear alone or, rather, say "yes" would not be desirable either, although there always must and ought to be an element of fear that will definitely smother the prophetic. On the strength of my intellectual superiority over her, I may expect a "yes," but since precisely in my superiority she sees the possibility of her freedom, fear alone will not determine her.—*Pap*. III B 58:6 *n.d*., 1841-42

From final draft; see 373:15-18:

And why do I enjoy this confidence, because I am not a cavalier, because I am utterly indifferent, a purely intellectual creature, the most neutral salt in the world. Indeed, here it pays off. I say with Per Degn, I would not do without the Latin for one hundred rix-dollars.*[132]
In margin: *In fact, how poor my income was in the old days, when I was cavalier, compared with my present one.—*Pap*. III B 58:7 *n.d*., 1841-42

From draft; see 373:20-21:

The moment had arrived—it was otherwise devoid of all fuss, kneeling, etc., which at this point would have been inexpedient.—*Pap*. III B 61:1 *n.d*. 1841-42

Sidelined in margin of copy of Either/Or, *I; see 374:26-27:*

That is, a book has the remarkable characteristic that it can be interpreted as one pleases. If a person talks like a book, his talking also has the same characteristic.—*Pap.* IV A 233 *n.d.*, 1843

From draft; see 374:29-30:

She was completely surprised, thought I was mad.—*Pap.* III

B 61:2 *n.d.*, 1841-42

From final draft; see 375:19-28:
So now I am engaged. Who would have said that about me.
In margin: . . . . . if Cordelia had a girl friend and would be honest, she would have to say: God knows what will come of the whole affair. There is something about him that tempts— and yet I am not in love—*Pap.* III B 63:1 *n.d.*, 1841-42

From final draft; see 375:31-32:

It is manifest again here; something that has divine origin always retains a meaning, however much one hardens oneself against it. Marriage, for example, contains a truth, even though to me at least it is rather uncomfortable;—*Pap.* III B 63:2 *n.d.*, 1841-42

From draft; see 376:1-4:

I have always made fun of engaged people;* therefore it will have significance to be engaged myself.
In margin: *That it is as ridiculous as it actually is I never realized so well until now when I myself am wearing the straitjacket.—*Pap.* III B 63:3 *n.d.*, 1841-42

From final draft; see 376:1-4:

. . . . . for an engaged person is actually an artist in the same sense as the virtuosos at Dyrehaugen, and an engagement is related to erotic love as the displays at Dyrehaugen to art. I am really happy to make the acquaintance of my fellow artists.

Since my engagement is the only job I have in life, I can totally devote myself to it; I can live solely for my engagement, undisturbed even by consideration of my promotion in the Customs Department.—*Pap.* III B 63:4 *n.d.*, 1841-42

In margin of Pap. III 63:4:

Incidentally, it has interested me for a long time to come to see the world from the standpoint of an engaged person; I thought one might make excellent observations, that one would be regarded as more harmless, would dare to permit oneself many liberties. I had thought of hiring a girl to be engaged to me for half a year; now it happens otherwise.—*Pap.* III B 63:5 *n.d.*, 1841-42

From final draft; see 376:13-21:

All such things I am willing to allow him, now that I am over the dangerous part. Prior to my having secured Cordelia for myself, he could not be allowed to confess his love; now it can do no harm. Now I have taken command; I can interpret everything. Her sympathy cannot be awakened to any significant degree, for now it is an external impossibility for her to return to him. Indeed, why should I tear away the last hope. He is a good man; I like him, and who knows, he perhaps could be useful once again, he could always be really acceptable as a home for a widow.—*Pap.* III B 63:6 *n.d.*, 1841-42

From final draft; see 379:25:

Silent, yes, of course; who talks aloud when walking alone on the street. Silent, but not every young girl appears silent because she keeps silent. And yet this is the first, the deepest quality in a young girl; it actually is her deeper nature, which can very well be united with a cheerful, lively, innocently happy talkativeness on the surface—silent—thoughtfully she looks down at her feet, her head is, as it were, too heavy, and yet she holds it lightly, her blonde heavy hair weighs down

heavily—she is like a ripe ear of corn.—*Pap.* III B 81 *n.d.*,
1841–42

In margin of final draft; see 379:25:

First polemic

—*Pap.* III 63:7 *n.d.*, 1841–42

Deleted from sketch; see 379:26-32:

Fortunately I have my uncle's house. It perhaps would be
difficult to find its equal in a short time. It is usually called a
hospitable house; I would rather call it a public house, that is,
the kind that only a particular group frequents—for example,
the tailors' guildhall—here only engaged people come. I always come here fairly often in order to have the pleasure of the
company of the engaged—the fact that I myself have become
engaged has created quite a sensation in the club. —I shall soon
make my entry now. —This house is just like a certain area in
Jylland that people call the Dry Goods Merchants' Jerusalem,
the Jerusalem of the engaged. If I wanted to impart to a young
man a distaste for tobacco, I would take him to Regensen; if I
want to impart to a young girl a distaste for being engaged, I
would introduce her here.—*Pap.* III B 99 *n.d.*, 1841–42

Deleted from draft; see 379:37-380:1:

One cannot blame Cordelia for finding distasteful the amorous tangibilities of these engaged people, these bunglings of
lovesick workmen.—*Pap.* III B 115 *n.d.*, 1841–42

Deleted addition to Pap. III B 99; *see 380:2-15:*

Incessantly one hears a sound as if someone were going
around with a flyswatter—it is the lovers' kissing—I make a
move to do something similar, however much I almost have
to force myself, merely to upset Cordelia. —On the whole, I
can guarantee perfect esthetic treatment to any girl who en-

trusts herself to me—it only ends with her being deceived, but this, too, is part of my esthetics.—*Pap.* III B 100 *n.d.*, 1841–42

From final draft; see 380:14-17:

It would be interesting if some literary drudge could be found to count up—see the blue book.—*Pap.* III B 136 *n.d.*, 1842

Deleted from sketch; see 380:34:

I am having *apparte* [unusual] enjoyment these days from the good folks who believe that I am an utterly new beginner in the realm of the erotic. These situations are priceless—experienced married men who are no longer able to make conquests now revive themselves by fastening themselves to the newly engaged in order to feel how far along one is in it etc. I thank them for good advice—I also perceive from this that the more concrete one becomes in life the more ridiculous the whole of life becomes. Hitherto I have always been secretive about my affairs; it has its advantages, but now I simultaneously have secrecy and its aroma and the ludicrousness of publicity.—*Pap.* III B 102 *n.d.*, 1841–42

From final draft; see 381:10-12:

And although I no doubt have lived a fairly interesting life and could easily make it tempting for a young girl, I shall, however, always reject this means, for if such means were necessary I would be convinced that love itself is not the absolute.

In margin: At any rate, what I seek is, namely, not a history—of that I have had enough—but immediacy.—*Pap.* III B 64:1 *n.d.*, 1841–42

From final draft; see 381:12-13:

. . . . . not until that moment do they exist for each other, and while nature gives birth only piecemeal, erotic love gives birth in pairs, wholes, totalities. So it always ought to be in the beginning; later on one can use past life as a tempting secret.— *Pap.* III B 64:2 *n.d.*, 1841–42

From sketch: see 383:24-28:

 . . . . . you become angry with me, although wrongly so, since you do not know how guilty I am—I prefer to begin with a girl's being angry with me— —*Pap.* III B 79 *n.d.*, 1841–42

From final draft; see 383:37-384:5:

I owe it to friends and relatives—in short, to the whole human race. It is indeed glorious to work for the whole; such a general power of attorney in the name of humanity gives one's personality a high degree of meaning.—*Pap.* III B 80 *n.d.*, 1841–42

Deleted from sketch; see 384:23-385:4:

Right now I am concentrating on making the engagement [*Forlovelse*] ludicrous—I certainly am no good as an engaged person, and yet I *engage* [*forlove*] to bring her to the point of never again becoming *engaged.* —Meanwhile it is a matter of luring it out of her, after putting it in myself, lest she become suspicious and seesaw all the higher the more strength she feels within herself. To become engaged means only to say: By your leave.—*Pap.* III B 98 *n.d.*, 1841–42

From final draft; see 385:17:

In this way we are suited to each other.
In margin: Charlotte Hahn
                                        —*Pap.* III B 65 *n.d.*, 1841–42

From final draft; see 387:5-6:
In this respect I must see to acquiring a caricature.

In margin: In my uncle's house I have a caricature—*Pap.* III
B 66:1 *n.d.* 1841-42

In margin of final draft; see 388:7-15:

Today I have written her a little epistle, as aphoristic and
tangential as possible. It requires to quite an extent my interpretation, and that is also the intention. —What she receives in
writing from me she very likely rereads often; thus it must be
of such a nature that it provides no sure footing, but it can be
what it will, depending on how her own mood interprets it. I
place the accent upon her and her art. When in the fullness of
time I make it impossible for her in every way, then she herself
will become the one who first loses interest.—*Pap.* III B 66:2
n.d., 1841-42

In margin of final draft; see 388:19-20:

. . . . . this position has sympathy, but still not the erotic.—
Pap. III B 66:3 *n.d.*, 1841-42

In margin of final draft; see 390:29-391:5:

N.B. with respect to *actio in distans*, in which he appears to
have an eye on the time— —*Pap.* III B 137 *n.d.*, 1842

Deleted from sketch; see 392:31-37:

When we were leaving my uncle's last night, she shook my
hand with unusual passion—she has really felt distressed there,
and no wonder; if I did not always find amusement in observing these remarkable unnatural affectations, I could not possibly hold out. Consequently, I am now beginning to elicit the
idea from her that it would be best to break the engagement. It
must be her idea, for otherwise she will not have sufficient
elasticity, and in another way her erotic love will not react so

strongly. —The handshake sufficiently demonstrates to me what I dare to hope.—*Pap.* III B 101 *n.d.*, 1841-42

In margin of final draft; see 393:3:

No. 4

—*Pap.* III B 71:1 *n.d.*, 1841-42

From final draft; see 394:36:

. . . . . he actually reminds me of the steadfast tin soldier, and I cannot help laughing every time I think of their common fate of falling under a gutter plank.—*Pap.* III B 71:2 *n.d.*, 1841-42

From final draft; see 395:3-9:

On the contrary, the more I see the girl, the more she pleases me. I now go slowly to the pastry shop on the other side; until shortly before twelve she attends to her job. She is diligent; I like that. The last five minutes before twelve, she is a bit restless.—*Pap.* III B 71:3 *n.d.*, 1841-42

From draft; see 396:14-35:

To wait in vain this way is almost too much. Now my servant has waited six hours, I myself two, in rain and wind, and we have found nothing. Every trace of her has vanished. It is due to not being sufficiently attentive; when one is dealing with girls one has to have an eye on every finger. There was a nymph, Cardea [*similar to 396:32-35*]. On the whole, it could be quite interesting if some literary hack could be found to count up in all the various folk legends, tales, and myths in which it is a girl who deceives a man how often it is a man who deceives a girl, in order to determine which sex in the judgment of centuries is the faithful one.—*Pap.* III B 74 *n.d.*, 1841-42

In margin of Pap. III B 74; *see 385:18-22; 396:14-28:*

. . . . . just to get a smile from Charlotte Hahn (consequently, this *actio in distans* must be used in the previous part). It lends itself superbly, evokes a mood that I owe to Cordelia.—*Pap.* III B 75 *n.d.*, 1841-42

From sketch; see 356:19-24; 396:14-28:

> Sie singen schön und geigen
> Ob nicht eine süssverträumtes Kind
> Am Fenster mocht erscheinen
> [They sing beautifully and play the
> violin
> To see whether a sweet dreamy
> child
> Might appear at the window].[133]

Then the little maiden is up before the devil gets his shoes on.

— — —

and what is the entire reward that I am asking—a smile from her, she is so beautiful when she smiles. —I do not ask more and would not accept it if it were offered me. Thus one ought to see immediately what each person is able to give and not ask for more. It is another matter with my Cordelia; with regard to her, I am unable to give up anything, but that is because she is able to give everything.—*Pap.* III B 90 *n.d.*, 1841-42

See 405:9:

There is a place out in Gribs forest that is called the Nook of Eight Paths.[134] The name is very appealing to me.—*JP* V 5643 (*Pap.* IV A 81) *n.d.*, 1843

From final draft; see 406:26:

. . . . . the bass voice in *The White Lady*[135]
—*Pap*. III B 155 *n.d.*, 1842

From final draft; see 407:33:

III
B 156
180

To be omitted

M.C.

III
B 156
181

What a long time it is since I saw you. In the finite sense, it surely is not so, but then what is the finite understanding able to grasp? It does not comprehend that it is long when I have not seen you for half a day; it comprehends equally little that the minute in which I do see you is long. But patience, and yet how does one learn patience? By praying. So this is my ritual. You know that a rosary has two kinds of pearls, large and small; a paternoster is prayed for each large pearl, and for each small one an Ave Maria. My rosary likewise has large and small [pearls]. For every large pearl on a rosary, there are ten small ones. I let the string of pearls run through my fingers; for every small pearl I say "Your"; for every large one "My." Is that not right? Should it not be so? My distracted, multiple soul, unlike yours, cannot concentrate on one thing; therefore I must say "Your" ten times for every time I say "My," for when I say "My," I know that it is something much more complete and whole when I say "Your." Not as if I or the least part of me should belong to another; no, but I, unfortunately, am intrinsically multiple. When you, however, call yourself "My," your whole soul is concentrated in it, and I am amazed only that you have chosen me among the multiplicity of human beings; it is as amazing as God's having chosen the earth among the multiplicity of worlds.

However, since each prayer is not especially long, does not demand any time, I am able to run through my rosary much faster, yet not in the sense of my not reflecting on my prayer; on the contrary I do a lot of reflecting, either by sinking into contemplation when I say "My" or cheering myself up when I say "Your." But since the words also resemble each other, it sometimes happens that the sameness of the motion makes me dizzy. "My" and "Your" become confused for me. In this blessed intoxication, I cannot distinguish between "My" and "Your." It is in this condition that I write this letter—and yet there is a higher intoxication.

Your Joh.
—*Pap.* III B 156 *n.d.*, 1842

From sketch; see 409:12-14:

. . . . . it is annoying to ride backwards that way in a carriage and down such a long street—the position cannot be changed—you cannot avoid my glance.—*Pap.* III B 96 *n.d.*, 1841-42

See 410:29-36:

Situation:

A seducer who already has the love of several girls on his conscience becomes enamored of a girl whom he loves to the extent that he does not have the heart to seduce her, but neither can he really decide to take up with her. He happens to see someone with a striking resemblance to her; he seduces her in order that in this pleasure he can enjoy the other.—*JP* V 5540 (*Pap.* III A 187) *n.d.*, 1841

From sketch; see 410:29-36:

This is the interesting aspect of the beginning; one looks down the main road, as it were, and sees how this side road turns and twists. I had the good fortune once of paying my respects to a dancer. I did not love her, but she had a striking resemblance to someone else—I saw her the first time—speedily found out her address—forgot her—after a month discovered that since that time I had seen her every time she danced—indeed, had paid triple the theater price in order to see her. — Now I looked down the main road.—*Pap.* III B 179:16 *n.d.*, 1841-42

From journal; see 410:29-36:

Here in Berlin, a Demoiselle Hedevig Schulze, a singer from Vienna, performs the part of Elvira.[136] She is very beautiful, decisive in bearing; in height, in the way she walks and dresses (black silk dress, bare neck, white gloves), she strikingly resembles a young lady I knew. It is a strange coincidence. I must really use a little power against myself in order to dislodge this impression.—*JP* V 5541 (*Pap.* III A 190) *n.d.*, 1841

From final draft; see 410:31:

At a theater in Vienna

　　　　　　　　　—*Pap.* III B 76:1 *n.d.*, 1841-42

From final draft; see 412:5-6:

. . . . . attaching itself firmly, dialectically, around its one and only object, more inflexibly than an evil conscience embraces a sinner's soul. Her embrace will not be hiatic, nor her kiss sibilant.—*Pap.* III B 160:2 *n.d.*, 1842

From final draft; see 412:17:

. . . . . insofar as she would wish any other reading; I generally am extremely careful in this respect as in every other, lest she suspect any design on my part.—*Pap.* III B 160:4 *n.d.*, 1842

From draft; see 412:18-415:16:

　　　　　　　　　　　　Fredriksberg.
　　　　　　　　　　　　Gold and money
　　　　　　　　　　　　dazzle the eyes
　　　　　　　　　　　　that I must understand.
Perhaps a little rendezvous can be arranged in a little side street where no one but the echo of the distant music knows

about it. —You are really dressed up, aren't you; that little scarf, true there is a little spot on it, but you have prudently concealed it—for a maidservant you are really beautiful—Do you think that I insult you by saying for a maidservant—on the contrary, I am very fond of maidservants—If you accompany me, I will explain many things about fine ladies to you; you surely have often wished that you were a fine and rich lady— It will be easy to make arrangements for a clergyman—*Pap.* III B 86 *n.d.*, 1841–42

From sketch; see 412:18-415:16:

A few scenes from Charlottenlund, from Dyrehaug life— evening light—the dancing scenes out there would also be very usable. —A rendezvous in the remote areas of the forest that is disturbed; it is lacking in taste that maidservants always have to wear hats when they go to the forest. It is better at Fredriksberg. There they are bareheaded; that is the way a maidservant should be. How gorgeous she is otherwise.— *Pap.* III B 94 *n.d.*, 1842–43

From sketch; see 412:18-413:30:

. . . . . it is summer time
she slips, lightly and properly dressed—she
struggles—what grace—modesty—
is it comic or tragic that a
young girl falls.
—*Pap.* III B 88 *n.d.*, 1841–42

From sketch; see 412:35-413:3:

Be careful girls. Because it is night and the forest is illuminated, you believe it is all right to look boldly at us men. Watch out. I know how to reimburse myself for a look like that.—*Pap.* III B 82 *n.d.*, 1841–42

Addition to Pap. III B 86; *see 414:12-25:*

. . . . . such a little miss. She is thinking about her sweet-heart; she is engaged to a servant in an aristocratic family or perhaps even to a coachman who has served in the cavalry; the cleverest fellows are that. —Or she is thinking about becoming engaged to a handsome fellow like that, and then she thinks about getting married. She even goes to hear the pastor read the marriage banns from the pulpit—he may become a policeman, a street commissioner, perhaps a fireman, a porter, etc.—if not these, a watchman. But a watchman has the defect that he must not live on the street where he calls—as long as he is engaged, there can be no harm in such an innocent infatuation—I realize very well that such things happen, but then the watchman lieutenant is ignorant of—*Pap*. III B 87 *n.d.*, 1841-42

From final draft; see 416:2:

Therefore, the person who is unable to write letters and notes never becomes a dangerous seducer.—*Pap*. III B 161:1 *n.d.*, 1842

Deleted from sketch; see 416:13-417:23:

A Contribution to a Theory of the Kiss
a prize essay
dedicated to
all doting lovers
by
the author.

There are many things between heaven and earth, they say, which no philosopher has explored. Among those things is also this realm. This might be because philosophers do not think about such things. More likely there are other reasons.

The most ambiguous kiss is the one given in the Christmas game of forfeit—it can be all or nothing—
the masculine kiss
a stolen kiss
the conjugal domestic kiss with which married people wipe each other's mouth.
—*JP* III 2393 (*Pap.* III B 106) *n.d.*, 1841–42

From sketch; see 417:3-23:

The kiss can be classified according to duration. Musical tones are also classified in this way. Here we see the different meanings of time. In the tonal world, time is also asserted, but abstractly; it enters into no relationship to the idea, and the historical does not manifest itself. With respect to the kiss, the first one, for example, the fact that it is the first one, has enormous significance, and the last one, the fact that it is the last one. This has no place in the tonal world; it would be ridiculous.—*JP* III 2394 (*Pap.* III B 114) *n.d.*, 1841-42

Deleted from sketch; see 417:25-33:

My
Solomon says: A good answer is like a sweet kiss. You know that I am well known, yes, almost unpopular, because I am always asking questions. Ah, they do not know what I am asking about. Only you know what I am asking about, only you can answer. O, give me an answer. Only you can give me a good answer, for a good answer, says Solomon, is like a sweet kiss.   Your
—*JP* V 5539 (*Pap.* III A 183) *n.d.*, 1841

From final draft; see 418:3-6:

What Plato emphasizes here especially is the significance of touch.—*Pap.* III B 162:1 *n.d.*, 1842

See 418:8-11:

My girl—the Latinist says of an alert listener: *pendet ex ore
alicujus* [hangs on someone's lips]. He is thinking particularly
of the ear that picks up what it hears, carries it through the secret passage of the ear, and hides it deep within. We say it with
a completely different meaning, for how do I hang continually
on your lips, how alert I am, yes, an exceptionally alert listener, so that even if nothing is said, I still hear the beating of
your heart.—*JP* V 5502 (*Pap*. III A 134) *n.d.*, 1841

From final draft; see 418:8-11:

Like a pupil, I hang on your lips, not on your words, but I
imbibe your being.—*Pap*. III B 162:2 *n.d.*, 1842

From final draft; see 418:31-33:

. . . . . *dos est uxoria, lites* [the dowry of a wife is quarreling]
de arte amandi, Lib. II, *v*. 155[137]

Quos humeros, quales vidi tetigique lacertos!
    Forma papillarum quam fuit apta premi!
Quam castigato planus sub pectore venter!
    Quantum et quale latus! quam juvenile femur

[What shoulders, what arms did I see—and
touch! How suited for caress the form of her
breasts! How smooth her body beneath the fault-
less bosom! What a long and beautiful side! How
youthfully fair the thigh]!

somewhere in Ovid.[138]
—*Pap*. III B 44 *n.d.*, 1841

From final draft; see 419:21-25:

. . . . . let this parenthesis, which for me contains the whole
world, be ended—*Pap*. III B 162:4 *n.d.*, 1842

From final draft; see 419:27:

Is it two wrestlers locked in an embrace? Are they so close to each other because the one continually wants to tear loose, the other continually wants to prevent it? Is it in farewell that the lips touch each other?—*Pap.* III B 162:5 *n.d.*, 1842

From final draft; see 420:25-32:

M. C.

You are sitting on my lap; we form one figure; from one trunk shoot two branches—*Pap.* III B 162:6 *n.d.*, 1842

From sketch; see 421:18-22; 423:7-10:

What are the acceptable grounds for breaking an engagement? On this point every little miss is a shrewd casuist—if the girl was too small,* as a certain man said, if one had not knelt before his fiancée in the momentous moment, consequently, if the most important formalities were disregarded
*or too big.
　　　　　　　　　　　　　　　　—*Pap.* III B 104 *n.d.*, 1841-42

Addition to Pap. IV B 104:

I know a man who actually cited these two grounds. When I protested to him that they could not possibly be regarded as adequate, he answered: Indeed, they are quite adequate. That is, if I had cited what one calls adequate grounds, I would have had to become involved in the endless pro and contra deliberations that I have avoided here, for it is impossible for anyone to reply to them.—*Pap.* III B 105 *n.d.*, 1841-42

In margin of final draft; see 421:18-20:

On the subject of breaking an engagement, every little miss is a born casuist—see the little book.[139]—*Pap.* III B 162:7 *n.d.*, 1842

From draft; see 421:31:

. . . . . of this kind, and it is the most beautiful day in my life.—*Pap*. III B 107:1 *n.d*., 1841-42

From draft; see 422:10-38:

III
B 107:2
162

I found my place in the middle of this cluster. Tossed about on this sea such as eight young girls are when they are alone like this, if one is sufficiently careful not to curb them too much by being far too much the cavalier, I was almost beside myself. And now I managed to direct their thoughts to the important question, under what circumstances should an engagement be broken. (The situation itself was so beautiful— the young girls—the sun shining in—the coffee) and now this conversation, just as my outer eyes reveled in enjoyment, so also my inner eyes reveled in the wealth of observations; a single word showed just about how far along they were on the road of love. I continually fanned the flames; brilliance and the esthetic removed the wall between us, and the whole situation took on a somewhat bacchantic tone, yet remained within the bounds of strictest propriety. I have often delighted in Retz's [*sic*] etching of Faust,[140] where Faust is dreaming and over him

III
B 107:2
163

arch the heavens, filled with female figures, just as here. — And now the subject being discussed. By means of it, I had as it were, undermined the whole company; I held them in the palm of my hand, and if I withdrew it, the confusion would have been dreadful.—*Pap*. III B 107:2 *n.d*., 1841-42

Continuation of Pap. III B 107:2; *see 423:14-28:*

I submitted a very difficult case for the assembly's deliberation. Someone had broken the engagement because they were not compatible. He was urged to give up this plan and was assured that the girl was very fond of him, to which he answered: Either we are compatible, and then she will perceive that we are not compatible, or we are not compatible, and then

she will perceive that we are not compatible.—*Pap*. III B 108
n.d., 1841-42

Deleted from sketch; see 423:5:

. . . . . if one could only acquire a new ring, that is, keep the
ring of the one with whom one breaks up, then one could collect trophies, but one does not do that and only receives one's
own again—it is very tautological.—*Pap*. III B 103 *n.d.*, 1841-
42

From final draft; see 424:4:

There was a side I forgot to emphasize for her yesterday; it
occurred to me immediately after I left, and I kept on thinking
about it constantly.—*Pap*. III B 163:1 *n.d.*, 1842

Deleted from draft:

Ordinarily I am able to think rather consistently, but the
conclusion that a baby appears because I love a girl is beyond
my comprehension; I could speculate myself mad on that—
Pap. III B 109 *n.d.*, 1841-42

Deleted from draft:

I knew a man who took great pride in the fact that no one
could have been more watchful over his fiancée than he, just
like that Roman consul who never slept during his consul-
ship—he had, you see, been engaged only four hours.—*Pap*.
III B 113 *n.d.*, 1841-42

In margin of final draft; see 427:1-4:

Moreover, I now acquire a decisive voice for putting in a
word about engagements. Those who are engaged are biased,
as are married people also, since marriage is a continuation of

it, but I and my kind, we are the competent ones.—*Pap.* III B 163:2 *n.d.*, 1842

From draft; see 427:4-8:

So I am free again and also have the advantage of being the object of the young girls' sympathy. I am a big hit; I am in the position of experiencing that a melancholy-tasting cake has been named after me—I have practiced a sentimental look one sometimes finds in old maids, and I have also noticed it in market horses, really worn-out nags, whose eyes sometimes have a wildness, a sentimental wildness—*Pap.* III B 118 *n.d.*, 1841-42

In margin of final draft; see 427:9:

No. 4.

—*Pap.* III B 146 *n.d.*, 1842

In margin of final draft; see 427:27:

No. 4.

—*Pap.* III B 164 *n.d.*, 1842

Heading of final draft; see 428:10-433:12:

Some journal remarks that must be included in appropriate places in the eroticist's diary.—*Pap.* III B 143:1 *n.d.*, 1842

In margin of final draft; see 428:10:

No. 1.

—*Pap.* III B 143:2 *n.d.*, 1842

In margin of final draft; see 433:12:

No. 1

—*Pap.* III B 165 *n.d.*, 1842

In margin of final draft; see 434:12:

> No. 3
>
> —*Pap*. III B 145 *n.d.*, 1842

In margin of final draft; see 435:18:

> No. 3
>
> —*Pap*. III B 166 *n.d.*, 1842

From draft of Anxiety; *see 435:32-437:28:*

In a way it has always seemed remarkable to me that the story of Eve has been completely opposed to all later analogy, for the expression "to seduce" used for her generally refers in ordinary language to the man, and the other related expressions all point to the woman as weaker (easier to infatuate, lure to bed, etc).* This, however, is easy to explain, for in Genesis it is a third power that seduces the woman, whereas in ordinary language the reference is always only to the relationship between man and woman and thus it must be the man who seduces the woman.

*Note. If anyone has any psychological interest in observations related to this, I refer him to "The Seducer's Diary" in *Either/Or.* If he looks at it closely, he will see that this is something quite different from a novel, that it has completely different categories up its sleeve, and, if one knows how to use it, it can serve as a preliminary study for a very serious and not exactly superficial research. The Seducer's secret is simply that he knows that woman is anxious.—*JP* V 5730 (*Pap*. V B 53:26) *n.d.*, 1844

See 436:2-14:

It takes courage to get married, and we ought not extol virginity—for Diana herself did not remain a virgin because she felt the superiority of the state but because she feared the pains of giving birth. Indeed, Euripides declares somewhere that he would rather go into battle three times than give birth once.— *JP* III 2587 (*Pap*. III A 144) *n.d.*, 1841

In margin of final draft; see 436:24:

No. 2

—*Pap*. III B 144 *n.d.*, 1842

In margin of final draft; see 437:29:

No. 2

—*Pap*. III B 167:1 *n.d.*, 1842

Deleted from journal; see 441:12-17:

And when the sun shuts its vigilant eye, when history is over, I will not only wrap up in my cloak but I will throw the night around me like a veil, and I will come to you—I will listen as the savage listens—not for your footsteps but for the beating of your heart.—*JP* V 5525 (*Pap*. III A 170) *n.d.*, 1841

From sketch; see 441:32-35:

. . . . . it is altogether right that Margaret catechizes Faust, but he has also appeared as a knight—must poetize himself out and in—*Pap*. III B 127 *n.d.*, 1841-42

From final draft; see 443:24:

If it were important to me to evoke a religious impression in her, then at such a moment I would have laid the Bible on the table, and it would never have occurred to me to offer her a sermon.—*Pap*. III B 167:3 *n.d.*, 1842

From sketch; see 444:8-14:

All is still—the bugler at Nørreport pronounces his benediction over the country; it echoes far away*—everything sleeps—only love [*Kærlighed*] is awake, either beside the sick bed or alone waiting or blissful, dreamy, watchful—people think that love sleeps at night—on the contrary, like other ghosts, it is awake only during the night hours—it has become a ghost—a light beckons me; she hears the signal—the hunter's call—it is also my call—this call seems to call people into the city; no, it is a blessing I take with me—the light moves—She is setting it in another room so that undisturbed she can look out into the darkness—it is a quarter after eleven—it is still day. Soon it will be night—

he goes inside the gate and his notes echo even farther away than when he stood outside the gate—

*they set the still spirits of the night in motion, and the one generation repeats it to the next—*Pap.* III B 32 *n.d.*, 1841

In margin of final draft; see 444:12:

. . . . . indeed, the love that lives for a scrupulous performance of its domestic duties is not served by the darkness of night; it demands the light of day or a lamp.—*Pap.* III B 168:1 *n.d.*, 1842

In margin of final draft; see 445:23:

Therefore I do not believe such things. I knew a man. He loved a girl, not so much for herself but rather because her clinging so hard to him moved him deeply. He realized that a union was unthinkable at the moment because many difficulties stood in the way. He left her; she declared that she could not live without him. He did not allow himself rest night or day until he had everything in order. Then he happily turned his thoughts to her, and lo, she was engaged to someone else. Then he swore eternal hatred of all girls, and if I am not mis-

III
B 32
125

III
B 32
126

III
B 32
125

taken about him he has avenged himself many times.—*Pap*. III
B 168:2 *n.d.*, 1842

From final draft; see 445:32:

The attempt would be well worth making, but in that case
the beginning would have to be arranged quite differently,
since the ending, the retreat, would become the interesting
factor upon which everything depended.—

April 14
—*Pap*. III B 168:3 April 14, 1842

EDITORIAL APPENDIX

ACKNOWLEDGMENTS

Preparation of manuscripts for *Kierkegaard's Writings* is supported by a genuinely enabling grant from the National Endowment for the Humanities. The grant includes gifts from the Dronning Margrethe og Prins Henrik Fond, the Danish Ministry of Cultural Affairs, the Augustinus Fond, the Carlsberg Fond, the Konsul George Jorck og Hustru Emma Jorcks Fond, and the A. P. Møller og Hustru Chastine Mc-Kinney Møllers Fond.

The translators-editors are indebted to Grethe Kjær and Julia Watkin for their knowledgeable observations on crucial concepts and terminology.

John Elrod, Per Lønning, and Sophia Scopetéa, members of the International Advisory Board for *Kierkegaard's Writings*, have given valuable criticism of the manuscript on the whole and in detail. Jack Schwandt, Pamela Schwandt, Michael Daugherty, Steven Knudson, and Craig Mason have helpfully scrutinized all or parts of the manuscript. The index has been prepared by Kennedy Lemke and Jennie Myers. The entire work has been facilitated by George Coulter and Lavier Murray.

Acknowledgment is made to Gyldendals Forlag for permission to absorb notes to *Søren Kierkegaards Samlede Værker*.

Inclusion in the Supplement of entries from *Søren Kierkegaard's Journals and Papers* is by arrangement with Indiana University Press.

The book collection and the microfilm collection of the Kierkegaard Library, St. Olaf College, have been used in preparation of the text, Supplement, and Editorial Appendix.

The manuscript, typed by Dorothy Bolton and Kennedy Lemke, has been guided through the press by Cathie Brett-schneider.

COLLATION OF *EITHER/OR*, PART I,
IN THE DANISH EDITIONS OF
KIERKEGAARD'S COLLECTED WORKS

Vol. I *Ed. 1* *Pg.*	*Vol. I* *Ed. 2* *Pg.*	*Vol. 2* *Ed. 3* *Pg.*	*Vol. I* *Ed. 1* *Pg.*	*Vol. I* *Ed. 2* *Pg.*	*Vol. 2* *Ed. 3* *Pg.*
v	*vii*	9	23	26	40
vi	*viii*	9	24	27	41
vii	*ix*	10	25	28	42
viii	*x*	11	26	29	42
ix	*xi*	13	27	30	43
x	*xiii*	14	31	35	47
xi	*xiv*	14	32	36	47
xii	*xv*	15	33	37	48
xiii	*xvi*	16	34	38	49
xiv	*xvii*	17	35	39	50
xv	*xix*	18	36	40	51
xvi	*xx*	19	37	42	52
2	2	22	38	43	53
3	3	23	39	44	54
4	4	23	40	45	55
5	5	24	41	47	56
6	6	25	42	48	57
7	7	26	43	49	58
8	8	27	44	50	59
9	10	28	45	51	60
10	11	28	46	53	61
11	12	29	47	54	62
12	13	30	48	55	63
13	14	31	49	56	64
14	15	32	50	57	65
15	17	33	51	59	66
16	18	34	52	60	67
17	19	35	53	61	68
18	20	35	54	62	69
19	21	36	55	63	70
20	22	37	56	65	71
21	24	38	57	66	72
22	25	39	58	67	73

Vol. I Ed. 1 Pg.	Vol. I Ed. 2 Pg.	Vol. 2 Ed. 3 Pg.	Vol. I Ed. 1 Pg.	Vol. I Ed. 2 Pg.	Vol. 2 Ed. 3 Pg.
59	68	74	102	119	115
60	69	75	103	120	116
61	70	76	104	121	117
62	71	77	105	122	118
63	72	78	106	123	119
64	74	79	107	125	120
65	75	80	108	126	121
66	76	80	109	127	122
67	77	81	110	128	123
68	78	82	111	130	124
69	79	83	112	131	125
70	80	84	113	132	126
71	82	85	117	135	129
72	83	86	118	136	129
73	84	87	119	137	130
74	85	88	120	138	131
75	86	89	121	139	132
76	88	90	122	140	133
77	89	91	123	141	134
78	90	92	124	143	135
79	91	93	125	144	136
80	92	94	126	145	137
81	94	95	127	146	138
82	95	96	128	148	139
83	96	97	129	149	140
84	97	98	130	150	141
85	98	99	131	151	142
86	99	99	132	152	143
87	100	100	133	153	144
88	102	101	134	155	145
89	103	102	135	156	146
90	104	103	136	157	147
91	105	104	137	158	148
92	106	105	138	159	149
93	108	106	139	160	150
94	109	107	140	161	151
95	110	108	141	163	152
96	111	109	144	166	154
97	112	110	145	167	155
98	113	111	146	167	155
99	115	112	147	169	156
100	116	113	148	170	157
101	117	114	149	171	158

Vol. I	*Vol. I*	*Vol. 2*	*Vol. I*	*Vol. I*	*Vol. 2*
Ed. 1	*Ed. 2*	*Ed. 3*	*Ed. 1*	*Ed. 2*	*Ed. 3*
Pg.	*Pg.*	*Pg.*	*Pg.*	*Pg.*	*Pg.*
150	172	159	196	226	203
151	174	160	197	227	204
152	175	161	198	228	205
153	176	162	199	229	206
154	177	163	200	230	207
155	178	164	201	232	208
156	179	165	202	233	209
157	181	166	203	234	210
158	182	167	203	235	211
159	183	168	206	238	214
160	184	169	207	239	215
161	186	170	208	240	215
162	187	171	209	241	216
163	188	172	210	242	217
164	189	173	211	243	218
165	190	174	212	244	219
166	192	175	213	246	220
167	193	176	214	247	221
168	194	177	215	248	222
169	195	178	216	249	223
170	196	179	217	251	224
171	198	180	218	252	226
172	199	181	219	253	227
173	200	182	220	254	228
174	201	183	221	256	228
175	202	184	222	257	229
176	203	185	223	258	230
177	205	186	224	259	231
178	206	187	225	260	232
179	207	188	226	261	233
180	209	189	227	262	234
181	210	190	228	263	235
182	211	191	229	265	236
183	212	192	230	266	237
184	213	193	231	267	238
185	215	194	232	268	239
186	216	195	233	269	240
187	217	196	234	271	241
188	218	197	235	272	242
189	219	198	236	273	243
193	223	201	237	274	244
194	224	201	238	275	245
195	225	202	239	276	246

Vol. I Ed. 1 Pg.	Vol. I Ed. 2 Pg.	Vol. 2 Ed. 3 Pg.	Vol. I Ed. 1 Pg.	Vol. I Ed. 2 Pg.	Vol. 2 Ed. 3 Pg.
240	278	247	286	330	291
241	279	248	287	331	291
242	280	249	288	332	292
243	281	250	289	333	293
244	282	250	290	334	294
245	283	251	291	335	295
246	284	252	292	337	296
247	286	253	293	338	297
248	287	254	294	339	298
249	288	255	295	340	299
250	289	256	296	341	300
251	291	257	297	343	301
254	294	260	298	344	302
255	295	261	299	345	303
257	297	263	300	346	304
258	298	263	301	347	305
259	299	264	302	348	306
260	300	265	303	350	307
261	301	266	304	351	308
262	302	267	305	352	309
263	303	268	306	353	310
264	305	269	307	354	311
265	306	270	308	356	312
266	307	271	309	357	313
267	308	272	310	358	314
268	309	273	311	359	315
269	310	274	312	360	316
270	312	275	313	362	317
271	313	276	314	363	318
272	314	277	315	364	319
274	316	280	316	365	320
275	317	281	317	366	321
276	318	281	318	368	322
277	319	282	319	369	323
278	320	283	320	370	324
279	321	284	321	371	325
280	322	285	322	372	326
281	324	286	323	373	327
282	325	287	324	375	328
283	326	288	325	376	329
284	327	289	326	377	330
285	329	290	327	378	331

Vol. 1	*Vol. 1*	*Vol. 2*	*Vol. 1*	*Vol. 1*	*Vol. 2*
Ed. 1	*Ed. 2*	*Ed. 3*	*Ed. 1*	*Ed. 2*	*Ed. 3*
Pg.	*Pg.*	*Pg.*	*Pg.*	*Pg.*	*Pg.*
328	379	332	371	431	372
329	381	333	372	432	373
330	382	334	373	433	374
331	383	335	374	434	375
332	384	336	375	435	376
333	385	336	376	436	376
334	386	337	377	438	377
335	387	338	378	439	378
336	389	339	379	440	379
337	390	340	380	441	380
338	391	341	381	443	381
339	392	342	382	444	382
340	394	343	383	445	383
341	395	344	384	446	384
342	396	345	385	447	385
343	397	346	386	448	386
344	398	347	387	449	387
345	400	348	388	451	387
346	401	349	389	452	388
347	402	350	390	453	389
348	403	351	391	454	390
349	404	352	392	455	391
350	406	353	393	456	392
351	407	354	394	457	393
352	408	355	395	459	394
353	409	356	396	460	395
354	411	357	397	461	396
355	412	358	398	462	397
356	413	359	399	464	398
357	414	360	400	465	399
358	415	361	401	466	400
359	417	362	402	467	401
360	418	363	403	468	402
361	419	364	404	470	403
362	420	365	405	471	404
363	421	366	406	472	405
364	422	366	407	473	405
365	424	367	408	474	406
366	425	368	409	475	407
367	426	369	410	476	408
368	427	370	411	478	409
369	428	371	412	479	410
370	429	371			

NOTES

EPIGRAPH. *Young.* Edward Young, *The Complaint or Night-Thoughts on Life, Death, and Immortality* (1742-44), IV, 629:

Are passions, then, the pagans of the soul? Reason alone baptized?

Kierkegaard had *Einige Werke von Dr. Eduard Young*, I-III, tr. J. A. Ebert, (Braunschweig, Hildesheim: 1767-72; *ASKB* 1911). There were two Danish translations at the time, *Forsøg til en Oversættelse af Dr. Edward Youngs Klager eller Nattetanker*, tr. Emanuel Balling (Helsingør: 1767), and *Dr. Edward Youngs Klage eller Natte-tanker*, tr. Barthold J. Lodde (Copenhagen: 1783). The Danish translation in *Either/Or* does not strictly follow Ebert (I, p. 95), Balling (p. 112), or Lodde (p. 108).

PREFACE

1. See Supplement, pp. 496-99 (*Pap.* III B 185:1-3, 187:1, 2).

2. See, for example, G. W. F. Hegel, *Wissenschaft der Logik*, I, *Georg Wilhelm Friedrich Hegel's Werke. Vollständige Ausgabe*, I-XVIII, ed. Philipp Marheineke et al. (Berlin: 1832-45; *ASKB* 549-65), p. 178; *Sämtliche Werke. Jubiläumsausgabe* [*J.A.*], I-XXVI, ed. Hermann Glockner (Stuttgart: 1927-40), IV, p. 656; *Hegel's Science of Logic* (tr. of *W.L.*, Lasson ed., 1923; Kierkegaard had 2 ed., 1833-34), tr. A. V. Miller (New York: Humanities Press, 1969), p. 524:

The inner is determined as the form of *reflected immediacy* or of essence over against the outer as the form of being, but the two are only one identity. This identity is first, the substantial unity of both as a substrate pregnant with content, or the *absolute fact* [*Sache*], in which the two determinations are indifferent, external moments. By virtue of this, it is a content and that totality which is the inner that equally becomes external, but in this externality is not the result of becoming or transition but is identical with itself. The outer, according to this determination, is not only *identical* with the inner in respect of content but both are only *one fact*.

See *Fear and Trembling*, p. 69, *KW* VI (*SV* III 118); *Pap.* III B 28.

3. See John 3:8.

4. See Herodotus, *History*, VII, 34-35; *Die Geschichten des Herodotos*, I-II, tr. Friedrich Lange (Berlin: 1811; *ASKB* 1116-17), II, pp. 159-60; *Herodotus*, I-IV, tr. A. D. Godley (Loeb, New York: Putnam, 1921-24), III, pp. 347-49:

Beginning then from Abydos they whose business it was made bridges across to that headland, the Phoenicians one of flaxen cables, and the Egyptians the second, which was of papyrus. From Abydos to the opposite shore it is a distance of seven furlongs. But no sooner had the strait been bridged than a great storm swept down and broke and scattered all that work.

When Xerxes heard of that, he was very angry, and gave command that the Hellespont be scourged with three hundred lashes, and a pair of fetters be thrown into the sea; nay, I have heard ere now that he sent branders with the rest to brand the Hellespont. This is certain, that he charged them while they scourged to utter words outlandish and presumptuous: "Thou bitter water," they should say, "our master thus punishes thee, because thou didst him wrong albeit he had done thee none. Yea, Xerxes the king will pass over thee, whether thou wilt or no; it is but just that no man offers thee sacrifice, for thou art a turbid and a briny river." Thus he commanded that the sea should be punished, and that they who had been overseers of the bridging of the Hellespont should be beheaded.

5. A town about twenty miles northwest of Copenhagen.

6. Holland-made paper with a beehive watermark.

7. The term as used by Kierkegaard, who constructed the plural form from the Greek singular used in translating the Psalms, where the Hebrew *Selah* probably indicates a liturgical or musical pause, means aphoristic, lyrical reflections in a range of substantive refrains. See Supplement, pp. 504-05 (*Pap*. III B 175, 176, 178; IV A 216).

8. A phrase from the Latin title of *Meditations* by Emperor Marcus Aurelius Antoninus. The auction-catalog of Kierkegaard's library lists *M. Antoninus Commentarii libri XIII*, ed. Johann M. Schulz (Leipzig: 1829; *ASKB* 1218), and *Marc. Aurel. Antonin's Unterhaltungen mit sich selbst*, tr. Johann M. Schulz (Schleswig: 1799; *ASKB* 1219). The phrase appears at the beginning of Kierkegaard's journal notebook EE (February 1, 1839). See *JP* V 5365 (*Pap*. II A 340).

9. With reference to the following sentence, see Supplement, p. 504 (*Pap*. III B 176).

10. With reference to the following two paragraphs, see Supplement, pp. 500-02 (*Pap*. III B 188:1, 188:2).

11. With reference to the remainder of the sentence, see Supplement, p. 502 (*Pap*. III B 188:3).

12. In a discussion of Greek tragedy (in a review of Adam Gottlob Oehlenschläger's *Dina*, *Intelligensblade*, II, 16-17, November 15, 1842, p. 80), Johan Ludvig Heiberg wrote that the word "interesting" is a "modern concept, for which the ancient languages do not have an equivalent expression" (ed. tr.). See Heiberg, *Prosaiske Skrifter*, I-III (Copenhagen: 1841-43; *ASKB* 1560[III]), III, p. 371. For an interpretation of "the interesting," see *Fear and Trembling*, pp. 82-83, *KW* VI (*SV* III 131).

13. The foolish Wise Men of Gotham put an eel in water in order to drown it and regarded the movements of the eel as signs of the death struggle. In Danish, such stories are associated with the *Molboer*, residents of Mols, a peninsular area northeast of Aarhus in Jutland.

14. See *Either/Or*, II, p. 207, *KW* IV (*SV* II 186).

15. Ibid., p. 320 (287).

16. See Diogenes Laertius, *Lives of Eminent Philosophers*, I, 13, 106-08; *Diogenis Laertii de vitis philosophorum*, I-II (Leipzig: 1833; *ASKB* 1109), I, pp. 6, 51-53; *Diogen Laërtses filosofiske Historie*, I-II, tr. Børge Riisbrigh (Copenhagen: 1812; *ASKB* 1110-11), I, pp. 5, 48-50; *Lives of Eminent Philosophers*, I-II, tr. R. D. Hicks (Loeb, New York: Putnam, 1925), I, pp. 15, 111-13.

17. *Allgemeines Gelehrten-Lexicon*, I-IV, ed. Christian Gottlieb Jöcher (Leipzig: 1750-51; *ASKB* 948-51); *Fortsetzung und Ergänzungen*, ed. Johann Christoph Adelung (Leipzig: 1784-87; *ASKB* 952-53).

18. *Le Grand Dictionnaire historique*, I-VI, ed. Louis Morèri (Basel: 1731-32; *ASKB* 1965-69).

19. Francois Boieldieu's opera *La Dame blanche*, text (based on Walter Scott's *The Monastery*) by Eugene Scribe, tr. Thomas Overskou (Copenhagen: 1826), p. 12. See *Kierkegaard: Letters and Documents*, Letters 62, 239, pp. 126, 336, *KW* XXV.

20. With reference to the remainder of the sentence, see Supplement, p. 502 (*Pap*. III B 187:3).

21. With reference to the remainder of the sentence, see Supplement, p. 502 (*Pap*. III B 187:6).

22. With reference to the following four sentences, see Supplement, pp. 502-03 (*Pap*. III B 187:5).

23. Cf. I Corinthians 7:29-31.

24. See Supplement p. 503 (*Pap*. III B 169, 171).

DIAPSALMATA

1. See Supplement, p. 504 (*Pap*. III B 178).

2. See Supplement, p. 504 (*Pap*. II A 340, III B 175).

3. By Paul Pelisson (1624-1693), possibly found by Kierkegaard in Lessing's *Zerstreute Anmerkungen über das Epigramm*. See *Gotthold Ephraim Lessing's sämmtliche Schriften*, I-XXXII (Berlin: 1825-28; *ASKB* 1747-62), XVII, p. 82.

4. With reference to the following paragraph, see Supplement, p. 504 (*Pap*. III B 179:2, 187:4).

5. Phalaris (570/65-554/49 B.C.), tyrant of Agrigentum. See Lucian, *Phalaris I*, 11-12; *Luciani Samosatensis opera*, I-IV (Leipzig: 1829; *ASKB* 1131-34), II, pp. 256-57; *Lucian*, I-VIII, tr. A. M. Harmon (Loeb, New York: Macmillan, 1913), I, pp. 17-19:

As for my gift, it is time you heard where and how I got this bull. I did not order it of the sculptor myself—I hope I may never be so insane as to want such things!—but there was a man in our town called Perilaus, a good metal-worker but a bad man. Completely missing my point of view, this fellow thought to do me a favour by inventing a new punishment, imagining that I wanted to punish people in any and every way. So he made the bull and came to me with it, a very beautiful thing to look at and a very close copy of nature; motion and voice were all it needed to make it seem actually alive. At the sight of it I cried out at once: "The thing is good enough for Apollo; we must send the bull to the god!" But Perilaus at my elbow said: "What if you knew the trick of it and the purpose it serves?" With that he opened the bull's back and said: "If you wish to punish anyone, make him get into this contrivance and lock him up; then attach these flutes to the nose of the bull and have a fire lighted underneath. The man will groan and shriek in the grip of unremitting pain, and his voice will make you the sweetest possible music on the flutes, piping dolefully and lowing piteously; so that while he is punished you are entertained by having flutes played to you." When I heard this, I was disgusted with the wicked ingenuity of the fellow and hated the idea of the contrivance, so I gave him a punishment that fitted his crime. "Come now, Perilaus," said I, "if this is not mere empty boasting, show us the real nature of the invention by getting into it yourself and imitating people crying out, so that we may know whether the music you speak of is really made on the flutes." Perilaus complied, and when he was inside, I locked him up and had a fire kindled underneath saying: "Take the reward you deserve for your wonderful invention, and as you are our music-master, play the first tune yourself!" So, he, indeed, got his deserts by thus having the enjoyment of his own ingenuity. But I had the fellow taken out while he was still alive and breathing, that he might not pollute the work by dying in it; then I had him thrown over a cliff to lie unburied, and after purifying the bull, sent it to you to be dedicated to the god. I also had the whole story inscribed on it—my name as the giver; that of Perilaus, the maker; his idea; my justice; the apt punishment; the songs of the clever metal-worker and the first trial of the music.

See *Practice in Christianity, KW* XX (*SV* XII 233).

6. An island across the ship channel from Copenhagen proper. In Kierkegaard's time, the truck gardens and small farms of Amager produced considerable foodstuffs for the city.

7. See Supplement, p. 505 (*Pap.* IV A 216).

8. In Danish, the infant's babbling utterance *da-da* also means "spanking."

9. See Supplement, pp. 460-67 (*Pap.* I A 331, pp. 145-46).

10. See Supplement, pp. 472, 505-07 (*Pap.* I A 339; III B 191:4).

11. With reference to the following paragraph, see Supplement, pp. 507-08 (*Pap.* II A 637).

12. See *JP* I 805 (*Pap.* III A 96); *Repetition*, p. 173, *KW* VI (*SV* III 210-11).

13. Cf. Ernst Theodor Amadeus Hoffmann, *Lebens-Ansichten des Katers Murr, E.T.A. Hoffmann's ausgewählte Schriften*, I-X (Berlin: 1827-28; *ASKB* 1712-16), VIII, pp. v-vi, viii. See Supplement, p. 508 (*Pap.* III A 111).

14. Cf. *Sickness unto Death*, p. 74, *KW* XIX (*SV* XI 185).

15. With reference to the following paragraph, see Supplement, p. 508 (*Pap.* III A 112).

16. With reference to the following paragraph, see Supplement, p. 509 (*Pap.* III A 114).

17. The Danish text has the masculine pronoun; the similar journal entry has the feminine pronoun. See Supplement, p. 509 (*Pap.* III A 114).

18. Cf. *Two Ages*, pp. 97-99, 103, and notes 69 and 72, *KW* XIV (*SV* VIII 91-92, 96).

19. Jonathan Swift (1667-1745), Anglican dean, English writer, author of *Gulliver's Travels*, etc. He gave his fortune for the founding of a hospital for the insane in Dublin, and during the few last years of his life he was severely debilitated. See, for example, Jonathan Swift, *Satyrische und ernsthafte Schriften*, I-VIII (Zurich: 1756-66; *ASKB* 1899-1906), *Vorrede*, I [pp. xxxvii-xxxviii]; Carl Friedrich Flögel, *Geschichte der komischen Litteratur*, I-IV (Liegnitz, Leipzig: 1784-87; *ASKB* 1396-99), II, p. 395.

20. With reference to the following paragraph, see Supplement, p. 509 (*Pap.* II A 373).

21. David Hartley (1705-1757), English philosopher and physician.

22. See Supplement, p. 509 (*Pap.* II A 373).

23. With reference to the following paragraph, see Supplement, pp. 509-10 (*Pap.* II A 400, 401).

24. With reference to the following paragraph, see Supplement, p. 510 (*Pap.* II A 414).

25. Cornelius Nepos (c. 1 B.C.), Roman historian. See his "Eumenes," V, 4-5, *The Book of Cornelius Nepos on the Great Generals of Foreign Nations*, XVIII; *Cornelii Nepotis vitae excellentium imperatorum* (Paris: n.d.), p. 99; *Cornelius Nepos*, together with *Lucius Anneaus Florus*, tr. John C. Rolfe (Loeb, New York: Putnam, 1929), p. 583.

26. With reference to the following paragraph, see Supplement, p. 510 (*Pap.* II A 421).

27. The italicized words are in italicized English in the Danish text.

28. With reference to the following paragraph, see Supplement, p. 510 (*Pap.* II A 435).

29. With reference to the following paragraph, see Supplement, p. 510 (*Pap.* II A 451).

30. Adam Gottlob Oehlenschläger, *Aladdin, eller Den forunderlige Lampe, Poetiske Skrifter*, I-II (Copenhagen: 1805; *ASKB* 1598), II; *Aladdin or the Wonderful Lamp*, tr. Henry Meyer (Copenhagen: Gyldendal, 1968). See *JP* I 973; IV 4928 (*Pap.* X¹ A 393; II A 451). In 1839, eleven performances of *Aladdin* were given in Copenhagen over a period of five weeks, beginning on April 17. Noureddin, mentioned later in the paragraph, is a sorcerer in the play.

31. With reference to the following paragraph, see Supplement, p. 511 (*Pap.* II A 540).

32. In Hebrew, a marking of a consonant that is to be pronounced with a suggestion of a vowel.

33. In Hebrew, a marking of a consonant to denote pronunciation more as a stop than as a spirant.

34. Certain dignitaries of the Ottoman empire were preceded by a banner bearing three horse tails.

35. Cf. *Repetition*, p. 170, *KW* VI (*SV* III 208).

36. Popular German printed pictures and picture cards. See *Repetition*, p. 158, *KW* VI *Sickness unto Death*, p. 79, *KW* XIX.

37. With reference to the following sentence, see Supplement, p. 511 (*Pap.* III B 179:3).

38. With reference to the following paragraph, see Supplement, p. 512 (*Pap.* III A 218).

39. Cf. *JP* V 5372 (*Pap.* II A 382).

40. With reference to the following two sentences, see *Letters*, Letter 8, *KW* XXV.

41. In Greek mythology, Lynceus of Messina was one of the Argonauts who accompanied Jason in the search for the Golden Fleece and was noted for his keenness of sight.

42. In Greek mythology, the giants, vanquished by the gods, were imprisoned in the volcanoes and were the cause of volcanic eruptions and noise.

43. See *The Concept of Irony, with Continual Reference to Socrates, KW* II (*SV* XIII 329).

44. With reference to the remainder of the paragraph, see *Letters*, Letter 11, *KW* XXV.

45. With reference to the following paragraph, see Supplement, p. 512 (*Pap.* II A 273).

46. With reference to the following paragraph, see Supplement, pp. 512-13 (*Pap.* II A 203; III A 49).

47. A term used in the Greek translation of Job 15:11 in the sense of discipline.

48. See *Letters*, Letter 72, *KW* XXV.

49. See Supplement, p. 513 (*Pap.* II A 112).

50. A drawbridge across the ship channel between Copenhagen and Amager. See *Letters*, Letter 17, *KW* XXV.

51. See Supplement, p. 513 (*Pap.* I A 158).

52. With reference to the following paragraph, see Supplement, pp. 513-14 (*Pap.* III B 179:8).

53. During the Middle Ages, some students wandered from university to university. See, for example, Johann Wolfgang von Goethe, *Faust*, I, l. 968, stage directions, *Goethe's Werke. Vollständige Ausgabe letzter Hand*, I-LX (Stuttgart, Tübingen: 1828-42; *ASKB* 1641-68 [I-LV]), XII, p. 69; *Faust*, tr. Bayard Taylor (New York: Random House, 1950), p. 45.

54. With reference to the following paragraph, see Supplement, p. 514 (*Pap.* III B 179:9).

55. With reference to the following paragraph, see Supplement, p. 514 (*Pap.* III B 179:10).

56. With reference to the following paragraph, see Supplement, p. 514 (*Pap.* II A 415).

57. With reference to the following paragraph, see Supplement, p. 515 (*Pap.* III B 179:13).

58. With reference to the following paragraph, see Supplement, p. 515 (*Pap.* III B 179:14).

59. See Genesis 25:20-34.

60. With reference to the following paragraph, see Supplement, pp. 515-16 (*Pap.* II A 152; III B 179:15). Here and elsewhere Kierkegaard spells the name Vergilius or Virgilius.

61. In the Middle Ages, the Roman poet Virgil (70-19 B.C.) was regarded as a sorcerer. See Supplement, pp. 515-16 (*Pap.* II A 152; III B 41:7, 179:15).

62. See Jens Immanuel Baggesen, *Jeppe, et sjællandsk Eventyr, Jens Baggesens danske Værker*, I-XII (Copenhagen: 1827-32; *ASKB* 1509-20), I, p. 201.

63. With reference to the remainder of the paragraph, see Supplement, p. 516 (*Pap.* III B 179:17).

64. With reference to the following paragraph, see Supplement, p. 517 (*Pap.* III B 179:18).

65. A reference to the sacred bull of Egypt. See Paul Friedrich A. Nitsch, *neues mythologisches Wörterbuch*, I-II, rev. Friedrich Gotthilf Klopfer (Leipzig, Sorau: 1821; *ASKB* 1944-45), I, p. 238.

66. With reference to the following paragraph, see Supplement, p. 517 (*Pap.* III B 179:24).

67. With reference to the following paragraph, see Supplement, p. 517 (*Pap.* III B 179:26).

68. See Psalm 90:4.

69. With reference to the following paragraph, see Supplement, p. 518 (*Pap.* III B 179:30, 32).

70. With reference to the following paragraph, see Supplement, pp. 518-19 (*Pap.* III B 179:34).

71. See Acts 3:2.

72. See pp. 125-28.

73. *Apuleius: Amor und Psyche*, tr. Joseph Kehrein (Giessen: 1834; *ASKB* 1216), p. 40; *Amor and Psyche*, tr. Ralph Mannheim (New York: Pantheon, 1956), p. 18: ' "For soon we shall have issue, and even now your womb, a child's as yet, bears a child like to you. If you keep my secret in silence, he shall be a god; if you divulge it, a mortal.' "

74. With reference to the following paragraph, see Supplement, p. 519 (*Pap.* III B 128).

75. Danish: *gennemlide*. The definitive Danish dictionary, *Ordbog over det danske Sprog*, VI, col. 841, states that the word was coined by Kierkegaard.

76. With reference to the following paragraph, see Supplement, p. 552 (*Pap.* III B 122:20).

77. See, for example, *JP* V 5535 (*Pap.* III A 179); *Letters*, Letters 62, 68, 69, pp. 125, 136, 139, *KW* XXV, which Kierkegaard wrote in Berlin while he was attending lectures by Friedrich Wilhelm Joseph Schelling.

78. With reference to the following paragraph, see Supplement, p. 520 (*Pap*. III B 179:46).

79. On recollection (and the distinction between recollection and memory), see *Stages on Life's Way, KW* XI (*SV* VI 15-21).

80. With reference to the following paragraph, see Supplement, pp. 520-21 (*Pap*. III B 179:47).

81. See note 79 above.

82. With reference to the following paragraph, see Supplement, p. 521 (*Pap*. III B 186).

83. With reference to the following paragraph, see Supplement, p. 521 (*Pap*. III B 179:51).

84. Trophonius was a legendary Greek architect of the first temple at Delphi; the site of the oracle of Lebradea was the Trophonean cave. The story of Parmeniscus is told by the Greek antiquarian Athenaeus in *The Deipnosophists*, XIV, 614; *Athenaeus*, I-VII, tr. Charles Burton Gulick (Loeb, New York: Putnam, 1927-51), VI, pp. 307-09.

85. Danish: *Velbekomme*, literally "May it do you good," the customary reply by the hostess upon being thanked for the meal.

86. Cf. p. 295.

87. With reference to the following paragraph, see Supplement, pp. 521-23 (*Pap*. II A 36; III B 179:52).

88. In Norse mythology, Fenris, a great wolf, the son of Loki, was chained until Ragnarok (the final destruction of the world in the conflict between Aesir, the gods, and the powers of Hel, led by Loki), when it would devour Odin, the chief of the gods.

89. A modified quotation from Jacob Bærent Møinichen, *Nordiske Folks Overtroe, Guder, Fabler og Helte* (Copenhagen: 1800; *ASKB* 1947), p. 101. The preceding list of materials used in making the chain follows Møinichen in part and in part Nicolai Frederik Severin Grundtvig, *Nordens Mythologi* (Copenhagen: 1832; *ASKB* 1949), pp. 518-19. Instead of Møinichen's *Kvinders Skrig* (cries of women) and *Biørnens Seener* (sinews of bears), Kierkegaard uses versions of Grundtvig's *Kvinde-Skiæg* (beards of women) and *Björne-Græs* (grass of bears). Grundtvig states that his reading of *Seener* as *sina (Græs)* or *Senegræs* (quitch grass) conforms to the requirement that the list contain "altogether *unknown* things."

90. General education or diploma examination at the end of the gymnasium or high school course, a prerequisite for entering the university.

91. See *Letters*, Document VII (transcript of Kierkegaard's *examen artium*), *KW* XXV.

92. With reference to the following paragraph, see Supplement, p. 523 (*Pap*. III B 179:53).

93. See I Timothy 2:4; *Pap*. III A 44. The passage may be an allusion to J. G. Fichte, *Die Anweisung zum seligen Leben, oder auch die Religionslehre, Johann Gottlieb Fichte's sämmtliche Werke*, I-XI (Berlin, Bonn: 1834-46; *ASKB* 489-99), for example, V, pp. 410-12.

94. Giovanni Domenico Cassini (1625-1712), Italian astronomer and first astronomer of the Paris Observatory.

95. With reference to the following paragraph, see Supplement, pp. 523-24 (*Pap.* III B 179:55).

96. Hans Peter Rohde, in *Gaadefulde Stadier paa Kierkegaards Vej* (Copenhagen: 1974), p. 85, has identified this elusive line as an Aeschylus fragment included in *Aeschylos' Werke*, tr. Johann Gustav Droysen (Berlin: 1842; *ASKB* 1046), p. 498 (ed. tr.).

97. With reference to the following paragraph, see Supplement, p. 524 (*Pap.* III B 123).

98. With reference to the following paragraph, see Supplement, p. 524 (*Pap.* 179:56; IV A 217).

99. See *Repetition*, pp. 131-33, *KW* VI (*SV* III 174-75).

100. With reference to the following paragraph, see Supplement, p. 525 (*Pap.* IV A 218).

101. *Aristophanis Comoediae*, I-II, ed. Wilhelm (Guilielm) Dindorf (Leipzig: 1830; *ASKB* 1051), I, pp. 69-70; *Aristophanes*, I-III, tr. Benjamin Bickley Rogers (Loeb, New York: Putnam), I, pp. 127-29. For a German translation of Aristophanes by J. G. Droysen, see *Pap.* III B 179:57.

102. With reference to the following paragraph, see Supplement, p. 525 (*Pap.* III B 179:58).

103. In Greek mythology, Prometheus was chained to a rock because of his violation in giving fire to mankind. By day, a vulture or eagle ate his liver, which healed during the night.

104. In Norse mythology, Loki (or Loke) was a personification of evil. His punishment for the death of Balder, god of light, consisted of being chained to a cliff. Over his head hung a serpent, whose poison dripped on Loki's face. His wife Signe held a bowl over his head, but when she emptied it, poison dripped upon him. This would continue until Ragnarok. See note 88 above.

105. Cf. *Sickness unto Death*, p. 18, *KW* XIX (*SV* XI 132).

106. See Mark 11:23.

107. With reference to the following paragraph, see Supplement, pp. 525-26 (*Pap.* III B 179:59).

108. With reference to the following paragraph, see Supplement, pp. 526-27 (*Pap.* IV A 219).

109. Stilpo of Megara (c. 4 B.C.), teacher of Zeno the Stoic, maintained that universal concepts have no objects and that consequently there are only identical or tautological propositions. Every perception has only a particular object, and no universal predicates can be applied. See Supplement, p. 527 (*Pap.* IV A 219). See, for example, G.W.E. Hegel, *Wissenschaft der Logik*, I, *Georg Wilhelm Friedrich Hegel's Werke. Vollständige Ausgabe*, I-XVIII, ed. Phillip Marheineke et al. (Berlin: 1832-45; *ASKB* 549-65), IV, pp. 30, 32, 34; *Sämtliche Werke. Jubiläumsausgabe* [*J.A.*], I-XXVI, ed. Hermann Glockner (Stuttgart: 1927-40), IV, pp. 508, 510, 512; *Hegel's Science of Logic*, (tr. of *W.L.*

Lasson ed., 1923; Kierkegaard had 2 ed., 1833-34) tr. A. V. Miller (New York: Humanities Press, 1969), pp. 411, 413, 414:

A. IDENTITY

1. Essence is simple immediacy as sublated immediacy. Its negativity is its being; it is self-equal in its absolute negativity, through which otherness and relation-to-other has vanished in its own self into pure equality-with-self. Essence is therefore simple identity-with-self.
2. This identity-with-self is the *immediacy* of reflection. It is not that equality-with-self that *being* or even *nothing* is, but the equality-with-self that has brought itself to unity, not a restoration of itself from an other, but this pure origination from and within itself, *essential* identity.

Remark 2: First Original Law of Thought

In this remark, I will consider in more detail identity as the law of identity which is usually adduced as the first law of thought.

This proposition in its positive expression $A = A$ is, in the first instance, nothing more than the expression of an empty *tautology*. It has therefore been rightly remarked that this law of thought has *no content* and leads no further.

Now as regards other confirmation of the absolute *truth of the law* of identity, this is based on *experience* in so far as appeal is made to the experience of every consciousness; for anyone to whom this proposition $A = A$, *a tree is a tree*, is made, immediately admits it and is satisfied that the proposition as immediately self-evident requires no further confirmation or proof.

110. See Niels Treschow, *Almindelig Logik* (Copenhagen: 1813), pp. 157-59; Hegel, *Wissenschaft der Logik*, II, *Werke*, V, pp. 90-91; *J.A.*, V, pp. 90-91; *Science of Logic*, pp. 641-43:

(c) *The Infinite Judgement . . .*

The *positive* moment of the infinite judgement, of the negation of the negation, is the *reflection of individuality* into itself, whereby it is posited for the first time as a *determinate determinateness*. According to that reflection, the expression of the judgement was: *the individual is individual*. In the judgement of existence, the subject appears as an *immediate* individual and consequently rather as a mere *something* in general. It is through the mediation of the negative and infinite judgements that it is for the first time *posited* as an individual.

The individual is hereby *posited* as continuing itself *into its predicate*, which is identical with it; consequently, too, the universality no longer appears as *immediate* but as a *comprehension* of distinct terms. The positively infinite judgement equally runs: *the universal is universal*, and as such is equally posited as the return into itself.

111. See Hegel, *Wissenschaft der Logik*, II, *Werke*, V, p. 139; *J.A.*, V, p. 139; *Science of Logic*, p. 679:

> As the immediate result of this bare abstraction, we obtain, of course, a *fourth figure* of the syllogism, namely that of the *relationless* syllogism *U-U-U*, which abstracts from the qualitative difference of the terms and consequently has for its determination their merely external unity, namely their *equality*.
>
> (d) *The Fourth Figure: U-U-U, or the Mathematical Syllogism*
>
> 1. The mathematical syllogism runs: if two things or determinations are equal to a third, they are equal to each other. Here the relationship of inherence or subsumption of the terms is extinguished.

112. With reference to the following paragraph, see Supplement, p. 527 (*Pap.* II A 510).

113. The Australian kangaroo.

114. With reference to the title and the following paragraph, see Supplement, pp. 527-29 (*Pap.* III B 179:27, 62, 63, A 117; IV A 220).

115. See Diogenes Laertius, *Lives of Eminent Philosophers*, II, 33; *Diogenis Laertii de vitis philosophorum*, I-II (Leipzig: 1833; *ASKB* 1109), I, p. 76; *Diogen Laërtses filosofiske Historie*, I-II, tr. Børge Riisbrigh (Copenhagen: 1812; *ASKB* 1110-11), I, p. 71; *Lives of Eminent Philosophers*, I-II, tr. R. D. Hicks (Loeb, New York: Putnam, 1925), I, p. 163: "Someone asked him [Socrates] whether he should marry or not, and received the reply, 'Whichever you do you will repent it.' " Cf. Baggesen, "*Ja og Nei*," *Værker*, I, p. 304. See Supplement, p. 529 (*Pap.* III A 117; IV A 220); *Stages, KW* XI (*SV* VI 149-50).

116. See Benedict (Baruch) Spinoza, *Ethics*, V, prop. 36, 40 ("*sub specie aeternitatis*"); *Opera philosophica omnia*, ed. August Gfroerer (Stuttgart: 1830; *ASKB* 788), pp. 427, 429; *The Chief Works of Benedict de Spinoza*, I-II, tr. R.H.M. Elwes (London: Bell, 1912), II, pp. 264-65, 268:

> PROP. XXXVI. *The intellectual love of the mind towards God is that very love of God whereby God loves himself, not in so far as he is infinite, but in so far as he can be explained through the essence of the human mind regarded under the form of eternity; in other words, the intellectual love of the mind towards God is part of the infinite love wherewith God loves himself.*
>
> PROP. XL. *In proportion as each thing possesses more of perfection, so is it more active, and less passive; and, vice versa, in proportion as it is more active, so is it more perfect.*
>
> *Proof.*—In proportion as each thing is more perfect, it possesses more of reality (II, Def. vi.), and, consequently (III.iii. and note), it is to that extent more active and less passive. This demonstration may be reversed, and thus prove that, in proportion as a thing is more active, so is it more perfect. Q.E.D.
>
> *Corollary.*—Hence it follows that the part of the mind which endures, be it great or small, is more perfect than the rest. For the eternal part of the

mind (V.xxiii. xxix.) is the understanding, through which alone we are said
to act (III.iii.); the part which we have shown to perish is the imagination
(V.xxxi.), through which only we are said to be passive (III.iii. and general
Def. of the emotions); therefore, the former, be it great or small, is more
perfect than the latter. *Q.E.D.*

Note.—Such are the doctrines which I had purposed to set forth concerning the mind, in so far as it is regarded without relation to the body; whence,
as also from I.xxi. and other places, it is plain that our mind, in so far as it
understands, is an eternal mode of thinking, which is determined by another eternal mode of thinking, and this other by a third, and so on to infinity; so that all taken together at once constitute the eternal and infinite
intellect of God.

117. See Hegel, *Wissenschaft der Logik*, I, *Werke*, III, pp. 59, 63, 66-67, 68;
J.A. IV, pp. 69, 73, 76-77, 78; *Science of Logic*, pp. 67, 70, 72, 73:

WITH WHAT MUST THE SCIENCE BEGIN?

It is only in recent times that thinkers have become aware of the difficulty
of finding a beginning in philosophy, and the reason for this difficulty and
the possibility of resolving it has been much discussed. What philosophy
begins with must be either *mediated* or *immediate*, and it is easy to show that
it can be neither the one nor the other; thus either way of beginning is re-
futed.

But if no presupposition is to be made and the beginning itself is taken *immediately*, then its only determination is that it is to be the beginning of
logic, of thought as such. All that is present is simply the resolve, which can
also be regarded as arbitrary, that we propose to consider thought as such.
Thus the beginning must be an *absolute*, or what is synonymous here, an
abstract beginning; and so it may not presuppose anything, must not be mediated
by anything nor have a ground; rather it is to be itself the ground of the entire science. Consequently, it must be purely and simply *an* immediacy, or
rather merely *immediacy* itself.

If it were not this pure indeterminateness, if it were determinate, it would
have been taken as something mediated, something already carried a stage
further: what is determinate implies an other to a first. Therefore, it lies in
the *very nature of a beginning* that it must be being and nothing else. To enter
into philosophy, therefore, calls for no other preparations, no further reflections or points of connection.

But the determination of *being* so far adopted for the beginning could also
be omitted, so that the only demand would be that a pure beginning be
made. In that case, we have nothing but the *beginning* itself, and it remains
to be seen what this is. . . .

As yet there is nothing and there is to become something. The beginning
is no pure nothing, but a nothing from which something is to proceed;

therefore being, too, is already contained in the beginning. The beginning, therefore, contains both, being and nothing, is the unity of being and nothing; or is non-being which is at the same time being, and being which is at the same time non-being.

118. See Christian F. Sintenis, *Stunden für die Ewigkeit gelebt* (Berlin: 1791-92); *Timer levede for Evigheden* (Copenhagen: 1795).

119. With reference to the following paragraph, see Supplement, p. 529 (*Pap.* III B 179:64).

120. A series of row houses built by Christian IV early in the eighteenth century as quarters for families of men in the Royal Navy. In 1817, an orphanage in the area was destroyed by fire.

121. See Virgil, *Aeneid*, VI, 424-29; *Virgils Æneide*, I-II, tr. Johan H. Schønheyder (Copenhagen: 1812), I, p. 274; *Virgil*, I-II, tr. H. Rushton Fairclough (Loeb, New York: Putnam, 1918-20), I, pp. 535-37: "The warder buried in sleep, Aeneas wins the entrance, and swiftly leaves the bank of that stream whence none return. At once are heard voices and wailing sore—the souls of infants weeping, whom, on the very threshold of the sweet life they shared not, torn from the breast, the black day swept off and plunged in bitter death."

122. With reference to the remainder of the paragraph, see Supplement, p. 530 (*Pap.* II A 649; III B 179:66).

123. With reference to the following paragraph, see Supplement, p. 530 (*Pap.* III B 179:67).

124. See Exodus 12:22-23.

125. See Supplement, pp. 530-31 (*Pap.* I A 169).

126. With reference to the following paragraph, see Supplement, p. 531 (*Pap.* III B 179:70).

127. See Supplement, p. 505 (*Pap.* IV A 216).

THE IMMEDIATE EROTIC STAGES

1. See Supplement, pp. 531-32 (*Pap.* IV A 222, 223).

2. See Adam Gottlob Oehlenschläger, *Axel og Valborg* (1808), *Oehlenschlägers Tragødier*, I-X (Copenhagen: 1841-44; *ASKB* 1601-05 [I-IX]), V, pp. 3-111.

3. For continuation of this sentence, see Supplement, p. 532 (*Pap.* III B 172:1).

4. "Optimate" (aristocrat) is used here in conjunction with "optimism."

5. Don Juan Tenorio was the fourteenth-century Spanish libertine who became a legendary figure and the leading character in dramas by Molina, Molière, Corneille, and Goldoni, in a ballet by Glück, and in an opera by Mozart. The Italian form "Don Giovanni" is used for the title and for the leading character in Mozart's opera. The opera libretto in Danish translation (text by Lorenzo da Ponte, based on Molière) by Laurids Kruse (Copenhagen: 1807) bears the title *Don Juan*.

6. With reference to the following sentence, see Supplement, p. 532 (*Pap.* IV A 224).

7. For example, Christian H. Weisse, *System der Aesthetik von der Idee der Schönheit*, I-II (Leipzig: 1830; *ASKB* 1379-80).

8. See, for example, G.W.F. Hegel, *Vorlesungen über die Aesthetik*, I, *Georg Wilhelm Friedrich Hegel's Werke. Vollständige Ausgabe*, I-XVIII, ed. Philipp Marheineke et al. (Berlin: 1832-45; *ASKB* 549-65), X¹, pp. 99-101; *Sämtliche Werke. Jubiläumsausgabe [J.A.]*, I-XXVI, ed. Hermann Glockner (Stuttgart: 1927-40), XII, pp. 115-17; *The Philosophy of Fine Art*, I-IV (tr. of *V.A.*, 1 ed., 1835-38; Kierkegaard had this ed.), tr. F.P.B. Osmaston (London: Bell, 1920), I, pp. 103-05:

(*a*) *First*, the origin of artistic creation proceeds from the Idea when, being itself still involved in defective definition and obscurity, or in vicious and untrue determinacy, it becomes embodied in the shapes of art. As indeterminate it does not as yet possess in itself that individuality which the Ideal demands. Its abstract character and one-sidedness leaves its objective presentment still defective and contingent. Consequently this first type of art is rather a mere search after plastic configuration than a power of genuine representation. The Idea has not as yet found the formative principle within itself, and therefore still continues to be the mere effort and strain to find it. We may in general terms describe this form as the *symbolic* type of art. . . .

(*b*) In the *second* type of art, which we propose to call "*Classical*," the twofold defect of symbolic art is annulled. Now the symbolic configuration is imperfect, because, first, the Idea here only enters into consciousness in abstract determinacy or indeterminateness: and, secondly, by reason of the fact that the coalescence of import with embodiment can only throughout remain defective, and in its turn also wholly abstract. The classical art-type solves both these difficulties. It is, in fact, the free and adequate embodiment of the Idea in the shape which, according to its notional concept, is uniquely appropriate to the Idea itself. The Idea is consequently able to unite in free and completely assonant concord with it. For this reason the classical type of art is the first to present us with the creation and vision of the complete Ideal, and to establish the same as realized fact.

9. *The Battle of the Frogs and the Mice*, a mock-epic attributed to Homer. Kierkegaard may have known of the work through conversations with Poul Martin Møller, his favorite university professor, who made a Danish translation. See *Efterladte Skrifter*, I-VI (2 ed., Copenhagen: 1848), I, pp. 254-64. The piece is not included in 1 ed. (Copenhagen: 1839-43; *ASKB* 1574-76).

10. A term applied to the painting that qualified a painter for admission as a member of the Academy of Art.

11. See Acts 1:9.

12. See Supplement, p. 532 (*Pap.* II A 260).

13. The Danish *sandselig* means "sensate" (an elemental, purely neutral word meaning endowed with sensation, perceived or perceivable through the

senses, "sens-ible"), "sensuous" (pertaining to the senses, susceptible to influences through the senses and imagination related to the senses), or "sensual" (unduly indulgent to the appetites, carnal). Only the context can suggest which English term is to be used in the translation. John Milton coined the word "sensuous" as a neutral term meaning "perceivable through the senses" in contradistinction to "sensual" (see *OED*, "sensuous"). With time, however, the distinction has become blurred, and the two words are frequently, albeit erroneously, used synonymously.

14. The Danish *Genialitet* cannot, of course, be rendered as "geniality." Neither can it be translated as "genius," in the sense of an extraordinarily gifted individual. Here it means defining characteristic, particular qualification, or elemental originality.

15. Horace, *Epistles*, I, 6, 45; Q. *Horatii Flacci opera* (Leipzig: 1828; *ASKB* 1248), p. 563; *Horace Satires, Epistles and Ars Poetica*, tr. H. Rushton Fairclough (Loeb, New York: Putnam, 1929), p. 289.

16. Cf. Hebrews 1:1.

17. An enclitic is a word that loses its accent in being attached to another word, as "not" in "cannot."

18. See *Irony, KW* II (*SV* XIII 273, 292).

19. Eros and Psyche. See p. 31 and note 73.

20. Cf. *Fragments*, p. 72, *KW* VII (*SV* IV 235).

21. The elder Cato (234-149 B.C.) was accustomed to conclude his speeches in the Roman senate with "*Ceterum* [or *Praeterea*] *censeo Carthaginem esse delendam* [Furthermore I am of the opinion that Carthage must be destroyed]."

22. See Paul Friedrich A. Nitsch, *neues mythologisches Wörterbuch*, I-II, rev. Friedrich Gotthilf Klopfer (Leipzig, Sorau: 1821; *ASKB* 1944-45), I, p. 619; II, p. 143. Kierkegaard extends to Diana's own birth the help she gave her mother, Latona, in the birth of her twin brother Apollo.

23. Henrich Steffens, *Caricaturen des Heiligsten*, I-II (Leipzig: 1819-21; *ASKB* 793-94), II, pp. 82-120. In the text, the spelling of the first word in the title is a Danish modification.

24. See Luke 19:40.

25. Achim von Arnim, *Owen Tudor, Novellen*, I-VI (Berlin: 1839-42; *ASKB* 1612-17), II, p. 260 (ed. tr.).

26. *Irische Elfenmärchen* (Thomas Crofton Croker, *Fairy Legends and Traditions of the South of Ireland*; London: 1825), tr. Grimm Brothers (Leipzig: 1826; *ASKB* 1423); Croker, "The Young Piper," *Fairy Legends* (London: 1906), pp. 43, 46-50. The portions cited are in "*Der kleine Sackpfeifer*," a story about a little bagpipe player who bewitches the living and the inanimate with his playing.

27. With reference to the remainder of the chapter, see Supplement, pp. 533-36 (*Pap.* I C 125). See also *JP* I 133 (*Pap.* II A 180).

28. Serious opera or grand opera, opera without spoken lines.

29. Cf. Virgil, *Georgics*, I, 404; *Virgil*, I-II, tr. H. Rushton Fairclough (Loeb, New York: Putnam, 1920), I, pp. 108-09.

30. In Norse mythology, Thor was challenged to a drinking feat by Loki, who had arranged to have Thor's drinking horn connected with the ocean. See, for example, Adam Oehlenschläger, *Thors Reise til Jothunheim*, IV, 34-40, V, 24-29, *Nordiske Digte* (Copenhagen: 1807; *ASKB* 1599), pp. 86-88.

31. *Figaros Givtermaal eller den gale Dag. Syngestykke i fire Akter oversat til Musik af Mozart efter den italiensk Omarbeidelse af Beaumarchais' franske Original*, tr. Niels Thoroup Bruun (Copenhagen: 1817), I, 5, p. 21; *Le Nozze di Figaro (The Marriage of Figaro)*, tr. Ruth and Thomas Martin (New York: G. Schirmer, 1951), I, 5, p. 67 (the Page's lines are lacking).

32. From Leporello's list of his master's conquests, *Don Juan. Opera i tvende Akter bearbeidet til Mozarts Musik*, tr. Laurids Kruse (Copenhagen: 1807), I, 6, p. 23; *Don Giovanni*, tr. Ellen H. Bleiler (New York: Dover, 1964), I, 2, p. 102.

33. See Bruun, *Figaro*, III, 13, p. 109; Martin, *Figaro*, IV, 21, p. 351. Cherubino, dressed as a girl, is kissed on the forehead by the countess, who therefore knows about the "mark," invisible to others.

34. *Tryllefløiten. Oversat efter Schickanders Syngespil die Zauberflöte og lagt under Mozarts Musik til samme*, tr. Niels Thoroup Bruun (Copenhagen: 1816).

35. See note 102 below.

36. Julius Caesar's summary report of the battle against King Pharanaces of Pontus at Zela in 47 B.C.

37. Horace, *Epistles*, I, 2, 42; *Opera*, p. 552; Loeb, p. 265.

38. See I Samuel 16:14-23.

39. Probably an allusion to Johannes Carsten Hauch's "*Bjergpigen*," *Lyriske Digte* (Copenhagen: 1842), p. 164.

40. See note 34 above. Presumably the reference is to the second edition (1826), which does not bear the translator's name, as does the first edition (1816).

41. Bruun, *Tryllefløiten*, II, 3, p. 59; *The Magic Flute*, tr. Judith A. Eckelmeyer (New York: Mellen Press, 1979), II, 3, p. 30.

42. Bruun, *Tryllefløiten*, I, 2, p. 9; Eckelmeyer, *Magic Flute*, II, 2, p. 30.

43. Bruun, *Tryllefløiten*, II, 29, p. 107; Eckelmeyer, *Magic Flute*, II, 29, p. 55.

44. See Heinrich Gustav Hotho, *Vorstudien für Leben und Kunst* (Stuttgart, Tübingen: 1835; *ASKB* 580), pp. 92-147.

45. The two Latin phrases traditionally referred to the two elements, the bread and the wine, in Holy Communion.

46. *Den i den ganske Verden bekjendte Ertz-Sort-Kunstner og Trold-Karl Doctor Johan Faust, og Hans med Djevelen oprettede Forbund, Forundringsfulde Levnet og skrækkelige Endeligt* (Copenhagen: n.d.; *ASKB* U35). See Supplement, p. 537 (*Pap.* I C 107); *Pap.* I C 107, pp. 278-92; XII, pp. 242-60. Kierkegaard's marked copy is in the Kierkegaard Archives, Royal Library, Copenhagen.

47. E. M. Tribler, bookbinder, Holmensgade 114, Copenhagen, published many folk books between 1818 and 1839. See Supplement, p. 537 (*Pap.* I C 107).

48. Literally, "straw market," in Kierkegaard's time just outside the Copenhagen city wall at Vesterport.

49. Part Two of *Faust* was first published in volume XII of *Goethe's Werke. Vollständige Ausgabe letzter Hand*, I-LX (Stuttgart, Tübingen: 1828-42; *ASKB* 1642-68 [I-LV]).

50. An allusion to the practice of omitting the actual publication date from some ballads and books and substituting "*Trykt i dette Aar* [Printed this year]."

51. Gottfried August Bürger, *Lenore* (1773), *Bürgers Gedichte* (Gotha, New York: 1828), pp. 48-57.

52. The current number in Leporello's list of his master's conquests. See Kruse, *Don Juan*, I, 6, p. 23; Bleiler, *Don Giovanni*, I, 2, p. 102.

53. Cf. *Letters*, Letter 21, p. 68, *KW* XXV.

54. The daughters of Thespius, founder of the city Thespia in Boeotia. See Nitsch, I, pp. 815-16; II, p. 586.

55. Possibly a reference to the poem *Don Juan* by George Gordon Byron, which he worked on intermittently until his death in 1824. Kierkegaard had *Lord Byron's sämmtliche Werke. Nach den Anforderungen unserer Zeit neu übersetzt von Mehreren*, I-X (Stuttgart: 1839; *ASKB* 1868-70).

56. *Repellerende* is a Latin word in Danish form (present participle) meaning "incoherent," "discrete," "separate." *Momenter* means "moments" in the temporal sense and "elements."

57. See, for example, *Vorstudien*, pp. 109-10.

58. From Leporello's list aria. See Kruse, *Don Juan*, I, 6, p. 23, which does not have lines directly corresponding to the Italian lines; Bleiler, *Don Giovanni*, p. 102.

59. See note 34 above.

60. Cf. Ephesians 6:11.

61. In Greek mythology, Nemesis was the goddess of vengeance.

62. *Armuth, Reichthum und Busse der Gräfin Dolores*, I-II (Berlin: 1810; *ASKB* 1621-22, 1840 ed.), II, p. 21. See Supplement, p. 537 (*Pap.* II A 70).

63. This characterization is the main clue to "The Seducer's Diary," pp. 313-445.

64. See, for example, *Fear and Trembling*, pp. 82-83, *KW* VI (*SV* III 131); *Postscript, KW* XII (*SV* VII 221); *JP* II 2105-09 and p. 603; VII, p. 51.

65. Bruun, *Figaro*, II, 6, p. 58; Martin, *Figaro*, II, 14, p. 186.

66. Kruse, *Don Juan*, I, 8, p. 26; Bleiler, *Don Giovanni*, I, 3, p. 104.

67. Presumably an allusion to the old custom whereby the ruler had a right to the bride before the groom.

68. In Greek legend, Endymion, a young shepherd, was loved by Selene (the moon).

69. The Don Juan dramatization of Molière (pseudonym of Jean Baptiste Poquelin, 1622-1673), *Le festin de Pierre*, was first presented in 1665. Before 1842, Kierkegaard had some of Molière's plays in Danish, including *Don Juan*, in *J.B.P. Molières udvalgte Skuespil*, tr. Knud Lyne Rahbek (Copenhagen: 1813; *ASKB* 1921).

70. Johann Karl August Musäus (1735-1787). Kierkegaard had his *Volksmärchen der Deutschen*, I-V (Vienna: 1815; *ASKB* 1434-38).

71. Johann Ludwig Tieck (1773-1853). Among various works by Tieck, Kierkegaard had *Sämmtliche Werke* I-II (Paris: 1837; *ASKB* 1848-49).

72. Johan Ludvig Heiberg (1791-1860), the leading Danish writer, literary critic, dramatist, and Hegelian philosopher. His *Don Juan*, first presented in 1814, was published in *Skuespil af J. L. Heiberg*, I-VII (Copenhagen: 1833-41; *ASKB* 1553-59).

73. The *Don Juan* of the Danish poet, esthetician, and zoologist Johannes Carsten Hauch (1790-1872) was published in *Gregorius den Syvende og Don Juan. To Dramaer* (Copenhagen: 1829). See Supplement, p. 537 (*Pap*. III B 172:2).

74. The ballet *Don Juan*, based on Molière and with music by Christoph Willibald Glück (1714-1787), was first performed in Vienna in 1761.

75. See note 55 above.

76. The theme of the last part of volume I of *Either/Or*, "The Seducer's Diary."

77. See Rahbek, *Don Juan*, IV, 3, pp. 231-37, the episode with the creditor Monsieur Dimanche; *Don Juan, Six Prose Comedies of Molière*, tr. George Graveley (London: Oxford University Press, 1968), pp. 79-83. This scene is not included in Kruse's version of the opera.

78. See Supplement, p. 538 (*Pap*. I C 109).

79. See Rahbek, *Don Juan*, IV, 6, pp. 237-39; Graveley, *Don Juan*, pp. 83-85.

80. See Rahbek, *Don Juan*, II, 3, pp. 202-05; Graveley, *Don Juan*, pp. 55-57.

81. The wide part of the channel between Amager and Sjælland at Copenhagen is now called Kalveboderne.

82. Rahbek, *Don Juan*, II, 1, pp. 190-92; Graveley, *Don Juan*, pp. 46-47.

83. See Rahbek, *Don Juan*, I, 1, pp. 175-76; Graveley, *Don Juan*, p. 35.

84. See Rahbek, *Don Juan*, III, 1, p. 214; Graveley, *Don Juan*, p. 64.

85. In Heiberg's version, Mr. Paaske corresponds to Monsieur Dimanche in Molière.

86. In Hegel's thought, reproduction is a level above the immediate, the sensate, the ability to have sensation. See, for example, Hegel, *Encyclopädie der philosophischen Wissenschaften*, II, *Die Naturphilosophie*, para. 353, *Zuzatz, Werke*, VII[1], p. 559; *J.A.*, IX, p. 585; *Hegel's Philosophy of Nature* (tr. of *E.P.W.*, Nicolin and Pöggeler ed., 1959; Kierkegaard had 3 ed., 1841), tr. A. V. Miller (Oxford: Oxford University Press, 1970), p. 358:

> The simple identity of the universal subjectivity of the Notion with itself, the sentient creature—which in the sphere of spirit is the ego—is sensibility; if an other is brought into contact with it, it transforms this directly into itself. The particularity, which in sensibility is at first only ideally posited, receives its due in irritability, where the activity of the subject consists in repelling the other with which it is in relation. Irritability is also sensation, subjectivity, but in the form of relation. But whereas sensibility is only this

negative relationship to other, reproduction is this infinite negativity of transforming what is outside me into myself, and myself into externality. Only then is universality real and not abstract—developed sensibility. Reproduction passes through sensibility and irritability and absorbs them; it is thus derived, posited universality which, however, as self-producing, is at the same time concrete singularity. It is reproduction which is first the whole—the immediate unity-with-self in which the whole has at the same time entered into relationship with itself.

87. Rahbek, *Don Juan*, II, 2, pp. 197-202; Graveley, *Don Juan*, pp. 51-55.

88. Rahbek, *Don Juan*, II, 2, p. 198; Graveley, *Don Juan*, p. 52.

89. Rahbek, *Don Juan*, II, 4, pp. 206-11; Graveley, *Don Juan*, pp. 57-61.

90. In the temple in Jerusalem, alms, contributions, and the temple tax were presented not in gentile coinage but in Jewish coinage. See, for example, Matthew 21:12; Mark 11:15; John 2:14-15.

91. The Danish *sætte* is used in the sense in which Fichte and Hegel use *setzen:* to posit. See, for example, Hegel, *Wissenschaft der Logik, Werke*, V, p. 16; *J.A.*, V, p. 16; *Science of Logic*, pp. 584-85:

In point of fact, the *comprehension* of an object consists in nothing else than that the ego makes it *its own*, pervades it and brings it into *its own form*, that is, into the *universality* that is immediately a *determinateness*, or a determinateness that is immediately universality. As intuited or even in ordinary conception, the object is still something *external* and *alien*. When it is comprehended, the being-in-and-for-self which it possesses in intuition and pictorial thought is transformed into a *positedness*; the *I* in *thinking* it pervades it. But it is *only* as it is in thought that the object is truly *in and for itself*; in intuition or ordinary conception it is only an *Appearance*. Thought sublates the *immediacy* with which the object at first confronts us and thus converts the object into a positedness; but this its *positedness* is *its being-in-and-for-itself*, or its *objectivity*.

92. See Kierkegaard's letter to Emil Boesen, *Letters*, Letter 60, *KW* XXV.

93. See *Irony, KW* II (*SV* XIII 390).

94. See Kruse, *Don Juan*, II, 20, pp. 123-26; Bleiler, *Don Giovanni*, II, 6, pp. 196-99.

95. See Jens Baggesen, *"Kallundborgs Krønike," Jens Baggesens danske Værker*, I-XII (Copenhagen: 1827-32; *ASKB* 1509-20), I, p. 236 (ed. tr.):

And no one, not any mother's wight,
Can slay with vengeance one who has died;
Though the thief himself the dust must bite,
All advantage was on his side.

See *Irony, KW* II (*SV* XIII 179).

96. See Kruse, *Don Juan*, I, 10, p. 35; Bleiler, *Don Giovanni*, I, 3, pp. 111-12.

97. See Supplement, p. 538 (*Pap.* I A 240).

98. With reference to the following three sentences, see Supplement, pp. 538-39 (*Pap.* I A 111).

99. *Expectorere*, a loan word literally meaning "to expectorate," comes from the Latin *ex* + *pectus* (from + heart, breast). See *Fear and Trembling*, p. 27, *KW* VI (*SV* III 79); *Repetition*, p. 157, *KW* VI (*SV* III 196).

100. The Danish *Mellemhverandre*, literally, "between each other," is not found in *Ordbog over det danske Sprog*. It is very rarely used in the *Værker* and *Papirer*, and the contexts seem to require a variety of translations. See, for example, *Irony, KW* II (*SV* XIII 232, 262, 362); *Two Ages*, p. 39, *KW* XIV (*SV* VIII 36); *JP* V 5659 (*Pap.* IV B 78).

101. See Diogenes Laertius, *Lives of Eminent Philosophers*, I, 33; *Diogenis Laertii de vitis philosophorum*, I-II (Leipzig: 1833; *ASKB* 1109), I, p. 15; *Diogen Laërtses filosofiske Historie*, I-II, tr. Børge Riisbrigh (Copenhagen: 1812; *ASKB* 1110-11), I, p. 14; *Diogenes Laertius Lives of Eminent Philosophers*, I-II, tr. R. D. Hicks (Loeb, New York: Putnam, 1925), I, p. 35: "Hermippus in his *Lives* refers to Thales the story which is told by some of Socrates, namely, that he used to say there were three blessings for which he was grateful to Fortune: 'first, that I was born a human being and not one of the brutes; next, that I was born a man and not a woman; thirdly, a Greek and not a barbarian.' "

102. The distinction between subject (being-for-itself) and substance (being-in-itself) is found in Hegel; see, for example, in *Wissenschaft der Logik*, II, *Werke*, V, pp. 8-9; *J.A.*, V, pp. 8-9; *Science of Logic*, pp. 579-80:

> Active substance, through the act of positing itself as the opposite of itself, an act which is at the same time the sublating of its *presupposed otherness*, of passive substance, is manifested as cause or originative substantiality. Conversely, through being acted on, posited being is manifested *as* posited, the negative *as* negative, and therefore passive substance as *self-related* negativity, the cause meeting in this other simply and solely with its own self. Through this positing, then, the *presupposed* or *implicit* originativeness becomes *explicit* or *for itself*, yet this being that is in and for itself is such only in so far as this positing is equally a *sublating* of what was presupposed; in other words, absolute substance has returned to itself and so become absolute, only *out of* and *in* its *positedness*. Hence this reciprocity is the appearance that again sublates itself, the revelation that the *illusory being* of causality in which the cause appears *as* cause, *is illusory being*. This infinite reflection-into-self, namely, that being is in and for itself only in so far as it is posited, is the *consummation of substance*. But this consummation is no longer *substance* itself but something higher, the *Notion*, the *subject*. *The transition of the relation of substantiality* takes place through its own immanent necessity and is nothing more than the manifestation of itself, that the Notion is its truth, and that freedom is the truth of necessity.

See also, for example, *Anxiety*, p. 409, *KW* VI (*SV* IV 408).

103. See Kruse, *Don Juan*, I, 1, p. 3; Bleiler, *Don Giovanni*, I, 1, pp. 85-86. At the end of the sentence, 2 ed. of *SV* (I, p. 127) has an interpolated passage

from a draft of *Either/Or*, I: "This is something that rarely occurs; here it is entirely in order and casts a new light on the structure of the overture. The overture seeks to stoop down to find a foothold in the theatrical actuality. We have already heard the Commendatore and Don Giovanni in the overture; after them, Leporello is the most important character. He cannot, however, be elevated into that battle in the regions of the atmosphere, and yet he belongs there more than anyone else."

104. For continuation of the paragraph, see Supplement, p. 539 (*Pap.* III B 172:3).

105. See Kruse, *Don Juan*, I, 1, p. 3; Bleiler, *Don Giovanni*, I, 1, p. 85.

106. See Kruse, *Don Juan*, I, 6, pp. 22-23; Bleiler, *Don Giovanni*, I, 3, pp. 100-02.

107. Kruse, *Don Juan*, I 6, p. 22; Bleiler, *Don Giovanni*, I, 3, p. 100. Cf. "A Cursory Observation Concerning a Detail in *Don Giovanni*," *The* Corsair *Affair*, p. 30, *KW* XIII (*SV* XIII 449).

108. A character in Ludvig Holberg, *Barselstuen, Den Danske Skue-Plads*, I-VII (Copenhagen: 1788; *ASKB* 1566-67), II, n.p. See, for example, V, 6.

109. In the German text of the edition (not located) of *Don Giovanni* used by Kierkegaard, a portion of the list aria reads, according to the Danish editors: "Tausend und zwei—nein, Tausend und drei; Sie sind auch dabei [Thousand and two—no, thousand and three; you are also included]."

110. See Kruse, *Don Juan*, II, 18, p. 120; Bleiler, *Don Giovanni*, II, 6, pp. 189-94.

111. See Kruse, *Don Juan*, I, 15, pp. 49-50; Bleiler, *Don Giovanni*, I, 3, pp. 123-24.

112. For an account of another banquet, see "*In Vino Veritas*," *Stages*, *KW* XI (*SV* VI 13-83, especially 78-79).

113. For the dating of the chapter, see Supplement, p. 539 (*Pap.* III B 172:4).

THE TRAGIC IN ANCIENT DRAMA
REFLECTED IN THE TRAGIC IN MODERN DRAMA

1. A coinage by Kierkegaard, which could also be rendered as the "Society of Buried Lives." See p. 137; Supplement, p. 539 (*Pap.* II A 690; IV A 225).

2. See, for example, G.W.F. Hegel, *Vorlesungen über die Aesthetik*, III, *Georg Wilhelm Friedrich Hegel's Werke. Vollständige Ausgabe*, I-XVIII, ed. Philipp Marheineke et al. (Berlin: 1832-45; *ASKB* 549-65), X³, pp. 506-07; *Sämtliche Werke. Jubiläumsausgabe* [*J.A.*], I-XXVI, ed. Hermann Glockner (Stuttgart: 1927-40), XIV, pp. 506-07; *The Philosophy of Fine Art* (tr. of *V.A.*, 1 ed., 1835-38; Kierkegaard had this ed.), I-IV, tr. F.P.B. Osmaston (London: Bell, 1920), IV, p. 275:

In the Epos play may be permitted to the breadth and variety of character, external conditions, occurrences and events; in the drama, on the contrary, the self-concentration of its principle is most asserted relatively to the particular collision and its conflict. It is thus that we recognize the truth of Aristotle's dictum, that tragic action possesses two sources (αἴτια δύο), opinion and character (διάνοια καὶ ἦθος), but what is most important is the end (τέλος), and individuals do not act in order to display diverse characters, but these latter are united with a common bond of imaginative conception to the former in the interest of the action.

See *Pap.* III C 34.

3. See Aristotle, *Poetics*, 1449 b ; *Aristoteles graece*, ed. Immanuel Bekker, I-II (Berlin: 1831; *ASKB* 1074-75), II, p. 1449; *Aristoteles Dichtkunst*, tr. Michael Conrad Curtius (Hanover: 1753; *ASKB* 1094), pp. 11-12; *The Works of Aristotle*, I-XII, ed. J. A. Smith and W. D. Ross (Oxford: Oxford University Press, 1908-52), XI:

> Reserving hexameter poetry and Comedy for consideration hereafter, let us proceed now to the discussion of Tragedy; before doing so, however, we must gather up the definition resulting from what has been said. A tragedy, then, is the imitation of an action that is serious and also, as having magnitude, complete in itself; in language with pleasurable accessories, each kind brought in separately in the parts of the work; in a dramatic, not in a narrative form; with incidents arousing pity and fear, wherewith to accomplish its catharsis of such emotions. Here by 'language with pleasurable accessories' I mean that with rhythm and harmony or song superadded; and by 'the kinds separately' I mean that some portions are worked out with verse only, and others in turn with song.

4. See, for example, G. E. Lessing, *Hamburgische Dramaturgie*, xxxvii-xxxix (1767), *Gotthold Ephraim Lessing's sämmtliche Schriften*, I-XXXII (Berlin: 1825-28; *ASKB* 1747-62), XXIV, pp. 267-84; *Hamburg Dramaturgy*, tr. Helen Zimmern (New York: Dover, 1962), pp. 105-14.

5. See, for example, Aristotle, *Poetics*, 1449 b-1450 a; Bekker, IV, pp. 1449-50; Curtius, pp. 12-13; *Works*, XI:

> As they act the stories, it follows that in the first place the Spectacle (or stage-appearance of the actors) must be some part of the whole; and in the second Melody and Diction, these two being the means of their imitation. Here by 'Diction' I mean merely this, the composition of the verses; and by 'Melody', what is too completely understood to require explanation. But further: the subject represented also is an action; and the action involves agents, who must necessarily have their distinctive qualities both of character and thought, since it is from these that we ascribe certain qualities to their actions. There are in the natural order of things, therefore, two causes, Thought and Character, of their actions, and consequently of their success or failure in their lives. Now the action (that which was done) is represented in the play by the Fable or Plot. The Fable, in our present sense of the term, is simply this, the combination of the incidents, or things done in the story; whereas Character is what makes us ascribe certain moral qualities to the agents; and Thought is shown in all they say when proving a particular

point or, it may be, enunciating a general truth. There are six parts consequently of every tragedy, as a whole (that is) of such or such quality, viz. a Fable or Plot, Characters, Diction, Thought, Spectacle, and Melody; two of them arising from the means, one from the manner, and three from the objects of the dramatic imitation; and there is nothing else besides these six. Of these, its formative elements, then, not a few of the dramatists have made due use, as every play, one may say, admits of Spectacle, Character, Fable, Diction, Melody, and Thought.

The most important of the six is the combination of the incidents of the story. Tragedy is essentially an imitation not of persons but of action and life, of happiness and misery. All human happiness or misery takes the form of action; the end for which we live is a certain kind of activity, not a quality. Character gives us qualities, but it is in our actions—what we do—that we are happy or the reverse. In a play accordingly they do not act in order to portray the Characters; they include the Characters for the sake of the action. So that it is the action in it, i.e. its Fable or Plot, that is the end and purpose of the tragedy; and the end is everywhere the chief thing. Besides this, a tragedy is impossible without action, but there may be one without Character.

6. With reference to the remainder of the paragraph, see Supplement, p. 540 (*Pap*. III B 130).

7. See II Samuel 24:1-10; I Chronicles 21:1-8.

8. Political clubs and other associations in Athens at the close of the fifth century B.C.

9. See Cicero, *On Divination*, II, 24; *On the Nature of the Gods*, I, xxvi, 71; *M. Tullii Ciceronis opera omnia*, I-IV and index, ed. Johann August Ernesti (Halle: 1756-57; *ASKB* 1224-29), IV, pp. 491, 678; *Cicero De natura deorum, Academica*, tr. H. Rackham (Loeb, New York: Putnam, 1933), p. 69; *Cicero De senectute, De amicitia, De divinatione*, tr. William Armistead Falconer (Loeb, Cambridge: Harvard University Press, 1953), p. 429: ' "But indeed, that was quite a clever remark which Cato made many years ago: 'I wonder,' said he, 'that a soothsayer doesn't laugh when he sees another soothsayer.' For how many things predicted by them really come true?' " See also *Either/Or*, II, *KW* IV (*SV* II 286).

10. In the Copenhagen newspaper *Berlingske Tidende*, March 22, 1839, there was a report of a proposal somewhat along this line made by Louis Adolphe Thiers, French historian and statesman, who became prime minister and foreign minister in March of 1840, after a period of absence from the two posts because of disagreements with the king.

11. See note 5 above.

12. Cf. Hegel, *Aesthetik*, III, *Werke*, X³, pp. 562-64; *J.A.*, XIV, pp. 562-64; *Philosophy of Fine Art*, IV, pp. 330-32:

Tragedy, in the nobility which distinguishes it in its ancient plastic form, is limited to the partial point of view that for its exclusive and essential basis it only enforces as effective the ethically substantive content and its necessary laws; and, on the other hand, leaves the individual and subjective self-penetration of the dramatic characters essentially unevolved; while comedy on its part, to complete what we may regard as the reversed side of such plastic construction, exhibits to us the personal caprice of soul-life in the unfettered abandonment of its topsy-turvydom and ultimate dissolution.

Modern tragedy accepts in its own province from the first the principle of subjectivity or self-assertion. It makes, therefore, the personal intimacy of character—the character, that is, which is no purely individual and vital embodiment of ethical forces in the classic sense—its peculiar object and content. It, moreover, makes, in a type of concurrence that is adapted to this end, human actions come into collision through the instrumentality of the external accident of circumstances in the way that a contingency of a similar character is also decisive in its effect on the consequence, or appears to be so decisive.

See also *Pap*. III C 34, reading notes on Hegel's *Aesthetik*.

13. See, for example, Hegel, *Grundlinien der Philosophie des Rechts*, para. 124, *Werke*, VIII, p. 166; *J.A.*, VII, p. 182; *Hegel's Philosophy of Right* (tr. of *G.R.*, 1 ed., 1821; Kierkegaard had 2 ed., 1833), tr. T. M. Knox (London: Oxford University Press, 1967), p. 84:

> The right of the subject's particularity, his right to be satisfied, or in other words the right of subjective freedom, is the pivot and centre of the difference between antiquity and modern times. This right in its infinity is given expression in Christianity and it has become the universal effective principle of a new form of civilization. Amongst the primary shapes which this right assumes are love, romanticism, the quest for the eternal salvation of the individual, &c.; next come moral convictions and conscience; and, finally, the other forms, some of which come into prominence in what follows as the principle of civil society and as moments in the constitution of the state, while others appear in the course of history, particularly the history of art, science, and philosophy.

14. See, for example, Aristotle, *Poetics*, 1452 b-1453 a; Bekker, II, pp. 1452-53; Curtius, pp. 25-26; *Works*, XI:

> We assume that, for the finest form of Tragedy, the Plot must be not simple but complex; and further, that it must imitate actions arousing fear and pity, since that is the distinctive function of this kind of imitation. It follows, therefore, that there are three forms of Plot to be avoided. (1) A good man must not be seen passing from happiness to misery, or (2) a bad man from misery to happiness. The first situation is not fear-inspiring or piteous, but simply odious to us. The second is the most untragic that can be; it has not one of the requisites of Tragedy; it does not appeal either to the human feeling in us, or to our pity, or to our fears. Nor, on the other hand, should (3) an extremely bad man be seen falling from happiness into misery. Such a story may arouse the human feeling in us, but it will not move us to

either pity or fear; pity is occasioned by undeserved misfortune, and fear by that of one like ourselves; so that there will be nothing either piteous or fear-inspiring in the situation. There remains, then, the intermediate kind of personage, a man not preeminently virtuous and just, whose misfortune, however, is brought upon him not by vice and depravity but by some error of judgement, of the number of those in the enjoyment of great reputation and prosperity; e.g. Oedipus, Thyestes, and the men of note of similar families. The perfect Plot, accordingly, must have a single, and not (as some tell us) a double issue; the change in the hero's fortunes must be not from misery to happiness, but on the contrary from happiness to misery; and the cause of it must lie not in any depravity, but in some great error on his part; the man himself being either such as we have described, or better, not worse, than that.

15. Pelagius (?-420), opposed by Augustine, denied original sin and stressed the freedom of the individual, the individual's capacity (unaided by divine grace) for achieving good, and his responsibility for his life.

16. Christian D. Grabbe, *Don Juan und Faust* (Frankfurt: 1829; *ASKB* 1670). See Supplement, p. 540 (*Pap.* II A 733).

17. See Matthew 16:26; Mark 8:36; Luke 9:25.

18. The word "sometimes" in this sentence is an example of the narrowed adverbial use of a term. The reference below to five cases indicates that the writer has Greek in mind primarily. Latin has six cases and Sanskrit eight.

19. The ancient Greeks.

20. See note 14 above.

21. See Hegel, *Aesthetik*, III, *Werke*, X³, pp. 531-32; *J.A.*, XIV, pp. 531-32; *Philosophy of Fine Art*, IV, pp. 298-300:

We are reminded of the famous dictum of Aristotle that the true effect of tragedy is to excite and purify *fear* and *pity*. By this statement Aristotle did not mean merely the concordant or discordant feeling with anybody's private experience, a feeling simply of pleasure or the reverse, an attraction or a repulsion, that most superficial of all psychological states, which only in recent times theorists have sought to identify with the principle of assent or dissent as ordinarily expressed. For in a work of art the matter of exclusive importance should be the display of that which is conformable with the reason and truth of Spirit; and to discover the principle of this we have to direct our attention to wholly different points of view. And consequently we are not justified in restricting the application of this dictum of Aristotle merely to the emotion of fear and pity, but should relate it to the principle of the *content*, the appropriately artistic display of which ought to purify such feelings. Man may, on the one hand, entertain fear when confronted with that which is outside him and finite; but he may likewise shrink before the power of that which is the essential and absolute subsistency of social phenomena. That which mankind has therefore in truth to fear is not the external power and its oppression, but the ethical might which is self-defined in its own free rationality, and partakes further of the eternal and inviolable, the power a man summons against his own being when he turns his back upon it. And just as fear may have two objectives, so also too compassion. The first is just the ordinary sensibility—in other words, a sympathy with the misfortunes and sufferings of another, and one which is experienced as something finite and negative. Your countrified cousin is ready enough with compassion of this order. The man of nobility and greatness, however, has no wish to be smothered with this sort of pity. For just to the extent that it is merely the nugatory aspect, the negative of misfortune which is asserted, a real depreciation of misfortune is implied. True sympathy, on the contrary, is an accordant feeling with the ethical claim at the same time associated with the sufferer—that is, with what is necessarily implied in his condition as affirmative and substantive. . . .

Over and above mere fear and tragic sympathy we have therefore the feeling of *reconciliation*, which tragedy is vouched for in virtue of its vision of eternal justice, a justice which exercises a paramount force of absolute constringency on account of the relative claim of all merely contracted aims and passions; and it can do this for the reason that it is unable to tolerate the victorious issue and continuance in the truth of the objective world of such a conflict with and opposition to those ethical powers which are fundamentally and essentially concordant.

See also *Pap*. III C 34, reading notes on Hegel's *Aesthetik*.

22. Hegel, *Aesthetik*, III, *Werke*, X³, p. 532; *J.A.*, XIV, p. 532; *Philosophy of Fine Art*, p. 299.

23. See p. 80 and note 102.

24. With reference to the remainder of the paragraph, see Supplement, p. 540 (*Pap*. III B 124).

25. See Hebrews 10:31.

26. On the Danish *Virkelighed* and *Realitet* in Kierkegaard's writings, see *JP* III 3651-55 and pp. 902-03.

27. With reference to the remainder of the sentence, see Supplement, p. 540 (*Pap*. III B 132:2).

28. Cf., for example, *Anxiety*, pp. 35-38, *KW* VIII (*SV* VI 306-09); " 'Guilty?'/'Not Guilty?' " *Stages, KW* XI (*SV* VI 175-459).

29. A loan word from Greek, meaning equivocality, ambiguity; it is used only three times in Kierkegaard's writings, all in *Either/Or*, I. See note 36 below.

30. See Exodus 20:5.

31. A tragedy also by Sophocles.

32. See Supplement, p. 540 (*Pap*. III C 40).

33. See Supplement, p. 541 (*Pap*. III C 39).

34. *Philoctetes*, 691-707; *Sophoclis Tragoediae*, I-II, ed. C. H. Weise (Leipzig: 1841; *ASKB* 1201), II, pp. 255-56; *Sophokles's Tragoedier*, I-II, tr. Peder Grib Fibiger (Copenhagen: 1821-22), II, p. 288; *The Complete Greek Tragedies*, I-IV,

ed. David Grene and Richmond Lattimore (Chicago: University of Chicago Press, 1959), II, p. 427:

> He was lame, and no one came near him.
> He suffered, and there were no neighbors for his sorrow
> with whom his cries would find answer,
> with whom he could lament the bloody plague
> that ate him up.
> No one who would gather
> fallen leaves from the ground
> to quiet the raging, bleeding sore,
> running, in his maggot-rotten foot.
> Here and there he crawled
> writhing always—
> suffering like a child
> without the nurse he loves—
> to what source of ease he could find
> when the heart-devouring suffering gave over.

35. See p. 115.

36. A loan word in Danish, meaning a sudden flashing (for example, the flashing of molten gold or silver), and used only once, here, in Kierkegaard's authorship. See also *Sølvblink* (silver flash), *Irony, KW* II (*SV* XIII 272); *Stages, KW* XI (*SV* VI 61). "Officiality" and "anacoluthic" (pertaining to a changing from one grammatical construction to another without completing the former) a few lines down are also loan words. The first is used only three times in the authorship (twice in *Either/Or* and once in *Point of View*) and the second only here. If the three words (and "amphiboly" on p. 127) seem odd in English, they make the impression intended, for they are still more odd in Danish and in the entire authorship. They are in keeping with this periodic tour de force in the paragraph.

37. With reference to the remainder of the sentence, see Supplement, p. 541 (*Pap.* III B 83).

38. German *verlieben sich* in Danish form.

39. See Supplement, p. 541 (*Pap.* IV A 114).

40. See Supplement, p. 541 (*Pap.* I A 207).

41. See p. 80 and note 102.

42. Labdakos was the grandfather and Jocasta the mother, and later the wife, of Oedipus.

43. See Supplement, p. 542 (*Pap.* III C 37).

44. The well-known Latin gloss on lines 621-22 of *Antigone* by Sophocles. See *Complete Greek Tragedies*, II, p. 180: ' "The bad becomes the good to him a god would doom.' "

45. With reference to the following sentence, see Supplement, p. 542 (*Pap.* III B 132:3).

46. Also the title of a French poem in Gustav Schwab, *Buch der schönsten*

Geschichten und Sagen, I-II (Stuttgart: 1836; *ASKB* 1429-30), I, p. 347. See Supplement, pp. 542-43 (*Pap.* II A 584).

47. Son of Queen Grimhild, wife of King Gjuke, and a troll. See *Oldnordiske Kæmpe-Historier*, I-III, tr. C. C. Rafn (Copenhagen: 1821-26; *ASKB* 1993-95), II, pp. 242-44. See Supplement, p. 543 (*Pap*, II A 584).

48. With reference to the following six sentences, see Supplement, p. 543 (*Pap.* III B 129).

49. See Proverbs 25:11.

50. See Matthew 6:19-20; James 5:2-3.

51. With reference to the following five sentences, see Supplement, p. 543 (*Pap.* III B 126).

52. See Luke 1:34.

53. Weise, II, p. 44; *Complete Greek Tragedies*, II, p. 188.

54. *Sophokles Tragoedien*, tr. Johann Christian Donner (Heidelberg: 1839), p. 186. See *Pap.* III C 35-36.

55. See I Corinthians 12:26.

56. Not a quotation.

57. See notes 29 and 36 above.

58. See Supplement, p. 543 (*Pap.* III B 132:4).

59. With reference to the following two sentences, see Supplement, p. 544 (*Pap.* B 179:40).

60. Epaminondas (d. 362 B.C.), Greek general of Thebes. See Cornelius Nepos, "Epaminondas," IX, 3; *Cornelius Nepos*, tr. John C. Rolfe (Loeb, together with *Lucius Annaeus Florus*, New York: 1929), p. 547:

> Finally, when commander at Mantinea, in the heat of battle he charged the enemy too boldly. He was recognized by the Lacedaemonians, and since they believed that the death of that one man would ensure the safety of their country, they all directed their attack at him alone and kept on until, after great bloodshed and the loss of many men, they saw Epaminondas himself fall valiantly fighting, struck down by a lance hurled from afar. By his death the Boeotians were checked for a time, but they did not leave the field until they had completely defeated the enemy. But Epaminondas, realizing that he had received a mortal wound, and at the same time that if he drew out the head of the lance, which was separated from the shaft and fixed in his body, he would at once die, retained it until news came that the Boeotians were victorious. As soon as he heard that, he cried: "I have lived long enough, since I die unconquered." Then he drew out the iron and at once breathed his last.

See Supplement, p. 544 (*Pap.* III B 179:40).

61. With reference to the following sentence, see Supplement, p. 544 (*Pap.* III B 179:41).

62. Hercules was killed by the poisoned blood of the centaur Nessus after being slain by Hercules. See Paul Friedrich A. Nitsch, *neues mythologisches*

Wörterbuch, I-II, rev. Friedrich Gotthilf Klopfer (Leipzig, Sorau: 1821; *ASKB* 1944-45), I, p. 842.

63. See Supplement, p. 544 (*Pap.* III B 132:5).

SILHOUETTES

1. See Supplement, p. 544 (*Pap.* III B 173:1).
2. See p. 137 and note 1.
3. Gotthold Ephraim Lessing, "Lied aus dem Spanischen," *G. E. Lessing's sämmtliche Schriften*, I-XXXII (Berlin: 1825-28; *ASKB* 1747-62), XVII, p. 281 (ed. tr.). See Supplement, p. 544 (*Pap.* III A 200). The source of the first four lines has not been located.
4. Cf. I Kings 19:11-12.
5. Democritus (440-357? B.C.) and Leucippus (fl. 450 B.C.), Greek pre-Socratic philosophers, held that all is atoms in motion (vortex) in a void. In this, they followed in part Anaxagoras (500-428 B.C.), who taught that the universe is qualitative particles in motion (vortex) and cosmic mind (nous), which initiated the motion.
6. Lessing, *Laokoon, oder, über die Grenzen Malerei und Poesie*; *Schriften*, II, pp. 121-397. *Laocoön . . .* , tr. W. A. Steel (Everyman, New York: Dutton, 1949), pp. 1-110. In this section, the terms "art," "artist," and "artistic" are used, in conformity with Lessing's distinction, for painting and sculpture.
7. See Lessing, *Laokoon, Schriften*, II, III-IV, XV-XVIII, pp. 147-87, 265-98; Everyman, pp. 14-24, 53-69.
8. According to tradition, Veronica dried the sweat on Christ's face as he went to Golgotha, and the cloth retained his image. "Veronica" means "true image."
9. Literally, "shadow outlines."
10. Watermark, such as is found in high-grade paper.
11. Proteus, a sea god who sought to escape foretelling the future by constantly changing form. See Homer, *Odyssey*, IV, 450-59; *Homers Odyssee*, tr. Christian Wilster (Copenhagen: 1837), p. 54; *Homer The Odyssey*, I-II, tr. A. T. Murray (Loeb, New York: Putnam, 1919), I, pp. 139-41.
12. Danish: *randsage Nyrer* (as in the Danish Bible); literally, "ransack the kidneys." See I Corinthians 2:10; Revelation 2:23.
13. See I Samuel 28:8-14.
14. Johann Wolfgang v. Goethe, *Clavigo, Goethe's Werke. Vollständige Ausgabe letzter Hand*, I-LX (Stuttgart, Tübingen: 1828-42; *ASKB* 1641-68 [I-LV]), X, pp. 49-124; *Goethe's Works*, I-V, tr. Hjalmar H. Boyesen (Philadelphia: George Barrie, 1885), III, pp. 155-82.
15. See Homer, *Odyssey*, XI, 582-601; Wilster, pp. 162-63; Loeb, I, pp. 427-29.
16. See *Clavigo*, I, 2, *Werke*, X, pp. 59-60; *Works*, III, p. 159.
17. See Mark 11:22-23; I Corinthians 13:2.
18. See *Clavigo*, III, 1, *Werke*, X, p. 83; *Works*, III, p. 167.

19. Simonides. See Cicero, *On the Nature of the Gods*, I, xxi, 60; *M. Tullii Ciceronis opera omnia*, I-IV and index, ed. Johann August Ernesti (Halle: 1756-57; *ASKB* 1224-29), IV, pp. 487-88; *Cicero De natura deorum, Academica*, tr. H. Rackham (Loeb, New York: Putnam, 1933), p. 59.

20. See I Peter 3:4.

21. See Matthew 6:30, 8:26, 14:31, 16:8; Luke 12:28.

22. Cf. Genesis 8:11.

23. See *Stages, KW* XI (*SV* VI 253-54).

24. See Mozart, *Don Juan*, tr. Laurids Kruse (Copenhagen: 1807), I, 6, pp. 18, 20; *Don Giovanni*, tr. Ellen H. Bleiler (New York: Dover, 1964), I, 2, pp. 98-100.

25. Adam Gottlob Oehlenschläger, *Aladdin*, IV (the jinni of the lamp speaking to Noureddin), *Poetiske Skrifter*, I-II (Copenhagen: 1805; *ASKB* 1597-98), II, p. 275; *Aladdin or the Wonderful Lamp*, tr. Henry Meyer (Copenhagen: Gyldendal, 1968), p. 171.

26. Danish: *Taleværelse*, literally, "speaking room" or "conversation room." The English "parlor" comes from the French *parler*, "to speak."

27. Kruse, *Don Juan*, I, 6, pp. 20-21.

28. Elvira carries a dagger in Kruse, *Don Juan*, I, 5, p. 18.

29. Virgil, *Aeneid*, VI, 469-74; *Virgils Aeneide*, tr. Johan Henrik Schønheyder (Copenhagen: 1812), pp. 276-77; *Virgil*, I-II, tr. H. Rushton Fairclough (Loeb, New York: Putnam, 1920), I, p. 539.

30. See, for example, Hegel, *Wissenschaft der Logik, Werke*, IV, pp. 70-71; *J.A.*, IV, pp. 548-49; *Science of Logic*, pp. 441-42:

> Therefore though ordinary thinking everywhere has contradiction for its content, it does not become aware of it, but remains an external reflection which passes from likeness to unlikeness, or from the negative relation to the reflection-into-self, of the distinct sides. It holds these two determinations over against one another and has in mind *only them*, but not their *transition*, which is the essential point and which contains the contradiction. *Intelligent* reflection, to mention this here, consists, on the contrary, in grasping and asserting contradiction. Even though it does not express the Notion of things and their relationships and has for its material and content only the determinations of ordinary thinking, it does bring these into a relation that contains their contradiction and allows *their Notion to show or shine through* the contradiction. Thinking reason, however, sharpens, so to say, the blunt difference of diverse terms, the mere manifoldness of pictorial thinking, into *essential* difference, into *opposition*. Only when the manifold terms have been driven to the point of contradiction do they become active and lively towards one another, receiving in contradiction the negativity which is the indwelling pulsation of self-movement and spontaneous activity [*Lebendigkeit*].

31. Heraclitus (c. 500 B.C.) on the oracle at Delphi. See *Ancilla to the Pre-Socratic Philosophers*, tr. Kathleen Freeman (Oxford: Blackwell, 1948), Hera-

cleitus, 93, p. 31: "The lord whose oracle is that at Delphi neither speaks nor conceals, but indicates."

32. Cf. Psalm 92:12; Song of Solomon 5:15; Ezekiel 31:3.

33. A small Greek coin placed in the mouth of the corpse as payment to Charon, the Hades boatman, for the ferry ride across the River Styx to the realm of the dead.

34. With reference to the remainder of the paragraph, see Supplement, p. 545 (*Pap*. III A 116).

35. Goethe, *Faust*, I, 3781-82, *Werke*, XII, p. 199; *Faust*, tr. Bayard Taylor (New York: Random House, 1950), p. 146. See *JP* V 5412, 5427 (*Pap*. II A 557, 802).

36. *Faust*, I, 3182, *Werke*, XII, p. 156; Taylor, p. 121.

37. See *Faust*, I, 3413-68, *Werke*, II, pp. 60-61; Taylor, pp. 130-33.

38. See *Faust*, I, 3211-16, *Werke*, XII, p. 169; Taylor, p. 124.

39. See *Wilhelm Meisters Lehrjahre*, IV, 13, *Werke*, XIX, p. 76; *Works*, IV, p. 197.

40. Cf. Matthew 25:35-36.

41. Cf., for example, Psalms 119:36, 141:4.

42. See Romans 9:10-21.

43. See Genesis 2:21-24.

44. *Opelske* literally means "to love forth." See, for example, *Eighteen Upbuilding Discourses*, *KW* V (*SV* IV 99); *Works of Love*, *KW* XVI (*SV* IX 208).

45. *"Den blaa Fugl"* in Scandinavia; in France, *"L' Oiseau bleu,"* in Marie Cathérine d'Aulnoy, *Les Contes de Fées*, I-IV (Paris: 1810), I, pp. 88-96. See *JP* V 5287 (*Pap*. II A 207).

46. For date of draft, see Supplement, p. 545 (*Pap*. III B 173:2).

THE UNHAPPIEST ONE

1. In Worcester Cathedral there is a tomb with the inscription *Miserrimus* [the most pitiable]. See Supplement, p. 545 (*Pap*. III A 40).

2. See *JP* III 3271 (*Pap*, II A 356).

3. Christian Henriksen Pram, *Stærkodder*, VII (Copenhagen: 1785), p. 142 (ed. tr.): "O friendly grave, in your shadow dwells peace, Your silent occupants knows not of sorrow."

4. In *The Eumenides* (Furies) by Aeschylus, the murderer Orestes is pursued by the Furies until he finds asylum in the temple at Delphi.

5. The Latin *segregati* is a translation of the Greek ἀφωρισμένοι, which means "separated," "set apart," "cut off," "expelled" (for example, from the synagogue). Cf. Romans 1:1, where Paul applies the term to himself and his task.

6. See Matthew 22:14.

7. See, for example, Cicero, *Cato the Elder on Old Age*, XX, 75; *M. Tullii Ciceronis opera omnia*, I-IV and index, ed. Johann August Ernesti (Halle: 1756-57; *ASKB* 1224-29), IV, p. 956; *Cicero De senectute, De amicitia, De divinatione*,

tr. William Armistead Falconer (Loeb, Cambridge: Harvard University Press, 1953), p. 87.

8. On Solon and Croesus, see Herodotus, *History*, I, 32, 34, 86; *Die Geschichten des Herodotos*, I-II, tr. Friedrich Lange (Berlin: 1824; *ASKB* 1117), I, pp. 18-19, 20, 49-50; *Herodotus*, I-IV, tr. A. D. Godley (Loeb, New York: Putnam, 1921-24), I, pp. 39, 41, 109-11:

> Thus then, Croesus, the whole of man is but chance. Now if I am to speak of you, I say that I see you very rich and the king of many men. But I cannot yet answer your question, before I hear that you have ended your life well. . . . If then such a man besides all this shall also end his life well, then he is the man whom you seek, and is worthy to be called blest; but we must wait till he be dead, and call him not yet blest, but fortunate.

> But after Solon's departure, the divine anger fell heavily on Croesus: as I guess, because he supposed himself to be blest beyond all other men.

> So the Persians took Sardis and made Croesus himself prisoner, he having reigned fourteen years and been besieged fourteen days, and, as the oracle foretold, brought his own great empire to an end. Having then taken him they led him to Cyrus. Cyrus had a great pyre built, on which he set Croesus, bound in chains, and twice seven Lydian boys beside him: either his intent was to sacrifice these first-fruits to some one of his gods, or he desired to fulfil a vow, or it may be that, learning that Croesus was a god-fearing man, he set him for this cause on the pyre, because he would fain know if any deity would save him from being burnt alive. It is related then that he did this; but Croesus, as he stood on the pyre, remembered even in his evil plight how divinely inspired was that saying of Solon, that no living man was blest. When this came to his mind, having till now spoken no word, he sighed deeply and groaned, and thrice uttered the name of Solon. Cyrus heard it, and bade his interpreters ask Croesus who was this on whom he called; they came near and asked him; Croesus at first would say nothing in answer, but presently, being compelled, he said, "It is one with whom I would have given much wealth that all sovereigns should hold converse." This was a dark saying to them, and again they questioned him of the words which he spoke. As they were instant, and troubled him, he told them then how Solon, an Athenian, had first come, and how he had seen all his royal state and made light of it (saying thus and thus), and how all had happened to Croesus as Solon said, though he spoke with less regard to Croesus than to mankind in general and chiefly those who deemed themselves blest. While Croesus thus told his story, the pyre had already been kindled and the outer parts of it were burning. Then Cyrus, when he heard from the interpreters what Croesus said, repented of his purpose.

9. G. W. F. Hegel, *Phänomenologie des Geistes, Georg Wilhelm Friedrich Hegel's Werke. Vollständige Ausgabe*, I-XVIII, ed. Philipp Marheineke et al. (Berlin: 1832-45; *ASKB* 549-65), II, pp. 158-73; *Sämtliche Werke. Jubiläumsausgabe*

[*J.A.*], I-XXVI, ed. Hermann Glockner (Stuttgart: 1927-40), II, pp. 166-81; *The Phenomenology of Mind* (tr. primarily based on 3 ed. of *P.G.*, 1841; Kierkegaard had 2 ed., 1832), tr. J. B. Baillie (New York: Harper, 1967), pp. 251-67.

10. Clemens Brentano, *Die drei Nüsse* (Berlin, Königsberg: 1834).

11. Cf. *Repetition*, pp. 131-33, *KW* VI (*SV* III 173-75); *Stages, KW* XI (*SV* VI 15-21).

12. For a consideration of actuality (*Virkelighed*) and reality (*Realitet*) in Kierkegaard's journals and writings, see *JP* III 3651-55 and pp. 900-03.

13. Ancaeus, son of the sea god Neptune, was king of Samos. When told the prophecy that he would never taste wine in his own vineyard, he defiantly lifted a cup of wine to his lips, but upon hearing that a wild boar was near, he went hunting and was killed. See Paul Friedrich A. Nitsch, *neues mythologisches Wörterbuch*, I-II, rev. Friedrich Gotthilf Klopfer (Leipzig, Sorau: 1821; *ASKB* 1944-45), I, p. 194.

14. In Greek mythology, Leto (Roman Latona) was the daughter of the Titans Coeus and Phoebe and mother of Zeus's children Artemis (Roman Diana) and Apollo, before whose birth she was obliged to roam around the earth, pursued by Hera (Roman Juno). See Nitsch, II, pp. 142-48.

15. In Greek mythology, a mythical people in the northernmost regions of the earth (dwellers beyond the North Wind).

16. See Supplement, p. 545 (*Pap*. III B 174:1).

17. Cf. Matthew 22:37; Mark 12:33; Luke 10:27.

18. In Greek mythology, a queen of Thebes, daughter of Tantalus, and wife of Amphion. Having boasted that she had twelve children and Leto (L. Latona) only two, she was slain by Leto's children, Artemis and Apollo. Niobe was turned into a stone image (on Mt. Sipylos, named after one of her children) that wept continually. See Nitsch, II, pp. 326-30.

19. In Greek mythology and literature, Oedipus, as foretold, killed his father, Laius, and married his mother, Jocasta. Antigone, his daughter, followed him in his banishment and disgrace.

20. See Job 1:21. See *Repetition*, pp. 197-99, 204-13, *KW* VI (*SV* III 231-33, 238-46).

21. See Job 2:9-10.

22. For continuation of the sentence, see Supplement, p. 545 (*Pap*. III B 174:2).

23. See Deuteronomy 6:5; Matthew 22:27.

24. With reference to the following sentence, see Supplement, pp. 545-46 (*Pap*. IV A 227).

25. Cf. Ecclesiastes 1:1-11.

THE FIRST LOVE

1. *Den første Kjærlighed* (hereafter *K.*), Johan Ludvig Heiberg's translation of Augustin Eugène Scribe's *Les Premières Amours ou Les Souvenirs d'enfance*,

was first presented June 10, 1831, and was published with separate pagination as no. 45 in the *Repertoire* (hereafter *R.*) of the Royal Theater in 1832.

2. With reference to the following sentence, see Supplement, p. 546 (*Pap. III B 40*).

3. Johan Herman Wessel, Norwegian-Danish writer (1742-85), "*Om en Jødepige,*" *Samtlige Skrivter*, I-II (Copenhagen: 1787), II, p. 130 (ed. tr.):

> You, god of all skalds, and judge of witticisms,
> Who are invoked so often, and who so rarely come . . ..

4. See, for example, Plato, *Phaedo*, 60 b-c; *Platonis quae exstant opera*, I-XI, ed. Friedrich Ast (Leipzig: 1819-32; *ASKB* 1144-54), I, pp. 478-81; *Udvalgte Dialoger af Platon*, I-VIII, tr. Carl Johan Heise (Copenhagen: 1830-38; *ASKB* 1164-66, 1169 [I-VII]), I, pp. 6-7; *The Collected Dialogues of Plato*, ed. Edith Hamilton and Huntington Cairns (Princeton: Princeton University Press, 1963), p. 43:

> Socrates sat up on the bed and drew up his leg and massaged it, saying as he did so, What a queer thing it is, my friends, this sensation which is popularly called pleasure! It is remarkable how closely it is connected with its conventional opposite, pain. They will never come to a man both at once, but if you pursue one of them and catch it, you are nearly always compelled to have the other as well; they are like two bodies attached to the same head. I am sure that if Aesop had thought of it he would have made up a fable about them, something like this—God wanted to stop their continual quarreling, and when he found that it was impossible, he fastened their heads together; so wherever one of them appears, the other is sure to follow after. That is exactly what seems to be happening to me. I had a pain in my leg from the fetter, and now I feel the pleasure coming that follows it.

5. Cf. I Corinthians 1:23.

6. See "*Von dem Machandelboom,*" *Kinder- und Haus-Märchen Gesammelt durch die Brüder Grimm*, I-III (2 ed., Berlin, 1819-22; *ASKB* 1425-27), no. 47, I, p. 236; "The Juniper Tree," *The Complete Grimm's Fairy Tales*, tr. Margaret Hunt, rev. James Stern (New York: Pantheon, 1972), p. 226.

7. See, for example, Plato, *Phaedo*, 97 b-99 b; *Opera*, I, pp. 570-75; Heise, I, pp. 82-86; *Dialogues*, pp. 79-80.

8. Danish: *Anledning*, verb *anlede*, "to lead to." The word itself has a very modest meaning, inasmuch as it only leads to something else.

9. See, for example, Aristotle on Empedocles, *Metaphysics*, 1000 b; *Aristoteles graece*, I-II, ed. Immanuel Bekker (Berlin: 1831; *ASKB* 1074-75), II, p. 1000; *The Works of Aristotle*, I-XII, ed. J. A. Smith and W. D. Ross (Oxford: Oxford University Press, 1908-52), VIII:

> Hence it also follows on his theory that God most blessed is less wise than all others; for he does not know all the elements; for he has in him no strife, and knowledge is of the like by the like. 'For by earth,' he says,

we see earth, by water water,
By ether godlike ether, by fire wasting fire,
Love by love, and strife by gloomy strife [Fragment 109].

A popular version would be "It takes a thief to know (to catch) a thief," or "It takes one to know one."

10. See p. 144 and note 15.

11. See II Corinthians 12:7; *Eighteen Discourses, KW* V (*SV* V 106-23).

12. In Hegelian terms, the concrete is the Idea in itself and the Idea as systematically developed in history and in thought. The particular actuality is abstract because the concrete is the whole. See, for example, G.W.F. Hegel, *Vorlesungen über die Geschichte der Philosophie, Georg Wilhelm Friedrich Hegel's Werke. Vollständige Ausgabe,* I-XVIII, ed. Philipp Marheineke et al. (Berlin: 1832-45; *ASKB* 549-65), XIII, p. 37; Sämtliche Werke, *Jubiläumsausgabe* [*J.A.*], I-XXVI, ed. Hermann Glockner (Stuttgart: 1927-40), XVII, p. 53; *Hegel's Lectures on the History of Philosophy,* I-III (tr. of 2 ed. of *G.P.*, 1840; Kierkegaard had 1 ed., 1833-36), tr. E. S. Haldane and Frances H. Simson (New York: Humanities Press, 1955), I, pp. 23-25:

The Notion of the Concrete . . .

It is a common prejudice that the science of Philosophy deals only with abstractions and empty generalities, and that sense-perception, our empirical self-consciousness, natural instinct, and the feelings of every-day life, lie, on the contrary, in the region of the concrete and the self-determined. As a matter of fact, Philosophy is in the region of thought, and has therefore to deal with universals; its content is abstract, but only as to form and element. In itself the Idea is really concrete, for it is the union of the different determinations. It is here that reasoned knowledge differs from mere knowledge of the understanding, and it is the business of Philosophy, as opposed to understanding, to show that the Truth or the Idea does not consist in empty generalities, but in a universal; and that is within itself the particular and the determined. If the Truth is abstract it must be untrue. Healthy human reason goes out towards what is concrete; the reflection of the understanding comes first as abstract and untrue, correct in theory only, and amongst other things unpractical. Philosophy is what is most antagonistic to abstraction, and it leads back to the concrete.

If we unite the Notion of the concrete with that of development we have the motion of the concrete. Since the implicit is already concrete within itself, and we only set forth what is implicitly there, the new form which now looks different and which was formerly shut up in the original unity, is merely distinguished. The concrete must become for itself or explicit; as implicit or potential it is only differentiated within itself, not as yet explicitly set forth, but still in a state of unity. The concrete is thus simple, and yet at the same time differentiated. This, its inward contradiction, which is indeed the impelling force in development, brings distinction into being. But thus, too, its right to be taken back and reinstated extends beyond the difference; for its truth is only to be found in unity. Life, both that which is in Nature and that which is of the Idea, of Mind within itself, is thus manifested. Were the Idea abstract, it would simply be the highest conceivable existence, and that would be all that could be said of it; but such a God is the product of the understanding of modern times. What is true is rather found in motion, in a process, however, in which there is rest; difference, while it lasts, is but a temporary condition, through which comes unity, full and concrete.

See *JP* II 1606 (*Pap.* V B 41).

13. See J. L. Heiberg, *Alferne* (Copenhagen; 1835).

14. See, for example, Hegel, *Wissenschaft der Logik*, I, *Werke*, IV, pp. 75-76; *J.A.*, IV, pp. 553-54; *Hegel's Science of Logic* (tr. of *W.L.*, Lasson ed., 1923; Kierkegaard had 2 ed., 1833-34), tr. A. V. Miller (New York: Humanities Press, 1969), pp. 445-46:

Ground is first, *absolute ground*, in which essence is, in the first instance, a substrate for the ground relation; but it further determines itself as *form* and *matter* and gives itself a *content*.

Secondly, it is a *determinate ground* as ground of a determinate content; in that the ground relation in its realization as such becomes external to itself, it passes over into *conditioning* mediation.

Thirdly, ground presupposes a condition; but the condition no less presupposes the ground; the unconditioned is their unity, the *fact in itself*, which through the mediation of the conditioning relation passes over into Existence.

15. See note 1 above.

16. Johanne Luise Pätges Heiberg (1812-1890), wife of Johan Ludvig Heiberg, was the leading Danish actress at the time. See *Crisis in the Life of an Actress, KW* XVII (*SV* X 319-44). Peter Jørgen Frydendahl (1766-1836) was noted for both his talent and the range of his roles. Johan Adolph Gottlob Stage (1791-1845) was preeminent in creating an ironical effect. Joachim Ludvig Phister (1807-1896) is the admired subject of *Herr Phister as Captain Scipio, KW* XVII (*Pap.* IX B 67-73).

17. A review of Thomasine Gyllembourg's novel by Poul Martin Møller in *Maanedsskrift for Litteratur*, XV, 1836, p. 145; *Efterladte Skrifter*, I-III (Copenhagen: 1839-43; *ASKB* 1574-76), II, p. 137.

18. With reference to the following two paragraphs, see Supplement, p. 546 (*Pap.* III B 95).

19. See *K.*, 1; *R.*, p. 2.

20. See Johann Georg Hamann, "*Leser und Kunstrichter; nach perspectivischem Unebenmasse*," *Hamann's Schriften*, I-VIII, ed. Friedrich Roth and G. A. Wiener (Berlin, Leipzig: 1821-43; *ASKB* 536-44), II, p. 397 ("*aus Lesern entstehen Schriftsteller*") (ed. tr.).

21. Danish: *fra Leveren*, literally, "from the liver."

22. *K.*, 1; *R.*, p. 1. The quotations (ed. tr.) from the work are not always exact, usually because of the need to accommodate a brief quotation grammatically to the text of the review.

23. *K.*, 1; *R.*, p. 1.

24. *K.*, 6; *R.*, p. 5.

25. See *K.*, 1; *R.*, p. 1.

26. See *K.*, 3; *R.*, p. 3.

27. *K.*, 1; *R.*, p. 2.

28. See *K.*, 7; *R.*, p. 6.

29. *K.*, 12; *R.*, pp. 9-10.

30. See *K.*, 12; *R.*, p. 10.

31. *K.*, 16; *R.*, p. 12.

32. According to Charles's report (*K.*, 16; *R.*, pp. 12-13), Pamela, a seamstress, had forced Charles to marry her by threatening suicide with "a monstrous pair of tailor's shears."

33. *K.*, 12; *R.*, p. 9.

34. *R.*, p. 4.

35. *K.*, 12; *R.*, p. 9.

36. *K.*, 18; *R.*, p. 14.

37. See *K.*, 5; *R.*, p. 4.

38. See *K.*, 1; *R.*, p. 1.

39. See *K.*, 1; *R.*, p. 2.

40. *K.*, 18; *R.*, p. 14, the last line of the play.

41. *K.*, 14; *R.*, p. 11.

42. The main character in Ludvig Holberg's play with that title. See *Den Danske Skue-Plads*, I-VII (Copenhagen: 1788; *ASKB* 1566-67) V, no pagination; *Comedies by Holberg*, tr. Oscar James Campbell and Frederic Schenk (New York: American-Scandinavian Foundation, 1914), pp. 119-78.

43. *R.*, p. 11.

44. A character in Clemens Brentano, *Die mehreren Wehmüller und ungarischen Nationalgesichter* (Berlin: 1833; *ASKB* 1850). See Supplement, p. 546 (*Pap.* I A 337).

45. *K.*, 8; *R.*, p. 7. Rinville and Emmeline alternate in singing (ed. tr.):

> It may be said at times
> A man deserts his girl;
> Yet still the heart does cling
> To love that first was his.

46. See "*Miguel de Cervantes Saavedras Levnet*," by Don Gregoria Mayans y Siscar, in Cervantes, *Don Quixote*, I-IV, tr. Charlotta Dorothea Biehl (Copenhagen: 1776-77; *ASKB* 1937-40), I, p. 21. King Philip III, upon seeing a student frequently laughing and clapping his hand to his forehead while reading a book, exclaimed that the student either must not be very bright or must be reading *Don Quixote*.

47. Goethe, *Egmont*, V, 1, *Werke*, VIII, pp. 268-72; *Works*, II, pp. 228-30.

48. See *K.*, 6; *R.*, p. 4.
49. A usurer to whom Charles owes money.
50. See *K.*, 7; *R.*, p. 5.
51. *K.*, 7; *R.*, p. 6.
52. An aside; *K.*, 8; *R.*, p. 7.
53. *K.*, 9; *R.*, p.8.
54. See *K.*, 9; *R.*, p. 8.
55. Cf. Adam Gottlob Oehlenschläger, *Aladdin, eller Den forunderlige Lampe. Et Lystspil*, IV, *Adam Oehlenschlägers Poetiske Skrifter*, I-II (Copenhagen: 1805; *ASKB* 1597-98), II, p. 274; *Aladdin or the Wonderful Lamp*, tr. Henry Meyer (Copenhagen: Gyldendal, 1968), p. 170.
56. *K.*, 10; *R.*, p. 8.
57. *R.*, p. 9.
58. See *K.*, 12; *R.*, p. 12.
59. *R.*, p. 11.
60. See *K*, 8; *R.*, p. 6.
61. News of Charles's marriage.
62. Terence, *Andria*, 99; *P. Terentii Afri Comoediae sex*, ed. M.B.F. Schmieder and F. Schmieder (Halle: 1819; *ASKB* 1291), p. 16; *The Lady of Andros, Terence*, I-II, tr. John Sargeaunt (New York: Macmillan, 1912), I, pp. 14-15.
63. See *K.*, 16; *R.*, p. 12.
64. See *K.*, 16; *R.*, p. 13.
65. See *Kong Olaf Tryggvesøns Saga*, 251; *Oldnordiske Sagaer*, I-XII, tr. Carl Christian Rafn (Copenhagen: 1826-37; *ASKB* 1996-2007), II, pp. 280-83; Snorre Sturlason, *Heimskringla or the Lives of the Norse Kings*, tr. Erling Monsen (Cambridge, Mass.: Heffer, 1932), pp. 212-13 (the climax in a sea battle between Olav's Norwegian forces and Swedish, Danish, and rebel Norwegian forces):

> Einar Tambarskelver was aft in the middle hold (by the mast) of the *Serpent*; he was shooting with his bow and shot harder than all others. He shot at Eric the Jarl and struck the tillerhead right above the jarl's head, and the arrow went as far in as its own bands. The jarl looked at it and asked if they knew who had shot it; but at the same time there came a second arrow so near the jarl that it flew between his side and his arm and struck so deeply into the headboard that the point stuck out on the other side. Then the jarl said to a man who was called Finn and who was said by some to be a Finn— he was an outstanding bowman: "Shoot the big man in the middle hold". Finn shot and the arrow struck the middle of Einar's bow at the moment when he was drawing his bow for the third time. The bow burst into two parts. Then said King Olav, "What burst there so loudly?" Einar answered: "Norway from thine hand, O king!" "So great a burst has not yet befallen," said the king; "take my bow and shoot with it", and he threw his bow to him. Einar took the bow and straightway drew it beyond the point of the

arrow; he shouted, "Too weak, too weak is the king's bow". He threw the bow back, took up his shield and sword, and fought.

66. Those named in the last four paragraphs of the chapter were in twenty-five performances of *The First Love* between June 10, 1831, and March 5, 1835 (except for the performance of February 17, 1835, in which Adolf Marius Rosenkilde [1816-1882] played Charles).

67. Quite likely a reference to Karl Werder (1806-1893), German Hegelian philosopher, whose lectures on logic and metaphysics Kierkegaard attended while in Berlin for the Schelling lectures during the winter of 1841-1842. See *Letters*, Letters 55, 61, *KW* XXV.

68-71. See note 16 above.

ROTATION OF CROPS

1. See *Aristophanis Comoediae*, I-II, ed. Wilhelm (Guilielm) Dindorf (Leipzig: 1830; *ASKB* 1051), I, pp. 149-50; *Aristophanes*, I-III, tr. Benjamin Bickley Rogers (Loeb, New York: Putnam, 1924), III, pp. 379-81:

CHR.   O yes, by Zeus, and many more than these. So that none ever has
       enough of thee. Of all things else a man may have too much,
       Of love,
CA.   Of loaves,
CHR.   Of literature,
CA.   Of sweets,
CHR.   Of honour,
CA.   Cheesecakes,
CHR.   Manliness,
CA.   Dried figs,
CHR.   Ambition,
CA.   Barley-meal,
CHR.   Command,
CA.   Pea soup.

2. *Des Aristophanes Werke*, I-III, tr. Johann Gustav Droysen (Berlin: 1835-38; *ASKB* 1052-54), I, pp. 149-50. In the first line of the quoted text, the word *Andern* (else), which appears after *Allem* (everything), is omitted.

3. See, for example, G.W.F. Hegel, *Wissenschaft der Logik*, II, *Georg Wilhelm Friedrich Hegel's Werke. Vollständige Ausgabe*, I-XVIII, ed. Philipp Marheineke et al. (Berlin: 1832-45; *ASKB* 549-65), V, p. 342; *Sämtliche Werke. Jubiläumsausgabe* [*J.A.*], I-XXVI, ed. Hermann Glockner (Stuttgart: 1927-40), V, p. 342; *Hegel's Science of Logic* (tr. of *W.L.*, Lasson ed., 1923; Kierkegaard had 2 ed., 1833-34), tr. A. V. Miller (New York: Humanities Press, 1969), p. 835:

Now the negativity just considered constitutes the *turning point* of the movement of the Notion. It is the *simple point of the negative relation* to self, the innermost source of all activity, of all animate and spiritual self-movement, the dialectical soul that everything true possesses and through which alone it is true; for on this subjectivity alone rests the sublating of the opposition between Notion and reality, and the unity that is truth.

4. See Genesis 2:20-22.

5. See Genesis 11:4-9.

6. The only desire of the Roman people, according to Juvenal, *Satires*, X, 80-81; *Die Satiren des Decimus Junius Juvenalis*, tr. F. G. Findeisen (Berlin, Leipzig: 1777; *ASKB* 1250), p. 374; *Juvenal and Persius*, tr. G. G. Ramsay (Loeb, New York: Putnam, 1928), p. 199: "Bread and Games!"

7. With reference to the following sentence, see Supplement, pp. 546-47 (*Pap*. III B 122:1).

8. *Dyrehave*, a large wooded park north of Copenhagen.

9. With reference to the following two paragraphs, see Supplement, p. 547 (*Pap*. III B 122:2).

10. Told of King Hjarne, King Frode's successor, in Scandinavian legendary history. See *Den danske Krønike af Saxo Grammaticus*, tr. Anders Sørensen Vedel (Copenhagen: 1851; *ASKB* 2008-10), VI, 25, p. CXII.

11. See Plato, *Gorgias*, 511 e-512 b; *Platonis quae exstant opera*, I-XI, ed. Friedrich Ast (Leipzig: 1819-32; *ASKB* 1144-54), I, pp. 428-31; *Udvalgte Dialoger af Platon*, I-VIII, tr. Carl Johan Heise (Copenhagen: 1830-59; *ASKB* 1164-67, 1169 [I-VII]), III, p. 165; *The Collected Dialogues of Plato*, ed. Edith Hamilton and Huntington Cairns (Princeton: Princeton University Press, 1963), pp. 293-94 (Socrates speaking):

> For I suppose he [the pilot of a ship] is capable of reflecting that it is uncertain which of his passengers he has benefited and which he has harmed by not suffering them to be drowned, knowing as he does that those he has landed are in no way better than when they embarked, either in body or in soul. He knows that if anyone afflicted in the body with serious and incurable diseases has escaped drowning the man is wretched for not having died and has received no benefit from him; he therefore reckons that if any man suffers many incurable diseases in the soul, which is so much more precious than the body, for such a man life is not worth while and it will be no benefit to him if he, the pilot, saves him from the sea or from the law court or from any other risk. For he knows it is not better for an evil man to live, for he must needs live ill.

See *Irony, KW* II (*SV* XIII 268).

12. See, for example, Aristotle, *Politics*, 1253 a; *Aristoteles graece*, ed. Immanuel Bekker, I-II (Berlin: 1831; *ASKB* 1074-75), II, p. 1253; *The Works of Aristotle*, I-XII, ed. J. A. Smith and W. D. Ross (Oxford: Oxford University Press, 1908-52), X:

> Hence it is evident that the state is a creation of nature, and that man is by nature a political [social] animal. And he who by nature and not by mere

accident is without a state, is either a bad man or above humanity; he is like the

'Tribeless, lawless, heartless one,'

whom Homer denounces—the natural outcast is forthwith a lover of war; he may be compared to an isolated piece at draughts.

Now, that man is more of a political animal than bees or any other gregarious animals is evident.

13. With reference to the following sentence, see Supplement, p. 547 (*Pap.* III B 122:3).

14. With reference to the following sentence, see Supplement, p. 547 (*Pap.* III B 122:4).

15. See Supplement, p. 512 (*Pap.* II A 382).

16. See "acquired immediacy" in the first sentence of the preceding paragraph.

17. With reference to the following sentence, see Supplement, p. 547 (*Pap.* III B 122:5).

18. With reference to the remainder of the paragraph, see Supplement, p. 548 (*Pap.* III B 122:6).

19. Nero (37-68), emperor of Rome, burned the city in the year 64. See Suetonius, "Nero," 38; *Caji Suetonii Tranquilli Tolv første Romerske Keiseres Levnetsbeskrivelse*, I-II, tr. Jacob Baden (Copenhagen: 1802-03; *ASKB* 1281), II, pp. 102-04; *Suetonius*, I-II, tr. J. C. Rolfe (Loeb, New York: Macmillan, 1914), II, pp. 155-57.

20. See, for example, Hegel, *Wissenschaft der Logik*, I, *Werke*, III, pp. 147-48, 154; *J.A.*, IV, pp. 157-58, 164; *Science of Logic*, pp. 137, 142:

The infinite in its simple Notion can, in the first place, be regarded as a fresh definition of the absolute; as indeterminate self-relation it is posited as *being* and *becoming*. The forms of *determinate being* find no place in the series of those determinations which can be regarded as definitions of the absolute, for the individual forms of that sphere are immediately posited only as determinatenesses, as finite in general. The infinite, however, is held to be absolute without qualification for it is determined expressly as negation of the finite, and reference is thus expressly made to limitedness in the infinite—limitedness of which being and becoming could perhaps be capable, even if not possessing or showing it—and the presence in the infinite of such limitedness is denied.

But even so, the infinite is not yet really free from limitation and finitude; the main point is to distinguish the genuine Notion of infinity from spurious infinity, the infinite of reason from the infinite of the understanding; yet the latter is the *finitized* infinite, and it will be found that in the very act of keeping the infinite pure and aloof from the finite, the infinite is only made finite.

What we have here is an abstract transcending of a limit, a transcending which remains incomplete because *it is not itself transcended*. Before us is the infinite; it is of course transcended, for a new limit is posited, but the result is rather only a return to the finite. This spurious infinity is in itself the same thing as the perennial ought; it is the negation of the finite it is true, but it cannot in truth free itself therefrom. The finite reappears *in the infinite itself* as its other, because it is only in its *connection* with its other, the finite, that the infinite is. The progress to infinity is, consequently, only the perpetual repetition of one and the same content, one and the same tedious *alternation* of this finite and infinite.

21. Marcus Aurelius, *Meditations*, VII, 2; *M. Antoninus Commentarii libri XII*, ed. J. M. Schultz (Leipzig: 1829; *ASKB* 1218), p. 179; *The Communings with Himself of Marcus Aurelius Antoninus*, tr. C. H. Haines (Loeb, Cambridge: Harvard University Press, 1953), p. 165.

22. See Supplement, p. 548 (*Pap*. III B 122:7).

23. With reference to the following sentence, see Supplement, p. 548 (*Pap*. III B 122:8).

24. See, for example, Aeschylus, *Prometheus Bound*, 250-54; *Aeschylos Werke*, tr. Johann Gustav Droysen (Berlin: 1842; *ASKB* 1046), pp. 419-20; *The Complete Greek Tragedies*, I-IV, ed. David Grene and Richmond Lattimore (Chicago: University of Chicago Press, 1958-60), I, p. 320:

> *Prometheus*
> I caused mortals to cease foreseeing doom.
> *Chorus*
> What cure did you provide them with against that sickness?
> *Prometheus*
> I placed in them blind hopes.
> *Chorus*
> That was a great gift you gave to men.
> *Prometheus*
> Besides this, I gave them fire.

25. With reference to the following sentence, see Supplement, p. 548 (*Pap*. III B 122:9).

26. See Horace, *Epistles*, I, 6, 1; *Q. Horatii Flacci Opera* (Leipzig: 1828; *ASKB* 1248), p. 217; *Satires, Epistles and Ars Poetica*, tr. H. Rushton Fairclough (Loeb, New York: Putnam, 1929), p. 287. See also *Eighteen Upbuilding Discourses*, *KW* V (*SV* IV 113); *Fragments*, p. 80 and note 35, *KW* VII (*SV* IV 244).

27. In Greek mythology, the river of forgetfulness or oblivion in the underworld, to be crossed by those entering the realm of the dead.

28. In Greek mythology, the three-headed dog that guarded the gate of Hades. See, for example, Virgil, *Aeneid*, VI, 417-24; *Virgils Æneide*, I-II, tr. Johan Henrik Schønheyder (Copenhagen: 1812; not listed in *ASKB*), pp. 273-74; *Virgil*, I-II, tr. H. Rushton Fairclough (Loeb, New York: Putnam, 1920), I, p. 535.

29. See Plutarch, "Marcellus," 14, *Lives*; *Plutark's Levnetsbeskrivelser*, I-IV, tr. Stephan Tetens (Copenhagen: 1800-11; *ASKB* 1197-1200), III, p. 272; *Plu-*

tarch's Lives, I-XI, tr. Bernadotte Perrin (Loeb, New York: Putnam, 1914-26), V, p. 473: ". . . Archimedes, who was a kinsman and friend of King Hiero, wrote to him that with any given force it was possible to move any given weight; and emboldened, as we are told, by the strength of his demonstration, he declared that, if there were another world, and he could go to it, he could move this." See Supplement, p. 549 (*Pap.* III B 122:10).

30. With reference to the following sentence, see Supplement, p. 549 (*Pap.* III B 122:11).

31. With reference to the following three sentences, see Supplement, p. 549 (*Pap.* III B 122:12, A 19).

32. See, for example, Hegel, *Wissenschaft der Logik*, I, *Werke*, III, pp. 122-24; *J.A.*, IV, pp. 132-34; *Science of Logic*, pp. 117-18:

Something and other are, in the first place, both determinate beings or somethings.

Secondly, each is equally an other. It is immaterial which is first named and solely for that reason called *something*; (in Latin, when they both occur in a sentence, both are called *aliud*, or 'the one, the other', *alius alium*; when there is reciprocity the expression *alter alterum* is analogous). If of two things we call one A, and the other B, then in the first instance B is determined as the other. But A is just as much the other of B. Both are, in the same way, *others* . . ..

Otherness thus appears as a determination alien to the determinate being thus characterized, or as the other *outside* the one determinate being; partly because a determinate being is determined as other only through being *compared* by a Third, and partly because it is only determined as other on account of the other which is outside it, but is not an other on its own account. At the same time, as has been remarked, every determinate being, even for ordinary thinking, determines itself as an other, so that there is no determinate being which is determined only as such, which is not outside a determinate being and therefore is not itself an other.

Both are determined equally as something and as other, and are thus the same, and there is so far no distinction between them. But this self-sameness of the determinations likewise arises only from external reflection, from the *comparing* of them; but the other as at first posited, although an other in relation to the something, is nevertheless also an other on its own account, apart from the something.

33. The ritual of pledging friendship (and the use of the familiar second-person singular *du* instead of the formal plural *De*). The use of *De* has more or less disappeared in recent years.

34. A scene in Holberg, *Mester Gert Westphaler*, II, 4; *Den Danske Skue-Plads*, I-VII (Copenhagen: 1788; *ASKB* 1566-67), I, no pagination.

35. See Sallust, *The War with Cataline*, XX; *C. Sallusti Crispi opera quae supersunt*, I-IV, ed. Friedrich Kritzius (Leipzig: 1828; *ASKB* 1269-72), I, p. 98;

Sallusts Catilinariske Krig, tr. Rasmus Møller (Copenhagen: 1811; *ASKB* 1273), p. 25; *Sallust*, tr. J. C. Rolfe (Loeb, New York: Putnam, 1921), p. 35.

36. With reference to the following sentence, see Supplement, p. 549-50 (*Pap*. III B 122:13).

37. With reference to the following sentence, see Supplement, p. 550 (*Pap*. III B 122:14).

38. With reference to the following sentence, see Supplement, p. 550 (*Pap*. III B 122:15).

39. With reference to the following two sentences, see Supplement, p. 550 (*Pap*. III A 124).

40. With reference to the following paragraph, see Supplement, pp. 550-51 (*Pap*. III B 122:16).

41. See Steen Steensen Blicher, *"Kjeltringliv,"* *Samlede Noveller*, I-V (Copenhagen: 1833-36; *ASKB* 1521-23), I, pp. 240-42.

42. With reference to the following paragraph, see Supplement, p. 551 (*Pap*. III B 122:17).

43. With reference to the following sentence, see Supplement, p. 552 (*Pap*. III B 122:18).

44. See Jens Immanuel Baggesen, *"Theateradministratoriade,"* *Jens Baggesens danske Værker*, I-XII (Copenhagen: 1827-32; *ASKB* 1509-20), I, p. 421. The name was Hassing, for which Baggesen found no suitable rhyme except "two-thirds of Washington—which is as good as nothing" (ed. tr.).

45. With reference to the following sentence, see Supplement, p. 552 (*Pap*. III B 122:19).

46. See Plotinus, *Enneads*, III, 4, 2; *Plotinus*, I-VI, tr. A. H. Armstrong (Loeb, Cambridge: Harvard University Press, 1966-67), III, pp. 145-47. Cf. Plato, *Phaedo*, 81 c-82 b; Heise, I, pp. 49-52; *Collected Dialogues*, pp. 64-65.

47. Johann Heinrich Wilhelm Tischbein (1751-1829), a friend of Goethe's. See Johann Wolfgang v. Goethe, *"An Denselben,"* *Goethe's Werke. Vollständige Ausgabe letzter Hand*, I-LX (Stuttgart, Tübingen: 1828-42; *ASKB* 1641-68 [I-LV]), II, p. 168.

THE SEDUCER'S DIARY

1. See Supplement, pp. 552-53 (*Pap*. IV A 231).

2. See Supplement, p. 553 (*Pap*. III B 67).

3. See Supplement, p. 553 (*Pap*. III B 170).

4. For continuation of the sentence, see Supplement, p. 553 (*Pap*. III B 45:1).

5. See *Irony*, *KW* II (*SV* XIII 351-54, 360, 362, 364-68); Supplement, p. 555 (*Pap*. III B 33).

6. See *JP* V 5772; VI 6713 (*Pap*. V A 12; X³ A 769).

7. With reference to the following sentence, see Supplement, p. 553 (*Pap*. III B 45:2).

8. With reference to the following paragraph, see Supplement, pp. 554-55 (*Pap*. III B 45:3).

9. See *Letters*, Letter 8, *KW* XXV; *Pap.* II A 801.

10. With reference to the remainder of the sentence and the following three sentences, see Supplement, p. 555 (*Pap.* III B 45:4).

11. With reference to the following paragraph, see Supplement, p. 555-56 (*Pap.* III B 33, 34, 35).

12. See Supplement, p. 556 (*Pap.* III B 45:5).

13. With reference to the following sentence, see Supplement, pp. 556-57 (*Pap.* III B 45:7, 38).

14. When Ixion, king of Thessaly, who had been given refuge on Olympus by Zeus, sought to embrace Hera (Roman Juno), Zeus substituted a cloud in her shape. A monster, Centaur, was born from this union. Ixion was chained to a fiery wheel in Hades as punishment for his act. See Paul Friedrich A. Nitsch, *neues mythologisches Wörterbuch*, I-II, rev. Friedrich Gotthilf Klopfer (Leipzig, Sorau: 1821; *ASKB* 1944-45), II, pp. 122-23; *JP* V 5100 (*Pap.* I A 75).

15. With reference to the remainder of the paragraph, see Supplement, p. 557 (*Pap.* III B 47:1).

16. With reference to the remainder of the paragraph, see Supplement, p. 557 (*Pap.* III B 47:2, 48, 49).

17. See, for example, Aristotle's denial of action at a distance, *Physics*, 244 b-245 b; *Aristoteles graece*, ed. Immanuel Bekker, I-II (Berlin: 1831; *ASKB* 1074-75), I, pp. 244-45; *The Works of Aristotle*, I-XII, ed. J. A. Smith and W. D. Ross (Oxford: Oxford University Press, 1908-52), II:

> Now it is impossible to move anything either from oneself to something else or from something else to oneself without being in contact with it: it is evident, therefore, that in all locomotion there is nothing intermediate between moved and movent.
>
> Nor again is there anything intermediate between that which undergoes and that which causes alteration: this can be proved by induction: for in every case we find that the respective extremities of that which causes and that which undergoes alteration are adjacent. . . .
>
> Nor, again, can there be anything intermediate between that which suffers and that which causes increase: for the part of the latter that starts the increase does so by becoming attached in such a way to the former that the whole becomes one. Again, the decrease of that which suffers decrease is caused by a part of the thing becoming detached. So that which causes increase and that which causes decrease must be continuous with that which suffers increase and that which suffers decrease respectively: and if two things are continuous with one another there can be nothing intermediate between them.
>
> It is evident, therefore, that between the extremities of the moved and the movement that are respectively first and last in reference to the moved there is nothing intermediate.

See Supplement, pp. 557-58 (*Pap.* III B 51, 52; IV A 232).

18. With reference to the following four paragraphs, see Supplement, pp. 558-59 (*Pap.* III B 50:1-4).

19. *Jery und Bätely, Goethe's Werke. Vollständige Ausgabe letzter Hand,* I-LX (Stuttgart, Tübingen: 1828-42; *ASKB* 1641-68 [I-LV]), XI, p. 10 (ed. tr.).

20. Cf. Psalm 139:7-9.

21. See II Samuel 12:1-9.

22. See Supplement, p. 559 (*Pap.* III B 68:1).

23. With reference to the following three paragraphs, see Supplement, pp. 557-59 (*Pap.* III B 51, 52, 68:1).

24. Johann Ludwig Tieck, "*Die wilde Engländerin,*" in *Das Zauberschloss, Ludwig Tieck's gesammelte Novellen,* I-X (Breslau: 1835), II, pp. 144-69.

25. The French paleontologist Georges Léopold Cuvier (1769-1832), in his *Recherches sur les ossements fossiles des quadrupèdes,* I-V (Paris: 1821-24), I, p. III, states that his aim is to show that an entire species can be reconstructed from a single bone.

26. With reference to the following sentence, see Supplement, p. 559 (*Pap.* III B 68:2).

27. According to Danish custom, the engagement ring is ordinarily worn on the fourth finger of the right hand.

28. For continuation of the sentence, see Supplement, p. 559 (*Pap.* III B 68:3).

29. See Supplement, p. 559 (*Pap.* 70:1).

30. With reference to the following two sentences, see Supplement, pp. 559-60 (*Pap.* III 70:2).

31. See Supplement, p. 560 (*Pap.* III B 70:3).

32. With reference to the following four sentences, see Supplement, p. 560 (*Pap.* III B 73).

33. Cf. G.W.F. Hegel, *Grundlinien der Philosophie des Rechts, Georg Wilhelm Friedrich Hegel's Werke. Vollständige Ausgabe,* I-XVIII, ed. Philipp Marheineke et al. (Berlin: 1832-45; *ASKB* 549-65), VIII, p. 17; *Sämtliche Werke. Jubiläumsausgabe [J.A.],* I-XXVI, ed. Hermann Glockner (Stuttgart: 1927-40), VII, p. 33; *Hegel's Philosophy of Right* (tr. of *P.R.*, 1 ed., 1821, also with reference to 2 ed., 1833, and later editions; Kierkegaard had 2 ed.), tr. T. M. Knox (Oxford: Oxford University Press, 1978), p. 10: "*What is rational is actual and what is actual is rational.*"

34. See Wolfgang Amadeus Mozart, *Don Juan,* tr. Laurids Kruse (Copenhagen: 1807), I, 16, p. 52; *Don Giovanni,* tr. Ellen H. Bleiler (New York: Dover, 1964), I, 3, p. 104.

35. Ludvig Holberg, *Erasmus Montanus,* V, 5; *Den Danske Skue-Plads,* I-VII (Copenhagen: 1788; *ASKB* 1566-67), V, no pagination; *Comedies by Holberg,* tr. Oscar James Campbell and Frederic Schenck (New York: American-Scandinavian Foundation, 1914), p. 178.

36. A long promenade running along the harbor northward from the center of Copenhagen.

37. See note 14 above.

38. See Genesis 39:12.

39. Cf., for example, Johan Ludvig Heiberg, *Elverhøi*, I, 5; *Skuespil*, I-VII (Copenhagen: 1853-41; *ASKB* 1533-59), III, p. 313.

40. At one time, the *alcedo ispida* (European kingfisher) was thought to build its nest on the water. See Supplement, p. 560 (*Pap.* II A 612; III B 55:1). The *alcedinae* comprise ninety species. The alcidae (auks, murres, puffins, 22 species) spend their winter at sea, where they dive for their food.

41. See Supplement, p. 560 (*Pap.* III B 55:2).

42. With reference to the following four sentences, see Supplement, p. 561 (*Pap.* III B 84).

43. With reference to the following paragraph, see Supplement, pp. 561-62 (*Pap.* III B 179:28).

44. With reference to the remainder of the sentence, see Supplement, p. 562 (*Pap.* III B 55:3).

45. In Greek mythology, Orpheus went to Hades in search of Eurydice, his wife. She was restored to him on the condition that he would not look at her before they returned to earth. He disobeyed, and she vanished.

46. See John 5:2.

47. Ovid, *The Art of Love*, II, 235-36; *P. Ovidii Nasonis opera quae supersunt*, I-III, ed. Antonius Richter (Leipzig: 1828; *ASKB* 1265), I, p. 237; *Ovid The Art of Love and Other Poems*, tr. J. H. Mozley (Loeb, Cambridge: Harvard University Press, 1957), p. 83. See Supplement, p. 562 (*Pap.* III B 55:4).

48. See Pius Alexander Wolff, *Preciosa* (music by Carl Maria von Weber), tr. Caspar Johan Boye (Copenhagen: 1822), I, p. 15.

49. With reference to the following five sentences, see Supplement, pp. 562-63 (*Pap.* III B 78).

50. With reference to the following sentence, see Supplement, p. 563 (*Pap.* III B 56:1).

51. With reference to the remainder of the sentence, see Supplement, p. 563 (*Pap.* III B 36).

52. See Supplement, p. 563 (*Pap.* III B 56:2).

53. The northern and eastern gates of the Copenhagen wall, now the names of city railway stations.

54. An area on the far side of Sortedams Lake, one of a string of three small lakes to the northwest of the city wall of Copenhagen.

55. See Supplement, p. 563 (*Pap.* III B 56:3).

56. With reference to the following sentence, see Supplement, p. 563 (*Pap.* III B 56:4).

57. In Greek mythology, Pallas Athena (Roman Minerva) sprang full-grown, and fully armed, from the head of Zeus (Roman Jupiter) after Zeus had swallowed her mother, Metis. See Nitsch, II, p. 251.

58. In Greek mythology, Aphrodite (Roman Venus), daughter of Zeus and Dione, sprang, according to some accounts, from the sea into which the blood of Uranus was shed when he was wounded by Cronus. See Nitsch, II, p. 613.

59. For continuation of the sentence, see Supplement, p. 564 (*Pap.* III B 56:5).

60. In Greek mythology, the parents of Psyche were ordered to take her and her two sisters in bridal attire to a crag and leave them there alone. Zephyr, the west wind, softly wafted them to a castle on the far side of the mountain. See Nitsch, II, p. 506. Raphael's painting has Psyche carried away by cupids.

61. See Genesis 41:32.

62. A street on the canal alongside Christiansborg, the parliament building.

63. See Shakespeare, *King Lear*, I, 1, 78-80; *Shakspeare's dramatische Werke*, I-XII, tr. August Wilhelm v. Schlegel and Johann Ludwig Tieck (Berlin: 1839-41; *ASKB* 1883-88), XI, p. 6; *The Complete Works of Shakespeare*, ed. George Lyman Kittredge (Boston: Ginn, 1936), p. 1198 (Cordelia speaking):

> Then poor Cordelia!
> And yet not so; since I am sure my love's
> More richer than my tongue.

64. See Supplement, p. 564 (*Pap*. III B 56:7).

65. See Supplement, p. 564 (*Pap*. III B 56:8).

66. A large woods and park west of Copenhagen containing a royal residence. King Frederik VI (1768-1839) opened the gardens to the public.

67. Cf. Genesis 2:18-23.

68. A reference to an earlier, especially medieval, family practice according to which the unmarried women had a separate room or building in which they worked and lived.

69. See Mozart, *Figaros Givtermaal*, tr. Niels Thoroup Bruun (Copenhagen: 1817), II, 2, p. 41; *Le Nozze di Figaro* (*The Marriage of Figaro*), tr. Ruth and Thomas Martin (New York: G. Schirmer, 1951), II, 10, p, 136. The lines are at variance with the Danish version.

70. See p. 295 and note 33.

71. Perhaps an allusion to Sidsellille and her loom in the medieval Danish ballad "*Herr Medelvold*." See *Udvalgte Danske Viser fra Middelalderen*, I-V, ed. Werner Hans Abrahamson, Rasmus Nyerup, and Knud Lyne Rahbek (Copenhagen: 1812-14; *ASKB* 1477-81), III, p. 361.

72. See Psalm 90:4.

73. With reference to the following paragraph, see Supplement, p. 564 (*Pap*. III B 56:9).

74. See Supplement, pp. 564, 566 (*Pap*. III B 56:10; 92).

75. Ovid, *The Remedies of Love*, 10; *Opera*, I, p. 321; Loeb, p. 179.

76. See, for example, Hegel, *Wissenschaft der Logik*, I, *Werke*, IV, pp. 156-58; *J.A.*, IV, pp. 634-36; *Hegel's Science of Logic* (tr. of *W.L.*, Lasson, ed., 1923; Kierkegaard had 2 ed., 1833), tr. A. V. Miller (New York: Humanities Press, 1969), pp. 507-09:

> The world in and for itself is the totality of Existence; outside it there is nothing. But since it is in its own self absolute negativity or form, its reflection-into-self is a *negative relation* to itself. It contains opposition and repels itself within itself into the essential world and into the world of otherness or

the world of Appearance. Thus, because it is totality, it is also only *one side* of it, and in this determination constitutes a self-subsistence distinct from the world of Appearance. The world of Appearance has in the essential world its negative unity in which it falls to the ground and into which it withdraws as into its ground. Further, the essential world is also the positing ground of the world of Appearance; for, containing the absolute form in its essentiality, its identity sublates itself, makes itself into positedness and as this posited immediacy is the world of Appearance. . . . Now since the realm of Laws contains within it this negative moment and opposition, and hence as totality repels itself from itself into a world in and for itself and a world of Appearance, the identity of both is thus the *essential relation of opposition*. The ground relation as such is the opposition which, in its contradiction, has fallen to the ground; and Existence is the ground that has united *with itself.* But Existence becomes Appearance; ground is sublated in Existence; it reinstates itself as the return of Appearance into itself, but at the same time as sublated ground, namely, as ground relation of opposed determinations; but the identity of such determinations is essentially a becoming and a transition, no longer the ground relation as such.

77. See Supplement, p. 564 (*Pap.* III B 56:10, 92).

78. Augustin Eugène Scribe, *Bruden,* tr. Johan Ludvig Heiberg, first presented at the Royal Theater in Copenhagen in 1831; *Det Kongelige Theaters Repertoire,* I-VI (Copenhagen: 1830-42), II, no. 11. Fritz, a corporal, loses a bride through his own fault; she marries a count instead.

79. With reference to the following six lines, see Supplement, pp. 564-65 (*Pap.* III B 89, 85, 72).

80. Joseph Freiherr v. Eichendorff, *"Vor der Stadt,"* *Gedichte* (Berlin: 1837; *ASKB* 1634), p. 24 (ed. tr.). See *Letters,* Letter 21, *KW* XXV; Supplement, p. 565 (*Pap.* III B 72).

81. With reference to the remainder of the sentence, see Supplement, p. 565 (*Pap.* III B 135:1).

82. See I Peter 4:8.

83. See Supplement, pp. 565-66 (*Pap.* III B 69).

84. From a Norwegian peasant ballad. See *Brage og Idun, et nordisk Fjærdingsaarsskrift,* ed. Povl Frederik Barfod, II, 1839, p. 445.

85. With reference to the remainder of the sentence, see Supplement, p. 566 (*Pap.* III B 93).

86. See, for example, Gottfried Wilhelm Leibniz, *Monadology,* para. 78-79; *Guil. Leibnitii opera philosophica,* I-II, ed. Johann Eduard Erdmann (Berlin: 1840; *ASKB* 620), II, p. 711; *The Monadology and Other Philosophical Writings,* tr. Robert Latta (London: Oxford University Press, 1965), pp. 262-63:

78. These principles have given me a way of explaining naturally the union or rather the mutual agreement [*conformité*] of the soul and the organic body. The soul follows its own laws, and the body likewise follows its own laws; and they agree with each other in virtue of the pre-established har-

mony between all substances, since they are all representations of one and the same universe.

79. Souls act according to the laws of final causes through appetitions, ends, and means. Bodies act according to the laws of efficient causes or motions. And the two realms, that of efficient causes and that of final causes, are in harmony with one another.

87. With reference to the following three sentences, see Supplement, p. 566 (*Pap.* III B 91).

88. With reference to the following sentence, see Supplement, p. 566 (*Pap.* III B 135:2).

89. Ovid, *The Art of Love*, II, 123-24; *Opera*, I, p. 233; Loeb, p. 75. See Supplement, p. 567 (*Pap.* III B 43).

90. Perhaps a blending of two orally perpetuated children's rhymes, "*Munken gaaer i Enge*" and "*Skjøn Ridder han drager sit røde Guldbaand.*" See *Börnerim, Remser og Lege, Samlede og tildels optegnede af Ewald Tang Christensen*, ed. Jens Sigsgaard (Copenhagen: [1981]), pp. 67-68, 74.

91. See I Samuel 3:1-18.

92. See Supplement, p. 567 (*Pap.* III B 58:1).

93. With reference to the following sentence, see Supplement, p. 567 (*Pap.* III B 58:2).

94. See Johann Christoph Friedrich v. Schiller, *Die Piccolomini*, III, 7; *Schillers sämmtliche Werke*, I-XII (Stuttgart, Tübingen: 1838; *ASKB* 1804-15), IV, p. 145.

95. See p. 91 and note 51. Vilhelm is the dead lover in the poem.

96. With reference to the remainder of the paragraph, see Supplement, pp. 567-68 (*Pap.* III B 58:3).

97. See Supplement, p. 568 (*Pap.* III B 58:4).

98. A German word with a Danish ending.

99. With reference to the remainder of the paragraph, see Supplement, pp. 568-69 (*Pap.* III B 58:5).

100. See, for example, Plato, *Apology*, 39 c; *Platonis quae exstant opera*, I-XI, ed. Friedrich Ast (Leipzig: 1819-32; *ASKB* 1144-54), pp. 152-55; *The Collected Dialogues of Plato*, ed. Edith Hamilton and Huntington Cairns (Princeton: Princeton University Press, 1963), p. 24 (Socrates speaking):

> Having said so much, I feel moved to prophesy to you who have given your vote against me, for I am now at that point where the gift of prophecy comes most readily to men—at the point of death. I tell you, my executioners, that as soon as I am dead, vengeance shall fall upon you with a punishment far more painful than your killing of me. You have brought about my death in the belief that through it you will be delivered from submitting your conduct to criticism, but I say that the result will be just the opposite. You will have more critics, whom up till now I have restrained without your knowing it, and being younger they will be harsher to you and will cause you more annoyance. If you expect to stop denunciation of your

wrong way of life by putting people to death, there is something amiss with your reasoning. This way of escape is neither possible nor creditable. The best and easiest way is not to stop the mouths of others, but to make yourselves as good men as you can. This is my last message to you who voted for my condemnation.

101. With reference to the remainder of the sentence, see Supplement, p. 569 (*Pap.* III B 58:6).

102. With reference to the remainder of the paragraph, see Supplement, p. 569 (*Pap.* III B 58:7).

103. With reference to the following sentence, see Supplement, p. 569 (*Pap.* III B 61:1).

104. With reference to the following sentence, see Supplement, pp. 569-70 (*Pap.* IV A 233).

105. With reference to the following sentence, see Supplement, p. 570 (*Pap.* III B 61:2).

106. With reference to the following four sentences, see Supplement, p. 570 (*Pap.* III B 63:1).

107. With reference to the following sentence, see Supplement, p. 570 (*Pap.* III B 63:2).

108. With reference to the remainder of the paragraph, see Supplement, pp. 570-71 (*Pap.* III B 63:3,4,5).

109. See J. L. Heiberg, *Recensenten og Dyret*, V, *Skuespil*, III, p. 210.

110. A performer at Bakken summer amusement park in Deer Park north of Copenhagen. See Supplement, pp. 570-71 (*Pap.* III B 63:4).

111. With reference to the remainder of the paragraph, see Supplement, p. 571 (*Pap.* III B 63:6).

112. See Ovid, *Loves*, I, iv, 16, 35-46; *Opera*, I, p. 148; *Ovid Heroides and Amores*, tr. Grant Showerman (Loeb, Cambridge: Harvard University Press, 1958), p. 331.

113. Cf. *Repetition*, p. 189, *KW* VI (*SV* III 224).

114. The source has not been located.

115. For additions, see Supplement, pp. 571-72 (*Pap.* III B 81, 63:7).

116. With reference to the following three sentences, see Supplement, p. 572 (*Pap.* III B 99).

117. The oldest student dormitory of the University of Copenhagen. It is located on Købmagergade, near the Round Tower.

118. With reference to the following sentence, see Supplement, p. 572 (*Pap.* III B 115).

119. With reference to the following seven sentences, see Supplement, pp. 572-73 (*Pap.* III B 100).

120. With reference to the following sentence, see Supplement, pp. 573, 576-77 (*Pap.* III B 136, 74).

121. See Supplement, p. 573 (*Pap.* III B 102).

122. With reference to the following sentence, see Supplement, p. 573 (*Pap.* III B 64:1).

123. With reference to the remainder of the sentence, see Supplement, pp. 573-74 (*Pap.* III B 64:2).

124. With reference to the following two sentences, see Supplement, p. 574 (*Pap.* III B 79).

125. With reference to the remainder of the paragraph, see Supplement, p. 574 (*Pap.* III B 80).

126. With reference to the following paragraph, see Supplement, p. 574 (*Pap.* III B 98).

127. See Supplement, p. 574 (*Pap.* III B 65).

128. Cf. *Fear and Trembling*, pp. 36, 119, *KW* VI (*SV* III 87, 164).

129. With reference to the following sentence, see Supplement, pp. 574-75 (*Pap.* III B 66:1).

130. An allusion to Don Giovanni's response to the knocking on the door by the Commendatore's statue. See Kruse, *Don Juan*, II, 19, pp. 122-23; Bleiler, *Don Giovanni*, II, 6, pp. 195-96.

131. Cf. *Repetition*, p. 152, *KW* VI (*SV* III 192).

132. With reference to the following letter, see Supplement, p. 575 (*Pap.* III 66:2).

133. See *JP* II 2240 (*Pap.* I A 1).

134. With reference to the following three sentences, see Supplement, p. 575 (*Pap.* III B 66:3).

135. See Genesis 31:34.

136. On memory [*Hukommelse*] and recollection [*Erindring*], see, for example, *Stages, KW* XI (*SV* VI 15-21).

137. With reference to the following paragraph, see Supplement, p. 575 (*Pap.* III B 137).

138. On this important category, see, for example, *JP* III 2338-59 and p. 794; VII, p. 56.

139. With reference to the following paragraph, see Supplement, p. 576 (*Pap.* III B 101).

140. See Supplement, p. 576 (*Pap.* III B 71:1).

141. Jens Immanuel Baggesen, "*Agnete fra Holmegaard,*" *Jens Baggesens danske Værker*, I-XII (Copenhagen: 1827-32; *ASKB* 1509-20), II, p. 358 (ed. tr.): "Agnes, she staggered, she drooped, she fell."

142. For continuation of the sentence, see Supplement, p. 576 (*Pap.* III B 71:2).

143. See J. L. Heiberg, "*Moralsk Læseøvelse i Vers,*" *Ny A-B-C-Bog . . . for den unge Grundtvig* (Copenhagen: 1817), p. 21; *Johan Ludvig Heibergs Prosaiske Skrifter*, I-XI (Copenhagen: 1861-62), X, p. 25.

144. With reference to the remainder of the paragraph, see Supplement, p. 576 (*Pap.* III B 71:3).

145. A Pythagorean concept (sometimes rendered as "the music of the spheres") based on the coincidence of the musical octave and the number (8) of planets.

146. With reference to the following paragraph, see Supplement, pp. 576-77 (*Pap.* III B 74, 75, 90).

147. In Roman mythology, Cardea was a goddess who watched over door hinges (Latin *cardo*). See Nitsch, I, p. 465; Ovid, *Calendar*, VI, 101-30; *Opera*, III, pp. 157-58; *Ovid's Fasti*, tr. James George Frazer (Loeb, New York: Putnam, 1931), pp. 324-27.

148. See, for example, Sallust, *The War with Cataline*, 22; *Sallusts Catalinariske Krig*, tr. Rasmus Møller (Copenhagen: 1811, *ASKB* 1273), pp. 27-28; *Sallust*, tr. J. C. Rolfe (Loeb, New York: Putnam, 1921), pp. 38-41.

149. In Greek and Roman mythology, Aeolus was the wind god, who kept the winds (his sons) in a cave on the island of Aeolia. See Nitsch, I, pp. 75-78.

150. In Greek legend, Ariadne, the daughter of Minos and Pasiphaë, loved Theseus and helped him slay the monster Minotaur, imprisoned in the labyrinth on the isle of Crete. Ariadne gave Theseus a thread to guide him out of the labyrinth. See Nitsch, I, pp. 309-13.

151. See Mark 3:24.

152. See Genesis 30:31-43.

153. See note 150 above. Theseus carried Ariadne off to Naxos, where he left her. See Nitsch, I, p. 310. The painting, in the Naples museum, is a mural from Herculaneum.

154. In Greek mythology, Nemesis was the goddess of retributive justice. See Nitsch, II, pp. 304-09.

155. *Gribs-Skov (Gribskov)*, Denmark's largest forest, which lies northwest of Copenhagen. See Supplement, p. 577 (*Pap.* IV A 81); *JP* V 5096, 5643, 5746 (*Pap.* I A 65; IV A 81; V A 84).

156. See Supplement, p. 578 (*Pap.* III B 155).

157. In Greek legend, this was the fate of the nymph Echo, who fell in love with Narcissus. See Nitsch, I, p. 656.

158. See pp. 440-41.

159. See Supplement, pp. 578-79 (*Pap.* III B 156).

160. With reference to the following two sentences, see Supplement, p. 579 (*Pap.* III B 96).

161. With reference to the following paragraph, see Supplement, pp. 579-80 (*Pap.* III A 187, B 179:16, A 190).

162. See Supplement, p. 580 (*Pap.* III B 76:1); cf. *Letters*, Letter 54, p. 105, *KW* XXV.

163. With reference to the remainder of the sentence, see Supplement, p. 580 (*Pap.* III B 160:2).

164. For continuation of the sentence, see Supplement, p. 580 (*Pap.* III B 160:4).

165. With reference to the following three paragraphs, see Supplement, pp. 580-81 (*Pap.* III B 86, 94, 82, 88).

166. The Copenhagen city council members.

167. With reference to the following two sentences, see Supplement, p. 581 (*Pap.* III B 82).

168. *Politivennen*, 86, 1837, pp. 219-21, 235-38, carried a satirical piece on the extravagant dress of "the modern servant girl."

169. "Matchless" and "golden age" were favorite expressions of Nicolai Frederik Severin Grundtvig (1783-l872), Danish historian, poet, preacher, and politician. See p. 415 and note 171 below.

170. With reference to the following three sentences, see Supplement, p. 582 (*Pap*. III B 87).

171. Probably an allusion to N.F.S. Grundtvig and his emphasis on the spoken word, a "matchless discovery." See, for example, *Postscript, KW* XII (*SV* VII 28-30); *JP* V 5089-90 (*Pap*. I A 60-61).

172. See Supplement, p. 582 (*Pap*. III B 161:1).

173. The specific source has not been located.

174. See Supplement, pp. 582-83 (*Pap*. III B 106).

175. With reference to the following three paragraphs, see Supplement, p. 583 (*Pap*. III B 114).

176. See Proverbs 24:26. The text is closest to Luther's German translation: "*Eine richtige Antwort ist wie ein lieblicher Kusz*," *Die Bibel* (Carlsruhe, Leipzig: 1836; *ASKB* 3). See Supplement, p. 583 (*Pap*. III A 183).

177. Socrates' analogy of the soul with two steeds and a charioteer. See Plato, *Phaedrus*, 253 c-256 e; *Opera*, I, pp. 186-95; *Dialogues*, pp. 499-502. See Supplement, p. 583 (*Pap*. III B 162:1); *JP* III 3323 (*Pap*. III B 26).

178. See Supplement, p. 584 (*Pap*. III B 162:1).

179. With reference to the following letter, see Supplement, p. 584 (*Pap*. A 134, B 162:2).

180. A design produced in sand on a vibrating plate. Named after Ernst Florens Friedrich Chladni (1756-1827), German physicist. See, for example, *JP* IV 4966; V 5393, 5923 (*Pap*. X² A 557; II A 482; VII¹ A 53).

181. An Egyptian statue that the Greeks assumed to be a representation of Memnon, a king of Ethiopia and son of Eos, the goddess of dawn. It was said to make a musical sound when the rays of the morning sun fell upon it.

182. Ovid, *Art of Love*, II, 155; *Opera*, I, p. 269; Loeb, p. 77. See Supplement, p. 584 (*Pap*. III B 44).

183. In Roman mythology, Venus (Greek Aphrodite), goddess of vegetation and protector of feminine chastity, has a girdle of beauty, into which were worked longing and deceptive speech and flattering entreaty that beguiled even the wise. See Homer, *Iliad*, XIV, 214-27; *Homers Iliade*, I-II, tr. Christian Frederik Emil Wilster (Copenhagen: 1836), II, p. 34; *Homer The Iliad*, I-II, tr. A. T. Murray (Loeb, Cambridge: Harvard University Press, 1939-42), II, p. 83.

184. With reference to the following sentence, see Supplement, p. 585 (*Pap*. III B 162:4).

185. For continuation of the paragraph, see Supplement, p. 585 (*Pap*. III B 162:5).

186. For postscript, see Supplement, p. 586 (*Pap*. B 162:6).

187. Said by Caesar in 49 B.C. when he crossed the river Rubicon (dividing

ancient Italy and Gaul) to attack Pompey in defiance of the senate's orders. See Suetonius, *Julius Caesar*, 32; *Caji Suetonii Tranquilli Tolv første Romerske Keiseres Levnetsbeskrivelse*, I-II, tr. Jacob Baden (Copenhagen: 1802-03; *ASKB* 1281), I, p. 31; *Suetonius*, I-II, tr. J. C. Rolfe (Loeb, New York: Macmillan, 1914), I, p. 45.

188. With reference to the following sentence, see Supplement, p. 585 (*Pap*. III B 104, 105, 162:7).

189. With reference to the remainder of the sentence, see Supplement, p. 586 (*Pap*. III B 107:1).

190. With reference to the following paragraph, see Supplement, pp. 586-87 (*Pap*. III B 107:2, 108).

191. In *Arabian Nights* or *Thousand and One Nights*, Queen Scheherazade, by telling stories for 1,001 nights, keeps in suspense the Sultan's resolve to take a new bride each night and to have her beheaded in the morning. He finally relents and abandons his plan. See *Tausend und eine Nacht*, I-IV, tr. Gustav Weil (Stuttgart, Pforzheim: 1838-41; *ASKB* 1414-17), I, p. 12; *The Arabian Nights' Entertainments*, tr. Richard F. Burton (New York: Random House, 1959), pp. 21-23.

192. See Supplement, p. 587 (*Pap*. III B 103).

193. For continuation of the paragraph, see Supplement, p. 587 (*Pap*. III B 163:1).

194. Caligula (Caius Caesar Germanicus, 12-41) was known for his cruel and ruthless tyranny. See Suetonius, *Caligula*, 30, 3; Baden, I, p. 312; Loeb, I, p. 453.

195. In classical legend, Pyramus and Thisbe, whose parents opposed their marriage, conversed through a crevice in the wall separating the two parental properties. See Ovid, *Metamorphoses*, IV, 55-166; *Opera*, II, pp. 99-102; *Ovid Metamorphoses*, I-II, tr. Frank Justus Miller (Loeb, New York: Putnam, 1916), I, pp. 183-91.

196. With reference to the following sentence, see Supplement, pp. 587-88 (*Pap*. III B 163:2).

197. With reference to the remainder of the paragraph, see Supplement, p. 588 (*Pap*. III B 118).

198. With reference to the following paragraph, see Supplement, p. 588 (*Pap*. III B 146).

199. Horace, *Odes*, II, 8, 3; *Q. Horatii Flacci opera* (Leipzig: 1828; *ASKB* 1248); *Horace The Odes and Epodes*, tr. C. F. Bennett (Loeb, New York: Putnam, 1930), p. 127. See *Repetition*, Supplement, p. 280.

200. Adam Gottlob Oehlenschläger, *Palnatoke*, V, 2 ("*Jeg gnider den ved Dag ved Nat—og kan / ei faae den ud!*"); *Oehlenschlägers Tragødier*, I-IX (Copenhagen: 1841-44; *ASKB* 1601-05), II, p. 298.

201. With reference to the following paragraph, see Supplement, p. 588 (*Pap*. III B 164).

202. With reference to the following paragraph, see Supplement, p. 588 (*Pap*. III B 143:1,2).

203. An expression attributed to Valdemar IV concerning his castle Gurre near a lake of the same name in north Sjælland. See *JP* V 5095 (*Pap.* I A 64).

204. See, for example, Hegel, *Wissenschaft der Logik*, I, *Werke*, III, pp. 124-25; *J.A.*, IV, pp. 134-35; *Science of Logic*, p. 119:

> Something *preserves* itself in the negative of its determinate being [*Nicht-dasein*]; it is essentially *one* with it and essentially *not one* with it. It stands, therefore, in a *relation* to its otherness and is not simply its otherness. The otherness is at once contained in it and also still *separate* from it; it is a *being-for-other.*
>
> Determinate being as such is immediate, without relation to an other; or, it is in the determination of *being*; but as including within itself non-being; it is *determinate* being, being negated within itself, and then in the first in-stance an other—but since at the same time it also preserves itself in its ne-gation, it is only a *being-for-other.*
>
> It preserves itself in the negative of its determinate being and is being, but not being in general, but as self-related in *opposition* to its relation to other, as self-equal in opposition to its inequality. Such a being is *being-in-itself.*
>
> Being-for-other and being-in-itself constitute the two moments of the something. There are here present *two pairs* of determinations: 1. Some-thing and other, 2. Being-for-other and being-in-itself. The former contain the unrelatedness of their determinateness; something and other fall apart. But their truth is their relation; being-for-other and being-in-itself are, therefore, the above determinations posited as *moments* of one and the same something, as determinations which are relations and which remain in their unity, in the unity of determinate being. Each, therefore, at the same time, also contains within itself its other moment which is distinguished from it.

205. See Ovid, *Calendar*, VI, 295-98; *Opera*, III, p. 143; *Fasti*, Loeb, p. 341; Nitsch, II, p. 622.

206. See, for example, Exodus 20:5; Deuteronomy 4:24.

207. The elemental meaning of "existence" is apparent in the etymology: *exsisto* (stand forth), *ex* (out) + *sto* (stand), understood here in the sense of hav-ing continuance in and through itself. In *Either/Or*, II, and in other Kierke-gaard works, "to exist" has a qualitative meaning related to the ethical and religious levels of becoming, "to stand out" beyond immediacy, beyond the givenness of subsistence.

208. See, for example, Heinrich Heine, *"Du bist wie eine Blume," Buch der Lieder* (Hamburg: 1837), p. 217; *The Complete Poems of Heinrich Heine*, tr. Suhr Draper (Boston: Suhrkamp/Insul, 1982), p. 96.

209. See, for example, *Anxiety*, pp. 82-91, *KW* VIII (*SV* IV 351-60); *JP* III 2739-44 and pp. 821-22; VII, p. 12.

210. See Supplement, p. 588 (*Pap.* III B 165).

211. See Supplement, p. 589 (*Pap.* III B 145).

212. Two beautiful peasant girls argued on the road about which one had the more beautiful posterior. A passerby was impressed as judge, and he de-

clared in favor of the elder sister and also promptly declared his love for her. Upon returning home, he told of the episode, and his younger brother sought out the younger sister. The father of the girls finally agreed. The citizens of Syracuse called the two Kallipygos (with beautiful posterior) and built a temple to Venus (Greek Aphrodite) with a statue of the goddess. The statue Venus Callipygus (Kallipygos) is in the National Museum in Naples. See Nitsch, I, p. 449.

213. Cf. Virgil, *Aeneid*, II, 204 (*horresco referens*); *Virgils Æneid*, I-II, tr. Johan H. Schønheyder (Copenhagen: 1812), I, p. 63; *Virgil*, I-II, tr. H. Rushton Fairclough (Loeb, New York: Putnam, 1918-20), I, pp. 308-09.

214. See Supplement, p. 589 (*Pap.* III B 166).

215. With reference to the following two paragraphs,, see Supplement, p. 589 (*Pap.* V B 53:26).

216. With reference to the following five sentences, see Supplement, p. 590 (*Pap.* III A 144).

217. In Roman mythology, Diana (Greek Artemis), the twin sister of Apollo, was a virgin huntress, the guardian of forests, and the protector of woman, especially in childbirth. See Nitsch, I, pp. 615-25.

218. See Euripides, *Medea*, 250-51; *Euripides*, tr. Christian Frederik Wilster (Copenhagen: 1840; *ASKB* 1115), p. 58; *The Complete Greek Tragedies*, I-IV, ed. David Grene and Richmond Lattimore (Chicago: University of Chicago Press, 1958-60), III, p. 67 (Medea speaking):

> A man, when he's tired of the company in his home,
> Goes out of the house and puts an end to his boredom
> And turns to a friend or companion of his own age.
> But we are forced to keep our eyes on one alone.
> What they say of us is that we have a peaceful time
> Living at home, while they do the fighting in war.
> How wrong they are! I would very much rather stand
> Three times in the front of battle than bear one child.

219. See Supplement, p. 590 (*Pap.* III B 144).

220. A character in Mozart's *Don Giovanni*. See pp. 96-98, 124-25.

221. The etching has not been identified.

222. See Supplement, p. 590 (*Pap.* III B 167:1).

223. See Judges 16:13-19.

224. "*Flyv, Fugl, flyv!*" the title of a poem by Christian Frederik Winther, *Digte* (Copenhagen: 1828), pp. 40-41.

225. See Ovid, *Metamorphoses*, X, 243-97; *Opera*, II, pp. 220-23; Loeb, II, pp. 81-85.

226. An allusion to the geese whose noise awakened the garrison on Capitoline Hill in Rome when the Gauls were about to overrun it.

227. See Matthias Claudius, *ASMUS omnia sua SECUM portans oder Sämmtliche Werke des Wandsbecker Bothen, Werke*, I-IV (1-8) (Hamburg: 1838; *ASKB* 1631-32), I, pp. 68-80.

228. Ibid., p. 69, a long-nosed caricature by Daniel Nikolaus Chodowiecki (1726-1801).

229. In Greek mythology, Alpheus, son of Oceanus, was the personification of the river Alpheus (now Rouphia). The island Ortygia, off the southeast coast of Sicily, was the site of ancient Syracuse. See Nitsch, I, p. 413.

230. With reference to the remainder of the paragraph, see Supplement, p. 590 (*Pap.* III A 170).

231. With reference to the following sentence, see Supplement, p. 590 (*Pap.* III B 127).

232. See Goethe, *Faust*, I, 3058-3173; *Werke*, XII, pp. 178-84; *Faust*, tr. Bayard Taylor (New York: Modern Library, 1950), pp. 130-35.

233. See Genesis 2:8.

234. See p. 31 and note 73.

235. For addition, see Supplement, p. 590 (*Pap.* III B 167:3).

236. In Roman mythology, Jupiter was identified with Zeus, the ruler of gods and men. The best known version of the gods' rebuff to the arrogance of men is in Plato. See *Symposium*, 189 d-191 a; *Opera*, III, pp. 468-73; *Udvalgte Dialoger af Platon*, I-VIII, tr. Carl Johan Heise (Copenhagen: 1830-59; *ASKB* 1164-67 [I-VII]), IV, pp. 37-43; *Collected Dialogues*, pp. 542-43 (Aristophanes speaking):

> First of all I must explain the real nature of man, and the change which it has undergone—for in the beginning we were nothing like we are now. For one thing, the race was divided into three; that is to say, besides the two sexes, male and female, which we have at present, there was a third which partook of the nature of both, and for which we still have a name, though the creature itself is forgotten. For though 'hermaphrodite' is only used nowadays as a term of contempt, there really was a man-woman in those days, a being which was half male and half female.
>
> And secondly, gentlemen, each of these beings was globular in shape, with rounded back and sides, four arms and four legs, and two faces, both the same, on a cylindrical neck, and one head, with one face one side and one the other, and four ears, and two lots of privates, and all the other parts to match. They walked erect, as we do ourselves, backward or forward, whichever they pleased, but when they broke into a run they simply stuck their legs straight out and went whirling round and round like a clown turning cartwheels. And since they had eight legs, if you count their arms as well, you can imagine that they went bowling along at a pretty good speed.
>
> The three sexes, I may say, arose as follows. The males were descended from the Sun, the females from the Earth, and the hermaphrodites from the Moon, which partakes of either sex, and they were round and they *went* round, because they took after their parents. And such, gentlemen, were their strength and energy, and such their arrogance, that they actually tried—like Ephialtes and Otus in Homer—to scale the heights of heaven and set upon the gods.
>
> At this Zeus took counsel with the other gods as to what was to be done.

They found themselves in rather an awkward position; they didn't want to blast them out of existence with thunderbolts as they did the giants, because that would be saying good-by to all their offerings and devotions, but at the same time they couldn't let them get altogether out of hand. At last, however, after racking his brains, Zeus offered a solution.

I think I can see my way, he said, to put an end to this disturbance by weakening these people without destroying them. What I propose to do is to cut them all in half, thus killing two birds with one stone, for each one will be only half as strong, and there'll be twice as many of them, which will suit us very nicely. They can walk about, upright, on their two legs, and if, said Zeus, I have any more trouble with them, I shall split them up again, and they'll have to hop about on one.

So saying, he cut them all in half just as you or I might chop up sorb apples for pickling, or slice an egg with a hair. And as each half was ready he told Apollo to turn its face, with the half-neck that was left, toward the side that was cut away—thinking that the sight of such a gash might frighten it into keeping quiet—and then to heal the whole thing up. So Apollo turned their faces back to front, and, pulling in the skin all the way round, he stretched it over what we now call the belly—like those bags you pull together with a string—and tied up the one remaining opening so as to form what we call the navel. As for the creases that were left, he smoothed most of them away, finishing off the chest with the sort of tool a cobbler uses to smooth down the leather on the last, but he left a few puckers round about the belly and the navel, to remind us of what we suffered long ago.

Now, when the work of bisection was complete it left each half with a desperate yearning for the other, and they ran together and flung their arms around each other's necks, and asked for nothing better than to be rolled into one.

237. With reference to the following paragraph, see Supplement, p. 591 (*Pap.* III B 32).

238. See Supplement, p. 591 (*Pap.* III B 168:1).

239. Cicero, *On Divination*, I, xlv, 103; *M. Tullii Ciceronis opera omnia*, I–IV and index, ed. Johann August Ernesti (Halle: 1756-57; *ASKB* 1224-29), IV, p. 644; *Cicero De senectute, De amicitia, De divinatione*, tr. William Armistead Falconer (Cambridge: Harvard University Press, 1953), pp. 334-35.

240. In Greek mythology, Alectryon, a friend of Ares, went to sleep while on watch at the tryst of Ares and Aphrodite (Roman Mars and Venus) and was surprised by Apollo (the sun god) and Hephaestus (Roman Vulcan). See Nitsch, I, p. 137.

241. In Greek mythology, Clytie was a nymph who fell in love with Apollo and was changed into a sunflower. See Nitsch, I, p. 535.

242. See Supplement, pp. 591-92 (*Pap.* III B 168:2).

243. In Greek mythology, Kainis was changed by her lover, Poseidon (Roman Neptune), into a man (Kaineus). See Nitsch, I, p. 444.

244. For addition, see Supplement, p. 592 (*Pap.* B 168:3).

SUPPLEMENT

1. In his *Kierkegaard-Studien*, I¹⁻²-II³ (Gutersloh: 1933; repr., Vaduz, Liechtenstein: Topos Verlag, 1978), II, pp. 490-92 (serial pagination), Emanuel Hirsch makes a good case for the idea that Kierkegaard's first writing plan was a series of letters by a pseudonymous Faustian doubter. The present entry and most of the remaining entries from *Papirer* I A-II A represent Kierkegaard's initial work on this projected series, which was never completed. There is, however, an obvious relation in substance, tone, and form to the "Diapsalmata" written by the sardonic young Mr. A in *Either/Or*, I, pp. 19-43. The back part of a notebook, marked CC by Kierkegaard and with pagination beginning from the back (the front and major portion was used for translations into Latin; see *Pap.* I C 11-12), contains entries I A 328-41. These are the core of the "Faustian letters." *Pap.* I A 329 touches on Gørres, *Die christliche Mystik*, and indicates that "the passage should be quoted"; this suggests that more than a journal style of writing was under way. *Pap.* II A 46 is titled "A Preface" and states that the book "should be called 'letters.' " Working on the basis of content and within the 1835-1837 time-span, Hirsch also includes the following entries in the "Faustian letters": *Pap.* I A 34, 72, 104, 158, 161, 292; II A 22-26, 29, 30, 46, 48-50, 53-57, 59. See *Erstlingsschriften*, ed. Emanuel Hirsch, Sören Kierkegaard, *Gesammelte Werke*, I-XXXVI Abt. (Düsseldorf, Köln: Eugen Diederichs Verlag, 1956-69), Abt. XXX, pp. 114-137.

That Kierkegaard had in mind a volume of pseudonymous letters by a fictive character not only has historical-literary importance but constitutes a warning of the continuing riskiness of attributing personally and directly the contents of his pseudonymous works and his writing "as a poet." See especially "First and Last Explanation," *Postscript*, end, and *Point of View, KW* XXII (*SV* XIII 540-42, 569-70 fn.).

2. Presumably Peter Wilhelm Lund (1801-1880), brother of Johan Christian Lund and Henrik Ferdinand Lund (married to Kierkegaard's sisters Nicoline Christine and Petrea Severine), paleontologist, natural scientist; he returned to Brazil in January 1833. Hirsch, however, considers the letter fictive and as a part of the "Faustian letters." See note 1 above.

3. See Prosper Merimée, *Les Ames du purgatoire* (Paris: 1834).

4. See Luke 12:16-21.

5. See Hans Christian Ørsted (1777-1851), *"Forsøg over Klangfigurerne,"* Det kongelige danske Videnskabernes Selskabs Skrifter, II, 1807-08, pp. 31-38.

6. Joakim Frederik Schouw (1789-1852) in his *Grundtræk til en almindelige Plantegeographie* (Copenhagen: 1822) gives names to the phytogeographical regions.

7. Jens Wilken Hornemann (1770-1841) in his *Forsøg til en dansk oeconomiske Plantelære* (Copenhagen: 1796) describes all the plants in Denmark, Holsten, Norway, Iceland, and Greenland, and discusses their range in those regions.

8. See *Fragments*, p. 108, *KW* VII (*SV* IV 269); G. Heinrich v. Schubert, *Die Symbolik des Traumes* (Bamberg: 1821; *ASKB* 776), p. 38.

9. See *Letters*, Letter 262, *KW* XXV.

10. Kierkegaard by this time had been a university student for four years, ostensibly in theology. Five years later, he completed doctoral work in philosophy (although in that faculty the degree was called Magister at the time).

11. See "*Om Naturhistoriens Studium i Danmark,*" *Kjøbenhavns flyvende Post,* 143, November 29, 1830, p. 578; *Prosaiske Skrifter,* I-XI (Copenhagen: 1861-62), X, p. 478.

12. Polyænus, *Strategemata,* VII, 9, relates the anecdote that Cambyses' army, during the siege of Pelusium, drove ahead of them animals sacred in Egypt in order to deter shooting by the besieged. See *Anxiety,* p. 40, *KW* VIII (*SV* IV 312).

13. Claudius Pulcher before the sea battle near Drepanum (249 B.C.). See Cicero, *On the Nature of the Gods,* II, 3 (7); *M. Tullii Ciceronis opera omnia,* I-IV and index, ed. Johann August Ernesti (Halle: 1757; *ASKB* 1224-29), IV, p. 514; *Cicero De natura deorum Academica,* tr. H. Rackham (Loeb, New York: Putnam, 1933), p. 129; Valerius Maximus, *Sammlung merkwürdiger Reden und Thaten,* I, 4, 3, tr. Friedrich Hoffmannn (Stuttgart: 1828-29; *ASKB* 1296), p. 32.

14. The basis for the text is *Efterladte Papirer,* I-VIII, ed. Hans Peter Barfod and Hermann Gottsched (Copenhagen: 1869-81), I, p. 43, in which the Latin phrase appears as a section title and is not in editorial brackets.

15. See Deuteronomy 34:1-4, with reference to Mt. Nebo rather than to Tabor, and Numbers 14:20-25.

16. The coastal road running north from Copenhagen, which was and is the main route to the amusement park at Bakken (Dyrehaugen or Dyrehavsbakken) in Dyrehaven, a large woods with many deer (therefore Deer Park).

17. The goddess Thetis sought in vain to prevent fulfillment of the prophecy of Achilles' death in the Trojan war by dressing him as a woman. See Paul Friedrich A. Nitsch, *neues mythologisches Wörterbuch,* I-II, rev. Friedrich Gotthilf Klopfer (Leipzig, Sorau: 1821; *ASKB* 1944-45), I, pp. 18-19 (Tethys).

18. See *Postscript, KW* XII (*SV* VII 314-15).

19. See note 16 above.

20. Cf. *Fragments* p. 6, *KW* VII (*SV* IV 177).

21. See Hans Lassen Martensen, review of Johan Ludvig Heiberg, "*Indledningsforedrag til den i November 1834 begyndte logiske Cursus paa denn kongelige militaire Høiskole,*" *Maanedsskrift for Litteratur,* XVI, 1836, pp. 515-28, especially p. 517.

22. The practice of beginning any historical discussion with creation.

23. The reference is to an epistemological view that explains the correspondence of object and perception by way of the interaction of body and soul.

24. The preceding lines touch lightly on Hegel's concept of movement and becoming in logic and time. In 1714, King Carl XII of Sweden made his famous ride from Turkey to the fortress Stralsund in Poland in sixteen days, averaging about seventy-five miles a day. When he arrived, his boots had to be cut off. See Karl Friedrich Becker, *Verdenshistorie,* I-XII (Copenhagen: 1822-

29; *ASKB* 1972-83), IX, pp. 78-79. To the shoemaker, the immediate is an abstraction: "boots without feet." The dialectical movement of boots and feet fitting each other is expressed by the squeaking. Unity is achieved when the boots have quit squeaking and fit the feet so perfectly that boots and feet can be separated only as they were in the case of Carl XII.

25. *Selskabet for Trykkefrihedens rette Brug* (The Society for the Right Use of Freedom of the Press), founded 1835. See *Kjøbenhavnsposten*, 105, May 2, 1835; *Dansk Folkeblad*, I, 1835, p. 1.

26. See *Fear and Trembling*, p. 69, *KW* VI (*SV* III 118).

27. See *Kjøbenhavnsposten*, 69, March 9, 1836; 88, March 25; 92, March 28; 94, March 29; 316, November 9; and, especially, 340, December 3.

28. The fictional object of address in a fictional epistolary exchange. See note 1 above.

29. See Nikolai Frederik Severin Grundtvig, *Christlige Prædikener eller Søndags Bog*, I-III (Copenhagen: 1827-30; *ASKB* 222-24), III, 26, especially pp. 584 and 592-95. See *Postscript, KW* XII (*SV* VII 28-33).

30. October 30, 1826. See *Kjendelse og Dom i Sagen Dr. Professor H. Clausen contra forhenværende residerende Capellan N.F.S. Grundtvig*, ed. Jens Diderik Roed (Copenhagen: 1826), pp. 21-22. Instead of replying to criticism in *Kirkens Gjenmæle* (1825) by N.F.S. Grundtvig, Henrik Nikolai Clausen had instituted an injury case in court. Grundtvig lost and was given a small fine and lifetime censorship (lifted in 1837).

31. Jakob Joseph von Görres, *Die christliche Mystik*, I-IV$^{1-2}$ (Regensburg, Landshut: 1836-42; *ASKB* 528-32), I, p. vii (ed. tr.): "Since he [Napoleon] disappeared and the restoration spun out its boring allegories and the *juste milieu* discharged its high-flown metaphors, everything has again become a romantic wilderness, and young Germany sits in the swamp, and young Switzerland and young Italy and young France and young Spain and Britannia, and carves whistles from the reeds and whistles and crows and cooes and wooes in all keys: apparently it is nothing but the stymphalic birds that wait for their Hercules to chase them away with his rattle. Thus all present time becomes myth; in the end even criticism will no longer be able to resist the mythologizing principle; it becomes a fly on the nose of the world giant and cleanses its wings with its legs and does spotwork backward for further cleansing."

32. See note 1.

33. A further characterization of the pseudonymous Faustian writer as a doubter, even to the point of radical doubt (suicide). See note 1 above.

34. The fictional recipient of the Faustian letter. See note 1 above.

35. Kierkegaard had a brother, Niels Andreas Kierkegaard (April 30, 1809), who died September 21, 1833, in Paterson, New Jersey, U.S.A., two years after he had emigrated.

36. Kierkegaard had a brother, Søren Michael Kierkegaard (March 23, 1807), who died September 14, 1819, from an accident while playing at school.

37. See *Works of Love, KW* XVI (*SV* XX 327-29).

38. See Matthew 10:30; Luke 12:7.

39. See p. 19.

40. See p. 32.

41. See G. J. Wenzel, *Manden af Verden eller Grundsætninger og Regler for Afstand, Tække, fiin Levensmaade og sand Høflighed,* tr. Niels Thoroup Bruun (Copenhagen: 1818), p. 98.

42. The long delayed letter from Brazil arrived on the day of the widow's remarriage. See note 1 above on the Faustian letters.

43. There is a shift in the relation of the visible pole-star to the true pole. Here the brother says that the movement of life from happiness to the sorrow of separation is an expression of a single, unchangeable love, just as the shifting position of the visible pole-star is an expression of its relation to the true pole. The metaphor is epitomized in the arithmetic symbol.

44. The manuscript of this entry is missing. Hans Peter Barfod (*E.P.*, I, pp. 18-20) gives the date as December 2, with no year, and places it together with entries from 1833. The editors of the *Papirer* place it in the period 1836-37. In his catalog of the journals and papers, Barfod calls this entry a draft of a letter. In tone and in some details, it is much like the "Diapsalmata" in *Either/Or,* I, pp. 19-43, and belongs together with *Pap.* I A 328 as a substantial element in Kierkegaard's projected pseudonymous work by a Faustian doubter. See note 1.

45. Cf. p. 33.

46. Cf. pp. 26, 28.

47. See Carl Christian Rafn, *Nordiske Kæmpehistorier,* I-III (Copenhagen: 1823; *ASKB* 1993-95), I, pp. 96-99.

48. A mysterious German youth who in 1828 appeared in Nürnberg without any knowledge of his past or awareness of his identity. See *Kjøbenhavns flyvende Post,* 65, 66, 70, 71, 73, August 15, 18, September 1, 5, 12, 1828, pp. 269-72, 273-76, 292, 295-96, 304.

49. See note 28 above.

50. See *Anxiety,* p. 51, *KW* VIII (*SV* IV 332); *Postscript, KW* XII (*SV* VII 138).

51. Cf. p. 33.

52. See p. 424 (where a saying of Caligula is used); *Either/Or,* II, pp. 99, 187, *KW* IV (*SV* II 91, 169).

53. The suffix *gal(e)* in the Danish *Nattergal* (nightingale) means "to sing" (hence night-singer), but *gal* also means "mad, insane" (hence English "gale," a furious or "mad" wind). The word-play here has been shifted to the relation between "moon" and "lunatic" as the best possible approximation in translation.

54. See II Samuel 11-12; *For Self-Examination, KW* XXI (*SV* XII 325-27).

55. Cf. p. 21.

56. Cf. pp. 26, 40.

57. A play by Ludvig Holberg, *Den Danske Skue-Plads,* I-VII (Copenhagen: 1788), V, no pagination; *Comedies by Holberg,* tr. Oscar James Campbell and

Frederic Schenck (New York: American-Scandinavian Foundation, 1914), pp. 119-78.

58. See *JP* III, NUMBERS, CROWD, MASS, PUBLIC.

59. See p. 20.

60. See, for example, pp. 26, 28; *Repetition*, pp. 173-74, *KW* VI (*SV* III 210-11); *Anxiety*, p. 99, *KW* VIII (*SV* IV 369).

61. See p. 25.

62. Cf. p. 19.

63. See Johann Georg Hamann, *Hamann's Schriften*, I-VII, ed. Friedrich Roth and G. A. Wiener (Berlin, Leipzig: 1821-43; *ASKB* 536-44), I, p. x.

64. St. Simeon Stylites (*c.* 390-459) was the first of the Stylites or pillar ascetics. See *From the Papers, KW* I (*SV* XIII 54).

65. See *Anxiety*, p. 51, *KW* VIII (*SV* IV 332); *Postscript, KW* XII (*SV* VII 138).

66. See Holberg, *Den honnette Ambition*, III, 1; *Danske Skue-Plads*, V, no pagination.

67. See p. 295 and note 34.

68. See *Works of Love, KW* XVI (*SV* IX 116-19).

69. "*Med Forlov, i hvilken Skole har Professor Sibbern lært dansk Stiil* (Excuse me, in what school has Professor Sibbern [one of Kierkegaard's esteemed professors of philosophy] learned how to write Danish)?" by C. F. Reiffenstein, editor and former pastrycook, in *Raketten med Stjerner*, ed. C. F. Reiffenstein, 141, December 10, 1836, pp. 169-74. J. K. Blok Tøxen (1776-1848) was a linguist and writer and Frederik Lange (1798-1862) a teacher.

70. See *Stages, KW* XI (*SV* 260-61).

71. See *Works of Love, KW* XVI (SV IX 104-05, 116-17). Love in its different varieties and their roots and manifestations is a constant theme in Kierkegaard's various works. *Works of Love* is the one volume that concentrates particularly on this theme.

72. Aristotle, *Metaphysics*, 993 b; *Politics* 1290 b-1291 a; *Aristoteles graece*, I-II, ed. Immanuel Bekker (Berlin 1831; *ASKB* 1074-75), II, pp. 993, 1290 b-1291 a; *The Works of Aristotle*, I-XII, ed. J. A. Smith and W. D. Ross (Oxford: Oxford University Press, 1908-52), VIII, X.

73. *Über Lenau's Faust. Von Johannes M. . . . . . .n.* (Stuttgart: 1836). Kierkgaard's reference is to *Perseus*, ed. J. L. Heiberg, I, June 1837, pp. 91-164, which has a Danish version (under the name H. Martensen) with the title *Betragtninger over Ideen af Faust, med Hensyn paa Lenaus Faust*. See Hans Lassen Martensen, *Af mit Levnet*, I-III (Copenhagen: 1882-83), I, pp. 183-87.

74. See *JP* V 5168 (*Pap.* I C 107).

75. See II Samuel 11-12; *For Self-Examination*, KW XXI (*SV* XII 325-27).

76. Omission indicated by editor H. P. Barfod in *E.P.*, I, pp. 127-28, the only extant text of this entry.

77. The Carpocratians (c. 2-6), who held that one ought to experience all forms of good and evil in the process of regaining union with the divine. See Karl Hase, *Kirkehistorie*, tr. Christian Winther and Theodor Schorn

(Copenhagen: 1837; *ASKB* 160-66), p. 88; *Anxiety*, p. 103, *KW* VIII (*SV* IV 372).

78. See *Visebog indeholdende udvalgte danske Selskabssange*, ed. Andreas Seidelin (Copenhagen: 1814; *ASKB* 1483), p. 400.

79. See p. 95.

80. See Nikolaus Lenau (pseud. of Nikolaus Niembsch), *Faust* (Stuttgart, Tübingen: 1836), pp. 49-51.

81. See note 73 above.

82. See note 77 above.

83-87. Presumably by the fictitious author of the "Faustian Letters." See note 1 above.

88. See *JP* V 5247 (*Pap.* II A 132).

89-93. See note 83 above.

94. Each of entries *Pap.* III A 220-26 is on a slip of paper and undated. Editor H. P. Barfod (*E.P.*) dates them uncertainly as 1842 (?) and editors P. A. Heiberg and V. Kuhr (*Pap.*) date them as 1840-42(?). Their contents seem to mark them as items for possible use in *Either/Or.*

95. The right of a feudal lord to sleep with a vassal's wife on the wedding night.

96. See Luke 7:11-15.

97. The Latin expression here is usually used in the form *disjecti membra poëtae*, literally, "the dismembered limbs of a poet." See Horace, *Satires*, I, 4, 62; *Horatii Flacci opera* (Leipzig: 1828; *ASKB* 1248), p. 401; *Horace Satires, Epistles and Ars Poetica*, tr. H. Rushton Fairclough (Loeb, New York: Putnam, 1929), pp. 52-53. Presumably this entry is the title for the following entries *Pap.* III A 228-41 (in the back of a green notebook marked JJ and containing entries III A 227-41), all of which belong together with III A 242 and 243, which are on a sheet inside a folder marked "The earliest rudiments of *Either/Or*. The green book, some items that were not used." This folder most likely contained III A 244-46 also. See *Stages, KW* XI (*SV* VI 64).

98. See, for example, *Fragments*, p. 36, *KW* VII (*SV* IV 203).

99. See ibid., pp. 26-33 (195-201); *Stages, KW* XI (*SV* VI 138).

100. See I John 2:17.

101. See note 97 above.

102. The motto is printed on the cover of Journal EE (*Pap.* II A 341-576), February 1-September 23, 1839.

103. See John 6:63.

104. Carl F. Flögel, *Geschichte der komischen Literatur*, I-IV (Liegnitz, Leipzig: 1784-87; *ASKB* 1396-99), I, p. 50, (ed. tr.).

105. The editors of the large Danish dictionary, *Ordbog over det danske Sprog*, do not know the origin of this expression either, but the editors of the German equivalent, Grimm, *Deutsches Wörterbuch*, claim a clue to the German cognate *mutterallein:* absolutely alone as in the mother's womb.

106. See *Berlingske Tidende*, 296, December 13, 1837: "*Hydro-Oxygen-Gas-Mikroskop.*"

107. See Hamann, *Schriften*, I, p. 497.

108. See *Mythologie der Feen und Elfen vom Urspringe dieses Glaubens bis auf die neuesten Zeiten, aus dem Englischen übersetzt v. O.L.B. Wolff*, I-II (Weimar: 1828), I, pp. 131-32.

109. See Genesis 25:29-34.

110. Friedrich Heinrich v. der Hagen, *Erzählungen und Märchen*, I-II (Prenzlau: 1825), I, pp. 147-52, 156-209.

111. See Ecclesiastes 1:9.

112. In Norse mythology, the Midgard-serpent, world-serpent, lay at the bottom of the sea, and its coils encircled the earth. See Adam Gottlob Oehlenschläger, "*Thors Fiskeri*," *Nordens Guder* (Copenhagen: 1837; *ASKB* 1600), pp. 100-05, especially p. 103; *The Gods of the North*, tr. William Edward Frye (London: 1845), pp. 117-21.

113. Cf. Genesis 2:17, 3:4; *Sickness unto Death*, p. 18, *KW* XIX (*SV* IX 132).

114. *Dionysius Longin vom Erhabenen*, tr. C. H. Heineken (Dresden: 1737; *ASKB* 1129).

115. See *JP* IV 4394 (*Pap.* I A 319).

116. Stephani the Younger, *Apothekeren og Doctoren* (music by Ditters v. Dittersdorf), tr. Lars Knudsen (Copenhagen: 1789).

117. In Norse mythology, Thor was challenged in various ways by Utgard Loki; each challenge involved an enormous deception, such as in the drinking bout. See, for example, Oehlenschläger, "*Gøgleriet i Utgard*," *Nordens Guder*, pp. 51-69; Frye, pp. 45-80.

118. Printed in Berlin in 1810.

119. According to the Danish editors, the word is not found in Lucian, who does, however, use ὁμόνεκρος (companion in death) in *Dialogues of the Dead*, II, 1; *Luciani samosatensis opera*, I-IV (Leipzig: 1829; *ASKB* 1131-34), I, p. 180; *Lucian*, I-VIII, tr. A. M. Harmon, K. Kilburn, et al. (Loeb, Cambridge: Harvard University Press, 1913-67), VII, p. 14: "fellow shade."

120. See Diogenes Laertius, *Lives of Eminent Philosophers*, II, 93-94; *Diogenis Laërtii de vitis philosophorum libri X*, I-II (Leipzig: 1833; *ASKB* 1109), I, pp. 102-03; *Diogen Lærtses filosofiske Historie*, I-II, tr. Børge Riisbrigh (Copenhagen: 1812; *ASKB* 1110 -11), I, p. 96; *Lives of Eminent Philosophers*, I-II, tr. R. D. Hicks (Loeb, New York: Putnam, 1925), I, p. 223:

> The school of Hegesias, as it is called, adopted the same ends, namely pleasure and pain. In their view there is no such thing as gratitude or friendship or beneficence, because it is not for themselves that we choose to do these things but simply from motives of interest, apart from which such conduct is nowhere found. They denied the possibility of happiness, for the body is infected with much suffering, while the soul shares in the sufferings of the body and is a prey to disturbance, and fortune often disappoints. From all this it follows that happiness cannot be realized. Moreover, life and death are each desirable in turn. But that there is anything naturally pleasant or unpleasant they deny; when some men are pleased and others pained by

the same objects, this is owing to the lack or rarity or surfeit of such objects. Poverty and riches have no relevance to pleasure; for neither the rich nor the poor as such have any special share in pleasure. Slavery and freedom, nobility and low birth, honour and dishonour, are alike indifferent in a calculation of pleasure. To the fool life is advantageous, while to the wise it is a matter of indifference.

121. Wilhelm Gottlieb Tennemann, *Geschichte der Philosophie,* I-VIII (Stuttgart: 1844-45; *ASKB* 827-30).

122. In the Danish game *Gnavspil,* if the one who has the counter with the picture of a house does not want to make an exchange, he says "Go to the next house." See *Fear and Trembling,* p. 100, *KW* VI (*SV* III 147); *Fragments,* p. 22, *KW* VII (*SV* IV 191).

123. Cf. Horace, *Epistles,* I, 1, 46; *Opera,* p. 541; Loeb, pp. 254-55.

124. Cf. *Den Romerske Keisers Mark. Aurel. Antonins Leveregler for sig selv,* tr. Christian Bastholm (Copenhagen: 1805), p. 272.

125. Horace, *Odes* I, 3, 9-16; *Opera,* pp. 9-11; *Horace The Odes and Epodes,* tr. C. E. Bennett (Loeb, New York: Putnam, 1930), pp. 12-13:

Oak and triple bronze must have girt the breast of him who first committed his frail bark to the angry sea, and who feared not the furious south-west wind battling with the blasts of the north, nor the gloomy Hyades, nor the rage of Notus, than whom there is no mightier master of the Adriatic, whether he choose to raise or calm the waves.

126. Cf. p. 32: "Pressing Done Here [*Her rulles*]." In the present entry, the sign painter has substituted "o" for "u" and thereby has not only coined a verb from the noun *Rolle* but has also capitalized it.

127. Bellerophon was a Greek legendary hero who tamed the winged horse Pegasus. He fell in an attempt to fly to Olympus on Pegasus. See Nitsch, I, p. 412.

128. Karl Rosenkranz, *Schelling Vorlesungen, gehalten in Sommer 1842 an der Universität zu Königsberg* (Danzig: 1843; *ASKB* 766).

129. Ovid, *The Art of Love; P. Ovidii Nasonis opera quae exstant,* I-III, ed. A. Richter (Leipzig; 1828; *ASKB* 1265), I, p. 237; *Ovid The Art of Love and Other Poems,* tr. J. H. Mozley (Loeb, Cambridge: Harvard University Press, 1957), p. 83, 235-36: "Night, storm, long journeys, cruel pains, all kinds of toil are in this dainty camp."

130. Jens Peder Tønder (1773-1836) was murdered by Petri Claudi F. E. Worm. See *Udvalg af danske og udenlandske Criminelsager,* I-IV, ed. F. M. Lange (Copenhagen: 1831-41; *ASKB* 926-31) IV, pp. 66-68, 97-99, 353-55, 374-79; V, pp. 113-15, 243-45, 267.

131. See Supplement, pp. 564-66 (*Pap.* III B 89, 85, 93, 91).

132. See Holberg, *Erasmus Montanus,* I, 3; *Danske Skue-Plads,* V, no pagination; *Comedies,* p. 124.

133. See p. 356 and note 80.

134. See *Stages, KW* XI (*SV* VI 21-23); *JP* V 5096; 5643; 5699 (*Pap.* I A 65; IV A 811, 170).

135. Augustin E. Scribe, *La Dame Blanche (Den hvide Dame)*, tr. Thomas Overskou (Copenhagen: 1826). See *Letters*, Letters 62, 239, pp. 126, 336, *KW* XXV.

136. See *Letters*, Letter 54.

137. Ovid, *The Art of Love; Opera*, I, p. 234; Loeb, pp. 76-77.

138. Ovid, *Amores*, I, 5, 19-22; *Opera*, I. p. 131; *Ovid Heroides and Amores*, tr. Grant Showerman (Loeb, Cambridge: Harvard University Press, 1858), pp. 334-35.

139. See Supplement, pp. 585-87 (*Pap.* III B 104, 105, 107, 108).

140. See F. A. Moritz Retzsch, *Umrisse zu Goethe's Faust* (Stuttgart: 1834-36; *ASKB* U91), II, plate 1.

BIBLIOGRAPHICAL NOTE

For general bibliographies of Kierkegaard studies, see:

Jens Himmelstrup, *Søren Kierkegaard International Bibliografi*. Copenhagen: Nyt Nordisk Forlag Arnold Busck, 1962.

Aage Jørgensen, *Søren Kierkegaard-litteratur 1961-1970, . . . 1971-1980*. Aarhus: Akademisk Boghandel, 1971, 1982; *Kierkegaardiana*, XII, 1982.

François Lapointe, *Søren Kierkegaard and His Critics: An International Bibliography of Criticism*. Westport, Connecticut: Greenwood Press, 1980.

Kierkegaard: A Collection of Critical Essays, ed. Josiah Thompson. New York: Doubleday (Anchor Books), 1972.

Søren Kierkegaard's Journals and Papers, I, ed. and tr. Howard V. Hong and Edna H. Hong, assisted by Gregor Malantschuk. Bloomington, Indiana: Indiana University Press, 1967.

For topical bibliographies of Kierkegaard studies, see *Søren Kierkegaards's Journals and Papers*, I-IV, 1967-75.

INDEX

A, 7
Abel, and Cain, 286
absence, and presence, 222-23
absolute, the, 300; erotic love as,
212, 381; and the relative, 513
abstraction, the abstract: and the
concrete, 55; human beings as,
546; the immediate as pure, 463;
of reflection, 95; world of, 559-60
accident, accidentality, the accidental, 47-48, 300, 419; and Don
Juan, 106; and occasion, 233-34
Achilles, 35
acorn, *see* analogy
act, engagement as, 372
action, 118; absolute, 150; dramatic,
247; in opera, 120; and knowledge, xiii; in tragedy, 142-44;
tragic, 150; unity of, 117-18
actress: in Dresden, 410
actual, actuality, 32, 249, 628; Cordelia's, 345; disappearing from,
306, 554; and idea, 238, 489; and
imagination, xiii; and novels, 249;
and other world, 306, 554; and
poetry, 305, 392; and possibility,
xii; secrecy implicit in, 234; and
theater, 466; and thought, xiii
Adam, 286, 430; ear of, 472; and
Eve, 286
Adelung, Johann Christoph, 605
admiration: absolute object of, 300;
highest, 290; and indifference, 290
ad se ipsum, 17
Aeneas, 197
Aeolus, 400
Aeschylus, *The Eumenides*, 633; *Prometheus Bound*, 644; *Werke*, 611
aeterno modo, 39, 40
affair(s): with Cordelia, 307-08;

love, 346, 532; with Pamela, 251-
52
age, the: conformity to, 472; desire
in, 22; nature of, 27; fallaciousness
of, 479; happy, 315. *See also* old
age; past age; present age
Agnes, 394
Aladdin, xi
Alcibiades, xviii
Alectryon, 445
Allah, 484
Allgemeines Gelehrten-Lexicon, 605
Alpheus: and Arethusa, 440-41
Amager, 19
America, 291, 548
amphiboly, 161
analogy: acorn, 210; bitter drink, 26;
bookkeeper, 32, 278; castle, 21,
510; cave, 483; clown and fire, 30;
country road, 248; distress at sea,
204; dwarf, 29; eagle's nest, 42;
egg and genius, xix; elephant,
524; farmer, 455; fishing, 482;
flash, 129; flies, 471, 513; Florine,
214; flower, 453; four-leaf clover,
239; galley slave, 482; geese and
ducks, 474; ghost(s), 206; genius
and egg, xix; harem, 32, 525;
hiker, 308; horse(s), 21, 41; kan-
garoos, 38; kingdom(s), 65; Kingfisher, 560; knight and cape, 363;
left hand and right hand, xvii; Lüneburger swine, 524; pasha, 22,
511; painting, 76; pebble, 129;
pendulum, 170; perspiration, 299;
plant, 80; pronoun, 22; prostitute,
518; Proteus, 175, 498-99; rain,
170; rich man and poor man, 412-
13; river, 407; road, 538-39; sea,
324; sheep, 403; sheva, 22; shoe-

Library of Congress Cataloging-in-Publication Data

Kierkegaard, Søren, 1813-1855.
  Either/or.

  (Kierkegaard's writings, 3-   )
  Translation of: Enten-eller.
  Bibliography: p.
  Includes index.
  I. Hong, Howard Vincent, 1912-   . II. Hong, Edna Hatlestad, 1913-   . III.
Title. IV. Kierkegaard, Søren, 1813-1855. Works. English. 1978; 3, etc.
PT8142.E57E5 1987   198′.9   86-25516
ISBN 0-691-07315-5 (v. 1 : alk. paper)
ISBN 0-691-02041-8 (v. 1 : pbk.)